ROUTLEDGE HANDBOOK OF HUMAN RIGHTS AND DISASTERS

The *Routledge Handbook of Human Rights and Disasters* provides the first comprehensive review of the role played by international human rights law in the prevention and management of natural and technological disasters.

Each chapter is written by a leading expert and offers a state-of-the-art overview of a significant topic within the field. In addition to focussing on the role of human rights obligations in disaster preparedness and response, the volume offers a broader perspective by examining how human rights law interacts with other legal regimes and by addressing the challenges facing humanitarian organizations.

Preceded by a foreword by the International Law Commission's Special Rapporteur on the Protection of Persons in the Event of Disasters, the volume is divided into four parts:

- Part I: Human rights law and disasters in the framework of public international law
- Part II: Role and application of human rights law in disaster settings
- Part III: (Categories of) rights of particular significance in a disaster context
- Part IV: Protection of vulnerable groups in disaster settings

Providing up-to-date and authoritative contributions covering the key aspects of human rights protection in disaster settings, this volume will be of great interest to scholars and students of humanitarianism, international law, EU law, disaster management and international relations, as well as to practitioners in the field of disaster management.

Flavia Zorzi Giustiniani is Assistant Professor of International Law at the International Telematic University Uninettuno, Italy.

Emanuele Sommario is Assistant Professor of International Law at the Scuola Superiore Sant'Anna of Pisa, Italy.

Federico Casolari is Associate Professor of European Union Law at the Alma Mater Studiorum – University of Bologna, Italy.

Giulio Bartolini is Associate Professor of International Law at the University of Roma Tre, Italy.

Routledge Studies in Humanitarian Action

Series editors: Andrej Zwitter, *University of Groningen*, Joost Herman, *University of Groningen* and Hassan Bashir, *Texas A&M University at Qatar*

This book series offers an interdisciplinary platform for the study of issues pertaining to humanitarianism, such as humanitarian principles, humanitarian space, resilience, safety and security, international law of humanitarian action, to mention but a few. It aims to broaden understanding of these issues and their interconnection from different angles – such as politics, law, economics, philosophy, psychology, sociology – brought together under the heading of Humanitarian Studies.

Routledge Handbook of Human Rights and Disasters
Edited by Flavia Zorzi Giustiniani, Emanuele Sommario, Federico Casolari and Giulio Bartolini

ROUTLEDGE HANDBOOK OF HUMAN RIGHTS AND DISASTERS

Edited by Flavia Zorzi Giustiniani, Emanuele Sommario, Federico Casolari and Giulio Bartolini

Routledge
Taylor & Francis Group
LONDON AND NEW YORK

First published 2018
by Routledge
2 Park Square, Milton Park, Abingdon, Oxon OX14 4RN

and by Routledge
52 Vanderbilt Avenue, New York, NY 10017

First issued in paperback 2020

Routledge is an imprint of the Taylor & Francis Group, an informa business

British Library Cataloguing-in-Publication Data
A catalogue record for this book is available from the British Library

Library of Congress Cataloging-in-Publication Data
Names: Zorzi Giustiniani, Flavia, editor.
Title: Routledge handbook of human rights and disasters / edited by Flavia Zorzi Giustiniani, Emanuele Sommario, Federico Casolari and Giulio Bartolini.
Other titles: Handbook of human rights and disasters
Description: Abingdon, Oxon ; New York, NY : Routledge, 2018. |
Series: Routledge studies in humanitarian action | Includes bibliographical references and index.
Identifiers: LCCN 2017049522 | ISBN 9781138069916 (hbk) | ISBN 9781315115238 (ebk)
Subjects: LCSH: International law and human rights. | Human rights. | Humanitarian assistance—Moral and ethical aspects. | Disasters—Social aspects. | Disaster relief—Social aspects.
Classification: LCC K3240 .R697 2018 | DDC 341.4/8—dc23
LC record available at https://lccn.loc.gov/2017049522

ISBN 13: 978-0-367-58079-7 (pbk)
ISBN 13: 978-1-138-06991-6 (hbk)

Typeset in Bembo
by Apex CoVantage, LLC

CONTENTS

CONTRIBUTORS

Giovanna Adinolfi is Associate Professor of International Law at the University of Milan. She has written on public international law, international economic law, and international disaster law. In this latter area, her research is focused on international legal disciplines concerning trade obstacles to relief consignments and access of affected population to foreign goods and equipment. She has also been the academic coordinator of the Summer School on 'EU Disaster Response Law in an International Context', funded by the European Union Jean Monnet Programme (European Module 2013–2016).

Giulio Bartolini is Associate Professor of International Law at the Department of Law, University of Roma Tre, where he is also responsible of the Jean Monnet Module on 'International and European Disaster Law' funded by the EU Commission. In the area of international disaster law he has been legal assistant to the ILC Special Rapporteur on the protection of persons in the event of disasters, and co-responsible of the FIRB-International Disaster Law Project and training courses organized with the IFRC and the Italian Red Cross. He has obtained the Diploma in Human Rights Law by the European University Institute, Academy of European Law.

Federico Casolari (PhD Bologna) is Associate Professor of European Union Law at the *Alma Mater Studiorum* – University of Bologna where he also teaches International Organizations Law. In 2015 he has been elected as member of the Executive Council of the Italian Society of International and European Law for the period 2015–2018. Federico Casolari has widely published on the relationship between European Union law and international law; the external relations of the European Union; the general principles of EU law (particularly the principles of equality, non-discrimination and loyalty); and the international & European disaster response law.

Annalisa Creta is Research Fellow in International Law at the Scuola Superiore Sant'Anna of Pisa where she focuses on issues related to civilian crisis management, with a particular emphasis on policy and training related matters. Her main interests lie in Human Rights law, the International Law on the Use of Force, Collective Security Law and International Disaster Response Law, and she is the author of several publications on the above topics.

Karen da Costa is Senior Lecturer in Human Rights at the School of Global Studies, University of Gothenburg, Sweden, where she teaches in the Erasmus Mundus Master Programme in Human Rights Policy and Practice. Her current research covers human rights and disasters, and her publications include the monograph 'The Extraterritorial Application of Selected Human Rights Treaties' (Brill/Martinus Nijhoff Publishers, 2013) and several peer-reviewed academic articles. Karen holds a PhD (2011) in International Studies (International Law) from the Graduate Institute of International and Development Studies, University of Geneva, Switzerland.

Gilles Giacca is Legal Adviser at the ICRC. He previously worked as a Research Fellow and Programme Coordinator at the Law Faculty of Oxford University and currently is Research Associate at the Oxford Institute for Ethics Law and Armed Conflict. Gilles Giacca has advised States, international organizations and NGOs on matters of international law, including arms trade. His most recent publications include 'Economic, Social and Cultural Rights in Armed Conflict' (Oxford University Press, 2014) and 'The Arms Trade Treaty: A Commentary' (Oxford University Press, 2016).

Lorenzo Guadagno manages the IOM programme on 'Reducing the vulnerability of migrants in emergencies'. He has published and worked at operational and policy level with various international and non-governmental organizations on disaster risk reduction and climate change adaptation. Specific professional interests include human mobility, ecosystem management and urbanization. He holds a Law degree from the Federico II University of Naples and a PhD in Sociology from the University of Sannio, Benevento.

Kristin Hausler is the Dorset Senior Research Fellow in Public International Law at the British Institute of International and Comparative Law, where she also provides training in international human rights law. She is a member of the ILA Cultural Heritage Committee and a principal investigator in a research project funded under the EU's Joint Programming Initiative on Cultural Heritage and Global Change. Previously, she worked on a repatriation project with Indigenous communities in Canada.

Marlies Hesselman is Lecturer in International Law at the Department of International Law of the University of Groningen. She publishes widely in the area of disaster management and human rights protection, and teaches in International Disaster Law in the NOHA-Master Programme. As an Academic Member of the ETO-consortium on extra-territorial human rights obligation, Marlies research interests also include "transnational" or "extra-territorial" human rights obligations, and issues of (sustainable) development.

Marco Inglese is Postdoctoral Researcher at the University of Fribourg. Marco already carried out postdoctoral researches at the University College Dublin and the University of Sarajevo. He has been Assistant Professor of International and European Law at the China-Europe School of Law in Beijing. Marco Inglese holds a joint PhD in European and Public Law (Universities of Bologna and Strasbourg).

Walter Kälin is Professor Emeritus for international and (Swiss) constitutional law, University of Bern/Switzerland. He is the former Envoy of the Nansen Initiative on disaster-induced cross-border displacement (2012–2015) and present legal advisor to the Chair of the Platform on Disaster Displacement. Prof. Kälin also served as a member of the UN Human Rights Committee

(2003–2008 and 2012–2014) and Representative of the UN Secretary-General on the Human Rights of Internally displaced persons (2004–2010).

Rónán McDermott is Researcher within the Centre for Humanitarian Action at University College Dublin. Rónán's research to date has been conducted from the perspective of the inter-disciplinary field of socio-legal studies. He is currently engaged in a research project concerning urban preparedness and resilience, which focuses on the cities of Bogotá, Nairobi and Jakarta.

Tommaso Natoli is Research Fellow of International Law at Roma Tre University. Tommaso research interests focus on International Human Rights Law, International Humanitarian Law and International and European Disaster Law. He has obtained a PhD in International Law and Human Rights (Sapienza University of Rome) with a thesis on 'The Humanitarian Response to Major Disasters: Legal Issues and Normative Dynamics'. In the context of his researches and teaching activities dealing with disaster law, he investigated legal instruments and case law on the human rights protection in disaster scenarios as well as within universal and regional protection systems.

Ingrid Nifosi-Sutton is Adjunct Professor of law at the American University Washington College of Law where she has designed and taught courses on international disaster response law. She has authored various essays on international human rights law, and conducted research on the import of the protection available to persons affected by disasters under international human rights law. Her book 'The Protection of Vulnerable Groups under International Human Rights Law' (Routledge, 2017) contains analysis of human rights monitoring bodies' conceptualization of the vulnerability of disaster victims and ensuing legal implications.

Ellen Nohle works in the field of international humanitarian law. She has a BCL from the University of Oxford, and has previous experience from the Swedish Armed Forces and from the field of migration and refugee law. Other publications include 'Proportionality and precautions in attack: The reverberating effects of using explosive weapons in populated areas' in *IRRC* (2016) and 'Positive Obligations of the Occupying Power: Economic, Social and Cultural Rights in the Occupied Palestinian Territory' in *Human Rights Law Review* (forthcoming).

Eleni Polymenopoulou is Lecturer in Law at Brunel University and visiting lecturer at the University of Grenoble2 (France). She has published several book chapters and articles in leading peer-reviewed journals of international and international human rights law. Her research focuses on the intersections between culture and the law, as well as the work of human rights courts. Alongside her academic appointment, she has also worked as a practicing lawyer and has collaborated with a number of NGOs, such as the Greek Council for Refugees and the international organization Article19.

Alice Riccardi is Research Fellow of International Law at Roma Tre University. Previously, she was Research Fellow (2013–2016) at Uninettuno University, i.e. the research unit coordinating the project on 'IDRL: Rules and Principles of International and EU Law' funded by the Italian Ministry of Education, University and Research. In that context she investigated international hard- and soft-law instruments dealing with IDL. She continues to research and teach IDL to Law School students and staff of humanitarian actors. Her interests also cover ICL, IHRL and

IHL. She is the author of 'Sentencing at the International Criminal Court: From Nuremberg to the Hague' (Eleven International Publishing, 2016).

Raquel Rolnik is a professor, architect and urban planner with over 35 years of scholarship, activism and practical experience in planning, urban land policy and housing issues. Based in São Paulo, she is a professor at the Faculty of Architecture and Urbanism of the University of São Paulo. In her career, she has held various government positions including Director of the Planning Department of the city of São Paulo (1989–1992) and National Secretary for Urban Programs of the Brazilian Ministry of Cities (2003–2007) as well as NGO activities, such as Urban Policy Coordinator of the Polis Institute (1997–2002). From May 2008, Ms. Raquel Rolnik was appointed by the UN Human Rights Council as UN Special Rapporteur on adequate housing for a six years mandate, ending June 2014. She is the author of several books, including *Guerra dos Lugares: A colonização da terra e da moradia na era das finanças* (to be launched in English by VERSO in 2018) and 'A cidade e a lei' among others.

Gabrielle Simm is Chancellor's Postdoctoral Research Fellow, Faculty of Law, University of Technology Sydney and a Visiting Fellow, Australian Human Rights Centre, University of New South Wales Law. She is the author of 'Sex in Peace Operations' (Cambridge University Press, 2013) and has research interests in international law, disasters, humanitarianism, refugee and migration law, and international law and film. Prior to becoming an academic, she was an international lawyer in the Australian government, a diplomat in Southeast Asia, and a refugee lawyer in Melbourne.

Alice Sironi is Migration Law Specialist at IOM (Geneva). She trains governments officials and other stakeholders on international migration law, reviews national legislation in this area and advises IOM offices to ensure that the activities of the Organization comply with international standards. Her current research interests are environmental migration, the protection of migrants in disasters and migration detention. She holds a Law degree of the Sorbonne University in Paris and of the University of Florence and a PhD in International Law and Human Rights of the University of Naples.

Emanuele Sommario is Assistant Professor of International Law at the Scuola Superiore Sant'Anna of Pisa. He has written on human rights law, international humanitarian law and international disaster law. In this latter area, he has been an advisor to the ILC Special Rapporteur on the protection of persons in the event of disasters, and one of the coordinators of a government-funded project on international disaster law. He is also a consultant and trainer for various operational agencies, such as the EU Civil Protection Mechanism and the Italian Civil Protection.

Mirko Sossai (PhD Siena) is Associate Professor of international law at the Law Department of the Roma Tre University, where he teaches international human rights law and law of international organisations. Co-rapporteur of the ILA study group on UN sanctions and international law. Member of the Editorial Board of the Journal of Conflict and Security Law. He published a monograph in Italian on the prevention of terrorism in international law and edited with Christine Bakker the book 'Multilevel Regulation of Military and Security Contractors: the Interplay between International, European, and Domestic norms' (Hart, 2012).

Gabriella Venturini is Professor Emerita of International Law, University of Milan, Italy. She is the President of the Italian Branch of the International Law. She taught and wrote extensively in the field of public international law and EU law and collaborated with the Italian Ministry of Foreign Affairs as a member of the Italian delegation at several international meetings, conferences and negotiations.

Sarah Williams is Professor of International Law in the Faculty of Law, UNSW Sydney and an Associate of the Australian Human Rights Centre, UNSW Sydney. She is the author of *Hybrid and Internationalized Criminal Tribunals* (Hart, 2012) and of a forthcoming text on the role of the *Amicus curiae in international criminal justice* (Hart, 2018). Her research interests include international criminal law, international humanitarian law and disaster response, and she is involved in two Australian Research Council projects, one on civil society in international criminal justice and one on reparations.

Flavia Zorzi Giustiniani is Assistant Professor of International Law and also a lecturer in European Union Law at Uninettuno University. In January 2014 she has been awarded the *National Habilitation* to the position of *Associate Professor in International Law.* She holds a PhD in International Law (2006), a Diploma in International Humanitarian Law awarded by the ICRC (2003) and two J.D.s in Political Science (2002) and Law (2011). Since 2010 she has been an appointed member of the Scientific Committee of the Italian Red Cross Commission for International Humanitarian Law. She was national coordinator of the FIRB-International Disaster Law Project.

FOREWORD

It constitutes for me a signal honor to have been invited to write the Foreword to this Handbook by its Editors, Giulio Bartolini, Federico Casolari, Emanuele Sommario and Flavia Zorzi Giustiniani. The Handbook is the felicitous result of the pioneering work carried out by them in the context of the joint 'International Disaster Law Project' of their respective Italian Universities, to wit, Roma Tre, Bologna, Scuola Superiore Sant'Anna of Pisa and Uninettuno of Rome. Their invitation carries for me a very special meaning as all four Editors, acting within the confines of the same Project, rendered me valuable assistance in the discharge of my functions as the Special Rapporteur of the United Nations (UN) International Law Commission (ILC) on the topic 'Protection of Persons in the Event of Disasters'.

As it is well known, the ILC was established by the UN General Assembly as a means of implementing the task imposed on it by Article 13(1)(a) of the UN Charter 'to initiate studies and make recommendations for the purpose of . . . encouraging the progressive development of international law and its codification'. In fulfilment of its mandate and on the proposal of the UN Secretary-General, the ILC in 2007 included in its program of work the topic 'Protection of Persons in the Event of Disasters' as one that 'reflected new developments in international law and pressing concerns of the international community as a whole' and appointed me to be its Special Rapporteur thereon.

The ILC having considered since 2008 eight consecutive reports by the Special Rapporteur, brought in 2016 to a successful conclusion its uninterrupted work on the topic with the adoption by consensus of a final set of 18 Draft Articles and a Preamble, accompanied by their corresponding Commentaries. The whole was then submitted to the UN General Assembly together with the recommendation, also approved by consensus, that an international convention be elaborated on the basis of the Draft Articles. By Resolution 71/141 of 13 December 2016 the UN General Assembly decided to include in the provisional agenda of its 2018 regular session an autonomous item to consider the comments of Governments on the ILC's recommendation.

The publication of this Handbook could, therefore, not have been more timely. Its comprehensive and systematic coverage of disasters from the perspective of Human Rights Law, fully described in the Introduction, will certainly furnish a most relevant conceptual framework to aid the UN General Assembly in assessing the political viability of the ILC's recommendation to elaborate, for the first time at the universal level, a 'hard law' framework international instrument on the basis of its final product.

After all, as the Special Rapporteur explicitly stated already in his First, Preliminary report: '[t]he title of the topic also imports a distinctive perspective, that is, of the individual who is a victim of a disaster, and, therefore, suggests a definite rights-based approach to the treatment of the topic'. The essence of such an approach, concretized in many of the provisions of the ILC's final Draft, is the identification of a specific standard of treatment to which the individual, the victim of a disaster, *in casu*, is entitled. To paraphrase the UN Secretary-General, a rights-based approach deals with situations not simply in terms of human needs, but in terms of society's obligation to respond to the inalienable rights of individuals, empowers them to demand justice as a right, not as charity, and gives communities a moral basis from which to claim international assistance when needed.

But the Handbook's unquestionable value goes well beyond its impact on the action that the UN General Assembly may take. This remarkable work represents the first instance in the existing legal literature of a thorough treatment being given to all aspects of the crucial role played by International Human Rights Law in defining the rights and duties of States and other actors in the 'disaster cycle', encompassing the pre-disaster, the disaster proper and the post-disaster stages. The Handbook extends in a similar vein its in-depth treatment to the important question of the relationship of disasters with, *inter-alia*, International Humanitarian Law and International Law on Displaced Persons.

The Handbook, therefore, not only fills a void but it does so in a manner that makes it, at the same time, the indispensable point of reference on the subject, thanks to the high scholarly merit of the many and diverse contributions highlighted in the almost exhaustive Table of Contents. It, thus, represents a well-deserved tribute to the foresight and enterprise of its distinguished Editors.

Eduardo Valencia-Ospina
ILC Special Rapporteur on the 'Protection of
Persons in the Event of Disasters'
Geneva

LIST OF ABBREVIATIONS

ACHR	American Convention on Human Rights
ACHPR	African Charter on Human and Peoples' Rights
ACommHPR	African Commission on Human and Peoples' Rights
ACtHPR	African Court on Human and Peoples' Rights
ASEAN	Association of East Asian Nations
AU	African Union
CBH	Cultural Built Heritage
CEDAW	Convention on the Elimination of All Forms of Discrimination against Women
CERD	Convention on the Elimination of All Forms of Racial Discrimination
CESCR	United Nations Committee on Economic, Social and Cultural Rights
CHR	Commission on Human Rights
CHS	Core Humanitarian Standard on Quality and Accountability
CoE	Council of Europe
CommEDAW	Committee on the Elimination of All Forms of Discrimination against Women
CommERD	Committee on the Elimination of Racial Discrimination
CommRC	Committee on the Rights of the Child
CommRPD	Committee on the Rights of Persons with Disabilities
CSOs	Civil Society Organizations
CRC	Convention on the Rights of the Child
CRPD	Convention on the Rights of Persons with Disabilities
CSR51	Convention relating to the Status of Refugees
DG ECHO	Directorate General European Civil Protection and Humanitarian Aid Operations
DRR	Disaster Risk Reduction
ECHR	European Convention on Human Rights
ECJ	Court of Justice of the European Union
ECOWAS	Economic Community of Western African States
ECtHR	European Court of Human Rights
EMC	European Medical Corps
ESCRs	Economic, Social and Cultural Rights
ETS	European Treaty Series

EU	European Union
FPIC	Free, Prior and Informed Consent
GHG	Greenhouse Gas
HFA	Hyogo Framework for Action
HRBA	Human Rights-Based Approach
HRC	United Nations Human Rights Council
HRComm	United Nations Human Rights Committee
IACtHR	Inter-American Court of Human Rights
IAEA	International Atomic Energy Agency
IASC	Inter-Agency Standing Committee
ICBL	International Campaign to Ban Landmine
ICCPR	International Covenant on Civil and Political Rights
ICESCR	International Covenant on Economic, Social and Cultural Rights
ICJ	International Court of Justice
ICRC	International Committee of the Red Cross
ICRMW	International Convention on the Rights of All Migrant Workers and Members of Their Families
IDL	International Disaster Law
IDPs	Internally Displaced Persons
IDRL	International Disaster Response Law
IFRC	International Federation of the Red Cross and Red Crescent Societies
IGOs	Intergovernmental Organisations
IHL	International Humanitarian Law
IHRL	International Human Rights Law
ILC	International Law Commission
ILO	International Labour Organization
IOM	International Organization for Migration
IPCC	Intergovernmental Panel on Climate Change
IRU	International Relief Union
LNTS	League of Nations Treaty Series
NGOs	Non-Governmental Organisations
NOAA	National Oceanic and Atmospheric Administration
NSAs	Non-State Actors
NSHAs	Non-State Humanitarian Actors
OAS	Organization of American States
OAU	Organization of African Unity
OHCHR	United Nations Office of the High Commissioner for Human Rights
PAHO	Pan American Health Organization
PDD	Platform on Disaster Displacement
SAARC	South Asian Association for Regional Cooperation
SCHR	Steering Committee for Humanitarian Response
TEK	Traditional Ecological Knowledge
TFEU	Treaty on the Functioning of the European Union
TPS	Temporary Protected Status
TRIPs	Trade-Related Aspects of Intellectual Property Rights
UN	United Nations
UNDP	United Nations Development Programme
UNDRIP	United Nations Declaration on the Rights of Indigenous Peoples

UNESCO	United Nations Educational, Scientific and Cultural Organization
UNFCCC	United Nations Framework Convention on Climate Change
UNGA	United Nations General Assembly
UNICEF	United Nations Children's Fund
UNISDR	United Nations Office for Disaster Risk Reduction
UNOCHA	United Nations Office for the Coordination of Humanitarian Affairs
UNSC	United Nations Security Council
UNSG	United Nations Secretary-General
UNTS	United Nations Treaty Series
VCLT	Vienna Convention on the Law of Treaties
WHO	World Health Organization

PART I

Human rights law and disasters in the framework of public international law

1

INTRODUCTION AND ACKNOWLEDGMENTS

Flavia Zorzi Giustiniani, Emanuele Sommario, Federico Casolari, and Giulio Bartolini

Empirical evidence points to the increased frequency and destructive potential of natural and technological disasters. From data collected at Leuven University by the Centre for Research on the Epidemiology of Disasters (CRED),[1] we know that 11,713 disasters have taken place between 2000 and 2016, killing more than 1.4 million people, injuring almost 5 million, and leaving almost 38 million homeless. More than 3.6 billion people have been affected, and the material damage has exceeded USD 2 trillion.[2] Notwithstanding a slight decrease in the number of catastrophic events over the last few years, the overall trend shows a clear surge in their incidence and in the economic damage caused.

Against this background, it may seem surprising that the existence of disaster-risk drivers – and more broadly the role of humans in transforming a natural hazard into a disaster – had already been anticipated by Jean-Jacques Rousseau in the wake of the Lisbon earthquake of 1755, with the ensuing tsunami and massive fire. This event set off the first major debate on natural catastrophes and their effects on human beings. The human toll and material damage caused by the event were terrific. Nonetheless, the fact that it struck on All Saints' Day, in a city that was deeply Catholic but also wealthy and awash with corruption and vice, prompted many at that time – including the great Enlightenment philosopher Voltaire – to attribute the event to the will of God. This stood in stark contrast to the position of Rousseau, who, categorically rejecting the notion that human behaviour had nothing to do with the event, keenly observed that

> it was hardly nature who assembled there twenty-thousand houses of six or seven stories. If the residents of this large city had been more evenly dispersed and less densely housed, the losses would have been fewer or perhaps none at all.[3]

He then noted how, after the quake, many lives were lost to a disorganised evacuation: '[h]ow many unfortunates perished in this disaster for wanting to take – one his clothing, another his papers, a third his money?'.[4]

History has proven Rousseau right. For it is now apparent that human activity weighs significantly in shaping the types of disasters that take place and their number. Leaving aside technological disasters – whose impact, though substantial, is negligible compared to that of natural disasters – statistics show that floods, storms, and droughts are the phenomena that most severely affect individuals and property.[5] As is known, all three types of hazards are considered to be linked to climate change, which in turn finds its primary cause in (human-made) greenhouse gas emissions. In its 5th Assessment Report, the Intergovernmental Panel on Climate Change (IPCC)[6] unequivocally confirmed this connection, stating that: '[h]uman influence on the climate system is clear, and recent anthropogenic emissions of greenhouse gases are the highest in history. Recent climate changes have had widespread impacts on human and natural systems'.[7]

The Assessment Report went on to identify the rising frequency of natural disasters as contributing to the adverse impact of climate change and pointed out that the vulnerability of human and natural systems will multiply the impact of extreme events. According to the report, vulnerability 'is the product of intersecting social processes that result in inequalities in socio-economic status and income, as well as in exposure. Such social processes include, for example, discrimination on the basis of gender, class, ethnicity, age and (dis)ability'.[8] It is now evident that disasters disproportionately affect poorer communities because of their greater vulnerability and 'significantly impede progress towards sustainable development'.[9] This situation is exacerbated by other disaster-risk drivers, such as unplanned and rapid urbanisation and poor land management, along with various compounding factors (demographic change, weak institutions, policies that do not take risk into account, etc.).[10]

It is now established beyond doubt that disasters are never completely 'natural' and that human behaviour plays a role in both their occurrence and their consequences. For a long time, however, the kind of response these events have been regarded as calling for was humanitarian. Many of the treaties concluded over the last few decades to facilitate cooperation between States in times of disaster – and forming what is now commonly referred to as International Disaster Law (IDL) – were exclusively predicated on this assumption, and little or no consideration was given to the human rights ramifications of disaster events. However, in recent years it has come to be recognised that human rights need protection even in these contexts and that relief aid is but one of the means that States have at their disposal to meet their international obligation to respect and protect human rights. In addition, it is now widely accepted that the role of human rights is not limited to disaster response. In fact, States have positive obligations to ensure effective disaster prevention and preparedness activities, so as to minimise the harm that disasters can do to a population.

The extent to which disasters exacerbate the inequalities inherent in life and society significantly turns on the question of how governments and humanitarian actors integrate human rights into their disaster preparedness and response plans. The purpose of this volume is precisely to consider whether and to what extent the human rights discourse has been mainstreamed into disaster prevention and response activities. It is widely recognised that appropriate actions at all stages in the so-called disaster management cycle lead to greater preparedness, better warnings, and reduced vulnerability and that an approach that is sensitive human rights can mitigate the effects of disasters on people, property, and the environment. It is in framing and implementing these policies that international law – as interpreted by international bodies – should play a role in ensuring that human rights concerns are given due weight in the process.

In this volume, the editors and authors have approached disaster management through the lens of international law, looking at human rights treaties and at the practice of their monitoring bodies and of other authorities to assess the extent to which these bodies and authorities have held States and other relevant actors to account in matters involving natural and technological disasters and to determine how international law is likely to influence the conduct of such actors in these matters in the future.

In particular, the present volume seeks to provide a comprehensive assessment of the main legal issues and challenges concerning the application of International Human Rights Law (IHRL) in disaster situations and the role this body of law can play in shaping the obligations of States and other actors involved in preventing and responding to natural and human-made disasters and in ensuring preparedness. Significantly, over the last few years many treaty-monitoring bodies and other human rights protection mechanisms (UN Special Rapporteurs, the Universal Periodic Review, international courts, etc.) have focused their attention on disaster-related issues, highlighting the central role of human rights in this domain. In addition, in 2016 the International Law Commission (ILC) adopted the final version of its Draft Articles on the Protection of Persons in the Event of Disasters (ILC Draft Articles),[11] where provisions dealing with human dignity and human rights have been included, and a full range of soft law instruments on the rights of disaster victims have been adopted at the global and regional levels. There is therefore abundant material deserving careful study.

Despite the many developments in the practice of human rights bodies, relief agents, and other stakeholders, we still lack a thorough academic investigation of these topics, as shown by the absence of monographs or edited volumes specifically devoted to them. This stands in stark contrast to the increasing attention the humanitarian and academic communities accord to the subject of disasters. This volume thus intends to bridge this gap and provide a careful appraisal of the important role that human rights play in disaster situations, while addressing the main legal issues involved in their implementation in such contexts.

Yet IHRL is not the only branch of international law that comes to bear in disaster settings. Issues concerning state sovereignty and the principle of non-intervention in the internal affairs of States have been central to the debate on disaster response. In addition, the International Humanitarian Law (IHL) applicable to armed conflicts may also become relevant, both because of the possibility that a disaster should strike a war-beleaguered State and because of the numerous provisions on humanitarian aid contained in IHL treaties. These and other general topics (starting from the legal definition of the term *disaster* in international law) are addressed in the present volume.

At the same time, it is necessary to consider how IHRL operates in disaster settings. More to the point, the questions that need to be considered are how and to what extent this body of law entitles disaster victims to additional protection and what the role of States and non-state actors is in implementing disaster prevention and response measures. Equally important is an appraisal of the circumstances and conditions under which States can limit or suspend the enjoyment of certain rights and take extraordinary measures to deal with an emergency.

A comprehensive survey of the way in which the human rights discourse is likely to shape IDL cannot ignore how IHRL affects the enjoyment of specific rights or categories of rights in disaster scenarios. In this respect, the volume takes on important questions such as the content of minimum guarantees that need to be ensured for affected individuals and their right not to suffer discrimination in the provision of aid, as well as certain specific rights that become particularly critical in disaster contexts, such as the right to shelter or the right to be informed. At the same time, attention needs to be devoted to the role of certain rights whose function in disaster settings has not been as extensively explored: this applies to economic and social rights, cultural rights, and rights that are functional to the enjoyment of other rights (e.g. the right to know). Humanitarian agents have highlighted that certain classes of individuals are more exposed to the ravaging effects of disasters and stand to suffer more in their aftermath. This applies to vulnerable groups in general, but particularly to groups that suffer from specific types of disadvantages that make them especially vulnerable to disasters. In this respect, it is particularly important to inquire into the legal protections available to those who have been displaced by a disaster, both internally and across international borders.

The analysis carried out in this volume is structured into four complementary parts preceded by a foreword by the ILC Special Rapporteur Eduardo Valencia-Ospina: 'Human Rights Law and Disasters in the Framework of Public International Law' (Part I), 'Role and Application of Human Rights Law in Disaster Settings' (Part II), '(Categories of) Rights of Particular Relevance in a Disaster Context' (Part III), and 'Protection of Vulnerable Groups in Disaster Settings' (Part IV).

Part I (Chapters 1–4) sets the stage for the other contributions, as it explains the topicality of the subject and describes how the international rules involved may interact with other principles and bodies of international law, such as the principle of state sovereignty and International Humanitarian Law. In the first chapter, Giulio Bartolini explores the preliminary question of the contours of the notion of *disaster* in international law so as to identify the material scope of the relevant sets of rules and thus ascertain who and what is entitled to legal protection. Subsequently, Karen da Costa provides an overview of the 'responsibility to protect' doctrine and reflects on the suitability of extending this doctrine to the area of disasters, thereby identifying the main advantages and shortcomings at both the conceptual and the practical levels. The contribution by Sarah Williams and Gabrielle Simm consequently outlines the way that IHL bears on the provision of aid to disaster victims in armed conflicts and the relation between IDL and IHL in such mixed contexts.

Part II (Chapters 5–10) then focuses on the role and application of IHRL in disaster settings. We start out with Marlies Hesselman, who looks at the purported existence of a right to receive international (humanitarian) aid in a disaster context under IHRL by analysing some recent key legal initiatives and developments concerned with this issue. An appraisal of the ILC's approach to human rights in its work on the protection of persons in the event of disasters is then carried out by Rónán McDermott, who among other questions addresses the ambiguous concept of protection deployed by the ILC and illustrates the tensions between sovereignty and human rights that can be discerned in the ILC Draft Articles. Providing assistance to disaster victims can be controversial, particularly when the disaster takes place in a situation of international or non-international armed conflict. Emanuele Sommario's chapter then focuses on the international legal framework on limitations on human rights and derogations from human rights treaties in disaster situations and then – looking at the practice of the main relevant judicial treaty bodies – proceeds to assess how these prerogatives have been employed in such contexts. The relevance of a human rights approach in the context of prevention and disaster risk reduction is then analysed by Mirko Sossai, who specifically evaluates the implications of this approach by reference to the relevant case law and to the solutions adopted by the ILC Draft Articles. In the next chapter, Annalisa Creta illustrates how human rights standards and principles can be integrated into disaster management policies in order to strengthen prevention, response, and recovery efforts, while increasing the protection of the affected individuals and communities. Lastly, Tommaso Natoli's contribution turns to the practices of humanitarian actors (intergovernmental and non-governmental humanitarian bodies) so as to assess how a consistent implementation of these practices can confer legitimacy on the work of these bodies, in such a way as to ultimately complement the States' monopoly over the production and implementation of international norms on the protection of individual rights in disaster situations.

Subsequently, Part III (Chapters 11–17) 'zooms in' and assesses how certain rights or categories of rights may become relevant in disaster scenarios. Specific attention is here devoted to those sets of guarantees which become critical in disaster settings and the specific challenges and problems posed by their implementation are thoroughly analysed. The discussion starts with Marco Inglese, who lays out the concept of the 'basic subsistence rights' that need to be ensured in the aftermath of a disaster, and through a top-down method, he sets out to identify these rights through a survey of universal instruments. Raquel Rolnik then addresses the particular challenges encountered in guaranteeing the right to housing in a disaster context and highlights the need for an extensive interpretation of this right, arguing that it should be implemented in keeping with the principle of non-discrimination. An assessment of this principle's legal scope of application in disaster scenarios is then offered by Federico Casolari, who analyses the different approaches taken in the relevant legal instruments and then focuses on the solution adopted by the ILC and on its possible added value. Giovanna Adinolfi's chapter is instead concerned with the right to a healthy environment within the specific context of IDL. Her chapter discusses the impact of the measures that States take to protect and promote this right in the prevention phase as well as in a post-disaster situation. In the following chapter, Alice Riccardi investigates the nature of the right to know prior to a disaster, examining in particular whether this right can be deemed a freestanding right or whether it is an instrumental obligation functional to the prevention of other human rights violations. The focus then shifts to economic and social rights. Ellen Nohle and Gilles Giacca survey the practice of human rights treaty-monitoring bodies and of other national and international courts and that of UN special procedures in order to illustrate how and to what extent economic and social rights remain applicable in disaster settings to afford legal protection to affected groups and individuals. The last contribution of Part III is instead devoted to the little-examined area of culture and cultural rights in times of disaster: by insisting on those cultural rights that seem more pertinent when a disaster strikes, Eleni Polymenopoulou explores the role of culture in disaster risk prevention and management from a legal perspective.

Finally, Part IV (Chapters 18–22) looks at groups of persons who (a) may be particularly vulnerable in disaster-stricken areas or (b) have been displaced as a consequence of a disaster. Ingrid Nifosi-Sutton starts us off by laying out the way the vulnerability of disaster-affected people has been conceptualised by the UN Committee on Economic, Social and Cultural Rights (CESCR) and applying this vulnerability paradigm to the housing situation of internally displaced women in post-quake Haiti. Subsequently Kristin Hausler analyses the changing role of indigenous communities in disaster management, looking in particular at the case law of human rights bodies that have upheld the rights of indigenous groups in the context of disaster risk reduction and prevention. Alice Sironi and Lorenzo Guadagno then address the specific condition of vulnerability that migrants are exposed to in disaster situations. They begin with a critical study of the role played by States of origin and destination and then turn to recent initiatives, notably the ongoing Migrants In Countries In Crisis (MICIC) Initiative, so as to assess their role in effectively reducing such vulnerability. Flavia Zorzi Giustiniani then provides an overview of a significant number of representative temporary-protection measures which are or may be applied at the national, regional, and international levels to protect migrants struck by disaster. Her aim is to assess the current attitudes of States and to explore the advantages and shortcomings of the measures identified. Lastly, Walter Kälin discusses how the international community has tried to cope with the reality of disaster displacement under the Nansen Initiative's Protection Agenda for People Displaced by Disasters across Borders: the discussion covers the process that led to the adoption of this instrument, the key legal issues it addresses, and its achievements so far.

The volume closes with a final chapter in which Gabriella Venturini, in light of the preceding analyses, offers a broad assessment of the role of human rights in disaster scenarios.

This volume is the final research output of the IDL Project,[12] financed by the Italian Ministry of Education, University, and Research under the FIRB funding scheme Futuro in Ricerca 2012. The Project was brought to completion between 2013 and 2016 by four research units coordinated by Giulio Bartolini (Roma Tre University), Federico Casolari (University of Bologna), Emanuele Sommario (Scuola Superiore Sant'Anna), and Flavia Zorzi Giustiniani (Uninettuno University), who also served as the Project's national coordinator. Its focus was on international law mechanisms dealing with disaster prevention and management, and its purpose was to make these mechanisms more effective in the belief that a more thorough legal regulation may help reduce the destructive potential these phenomena have on humans and on the material resources they rely on.

Several activities carried out under the IDL Project have been instrumental in bringing out this volume. In particular, the initial research results were presented and discussed at the international conference titled 'The Protection of Persons in Times of Disasters: International and European Perspectives', held on 3–4 March 2016 in Rome at the Representations of the European Commission and the European Parliament in Italy. The authors of many of the chapters included in this volume presented their interim findings at the conference, drawing great benefit from the ensuing discussions.

In addition, the authors were able to take advantage of two innovative open-access databases created and managed by the project's team. One is the International Disaster Law Database,[13] which collects international instruments (treaties, secondary law produced by international organisations, and soft law documents) relating to the various phases of the disaster cycle and making it possible to perform full-text searches on all the content. The second is the Human Rights Protection and Disasters Database,[14] systematising the practice of international and regional human rights bodies dealing with disasters and their impact on the enjoyment of the relative human rights.

The editors wish to thank all partners of the IDL Project for their invaluable contribution in making this volume possible. These are the International Federation of Red Cross and Red Crescent Societies, the Italian Red Cross, the International Institute of Humanitarian Law (Sanremo), the Italian Department of Civil Defence, and the Active Learning Network for Accountability and Performance in Humanitarian Action (ALNAP). We also owe a debt of gratitude to all research fellows involved in the IDL Project – Mauro Gatti, Chiara Macchi, Claudia Morini, Tommaso Natoli, Alice Riccardi, and Susanna Villani – for their precious support at all stages of the research.

Many thanks go as well to the academic and research institutions that hosted us in the course of the research project, providing working environments that proved very fruitful in conceiving and finalising the present volume, namely, the Australian National University (Canberra), the British Institute of International and Comparative Law (London), the Geneva Centre for Security Policy (Geneva), the Graduate Institute of International and Development Studies (Geneva), and the Kalshoven-Gieskes Forum on IHL at Leiden University (Leiden).

A debt of gratitude is owed to all those who have contributed to this study and to all the chairs and speakers who, while not appearing in this volume, have taken part in the events that made it possible. We are deeply grateful to Eduardo Valencia-Ospina, who agreed to write the foreword to this volume.

A special thank goes to Claudia Morini and Alice Riccardi for their assistance in the editorial process leading to the completion of this edited volume, and to Chris Callan, Anna Riddell, Emma Thorley, and Filippo Valente for the language revision of the manuscript. We also acknowledge that the language revision of the volume was partly funded under the Jean Monnet module 'International and European Disaster Law' of the Erasmus+ Programme managed at Roma Tre University by Giulio Bartolini.[15] The publication process has been greatly facilitated by the smooth cooperation with Routledge.

Last but not least, we are indebted to Professors Andreas de Guttry (Scuola Superiore Sant'Anna), Marco Gestri (University of Modena and Reggio Emilia), and Gabriella Venturini (University of Milan), whose work, especially in International Disaster Response Law,[16] has earned them a place among the academic pioneers of the discipline of International Disaster Law and who have encouraged us to continue our research on these stimulating and constantly evolving subjects.

Notes

1 The CRED runs the Emergency Events Database (EM DAT), a global database on natural and technological disasters that contains core data on the occurrence and effects of more than 21,000 disasters starting from 1900. For a disaster to be entered into the database, at least one of the following criteria need to be satisfied: (a) 10 or more people are reported killed, (b) 100 or more are reported as having been affected, (c) a state of emergency has been declared, or (d) a call for international assistance has been made. Affected people comprise all individuals requiring immediate assistance during an emergency, including displaced or evacuated people. More information available at www.emdat.be/, accessed on 10 July 2017.

2 All data are extrapolated from the EM DAT research engine, available at www.emdat.be/database, accessed on 10 July 2017.

3 J.-J. Rousseau, 'Rousseau to Voltaire, 18 August 1756' in R.A. Leigh (ed), *Correspondance complète de Jean-Jacques Rousseau*, vol. 4 (Institut Musée Voltaire, 1967) 37–50, translated by R. Spang.

4 Ibid.

5 In 2016, out of 344 natural disasters reported, 260 (75%) were either droughts, floods, or storms, which affected over 110 million people and caused over USD 100 billion in damages. By comparison, 50 years earlier (in 1966) the total number of individuals affected by all types of natural disasters was 12 million, and the material damage was estimated at USD 19 billion (inflation-adjusted).

6 The IPCC is the international body entrusted with assessing scientific advancements related to climate change. Established in 1988 under the UN umbrella, it provides policymakers with regular assessments of the scientific basis of climate change, its impacts and future risks, and options for adaptation and mitigation. For its 5th Assessment Report, see IPCC, Climate Change 2014: Synthesis Report. Contribution of Working Groups I, II and III to the Fifth Assessment Report of the Intergovernmental Panel on Climate Change (2014).

7 Ibid 2.

8 Ibid 54.

9 Sendai Framework for Action, art 4.

10 Ibid art 6.

11 ILC, Report of the International Law Commission, Sixty-Eighth Session, UN Doc. A/71/10 (2016) (2 May–10 June and 4 July–12 August 2016) 12.

12 The full title of the Project is 'International Disaster Law: Rules and Principles of International and EU Law Concerning the Prevention and Management of Natural and Manmade Disasters' (reference No. RBFR12Y56K). An overview of the activities carried out under the project is available at http://disasterlaw.sssup.it/, accessed on 22 July 2017.

13 Available at http://disasterlaw.sssup.it/disasters-database/, accessed on 22 July 2017.

14 Available at http://disasterlaw.sssup.it/human-rights-protection-and-disasters-list-of-documents/, accessed on 22 July 2017.

15 An overview of the Project is available at www.ieudl.eu/, accessed on 22 July 2017.

16 A. de Guttry, M. Gestri and G. Venturini (eds), *International Disaster Response Law* (Springer, 2012).

2

A TAXONOMY OF DISASTERS IN INTERNATIONAL LAW

Giulio Bartolini

Introduction

As the purpose of this volume is to address the legal challenges posed to the protection of human rights by events loosely qualified as 'disasters', a preliminary question to be explored is the identification of the term's legal contours under international law. However, as emphasised by the International Law Commission (ILC) Special Rapporteur Eduardo Valencia-Ospina, within the framework of activities related to the Draft Articles on the protection of persons in the event of disasters (ILC Draft Articles):[1] '[t]here is no generally accepted legal definition of the term in international law'.[2] Indeed, it would be challenging to pinpoint a single instrument of international law capable of providing the authoritative and guiding legal parameter for this term. In this regard we are experiencing similar challenges to other areas of law in which standardised definitions are lacking and significant interpretative efforts are consequently required to navigate among different instruments towards the identification of common criteria.[3] The relevance of this interpretative exercise should not be underestimated, as

> [s]uch a definition will help identify the situations in which protection may or shall be invoked, as well as the circumstances under which protection will no longer be necessary. Describing the contours of 'disaster' will also help identify the persons in need of protection and thus ascertain who is entitled to protection.[4]

Hence, with the aim of providing a pertinent terminological framework for this volume, in the subsequent paragraphs, we will explore the taxonomy[5] of disasters and seek to better identify the legal contours and implications of this notion.

A first brief reference will be made to the terminology issues addressed by disaster studies, in which specific emphasis is placed on the social and sociological dimensions of events that might represent a disaster, our aim being to verify to what extent such references could be translated into legal paradigms or capable of influencing them. Subsequently we will focus our attention on the international legal dimension of this term, conducting a critical assessment of the main approaches in this area as identifiable in relevant practice. In particular, the law-making techniques adopted in treaties and soft-law documents could be grouped according to two diverging perspectives: (a) international instruments avoiding the terminology challenge, hence addressing relevant legal issues arising in the event of disaster without trying to define this term or, conversely, (b) documents illustrating the distinctive features events should possess in order to be qualified as a disaster. This second approach can be traced back to one of the earliest definitions of disaster in international law, namely that provided in the Convention establishing the International Relief Union in 1927 (IRU Convention). In this latter context attention will be paid to current and recurring key issues in the terminology dilemma, thus permitting us to identify trends and converging elements. This analysis will also take advantage of the definitions of disaster included in the most recent and relevant documents in this area, namely the abovementioned ILC Draft Articles and the Report of the open-ended intergovernmental expert working group on indicators and terminology relating to disaster risk reduction, elaborated to measure global progress in the implementation of the Sendai Framework on Disaster Risk Reduction (Sendai Framework), as endorsed by the United Nations (UN) General Assembly in February 2017 (Report on DRR terminology).[6] Finally, some concluding remarks will build upon this analysis in order to highlight the potential relevance of these terminology issues to the protection of individuals under human rights law.

A brief foray into the terminological challenges pertaining to disaster studies

Although our focus will be on the international law dimension of the term 'disaster', we should emphasise that the 'definitional minefield'[7] related to the notion of disaster is a contentious issue in disaster studies too. As recently recognised, indeed, 'the existing taxonomies of disaster matter . . . [as they] . . . might have far-reaching consequences for disaster policy'.[8] Over the last few decades[9] (and in advance compared to the terminology debate among international law scholars)[10] a vast array of writings have been produced with the primary aim of revising the traditional narrative according to which such events were 'an exteriority where God or Nature was to blame for the destruction caused by disasters'.[11] The position that 'there is no such thing as a natural disaster'[12] is a current leitmotiv of disaster studies scholars and might now be considered as the starting point for our terminological analysis in this area.

This emphasis permits us to underline that it is 'hard to identify catastrophic events which result purely from "natural" causes',[13] as 'the human contribution to disasters must be understood and recognized'.[14] Based on such assumptions, disaster studies tend to emphasise that '[a] disaster event is the intersection of the physical and social environments',[15] and may conclude that '[i]t is also now well established that disaster risk and eventual disaster are social constructs based on the presence of potentially damaging physical events but seriously and dominantly conditioned by society's perceptions, needs, demands, decisions and practices'.[16] From this viewpoint, therefore, disasters appear to be the consequences of hazards or hazardous events[17] whose final adverse effects on the inventory of elements present in the affected area are primarily determined by the combination of the abovementioned event(s) with human, environmental, social and structural vulnerabilities, as well as the capacity of affected communities to be resilient and cope with them. In brief, the consequences of a hazard 'are at least as much a function of where and how we live as a function'[18] of the hazard itself. Such positions have also been expressed through various hypotheses of equations seeking to capture the distinguishing elements of disaster risk and hence predict the possibility of adverse effects caused by a hazard. For instance, according to some,

$$\textit{Disaster Risk}(R) = \frac{\text{Vulnerability}(\text{V}) \times \text{Hazard}(\text{H})}{\textit{Capacity}(C)}$$ [19]

or

$$Disaster\ Risk(R) = \frac{\text{Hazard}(\text{H}) \times \text{Exposure}(\text{E}) \times \text{Vulnerability}(\text{V})}{Coping\,Capacity(C)}$$ [20]

Such nuanced elements focus in particular on the social and sociological implications of such events, as emphasised by scholars who have emblematically and succinctly qualified disasters as 'social events in social time'.[21] However, the translation of such elements into legal terminology remains complex. First, it should be recognised that even within disaster studies the possibility of identifying a common terminology is far from being accepted, as recognised by leading treaties in this area.[22] The never-ending nature of the process of refining this term has been captured by Kroll-Smith and Gunter, according to whom 'the more we know about specific disasters, the more definitions of disaster are registered in the literature'.[23] Second, even if it were accepted that the abovementioned 'shift in focus has obvious implications for law in general and human rights in particular',[24] it must also be recognised that international law practice dealing with the terminology issue appears to have evolved primarily according to its own trend and regardless of the concomitant debate in disaster studies, as can be revealed through an assessment of such practice.

As a result, even if current international legal terminology could be criticised as not being fully capable of fully reflecting the social implications of disasters and the need to address the causes underlying such events, it still represents the primary point of reference for the identification of a workable definition of disaster in this branch of law. For this same reason we will engage in the following paragraph in an empirical assessment of current definitions of disaster as provided by international law instruments, so as to grasp their main elements of reference. However, a plea could be made for a more osmotic approach among areas of research regarding disaster scenarios, as some elements of the current terminological reflections pertaining to disaster studies might also help to provide a broad theoretical picture and better address the same issue under a legal lens, for example regarding the thorny issue of separating natural or man-made disasters in relevant legal definitions.

The definition of 'disaster' in international law practice

As mentioned above, the terminology issue can also be addressed from the perspective of international law, according to solutions endorsed in treaties or soft-law documents. In this context the primary references for terminological analysis are provided by instruments pertaining to the emerging body of law qualified as international disaster law.[25] Although its legal contours are still under debate, this term can be said to include rules and policies aiming to comprehensively address the legal and operational issues pertaining to the cycles of a disaster – commonly distinguished into the phases of mitigation, preparedness, relief and recovery –[26] hence adopting a holistic approach towards the main legal, institutional and policy challenges raised by disasters in its temporal phases.[27]

Of particular relevance to our analysis are instruments in which, thanks to their specific focus, the large majority of general legal definitions of disaster can be found, as we shall explore later. For the purpose of our analysis, within the 'rather scattered and heterogeneous collection of instruments'[28] pertaining to this area of law, other instruments not addressing the terminology issue or having a limited scope of application and thus not contributing to the identification of common trends in this context are of little relevance.

In this latter regard, in fact, it could be underlined that the triggering mechanisms of several treaties and other documents have been tailored to their specific scope of application *ratione materiae*, and consequently a general definition of disaster is lacking in such instruments. These texts do not dwell on an abstract definition of the term but interpret it as a specific kind of event that warrants assistance activities in and of itself. Reference could be made, for instance, to the term 'disease'[29] included in the WHO International Health Regulations, 'oil pollution incident'[30] provided by the 1990 International Convention on Oil Pollution Preparedness, Response and Co-Operation, or 'nuclear accident or radiological emergency' in the 1986 Convention on Assistance in the Case of a Nuclear Accident or Radiological Emergency.[31] Even if related events might eventually lead to a situation of disaster according to the potential general definition emerging in international law, the limited scope of application of these instruments has an impact on the possible use of their constitutive elements to identify criteria for the more comprehensive term of art. Similarly, reference could be made to treaties pertaining to different subject matters but including specific provisions whose application is triggered by the occurrence of a 'disaster'. However, such documents do not provide autonomous definitions of the term, probably under the assumption that it is self-evident, or not wishing to embark on a lengthy law-making process in relation to definitions of less relevance for their purpose. An example of this latter trend may be provided by universal treaties regulating customs, such as Article 1(B) of Annex B.9 to the 1990 Istanbul Convention, intended to facilitate the temporary admission of relief consignments 'to those affected by natural disasters and similar catastrophes', or other treaty clauses making reference to 'natural disasters'[32] or 'disasters or natural calamities'[33] for their application, without however detailing such terms.

Consequently, for the purposes of this contribution, specific attention will be paid to international instruments that expressly include a general definition of disasters, so as to verify recent evaluations according to which '[a] closer examination of the content of several conventions makes it possible to argue that the definitions of the term "disaster", where provided in the treaties, are almost identical or at least do not differ in any significant manner'.[34] In this regard, looking at the genealogy of the legal definition of disaster, the first example may be provided by one of the earliest instruments in this area, namely Article 2(1) IRU Convention. According to this provision, the purpose of the organisation was

> [i]n the event of any disaster due to *force majeure*, the exceptional gravity of which exceeds the limits of the powers and resources of the stricken people, to furnish to the suffering population first aid and to assemble for this purpose funds, resources and assistance of all kinds.[35]

Hence this first general definition of disaster in international law does appear to focus on certain key elements in the debate.

First, the '[*f*]*orce majeure*'s more restrictive "Acts of God" emphasis'[36] provided by the IRU Convention apparently points to the unavoidable and unexpected character of disasters, a trend being reversed by the current mainstream in disaster studies. Second, for an event to be qualified as a disaster for the IRU's purposes it should be able to overwhelm the capacity of affected communities and States. This element is easily associated with the very *raison d'être* of the IRU, intended 'to co-ordinate as occasion offers the efforts made by relief organisations . . . and to induce all peoples to render mutual international assistance'.[37] This emphasis on the involvement of international assistance in tackling a calamitous event may be particularly significant for the application of treaties devoted to this area of cooperation, although it can hardly be prescribed as a requirement for the definition of a disaster, as emphasised by subsequent practice. Finally, it could also be argued that the IRU substantially considered the notion to be self-explanatory, taking into account that the treaty provides only basic indications on the characteristics events should have in order to be qualified as a disaster. While this early definition suffers somewhat the lapse of time since its original drafting, it is nonetheless significant as already able to highlight the difficulties and certain trends in the elaboration of a legal qualification of disaster.

Subsequent attempts at dealing with this definition in relevant international instruments have followed two diverging methodologies, namely: (a) avoidance of the terminology issue, thus addressing relevant problems without providing a definition of the term, or (b) a descriptive approach, aiming to illustrate the distinctive features events should present in order to be qualified as a disaster.

The first trend can be considered a minority one. Only in a few instances do treaties specifically addressing the disaster cycle provide no legal qualification of this term in the text. In this regard mention could be made of the 1991 Inter-American Convention to Facilitate Disaster Assistance[38] and certain bilateral treaties developed in the 1970s and 1980s.[39] It is not unusual in law-making processes to omit a detailed definition of key terms, with the implicit aim of maintaining some flexibility and preventing States from relying on a literal interpretation of the proposed criteria to escape from the application of relevant treaties. Examples are provided by the notions of 'armed conflict' in international humanitarian law or 'outstanding universal value'[40] in the 1972 World Heritage Convention. However, in the area of disaster law such a trend may be due to an opposing rationale. In particular, the fact that the application of such treaties of assistance depends primarily on the concrete willingness of States involved to act in a spirit of cooperation and solidarity has reduced the need to set stringent requirements regarding the exact definition of the treaty's *ratione materiae* scope of application. This element is particularly emphasised by the Inter-American Convention to Facilitate Disaster Assistance where, although a reference to disaster situations is made in the Preamble, its Article 1 devoted to '[a]pplicability' simply states that '[t]his Convention shall apply whenever a state party furnishes assistance in response to a request from another state party, except as they otherwise agree'.

While this radical approach has not been replicated in many contexts, significant room for flexibility has also been provided in treaties that do provide a definition of disaster. In some cases, for instance, even if the relevant document includes criteria to qualify certain events as a disaster, the definition includes clauses intended to potentially enlarge its scope of application according to the interests of parties involved. Reference could be made, for instance, to the 1997 Agreement between Argentina and Chile on cooperation in case of disasters, whose Article 1, apart from describing the characteristics events should have to be qualified as a disaster, also provides that '"[d]isaster" shall mean any event so described by the Party requiring assistance'.[41]

However, as mentioned above, the large majority of international instruments addressing disasters usually include a definition of this term through certain descriptive elements and general criteria. As a result, 'even if "disaster" is not a term of art and, as such, lacks one single accepted definition',[42] especially since the 1970s and 1980s an increasing body of practice has built up in this regard. Such practice comprises certain common elements and qualifiers, permitting the delineation of current converging trends in this area in light of recurring *topos* and cross-fertilisations. Hence, before looking at the recurring issues in practice over the last decades, it may be helpful to draw attention to the definitions of disaster included in the most recent and relevant documents in this area, namely the ILC Draft Articles and the Report on DRR terminology, which already emphasise current elements in the debate and highlight the shift that practice in this area has undergone since the early definition was provided in the 1927 IRU Convention.

According to Draft Article 3(a) of the ILC Draft Articles, '"disaster" means a calamitous event or series of events resulting in widespread loss of life, great human suffering and distress, mass displacement, or large-scale material or environmental damage, thereby seriously disrupting the functioning of society'.[43] Similarly, for the Report on DRR terminology, which has led the UN Office for Disaster Risk Reduction (UNISDR) to update its definition,[44] a disaster is

> [a] serious disruption of the functioning of a community or a society at any scale due to hazardous events interacting with conditions of exposure, vulnerability and capacity, leading to one or more of the following: human, material, economic and environmental losses and impacts.

These texts capture current trends and key converging elements in relation to terminology but nonetheless present some differences, for instance the emphasis in the Report on DRR terminology on elements such as pre-existing vulnerabilities and exposures, thus addressing aspects present in disaster studies but not international law practice. Such definitions obviously do not come out of the blue but are expressions of the significant practice developed over the last decades, permitting identification of the main and recurring complexities related to the terminology issue, as will be explored subsequently. In particular, the current definitions of disaster pivot on two main axes, upon which we can place the most frequently recurring features emphasised by practice, namely: the origin of disasters and the effects of such calamitous events. A series of sub-questions could also be formulated in relation to these features.

Origin of disasters

First, practice tends to categorise disasters according to their origins and causal elements, thus replicating in the normative arena the basic dilemma faced by disaster studies. As underlined above, disaster studies consider it almost impossible to make clear distinctions regarding the nature of disasters, namely to focus only on natural disasters as compared to those of man-made origin. In fact, disasters often result from a complex web of factors in which no single sufficient cause can be identified, especially once natural phenomena merge with human agency in the birth and expansion of calamitous events.

Despite this basic assumption, in some limited cases treaties have expressly restricted their scope of application to natural disasters, as mainly exemplified by Article 1.3 of the 2011 South Asian Association for Regional Cooperation Agreement on Rapid Response to Natural Disasters (SAARC Agreement).[45] Conversely, the very large majority of relevant instruments does not include a qualifier in this regard[46] (probably on the assumption that an explicit reference to causation may be unnecessary) or clearly affirm, through similar expressions,[47] that a disaster might be caused by exposure to 'the operation of the forces of nature or to human intervention'.[48] This approach is also confirmed by the Commentary to Draft Article 3(A) of the 2016 ILC Draft Articles, which emphasises that '[n]o limitation is included concerning the origin of the event, that is whether it is natural or human-made, in recognition of the fact that disasters often arise from complex sets of causes that may include both wholly natural elements and contributions from human activities',[49] according to the position already endorsed by the Special Rapporteur.[50] In a similar manner this approach can be inferred from the reference to 'hazardous events' included in the definition of disaster of the Report on DRR Terminology, as it makes explicit reference to this additional term of art. In fact, according to the Report, '[h]azards may be natural, anthropogenic or socio-natural in origin. Natural hazards are predominantly associated with natural processes and phenomena. Anthropogenic hazards, or human-induced hazards, are induced entirely or predominantly by human activities and choices'.[51]

The first element of this qualification also calls for the analysis of certain related issues. In particular, 'disasters of human-made origin' may apply to several scenarios, as exemplified by scholars seeking to include within this term 'financial,' 'natural' and 'man-made' events (including armed conflicts).[52] However, from our perspective, such a very broad interpretation risks completely undermining a potentially autonomous notion of disaster in international law and does not appear to be supported by international practice.

In particular, several instruments specify that armed conflict does not fit within the legal definition of disaster.[53] This approach has been expressly endorsed by treaties[54] and other relevant documents in this area. An early example is already included in the UN 1984 Draft Convention on Expediting the Delivery of Emergency Assistance[55] and subsequently reiterated by the International Federation of the Red Cross and Red Crescent Societies in their Guidelines for the Domestic Facilitation and Regulation of International Disaster Relief and Initial Recovery Assistance (IDRL Guidelines).[56] Even the ILC has confirmed that '[a] situation of armed conflict cannot be qualified *per se* as a disaster'.[57] Said approach is also shared by the Report on DRR terminology, which maintains, in relation to anthropogenic hazards, that '[t]his term does not include the occurrence or risk of armed conflicts and other situations of social instability or tension which are subject to international humanitarian law and national legislation'.[58] Such express limitations are especially relevant in identifying the contours of an autonomous definition of disaster, as armed conflicts could otherwise easily fulfill any proposed criteria due to their significant impact and negative consequences. The reasons behind this latter approach can clearly be justified by the desire to make a clear distinction from a branch of international law, namely the law of armed conflicts, that is already extensively regulated at the universal level according to its own rationale. Moreover, it reflects the recognition of 'important differences between the context of conflict and peacetime disaster',[59] according to a solution also endorsed by disaster studies.[60]

In a similar vein, with the aim of avoiding definitions which are too broad, the Commentary to Draft Article 3(a) of the ILC Draft Articles maintains that the term 'disaster' does not include 'other serious events, such as political and economic crises, which may also undermine the functioning of society, but which are outside the scope of the draft articles'.[61] Nonetheless, it could also be pointed out that, in certain circumstances, the relatively flexible approach adopted in some definitions has ultimately implied that mechanisms originally envisaged to deal with common scenarios related to disaster situations have effectively been used to address other public emergencies. In this regard the primary example is provided by the activation of the European Union (EU) Civil Protection Mechanism to deal with the recent migrant crisis and the phenomenon of internally displaced persons present in non-EU States in relation to scenarios of armed conflict. Such extensive use of the Mechanism has however met with criticism in the doctrine focusing on the ad hoc nature of this solution, which has responded mainly to internal EU policies rather than to the scope of the Civil Protection Mechanism itself.[62]

Effects of disasters

Second, definitions of disasters usually include references to the effects calamitous events should have in order to be qualified as such. In particular, reference is made to events capable of affecting three broad categories usually expressly specified in current practice, namely: people,[63] property[64] and the environment.[65] In a very limited number of instruments express reference is also made to 'cultural heritage'[66] as a distinctive element potentially suffering from the effects of disasters, with the clear intention of emphasising the relevance of cultural assets, their intangible relationship to human beings and the need to preserve them for future generations from the effects of disasters.[67] Hence events may well trigger a series of consequences, recently included through several broad examples in the ILC definition, such as loss of life, human suffering and distress, mass displacement, or material or environmental damage. This text has systematised similar terminology used in international practice, where reference is made, for instance, to prejudices to the 'health'[68] of humans and 'animals',[69] 'material damage',[70] 'economic losses',[71] 'human . . . losses',[72] 'environmental losses',[73] 'social . . . damage',[74] etc.

Such emphasis on different kinds of effects seeks to comprehensively underline the many significant impacts disasters might have on affected communities, not being limited to direct prejudices against human life but covering the entire 'disaster impact'.[75] For instance, the emphasis on environmental damage – an element that has more recently been routinely included in the definitions of disaster – should be welcomed as a recognition, also in this area, that 'the environment is not an abstraction but represents the living space, the quality of life and the very health of human beings, including generations unborn' according to the position maintained by the International Court of Justice.[76]

In order to avoid over-restrictive definitions, it should be emphasised that relevant provisions consider such criteria as being alternative ones. Therefore it is not necessary to ascertain the occurrence of all the abovementioned effects together, as the existence of one of them is sufficient to fulfill the criterion. Similarly, it can also be emphasised that a transboundary nature of disasters is not considered necessary in this practice. Therefore even if the events in question are of a solely domestic nature they can still be relevant for the definition of a disaster, as reiterated by the Commentary to Draft Article 3(a) of the ILC Draft Articles.[77]

As emphasised above, for a hazard to result in a disaster implies its capacity to impact people, property or the environment. However, in order to avoid classifying any sort of event as a disaster, international practice routinely employs certain qualifications so that only significant matters are contemplated: for instance, effects of hazards must be 'severe',[78] 'widespread',[79] 'significant'[80] or 'serious'.[81] Such elements clearly aim to differentiate between the common difficulties that communities may experience and a proper international legal definition of disaster. In fact, even if this term should be vested with some flexibility due to its mutable nature, the risk of its over-application or indefinite character is quite evident, as emphasised by some very outdated and isolated practice in this area seeking to deal with not only technological and natural disasters but also 'les accidents de la vie quotidienne et de la circulation routière'.[82]

However, it remains complex to effectively establish a threshold for such qualifications and effects of disasters. The difficulties are illustrated, for instance, by Draft Article 3(a) of the ILC Draft Articles, whose reference to events capable of 'seriously disrupting the functioning of society' has expressly been used to cover 'only extreme events'[83] and to fix 'a high threshold',[84] in order to ensure that the occurrence of severe detrimental effects alone, as exemplified in the first part of this same definition,[85] could not be considered sufficient to fulfill this term. This latter reasoning is expressly included in the Commentary, where it is specified that 'the nature of the event is further qualified by the requirement that any, or all, of the four possible outcomes, as applicable, result in the serious disruption of the functioning of society. In other words, an event that resulted in, for example, large-scale material damage, but did not seriously disrupt the functioning of society, would not, accordingly, satisfy the threshold requirement'.[86] However, the Commentary fails to spell out which criteria should be used to ascertain the disruption of a society. Accordingly, some scholars have suggested that this additional element should be deleted in order to avoid establishing too high a threshold,[87] or have underlined that the societal disruption element would not be fit for some types of disasters, such as environmental ones.[88]

Furthermore, it could be pointed out that the sole reference to 'society' in this definition could potentially be misleading. Even if this term is also present in other instruments, such as the Tampere Convention on the Provision of Telecommunication Resources for Disaster Mitigation and Relief Operations (Tampere Convention) or the IDRL Guidelines,[89] other trends are also identifiable. In particular, other treaties include an additional reference to the term 'community' along with 'society',[90] or make reference to more geographically defined notions such as disasters impacting local communities[91] or having a 'spatially limited' character,[92] for example occurring in 'a definite area'.[93] Similarly, several treaties use the terms 'disaster' or 'accidents'[94] in an interchangeable manner, with the implicit consequence of also addressing events with a more limited impact.

Presumably, this latter practice seeks to avoid the potential interpretative difficulties related to the term 'society', a notion not qualified in international instruments and one that might imply the assessment of the detrimental effects of hazards on a very large scale. The Report on DRR terminology, however, adopts a different solution: here the definition of disaster specifies '[a] serious disruption of the functioning of a community or a society at any scale' and the related *Annotations* emphasise that this criteria is satisfied when the events 'test or exceed the capacity of a community or society to cope using its own resources, and therefore may require assistance from external sources, which could include neighbouring jurisdictions, or those at the national or international levels'.[95] In this latter case, therefore, the disruption of a community or society is primarily linked to the presence of events of any scale that overwhelm the response capacity of the entities affected. This concept appears in several treaties, presumably with the aim of underlining the shortcomings among the descriptive criteria otherwise used for the identification of a disaster.[96]

It is clear that increased harmonisation should be favored in future international practice in order to clarify this element, which is largely motivated by different perspectives behind the two instruments: the definition provided by Draft Article 3(a) of the ILC Draft Articles has been accompanied by the usual caveat, according to which Draft Article 3 on the 'use of terms' has been provided '[f]or the purposes of the present draft articles'. As the purpose of the Draft Articles is primarily to regulate cooperation at the international level between the affected State and external assisting actors, usually driven by large-scale disasters, it does not appear unusual that the ILC moved toward a definition intended to identify international provisions with a high threshold in relation to events. Conversely, the Sendai Framework appears to adopt a very comprehensive approach, being intended to 'apply to the risk of small-scale and large-scale, frequent and infrequent, sudden and slow-onset disasters caused by natural or man-made hazards'.[97] From our perspective, and in the light of relevant practice, a broader definition should be favored in the identification of 'disaster' as a legal term of art, at least making reference to community along with society, in order to ensure that the interpretative challenges related to the societal disruption element do not result in an excessively limitative notion.

The abovementioned detrimental effects can be recorded and evaluated according to different time scales, and in this regard reference is usually made to notions such as sudden-onset (such as volcanic eruptions) or slow-onset emergencies (such as drought). Recognition of the different temporal context of disasters has progressively been encapsulated in legal definitions addressing this term. For instance, a very limited number of international treaties expressly limit their field of application to sudden-onset disasters, as was the case in the original version of the 1991 Treaty establishing the Caribbean Disaster Emergency Response Agency, which specified situations involving '[a] sudden event'.[98] However, this limitation has been deleted from the new 1998 treaty regulating this entity[99] and the majority of international instruments do not include this qualification. Conversely, certain relevant instruments now expressly include slow-onset disasters in their scope of application, such as the Tampere Convention[100] and the IDRL Guidelines.[101]

This position has recently been shared by the ILC in its Commentary to Draft Article 3(a), according to which 'the draft articles apply equally to sudden-onset events (such as an earthquake or tsunami) and to slow-onset events (such as drought or sea-level rise), as well as frequent small-scale events (floods or landslides)',[102] hence expanding the definition to a series of events 'that, on their own, might not meet the necessary threshold, but that, taken together would constitute a calamitous event for the purposes of the draft articles'.[103] In a similar vein the *Annotations* to the definition of disaster in the Report on DRR terminology make reference to both categories of disasters. While a slow-onset disaster is 'one that emerges gradually over time. Slow-onset disasters could be associated with, e.g. drought, desertification, sea-level rise, epidemic disease', a sudden-onset disaster is 'one triggered by a hazardous event that emerges quickly or unexpectedly. Sudden-onset disasters could be associated with, e.g. earthquake, volcanic eruption, flash flood, chemical explosion, critical infrastructure failure, transport accident'.[104]

Finally, it should also be emphasised that various definitions do not limit this notion to the effective occurrence of negative consequences. Indeed, several international instruments emphasise that this definition could be satisfied, in legal terms, even before the occurrence of the disaster scenarios hypothesised, mainly in order to permit the timely activation of relevant assistance treaties and reduce the negative consequences foreseen. In several treaties[105] a disaster is considered as such in the presence of an event which 'threatens'[106] or 'may cause'[107] the abovementioned detrimental effects, a position shared by Article 1(C) of the 2000 Framework Convention on Civil Protection Assistance, which requires only the threat of loss in order to identify a disaster,[108] by Decision 1313/2013/EU,[109] and by other treaties.[110] It appears clear, especially in relation to treaties on assistance, that the prompt activation of cooperation among States and other assisting actors may help to reduce potential detrimental effects. Similarly, the relevance of protection issues linked with human rights standards can hardly be limited to actual victims of disasters without paying attention to potential ones. However, this element has not been expressly included in the definition or the Commentary to Draft Article 3(a),[111] in line with the original proposal of the ILC Special Rapporteur.[112]

Conclusions

This taxonomy of the definitions of disaster provided by international law instruments allows us to identify several elements that converge toward the identification of this term of art, relating in particular to the origins of disasters, the effects such events might have and relevant limitations. As a result, even if certain criteria have yet to be properly addressed by practice, the legal boundaries of this notion are increasingly well defined.

As mentioned above, the protection of human rights in disaster scenarios obviously represents one of the key legal paradigms to be taken into account. Indeed, the same terminology issue may be of some relevance in this context, as will be explored in the following chapters.

First, the definition of the term 'disaster', according to international law practice, helps to clarify which events and related legal issues fall outside the parameters of this notion. A particular mention could be made of armed conflicts, which *per se* do not represent a disaster, according to relevant documents such as the ILC Draft Articles and the Report on DRR Terminology, as well as other practice. Also for the purpose of the present volume, armed conflicts have been excluded from any specific analysis, unless relevant international humanitarian law provisions might provide insights to help solve certain challenges, for example in the case of disasters occurring in complex emergencies, namely within a State already affected by an armed conflict.[113]

Second, defining the term 'disaster' can permit the identification of specific exigencies related to the protection and respect of human rights which arise in such particular scenarios. As rightly underlined by Kälin, '[h]uman rights are never more important for people than in times of particular need and vulnerability, and they therefore have an important role to play in times of disasters'.[114] The provision of this latter definition with clear contents could therefore help States, international organisations and non-state actors to better clarify the specific content of obligations inherent in general human rights guarantees as applied in disaster contexts. This perspective is endorsed by the ILC Special Rapporteur Valencia-Ospina, according to whom '[s]uch a definition will help identify the situations in which protection may or shall be invoked'[115] and clarify who needs protection in such specific circumstances. In particular, the context-based character of some challenges to the application of human rights obligations in the case of disasters implies that clarification of this definition might contribute to the better identification of situations where additional or specifically tailored measures could be requested as compared to common scenarios, as explored by the authors of this volume.[116] Even the integration of the rights-based approach into the disaster management perspective, as championed by some actors,[117] can obviously benefit from the identification of situations in which suggested actions and legal and operative paradigms should be considered relevant.

Furthermore, this link between the terminology issue and substantive human rights provisions could also be explored in relation to certain specific elements. For instance, while we have seen that the origin of a disaster, i.e. human-made or natural, is no longer appropriate for terminology purposes, as both typologies are commonly covered by relevant instruments, it could easily be shown that this distinction still has an impact in terms of the substantive human rights obligations States are expected to fulfill. Examples could be provided, for instance, in relation to different standards that States are requested to comply with, under a due diligence paradigm, in relation to the prevention of natural or anthropic disasters.[118] Conversely, on the basis of the abovementioned terminological analysis, criticisms could be made regarding the restricted scope of application of instruments specifically intended to address challenges to the protection of human rights solely in case of natural disasters, such as the Operational Guidelines on Human Rights and Natural Disasters drawn up by the Inter-Agency Standing Committee.[119] As discussed above, especially on the basis of analysis carried out within the framework of disaster studies and confirmed by relevant practice, such a distinction is hardly tenable, as similar challenges to human rights protection might also be expected to occur in the event of human-made disasters. Finally, terminology issues might also impact limitations and derogations to human rights treaties. In fact, especially in relation to events capable of fulfilling the high threshold criteria provided by Draft Article 3(a) of the ILC Draft Articles, States may be able to consider such disasters as situations representing public emergencies and hence demand extraordinary measures, as shall be explored subsequently.[120]

As a result, the possibility of qualifying an event as a disaster might have the added value of underlining the specific and multifaceted peculiarities that such situations can imply and therefore properly guarantee positive and negative human rights obligations. Even if human rights law is naturally not dependent, from the point of view of its relevance, upon the existence of a disaster, identifying the proper content of the latter term could nonetheless help to better frame the guarantees protecting fundamental values within this specific context.

Selected bibliography

G. Bartolini, 'Il progetto di articoli della Commissione del diritto internazionale sulla "Protection of Persons in the Event of Disasters"', *100 Rivista di diritto internazionale* (2017) 677 ff.

A. de Guttry, 'Surveying the Law' in de Guttry, Gestri and Venturini (eds), *International Disaster Response Law* (Springer, 2012), 3 ff.

IFRC, *Law and Legal Issues in International Disaster Response: A Desk Study* (IFRC, 2007).

R.W. Perry and E.L. Quarantelli (eds), *What Is a Disaster? New Answers to Old Questions* (International Research Committee on Disasters, 2005).

J.-M. Thouvenin, 'La définition de la catastrophe par la CDI: vers une catastrophe juridique?' in P. Sanjuán and J.-M. Thouvenin (eds), *International Law and Disasters* (Ibanez, 2011) 41 ff.

Notes

1 ILC, Report of the International Law Commission, Sixty-Eighth Session, UN Doc. A/71/10 (2016) (ILC Report 2016) (2 May–10 June and 4 July–12 August 2016) 12.
2 ILC, Preliminary Report on the Protection of Persons in the Event of Disasters by Mr. Eduardo Valencia-Ospina, UN Doc. A/CN.4/598 (5 May 2008) 152, para 46.
3 For similar problems see for instance: M. Di Filippo, 'The Definition(s) of Terrorism in International Law' in B. Saul (ed), *Research Handbook on International Law and Terrorism* (Edward Elgar Publishing, 2014) 105; A. Gilles, *La definition de l'investissement international* (Larcier, 2012); C. Dugard, 'The Problem of the Definition of Terrorism in International Law' in P. Eden and T. O'Donnel (eds), *September 11, 2001: A Turning Point in International and Domestic Law?* (Transnational Publishers, 2005) 187; V. Grammatikas, 'The Definition of Minorities in International Law: A Problem Still Looking for a Solution' 52 *Revue Hellénique de droit International* (1999) 321.
4 ILC, Second Report on the Protection of Persons in the Event of Disasters by Mr. Eduardo Valencia-Ospina, Special Rapporteur, UN Doc. A/CN.4/615 (7 May 2009) 193 (ILC Second Report) para 31.
5 Regarding this term and its use in classification exercises in international law see, of course, M. Milanovic and V. Hadzi-Vidanovic, 'A Taxonomy of Armed Conflict' in N.D. White and C. Henderson (eds), *Research Handbook on International Conflict and Security Law: Jus ad bellum, jus in bello, and jus post bellum* (Edward Elgar Publishing, 2013) 256.
6 UNGA, Report of the Open-Ended Intergovernmental Expert Working Group on Indicators and Terminology Relating to Disaster Risk Reduction, UN Doc. A/71/644 (1 December 2016) (Report on DRR terminology); for the relevant UNGA Resolution see UNGA, Res 71/276, UN Doc. A/RES/71/276 (13 February 2017) where, at its para 2, this body '[e]*ndorses* the recommendations contained in sections IV and V of the report', namely the recommendations on global indicators and terminology proposed by the working group.
7 D. Alexander, 'An Interpretation of Disaster in Terms of Changes in Culture, Society and International Relations' in R.W. Perry and E.L. Quarantelli (eds), *What Is a Disaster? New Answers to Old Questions* (International Research Committee on Disasters, 2005) 25, 27.
8 L.G. Sun, 'Climate Change and the Narrative of Disaster' in J. Peel and D. Fisher (eds), *The Role of International Environmental Law in Disaster Risk Reduction* (Brill, 2016) 27, 47–48.
9 See, for instance, A. Wijkman and L. Timberlake, *Natural Disasters: Acts of God or Acts of Man?* (Earthscan, 1984).
10 See, however, the early evaluation made by P. Macalister-Smith, *International Guidelines on Humanitarian Assistance* (Max Planck Institute for Comparative Public Law and International Law, 1991) 21 who maintains that previous attempts to define this term in international law resulted in short-lived and inadequate results.
11 K.C. Lauta, 'Human Rights and "Natural" Disasters' in S.C. Breau and K. Samuel (eds), *Research Handbook on Disasters and International Law* (Edward Elgar Publishing, 2016) 93.
12 C. Hartman and G.D. Squires (eds), *There Is No Such Thing as a Natural Disaster: Race, Class, and Hurricane Katrina* (Routledge, 2006).
13 D. Cubie, *The International Legal Protection of Persons in Humanitarian Crises Exploring the Acquis Humanitaire* (Hart, 2017) 245.
14 Sun (n. 8) 30.
15 B.L. Brown, 'Disasters Myth or Reality: Developing a Criminology of Disasters' in M. Deflem (ed), *Disasters, Hazards and Law* (Emerald, 2012) 3, 5.
16 A. Oliver-Smith, I. Alcántara-Ayala, I. Burton and A. Lavell, 'The Social Construction of Disaster Risk: Seeking Root Causes' 22 *International Journal of Disaster Risk Reduction* (2017) 469.
17 According to the Report on DRR terminology, 18, a hazard is '[a] process, phenomenon or human activity that may cause loss of life, injury or other health impacts, property damage, social and economic disruption or environmental degradation'. As for hazardous events, see ibid 20.
18 Sun (n. 8) 31.
19 USAID, 'Introduction to Disaster Risk Reduction' (2011) 15, available at www.preventionweb.net/files/26081_kp1concepdisasterrisk1.pdf, accessed on 7 July 2017.
20 B. Field et al. (eds), *Managing the Risks of Extreme Events and Disasters to Advance Climate Change Adaptation: Special Report of the Intergovernmental Panel on Climate Change* (Cambridge University Press, 2012) 69.
21 R.W. Perry, 'Disasters, Definitions and Theory Construction' in Perry and Quarantelli (eds) (n. 7) 311, 313.
22 E.L. Quarantelli (ed), *What Is a Disaster?* (Routledge, 1998); Perry and Quarantelli (eds) (n. 7).

23 S. Kroll-Smith and V.J. Gunter, 'Legislators, Interpreters and Disasters: The Importance of How as Well as What Is a Disaster' in Quarantelli (ed) (n. 22) 160–176.

24 Lauta (n. 11) 94. More extensively K.C. Lauta, *Disaster Law* (Routledge, 2014) 76 ff.

25 There is a growing body of literature on this topic, for instance: A. de Guttry, M. Gestri and G. Venturini (eds), *International Disaster Response Law* (Springer, 2012); D. Caron, M.J. Kelly and A. Telesetsky (eds), *The International Law of Disaster Relief* (Cambridge University Press, 2014); Breau and Samuel (eds) (n. 11).

26 Such terms are usually used by practitioners and researchers to identify the cyclical processes and patterns that disaster events follow. However, there is no agreement on the exact content of the different components. According to M. Nthakomwa, 'Cycles of a Disaster' in K.B. Penuel and M. Statler, *Encyclopedia of Disaster Relief* (Sage, 2011) 96–98: the mitigation phase pertains to activities intended to minimise or prevent the occurrence of non-imminent disaster; preparedness concerns actions carried out to minimise the impact of impeding disasters, usually on the basis of procedures developed during the mitigation phase; response deals with the actions immediately following a disaster; and recovery starts once the emergency is under control. Conversely, according to D.A. Farber, J. Chen, R. Verchick and L. Sun, *Disaster Law and Policy* (2nd edn, Aspen, 2009) 3, the disaster cycle consists of mitigation, emergency response, compensation and rebuilding, with the latter completing the circle by including (or failing to include) mitigation measures.

27 The need to comprehensively address legal issues pertaining to the disaster cycle has also been underlined by the ILC, according to which

> the scope of the draft articles *ratione temporis* is primarily focused on the immediate post-disaster response and early recovery phase, including the post-disaster reconstruction phase. Nonetheless . . . the pre-disaster phase falls within the scope of the draft articles, and is the subject of draft article 9, which deals with disaster risk reduction and disaster prevention and mitigation activities.

See ILC Report 2016 (n. 1) 19, para 4.

28 D. Fisher, 'Domestic Regulation of International Humanitarian Relief in Disasters and Armed Conflict: A Comparative Analysis' 866 *IRRC* (2007) 347, 353.

29 According to art 1 of the WHO Health Regulations '"disease" means an illness or medical condition, irrespective of origin or source, that presents or could present significant harm to humans'.

30 International Convention on Oil Pollution Preparedness, Response and Cooperation (adopted 30 November 1990, entered into force 13 May 1995) 1891 UNTS 78, art 2.2,

> 'Oil pollution incident' means an occurrence or series of occurrences having the same origin, which results or may result in a discharge of oil and which poses or may pose a threat to the marine environment, or to the coastline or related interests of one or more States, and which requires emergency action or other immediate response.

31 Convention on Assistance in the Case of a Nuclear Accident or Radiological Emergency (adopted 26 September 1986, entered into force 26 February 1987) 1457 UNTS 134.

32 See, along similar lines, the Annex to the Convention on Facilitation of International Maritime Traffic (adopted 9 April 1965, entered into force 5 March 1967) 591 UNTS 265, arts 5.11 and 5.12 according to which public authorities must facilitate the arrival and departure of vessels engaged in natural disaster relief work and to the greatest extent possible facilitate the entry and clearance of persons and cargo arriving in such vessels.

33 See Convention for the Protection of the World Cultural and Natural Heritage (adopted 16 November 1972, entered into force 17 December 1975) 1037 UNTS 152, art 21, according to which the World Heritage Committee is requested to provide priority consideration for international assistance to be arranged for the benefit of cultural heritage in such cases.

34 A. de Guttry, 'Surveying the Law' in de Guttry, Gestri and Venturini (eds) (n. 25) 6.

35 Convention Establishing an International Relief Union (IRU) (adopted 12 July 1927, entered into force 27 December 1932) 135 League of Nations Treaty Series 247 ff. As for the IRU see P. Macalister-Smith, 'The International Relief Union: Reflections on Establishing an International Relief Union of July 12, 1927' 54 *Legal History Review* (1986) 368–372; J. Hutchinson, 'Disasters and the International Order – II: The International Relief Union' 23 *International History Review* (2001) 253.

36 K.N. Bookmiller, 'Closing "the Yawning Gap"? International Disaster Response Law at Fifteen' in Breau and Samuel (eds) (n. 11) 50.

37 See art 2.2.

38 Inter-American Convention to Facilitate Disaster Assistance (adopted 7 June 1991, entered into force 16 October 1996) A-54 OAS.

39 See, in this regard: Convention on Mutual Assistance in the Event of Disasters or Serious Accidents (Federal Republic of Germany and Luxembourg, adopted 2 March 1978, entered into force 1 December 1981) 1320 UNTS 123; Convention on Mutual Assistance in the Event of Disasters or Serious Accidents (Federal Republic of Germany and Switzerland, adopted 28 November 1984, entered into force 1 December 1988) 1554 UNTS 155; Convention between the Kingdom of the Netherlands and the Kingdom of Belgium on Mutual Assistance in Combating Disasters and Accidents (adopted 14 November 1984, entered into force 1 November 1988) 1526 UNTS 42; Agreement on Cooperation on Disaster Preparedness and Prevention, and Mutual Assistance in the Event of Disasters (Argentina and Spain, adopted 3 June 1988, entered into force 1 September 1992) 1689 UNTS 23.
40 C. Forrest, *International Law and the Protection of Cultural Heritage* (Routledge, 2010) 232–233.
41 Agreement between the Argentine Republic and the Republic of Chile on Cooperation in Case of Disasters (adopted 8 August 1997) art 1.
42 ILC Second Report (n. 4) 193 para 31.
43 ILC Report 21, where the relevant Commentary is also present.
44 For the past version of the notion of disaster see UNISDR, *Terminology on Disaster Risk Reduction* (Geneva, 2009) 9: '[a] serious disruption of the functioning of a community or a society involving widespread human, material, economic or environmental losses and impacts, which exceeds the ability of the affected community or society to cope using its own resources', available at www.unisdr.org/files/7817_UNISDR TerminologyEnglish.pdf, accessed on 7 July 2017.
45 SAARC Agreement on Rapid Response to Natural Disasters (adopted 11 November 2011) art 1.3, makes reference to 'a natural hazard event'.
46 See, for instance, ASEAN Agreement on Disaster Management and Emergency Response (adopted 26 July 2005, entered into force 24 December 2009) art 1.3 (ASEAN Agreement).
47 Regarding this approach see, for instance: Agreement between the Republic of Austria and the Republic of Albania on Mutual Assistance in the Case of Disasters or Serious Accidents (adopted 27 January 2010, entered into force 1 July 2011) 2771 UNTS 307 art 2; Agreement establishing the Caribbean Disaster Emergency Management Agency (adopted 1 July 2008, provisional application 4 July 2008) art 1 (CDEMA Agreement); IFRC, Guidelines for the Domestic Facilitation and Regulation of International Disaster Relief and Initial Recovery Assistance (IFRC, 2007) art 2.1 (IDRL Guidelines); Agreement between the Government of the Republic of Lithuania and the Government of the Republic of Belarus on Cooperation in the Field of Prevention and Elimination of Consequences of Catastrophes, Natural Disasters and Serious Accidents (adopted 16 December 2003, entered into force 27 July 2004) 2339 UNTS 203, art 1.3; Institute of International Law, Sixteenth Commission: Humanitarian Assistance. Resolution (Bruges session, 2 September 2003) art I (Resolution on Humanitarian Assistance); Agreement on the Establishment of the Civil-Military Emergency Planning Council for Southeastern Europe (adopted 3 April 2001) art II; Tampere Convention on the Provision of Telecommunication Resources for Disaster Mitigation and Relief Operations (adopted 18 June 1998, entered into force 8 January 2005) 2296 UNTS 5, art 1.6 (Tampere Convention).
48 See CDEMA Agreement, art 1, according to which "'disaster' means the exposure of the human habitat to the operation of the forces of nature or to human intervention resulting in widespread destruction of lives or property, but excludes events occasioned by war or military confrontation'.
49 ILC Report 2016 (n. 1) 23, para 4.
50 ILC Second Report (n. 4) 194, para 37.
51 Report on DRR Terminology 18.
52 S.C. Breau and K.L.H. Samuel, 'Introduction' in S.C. Breau and K.L.H. Samuel (eds), Research Handbook on Disasters and International Law (Edward Elgar Publishing, 2016) 3.
53 However, see the Resolution on Humanitarian Assistance art I, intended to extend the scope of application of this document to calamitous events whether of natural origin, man-made disasters or caused by armed conflicts or violence.
54 See: CDEMA Agreement, art 1 according to which a disaster 'excludes events occasioned by war or military confrontation'; Accord entre le Gouvernement de la République française et le Gouvernement de la Malaisie sur la coopération dans le domaine de la prévention et de la gestion des catastrophes, et de la sécurité civile (adopted 25 May 1998) art 1.a, which qualifies as a disaster 'un événement autre que la guerre', available at www.ifrc.org/Docs/idrl/I392FR.pdf, accessed on 7 July 2017.
55 UNGA, Draft Convention on Expediting the Delivery of Emergency Assistance, UN Doc. A/39/267/Add.2-E/1984/96/Add.2 (1984) art 1.b, where the definition excluded 'an ongoing situation of armed conflict'.

56 IDRL Guidelines art 2.1, according to which the definition is aimed at 'excluding armed conflict'.
57 ILC Report 2016 (n. 1) 24, para 10.
58 Report on DRR Terminology 18.
59 IFRC, *Law and Legal Issues in International Disaster Response: A Desk Study* (IFRC, 2007) 24.
60 This approach has also been criticised in the area of disaster studies. For instance Sun (n. 8) 47, maintains

> [b]lurring the traditional lines between natural and technological disasters by recognizing that they exist along a continuum of human contribution might also open the door to grouping natural disasters, not just with technological disasters like toxic releases and industrial accidents, but with the intentional man-made crises such as terrorism and war. This blurring of the boundaries between disasters, terrorism, and war might prove problematic for a number of reasons.

61 ILC Report 2016 (n. 1) 22, para 2.
62 F. Casolari, 'La dimensione esterna dell'azione dell'Unione europea nella risposta a disastri naturali ed antropici: quale coerenza?' in M. Gestri (ed), *Disastri, protezione civile e diritto* (Giuffrè, 2016) 98–99.
63 With similar references made to situations affecting 'people', 'life', etc. see for example: Decision No. 1313/2013/EU of the European Parliament and of the Council on a Union Civil Protection Mechanism (Decision No. 1313/2013/EU) art 4.1; CDEMA Agreement, art. 1; Agreement between the Government of the Republic of Lithuania and the Government of the Republic of Belarus, art 1.3; Framework Convention on Civil Defence Assistance (Framework Convention) (adopted 22 May 2000, entered into force 23 September 2001) 2172 UNTS 213, art 1.c.; Tampere Convention, art 1.6.
64 See for instance: Decision No. 1313/2013/EU, art 4.1; Agreement between the Republic of Austria and the Republic of Albania, art 2; CDEMA Agreement, art 1; IDRL Guidelines, art 2.1; Agreement between the Government of the Republic of Lithuania and the Government of the Republic of Belarus, art 1.3; Tampere Convention, art 1.6.
65 Ibid.
66 See in particular: Decision No. 1313/2013/EU, art 4.1; Council Decision of 24 June 2014 2014/415/UE on the arrangements for the implementation by the Union of the solidarity clause, OJ L 192/53 (2014) art 3; Agreement among the Governments of the Participating States of the Black Sea Economic Cooperation (BSEC) on Collaboration in Emergency Assistance and Emergency Response to Natural and Man-Made Disasters (adopted 15 April 1998, entered into force 11 March 2003) art 2 (BSEC Agreement).
67 Concerning the relevance of these elements in the definition of cultural heritage see A.A. Yusuf, 'Article 1. Definition of Cultural Heritage' in F. Francioni (ed), *The 1972 World Heritage Convention: A Commentary* (Oxford University Press, 2008) 23, 27. See, similarly, Forrest (n. 40) 25–26.
68 See for instance: IDRL Guidelines, art 2.1; Agreement between the Government of the Republic of Lithuania and the Government of the Republic of Belarus, art 1.3; Tampere Convention, art 1.6.
69 Agreement between the Republic of Austria and the Republic of Albania, art 2.
70 See, for similar expressions making reference to economic or material losses: ASEAN Agreement, art 1.3.
71 See: SAARC Agreement, art 1.3; Agreement between the Republic of Austria and the Republic of Albania, art 2; ASEAN Agreement, art 1.3.
72 See, for instance, SAARC Agreement, art 1.3.
73 Regarding losses to the environment see, for instance: Decision No. 1313/2013/EU, art 4.1; SAARC Agreement, art 3; IDRL Guidelines, art 2; Agreement between the Republic of Austria and the Republic of Albania, art 2; Agreement between the Government of the Republic of Lithuania and the Government of the Republic of Belarus, art 1.3; Framework Convention, art 1.c; Tampere Convention, art 1.6; BSEC Agreement, art 2.
74 BSEC Agreement, art 2.
75 Regarding this term see the Report on DRR terminology, 13, where '[t]he term includes economic, human and environmental impacts, and may include death, injuries, disease and other negative effects on human physical, mental and social well-being'.
76 *Legality of the Threat or Use of Nuclear Weapons (Advisory Opinion)* [1996] ICJ Rep. (I) 257, 241, para 29.
77 ILC Report 2016 (n. 1) 19, para 5.
78 Decision No. 1313/2013/EU, art 4.1.
79 See: SAARC Agreement, art 1.3; CDEMA Agreement, art 1; ASEAN Agreement, art 1.3; IDRL Guidelines, art 2.1; Tampere Convention, art 1.6.
80 BSEC Agreement, art 2; Agreement between the Republic of Austria and the Republic of Albania, art 2.
81 Agreement between Argentina and Chile, art 1.

82 See Accord de coopération entre le Gouvernement de la République française et le gouvernement du Royaume de Maroc en matière de protection et de sécurité civiles (adopted 21 April 1981, entered into force 21 April 1981) 1264 UNTS 453, art 1.
83 ILC Report 2016 (n. 1) 22, para 4.
84 Ibid 24, para 10.
85 Such effects are 'widespread loss of life, great human suffering and distress, mass displacement, or large-scale material or environmental damage'.
86 ILC Report 2016 (n. 1) 23, para 5.
87 J.-M. Thouvenin, 'La définition de la catastrophe par la CDI: vers une catastrophe juridique?' in P. Sanjuán and J.-M. Thouvenin (eds), *International Law and Disasters* (Ibanez, 2011) 41, 46–49.
88 T. Stephens, 'Disasters, International Environmental Law and the Antrophocene' in Breau and Samuel (eds) (n. 11) 155, who criticises the ILC definition as, under international environmental law, calamities can involve damage to the environment per se and need not involve societal disruption (i.e. 'pure environmental harm').
89 IDRL Guidelines, art 2.1.
90 See: ASEAN Agreement, art 1.3, making reference to '[a] serious disruption of the functioning of a community or a society'; SAARC Agreement, art 1.3.
91 See art 1(a) of the 1998 Accord entre le Gouvernement de la République française et le Gouvernement de la Malaisie making reference to events which have a negative impact on the activities of 'collectivités locales'.
92 Agreement between the Republic of Austria and the Republic of Albania, art 2.
93 See BSEC Agreement, art 2.
94 As for this term see, for instance: Agreement between the Republic of Austria and the Republic of Albania, art 2; Agreement between the Republic of Austria and the Republic of Croatia on Mutual Assistance in the Event of Disasters or Serious Accidents (adopted 17 September 2004, entered into force 1 August 2006) 2486 UNTS 277, art 2; Agreement between the Government of the Republic of Lithuania and the Government of the Republic of Belarus, art 1.3.
95 Report on DRR Terminology 13.
96 See, for instance, SAARC Agreement, art 1.3, which makes reference to a situation 'which exceeds the ability of the affected community or society to cope using its own resources'. For similar criteria: Agreement between the Republic of Austria and the Republic of Albania, art 2.
97 Sendai Framework, para 15.
98 CDEMA Agreement, art 1.d.
99 Ibid art 1.
100 Tampere Convention, art 1.6 makes reference to events 'developing suddenly or as the result of complex, long-term processes'.
101 See IDRL Guidelines, art 2.1.
102 ILC Report 2016 (n. 1) 23, para 4.
103 Ibid.
104 Report on DRR Terminology 13.
105 Regarding this approach see, for instance, Agreement between the Government of the Republic of Lithuania and the Government of the Republic of Belarus, art 1.3.
106 Agreement between the Government of the Republic of Latvia and the Cabinet of Ministers of Ukraine on the Co-Operation in the Field of Prevention of Disasters and Elimination of Their Consequences (adopted 27 April 2006, entered into force 8 August 2008) 2619 UNTS 95.
107 Agreement between the Government of the Hellenic Republic and the Government of the Russian Federation on Co-Operation in the Field of Prevention and Response to Natural and Man-Made Disasters (adopted 21 February 2000, entered into force 19 June 2002) art 1.
108 Framework Convention, art 1(c), according to which a disaster is 'an exceptional situation in which life, property or the environment may be at risk'.
109 Decision 1313/2013/EU, art 4.1.
110 See: Tampere Convention, art 1.6; Agreement between the Republic of Austria and the Republic of Albania, art 2; Agreement between the Republic of Austria and the Republic of Croatia, art 2; BSEC Agreement, art 2; Agreement between Argentina and Chile, art 1.1.
111 For a criticism see Thouvenin (n. 87) 49–50.
112 ILC Second Report (n. 4) 195, para 47, where 'the Special Rapporteur underscores that some actual loss is required, as opposed to the mere threat of harm'.
113 See Williams and Simm's chapter in this volume.

114 W. Kälin, 'The Human Rights Dimension of Natural or Human-Made Disasters' 55 *GYIL* (2012) 119, 147.
115 ILC Second Report (n. 4) 193, para 31.
116 See the chapters by Hesselman, McDermott, Rolnik, Casolari, Adinolfi, Riccardi, Giacca, Polymenopoulou, Nifosi, Guadagno and Sironi in this volume.
117 See Creta's chapter in this volume.
118 See Sossai's chapter in this volume.
119 IASC, *Human Rights and Natural Disasters: Operational Guidelines and Field Manual on Human Rights Protection in Situations of Natural Disasters* (Brookings-Bern Project on Internal Displacement, 2008).
120 See Sommario's chapter in this volume.

3

R.I.P. R2P

On the controversial 'responsibility to protect' doctrine and why it adds no value to disasters

Karen da Costa[*]

Introduction

The assumption upon which the doctrine discussed in this chapter builds is that it is not morally acceptable for human beings and the international community to be aware of existing atrocities in the world, but not to take effective action to prevent or halt them, due to political differences blocking existing international mechanisms. The question is how to develop an alternative route to effectively bypass such blockages.

The 'responsibility to protect' (R2P) concept was meant to address this difficulty. It should allow the international community to act once confronted with ongoing atrocities despite eventual blockages in the United Nations (UN) system (especially veto by the UN Security Council permanent members against actions aimed at stopping atrocities).[1]

R2P links sovereignty to responsibility, making it clear that States have the *primary* responsibility to protect their own populations. However, when States are either unable or unwilling to protect their population from mass atrocities (identified as war crimes, crimes against humanity, ethnic cleansing, and genocide), this will give the *residual authorisation* for the international community to act to protect the lives at risk (secondary responsibility). Action under this framework is believed to enable the international community to halt widespread violence. Thus, arguably, this concept was meant to address the moral call of the international community. However, things are not as smooth as they may sound, and much debate entangles the R2P concept, as discussed later on.

Beyond analysing R2P, this chapter considers whether and how this doctrine may be used in disasters. The cyclone that hit Myanmar in 2008 is the closest example on the use of R2P in disasters, as illustrated later on. The question, however, is also worthy of being considered more generally in relation to further disasters. *Disaster* in this paper is understood as 'a calamitous event or series of events resulting in widespread loss of life, great human suffering and distress, mass displacement, or large-scale material or environmental damage, thereby seriously disrupting the functioning of society'.[2] The focus of the current chapter is on disasters linked to natural hazards (e.g. hurricanes, cyclones, earthquakes, tsunamis). Sometimes they are referred to as 'natural disasters', despite the fact that no disaster is fully natural, and even those relating to natural hazards combine human action or inaction (e.g. lack of action to adopt and implement building codes that should improve the earthquake resistance of buildings). Bearing in mind this terminological caveat, the chapter will also use the term 'natural disaster' as shorthand, and it will not cover purely 'human-made' disasters, especially situations of armed conflict.[3]

The chapter is organised as follows: the second section outlines the responsibility to protect doctrine; the third section considers the possibility of applying it in disasters; and the fourth section considers alternatives to the application of R2P in disasters.

The rise and fall of a concept

Who came up with the R2P idea and why? The North-South debate and the experiences of Rwanda and the Balkans

R2P is rooted in the idea of 'sovereignty as responsibility', a contribution of former Sudanese diplomat (later nominated as the UN Secretary-General's Special Representative on Internally Displaced Persons) Francis Deng and colleagues, when they addressed conflicts in Africa in the mid-1990s.[4] These ideas were later included in regional instruments, such as the African Union (AU) Constitutive Act of 2000, which mentions the AU's obligation to intervene in 'grave circumstances', together with a pledge of 'non-*indifference*' to the internal affairs of States. The same document also referred to three of the four R2P-triggering crimes (discussed later), apart from ethnic cleansing.[5] These ideas suggest that there is an international collective need to care for and assist people in danger, despite national borders.

On the other hand, by effectively discharging their obligations of good governance, including the observance of fundamental rights, national governments would demonstrate they were meeting their sovereignty-related responsibilities. Mass atrocities taking place in a given country would thus suggest a State's failure towards its population, leading to potential international community action to protect rights of the affected population.

Administrations in the Global North, the United States (US) (Clinton and Bush) and the United Kingdom (UK) (Blair), among others, have supported similar initial considerations but indicated that the concept should go further, also encompassing security concerns besides the need for global respect for human rights. Cooperation to halt terrorism and the non-proliferation of weapons of mass destruction were matters of concern for them.[6] The argument continued on the basis of the interdependency of the globalised world, in which egregious human rights violations or security threats in one country may jeopardise the stability and security of other countries. In such scenarios, the principle of non-interference in internal affairs was to be qualified, for genocide, for example, and could not be ignored as a purely internal matter.

Especially after the 2003 US/UK-led Iraq invasion, developing countries became very anxious with R2P and its possible future abuse in military interventions.[7]

This comes as no real surprise, for Global South countries are traditionally quite anxious about the prospect of being at the receiving end of ideas resembling military intervention. However, some authors, such as Luck, argue that it makes little sense to perceive R2P as a North-South divide and thus try to downplay the issue and how it affects the R2P idea.[8] He rather encourages Southern countries to participate in the conceptualisation and, notably, in the identification of the limits of the notion, so as to make sure the doctrine will not be abused later on.[9] This might be a realist (though somewhat unfortunate) take on the development of the concept, which does not question the limited possibilities of different States. Another aspect to bear in mind (later discussed) is that R2P is not limited to coercive military action but also includes milder measures.

In any event, being R2P grounded in the South or in the North, two shocking events are commonly linked to the further development of the concept: one that took place in the South (Rwanda) and one in the North (the Balkans).

In both situations the response of the international community was far from ideal. In Rwanda, in 1994, the international community was still healing its wounds from the then recent intervention in Somalia, which ended up with casualties among American troops and with local militias putting the bodies of US soldiers on display as trophies. The result was a very weak international action in Rwanda, which did not manage to effectively stop the genocide that took place over the course of one hundred days and ended up with the slaughtering of about a million people.[10]

In the Balkans, the international community acted after the situation escalated to a breaking point (notably the anti-Albanian discrimination campaign conducted by the Milosšević regime), though on dubious legal grounds. Despite not securing a UN Security Council (UNSC) authorisation, mostly because of the threat of veto by both Russia and China,[11] the NATO intervention in Kosovo was considered to be based on solid moral grounds, as it was meant to stop the bloodshed of the civilian population. As Simma put it, this extraordinary action could be exceptionally justified under very particular circumstances. However, the bypassing of authorisation to use force according to the UN Charter should never become the rule, for it would risk the collapse of the collective security system.[12]

What is R2P and has it ever been used?

Beyond the above-mentioned initial thoughts on the idea, the kickstart for the later R2P concept came with the 2001 Report of the International Commission on Intervention and State Sovereignty (ICISS), the result of a Canadian initiative.[13] The general framework for the R2P contained in the Report views States as having the primary responsibility to protect their population from mass atrocities, and the international community as having a secondary responsibility to protect if the States involved are unable or unwilling to do so. According to the Report, sovereignty means responsibility and is not a shield for committing mass atrocities. It advocates for a 'continuum of measures' in the R2P framework, comprising the responsibility to prevent, to react, and to rebuild.[14] It further suggests that, although the UNSC continues to play a central role in the collective security system, when it fails to act, the UN General Assembly (UNGA) should then take action, similarly to what it did in the 'Uniting for Peace Resolution of 1950' formula (securing a two-thirds majority approval of military action in an Emergency Special Session).[15]

The possibility of military action to be taken by the General Assembly may nudge the UNSC to think twice about its inaction. In extreme situations in which the UNSC fails to address a crisis, regional organisations may also consider taking action, but if they were to go that far, they would have to make sure they obtain ex post facto UNSC authorisation for backing up the measures taken.[16]

In 2004, the High-level Panel on Threats, Challenges and Change, appointed by the UN Secretary-General (UNSG), issued a further report on the subject.[17] It narrowed down the originally proposed framework, placing greater emphasis on the need to strengthen the existing international mechanism of collective security, which, if working properly, should be able to prevent mass atrocities. Here one may hint at the idea that R2P is a superfluous concept, for the UN Charter already carefully assigns powers and competencies to the main UN bodies, which, if they were acting according to plan, should be able to tackle mass atrocities in a timely manner. The problem is that the UN Charter system has not quite effectively functioned in such situations, especially due to political differences by the five UNSC permanent members (the P5). The development of the R2P concept, however, did not stop here.

The UNSG's 2005 report 'In Larger Freedom' was the third key document drawing the contours of R2P, and it was published in preparation for the world summit later in the same year. It emphasised the need to prevent mass atrocities, focusing on prevention as a key part of the R2P concept.[18]

Later on in 2005, UN members met and by consensus adopted the World Summit Outcome document, considered the most authoritative document in terms of legal grounding for R2P.[19] Since the 2005 World Summit Outcome document was unanimously adopted by more than 150 States, the corresponding UNGA Resolution adopted during the summit lent great legitimacy to the doctrine.[20]

This document fundamentally set out the key features of the R2P doctrine, namely, its components and pillars and the continuum of measures to be taken. Accordingly, R2P is understood to have two components, listed in paragraphs 138–139 of the World Summit Outcome document. The first of these relates to obligations of the affected State vis-à-vis its population, together with its efforts to prevent the selected heinous crimes:

> 138. *Each individual State has the responsibility to protect its populations from genocide, war crimes, ethnic cleansing and crimes against humanity.* This responsibility entails the *prevention* of such crimes, including their incitement, through appropriate and necessary means. We accept that responsibility and will act in accordance with it. The international community should, as appropriate, encourage and help States to exercise this responsibility and support the United Nations in establishing an early warning capability.
>
> (*emphasis added*)

In a second stage, R2P lays greater emphasis on the international community, indicating that it has the duty to assist States, which may include a duty to step in should the affected State be unwilling or unable to protect its own population against such crimes:

> 139. *The international community, through the United Nations, also has the responsibility to use appropriate diplomatic, humanitarian and other peaceful means, in accordance with Chapters VI and VIII* of the Charter, to help to protect populations from genocide, war crimes, ethnic cleansing and crimes against humanity. In this context, *we are prepared to take collective action, in a timely and decisive manner, through the Security Council, in accordance with the Charter, including Chapter VII, on a case-by-case basis and in cooperation with relevant regional organizations as appropriate, should peaceful means be inadequate and national authorities are manifestly failing to protect their populations from genocide, war crimes, ethnic cleansing and crimes against humanity.*
>
> (*emphasis added*)

A later report by the UNSG, assisted by Edward Luck, then Special Adviser on the Responsibility to Protect, proposed how to 'operationalise' the R2P concept, indicating how the UN, States, and the international community should act in the R2P framework in the event of mass atrocities that are underway or about to take place.[21]

The Report suggested three pillars for the R2P concept, which can without difficulty be linked to the World Summit Outcome document paragraphs just quoted: (1) 'protection responsibilities of the state', meaning that the primary protection responsibility lies with the affected State; (2) 'international assistance and capacity building', meaning that collective action may be taken by other States to support the affected State; and (3) 'timely and decisive response', meaning that when the affected State is failing its population the international community may act.[22]

Finally, the Report makes it clear that R2P implies a 'continuum of responses', military action being only one shade in the palette. R2P is therefore not to be understood as boiling down to 'sending the Marines'.[23] It rather encompasses a larger vision that includes prevention, reaction, and post-crisis rebuilding.

In 2006, the UNSC passed Resolution 1674, which endorsed R2P exactly as adopted by the UNGA. An important question to ask in this context is: what is the practical use of the doctrine to date?

R2P has already been used in practical situations, including in instances not involving coercive military action. One such example was the diplomatic mediation that diffused the post-election violence that erupted in Kenya between 2007 and 2008.[24]

An example of R2P in coercive military action was the reference made to the doctrine by the UNSC when it addressed the situation in Libya after the repression of opposition members by the Gaddafi government.[25] R2P success story, the chaos that descended upon the country following the toppling of Gaddafi has raised serious doubts about the practical use of the doctrine.[26]

Why is R2P flawed?

The basic flaw in the R2P doctrine as it stands, namely, as endorsed by the UNGA and later by the UNSC, is that military action under R2P can only be undertaken in accordance with the UN Charter. Therefore, beyond the possibility of acting in self-defence (grounded in Article 51 UN Charter), States do have to secure authorisation by the UNSC before taking coercive military action (even under the R2P doctrine). This raises the question of the added value of such a doctrine, which was originally meant to precisely address serious situations in which the international community fails to take action due to splits in the UNSC.

Beyond this technical and somewhat legalistic answer, a more worrying trend is that, in recent years, States seem to be very reluctant to assume responsibility for taking external military action but, more than that, for possibly being held legally accountable when taking such action.

The most serious (though pre-R2P) example of State action despite the lack of UNSC authorisation was the 2003 Iraq invasion led by the US and the UK. Together with references to previous UNSC resolutions authorising the use of force against Iraq, another debatable justification used was to oppose the threat posed by weapons of mass destruction held by the Iraqi regime, which later on proved not to exist, so as to pose such a feared threat. Humanitarian motives were included among various justifications given by the coalition to self-legitimise their action.[27] Nonetheless, the Iraq invasion became one leading example where States' actions hint not towards a responsibility to protect populations facing serious threats but, rather, towards their willingness to pursue nebulous interests, while avoiding legal accountability.

Even after the R2P doctrine came into being, there have been political statements suggesting that military action could be carried out despite the lack of authorisation by the UNSC (an issue broader than, but related to, R2P). For example, in the ongoing Syria crisis, the former UK prime minister David Cameron suggested that the UK would be prepared to take military action in Syria even if Russia should veto a UN resolution allowing States to take such action. Without entering into the merits of the discussion, the question is how to accommodate individual military State action without ruining the collective security system of the UN Charter.[28]

At the same time, the question regarding the selectivity of international actions is a recurrent issue to bear in mind in this context.

It is true that one can make the fair point that R2P is actually more than coercive military action. Be that as it may, less than coercive military actions can be undertaken without the need for such a doctrine. Cooperation existed before R2P and will continue regardless of the fate of this doctrine. It is thus also suggested that R2P adds no real value in 'cooperation' scenarios.[29]

On the other hand, it can also be argued that the main advantage of the R2P doctrine, as accepted in the World Summit Outcome, is to institutionalise the response to the gravest crimes through the UN and in particular the UNSC. Consequently, R2P cannot be used to justify unilateral military action claiming to be taken in pursuit of collective interests.

Considering R2P in disasters

Why and how to apply R2P in disasters?

One may ask why consider the application of R2P to disasters, for as illustrated in the previous section, R2P is a human-centric concept, aiming to protect populations from atrocities committed by other human beings.[30]

It is true that (unlike hazards) disasters are themselves also human-made (at least in part). But, beyond this point, the possible application of R2P in disasters had been discussed in early conceptual documents on this doctrine. This aspect of the debate is grounded in its first days, namely, in a reference to the subject made in the 2001 Report published by the Canadian-led initiative on R2P. In that document, among the 'conscience-shocking situations' that could trigger military action under the R2P doctrine figured 'overwhelming natural or environmental catastrophes, where the State concerned is either unwilling or unable to cope, or call for assistance, and significant loss of life is occurring or threatened'.[31]

However, later on, when the R2P concept was adopted in the UNGA, the reference to disasters was completely left out.[32] The General Assembly was adamant to limit the use of R2P to the four serious international crimes, and the language adopted in the 2005 World Summit Outcome document refers only to these four crimes. The phrasing adopted leaves little room for doubt, for the General Assembly repeats five times the exclusive reference to these four crimes as triggers for applying R2P.

Therefore, for the UNGA (and later on, for the UNSC, which endorsed R2P exactly as adopted by the UNGA), these are the only situations in which the doctrine could be used.

What would trigger R2P in disasters?

In an effort to evoke R2P in disasters, some authors have tried to identify whether the commission of one of the four R2P-triggering crimes can be linked to disasters.[33] The idea here would be to verify whether action or inaction by a disaster-affected government may amount to the commission, in particular, of crimes against humanity (the other crimes are less likely to be linked to natural disasters). This would arguably then justify the triggering of R2P, including any military action to be taken for the delivery of humanitarian aid.

The emblematic example referred to in this discussion is Myanmar after the Nargis cyclone, which hit the country in May 2008, devastating the Ayeyarwady Delta region and affecting about 2.4 million people. About 85,000 people were killed, and over 50,000 went missing.[34] Shortly after the cyclone hit the country, humanitarian aid was initially halted by the national government, despite the fact that the government in power was known to be unable to fully meet the needs of its population.

This led to criticism against the government for failing to protect its own population, a criticism that was voiced particularly strongly by France's minister of foreign affairs at the time, Bernard Kouchner.

What is more, in the Nargis situation, peaceful means were tried and at first did not succeed. Coercive military action was then considered, but it would have to pass through the UNSC, and China threatened a veto.[35] Such developments left the international community in a situation similar to the one it tried to avoid when it conceived the R2P doctrine, meaning not being able to prevent massive human tragedy from taking place due to the likely lack of agreement in the UNSC.

In this particular example, the situation improved within a month from the Nargis cyclone having hit Myanmar. Greatly due to diplomatic efforts at the international and regional levels (namely, concerted action by the then UNSG Ban Ki-Moon and the ASEAN delegation),[36] the national government allowed foreign humanitarian assistance to reach the country.

In any event, the episode in Myanmar triggered a discussion on whether the military junta's obstruction of international aid could potentially amount to crimes against humanity (especially murder, extermination, forcible transfer, persecution, and other inhumane acts).[37]

The appraisal of such allegation is not straightforward, however. This is so especially taking into account that humanitarian aid is mostly to be delivered shortly after a natural disaster hits a country, and so the gathering and checking of information on governmental policies during the humanitarian response might prove a difficult exercise to be undertaken under these circumstances. But even if one accepts a less stringent threshold for verifying the likelihood of the commission of crimes against humanity or other R2P-triggering crimes in a country hit by a natural disaster, the advantages of adopting such a strategy do not seem real, as discussed later on.

This is not to say that admitting that a crime against humanity (in particular as a result of a refusal to consent to humanitarian access) can also take place during a humanitarian emergency following a natural disaster would mean expanding the use of R2P. In practice, however, it seems that it is better not to resort to military force in such situations, especially due to reasons of political expediency. In relation to Myanmar, the conventional wisdom is that to force humanitarian aid through coercive military action would have made matters worse.[38] Besides, there was a lack of political will by Western States, especially the US and the UK, to take coercive military action.[39]

On a more general note, some argue that strategically it may be a wrong move to try to apply R2P in situations less obviously connected with the four international crimes triggering the application of this doctrine, with the risk of putting too much pressure on the concept and blasting it altogether. Since the R2P doctrine, as described in the World Summit Outcome, has not yet clearly consolidated as a norm of international law (it is based on a UNGA resolution which was later endorsed by the UNSC), it might be better not to try to stretch the concept too much, or everything can be lost.[40] It seems that, unless it can be clearly linked to the four R2P-triggering serious crimes, it is better to avoid attempting to apply R2P in disaster situations.[41] Embracing this position are high UN officials, including the UNSG, who opposed the idea of extending the application of R2P to situations beyond the four international crimes which the concept was originally linked to. For them, R2P should not be used to justify the response to natural disasters and environmental crises, including those linked to climate change, for this would arguably undermine the 2005 consensus.[42]

Moreover, and most relevant, is that the use of R2P in disasters has not attracted support from States or from the International Law Commission (ILC) when it addressed the protection of rights in disasters.[43]

Does R2P add value in disasters?

Despite the great opposition to the application of R2P in natural disasters, not everything is lost. Cooperation, which is also an important aspect of R2P, is very important in disasters as a way of enhancing relief action. This regularly takes place outside the development of the R2P concept, and various legal standards covering disasters already emphasise the importance of it.

As covered in the following section, the duty to cooperate is also an important feature in the ILC Draft Articles on the Protection of Persons in the Event of Disasters (ILC Draft Articles).[44]

On the other hand, coercive military action seems to be a very bad idea to be used in disasters. First of all, it is important to have access to places where disasters take place, and governmental institutions will normally have vital details about the geography, routes, and population of the affected area, as well as knowledge about the community itself and its institutional apparatus.[45]

Finally, coercively acting through military means may escalate an already difficult situation in a particular country, thus making it even more difficult for disaster victims to have access to humanitarian aid. If governmental institutions are busy upholding their sovereignty, it is very likely that human and material resources will be split to deal with the two 'crises'. Therefore, cooperation seems a much better approach than coercive military action in disasters.

Alternatives for the use of R2P in disasters

Having argued that R2P is of little value in disasters, particularly in natural disasters, this section identifies the key developments and standards relevant to disasters. It is divided in two parts. The first part covers the work of the ILC in developing articles for the protection of persons in the event of disasters.[46] The focus here is on how the ILC avoided R2P to permeate the Draft Articles and what phrasing it adopted instead. The second part covers regional treaties on disasters, particularly clauses relating to inter-State cooperation in disasters, and how they relate to R2P. It is argued that there is a growing body of legal standards and practices on disasters that can provide useful guidance for States and further actors.

The ILC Draft Articles on the protection of persons in the event of disasters and R2P

An important development is the work by the ILC on the subject, which started in 2006 and culminated in 2016 with the adoption of the eighteen the ILC Draft Articles, together with their Commentaries. This process led to fruitful reflections on the topic by many actors over the years, notably documented in eight reports by Mr Eduardo Valencia-Ospina, the ILC Special Rapporteur appointed for the subject, together with several inputs from governments, international organisations, and other entities. By the end of this process, the ILC recommended to the UNGA that a convention be drafted on subject on the basis of the Draft Articles.[47]

The UNGA took note of the ILC Draft Articles and invited governments to submit comments on the recommendation by the ILC to draft a convention on the basis of the Draft Articles.[48] The UNGA also decided to include in the provisional agenda of its 73rd session, in 2018, an item entitled 'Protection of persons in the event of disasters'.

It is interesting to note that, from the very beginning of its work on disasters, the ILC indicated that it would rather close the door to R2P, especially in terms of coercive military action.[49] Although we cannot look at the entire project in detail here, the focus will be on ILC Draft Articles 10–14, which, read together, suggest that they were phrased in such a way as to protect the ILC project from R2P intrusion.

Draft Article 10 (Role of the affected State) emphasises that the affected State has the duty to ensure the protection of persons and the provision of disaster relief assistance, but that it also has the primary role in relief efforts. It reads:

1. The affected State has the duty to ensure the protection of persons and provision of disaster relief assistance in its territory, or in territory under its jurisdiction or control.
2. The affected State has the primary role in the direction, control, coordination and supervision of such relief assistance.

This Draft Article seems broadly compatible with R2P, for it accommodates a rationale analogous to pillar 1 of that doctrine, namely, the principle that the affected State is the primary and main actor in addressing disaster relief efforts.

Furthermore, paragraph 2 of the same Draft Article 10 suggests that it is incumbent on the affected State to play the primary role in disaster relief operations, thus making it clear that the affected State shall take the lead. Whether this is good or bad it is not possible to say in abstract, but the assumption seems to be that the affected State is in the best position to know its country and population and arguably is the best actor to lead relief efforts in the affected country.[50]

The following Draft Article already departs from R2P. It reads:

> Article 11. Duty of the affected State to seek external assistance
>
> To the extent that a disaster manifestly exceeds its national response capacity, the affected State has the duty to seek assistance from, as appropriate, other States, the United Nations, and other potential assisting actors.

This provision places upon the affected State the duty to seek external support should the needs of its population manifestly exceed the national capacity to handle the disaster in question. The ILC commentary on this Draft Article emphasises that the affected State shall act in good faith in deciding whether a disaster manifestly exceeded its own capacity to handle the situation.[51] The Commentary also recalls different human rights obligations of States in the context of disasters, suggesting that the affected State's duty to seek assistance also derives from them.[52]

As the matter is to be decided solely by the affected State, this may pose problems especially if affected States are unwilling to admit they have reached the limit of their operations but do not want external assistance to enter the country, as was the case with Myanmar in the first weeks after the Nargis cyclone. The ILC Draft Articles leave the matter open. Sivakumaran suggests that the compromise formula aimed at solving this dilemma (addressing the needs of the affected population while preserving the sovereignty of the affected State) is that, once consent to external assistance is given, it cannot be arbitrarily withheld, as discussed below.[53]

Here one can already sense, perhaps unsurprisingly, bearing in mind that this is a legal drafting exercise discussed chiefly among States, that throughout the entire text of the ILC Draft Articles on disasters a compromise has been struck between the interests of States and those of disaster victims. The very title of the project, namely, the 'Protection of persons in the event of disasters', suggests this is the main rationale of this initiative. As stated in Draft Article 2, the purpose of the Articles is to 'facilitate the adequate and effective response to disasters and reduction of the risk of disasters, so as to meet the essential needs of the persons concerned, with full respect for their rights'. However, reading the entire eighteen Draft Articles, one can sense a less openly stated intention to make sure that the sovereignty of the affected State is protected.[54]

Draft Article 13 deals with the affected State's consent to external assistance, basically indicating that 'the provision of external assistance requires the consent of the affected State' but that such consent 'shall not be withheld arbitrarily'. The formula adopted here suggests a compromise between potential external aid providers and the affected State.

This formula excludes the more controversial use of R2P, namely, its use enabling the international community to intervene by coercive military force should the affected State refrain from discharging its obligations towards its population. Instead, the affected State preserves its sovereignty; in other words, no third State can come in and forcefully deliver aid (the discussion that followed Nargis in Myanmar). Issues pertaining to the 'arbitrary withdrawal of consent' to external assistance have given rise to much debate, including, among others, the debate held back in 2003 during the Bruges session of the Institut de Droit International. On that occasion, several possible justifications for a non-arbitrary refusal were proposed. One possible example in this regard is where a State is able and willing to use its own resources to adequately tackle a given disaster situation.[55]

Further provisions in the ILC Draft Articles suggest some tension between the interests of the affected States and those of other States, international organisations, and humanitarian NGOs.[56] Draft Article 14 covers 'Conditions on the provision of external assistance', stating that the affected State can set the conditions subject to which it will accept humanitarian assistance. This should take the needs of the affected population into account, and also the quality of assistance. This is an important and necessary provision, for disaster relief practice suggests anecdotal evidence of relief items that had to be discarded by the receiving States, such as expired food and medicine or clothing and food that was culturally inappropriate for the affected communities.[57]

Draft Article 14 further provides that the conditions placed on external assistance have to be compliant with applicable law, meaning both international law (including the ILC Draft Articles) and national law.[58] This can prove challenging especially in terms of national law provisions. It is important to read the Draft Articles in good faith and to consider the rationale behind them, including the duty of the affected State to facilitate external assistance, as pointed out in due course.

Also, Draft Article 12 covers 'Offers of external assistance', stating that external actors have a right to offer their assistance. It does deviate from the coercive rationale of military intervention under R2P. Here, assistance to the affected State may be offered by a range of external factors, such as States, the UN, NATO, UN Children's Fund, the International Federation of the Red Cross and Red Crescent Societies (IFRC), Médecins Sans Frontières, and Oxfam, to name but a few. This provision especially benefits the affected population, for it relates to their rights, too. It is also linked to a previous one, Draft Article 13, according to which the affected State has to decide on offers of assistance made.[59] These provisions benefit the affected population, for they may well speed up the process so that aid can more quickly reach those in need.

Finally, Draft Article 15 imposes on the affected State a duty to facilitate external assistance, this by reducing the red tape involved in humanitarian relief items sent to the country, as well as a duty to facilitate the entry of foreign aid workers to work in the country. In this lies a major contribution in the area, for anecdotal accounts suggest this is a very serious issue jeopardising a speedy and effective provision of aid in disasters.[60]

From the above discussion it can be appreciated that the ILC Draft Articles refer to 'duties' of international cooperation on the delivery and distribution of humanitarian aid.[61] The disaster-affected State has not only a duty to protect its own population but also the primary role in relief operations. This also suggests acknowledgement of the affected State's sovereignty, which ought to be respected by other actors cooperating or intending to cooperate with it.[62]

It is important to bear in mind the protection of disaster victims as the ultimate goal of the ILC initiative in drafting the Articles, as suggested by the Special Rapporteur back in the early days of the project, referring to the human rights-based approach as the focus of the project.[63] This rationale shall permeate the interpretation of all provisions therein, including the duties of the affected State, among which figure (1) the duty to seek assistance, and this is especially so when the affected State finds itself incapable of addressing the humanitarian needs linked to the disaster, and (2) the duty not to arbitrarily withhold consent to international assistance. On the other hand, the international community would have the right to offer humanitarian assistance. Under the ILC Draft Articles, the duty to cooperate applies to all actors involved in disaster assistance.

As indicated, the affected State shall give consent to foreign assistance, though it can set some criteria, so that truly needed items are to be delivered and that the assistance will be of quality (so as to make sure, for example, that the relief workers sent to the affected State are properly trained).

From this brief overview of the ILC Draft Articles there is a clear suggestion that the project does not wish to allow R2P to permeate its text. One possible reason for this is that States are generally no longer confident in this doctrine, bearing in mind, among other things, that R2P, as it stands, makes no reference to natural disasters. It therefore seems understandable that the ILC Special Rapporteur refrained from pushing to wedge this disputed concept into the ILC Draft Articles. This may be a sensible approach to take, for otherwise the inclusion of R2P in the Draft Articles could sabotage the whole project (including the possible future adoption of the Draft Articles as a treaty).[64]

But one point that R2P also uses and the ILC Draft Articles do not discard is the need for cooperation. In the ILC Draft Articles, the duty of cooperation applies not only to States but also to various other actors, such as international and regional organisations and humanitarian organisations such as the IFRC, the International Committee of the Red Cross, and NGOs. Indeed, cooperation permeates various standard-setting initiatives in disasters, ranging from regional treaties to soft law standards. Cooperation could be perceived as one aspect of the R2P doctrine which the ILC Draft Articles actually do not repeal. Be that as it may, this seems to reflect an incidental convergence of the two initiatives rather than a declared wish to preserve or accommodate the R2P doctrine in the ILC Draft Articles. The next section will briefly outline some examples of cooperation duties in disasters.

Regional treaties on disasters and R2P

Beyond the ILC Draft Articles, different treaties on disasters also do not address R2P (many predate this doctrine). What is more, many disaster treaties focus or contain provisions on cooperation and/or collaboration[65] among States, a principle that underpins the practice in this area.[66]

For example, the 2005 ASEAN Agreement on Disaster and Emergency Management emphasises the need for inter-State cooperation. This is reflected in the very objective of the treaty, which is

> to provide effective mechanisms to achieve substantial reduction of disaster losses in lives and in the social, economic and environmental assets of the Parties, and to jointly respond to disaster emergencies through concerted national efforts and intensified regional and international co-operation.[67]

Cooperation also figures among the principles of the treaty, according to which States shall, 'in the spirit of solidarity and partnership and in accordance with their respective needs, capabilities and situations, strengthen co-operation and coordination to achieve the objectives of this Agreement'.[68] Finally, inter-State cooperation is also emphasised in efforts to reduce disaster losses, to provide information to neighbouring States that might be affected by a disaster, and to promptly respond to requests for assistance by other States parties.[69]

This particular treaty clearly diverges from the R2P doctrine, emphasising that State action shall be guided by the respect for State sovereignty, territorial integrity, and national unity in accordance with the UN Charter.[70] It further indicates that the primary responsibility to respond to disaster lies with the affected State and that 'external assistance or offers of assistance shall only be provided upon the request or with the consent of the affected Party'.[71]

In the Caribbean, the Agreement establishing the Caribbean Disaster Emergency Management Agency (CDEMA) similarly alludes to the cooperation of States parties towards a timely and structured mobilisation of disaster relief resources[72] and to their obligation to participate in joint technical cooperation programmes on disaster management.[73] The same treaty contains a further provision relevant to R2P, which precludes external coercive military intervention, making it clear that no member of the 'disciplined forces' of another participant State shall be sent to the disaster-affected State without its prior express consent.[74]

Is cooperation only a formal commitment of States, or do they truly follow this rationale? In this brief overview, it was not possible to further investigate the practical reliance on these clauses. Despite this shortcoming, the reference to cooperation in different regional disaster treaties amounts to a positive trend that may be followed in a future international treaty, such as the treaty that may arise from the Draft Articles put together by the ILC.

Cooperation and collaboration are important features in disasters. States seem keen on cooperating/collaborating, but they also cherish their sovereignty, lending no support to coercive external intervention in natural disasters. In this sense, it is perhaps unsurprising that the majority of States did support the adoption of the UNGA resolution on R2P, but not the possibility of extending this concept to disasters (especially natural ones).[75]

Conclusion

R2P is dead. R.I.P. R2P. This is what arises from an assessment of the doctrine, especially considering its added value in natural disasters. As Ford puts it, R2P is a failure, for it has not lived up to its expectations.[76] Be that as it may, the increase in the use of R2P language by the UNSC may be considered a positive development. Especially by linking R2P to international crimes, the Security Council might act in a more systematic and less political fashion.[77] In any event, R2P seems more promising in relation to preventing mass violence from taking place,[78] but one can have prevention outside R2P, and so the added value of this doctrine in such situations is not clearly evident.

One needs to be careful when broadly advocating for the use of R2P in natural disasters. As Evans puts it, if R2P is to protect everybody from everything, it will end up protecting nobody from anything.[79] Thus, loosely applying R2P beyond mass atrocities might undermine the very utility of the concept, jeopardising how it can be effectively operationalised. Worse, it may dilute the concept and lead States not to act even in cases of blunt commission of the original four mass-atrocity crimes.[80]

It is important to also bear in mind that States were already reluctant to embrace the idea of R2P a few years after they adopted the 2005 World Summit Outcome document. That is why the UN is very careful not to expand its usage beyond the phrasing contained in that specific document.[81]

This chapter attempted to provide an account of this ambitious doctrine, which unfortunately boiled down to little once it entered the sphere of international organisations. It seems it is better for States and individuals, especially in the event of natural disasters, to instead rely on further initiatives and instruments, such as those emphasising the need for cooperation in disasters, as suggested by the work of the ILC and of different regional disaster treaties.

Selected bibliography

R. Barber, 'The Responsibility to Protect the Survivors of Natural Disaster: Cyclone Nargis, a Case Study' 14(1) *Journal of Conflict & Security Law* (2009) 3.

A.J. Bellamy, *Responsibility to Protect: The Global Effort to End Mass Atrocities* (Polity, 2009).

G. Evans, 'The Responsibility to Protect in Environmental Emergencies' 103 *Proceedings of the Annual Meeting (American Society of International Law)* (2009) 19.

S. Ford, 'Is the Failure to Respond Appropriately to a Natural Disaster a Crime against Humanity – the Responsibility to Protect and Individual Criminal Responsibility in the Aftermath of Cyclone Nargis' 38 *Denver Journal of International Law & Policy* (2009) 227.

C. Allan and T. O'Donnell, 'A Call to Alms? Natural Disasters, R2P, Duties of Cooperation and Uncharted Consequences' 17 *Journal of Conflict and Security Law* (2012) 337.

Notes

* The author would like to thank various persons that commented on earlier versions of this chapter, namely: Professor Maria Lee and the participants of the UCL Staff Seminar held on 16 December 2015 at the Faculty of Laws; the organisers and participants of the International Conference on the Protection of Persons in Times of Disasters: International and European Legal Perspectives, held in Rome, 3–4 March 2016; and the editors of the current volume. Any errors are the author's sole responsibility.

1 For the background to the R2P doctrine, including on disasters, see A.J. Bellamy, *Responsibility to Protect: The Global Effort to End Mass Atrocities* (Polity, 2009); S. Ford, 'Is the Failure to Respond Appropriately to a Natural Disaster a Crime against Humanity – the Responsibility to Protect and Individual Criminal Responsibility in the Aftermath of Cyclone Nargis' 38 *Denver Journal of International Law & Policy* (2009) 227; R. Barber, 'The Responsibility to Protect the Survivors of Natural Disaster: Cyclone Nargis, a Case Study' 14(1) *Journal of Conflict & Security Law* (2009) 3.

2 Definition contained in Draft Article 3(a). See ILC, Protection of Persons in the Event of Disasters: Titles and Texts of the Preamble and Draft Articles 1 to 18 of the Draft Articles on the Protection of Persons in the Event of Disasters Adopted, on Second Reading, by the Drafting Committee, UN Doc. A/CN.4/L.871 (27 May 2016) 2. For a detailed coverage and discussion of the notion of 'disaster' under international law, see Bartolini's chapter in this volume.

3 Some disaster-related treaties and documents expressly exclude from the disaster definition situations of war. See e.g. the Agreement Establishing the Caribbean Disaster Emergency Management Agency (adopted 1 July 2008, entered into force 4 July 2008) (CDEMA Agreement). Art 1 defines disaster as 'the exposure or the human habitat to the operation of the forces of nature or to human intervention resulting in widespread destruction of lives or property, but excludes events occasioned by war or military confrontation'. A similar position has been adopted in the IFRC International Disaster Relief Law Guidelines. See IFRC, 'Introduction to the Guidelines for the Domestic Facilitation and Regulation of International Disaster Relief and Initial Recovery Assistance' (2011), available at www.ifrc.org/PageFiles/125652/1205600-IDRL%20Guidelines-EN-LR%20(2).pdf, accessed on 6 May 2017 (IDRL Guidelines), Guideline 2.1. Initially, the ILC indicated that the focus of its attention would be 'natural disasters', but as its work developed it adopted a more encompassing notion of disasters. ILC, Report of the International Law Commission, Fifty-Eight Session, UN Doc. A/61/10 (2006) (1 May–9 June and 3 July–11 August 2006) 476.

4 E.C. Luck, 'Environmental Emergencies and the Responsibility to Protect: A Bridge Too Far?' 103 *Proceedings of the Annual Meeting (American Society of International Law)* (2009) 19, 36. Edward Luck was back then the Special Advisor to the UN Secretary-General on R2P. See also Bellamy (n. 1) 21–27.

5 Luck (n. 4) 38; Bellamy (n. 1) 78.

6 Bellamy (n. 1) 24–26.

7 See Ibid 26–27, for the position of China and Cuba.

8 Luck (n. 4) 37–38.

9 Ibid 38.

10 L. Melvern, *Conspiracy to Murder: The Rwandan Genocide* (Verso, 2004).

11 Bellamy (n. 1) 55.

12 B. Simma, 'NATO, the UN and the Use of Force: Legal Aspects' 10(1) *European Journal of International Law* (1999) 1. See also, in the same journal issue, Cassese's comments on Simma's article: A. Cassese, 'Ex Iniuria Ius Oritur: Are We Moving towards International Legitimation of Forcible Humanitarian Countermeasures in the World Community?' 10(1) *European Journal of International Law* (1999) 23.

13 International Development Research Centre, The Responsibility to Protect: Report of the International Commission on Intervention and State Sovereignty (ICISS) (December 2001), available at http://responsibilitytoprotect.org/ICISS%20Report.pdf, accessed on 6 May 2017 (ICISS Report).

14 Ibid para 2.29.

15 For the 'Uniting for Peace' resolution see UNGA, Res 377(V), UN Doc. A/RES/377(V) (3 November 1950).

16 Bellamy (n. 1) 57.

17 UNGA, A More Secure World: Our Shared Responsibility: Report of the High-Level Panel on Threats, Challenges and Change, UN Doc. A/59/565 (2 December 2004).

18 UNSG, Report of the Secretary-General: In Larger Freedom – towards Development, Security and Human Rights for All, UN Doc. A/59/2005 (21 March 2005).

19 UNGA, World Summit Outcome, UN Doc. A/Res/60/1 (16 September 2005) paras 138–39. See also Bellamy (n. 1) 67.

20 UNGA, Res A/60/1, UN Doc. A/RES/60/1 (24 October 2005). See G. Evans, 'The Responsibility to Protect in Environmental Emergencies' 103 *Proceedings of the Annual Meeting (American Society of International Law)* (2009) 19, 28.
21 UNGA, Report of the Secretary-General: Implementing the Responsibility to Protect, UN Doc. A/63/677 (12 January 2009).
22 See Evans (n. 20) 26. See also Luck (n. 4) 36. On the three pillars see the UNGA, Implementing the Responsibility to Protect: Report of the Secretary-General, UN Doc. A/63/677 (12 January 2009) (UNSG, Report on R2P).
23 See Evans (n. 20) 28.
24 See UNSG, Report on R2P, paras 11(c) and 51, referring to the Kenyan situation as an example of pillar three of the R2P doctrine. See also Evans (n. 20) 28.
25 UNSC, Res 1973, UN Doc. B/RES/1973 (17 March 2011).
26 D. Rieff, 'R2P R.I.P.' *New York Times, the Opinion Pages, OP-ED Contributor* (7 November 2011), available at www.nytimes.com/2011/11/08/opinion/r2p-rip.html?_r=0%3E, accessed on 6 May 2017, criticising the Global North for using R2P to promote regime change in the Global South. For a response, see G. Evans, 'Response to David Rieff's "R2P, RIP"' *The New York Times and International Herald Tribune* (10 November 2011), available at www.gevans.org/speeches/speech455.html, accessed on 6 May 2017, arguing that a greater effort should be made to further elaborate R2P, especially in regard to the need for the UN Security Council to apply objective criteria when considering the adoption of military intervention under R2P.
27 S. Murphy, 'Assessing the Legality of Invading Iraq' 92(4) *Georgetown Law Journal* (2004) 173.
28 According to media reports, when David Cameron was asked if he would wait for a UN resolution before taking action, he told the UK Parliament that 'Russia has different aims to us and they have repeatedly threatened to veto any such resolution'. He continued stating that

> Of course it is always preferable in these circumstances to have the full backing of the United Nations Security Council but I have to say what matters most of all is that any action we would take would both be legal and would help protect our country.

See A. Justice, 'David Cameron: Military Action in Syria without UN Backing Would Be "Legal"' *International Business Times* (18 November 2015), available at www.ibtimes.co.uk/david-cameron-military-action-syria-without-un-backing-would-be-legal-1529381, accessed on 6 May 2017.
29 On this issue, see J.B. Heath, 'Disasters, Relief, and Neglect: The Duty to Accept Humanitarian Assistance and the Work of the International Law Commission' 43 *New York University Journal of International Law & Politics* (2010) 419, 433, arguing that 'what it means to invoke RtoP remains unclear, especially where the principle is invoked to justify something other than forced intervention' (footnote omitted).
30 On R2P as a human-centric concept, see L. Malone, 'Green Helmets: Eco-Intervention in the Twenty-First Century' 103 *Proceedings of the Annual Meeting (American Society of International Law)* (2009) 19, 22, 26.
31 ICISS Report 32.
32 C. Allan and T. O'Donnell, 'A Call to Alms? Natural Disasters, R2P, Duties of Cooperation and Uncharted Consequences' 17 *Journal of Conflict and Security Law* (2012) 337, 344.
33 See e.g. Ford (n. 1); Barber (n. 1).
34 See IFRC, 'Myanmar: Cyclone Nargis 2008 Facts and Figures' (3 May 2011), available at www.ifrc.org/en/news-and-media/news-stories/asia-pacific/myanmar/myanmar-cyclone-nargis-2008-facts-and-figures/, accessed on 6 May 2017.
35 Ford (n. 1) 255–256.
36 Luck (n. 4) 36–37.
37 Ford (n. 1) 241; Barber (n. 1) 18–24. See also E. Schmid, 'Adverse Human Agency and Disasters: A Role for International Criminal Law?' in S. Breau and K. Samuel (eds), *The Elgar Research Handbook on Disasters and International Law* (Edward Elgar Publishing, 2016) 111.
38 Luck (n. 4) 36–37.
39 Ford (n. 1) 267.
40 Heath (n. 29) 432–433; Malone (n. 30) 27.
41 Ibid 27. See also F. Russo, 'Disasters through the Lens of International Criminal Law' in A. de Guttry, M. Gestri and G. Venturini (eds), *International Disaster Response Law* (TMC Asser Press, 2012) 441–462.
42 See the UNSG, Report on R2P para 10(b). Malone (n. 30) 27.

43 See UNGA, Sixth Committee, Agenda item 75: Report of the International Law Commission on the Work of Its Sixtieth Session, UN Doc. A/C.6/63/SR.23 (2008) para 10 (position of Austria); para 20 (position of India); para 31 (position of China); para 80 (position of Malaysia); para 86 (position of the USA). See also ILC, Report of the International Law Commission, Sixty-First Session, UN Doc. A/64/10 (2009) (4 May–5 June and 6 July–7 August 2009) para 164.

44 ILC, Report of the International Law Commission, Sixty-Eighth Session, UN Doc. A/71/10 (2016) (2 May–10 June and 4 July–12 August 2016), draft art 7.

45 Heath (n. 29) 436, argues that 'the [disaster-affected] state is in the best position to understand the needs of its citizens-it knows the infrastructure, understands the habits and special needs of the population, and knows what aid items might be inappropriate to the circumstances'. It is worth bearing in mind, however, that in many cases (uncoerced) foreign military aid is considered very helpful because the military generally has the necessary equipment and experience to speedily reach the affected areas. There are in fact several soft law instruments addressing the use of military assets in disaster scenarios (e.g. the 'Guidelines on the Use of Military and Civil Defense Assets in Disaster Relief', known as the 'Oslo Guidelines', first prepared in 1994 by a number of donor States and humanitarian agencies and last revised in 2007, available at https://docs.unocha.org/sites/dms/Documents/Oslo%20Guidelines%20 ENGLISH%20(November%202007).pdf, accessed on 7 May 2017).

46 In 2006, at its 58th session, the ILC decided to start working on the topic of the 'Protection of persons in the event of disasters'. See ILC, Report of the International Law Commission, Fifty-Eight Session, UN Doc. A/61/10 (2006) (1 May–9 June and 3 July–11 August 2006) para 257.

47 ILC, Report of the International Law Commission, Sixty-Eighth Session, UN Doc. A/71/10 (2016) (2 May–10 June and 4 July–12 August 2016) paras 43–46.

48 UNGA, Res 71/141: Protection of Persons in the Event of Disasters, UN Doc. A/71/141 (13 December 2016).

49 In the initial document outlining its future work on the topic the ILC made reference to the R2P, signalling the importance of prevention in the context of disasters. It indicated that it would be focusing on peaceful interaction between States, and thus it would not consider the responsibility to react in response, including through coercive measures, the most extreme of them being military intervention. ILC, Report of the International Law Commission, Fifty-Eight Session, UN Doc. A/61/10 (2006) (1 May–9 June and 3 July–11 August 2006) 468.

50 This principle is also reaffirmed in many instruments (binding and soft law alike) dealing with the role of the affected State.

51 ILC, Report of the International Law Commission, Sixty-Eighth Session, UN Doc. A/71/10 (2016) (2 May–10 June and 4 July–12 August 2016) 56.

52 Ibid 53–55.

53 S. Sivakumaran, 'Arbitrary Withholding of Consent to Humanitarian Assistance in Situations of Disaster' 64 *International & Comparative Law Quarterly* (2015) 501, 509.

54 See F. Zorzi Giustiniani, 'The Works of the International Law Commission on "Protection of Persons in the Event of Disasters": A Critical Appraisal' in A. de Guttry, M. Gestri and G. Venturini (eds) (n. 41) 65.

55 For more on the discussion in the framework of the Institut de Droit International, see ibid 79–80.

56 See especially ILC draft arts 14, 12, and 15.

57 IFRC, 'Law and Legal Issues in International Disaster Response: A Desk Study' (2007) 14, 99–100, 107, 137, available at www.ifrc.org/PageFiles/125639/113600-idrl-deskstudy-en.pdf, accessed on 7 May 2017 (IFRC Desk study). The issue of quality of relief is also covered in some regional treaties, such as the ASEAN Agreement on Disaster Management and Emergency Response (adopted 26 July 2005, entered into force 24 December 2009). Art 12(4) reads as follows: '[t]he relief goods and materials provided by the Assisting Entity should meet the quality and validity requirements of the Parties concerned for consumption and utilisation'.

58 Art 14 covers the conditions on the provision of external assistance, and it reads as follows:

> [t]he affected State may place conditions on the provision of external assistance. Such conditions shall be in accordance with the present draft articles, applicable rules of international law, and the national law of the affected State. Conditions shall take into account the identified needs of the persons affected by disasters and the quality of the assistance. When formulating conditions, the affected State shall indicate the scope and type of assistance sought.

59 The actual phrasing is as follows: '3. When an offer of external assistance is made in accordance with the present draft articles, the affected State shall, whenever possible, make known its decision regarding the offer in a timely manner.'

60 See e.g. IFRC Desk study 98–100, identifying different disaster settings in which relief operations have faced difficulties in the importation of food, medicines, ground vehicles, telecommunications equipment, and other relief items. Often as a result of lengthy customs and other clearance procedures, perishable items rot, medicine expires, and emergency relief items such as blankets and tents become redundant by the time clearance is finally obtained.
61 Allan and O'Donnell (n. 32) 339.
62 See Zorzi Giustiniani (n. 54) 76.
63 On this issue, see McDermott's chapter in this volume.
64 G. Bartolini, T. Natoli and A. Riccardi, 'Report of the Expert Meeting on the ILC's Draft Articles on the Protection of Persons in the Event of Disasters' 3 *International Law and Disasters Working Papers Series* (2015) 7, available at http://disasterlaw.sssup.it/wp-content/uploads/2014/01/Bartolini-Natoli-Riccardi-Report-of-the-Expert-Meeting-2015-DEF.pdf, accessed on 7 May 2017.
65 In the Oxford Dictionaries online thesaurus, the two words are listed as synonyms.
66 One example is the Preamble of the Agreement among the Governments of the Participating States of the Black Sea Economic Cooperation on collaboration in Emergency Assistance and Emergency Response in Natural and Man-Made Disasters (adopted on 15 April 1998), whose opening lines are as follows:

> [t]he Governments parties to the present Agreement, . . . Taking into account the probability of emergencies, which the Parties cannot eliminate by their own forces and facilities, and also the demand caused by this fact for coordinated actions of Parties aimed at emergency prevention and response; Desiring to further extend the developed regional *cooperation* to cover the assistance in case of emergencies and displaying joint efforts to provide coordinated assistance to the affected population; . . . Encouraging further *cooperation* in the field of international emergency assistance on the basis of the initiatives taken by the First Black Sea Red Cross and Red Crescent Societies Conference (1997).
>
> (*emphasis added*)

67 ASEAN Agreement on Disaster Management and Emergency Response, art 2.
68 Ibid art 3.
69 Ibid art 4.
70 Ibid art 3.
71 Ibid. See also art 11 (Joint Emergency Response through the Provision of Assistance).
72 See CDEMA Agreement, art XIII(1)(g).
73 Ibid art XIX(r).
74 Ibid art XXI(3).
75 For a discussion on the issue of cooperation in the Draft Articles adopted by the ILC, see McDermott's chapter in this volume.
76 Ford (n. 1) 268.
77 Ibid.
78 Luck (n. 4) 37.
79 Evans (n. 20) 29.
80 Ibid 32.
81 Luck (n. 4) 38.

4

ASSISTANCE TO DISASTER VICTIMS IN AN ARMED CONFLICT

The role of international humanitarian law

Sarah Williams and Gabrielle Simm

Introduction

This chapter considers the interaction between the sub-fields of International Humanitarian Law (IHL) and International Disaster Law (IDL) in governing humanitarian assistance to disaster victims in an armed conflict. Disasters are defined as 'a calamitous event or series of events resulting in widespread loss of life, great human suffering and distress, mass displacement, or large-scale material or environmental damage, thereby seriously disrupting the functioning of society'.[1]

As at March 2017, there were forty armed conflicts in or between States around the world.[2] The majority of these armed conflicts are non-international in nature. In several of those States, the armed conflict (or a series of conflicts) has been ongoing for decades, for example, the conflict between India and Pakistan regarding Kashmir.[3] Several States affected by armed conflict are also prone to disasters. Examples in the Asia-Pacific region include China, the Philippines, Nepal, India, Pakistan, Burma/Myanmar and Indonesia.[4] Therefore perhaps the most likely scenario in which to consider the overlap between IDL and IHL is where a disaster occurs in a State that is already experiencing armed conflict. The Philippines is an example of a State prone to geophysical disasters (such as volcanic eruptions and earthquakes) as well as meteorological disasters (such as storms). In 2014 the government of the Philippines concluded a peace deal with the Moro Islamic Liberation Front ending two decades of conflict, during which earthquakes and typhoons struck the island of Mindanao in addition to the cycles of drought and flood.[5] Within that scenario, the disaster may occur in the same region as the armed conflict or in a part of the State that is not affected by the armed conflict at all. An example of the latter situation is Cyclone Nargis, which struck the Ayeyarwady (Irawaddy) Delta and Yangon District of Myanmar/Burma in May 2008, removed from the site of ongoing conflict in Karen and Shan States.[6] Conflict and politicisation of aid may also lead to famine, a slow-onset disaster.[7]

A different scenario is where a disaster or series of disasters lead to the emergence of an armed conflict. This scenario is most likely to arise from what are called 'slow-onset disasters', which are distinct from 'sudden onset disasters' such as earthquakes or hurricanes. Examples of slow-onset disasters include sustained periods of flooding or drought that gradually reduce available resources and the resilience of communities to withstand further incidents. Slow-onset disasters may exacerbate existing inequalities and lead to increased tensions over scarce resources, eventually triggering an armed conflict. The mismanagement of sudden onset disasters can also lead to conflict. Cyclone Bhola hit East Pakistan in November 1970, leading to around 500,000 deaths. Existing tensions rose due to the government in West Pakistan's inadequate response, and by March 1971, a civil war had erupted, leading to the secession of East Pakistan and emergence of the independent State of Bangladesh.[8] As this brief discussion demonstrates, there is certainly scope for IHL to play a role in relation to disaster-related humanitarian assistance in many countries.

There are key differences between IHL and IDL. IHL has been established for approximately 150 years and applies in situations of armed conflict and occupation. This body of law includes some of the best-known and most widely ratified treaties and well-recognised rules of customary international law, although its implementation and enforcement are far from perfect. Amongst these treaty-based and customary international law provisions are several that regulate the provision of humanitarian assistance to civilian populations affected by an armed conflict, although there is no formal definition of humanitarian assistance in the IHL instruments.

The term IDL is relatively new and encompasses disaster risk reduction as well as disaster response, increasingly replacing International Disaster Response Law (IDRL).[9] The international legal definition of a disaster, outlined above, is more limited than the colloquial use of the term disaster, which sometimes refers to war and terrorism as well as natural, industrial or technological disasters and health emergencies. There is no overarching multilateral instrument that provides a comprehensive legal framework for disasters[10] and many IDL instruments are non-binding. Instead, IDL operates at mainly bilateral and regional levels[11] and, increasingly, through the incorporation of soft law standards, such as the IDRL Guidelines,[12] into domestic laws and procedures.[13] Nor is there consensus on the existence or content of any customary international law rules within IDL. Yet, where a disaster occurs in a country where an armed conflict is ongoing or emerges, there is a possible role for both IHL and IDL.

The relationship between the two bodies of law in situations of armed conflict, and how it might apply in practice, is unclear. As States, international organisations and other actors have attempted to provide greater clarity to the content and structure of IDL over the last decade or so, the relationship between these two bodies of law has proved difficult to define. The International Law Commission (ILC or the Commission) is charged with the codification and progressive development of international law. The ILC adopted its Draft Articles on the Protection of Persons in the Event of Disasters (ILC Draft Articles) at first reading in 2014.[14] After receiving comments from States, the ILC Drafting Committee adopted revised Draft Articles after second reading in May 2016, which, along with the associated commentaries, were included in the ILC's 2016 annual report.[15] The ILC recommended to the General Assembly 'the elaboration of a convention on the basis of the draft articles'.[16] The Sixth Committee considered the ILC Draft Articles from 24 to 26 October 2016.[17] Ultimately, the General Assembly, while expressing its appreciation to the ILC for finalising the topic,[18] took note of the ILC Draft Articles and invited States to submit comments concerning the Commission's recommendation that the ILC Draft Articles should form the basis of a convention.[19] Given the preference of the General Assembly for 'soft law' outcomes from previous ILC topics, it is currently uncertain whether the ILC Draft Articles will form the basis for a future legally binding instrument.

However, in the process of drafting the ILC Draft Articles, the ILC has had to consider the relationship between IHL and IDL,[20] and proposed a provision to address that relationship specifically. The final version of that provision (now Draft Article 18(2), formerly Draft Article 21) provides: '[t]he present draft articles do not apply to the extent that the response to a disaster is governed by the rules of international humanitarian law'.[21] This provision offers an improved approach to the relationship than previous versions of the Draft Article. However, it still reflects the view that IDL is displaced by IHL as the *lex specialis* legal regime.[22]

This chapter suggests that such an interpretation is overly simplistic and gives undue weight to the *lex specialis* principle. The chapter first outlines the principles of IHL relevant to the provision of humanitarian assistance and their potential relationship to disaster victims. Next, it considers how the ILC has approached the role of IHL in the Draft Articles, before examining how IHL and IDL may interact in practice. Finally, the chapter argues that a more nuanced understanding of the relationship between IHL and IDL is required, which takes into account the context in which a disaster has occurred and recognises that the two may be complementary.

Relevant provisions of IHL

The relevant provisions of IHL that may be relevant in a disaster are found in the Geneva Convention Relative to the Protection of Civilian Persons in Time of War 1949 (GCIV),[23] the Protocols Additional to the Geneva Conventions (API and APII),[24] as well as in customary international law.[25] For present purposes, the relevant rules of IHL include the 'applicability' provisions of IHL, that is, those provisions that specify *when* IHL will apply. The relevant rules also include those substantive provisions that concern *when*, *how* and *by whom* humanitarian assistance can be provided and the *substantive content* of the relevant legal obligations.

Applicability of IHL

IHL is a 'set of rules which seek, for humanitarian reasons, to limit the effects of armed conflict. It protects persons who are not or are no longer participating in the hostilities and restricts the means and methods of warfare'.[26] Accordingly, IHL is not a regime of general application and applies only during situations of armed conflict, both international and non-international in nature, and occupation. The question of whether an armed conflict or an occupation exists is an objective one, and the relevant treaties set out varying thresholds for the application of IHL. For international armed conflicts, there must be a use of armed force between States or a declaration of war,[27] while in non-international armed conflicts, minimum requirements of intensity of violence and organisation of armed groups must be satisfied so as to distinguish an armed conflict from internal disturbances that do not attract the application of IHL.[28] In the context of international armed conflicts, 'territory is considered occupied when it is actually placed under the authority of the hostile army'.[29] Humanitarian actors must therefore make important factual determinations before being certain that IHL will apply in a given context.

Consistent with IHL's limited focus, it contains important temporal, geographic and personal limitations. First, temporally, the majority of provisions apply only for the duration of the armed conflict.[30] For international armed conflicts, this is from the onset of hostilities until the end of hostilities.[31] For non-international armed conflicts, IHL applies from the point at which the threshold requirements of intensity and organisation are met until there is a peaceful settlement or other cessation of hostilities.[32] IHL provisions on occupation apply as soon as territory is placed under control of a hostile army and continue until the foreign forces withdraw or are forced from the territory, or authority is transferred to the legitimate authorities.[33] Otherwise IHL will cease to apply to the occupation 12 months from the close of military operations, although certain obligations may continue.[34]

Second, the relevant IHL conventions are silent as to their geographical application.[35] For international armed conflicts, this means that IHL applies at least throughout the territory of the

States party to the conflict[36] and areas of belligerent occupation.[37] For non-international armed conflicts, 'the whole territory under the control of a party to the conflict, whether or not actual combat takes place there'.[38] That is, the geographic application of IHL is not restricted to the territory in which hostilities are being conducted.

Finally, IHL is limited as to the persons to whom it applies. In terms of those protected by IHL, IHL applies to specific classes of 'protected persons', in particular, civilian populations affected by armed conflict, those no longer participating in hostilities, such as the sick and wounded and prisoners of war, and those under the control of an occupying force.[39] IHL has historically focused on the protection of those in the control of an adverse power to a conflict, and a strict interpretation of IHL would preclude a State's own nationals relying on its provisions.[40] However, Article 70 of API refers to humanitarian assistance provided by impartial humanitarian organisations to the civilian population, 'regardless of any criteria of nationality, and independently of the Party to which they belong'.[41] In terms of who is bound, IHL creates rights and obligations for a range of actors, including: States parties to the Conventions in the territory of which an armed conflict is occurring (here, States parties) who may also be parties to the conflict; armed groups that are parties to a conflict; third or 'neutral' States (also referred to as States parties); and international organisations and humanitarian actors.

Substantive IHL provisions on humanitarian assistance

The substantive provisions of IHL vary depending on whether a conflict is international or non-international in character and also on the nature of the parties to the conflict, which may include State and non-state actors. The distinction between international and non-international armed conflict is of decreasing relevance and many international lawyers consider that most provisions relevant to international armed conflict would now extend to non-international armed conflict as a matter of customary international law anyway.[42] However, given that this argument is not yet universally accepted, the discussion here will maintain this distinction.

International armed conflict

IHL contains several provisions related to the delivery of humanitarian assistance. In an international armed conflict, IHL recognises the right of humanitarian initiative of the International Committee of the Red Cross (ICRC) and 'other impartial humanitarian organisations', which may be undertaken 'for the protection of civilian persons and for their relief' but 'subject to the consent of the Parties to the conflict concerned'.[43] This is supplemented by Additional Protocol I (API), which requires the States party to the conflict to extend to the ICRC 'all facilities within their power so as to enable it to carry out the humanitarian functions assigned to it' and, as far as possible, to other humanitarian organisations authorised to perform humanitarian activities.[44] Third States and the States party to the conflict 'shall facilitate in every possible way the assistance' of the ICRC and national societies to the victims of conflicts.[45]

States parties must allow free passage 'as rapidly as possible' 'of all consignments of medical and hospital stores . . . intended only for civilians' of another State party, even where that State may be an adverse party to the conflict.[46] This duty to allow the passage of relief consignments is subject to limits: in particular, it only applies where the State is satisfied that there are no serious reasons for fearing that the consignments may be diverted or control over their distribution may not be effective or that 'a definite advantage may accrue to the military efforts or economy of the enemy' by allowing the consignment.[47] Moreover, the State concerned may make passage conditional on the protecting power supervising distribution of the relief consignments and may prescribe the technical conditions on which passage is permitted.[48]

API extends the provisions in GCIV on relief supplies to occupied territories (see below) to 'the civilian population of any territory under the control of a Party to the conflict, other than occupied territory'.[49] Control of territory is thus an important, and often complex, aspect of humanitarian assistance under IHL, particularly in situations where it may not be evident which (or if any) party to a conflict controls a particular territory or where the entity in control may change often. Where the affected civilian population is not adequately provided with food and medical supplies, clothing, bedding, means of shelter and other supplies essential to the survival of the civilian population, 'relief actions which are humanitarian and impartial in character and conducted without any adverse distinction shall be undertaken, subject to the agreement of the Parties concerned in such relief actions'.[50] The provision does not specify by whom such actions shall be carried out. States, including those States party to the conflict, 'shall allow and facilitate rapid and unimpeded passage of all relief consignments, equipment and personnel provided', even if such assistance is destined for the civilian population of an adverse Party.[51] This is a different obligation to that in Article 23 of GCIV, as it requires States to facilitate, rather than merely allow the passage of relief.[52] However, as with Article 23, this obligation is qualified by the right to prescribe the technical arrangements under which such passage is permitted and requiring a Protecting Power to supervise the local distribution.[53] Moreover, the parties to the conflict shall not divert relief consignments nor delay their delivery, except in cases of urgent necessity in the interest of the civilian population concerned.[54] The parties to the conflict must also protect relief consignments and facilitate their rapid distribution[55] and, together with States parties, encourage and facilitate effective international coordination of relief actions.[56]

API also includes provisions concerning (but not defining) relief personnel who may, where necessary, participate in relief operations subject to the approval of the Party in whose territory they will carry out their duties.[57] Such personnel 'shall be respected and protected', must be assisted by each party receiving consignments 'to the fullest extent practicable' and may only have their activities or movements temporarily restricted 'in case of imperative military necessity'.[58] Relief personnel must not exceed the terms of their mandate and shall take account of the security requirements of the Party in whose territory they are carrying out their duties or risk the termination of their mission.[59]

Occupied territory

GCIV contains the most specific provisions concerning humanitarian assistance. However, these provisions apply only in relation to relief consignments to the populations of occupied territories; thus their reach is limited. An occupying power has certain fundamental obligations towards the civilian population of the occupied territory. Article 55 of GCIV provides that:

> to the fullest extent of the means available to it, the Occupying Power has the duty of ensuring the food and medical supplies of the population; it should, in particular, bring in the necessary foodstuffs, medical stores and other articles if the resources of the occupied territory are inadequate.

GCIV also recognises the right of humanitarian initiative of national Red Cross and other relief societies, as well as other assistance organisations,[60] with respect to occupied territory, subject only 'to temporary and exceptional measures imposed for urgent reasons of security by the Occupying Power'.[61]

Where all or part of the population of an occupied territory is 'inadequately supplied', an occupying power 'shall agree to relief schemes on behalf of the said population, and shall facilitate them by all the means at its disposal'.[62] This equates to an unconditional duty on the part of the occupying power to accept relief in such circumstances. Relief 'shall consist, in particular, of the provision of consignments of foodstuffs, medical supplies and clothing' and may be undertaken by states or by impartial humanitarian organisations such as the ICRC.[63] Allowing relief consignments does not relieve the Occupying Power of its own obligations towards the population of the occupied territory, in particular, those under Article 55.[64] All States parties must 'permit the free passage of these consignments and shall guarantee their protection'. However, a State party to the conflict that grants free passage for relief supplies headed to territory occupied by an adverse party to the conflict has:

> the right to search the consignments, to regulate their passage according to prescribed times and routes, and to be reasonably satisfied through the Protecting Power that these consignments are to be used for the relief of the needy population and are not to be used for the benefit of the Occupying Power.[65]

Once relief consignments are allowed in, the Occupying Power cannot divert relief consignments, except 'in cases of urgent necessity, in the interests of the population of the occupied territory and with the consent of the Protecting Power'.[66] Relief consignments must be exempt from all charges, taxes or customs duties in the occupied territory, 'unless these are necessary in the interests of the economy of the territory'.[67] Further, the Occupying Power 'shall facilitate the rapid distribution of these consignments'[68] and must allow individuals within the occupied territory to receive the individual relief consignments sent to them, subject only 'to imperative reasons of security'.[69] All States parties shall 'endeavour to permit the transit and transport, free of charge, of such relief consignments on their way to occupied territories'.[70] Protecting powers play an important role in supervising the transfer and distribution of relief consignments to occupied territories.[71] However, in practice, this responsibility is usually delegated to a neutral State, to the ICRC or to another impartial humanitarian organisation.

Non-international armed conflict

There are fewer provisions regulating humanitarian assistance in non-international armed conflicts. Common Article 3 to the Geneva Conventions recognises that an impartial humanitarian body, such as the ICRC, 'may offer its services to the Parties to the conflict'. This is supplemented by Article 18 of Additional Protocol II (APII), which provides that relief organisations such as national societies may 'offer their services for the performance of their traditional functions in relation to the victims of the armed conflict'. Moreover, where:

> the civilian population is suffering undue hardship owing to a lack of the supplies essential for its survival, such as foodstuffs and medical supplies, relief actions for the civilian population which are of an exclusively humanitarian and impartial nature and which are conducted without any adverse distinction shall be undertaken.[72]

However, both the provision of services and relief actions are subject to the consent of the State.

Discussion of IHL provisions

This brief overview of the relevant IHL provisions suggests several key conclusions. First, IHL is limited in its application to situations of armed conflict or occupation with temporal, personal and geographic restrictions. To determine whether IHL will apply to a particular situation, location or individual requires important factual determinations, including as to the nature of an armed conflict and whether a particular actor is in control of territory. In certain situations, there may be more than one conflict in a territory, for example, an international armed conflict between two States and a non-international armed conflict within one of those States. Moreover, a disaster does not respect State boundaries and may affect the territory of States not involved in an armed conflict as well as those involved, thus potentially leading to differentiated legal regimes applying to one relief effort.

Second, IHL does not define what constitutes humanitarian assistance, although its content has been somewhat clarified by practice.[73] It suggests that the content of relief is 'consignments of foodstuffs, medical supplies and clothing',[74] although this is expanded by Article 69 of API to include 'the provision of clothing, bedding, means of shelter, other supplies essential to the survival of the civilian population of the occupied territory and objects necessary for religious worship', at least in respect of occupied territories. There are also suggestions that humanitarian assistance must have an element of urgency and be indispensable to the affected population.[75] However, IHL does indicate important principles that suggest whether assistance is humanitarian in nature, namely, assistance should be consistent with the principles of humanity (to prevent unnecessary suffering and without distinction), impartiality and – potentially – neutrality.[76] IHL also suggests the urgency of humanitarian assistance to respond to immediate and indispensable needs of the population, as distinct from development assistance, which has a longer-term focus. In the context of IDL, this means that IHL will not be suited (perhaps other than in situations of occupation) to addressing the recovery and rehabilitation phases of disasters.

Third, other than in the case of an occupying power, IHL does not set out clear obligations on the territorial State or the non-state actor in control of territory regarding the primary obligation to provide assistance to the population within its own territory. While there is a presumption that 'states are primarily responsible for organising relief' and relief societies 'play an auxiliary role by assisting the authorities in their task',[77] IHL does not specify that underlying obligation, which must be sourced elsewhere, for example in International Human Rights Law (IHRL) or national law. Obligations of States or parties to the conflict under IHL are limited to admitting and facilitating the distribution of external assistance and not withholding consent or interfering with external relief efforts. The focus of IHL appears to be on the provision of relief from *outside* the State or territory concerned, with key roles indicated for the ICRC and other impartial humanitarian organisations pursuant to the right of humanitarian initiative. The role of third or neutral States in relation to humanitarian assistance, separate from the concept of protecting powers that is rarely employed in current conflicts, is not clearly indicated. IHL certainly does not address directly the provision of humanitarian assistance by the militaries of third States. Although military assistance is meant to be the final option for international disaster response, the reality is that many States do rely on their own military to provide humanitarian assistance in disaster contexts.[78] Nor does IHL specifically refer to the International Federation of Red Cross and Red Crescent societies (IFRC), UN agencies, regional organisations or non-governmental organisations that are often primary responders in a disaster.[79]

Fourth, there is no single comprehensive regime in IHL concerning humanitarian assistance, as the legal framework varies depending on the nature of the conflict and includes more provisions concerning occupation. Moreover, provisions in IHL concerning humanitarian relief lack detail as to the legal, logistical and operational aspects of humanitarian assistance. The obligations to allow and to facilitate assistance are general, and the only specific – albeit important – provisions concerning distribution are those concerning the imposition of taxes or duties. Thus, IHL may not apply in all contexts, but even where it does apply, relevant IHL provisions may not be comprehensive or address all key issues. This is particularly so regarding non-international armed conflicts. Moreover, IHL provisions are subject to restrictions based on military necessity and security, for example the provisions on withholding relief supplies for imperative reasons of security.[80] While these limits reflect the tension between humanitarian protection and military concerns inherent in IHL, these provisions may be subject to manipulation by States or armed groups or different interpretations by various actors and their application to situations where such concerns are not justified should be treated with caution.

Finally, the significance of State consent to humanitarian assistance in IHL is clear. While IHL has focused on limiting the circumstances in which a State can withhold consent to humanitarian assistance, and the requirements vary depending on the relevant instrument, some degree of consent is still required for humanitarian actions.[81] This underlies the view, noted above, that States should be primarily responsible for providing assistance, rather than humanitarian actors.[82] Moreover, as Barber notes, at least under the express obligations in IHL, the 'obligation to consent to and facilitate humanitarian assistance is limited to situations in which the failure to do so may threaten the survival of a civilian population'.[83] Barber argues that the obligation not to withhold consent might extend to other circumstances under customary international law.[84] Yet, at least on its face and particularly in relation to a non-international armed conflict, IHL would require the impact of a disaster to reach the threshold whereby the survival of the population is threatened, which may not always be the case.[85] However, while recognising the 'ambiguities about the extent of the obligations of domestic actors to consent to and facilitate international relief', Fisher notes, 'there are substantially fewer conditions that may legitimately be imposed on international humanitarian organizations before allowing them access in conflict settings [under IHL] than in disasters'.[86]

The interaction between IHL and IHRL is also important. International human rights instruments may also operate in situations of armed conflict to the extent that such obligations have not been the subject of lawful derogation.[87] Even where there has not been a formal derogation, IHRL may still somehow 'override' IHL provisions, as seen in recent jurisprudence.[88] While IHL clearly remains the specialist legal framework applicable in armed conflict, IHRL continues to apply and in fact may supplement IHL where IHL is silent or does not comprehensively regulate a particular situation, as recognised by the International Court of Justice[89] and the European Court of Human Rights.[90] The focus has now turned to how to approach the interaction between the two applicable regimes. Examples of this interaction include looking to IHL to determine what constitutes a 'lawful death' and to give further substance to provisions on detention in non-international armed conflict.[91] Two key points arise from this brief discussion for the purposes of this chapter. First, although it is a specialist regime, IHL does not automatically displace other legal regimes, including IHRL. Second, IHRL will also continue to apply in armed conflict, including to those States in which a disaster has occurred, and is available as a further source of law.

The ILC's approach to the relationship between IHL and IDL

Provisions of IHL have clearly influenced the development of IDL. The ILC and the IFRC have recognised IHL as a source for many of the provisions in the IDRL Guidelines[92] and the ILC Draft Articles[93] that effectively attempt to extend some of the IHL provisions discussed above to peacetime IDL. Examples of common principles include the right of humanitarian initiative of humanitarian organisations, the obligation on States to facilitate humanitarian assistance, the principles governing the provision of assistance and the circumstances in which consent to assistance can be withheld.

However, the main question for this chapter is the extent to which IHL leaves any space for IDL to apply in situations of armed conflict. There have been two ways in which armed conflict and IHL have been considered in relation to the applicability of IDL instruments. The first is a definitional one, namely, whether the definition of disaster for a particular instrument includes or excludes situations of armed conflict. That is, whether an armed conflict per se is a 'disaster' for the purposes of IDL instruments. The second is the inclusion of a specific clause regulating the relationship between armed conflict and IHL and IDL.

Armed conflict and the definition of disaster

Approaches to the inclusion of armed conflicts in the definition of disaster have been mixed. The IDRL Guidelines[94] and the Oslo Guidelines[95] exclude armed conflicts as such from the definition of disaster, while other instruments do not.[96] The issue of definition also received attention in the ILC. The ILC Special Rapporteur initially proposed that the definition of disaster specifically exclude armed conflict from the definition of disaster,[97] on the basis that a 'well-developed body of law exists to cover such situations'.[98] Following discussion in the drafting committee and Sixth Committee, the exclusion of armed conflict shifted from being a definitional issue to being one for the substance of the Draft Articles.[99] Accordingly, Draft Article 3 [now 3(a)] as adopted does not specifically exclude armed conflict from the definition of disaster. While it was clear that States did not consider that an armed conflict would, of itself, constitute a disaster, the ILC did not wish automatically to exclude armed conflicts from the definition of disaster largely because of the concern, raised in the Committee, that a categorical exclusion would be counter-productive, particularly in situations of 'complex emergencies' where a disaster, whether emanating from natural or human causes, occurs in an area where there is an armed conflict. To simply exclude the applicability of the Draft Articles because of the co-existence of an armed conflict would be detrimental to the protection of the victims of the disaster, especially when the onset of the disaster pre-dated the armed conflict.[100]

The reluctance to exclude armed conflicts per se from the definition of disaster thus reflects two concerns. First, can an armed conflict itself, and its consequences, reach the threshold required for a disaster? Second, what would be the justification for excluding armed conflicts from the scope of a disaster, particularly where a natural disaster that would otherwise meet the definition of disaster occurs in the same territory?

States largely endorsed this approach in their comments on the Draft Articles.[101] However, Mexico and the United States expressed concern that armed conflicts and their consequences were not excluded from the scope of the definition of disasters.[102] The ICRC also maintained its 'concern' that the article did not expressly exclude armed conflict, which it suggested 'creates overlap and contradictions between rules of international humanitarian law and the draft articles, resulting in confusion and potential conflicts of norms'.[103] Despite these comments, the Special Rapporteur did not suggest any changes to Draft Article 3 to exclude armed conflict, and the final version adopted by the ILC in 2016 did not expressly exclude either armed conflicts per se or their consequences. The commentaries to Draft Article 18 confirms this approach, noting that a 'blank exclusion of the applicability of the Draft Articles because of the coexistence of an armed conflict would be detrimental to the protection of the persons affected by the disaster'.[104]

A relationship clause

The Special Rapporteur and the ILC dealt with the relationship between IHL and IDL by the inclusion of a 'relationship' clause. This was introduced initially as Draft Article 4, became Draft Article 21 and is currently Draft Article 18(2). Draft Article 21 was entitled 'Relationship to international humanitarian law' and remained substantively unchanged until its most recent iteration. It provided: 'The present draft articles do not apply to situations to which the rules of international humanitarian law are applicable'. The provision followed on from Article 20 [now 18(1)], which concerns the relationship of the Draft Articles to other rules of international law. It stated: 'The present draft articles are without prejudice to special or other rules of international law applicable in the event of disasters'.

The President of the Drafting Committee noted the distinction between the two clauses.[105] Draft Article 20 merely preserved the continued operation of both IDL and other areas of international law – including IHRL – that might be applicable in a disaster. In contrast, Draft Article 21 was intended 'to clarify the relationship between the draft articles and international humanitarian law, giving predominance to the latter set of rules in situations where they are applicable'.[106] While an initial reading of Draft Article 21 may suggest otherwise, it is clear from the drafting history of Article 21 that it was not intended to displace IDL completely where a disaster occurs in a situation where there is an armed conflict. This position is reaffirmed by the ILC commentary to Draft Article 21, which states that '[T]he provision is formulated in a manner intended to clarify the relationship by giving precedence to the rules of international humanitarian law'. Where a disaster coexists with an armed conflict

> international humanitarian law shall be applied as *lex specialis*, whereas the rules contained in the present draft articles would continue to apply 'to the extent' that legal issues raised by a disaster are not covered by the rules of international humanitarian law.[107]

Therefore, the ILC Draft Articles are not automatically displaced where a disaster occurs in a State experiencing armed conflict. Several States endorsed the approach reflected in Draft Article 21, namely that IDL would apply to the extent that IHL did not regulate a particular situation. However, States also noticed that there was inconsistency between the wording of the draft article and the commentary, with the commentary more clearly reflecting the intended relationship.[108] The ICRC and the IFRC argued that there should be an unambiguous statement that the Draft Articles do not apply in situations of armed conflict, while the UN Office for the Coordination of Humanitarian Affairs (UNOCHA) argued that the Draft Articles did not 'provide a clear understanding of the relationship between the draft articles and international humanitarian law'.[109] The Special Rapporteur endorsed the suggestion that a 'without prejudice' clause might better represent the relationship the Draft Articles sought to create.[110] However, the draft article that emerged from the Drafting Committee, Draft Article 18(2), which was now amalgamated with the provision on other rules of international law, is not a 'without prejudice' clause.[111] Instead, it provides: '[t]he present draft articles do not apply to the extent that the response to a disaster is governed by the rules of international humanitarian law'.

This provision represents a more nuanced approach to determining the applicable law in a given situation, which in many respects will require a similar approach to resolving the relationship between IHL and IHRL, as discussed above. However, the ILC, States and relevant international organisations have not considered fully how that relationship might work in practice. The next section explores this possible interaction.

Relationship between IHL and IDL in practice

The above discussion demonstrates four possible scenarios for the relationship between IHL and IDL where disasters occur in the context of armed conflict: (1) IDL does not or should not apply; (2) IHL does not or should not apply; (3) IHL applies, but is supplemented, complemented or interpreted by reference to IDL; and (4) IHL applies, but is supplemented or complemented by IDL. This section provides some initial thoughts on these various options.

Regarding the first scenario, IDL would not apply on the basis that IHL is the *lex specialis*. However, this overstates the role to be played by *lex specialis*, equating this to excluding the application of an entire body of law without any consideration of the extent to which there is necessarily any conflict or overlap of rules between the two regimes. This absolute approach is no longer accepted in the realm of IHRL and has not been adopted in the ILC's own study on the impact of armed conflict on treaty obligations.[112] Therefore, unless the relevant IDL instruments expressly preclude IDL from applying in an armed conflict situation, non-applicability should not be assumed merely because of IHL's specificity in relation to armed conflicts. As outlined above, the ILC has not adopted this approach in the ILC Draft Articles.

Similarly, although IDL is also a 'specialist' regime in the sense that it is – as a general rule – only relevant where a disaster has occurred, this does not mean that the *lex specialis* rule results in the non-applicability of IHL. This would be contrary to the long-standing importance and impact of IHL in addressing armed conflict. However, there are several possibilities where IHL does not or should not apply to a particular disaster situation.

An obvious situation is where IHL does not apply because there is no armed conflict or occupation that would trigger the application of IHL. That is, the thresholds for the application of IHL discussed above (inter-State use of force, intensity of violence, level of organisation or the occupation of territory) have not been met. The non-applicability of IHL may be evident; however, in some situations it will be unclear. For example, there may be significant unrest within a State, but whether the threshold for a non-international armed conflict has been met may be a matter of dispute. This is particularly the case where a government does not wish to recognise non-state actors as parties to a conflict, or the existence of a situation of non-international armed conflict and to accept that IHL, rather than domestic law, applies. Similar concerns may arise in relation to violence perpetrated by groups considered to be terrorist in nature. Where a disaster occurs in such a context, humanitarian responders will need to determine whether IHL applies so as to identify the relevant framework. This may place responders in direct conflict with government authorities that do not recognise the situation as one to which IHL applies.

As signalled above, the geographical location of the disaster and the armed conflict should also determine whether IHL applies. In principle, IHL will apply to *all* the territory of States parties to the conflict (in an international armed conflict), to all territory controlled by parties to a conflict (in a non-international armed conflict) and throughout an occupied territory. Yet where the disaster affects an area that is geographically removed from and does not impact, or is not impacted by, the armed conflict, IHL should not regulate the provision of humanitarian assistance. Rather, IDL, particularly as given effect in domestic law, would be the appropriate body of law. Gavshon refers to the example of Hurricane Katrina in 2005, which affected part of the US at a time when the US was engaged in a non-international armed conflict with Al Qaeda. She notes that no one suggested (or perhaps even contemplated) that IHL would be the relevant legal framework, although IHL technically applied to the entirety of US territory at the time.[113] Another example would be the international armed conflicts in which the US and other States have participated, but which are fought in other continents. The idea that relief operations in the US should be conducted in accordance with IHL, which technically applies to the entire territory of the US, is absurd.

This concern also ties to the personal limitations of IHL. While those affected by a disaster are likely to be civilians (in the sense that they are not participating in hostilities), where the disasters victims are remote from armed conflict and otherwise unaffected by it, it is hard to view disaster victims as also being victims of armed conflict and hence needing the protection of IHL.[114]

Further, a technical reading of IHL provisions may suggest that a State's own nationals cannot use IHL to access relief.[115]

One suggestion is that there must be a nexus to the armed conflict before IHL is considered the appropriate body of law for the provision of assistance after a disaster.[116] A requirement for a nexus is certainly not express, with the relevant IHL instruments addressing only the suffering of the affected populations and not stipulating that the suffering needs to have been *caused* by the armed conflict. That is, the provision of humanitarian assistance in response to suffering caused by other factors, such as a disaster, is not necessarily excluded. IHL includes a requirement for a connection to an armed conflict in some contexts. For example, the war crimes regime requires a nexus between the alleged crime and the armed conflict and excludes incidents that have no connection to the armed conflict, although admittedly the nexus requirement is interpreted somewhat loosely.[117] Similarly, where there is no connection between a disaster, the required humanitarian assistance and an armed conflict or occupation, even though IHL may technically apply, it may be more appropriate not to apply IHL. However, as with war crimes, a flexible approach to a nexus will be required so as to capture situations where the armed conflict might be indirectly affecting the disaster-related assistance, for example, where assistance would have to transit through areas controlled by non-state actors party to the conflict and its delivery might be affected.

Another possibility is that the parties to a conflict do not apply IHL to disaster-related humanitarian assistance, even though technically IHL applies. IHL provides a minimum set of standards and obligations that parties to the conflict must apply. It is open to the parties to a conflict, by agreement or practice, to not apply a more beneficial and detailed framework(s). IDL, which has been designed predominantly to apply in peacetime and may have been given effect in national law, avoids the need to balance military and security interests required by IHL. This means that IDL may offer a less tense and 'political' framework for the delivery of assistance than IHL. IDL may also facilitate the provision of assistance by military forces, both of the affected State and of third States.[118] In fact, Venturini suggests that IHL plays a more limited role in facilitating disaster assistance and relief in some mixed situations of disaster and armed conflict than might be expected.[119] It is, however, somewhat difficult to draw firm conclusions regarding the extent to which States have considered IDL to be a framework for the delivery of humanitarian assistance after a disaster within armed conflict, as many relevant examples, such as the 2004 Indian Ocean tsunami, pre-date the adoption of the main IDL instruments and their implementation in domestic law by many States.

Under the third scenario, both IDL and IHL would apply, and a decision would be taken on a case-by-case basis as to which provision should be adopted. Arguably the more specific, relevant or beneficial provision should be preferred.

The final scenario is where IHL applies to a situation, but the relevant IHL provisions are not comprehensive or do not address the issue in question. In this situation, the specific rules of IHL would be complemented or supplemented by IDL, or interpreted by reference to IDL, in much the same way that IHRL operates in relation to IHL.[120] The status of the IHL provisions on humanitarian assistance, in particular, the recognition of the right of humanitarian initiative, may aid in getting agreement to the provision of assistance in the first place. However, given that the IHL framework surrounding humanitarian assistance is not comprehensive or detailed, there is plenty of scope to draw on IDL to fill the gaps or address the uncertainties of IHL. For example, the IDRL Guidelines contain more detailed provisions addressing technical issues, such as visas, customs and qualifications of relief personnel, that are not fully addressed, or addressed at all, by IHL. Even though these instruments are non-binding and do not necessarily have customary international law status, they may have been given effect in the national law of the State(s) concerned or may be a useful guide that a State may elect to follow. This approach depends on the relevant governments, humanitarian organisations and other actors being familiar with the provisions of IDL, including those incorporated into national law. However, at present 'the point at which [IHL] gives way to other areas of law to set the standards of assistance is uncertain'.[121]

Another, more controversial, potential gap is that IHL does not regulate the provision of assistance to persons not protected by the conventions, in particular, combatants and those taking part in hostilities.[122] In a disaster situation, there may be a need to provide assistance to combatants, particularly within a non-international armed conflict. While recognising that this raises issues as to impartiality and neutrality, using IDL to complement IHL to deliver assistance to parties to the conflict affected by the disaster as well as civilian populations may provide a solution, particularly where a disaster has rendered that party unable to continue hostilities for a period.

Conclusion: is IHL appropriate to regulate humanitarian assistance in disasters?

There are clear advantages to applying IHL as the legal framework to regulate humanitarian assistance in the context of a disaster. IHL contains binding and well-accepted obligations on States and other parties to a conflict to accept and facilitate assistance, as well as obligations on third States, including those through which assistance may need to transit. In contrast, most IDL instruments are either limited in scope or non-binding. States do not yet accept their provisions as constituting rules of customary international law, although soft law guidelines are increasingly being incorporated into national laws and frameworks for disaster response. Despite its hard law status, IHL is not necessarily applicable to disaster relief as this chapter suggests. First, IHL has limited application (both as to the thresholds before IHL is triggered and its temporal, geographic and personal dimensions). Second, the disparate and non-comprehensive provisions that apply depend on the nature of the armed conflict or whether a situation amounts to an occupation. Third, IHL is potentially susceptible to political and military tensions, for example, the restrictions for military necessity or the prospect that the State concerned will dispute the existence of an armed conflict and the applicability of IHL. These represent some of the challenges to using IHL to regulate disaster relief.

Given these limits, it should certainly not be assumed that IDL is not relevant merely because a disaster occurs in a State(s) affected by an armed conflict or occupation, that is, that IHL should always play the exclusive or at least primary role in relation to humanitarian assistance. In fact, IDL might provide a more suitable, and perhaps less politicised, framework for regulating humanitarian assistance, although many government legal advisers may not be as familiar with its provisions. While its provisions may not be binding, they could provide the basis for negotiated practical arrangements. Moreover, IHL is itself acknowledged to have a weak enforcement mechanism, so simply because its obligations are 'hard law' does not necessarily mean they are respected and implemented.[123] As Stoffels concluded, 'the problem lies not in inadequate legal definitions, but in the context in which humanitarian assistance is implemented and in the interests involved'.[124] As more States take steps to give effect to instruments such as the IDRL Guidelines in their national disaster legal and policy frameworks, those provisions *will* bind, or at least must be considered by, national actors and may even give rise to rights under national law. It is therefore increasingly likely that these more comprehensive peacetime arrangements, rather than the provisions of IHL, will regulate, or be considered relevant to, the delivery of humanitarian assistance in disasters, even in those States affected by armed conflict.

The aim of IDL is to 'facilitate the adequate and effective response to disasters . . . so as to meet the essential needs of the persons concerned, with full respect for their rights'.[125] Applying

IHL to the exclusion of IDL potentially undermines a key emphasis of IDL, which is to reinforce the prerogative – and responsibility – of the affected State to lead the disaster response and to regulate, control and coordinate international assistance.[126] National authorities are the primary responders and international assistance is required only to the extent that national capacity is overwhelmed. The IFRC, which has been leading the push for recognition of IDL, emphasises building national capacity and resilience to disasters, including through improving domestic legal frameworks.[127] In contrast, IHL emphasises the right of international organisations and third States to provide relief and seems to be premised on the notion of an affected State that is unwilling or unable to provide humanitarian assistance to civilians in need. There is therefore a risk that IHL prioritises international rather than national responses inconsistently with the emphasis on building resilience through the development and implementation of national plans in IDL.[128] Prioritising the international (as IHL tends to do) over the national (where IDL constitutes 'hard law') could preclude national authorities from fulfilling their role as the primary responder and coordinator of assistance.

However, this is not to suggest that IHL has no role in relation to the provision of humanitarian assistance after a disaster. IHL contains key provisions such as those detailing the provision of assistance in situations where there are military and security threats to the delivery of assistance or relief personnel from ongoing hostilities. IHL recognises the risk of interference with, or partiality in the distribution of, assistance to certain groups. Further, IHL regulates assistance that is required in areas controlled by non-state actors and addresses a refusal by parties to the conflict to allow assistance. Rather, this chapter suggests that IHL should be the *lex specialis* where there is a truly complex emergency,[129] in particular, where the disaster and the armed conflict are connected and the armed conflict is interfering with the delivery of humanitarian assistance. Yet, as with IHL and IHRL, IDL remains relevant and could complement or supplement IHL where that body of law is silent or not comprehensive or provide an aid for interpretation. However, IDL would defer to IHL in relation to more specific IHL provisions, for example, when assistance might be considered to be aiding a party to the conflict. It should also be recalled that IHRL continues to apply where there is both an armed conflict and a disaster. While the relationship of IHRL to IDL and IHL has not been the main focus of this chapter, it may be that IHRL would provide an equally strong set of claims as IHL in respect of the right of initiative and the obligations of States and other actors to accept and facilitate assistance after a disaster, but also an equally challenging issue of enforcement. In this way, IHRL and IDL, particularly as they continue to develop and be implemented at the national level, may provide an alternative to relying on IHL.

Thus the ILC was right not to categorically exclude armed conflict from the definition of disaster. However, the relationship clause does little to address the complexities of this area of humanitarian assistance and the overlap and potential interaction between IHL and IDL. In fact, while aiming to produce text that was simple and elegant, the ILC gave fairly superficial consideration to this relationship. In this sense, it was a lost opportunity to collect State practice and to explore the issues fully in an attempt to provide more clarity, consistency and uniformity in this area. Differences in scope and application between the two regimes appear to have been assumed, rather than established by a careful review of the key provisions and their application in practice. This lack of analysis is unlikely to change when the Draft Articles are discussed in the Sixth Committee of the UN General Assembly. As it presently stands, the ILC Draft Articles leave responders to consider the applicability of each area of law on a case-by-case basis. This brings a real risk of delay and uncertainty in the applicable legal framework, which is not desirable in challenging conditions. Moreover, failing to examine the relationship between the two regimes fully does little to explore the gaps and inconsistencies across the two regimes and potentially leaves victims of disasters to face different rights and treatment depending on which regime is applied.

Selected bibliography

R. Barber, 'Facilitating Humanitarian Assistance in International Humanitarian and Human Rights Law' 91 *International Review of the Red Cross* (2009) 371.

D. Fisher, 'Domestic Regulation of International Humanitarian Relief in Disasters and Armed Conflict: A Comparative Analysis' 89 *International Review of the Red Cross* (2007) 345.

D. Gavshon, 'The Applicability of IHL in Mixed Situations of Disaster and Conflict' 14 *Journal of Conflict & Security Law* (2009) 243.

M. Milanovic, 'The Lost Origins of *Lex Specialis*: Rethinking the Relationship between Human Rights and International Humanitarian Law' in J.D. Ohlin (ed), *Theoretical Boundaries of Armed Conflict and Human Rights* (Cambridge University Press, 2016) 78.

G. Venturini, 'Disasters and Armed Conflict' in A. de Guttry, M. Gestri and G. Venturini (eds), *International Disaster Response Law* (TMC Asser Press, 2012) 251.

Notes

1 ILC, Report of the International Law Commission, Sixty-Eighth Session (2 May–10 June and 4 July–12 August 2016), Draft Articles and Commentaries on the Protection of Persons in the Event of Disasters (ILC Draft Articles), UN Doc. A/CN.4/871, draft art 3, in *Yearbook of the International Law Commission*, A/71/10 (2016), vol 2, Part Two. Note that this is not the accepted common definition of 'disaster', with many instruments adopting their own definition.

2 International Institute for Strategic Studies, 'Armed Conflict Database: Current Conflicts' (2015), available at https://acd.iiss.org, accessed on 17 March 2017.

3 See K. Mukherjee, 'The Kashmir Conflict in South Asia: Voices from Srinagar' 30(1) *Defense & Security Analysis* (2014) 44.

4 On disaster-prone Asia-Pacific States, see UN Economic and Social Commission for Asia and the Pacific, 'Asia-Pacific Disaster Report 2015' (27 October 2015), available at www.unescap.org/resources/asia-pacific-disaster-report-2015, accessed on 1 July 2016, xxii. On conflict in the Asia-Pacific, see International Institute for Strategic Studies, *Asia-Pacific Regional Security Assessment 2015* (Strategic Dossier, 29 May 2015).

5 On the ceasefire, see BBC News, 'MILF Rebels Hand Over Arms in the Philippines' (16 June 2015), available at www.bbc.com/news/world-asia-33144749, accessed on 1 July 2017. On disasters in the Philippines, see G. Bankoff, *Cultures of Disaster: Society and Natural Hazards in the Philippines* (Routledge Curzon, 2003) 124; J. Wingard and A.S. Brändlin, 'Philippines: A Country Prone to Natural Disasters' *Deutsche Welle* (10 November 2014), available at www.dw.com/en/philippines-a-country-prone-to-natural-disasters/a-17217404, accessed on 7 June 2017.

6 A. South, 'The Politics of Protection in Burma' 44 *Critical Asian Studies* (2012) 175.

7 A. de Waal, *Famine Crimes: Politics and the Disaster Relief Industry* (James Currey, 1997).

8 N. Ahmed, 'Entangled Earth' 27 *Third Text* (2013) 44, 45–47.

9 On disaster risk reduction, see UNGA, Sendai Framework for Disaster Risk Reduction 2015–2030, UN Doc. A/CONF.224/CRP.1 (18 March 2015) (Sendai Framework). On IDRL, see IFRC, Guidelines for the Domestic Facilitation and Regulation of International Disaster Relief and Initial Recovery Assistance (30 November 2007) (IDRL Guidelines).

10 Although a UNGA resolution provides the basis for international cooperation: UNGA, Res 46/182: Strengthening of the Coordination of Humanitarian Emergency Assistance of the United Nations, UN Doc. A/RES/46/182 (19 December 1991).

11 See the treaties cited in UN Secretariat Study Prepared to Assist the ILC Special Rapporteur: UNGA, Protection of Persons in the Event of Disasters: Memorandum by the Secretariat, UN Doc. A/CN.4/590 (11 December 2007).

12 IDRL Guidelines (n. 9). The UNGA has encouraged States to make use of the IDRL Guidelines: see UNGA, Res 63/139, UN Doc. A/RES/63/139 (5 March 2009); UNGA, Res 63/141, UN Doc. A/RES/63/141 (10 March 2009); and UNGA, Res 63/137, UN Doc. A/RES/63/137 (3 March 2009).

13 See the IFRC and national society reports analysing the extent to which IDRL Guidelines have been adopted: IFRC, 'Disaster Law Publications' (2015), available at www.ifrc.org/en/what-we-do/disaster-law/research-tools-and-publications/disaster-law-publications/, accessed on 7 June 2017.

14 See ILC Draft Articles (n. 1).

15 ILC, Report of the International Law Commission, Sixty-Eighth Session, UN Doc. A/71/10 (2016) (2 May–10 June and 4 July–12 August 2016).

16 Ibid para 46.
17 UNGA, Sixth Committee: Summary Record of the 20th Meeting – 24 October 2016, UN Doc. A/C.6/71/SR.20 (11 November 2016); UNGA, Sixth Committee: Summary Record of the 21st Meeting – 25 October 2016, UN Doc. A/C.6/71/SR.21 (16 November 2016); UNGA, Sixth Committee: Summary Record of 23th Meeting – 26 October 2016, UN Doc. A/C.6/71/SR.23 (14 November 2016).
18 UNGA, Res 71/140, UN Doc. A/RES/71/140 (19 December 2016).
19 UNGA, Res 71/141, UN Doc. A/RES/71/141 (19 December 2016).
20 The need to consider the overlap between IHL and the scope of the Draft Articles was evident from the first report prepared by the Special Rapporteur. See ILC, Preliminary Report on the Protection of Persons in the Event of Disasters, by Mr. Eduardo Valencia-Ospina, Special Rapporteur, UN Doc. A/CN.4/598 (5 May 2008).
21 ILC Draft Articles (n. 1).
22 For discussion of how *lex specialis* operates, see: ILC, Fragmentation of International Law: Difficulties Arising from the Diversification and Expansion of International Law, Report of the Study Group of the International Law Commission, Finalized by Martti Koskenniemi, UN Doc. A/CN.4/L.682 (13 April 2006); ILC, Report of the International Law Commission, Fifty-Sixth Session, UN Doc. A/59/10 (16 September 2004) (3 May–4 June and 5 July–6 August 2004) paras 304–313.
23 Geneva Convention Relative to the Protection of Civilian Persons in Time of War (adopted 12 August 1949, entered into force 21 October 1950) 75 UNTS 287 (Geneva Convention IV).
24 Protocol Additional to the Geneva Conventions of 12 August 1949, and Relating to the Protection of Victims of International Armed Conflicts (adopted 12 December 1977, entered into force 7 December 1978) 1125 UNTS 3 (Additional Protocol I) and Protocol Additional to the Geneva Conventions of 12 August 1949, and Relating to the Protection of Victims of Non-International Armed Conflicts (adopted 8 June 1977, entered into force 7 December 1978) 1125 UNTS 609 (Additional Protocol II).
25 For relevant customary international law rules, see ICRC, *Customary International Humanitarian Law: Rules and Practice* (Cambridge University Press, 2005) and the online updates of State practice.
26 See, e.g., ICRC, Advisory Service on International Humanitarian Law, 'What Is International Humanitarian Law' (July 2004), available at www.icrc.org/eng/assets/files/other/what_is_ihl.pdf, accessed on 1 July 2017.
27 See common art 2 of the Geneva Conventions; Additional Protocol I, art 1; *The Prosecutor v. Dusko Tadić (Decision on the Defence Motion for Interlocutory Appeal on Jurisdiction)* (ICTY, Appeals Chamber, Case No IT-94–1-A, 2 October 1995) para 70. See also J. Pictet (ed), *Commentary III, Geneva Convention Relative to the Treatment of Prisoners of War* (ICRC, 1960) 23.
28 See common art 3 of the Geneva Conventions; *Tadić* para 70. For the application of Additional Protocol II, art 1 imposes the additional requirements that the conflict take place in the territory of a State party to Additional Protocol II between its armed forces and dissident armed forces or other organised armed groups which, under responsible command, exercise such control over a part of its territory as to enable them to carry out sustained and concerted military operations and to implement this Protocol.
29 Hague Convention (IV) Respecting the Laws and Customs of War on Land and its annex: Regulations concerning the Laws and Customs of War on Land (adopted 18 October 1907, entered into force 26 January 1910) 205 CTS 277 (Hague Regulations), Regulation 42. See also: common art 2 of the Geneva Conventions.
30 Both the commencement and end of application of IHL are based on the factual circumstances. For thorough discussion, see J. Grignon, 'The Beginning of Application of International Humanitarian Law: A Discussion of a Few Challenges' 96 *International Review of the Red Cross* (2014) 139; M. Milanovic, 'The End of Application of International Humanitarian Law' 96 *International Review of the Red Cross* (2014) 163.
31 Geneva Convention IV, arts 1 and 6; Additional Protocol I, arts 1 and 3.
32 Additional Protocol II, art 2. See also *Tadić* para 70.
33 Hague Regulations regulation, 42; Geneva Convention IV, art 2.
34 Geneva Convention IV, art 6. For further discussion, see T. Ferraro, 'Determining the Beginning and End of an Occupation under International Humanitarian Law' 94 *International Review of the Red Cross* (2012) 133.
35 This issue has become particularly relevant recently concerning the extra-territorial use of drones: see J. Pejic, 'Extraterritorial Targeting by Means of Armed Drones: Some Legal Implications' 96 *International Review of the Red Cross* (2014) 67.
36 See, e.g., J. Kleffner, 'Scope of Application of International Humanitarian Law' in D. Fleck (ed), *The Handbook of Humanitarian Law in Armed Conflicts* (3rd edn, Oxford University Press, 2013) 56–57;

Y. Dinstein, *War, Aggression and Self-Defence* (5th edn, Cambridge University Press, 2011) 19. IHL may also extend beyond the territory of the parties, in areas where there are actual hostilities outside the territory or territorial control of the parties to the conflict, for example, the high seas.

37 For an occupation, the 'occupation extends only to the territory where such authority has been established and can be exercised': Hague Regulations, art 42.

38 *The Prosecutor v. Dragoljub Kunarac, Radomir Kovač and Zoran Vuković (Judgement)* (ICTY, Appeals Chamber, Case No IT-96–23 & IT-96–23/1-A, 12 June 2002) para 57. Common art 3 of the Geneva Conventions refers to acts that are prohibited 'at any time and in any place whatsoever'. See also *Tadić* paras 68–70; *The Prosecutor v. Laurent Semanza (Judgement and Sentence)* (ICTR, Trial Chamber III, Case No. ICTR-97–20-T, 15 May 2003) para 367. (Their scope extends throughout the territory of the State where the hostilities are taking place without limitation to the 'war front' or to the 'narrow geographical context of the actual theatre of combat operations'.)

39 Art 4 of Geneva Convention IV (international armed conflict) states that

> [p]ersons protected by the Convention are those who, at a given moment and in any manner whatsoever, find themselves, in case of a conflict or occupation, in the hands of a Party to the conflict or Occupying Power of which they are not nationals.

In contrast, common art 3 of the Geneva Conventions refers to '[p]ersons taking no active part in the hostilities'. Art 4 of Additional Protocol II is for the protection of 'all persons who do not take a direct part or who have ceased to take part in hostilities'.

40 IHL appears to be shifting from this position: see *Tadić* paras 163–169.

41 Additional Protocol I, art 70. See also Y. Sandoz, C. Swinarski and B. Zimmermann (eds), *Commentary on the Additional Protocols of 8 June 1977 to the Geneva Conventions of 12 August 1949* (Martinus Nijhoff Publishers, 1987) 819.

42 This was the conclusion of the ICRC Customary International Humanitarian Law Study, which found that customary international law had developed to fill the gaps left by IHL treaty law, particularly regarding non-international armed conflicts: J.M. Henckaerts, 'Study on Customary International Humanitarian Law: A Contribution to the Understanding and Respect for the Rule of Law in Armed Conflict' 87 *International Review of the Red Cross* (2005) 175, 188. See n. 20.

43 Geneva Convention IV art 10. See also Geneva Conventions I, II and III, art 9.

44 Additional Protocol I, art 81.

45 Ibid art 81(3).

46 Geneva Convention IV, art 23. This duty also extends to 'free passage of all consignments of essential foodstuffs, clothing and tonics intended for children under fifteen, expectant mothers and maternity cases'.

47 Geneva Convention IV, art 23.

48 Ibid.

49 Additional Protocol I, art 70.

50 Ibid drawing on art 69.

51 Ibid art 70(2).

52 See also ICRC Customary International Humanitarian Law Study (n. 42) rule 55.

53 Ibid art 70(3).

54 Ibid.

55 Ibid art 70(4).

56 Ibid art 70(5).

57 Ibid art 71(1).

58 Ibid arts 71(2) and (3).

59 Ibid art 71(4).

60 Art 63 of Geneva Convention IV applies the same principles

> to the activities and personnel of special organizations of a non-military character, which already exist or which may be established, for the purpose of ensuring the living conditions of the civilian population by the maintenance of the essential public utility services, by the distribution of relief and by the organization of rescues.

61 Geneva Convention IV, art 63.

62 Ibid art 59.

63 Ibid.

64 Ibid art 60.

65 Ibid art 59.
66 Ibid art 60.
67 Ibid art 61.
68 Ibid.
69 Ibid art 62.
70 Ibid art 61.
71 Ibid.
72 Ibid art 18(2).
73 For a detailed examination of this issue, see E.E. Kuijt, *Humanitarian Assistance and State Sovereignty in International Law: Towards a Comprehensive Framework* (Intersentia, 2015) 32–38.
74 Geneva Convention IV, art 59. See also art 23, which refers to medical supplies and hospital stores.
75 See Kuijt (n. 73) 38–53.
76 These principles are drawn from the wording of the Geneva Conventions, in particular references to 'impartial humanitarian organisations' and relief actions 'of an exclusively humanitarian and impartial nature', as well as from the principles of the Red Cross movement itself.
77 Y. Sandoz, C. Swinarski and B. Zimmermann (eds), *Commentary on the Additional Protocols of 8 June 1977 to the Geneva Conventions of 12 August 1949* (Martinus Nijhoff Publishers, 1987).
78 Recent examples that included a significant component of assistance being provided by national and foreign military forces are the 2015 Nepal earthquake and Typhoon Haiyan in the Philippines in 2013.
79 Since 2005, humanitarian response has been coordinated by the UNOCHA through the cluster system, which designates certain agencies as lead for particular issues such as nutrition, water and sanitation, shelter and protection. See further: Humanitarian Response, 'Clusters' (2015), available at www.humanitarianresponse.info/en/coordination/clusters/what-cluster-approach, accessed on 7 June 2017.
80 Geneva Convention IV, art 63. See also other restrictions discussed in the previous section.
81 See ICRC Customary International Humanitarian Law (n. 42) Rule 55, and Commentary thereto. See also Kujit (n. 73).
82 R. Barber, 'Facilitating Humanitarian Assistance in International Humanitarian and Human Rights Law' 91 *International Review of the Red Cross* (2009) 371, 386.
83 Ibid 387.
84 Ibid.
85 In contrast, in an international armed conflict, it is enough that the population is 'inadequately supplied'.
86 D. Fisher, 'Domestic Regulation of International Humanitarian Relief in Disasters and Armed Conflict: A Comparative Analysis' 89 *International Review of the Red Cross* (2007) 345, 346.
87 IHRL instruments allow for derogation from specific articles in limited circumstances. For example, art 4 ICCPR allows for derogation 'in time of public emergency which threatens the life of the nation and the existence of which is officially proclaimed'.
88 E.g. *Hassan v. United Kingdom*, App. No. 29750/09 (ECtHR, Grand Chamber, Judgment of 16 September 2014).
89 *Legality of the Threat or Use of Nuclear Weapons (Advisory Opinion)* [1996] ICJ Rep. (I) 257, para 25; *Legal Consequences of the Construction of a Wall in the Occupied Palestinian Territory (Advisory Opinion)* [2004] ICJ Rep. 136 para 106; *Armed Activities on the Territory of the Congo (Democratic Republic of the Congo v. Uganda) (Judgment)* [2005] ICJ Rep. 168, paras 216–220.
90 See e.g. *Hassan v. United Kingdom*.
91 Both of these issues are discussed in M. Sassòli and L.M. Olson, 'The Relationship between International Humanitarian and Human Rights Law Where It Matters: Admissible Killing and Internment of Fighters in Non-International Armed Conflicts' 90 *International Review of the Red Cross* (2008) 599.
92 See e.g. D. Fisher, *Law and Legal Issues in International Disaster Response: A Desk Study* (IFRC, 2007) 36, recognising that 'it is instructive to look to IHL by way of analogy where it addresses the same issues confronted by IDRL, particularly in light of the fact that some of the origins of IDRL can be traced to the rise of IHL'.
93 The ILC Special Rapporteur noted IHL as one of three sources for IDL and indicated that '[o]n a wider conceptual level, IDRL shares with international humanitarian law a significant number of fundamental principles': ILC (n. 15) paras 20–21.
94 IDRL Guidelines art 2(1).

95 UNOCHA, *Guidelines on the Use of Foreign Military and Civil Defence Assets in Disaster Relief*, November 2007 (Oslo Guidelines) para 10: The Oslo Guidelines address the use of Military and Civil Defence Assets (MCDA) following natural, technological and environmental emergencies in times of peace. The principles, mechanisms and procedures concerning military forces participating in peacekeeping operations or the delivery of humanitarian assistance in situations of armed conflict are not encompassed by this document. The use of MCDA in armed conflict situations is covered in the UNOCHA, *Guidelines on the Use of Military and Civil Defence Assets to Support United Nations Humanitarian Activities in Complex Emergencies*, March 2003 (MCDA Guidelines).

96 E.g. Tampere Convention on the Provision of Telecommunication Resources for Disaster Mitigation and Relief Operations (adopted 18 June 1998, entered into force 8 January 2005) 2296 UNTS 5, art 1(6).

97 Draft art 3 initially provided: '"Disaster" means a serious disruption of the functioning of society, *excluding armed conflict*, causing significant, widespread human, material or environmental loss' (emphasis added).

98 ILC, Second Report on the Protection of Persons in the Event of Disasters, by Mr. Eduardo Valencia-Ospina, Special Rapporteur, UN Doc. A/CN.4/615 (7 May 2009) para 48.

99 ILC, Report of the International Law Commission, Sixty-First Session, UN Doc. A/64/10 (4 May–5 June and 6 July–7 August 2009) (2009) para 172; 'Statement of the Chairman of the Drafting Committee Mr. Marcelo Vázquez-Bermúdez' (31 July 2009), available at http://legal.un.org/ilc/sessions/61/pdfs/english/2009_dc_chairman_protection_31july2009.pdf, accessed on 7 June 2017.

100 Statement of Mr. Vázquez-Bermúdez (n. 99) 11.

101 ILC, Eighth Report on the Protection of Persons in the Event of Disasters, by Mr. Eduardo Valencia-Ospina, Special Rapporteur, UN Doc. A/CN.4/697 (17 March 2016); ILC, Protection of Persons in the Event of Disasters, Comments and Observations Received from Governments and International Organizations, UN Doc. A/CN.4/696 (14 March 2016).

102 ILC, Protection of Persons in the Event of Disasters, Additional Comments and Observations Received from Governments and International Organizations, UN Doc. A/CN.4/696/Add.1 (28 April 2016).

103 Eighth Report (n. 101).

104 Commentary to ILC draft art 18, para 8.

105 'Protection of Persons in the Event of Disasters, Statement of the Chairman of the Drafting Committee' (30 May 2014), available at http://legal.un.org/docs/?path=../ilc/sessions/66/pdfs/english/dc_chairman_statement_disasters.pdf&lang=E, accessed on 7 June 2017.

106 Statement of Mr. Vázquez-Bermúdez (n. 99).

107 Commentary to ILC Draft Articles (2016) art 18, para 9.

108 Eighth Report and Comments from States (n. 101 and 102).

109 Eighth Report (n. 101) para 379.

110 Ibid 101 and 381.

111 ILC Draft Articles (n. 1).

112 See ILC, Draft Articles on the Effects of Armed Conflicts on Treaties, with Commentaries, UN Doc. A/66/10 (2011).

113 D. Gavshon, 'The Applicability of IHL in Mixed Situations of Disaster and Conflict' 14 *Journal of Conflict & Security Law* (2009) 243, 247.

114 Ibid 251.

115 This is linked to 'protected persons' being required to be of different nationality. See ibid 256.

116 Ibid 248–252.

117 For example, arts 2 and 3 of the ICTY Statute require a nexus between the crime and the armed conflict, while the ICC Elements of Crime require for each war crime that the 'conduct took place in the context of and was associated with' an armed conflict. For further discussion, see R. Cryer, H. Frimar, D. Robinson and E. Wilmshurst, *An Introduction to International Criminal Law and Procedure* (3rd edn, Cambridge University Press, 2014) 281–282.

118 UNOCHA, 'Asia Pacific Regional Guidelines for the Use of Foreign Military Assets in Natural Disaster Response Operations, Asia Pacific Conferences on Military Assets in Natural Disaster Response Operations' (2014), available at http://reliefweb.int/sites/reliefweb.int/files/resources/Guidelines_FMA_Final.pdf, accessed on 7 June 2017. Cfr Oslo Guidelines.

119 G. Venturini, 'Disasters and Armed Conflict' in A. de Guttry, , M. Gestri and G. Venturini (eds), *International Disaster Response Law* (TMC Asser Press, 2012) 251, 264. Venturini considered conflict and disaster situations in Ethiopia/Eritrea, Colombia, the Democratic Republic of the Congo, Indonesia and Sri Lanka.

120 For an excellent discussion of the role of *lex specialis* in IHRL, see M. Milanovic, 'The Lost Origins of *Lex Specialis*: Rethinking the Relationship between Human Rights and International Humanitarian Law' in J.D. Ohlin, *Theoretical Boundaries of Armed Conflict and Human Eights* (Cambridge University Press, 2016) 78 ff.

121 Gavshon (n. 115) 254.

122 Ibid.

123 In 2015, the ICRC and the Swiss Government undertook a consultation on improving compliance with IHL, and recognised that rather than inadequate rules, '[i]nsufficient respect for applicable rules is the principal cause of suffering during armed conflicts': ICRC, 'Strengthening Compliance with International Humanitarian Law: The Work of the ICRC and the Swiss Government' (3 November 2015), available at www.icrc.org/en/document/strengthening-compliance-international-humanitarian-law-ihl-work-icrc-and-swiss-government, accessed on 7 June 2017.

124 R.A. Stoffels, 'Legal Regulation of Humanitarian Assistance in Armed Conflict: Achievements and Gaps' 86 *International Review of the Red Cross* (2004) 515, 544.

125 ILC Draft Articles, draft art 2.

126 This obligation is reflected in draft arts 10 [9, 12] and 11 [10, 13] of the ILC draft arts.

127 This is reflected in the aims of the IFRC IDRL Project, for example, which aim to enhance domestic capacity and provide technical assistance.

128 E.g. Sendai Framework: priority 3 of 4 is investing in disaster risk reduction for resilience and para 27 refers to national and local strategies and plans.

129 The Inter-Agency Standing Committee 1994 defined 'complex emergency' as

> a humanitarian crisis in a country, region or society where there is total or considerable breakdown of authority resulting from internal or external conflict and which requires an international response that goes beyond the mandate or capacity of any single agency and/or the ongoing United Nations country program.

PART II

Role and application of human rights law in disaster settings

5

A RIGHT TO INTERNATIONAL (HUMANITARIAN) ASSISTANCE IN TIMES OF DISASTER

Fresh perspectives from international human rights law

Marlies Hesselman

Introduction

The existence and content of a '(human) right to (international) humanitarian assistance' during disasters has seen much debate over the past two decades.[1] Although there is little explicit support for this right in treaty or customary international law,[2] there is broad agreement that the rights to life, health, water, food, housing, or social security, jointly and directly entitle individuals to receive various types of assistance, especially from their own States.[3]

What is less certain is whether International Human Rights Law (IHRL) also entitles individuals or their affected States to receive (particular types of) *international* assistance. This question is pertinent, since disasters typically overwhelm 'local response capacities' and can severely disrupt the functioning of disaster-struck societies.[4] Furthermore, it is a harsh reality that many disaster-struck States lack the adequate resources and expertise to protect the human rights of disaster-struck populations. Even today, many disasters are still 'forgotten', 'overlooked' or (severely) underfunded – an issue highlighted by the United Nations General Assembly (UNGA) more than two decades ago.[5] The Global Humanitarian Assistance (GHA) Reports reveal that in 2014 virtually all UN-coordinated appeals for international humanitarian assistance went (substantially) unmet, including those for disasters, whereas in 2015 no UN appeal was met.[6] The UN Coordinated Appeals for the Bohol earthquake and typhoon Haiyan in the Philippines, for example, were met only 50% and 60% respectively.[7] This global funding gap for humanitarian assistance (currently at 15 billion USD per year, for both conflict and disaster assistance) was recently condemned by the UN High-Level Panel on Humanitarian Financing as 'too important to fail'.[8]

In 2015, this UN High-Level Panel also underscored that improved assistance and cooperation in disaster risk reduction (DRR) prevents the 'much more expensive, long-term and recurring costs of humanitarian response'.[9] The 2015–2030 Sendai Framework on Disaster Risk Reduction also unambiguously calls for 'enhanced provision of coordinated, sustained and adequate international support for disaster risk reduction', particularly for vulnerable countries, through bilateral and multilateral channels. It specifically mentions 'enhanced *technical* and *financial support* and *technology transfer* on concessional and preferential terms, as mutually agreed, for the development and strengthening of their capacities'.[10]

From a perspective of IHRL, States clearly carry a *joint and individual* obligation to cooperate and assist internationally on human rights, including 'in providing disaster relief and humanitarian assistance in times of emergency'.[11] These obligations derive from Articles 55 and 56 of the UN Charter, a range of UNGA resolutions and Article 2(1) of the International Covenant on Economic, Social and Cultural Rights (ICESCR).[12] The latter provision, according to the Committee on Economic, Social and Cultural Rights (CESCR), requires States to contribute to human rights protection abroad to the maximum of their 'capacity', 'ability' or 'position',[13] while there rests a 'special responsibility and interest' on economically developed States to do so.[14] The CESCR emphasised 'for the avoidance of any doubt':

> it is particularly incumbent on States parties, and other actors in a position to assist, to provide 'international assistance and cooperation, especially economic and technical' which enables developing countries to fulfil their core obligations. . . . [I]n the absence of an active programme of international assistance and cooperation on the part of all those States that are in a position to undertake one, the full realization of economic, social and cultural rights will remain an unfulfilled aspiration in many countries.[15]

The key question addressed in this chapter is: what is the current state of these legal obligations in the context of disasters and, importantly, can any actor legally claim international assistance as a result of them?[16] In the past, commentators have argued that it is 'absurd to contend that every state in the world is duty bound to come up, on demand' with humanitarian relief to any particular State[17] or that there is 'a legally binding obligation upon *any particular* State to provide *any particular* form of assistance' to *any particular* actor;[18] yet, at the same time, it is 'unjustified to go further and suggest that the relevant commitment is meaningless' or that 'inescapably all international assistance and cooperation fundamentally rests upon charity'.[19] In particular circumstances, it may be possible to find obligations to assist that are mandatory, certainly for wealthy States or for those with particular resources.[20] In fact, the European Union's Instrument for Humanitarian Aid to third countries asserts in the preamble that: 'victims of natural disasters . . . have a right to international humanitarian assistance where their own authorities prove unable to provide effective relief'.[21]

As argued by Salomon recently, two types of benefits could derive from more clearly determining or 'disaggregating' the bases for international obligations in this area: first, it could compel States to actually effectuate them, and second, it could facilitate actually determining an internationally wrongful act.[22]

This chapter offers a fresh perspective on the above questions by analysing in particular four recent legal developments in international (human rights) law: (a) the recent adoption of the International Law Commission (ILC) Draft Articles on the Protection of Persons in the Event of Disasters (ILC Draft Articles); (b) recent interpretive practices of UN human rights treaty bodies; (c) the adoption of new complaints mechanisms to UN human rights treaties; and (d) the work of UN Charter-based human rights mechanisms.

The ILC Draft Articles

In 2016, the ILC adopted its Draft Articles after nearly 10 years of drafting and debate.[23] A possible 'right to (international) humanitarian assistance' was immediately considered, for example by the ILC Secretariat which noted that this right received considerable support in soft law, by scholars, and in some regional treaty law[24] but that general positive international law remained inconclusive.[25] In 2008, the ILC Special Rapporteur, Mr Valencia-Ospina continued to express initial support by considering that present international law might not account for 'all of the legitimate needs of persons affected by disaster'[26] and that the progressive formulation of a dedicated right could help prevent fragmented approaches, in comparison to a set of separate rights.[27] He also buttressed earlier remarks by the UN Secretary-General, stating that rights-based approaches underscore 'society's obligation to respond to the inalienable rights of individuals', demanding 'justice as a right, not as a charity'.[28] The ILC itself recalled the International Court of Justice (ICJ)'s *Nicaragua* judgment, stating that:

> [t]here can be no doubt that the provision of strictly humanitarian aid to persons or forces in another country, whatever their political affiliations or objectives, cannot be regarded as unlawful intervention, or as in any other way contrary to international law.[29]

Nevertheless, Valencia-Ospina, various responding States, and ILC members all expressed their doubts about an individual right to appeal for international relief, for it could raise tensions with State sovereignty, non-intervention, the primary protective responsibility of affected States, or with newly developing concepts at that time, such as the 'Responsibility to Protect'.[30] As a result, by 2010, it seems the idea of formulating any individual right to humanitarian assistance in the ILC Articles was abandoned. Instead, a so-called 'dual-axis approach' was favoured, i.e.:

> the Commission would focus first on the rights and obligations of *States vis-à-vis each other*, and then on the rights and obligations of *States vis-à-vis individuals.* It was further emphasized that State-to-State relations remained an important feature of disaster relief.[31]
>
> *(emphasis added)*

In the final draft, Draft Article 5 now affirms the general rights-based nature of the ILC Draft Articles, since '[p]ersons affected by disasters are entitled to the respect for and protection of their human rights in accordance with international law'.[32] The remainder of the Draft Articles is highly 'duty-based' and includes no further references to 'rights'. In particular, Draft Article 7 starts by setting out a *compulsory*, reciprocal duty of cooperation for all States: 'States shall, as appropriate, cooperate among themselves, with the UN, with the components of the Red Cross and Red Crescent Movement, and with other assisting actors' in the application of the Draft Articles.[33] This is followed by further specific *duties for affected States*, including a duty to ensure the protection of persons under their jurisdiction or control, a duty to seek external assistance when disasters manifestly exceed national response capacities, and the obligation not to arbitrarily withhold consent to offers of international assistance – even if giving consent is in principle a primary requirement for foreign aid to be brought in.[34]

On the part of *assisting actors*, the (corresponding) duties are decidedly weak however. Draft Article 12 merely provides that assisting actors 'may offer assistance' (i.e. are authorised to do so, but have no duty) and 'shall expeditiously give due consideration' to requests and 'inform the affected State of their reply', supposedly in good faith.[35] The Commentaries to the Draft Articles explicitly clarify that any offer of assistance, whether unilaterally or in response to requests, 'are essentially voluntary and should not be construed as recognition of the existence of a legal duty to assist'.[36] During the drafting of this article, several visions of Draft Article 12 were given, including recasting the provision as 'a positive duty on the international community to offer assistance'. Others considered this would 'go too far' and that a 'specific legal obligation on third States or other organizations' should not be recognised.[37] Again others asked that Draft Article 12 more clearly define under which circumstances assisting States could decline offers.[38]

The following paragraphs will attest that there is good reason to critique the ILC Draft Articles from a perspective of current IHRL, although the analysis also evidences that it may have been difficult for the ILC to operationalise specific duties of assistance through such a relatively abstract document.

Work of UN human rights treaty bodies

UN human rights treaty supervisory bodies have played a key role in the further articulation of duties of assistance under IHRL. General Comments/Recommendations have proven especially instructive, as highly 'authoritative' interpretative statements on the content of treaty provisions, even if these statements as such are non-binding;[39] yet Concluding Observations also play a role in concretising duties in respect of specific countries and settings.

This chapter focuses on the practice of the CESCR, the Committee on the Rights of the Child (CommRC), and the Committee on Rights of Persons with Disabilities (CommRPD), for they monitor treaties that include provisions on international cooperation and assistance.[40] It is immediately noted that the practice of the CommRPD is very young and includes few relevant statements.

General comments

First, while CESCR has taken the lead in clarifying obligations of international cooperation and assistance, recently the CommRC also affirmed in a fairly straightforward manner that:

> States parties have an obligation to cooperate with one another in the promotion of universal respect for, and observance of, human rights. . . . States that lack the resources needed to implement the rights enshrined in the Convention and its Optional Protocols are *obliged* to seek international cooperation, be it bilateral, regional, interregional, global or multilateral. States parties with resources for international cooperation have an *obligation* to provide such cooperation with the aim of facilitating the implementation of . . . rights in the recipient State.[41]
>
> *(emphasis added)*

The CommRC uses very strong, clear language here, and its work is consistent with earlier and ongoing work of the CESCR. The CESCR has held in several General Comments that:

> [d]epending on the availability of resources, States should facilitate the realization of the right to water [or health, or food] in other countries, for example through provision of water resources, financial and technical assistance, and provide the necessary aid when required. In disaster relief and emergency assistance, including assistance to refugees and displaced persons, priority should be given to Covenant rights, including the provision of adequate water [food aid, or health services]. . . . The economically developed States parties have a special responsibility and interest to assist the poorer developing States in this regard. . . . When examining the reports of States parties and their ability to meet the obligations to realize the right to water, the Committee will consider the effects of the assistance provided by all other actors.[42]

The manner in which the examination of State reports takes place through the adoption of 'Concluding Observations' is the subject of the next section. Yet, interestingly, as far back as General Comment 2 of 1990, CESCR concluded that Article 22 ICESCR provides an 'important opportunity to States parties . . . to identify in their reports any particular needs they might have for technical assistance or development cooperation'.[43] These needs may be directed at UN bodies and agencies,[44] but in view of the present author, there is no reason why these needs could not be addressed directly to fellow States Parties of the ICESCR too. The next section demonstrates how the CESCR has further built on these General Comments in Concluding Observations.

Finally, the CESCR also provides further guidance on *how* assistance should be delivered, notably in a safe, sustainable, and culturally appropriate manner; not adversely affecting local markets; and facilitating the return to self-reliance of the beneficiaries.[45] Aid should be based on the needs of the intended beneficiaries.[46]

Concluding Observations

Concluding Observations are the outcomes of the aforementioned State Reporting procedures at human rights treaty bodies. Through reporting procedures, States are required to periodically justify how they have implemented relevant human rights treaties (or not). General Comments provide general guidance on the duties of States, and the ICESCR-Reporting Guidelines further ask States to indicate in respect of implementing Article 2(1): 'the impact of international economic and technical assistance and co-operation', as *given* or *received*, for the 'full realization' of the ICESCR, including its impact 'in other countries, especially developing countries'.[47]

A very specific reference point in the practice of the Committees has become to assess whether States parties meet important, longstanding international financing commitments, such as the international target to devote 0.7% of Gross National Income (GNI) to Official Development Assistance (ODA) annually.[48] Presently, these ODA commitments *include* humanitarian assistance in the context of conflicts and disasters.[49] The Sendai Framework notes that meeting such ODA targets is 'essential for effective disaster management'.[50]

Unfortunately, Committees often have to reprimand States for not meeting these targets,[51] and seldom can they praise countries for spending sufficient resources.[52] In 2016, only 6 of 29 OECD-DAC countries met the target; the overall level of ODA expenditure by these countries was 0.32% of their GNIs.[53]

There remains some international scholarly debate about whether the 0.7% GNI/ODA target (by now) must be seen as a *legal* obligation under the ICESCR or CRC – even if most academics (and possibly even most States)[54] would now concede that cooperation and assistance follows a 'logic of obligations', rather than a 'logic of charity' in IHRL, or in other words, presents a 'legal obligation' as such.[55] In general, however, there is considerable support for the Committees' specific practice of appraising the 0.7% financing target as part of assessing whether Article 2(1) ICESCR is implemented,[56] and it can be seen as a (legal) key to assessing whether developed States have exhausted their legal 'responsibilities', 'capacities', 'abilities', or 'positions to assist' under IHRL (or not). Several authors stress that the obligation to assist in times of disasters is more clearly pronounced in IHRL, because of specific circumstances.[57]

The key challenge in IHRL, in fact, may not be a lack of *duty*-bearers, but a lack of clear *rights*-holders that can claim assistance. In other words, could the Philippines, Tuvalu, or Mauritius claim from countries like Spain, Belgium, or Japan (three countries that consistently fail to meet international ODA targets) that they be given (particular kinds of) disaster assistance, when they can prove they lack sufficient resources themselves? Of course, this question can be raised both for financial, technical, or technological assistance. Under which circumstances could developed States (still) legally refuse assistance requests?

Committees have generally not been reluctant to appraise efforts of *both affected* and *assisting* States in engaging in international cooperation and assistance.[58] On the part of affected States, CESCR for example, in 2000, asked Mongolia to continue to address with urgency the 'immediate nutritional needs of the population, including through international humanitarian assistance' as a result of droughts,[59] whereas CommRC encouraged the Ukraine to 'take all appropriate measures, including seeking international cooperation, to prevent and combat damaging effects of environmental degradation on children, including pollution of the environment and food products' with reference to the Chernobyl nuclear disaster.[60] Towards small island States, the CommRC is very specific and for example asks 'to continue and strengthen [their] cooperation with bilateral, multilateral, regional and international partners' including the UN Office of the High Commissioner for Human Rights, the UN Office for Disaster Risk Reduction and other relevant disaster agencies and 'to seek bilateral, multilateral, regional and international cooperation' in implementing a range of very specific DRR recommendations.[61] On another occasion, the CommRC asked Mozambique to redirect (any increases of) ODA to a list of highly specific 'high/quick impact' development programmes, mostly in the area of health and education.[62] This illustrates that the practice of monitoring can reveal and endorse specific assistance needs, including for disaster assistance.

Towards *assisting States*, the CESCR recommends for example, in addition to the 0.7% target comments, that South Korea further unties its bilateral aid and takes on board recommendations by DAC-OECD to increase 'the grant element of bilateral ODA commitments to least developed countries'.[63] With respect to Italy, the CommRC commented on multilateral aid expenditure, noting with concern that contributions to the UN Children's Fund (UNICEF) were consistently declining.[64] The CESCR reprimanded Japan for not only spending very little on development assistance but also observed that Japan devoted about 40% of its 0.27% GNI/ODA to socio-economic rights.[65] In 2010, the CommRC equally commented on Japan's funding priorities, noting with concern that Japan further reduced its GNI/ODA target to 0.2%, although noting with approval that Japan stepped up its commitments to finance climate change measures in developing countries, as well as support to African countries. Highly interesting for present purposes, Japan, but also other countries,[66] were requested by CommRC to:

> reconsider commitments to international ODA targets with a view to increasing the provided resources [and to] take into account the concluding observations and recommendations of the Committee on the Rights of the Child for the recipient country in question.[67]

This latter comment is of particular interest, since it shows how the practice of Concluding Observations can help steer ODA expenditures towards particular IHRL aims and underpin claims to particular kinds of assistance by affected States. It should be remembered that General Comment 2 of 1990 specifically indicated that reporting procedures should be used to this end.

Some concluding remarks

In summary, the above analysis clearly affirms that international assistance is considered a legal obligation under IHRL treaties. Committees have tried to give further meaning to these open-ended duties by refering to important (repeated) international agreements for cooperation, assistance, and financing, including the 0.7% GNI/ODA target – recently affirmed in the Addis Ababa Action Agenda, the Sustainable Development Goals, and the 2015–2030 Sendai Framework.

Monitoring bodies can further use such commitments, along with assessments of challenges in national human rights protection by affected States, to shape assistance requests and offers and to help affected States formulate clear, specific assistance needs. Of course, Committees do and should appraise the efforts of affected States themselves as well, in line with their obligations to mobilise and allocate maximum available resources domestically.

Drafting processes for optional protocols

This section addresses the question whether a lack of international assistance, e.g. under the 0.7% norm, or a particular refusal to honour a specific aid request can lead to a complaint before international supervisory bodies and to a determination of a violation of Article 2(1) ICESCR.

Such options were certainly entertained during the drafting processes of a number of new complaints mechanisms recently, notably the 2006 Optional Protocol to the CRPD (OP-CRPD) (adopted 2006, entered into force 2008); the 2008 Optional Protocol to the ICESCR (OP-ICESCR) (adopted 2008, entered into force 2013); and the 2011 Optional Protocol to the CRC on communication procedures (OP-CRC III) (adopted December 2011, entered into force 2014).[68] These drafting processes therefore merit closer consideration.[69]

CRPD and OP-CRPD

First, the CRPD is one of the latest additions to the corpus of substantive human rights treaties while OP-CRPD pre-dates OP-ICESCR and OP-CRC III; the drafting process of the CRPD in particular included debates on the inclusion of obligations of cooperation and assistance in this new treaty.

Although initially there were debates between those opposing and those favouring such obligations in the CRPD, it is remarkable that the original discussions focused on very specific and 'programmatic' text proposals regarding international cooperation and assistance.[70] Ultimately a highly detailed provision was not included, but a set of international obligations of cooperation and assistance were eventually included in Article 23. This is heralded in literature as a strong affirmation of the existence of international obligations in IHRL as such.[71] The OP-CRPD itself, unlike the later treaties discussed below, does not include further reference to international cooperation and assistance, nor saw debate on this.

OP-ICESCR

The drafting process of the OP-ICESCR in 2002–2007 is of great interest here, first of all, because only very few States disputed outright and explicitly throughout drafting that the ICESCR includes a *legal* obligation to cooperate or assist. Instead, what was challenged is whether obligations of international assistance are suitable for an international complaints procedure specifically. To illustrate this point further, only the United Kingdom, the Czech Republic, Canada, France, and Portugal were put on record, in 2005, as believing that 'international cooperation and assistance was an important moral obligation but not a legal entitlement' under the ICESCR or that the Covenant could not be interpreted to 'impose a legal obligation to provide development assistance or give a legal title to receive such aid'.[72] In 2006, Canada was the only state to repeat this position.[73] Other States took conflicting positions. For example, the Czech Republic had submitted in 2003 that, when 'core obligations under ICESCR are not met due to resource constraints, then international assistance and cooperation should be provided, in keeping with the Charter of the United Nations and article 2(1) ICESCR', thus contradicting its 2005 position.[74] Moreover, in 2005, both Portugal and Czech Republic also supported the inclusion of Article 2(1) ICESCR in the OP-ICESCR, with Portugal adding that this new 'procedural instrument' would be able to 'accommodate different views on obligations of international assistance'.[75]

On the other hand, Ecuador, Angola, Egypt, Ghana, Indonesia, Iran, Morocco (on behalf of the Group of African States), and Nigeria clearly supported a legal obligation of international assistance enshrined in the ICESCR and that these obligations should be reflected in the text of an optional protocol.[76] They submitted that Article 2(1) is 'central to any discussion on the implementation of the Covenant' and it needs to be considered in light of important political commitments, such as the Monterrey Declaration on Development Financing (which includes the 0.7% ODA target) or the Millennium Development Goals (MDGs).[77] Sweden contended that certain concepts of the ICESCR needed more clarity before a complaints mechanism would be acceptable but also 'emphasize[d] the importance of including a human rights approach to development assistance'.[78] The contribution on behalf of NGOs explicitly suggested that the 0.7% GNI/ODA target could play a role in assessing the implementation of Article 2(1) ICESCR.[79] Finally, on the suitability of claiming assistance under the new instruments, France, the UK, the Netherlands, China, and also Mr Riedel on behalf of the CESCR voiced some particular concerns.[80] The Netherlands observed that assistance would be most appropriately effectuated through genuine dialogue, partnerships, and technical assistance programmes and 'strongly doubted whether an inter-State complaints mechanism was compatible with this notion',[81] whereas, Mr Riedel saw some 'difficulty of invoking a right to international assistance under a[n individual] communications procedure, although it might be utilized in an inter-State procedure'.[82] The latter position appears to be supported by African States, who were put on record as stating that 'only an inter-State procedure should be applicable to international cooperation'.[83] NGOs also acknowledged the

> difficulty of establishing a causal link between the lack of international assistance and specific violations under an individual communications procedure, but that the lack of international assistance could be a mitigating factor in assessing States' ability to guarantee the rights in the Covenant.[84]

Ultimately, the African group maintained that different States simply had different capacities to realise rights and that an international trust fund had to become part of the new OP-ICESCR as a way of securing the fulfilment of rights. This was objected to by another sizable group of States for possible misuse of the fund, for it could be a reward for failing to implement human rights in the first place.[85] Again, the challenge was not to the obligation to assist as such but rather to the way it might be operationalised as a claimable right under ICESCR.

In the end, Article 14 of the OP-ICESCR came to include a trust fund, with voluntary contributions, aimed at 'providing expert and technical assistance'. The establishment of this fund was necessary to secure support for the OP-ICESCR by developing States, though it is not in operation yet. The Committee can try to seek to activate the fund to help a State lacking capacity (as evidenced through a complaint) to better protect human rights.[86] Similarly, the Committee shall, as appropriate, communicate its views and recommendations to UN agencies and other competent bodies – with the consent of the State concerned – as to what 'technical advice or assistance' might be helpful and help such bodies to decide which 'international measures likely to contribute' to achieving progress in implementing the ICESCR might be necessary.[87]

As a result, through the back door, it seems possible that an individual complaint of affected individuals against their own State, or an inter-State complaint, could lead to access to international assistance through the fund or from UN agencies with an appropriate mandate.[88] This assistance is ultimately geared towards *States*, not individuals directly, and it is mostly of an expert or technical nature. This is a very indirect, and somewhat limited, route, but disaster victims, or improperly protected persons in disaster-prone areas, could certainly try to formulate a claim before the CESCR, given that the OP-ICESCR has been in force since May 2013. Certainly in the area of DRR, and given the new Sendai Framework, such claims could be of great interest.

All in all, the drafting process of the OP-CESCR seems to firmly underscore that cooperation and assistance is a legal obligation but that further work is necessary for its operationalisation.

OP-CRC III

Finally, the drafting process of the OP-CRC III in 2009–2011 deserves brief discussion. The preparatory works for this treaty only reveal that drafters opined that 'the issue of international assistance and cooperation to States had been dealt with in the OP-ICESCR' and '[a]n appeal for resources in that respect could be made in the future in connection with the optional protocol to the Convention on the Rights of the Child if adopted'.[89] Two years later, during the second session, the drafting history demonstrates some views in favour and some against establishing a similar trust fund for the CRC,[90] but this fund was not ultimately created. Similar to OP-ICESCR, however, the OP-CRC III does include a mandate for the Committee to indicate a need for assistance to UN agencies. Buck and Wabwile have further argued that it would be 'properly within the mandate of the [CommRC] to adopt a Recommendation which creates an organisational framework for the Committee to operate a global trust fund similar to the one established under the terms of Article 14(3) of OP-ICESCR', i.e. a fund that can 'be applied to finance the work of the Committee and provide assistance to States where there is need'.[91] The authors also suggested that the trust fund could 'recruit and mobilize various actors in the global community including the corporate sector, civil society organisations, regional bodies and supportive States', in this way providing 'an alternative platform for global resource mobilisation' – i.e. one that would arguably more firmly recognise and give effect to a 'right to claim assistance' for States that lack capacity, although aimed at the international community more broadly.

Some concluding remarks

All in all, the drafting processes of the new instruments offer an interesting, more nuanced picture on the content of present human rights treaty law. Certainly, it seems possible to conclude that international cooperation and assistance is a matter of *international legal obligation* and that claims about failure to fulfil these obligations could be made before supervisory bodies,[92] and to some extent give rise to claims to be provided with assistance. At the same time, the manner in which the relevant provisions have been operationalised (i.e. at best through a voluntary fund so far) seems fairly poor. Time will tell us how bodies may deal with any complaints or requests regarding international assistance.

UN Charter-based mechanisms

Finally, this section briefly appraises the work of UN Charter-based mechanisms on international cooperation and assistance, with a special focus on disaster settings.

The work of special procedures

Over the previous years, a considerable range of disaster situations has been scrutinised by Special Rapporteurs with relevant thematic or country mandates (e.g. Haiti, Myanmar, internationally displaced persons (IDPs), housing, water, food, and health). The monitoring practice of Special Procedures typically includes annual reports, country visits, and communications mechanisms, though the latter are uncommon in the area of disaster management and international cooperation.[93] Another key feature of the work of Special Rapporteurs is standard setting initiatives, two of which are discussed below.

Standard setting initiatives

First, the UN Guiding Principles on Internal Displacement were adopted by the UN Secretary-General's Special Representative on IPDs in 1998. They are now 20 years old but still very much respected and referred to. Guiding Principle 3 affirms that *national authorities* have the primary duty and responsibility to protect IDPs and to provide them with humanitarian assistance. In addition, although IDPs 'have the right to request and to receive protection and humanitarian assistance', they can claim such assistance specifically *from their national authorities*. At the same time, 'humanitarian organizations and other appropriate actors have the right to offer their services', which 'shall not be regarded as an unfriendly act or an interference in a State's internal affairs and shall be considered in good faith'. Basically, the Guiding Principles reflect the ILC Draft Articles (or *vice versa*), with the exception that the ILC did not ultimately formulate any 'right' to receive assistance or to offer it. Instead the ILC underlined the applicability of IHRL generally and placed a general (though ill-defined) 'duty to cooperate' on *all* actors concerned.

Secondly, the former Special Rapporteur on housing and property restitution in the context of the return of refugees and internally displaced persons, Mr Pinheiro, drafted the UN Principles on Housing and Property Restitution for Refugees and IDPs in 2005 (Pinheiro Principles), which are also applicable to disasters. Pinheiro Principle 10.4 requires affected States, when necessary, to 'request from other States or international organisations the financial and/or technical assistance required to facilitate the effective voluntary return, in safety and dignity, of refugees and displaced persons'.[94] A 2007 UN Handbook further elaborates that States, as needed, ask for 'financial assistance from the international community to facilitate return if national resources are insufficient to achieve this'. Although seemingly inspired by situations of armed conflict, the Handbook equally answers the question of 'who should pay for voluntary repatriation and restitution programmes?' by providing that '[d]onor countries and UN and other agencies should consider earmarking funds for these purposes within their various funding strategies'.[95] Cooperation is also further supported in Pinheiro Principle 22: the 'international community should work with national Governments and share expertise on the development of national housing, land and property restitution policies and programmes'[96] in line with relevant I(HR)L standards. Of course, none of the work of Special Rapporteurs is formally binding; it is soft law.

Country visits

Special Procedures have also addressed specific disaster settings and international cooperation and assistance through country visits, sometimes in considerable detail.[97] For example, after a visit to the Maldives, the Special Rapporteur on the human rights of IDPs (SR on IDPs), for example, proposed a broad range of disaster risk-related measures to be implemented by the Government and called upon the international community to 'raise attention and provide increased international support in order to strengthen local and national capacities, as well as domestic legal frameworks and policies to address disaster risk reduction'.[98] This support includes particularly 'exchange of best practices and expertise'; 'technologies for addressing coastal erosion, protective measures against flooding, and reclamation projects'; or 'specific cooperation and assistance frameworks' supportive of climate change adaptation strategies, 'at the bilateral, multilateral and regional level'.[99] Specifically, cooperation agreements could pertain to humanitarian and emergency assistance during the initial phase of disasters or support durable solutions; moreover, 'with regard to all of the above, the international community should ensure coordination of international support at the national level'.[100]

This report clearly conveys a sense of urgency and the specificity of these recommendations is remarkable. Similarly detailed observations can be found in the SR on IDP's report regarding typhoon Haiyan in the Philippines, which considered that:

> [i]nternational assistance remains a vital component of the overall response and to ensuring durable solutions for internally displaced persons in the Philippines. The international community is urged to maintain its technical and financial support, particularly for environmental risk assessment and disaster management.[101]

In addition:

> [t]he international community should stand ready to respond effectively to disaster-related displacement in the Philippines, in line with the recommendations contained in the Nansen Initiative Agenda for the Protection of Cross-Border Displaced Persons in the Context of Disasters and Climate Change. It should equally provide support to the Philippines for the effective implementation of the Sendai Framework for Disaster Risk Reduction 2015–2030 as well as measures of adaptation to climate change under the 2015 Paris Agreement on climate change.[102]

It is clear that the Special Procedures here bring in a range of important international agreements for cooperation and assistance. It is recalled that the UN appeal target for typhoon Haiyan was only 60% met. In fact, Special Procedures have very critically remarked on poor responses to UN appeals and other essential funding needs for disaster assistance on other occasions.[103] The Special Rapporteur on the Right to Food reminded in a response to droughts in Niger that governments have an obligation to provide assistance, to the extent that their resources permit, when individuals are suffering in another country, such as a situation of widespread famine – this includes obligations 'to cooperate in providing disaster relief and humanitarian assistance in times of emergency'.[104]

Besides the above statements, the Special Rapporteur on adequate housing as a component of the right to an adequate standard of living, and on the right to non-discrimination in this context (SR on housing), also has considered disaster assistance in considerable detail.[105] For example, after a country visit to Algeria, she urged the international community (allegedly of States) 'to provide sufficient funding to ensure decent living conditions, including adequate housing, for Saharan refugees in the Tindouf camps', noting that tents in which the refugees live 'need to be replaced at least every five years, but the international organizations active there are unable to do so due to lack of funds'. The shelters that refugees now build themselves are very prone to regular flooding events in the region.[106] Furthermore, in 2006, the SR on housing observed that enormous disaster impacts in Iran required joint efforts of the Government, national non-governmental actors and the international community alike.[107] The international community was called upon to 'provide technical cooperation to facilitate an increase in the construction of earthquake-proof houses and cooperation in the area of disaster prevention across the Country'; 'to collaborate in the immediate improvement of the living conditions in the survivor camps in Bam and accelerate the reconstruction efforts in the city'; 'to increase funding to housing projects', especially for vulnerable groups; to monitor and report all funding provided; and to increase support for training and capacity building for civil society.[108] Again, the great specificity in these country recommendations, far beyond the detail included in Concluding Observations, stands out. In fact, the SR on IDPs also made further specific remarks in response to the situation in Haiti, such as requiring the harmonisation of 'funding cycles between humanitarian and development agencies' with a view 'to increase the chances of a smooth transition between the largely humanitarian approach adopted up to now in Haiti and a more development rights-based approach'.[109] Finally, in respect of Cabo Verde, the SR on housing observed very recently that '[g]iven that the country is highly reliant on aid and loans provided by the international community, including international financial institutions, the provision of loans and aid must be in line with the States human rights obligations and national priorities'.[110] The SR specifically added that '[t]he reconstruction and rehabilitation of communities affected by disasters is a challenge for authorities, both in terms of technical and financial resources', and Cabo Verde's situation became more complicated because it recently changed its status from Least Developed Country to Middle Income Country, resulting in difficulty in accessing international aid and loans.[111]

The argument can be made here that the monitoring work of Special Procedures adds to the clarification of assistance needs and provides in-depth instructions to both affected and assisting actors as to the modes, types, and extent[112] of cooperation and assistance needed, and perhaps even required, for the protection of human rights.

The Human Rights Council

Finally, the UN Human Rights Council (HRC) could perhaps not lag behind in addressing disasters, i.e. considering the ample engagement with this topic in other fora. Two aspects of the work of the UNHRC stand out: two recent reports/analytical studies on disasters and the considerations in the Universal Period Review (UPR) on disaster assistance.

Reports/analytical studies

In 2015 and 2016, the HRC published its first specific reports on human rights protection in disaster settings. The 2015 analytical study on 'human rights protection in post-conflict and post-disaster situations' does not amply address international cooperation, but the HRC submits in passing that affected States have the 'primary responsibility for coordinating humanitarian assistance, and are at least under the moral duty to accept bona fide offers of assistance by States or other relevant organizations'.[113] This report also includes a heading called 'Multi-Level Approaches', which further affirms that '[a] regional approach is also necessary given that regional organizations and mechanisms have significant expertise and resources to offer when dealing with disaster situations'.[114] The report does not speak of obligations to assist, or rights to be furnished with assistance.

These fairly careful statements stand in marked contrast with the HRC's 2015 study on 'climate change and the human right to health'. This study not only affirms the links between climate change and disasters, but also underscores that:[115]

> States should enhance cooperation and development assistance on the basis of principles of equity and common but differentiated responsibility to ensure adequate funding of, and research into, adaptation measures that help the poorest countries and those persons, groups and peoples most at risk. Specific measures could include: equitable access to technology, including, if necessary, the lowering of intellectual property standards and facilitation of technology transfer; targeted poverty reduction efforts; and establishment of a special climate justice fund to finance climate mitigation and adaptation policies with funds from both the public and private sectors.[116]

While none of the work of the HRC is legally binding, and the language employed is also not strongly legally worded, i.e. 'should' (perhaps for that reason), the Council's work nevertheless reaffirms the dire need for enhanced international cooperation and assistance for human rights in the context of disasters and for climate change as a related issue. International regulatory frameworks, such as the Sendai Framework, the UN Framework Convention on Climate Change or the 2015 Paris Climate Change Agreement, could bolster and provide further understanding about how burden sharing can be foreseen (e.g. through a fund, through common but differentiated responsibilities, through a principle of equity etc.) or what type of financing and technology sharing commitments are necessary – also per the Addis Ababa Action Agenda or Sendai Framework.

Universal Periodic Review

Finally, international disaster assistance has been addressed in several UPRs as well. For example, in Cuba's UPR, the Russian Federation and Bangladesh respectively recommended that Cuba provide 'humanitarian assistance at the extent possible to neighbouring countries which need assistance because of man-made or natural catastrophes' and to provide 'support to countries requesting assistance in case of natural disasters and other ravages of nature'.[117] In the UPR of Bhutan, the Solomon Islands recommended the development and submission of proposals for assistance to improve capacity for disaster management, which incidentally might include 'sound disaster management from a human rights perspective'.[118] Uganda also asked Bhutan to call for technical assistance in disaster management, and the Maldives recommended that it 'avail itself of technical assistance and international cooperation in its efforts relating to disaster management and preparedness as well as climate change mitigation'.[119] In turn, Bhutan recommended that Bangladesh 'continue and strengthen, with international support and cooperation, its efforts to mitigate the negative impact of climate change, as well as disaster management programmes'.[120] Finally, Kuwait received several positive encouragements to continue humanitarian disaster assistance to developing countries or to multilateral funds, e.g. from Mauritania, Bahrain, Qatar, Egypt, Pakistan, and Singapore.[121]

The UPR thus affirms a practice of requiring particular States to engage in particular types of cooperation and assistance for the protection of human rights, including very specifically for disaster settings.

Conclusions

In summary, this chapter analysed afresh whether individuals or States can claim international (humanitarian) assistance in disaster situations under current IHRL, as a legal entitlement.

Clearly, despite poor recognition of this fact in the final ILC Draft Articles, obligations of cooperation and assistance have long been acknowledged in IHRL, and in the UN Charter. To some extent they have been reflected in ILC Draft Article 7. Regrettably, and in contravention of IHRL, the ILC has generally placed the burden of human rights protection solely on the *affected* State. Although affected States have the primary duty to protect citizens and to seek assistance when needed, it is a problem that no corresponding 'specific duties of assistance' for assisting actors have been included. In addition, the ILC neglected to clarify under which circumstances developed States could refuse requests for assistance (or not), as called for by some drafters.

As recently considered by Salomon, positive IHRL does not consider cooperation and assistance discretionary, but a better delineation of what is required, when, and by which State(s), is needed for rights and obligations of assistance to be operationalised. She considers that the difficulties of determining breaches of these obligations stem from a 'paucity of judicial elucidation' regarding whether/when States are 'required to act in a particular situation, and how'.

Yet, this chapter has evidenced that IHRL monitoring mechanisms do actually – in a highly practical manner – provide elucidations of the legitimate needs of disaster assistance in *concrete* settings. Treaty bodies, Special Procedures, and States in the UPR all engage rather extensively and in considerable detail with efforts of international (disaster) assistance, and their monitoring outputs include clear instructions on the types and levels of assistance needed and what needs to be provided by international actors.

The argument is made here, backed up by repeated international assistance agreements, including specific disaster management regimes, that disaster-affected States are able to stake claims to specific international assistance, from specific States. Such claims are especially relevant when it can be adduced that States fail to (consistently) meet international assistance targets, and there is an obvious or 'objective' capacity to assist in some manner.[122]

In this sense, new IHRL complaints procedures offer unexplored potential to place the onus on assisting actors to justify why they do not or have not come forward with assistance in response to legitimate, reasonable requests for assistance. The same actually counts for a claim before the ICJ.

All in all, time will tell whether it is indeed possible to use IHRL monitoring mechanisms for colouring in/operationalising the open-ended legal obligations of international cooperation and assistance; yet, it seems there is reason to argue this could be a possible way to concretely effectuate assistance and to ensure that human rights protection does not 'remain an unfulfilled aspiration in many countries'.[123] For – in the words of the UN High-Level Panel on Humanitarian Financing – 'it is unacceptable that anybody should die or live without dignity because we cannot find the resources required to help people in need' . . . , when global resources are plenty.[124]

Selected bibliography

P. Alston and G. Quinn, 'The Nature and Scope of States Parties' Obligations under the International Covenant on Economic, Social and Cultural Rights' 9 *Human Rights Quarterly* (1987) 156–229.

A. Creta, 'A (Human) Right to Humanitarian Assistance in Disaster Situations? Surveying Public International Law' in A. de Guttry, M. Gestri and G. Venturini (eds), *International Disaster Response Law* (TMC Asser Press, 2012) 353–379.

M. Salomon, 'How to Keep Promises: Making Sense of the Duty among Multiple States to Fulfil Socio-Economic Rights in the World' in A. Nollkaemper and D. Jacobs (eds), *Distributing Responsibilities in International Law* (Cambridge University Press, 2015) 363–385.

M. Sepúlveda Carmona, 'The Obligations of "International Assistance and Cooperation" under the International Covenant on Economic, Social and Cultural Rights: A Possible Entry Point to a Human Rights based Approach to Millennium Development Goal 8' 13 *International Human Rights Journal* (2009) 86–109.

W. Vandenhole, 'Economic, Social and Cultural Rights in the CRC: Is There a Legal Obligation to Cooperate Internationally for Development?' *International Journal of Children's Rights* (2009) 23–63.

Notes

1 A. Creta, 'A (Human) Right to Humanitarian Assistance in Disaster Situations? Surveying Public International Law' in A. de Guttry, M. Gestri and G. Venturini (eds), *International Disaster Response Law* (TMC Asser Press, 2012) 353; ILC, Memorandum of the ILC Secretariat, UN Doc. A/CN.4/590 (2008) paras 257–258; IFRC, 'Law and Legal Issues in International Disaster Response: A Desk Study' (IFRC, 2007) 35, available at http://www.ifrc.org/PageFiles/125639/113600-idrl-deskstudy-en.pdf, accessed on 17 December 2017; Y. Dinstein, 'The Right to Humanitarian Assistance' 47 *Naval War College Review* (2000) 77–91; R. Hardcastle and A. Chua, 'Victims of Natural Disaster: The Right to Receive Humanitarian Assistance' 1 *The International Journal of Human Rights* (1997) 35–49; P. Walker, 'Victims of Natural Disasters and the Right to Humanitarian Assistance: A Practioner's View' 325 *International Review of the Red Cross* (1998) 611–617.

2 See for further debate (of the absence) of customary law in paragraph 2 below, and ILC, Preliminary Report of Special Rapporteur on the Protection of Persons in Event of Disasters, Mr Valencia-Ospina, UN

Doc. A/CN.4/598 (2008) paras 26, 257–258; Creta (n. 1); important exceptions in treaty law include: the 1996 EU 'Instrument for Humanitarian Aid', Council Regulation (EC) No 1257/96 of 20 June 1996, OJL 163/1996, preamble: 'victims of natural disasters . . . have a right to international humanitarian assistance where their own authorities prove unable to provide effective relief'; African Union Convention for the Protection and Assistance of Internally Displaced Persons in Africa (Kampala Convention) (adopted 23 October 2009, entered into force December 2012) AU Doc. Ext/Assembly/AU/PA/Draft/Decl.(I) Rev.1, art 5(9): 'States Parties shall respect the right of internally displaced persons to peacefully request or seek protection and assistance, in accordance with relevant and international laws, a right for which they shall not be persecuted, prosecuted or punished'; African Charter of Rights and Welfare of the Child (art 23) and the UN Convention on the Rights of Persons with Disabilities (CRPD) (art 11) also mention explicitly emergency assistance, though not necessarily as a 'right' of individuals.

3 See for thorough review: M. Hesselman, 'Establishing a Full "Cycle of Protection" for Disaster Victims: Preparedness, Response and Recovery According to International Human Rights Supervisory Bodies' 18 *Tilburg Law Review* (2013) 120–125, 129–130; and particularly CESCR, General Comment No. 14: The Right to the Highest Attainable Standard of Health, UN Doc. E/C.12/2000/4 (2000) para 12; CESCR, General Comment No. 1: The Right to Water, UN Doc. E/C.12/2002/11 (2003) paras 16(h), 22, 36–38, 44(c), 48, 61; CESCR, General Comment No. 12: The Right to Food, UN Doc. E/C.12/1999/5 (1999) paras 5, 6 13, 15, 19, 38; CESCR, General Comment No. 19: The Right to Social Security, UN Doc. E/C.12/GC/19 (2008) paras 27–28, 50, 52, 58, 61; see similarly ILC, Memorandum (2008) (n. 1) para 253; Creta (n. 1) 358–359.

4 See ILC, Second Report by the Special Rapporteur on the Protection of Persons in the Event of Disasters, UN Doc. A/CN.4/615 (2009) paras 31–46; ILC, Titles and Texts of the ILC Draft Articles on the Protection of Persons in the Event of Disasters, UN Doc. A/CN.4/L.871 (2016) draft arts 3(a) and 11.

5 GHA, Report 2016 (2016), available at www.globalhumanitarianassistance.org/report/gha2016, accessed on 1 March 2017, 57; OECD-DAC, 'The 22 Billion Challenge: Enough Quality Money to Deal with the Crises of the Future' (2014), available at www.oecd.org/dac/governance-peace/conflictfragilityandresilience/the22bnusdchallenge.htm, accessed on 1 March 2017; UNGA, Res 46/182, UN Doc. A/RES/46/182 (1991) para 12; see also S. Jansen-Wilhelm, *Accepting Assistance in the Aftermath of Disasters: Standards for States under International Law* (Intersentia, 2015) 90.

6 GHA, 'Report 2015' (2015), available at www.globalhumanitarianassistance.org/report/gha-report-2015, accessed on 17 March 2017; GHA Report 2016 (n. 5).

7 GHA Report 2015 (n. 6) 22–23.

8 UN High-Level Panel on Humanitarian Financing, 'Report to the Secretary-General: Too Important to Fail: Addressing the Humanitarian Financing Gap' (December 2015), available at www.un.org/news/WEB-1521765-E-OCHA-Report-on-Humanitarian-Financing.pdf, accessed on 1 March 2017. The international community presently leverages 'only' about 25–28 billion USD annually, of which 25–30 % is actually contributed by the private sector.

9 Ibid 6.

10 UNISDR, Sendai Framework for Disaster Risk Reduction 2015–2030, UN Doc. UNISDR/GE/2015 (2015) paras 24–27; see for definitions of 'cooperation' or 'assistance' in IHRL, M. Salomon, 'How to Keep Promises: Making Sense of the Duty among Multiple States to Fulfil Socio-Economic Rights in the World' in A. Nollkaemper and D. Jacobs (eds), *Distributing Responsibilities in International Law* (Cambridge University Press, 2015) 366, note 1, or ILC draft art 6.

11 See CESCR, General Comment 12 (n. 3) paras 38–39.

12 See such assertions in ILC, Second Report (2009) (n. 4) paras 50–70; CESCR, General Comment No. 3: The Nature of States Obligations (art. 2(1) of the Covenant), UN Doc. E/1991/23 (1990) para 14; CESCR, General Comment 12 (n. 3) paras 36, 38–39; CESCR, General Comment 14 (n. 3) paras 38, 40; similarly CESCR, General Comment 15 (n. 3) paras 30, 34.

13 CESCR, General Comment 14 (n. 3) paras 40, 65; CESCR, General Comment 12 (n. 3) para 38; CESCR, General Comment 15 (n. 3) para 38.

14 CESCR, General Comment 3 (n. 12) para 14; CESCR, General Comment 14 (n. 3) paras 40, 42, 45, 65; CESCR, General Comment 15 (n. 3) para 30, 34, 38.

15 CESCR, General Comment 15 (n. 3) para 37–38; CESCR, General Comment 3 (n. 12) paras 10, 14; similarly CESCR, General Comment 14 (n. 3) para 45.

16 Jansen-Wilhelm (n. 5) 138–140; Salomon (n. 10) 366–385; M. Hesselman, 'Sharing International Responsibility for the Protection of Poor Migrants? An Analysis of Extra-Territorial International and Regional Socio-Economic Human Rights Law' 15 *European Journal of Social Security* (2013) 187.

17 Dinstein (n. 1) 78.
18 P. Alston and G. Quinn, 'The Nature and Scope of States Parties' Obligations under the International Covenant on Economic, Social and Cultural Rights' 9 *Human Rights Quarterly* (1987) 156, 191; M. Sepúlveda Carmona, 'The Obligations of "International Assistance and Cooperation" under the International Covenant on Economic, Social and Cultural Rights: A Possible Entry Point to a Human Rights based Approach to Millennium Development Goal 8' 13 *International Human Rights Journal* (2009) 86; Hesselman (n. 16); Salomon (n. 10).
19 Dinstein (n. 1) 78; Jansen-Wilhelm (n. 5) 138–139. See also Hesselman (n. 16); Salomon (n. 10) 368; Alston and Quinn (n. 18) 191; HRC, Report of the Special Rapporteur on the Right to Health, Paul Hunt, UN Doc. A/HRC/7/11/Add.2 (2008) para 133, includes Hunt's now famous critique on Sweden's position that there is no legal obligation to assist.
20 Alston and Quinn (n. 18) 191.
21 Council Regulation (EC) No 1257/96 (n. 2).
22 Salomon (n. 10) 367.
23 See work of the ILC between 2007–2016 here, available at http://legal.un.org/ilc/guide/6_3.shtml; final draft articles and Commentaries adopted through: ILC, Report of the International Law Commission of Its Sixty-Eighth Session, UN Doc. A/71/10 (2016) ch IV.
24 See (n. 2) above, although the ILC Secretariat did not refer to all instances.
25 ILC Secretariat (n. 1) paras 257–258.
26 ILC Special Rapporteur (n. 2) para 54.
27 Ibid.
28 Ibid para 12; see McDermott's chapter in this book.
29 See ILC, Report of the International Law Commission of its Sixtieth Session, UN Doc. A/63/10 (2008) para 222; *Military and Paramilitary Activities in and against Nicaragua (Nicaragua v. United States of America) (Merits)* [1986] ICJ Rep. 14, 124. At the same time, the ICJ's pronouncement regarded a situation of armed conflict and not a disaster during peacetime.
30 ILC Special Rapporteur (n. 2) para 54; ILC (n. 29) paras 222, 242–243; ILC, Third Report on the Protection of Persons in the Event of Disasters, by Eduardo Valencia-Ospina, Special Rapporteur, UN Doc. A/CN.4/629 (31 March 2010) paras 5–6.
31 Ibid.
32 ILC, Draft art 5 (n. 23) 15.
33 Ibid art 7 (n. 23) 15. The word 'shall' was maintained, despite several States stressing unease with this compulsory formulation.
34 ILC, Draft arts 10, 11 and 13 (n. 23) 15–16. It seems that art 11 ICESCR also requires cooperation based on 'free consent'; see for an analysis of the obligation to accept assistance in IHRL, Jansen-Wilhelm (n. 5).
35 ILC, Draft art 12 (n. 23) 15–16.
36 ILC (n. 23) 57.
37 ILC, Report of the International Law Commission, Sixty-Third Session, UN Doc. A/66/10 (2011) (26 April–3 June and 4 July–12 August 2011) para 283.
38 Ibid para 279.
39 See further considerations on this point e.g. Hesselman (n. 23) 187, 189–190.
40 Arts 2(1) and 11 ICESCR, art 4 CRC and arts 4 and 32 CRPD.
41 CommRC, General Comment No. 19 (2016) on Public Budgeting for the Realization of Children's Rights (Art. 4), UN Doc. CRC/C/GC/19 (20 July 2016) paras 35, 65, 75; see also introduction, and e.g. CESCR, General Comment 15 (n. 3) paras 34, 60; See similarly CESCR, General Comment 14 (n. 3) paras 38–40.
42 CESCR, General Comment 15 (n. 3) paras 34, 60; see similarly CESCR, General Comment 14 (n. 3) paras 38–40; CESCR, General Comment 12 (n. 3) paras 5–6, 13, 15, 36, 38.
43 CESCR, General Comment No. 2 on International Technical Assistance, UN Doc. E/1990/23 (1990) para 10.
44 Ibid.
45 CESCR, General Comment 12 (n. 3) paras 38–39; CESCR, General Comment 14 (n. 3) 40, 65; CESCR, General Comment 15, paras 34, 60.
46 CESCR, General Comment 12 (n. 3) para 39.
47 CESCR, Reporting Guidelines ICESCR, UN Doc. E/CN.12/2008/22 (2009).
48 See W. Vandenhole, 'Economic, Social and Cultural Rights in the CRC: Is There a Legal Obligation to Cooperate Internationally for Development?' *International Journal of Children's Rights* (2009) 23–63; Hesselman (n. 16); Salomon (n. 10) 368; the target dates back to 1970 and has been repeatedly affirmed

by States. In 2005, 15 EU countries agreed to meet the target by 2015. Organization for Economic Cooperation and Development (OECD),'History of the 0.7% ODA Target', available at www.oecd.org/dac/stats/ODA-history-of-the-0-7-target.pdf, accessed on 1 March 2017.

49 OECD,'Definition of ODA', available at www.oecd.org/dac/stats/officialdevelopmentassistancedefinitionandcoverage.htm#Coverage, accessed on 1 March 2017; OECD,'Development Aid Rises again in 2015, Spending on Refugees Doubles', available at www.oecd.org/dac/development-aid-rises-again-in-2015-spending-on-refugees-doubles.htm, accessed on 1 March 2017; in 2015, of the total amount of ODA leveraged by OECD-DAC countries (at 131.6 billion USD), 13.6 billion was devoted to humanitarian assistance in conflicts and disasters. Also consider UNGA, Resolution 46/182, UN Doc. A/RES/46/182 (1991) para 11.

50 Sendai Framework (n. 10) para 19(1).

51 CESCR, Concluding Observations on the Sixth Periodic Report of Finland, UN Doc. E/C.12/FIN/CO/6 (16 December 2014); and in that same year also Slovenia, Romania, Portugal, Czech Republic, and Monaco received reprimands. See for an elaborate further analysis and discussion of this Concluding Observation practice, Hesselman (n. 16).

52 E.g. CESCR, Concluding Observations on the Fifth Period Report of Norway, UN Doc. E/C.12/NOR/CO/5 (13 December 2013) para 3. Norway devotes 1% of GNI to international development assistance.

53 OECD, 'Development Aid Rises again in 2016 but Flows to Poorest Countries Dip' (2016), available at www.oecd.org/dac/financing-sustainable-development/development-aid-rises-again-in-2016-but-flows-to-poorest-countries-dip.htm, accessed on 30 May 2017.

54 See for specific analysis Hesselman (n. 16), and paragraph 4 of this chapter.

55 See Hesselman (n. 16); Sepúlveda Carmona (n. 18) 89, 93 considering cooperation and assistance a legal obligation, but the 0.7% target as something that requires a 'timetable' – these timetables have repeatedly not been met though, hollowing out this observation; Salomon (n. 10) 368 instead considers it a 'general duty amongst developed states' to meet the 0.7% target.

56 E.g. Hesselman (n. 16) for further discussion; Jansen-Wilhelm (n. 5) 138–139; Vandenhole (n. 48) 23, 61–62; Sepúlveda Carmona (n. 18) 93, 102.

57 Sepúlveda Carmona (n. 18) 93–94; similarly Salomon (n. 10) 376.

58 See on this point also Sepúlveda Carmona (n. 18).

59 CESCR, Concluding Observations of the Committee on Economic, Social and Cultural Rights on Mongolia, UN Doc. E.C12./1/ADD.47 (1 September 2000) para 24.

60 CommRC, Concluding Observations: Ukraine, UN Doc. CRC/C/15/Add.191 (9 October 2002) paras 55–56.

61 CommRC, Concluding Observations on the Initial Report of Tuvalu, UN Doc. CRC/C/TUV/CO/1 (29 October 2013) paras 56, 67; CommRC, Concluding Observations on the Combined Second to Fourth Periodic Reports of Fiji, UN Doc. CRC/C/FJI/CO/2-4 (12 October 2014) paras 55–56; CommRC, Concluding Observations on the Combined Third to Fifth Periodic Reports of Mauritius, UN Doc. CRC/C/MUS/CO/3-5 (26 February 2015) paras 57–58, 75; see for similar questions raised, and evidence adduced, that general obligations of assisting States are discussed by CommRC, Vandenhole (n. 48) 44–45.

62 CommRC, Concluding Observations on Mozambique, UN Doc. CRC/C/MOZ/CO/2 (4 November 2009) paras 19–20.

63 CESCR, Concluding Observations of the Committee on Economic, Social and Cultural Rights: Republic of Korea, UN Doc. E/C.12/KOR/CO/3 (17 December 2009).

64 CommRC, Concluding Observations: Italy, UN Doc. CRC/C/ITA/CO/3-4 (30 October 2011).

65 CESCR, Concluding Observations of the Committee on Economic, Social and Cultural Rights: Japan, UN Doc. E/C.12/1/ADD.67 (24 September 2001).

66 CommRC, Concluding Observations: Singapore, UN Doc. CRC/C/SGP/CO/2-3 (4 May 2011) paras 23–24; CommRC, Concluding Observations: Norway, UN Doc. CRC/C/NOR/CO/4 (3 March 2010) para 12; CommRC, Concluding Observations: Australia, UN Doc. CRC/C/AUS/CO/4 (28 August 2012) para 22; CommRC, Italy (n. 64).

67 CommRC, Concluding Observation: Japan, UN Doc. CRC/C/JPN/CO/3 (20 June 2010) paras 29–30.

68 Open-Ended Working Group (OEWG) on OP-ICESCR, Report of the Open-Ended Working Group on Its First Session, UN Doc. E/CN.4/2004/44 (2004) paras 21, 45, in which the 'Committee experts noted that in theory such cases might arise'; OEWG on OP-ICESCR, Report of the Open-Ended Working Group on Its Second Session, UN Doc. E/CN.4/2005/52 (2005) paras 9, 63, 79–80, 99, 101, 105.

69 See on this topic earlier, e.g. Sepúlveda Carmona (n. 18).

70 See e.g. UNGA, Report of the Third Session of the Ad Hoc Committee on a Comprehensive and Integral International Convention on the Protection and Promotion of the Rights and Dignity of Persons

with Disabilities, UN Doc. A/AC.265/2004/5 (2004) 69–71; see debate and proposals via: Daily Summary of Afternoon Session of the Fourth Session of the Ad Hoc Commission (27 August 2004), available at www.un.org/esa/socdev/enable/rights/ahc4sumart24bis.htm, accessed on 17 March 2017.
71 Vandenhole (n. 48) 60–61.
72 OEWG on OP-ICESCR (2005) para 76.
73 OEWG on OP-ICESCR, Report of the Open-Ended Working Group to Consider Options Regarding the Elaboration of an Optional Protocol to the International Covenant on Economic, Social and Cultural Rights on Its Third Session, UN Doc. E/CN.4/2006/47 (2006) paras 80–82.
74 Ibid para 8.
75 OEWG on OP-ICESCR (2005) para 78.
76 Ibid para 77; OEWG on OP-ICESCR (n. 73) para 78.
77 OEWG on OP-ICESCR (n. 73) para 78.
78 Ibid paras 17, 40.
79 Ibid para 22.
80 OEWG on OP-ICESCR (n. 73) paras 80–81, 84; OEWG on OP-ICESCR (2005) paras 63, 76, 79–80, 105.
81 OEWG on OP-ICESCR (n. 73) para 81.
82 Ibid (2005) para 79.
83 Ibid para 105.
84 OEWG on OP-ICESCR (2005) para 80.
85 OEWG on OP-ICESCR (n. 73) para 79; OEWG on OP-ICESCR (2007) paras 127–130.
86 See for the manner in which the CESCR might approach this: CESCR, Statement on an Evaluation of the Obligation to Take Steps 'to the Maximum of Available Resources' under an Optional Protocol to the Covenant, UN Doc. E/C.12/2007/1 (2007).
87 Arts 14(1) and (2) OP-ICESCR.
88 The option seems also to have been specifically entertained by the Chair-Rapporteur of the Working Group.
89 HRC, Report of the Open-Ended Working Group to Explore the Possibility of Elaborating an Optional Protocol to the Convention on the Rights of the Child to Provide a Communications Procedure, UN Doc. A/HRC/13/43 (2009) para 87.
90 HRC, Report of the Open-Ended Working Group on an Optional Protocol to the Convention on the Rights of the Child to Provide a Communications Procedure, UN Doc. A/HRC/17/36 (2011) paras 90–91.
91 T. Buck and M. Wabwile, 'The Potential and Promise of Communications Procedures under the Third Protocol to the Convention on the Rights of the Child' 2 *International Human Rights Law Review* (2013) 205, 236–237.
92 See similarly Salomon (n. 10).
93 One example is the communication brought against Turkey about poor recovery and housing situations after earthquakes near the town of Van for 110 families. Issues of international assistance or lack of capacity were not part of the communication. HRC, Communications Report of Special Procedures, UN Doc. A/HRC/26/21 (2 June 2014) 88, available at www.ohchr.org/EN/Issues/Housing/Pages/Communications.aspx, accessed on 30 June 2017.
94 CHR, Final report of the Special Rapporteur, Paulo Sérgio Pinheiro on Internally Displaced Persons: Principles on housing and property restitution for refugees and displaced person, UN Doc E/CN.4/Sub.2/2005/17 (28 June 2005).
95 FAO/IDMC/OCHA/OHCHR/UN-Habitat/UNHCR, 'Handbook on Housing and Property Restitution for Refugees and Displaced Persons: Implementing the "Pinheiro Principles"' (March 2007), p. 56, available at www.ohchr.org/Documents/Publications/pinheiro_principles.pdf, accessed 17 December 2017.
96 Idem. p. 96.
97 E.g. see country visit reports of: HRC, Report of the Special Rapporteur on Adequate Housing as a Component of the Right to an Adequate Standard of Living, and on the Right to Non-Discrimination in This Context, Raquel Rolnik; HRC, Report of the Country Visit in Indonesia, UN Doc. A/HRC/25/54/Add.1 (26 December 2013); HRC, Report of the Special Rapporteur on the Human Rights of Internally Displaced Persons, Chaloka Beyani, Addendum, Mission to Haiti, UN Doc. A/HRC/29/34/Add.2 (8 May 2015); HRC, Report of the Special Rapporteur on the Human Rights of Internally Displaced Persons, Chaloka Beyani, Addendum, Follow-Up Mission to Georgia, UN Doc. A/HRC/26/33/Add.1 (4 June 2014); HRC, Report of the Special Rapporteur on the Right of Everyone to the Enjoyment of the Highest Attainable Standard of Physical and Mental Health, Addendum, Mission to Japan (15–26 November 2012), UN Doc. A/HRC/23/41/Add.3 (31 July 2013); HRC, Report of the Special Rapporteur on the

Right to Food on Her Mission to Philippines, UN Doc. A/HRC/31/51/Add.1 (29 December 2015) and as discussed below.

98 HRC, Report of the Special Rapporteur on the Human Rights of Internally Displaced Persons, Chaloka Beyani, Addendum, Mission to Maldives, UN Doc. A/HRC/19/54/Add.1 (30 January 2012) para 72(a).

99 Ibid 72(b).

100 Ibid 72(c).

101 See HRC, Report of the Special Rapporteur on the Human Rights of Internally Displaced Persons on His Mission to the Philippines, UN Doc. A/HRC/32/35/Add.3 (5 April 2016) paras 125–127.

102 Ibid para 126.

103 E.g. HRC, Report of the Special Rapporteur on the Human Rights of Internally Displaced Persons on His Mission to Afghanistan, UN Doc. A/HRC/35/27/Add.3 (12 April 2017) para 73.

104 HRC, Report of the Special Rapporteur on Right to Food, Jean Ziegler, UN Doc. E/CN.4/2006/44 (16 March 2006) paras 13, 15, 24.

105 See also Rolnik's chapter in this book.

106 See HRC, Report of the Special Rapporteur on Adequate Housing as a Component of the Right to an Adequate Standard of Living, and on the Right to Non-Discrimination in This Context, Raquel Rolnik, Addendum, Mission to Algeria, UN Doc. A/HRC/19/53/Add.2 (26 December 2011).

107 See HRC, Report of the Special Rapporteur on Adequate Housing as a Component of the Right to an Adequate Standard of Living, and on the Right to Non-Discrimination in This Context, Miloon Kothari – Mission to the Islamic Republic of Iran, UN Doc. E/CN.4/2006/41/Add.2 (21 March 2006) para 106.

108 Ibid.

109 HRC, Report of the Special Rapporteur on the Human Rights of Internally Displaced Persons, Chaloka Beyani, Addendum, Mission to Haiti, UN Doc. A/HRC/29/34/Add.2 (8 May 2015) para 83(e).

110 HRC, Report of the Special Rapporteur on Adequate Housing as a Component of the Right to an Adequate Standard of Living, and on the Right to Non-Discrimination in This Context on Her Mission to Cape Verde, UN Doc. A/HRC/31/54/Add.1 (23 December 2015) para 94(a)iv.

111 Ibid paras 9, 68.

112 In the case of Niger and Afghanistan, there were references to very specific amounts of funding asked for, see (n. 100 and 101).

113 HRC, Final Research-Based Report of the Human Rights Council Advisory Committee on Best Practices and Main Challenges in the Promotion and Protection of Human Rights in Post-Disaster and Post-Conflict Situations, UN Doc. A/HRC/28/76 (10 February 2015) para 46.

114 Ibid para 80.

115 HRC, Analytical Study on the Relationship between Climate Change and the Human Right of Everyone to the Enjoyment of the Highest Attainable Standard of Physical and Mental Health, Report of the UNHCHR, UN Doc. A/HRC/32/23 (6 May 2016) paras 4, 14–18, 22, 25, 28, 34–35, 46, 49, 58–59, 61, 63–64.

116 Ibid para 61.

117 HRC, Report of the Working Group on the Universal Periodic Review: Cuba, UN Doc. A/HRC/24/16 (8 July 2013) paras 170.81 and 170.83.

118 HRC, Report of the Working Group on the Universal Periodic Review: Bhutan, UN Doc. A/HRC/27/8 (2014) para 118.98.

119 Ibid paras 118.97, 118.102.

120 HRC, Report of the Working Group on the Universal Periodic Review: Bangladesh, UN Doc. A/HRC/11/18 (5 October 2009) para 94.41.

121 HRC, Report of the Working Group on the Universal Periodic Review: Kuwait, UN Doc. A/HRC/29/17 (13 April 2015) paras 157.169, 157.175, 157.176, 157.178, 157.272, 157, 270.

122 Salomon (n. 10) 280.

123 CESCR, General Comment 3, paras 10, 14.

124 UN High-Level Panel on Humanitarian Financing (n. 8) 4.

6

THE HUMAN RIGHTS APPROACH OF THE INTERNATIONAL LAW COMMISSION IN ITS WORK ON THE PROTECTION OF PERSONS IN THE EVENT OF DISASTERS

Rónán McDermott

Introduction

In order to address the fragmented and underdeveloped nature of international law pertaining to natural and technological disasters the International Law Commission (ILC or the Commission), at its fifty-ninth session in 2007, decided to include the topic 'Protection of persons in the event of disasters' in its programme of work. With Eduardo Valencia-Ospina as Special Rapporteur, the ILC ultimately produced a set of Draft Articles relating to the topic in 2016. The ILC claims that the objective of its work was to ultimately 'facilitate an adequate and effective response to disasters that meets the essential needs of the persons concerned, with full respect for their rights'.[1] As one of the most significant developments relating to disaster law in recent years, an appraisal of the ILC's approach to human rights is warranted. Such an appraisal is further justified by the ILC's claim that the individual, 'as a bearer of rights and as a person with essential needs, is at the centre of its work on the topic'.[2]

The chapter demonstrates that human rights are referenced throughout the entire set of Draft Articles and the Commentaries thereto. It assesses the human rights approach of the ILC to the Draft Articles from the appointment of the ILC of a Special Rapporteur through to their adoption on final reading. Thus, the first section addresses the scope of the ILC's work and its implications for human rights. The second through fourth sections address the Draft Articles concerning human dignity, human rights and humanitarian principles respectively. It is clear that these provisions, in particular the stand-alone human rights Draft Article (Draft Article 5) proposed by the ILC, are litmus tests for the approach to human rights adopted by the ILC. However, other Draft Articles are either inspired by consideration of international human rights obligations, are partly informed by them or have important human rights implications. Therefore, a brief overview of the human rights content of the Draft Articles will then be provided in the fifth section before a more general appraisal of the ILC's approach to human rights concerning the topic is submitted in the sixth section. This appraisal discusses the seemingly confused definition of protection adopted by the ILC and the implications this has for the approach to human rights that the

ILC has undertaken. The tension that the ILC encountered between promoting the protection of human rights on the one hand while respecting the principles of territorial sovereignty and non-intervention on the other is also highlighted. Finally, the human rights approach of the ILC is set in context and situated alongside parallel international developments in the law and policy of disaster management.

Scope of the ILC's work and its implications for human rights

The ILC has limited the scope of its work on the topic to protection in the context of natural and technological disasters. This is reflected in Draft Article 3 in which disaster is defined as:

> a calamitous event or series of events resulting in widespread loss of life, great human suffering and distress, mass displacement, or large-scale material or environmental damage, thereby seriously disrupting the functioning of society.[3]

Of interest from a human rights perspective, this definition includes disasters causing large-scale material or environmental damage that do not impact directly on human life or directly cause great human suffering and distress.[4] The Draft Articles address the applicability of the Draft Articles in armed conflict settings. Despite earlier confusion in the drafting of the Articles and the Commentaries thereto, it is recognised in the commentary to Draft Article 18 that the Draft Articles do apply in accordance with the principle of *lex specialis* to disasters that occur in the context of armed conflict to the extent that the specific legal issues raised by a disaster are not covered by international humanitarian law.[5]

While human rights issues are more likely to arise in conflict than in natural and/or technological disaster settings, recent decades have seen increased attention being paid by humanitarian actors and scholars from across disciplines to human rights issues in natural disaster settings.[6] This development has served to highlight the fundamental human rights dimension to both the generation of vulnerability to disaster and the perpetuation and exacerbation of human rights abuses arising from disasters. Despite this, the nexus between human rights and natural and technological disasters have been relatively neglected within international law. It was recognised early in the Commission's work on the topic that the 'link between international human rights law and disasters has not yet been generally reflected in existing hard-law instruments on either subject'.[7]

Only in recent years have legal scholars been exploring the relationship between human rights law and natural and technological disasters.[8] One focus of attention has been on exploring the existence of an independent human right to humanitarian assistance.[9] In considering the human rights approach of the ILC, it would be instructive to assess how it engages with this debate. The Special Rapporteur's Preliminary Report notes that there are no major international or regional human rights treaties that explicitly recognise the existence of such a right.[10] The existence of an implicit right is also unclear. The Special Rapporteur acknowledges that recognising such a right to assistance would counter the risk of fragmentation that would inevitably arise from the arbitrary selection of, or emphasis on, particular rights. However, he also recognises that the recognition of such a right would have broader ramifications for the international legal order, resulting in a potential tension with the principles of State sovereignty and non-intervention.[11]

The Preliminary Report examined two existing human rights instruments at the time that make explicit reference to disaster settings: the Convention on the Rights of Persons with Disabilities[12] and the African Charter on the Rights and Welfare of the Child.[13] Noting that these impose obligations to protect rather than bestow individual rights per se, it asserted that 'a rights-based approach to protection and assistance in the event of disasters contemplates those obligations as well'.[14] Rather, the Preliminary Report recognises the relevance of international human rights law of general application to the protection of persons in times of disaster. It lists a number of relevant rights, including the right to life, the right to food, the right to health and medical services, the right to the supply of water, the right to adequate housing, clothing and sanitation and the right not to be discriminated against.[15]

The temporal scope of the ILC's work on the topic is also important in assessing its human rights approach. Amongst social scientists focusing on disasters and humanitarian actors, the symbiotic relationship between human rights and disasters is recognised. On the one hand, human rights violations in times of normalcy can render those whose rights are violated more vulnerable to disasters where and when they occur. This would render greater attention to pre-disaster phases important. On the other hand, disasters can reinforce human rights violations, for example as a result of discrimination in disaster response. The increased recognition of human agency in generating and exacerbating, as well as alleviating the impact of disasters has complemented the hitherto emphasis within disaster management on disaster preparedness and response.

Turning to the extent that the ILC has adopted such an approach, it should be stressed that it was noted in the Special Rapporteur's Second Report on the topic that a number of delegates in the Sixth Committee suggested that the ILC should effectively limit its focus to disaster response solely, to the exclusion of other phases of the disaster management cycle.[16] In the same Report the Special Rapporteur stated that having a wider focus could be 'overly ambitious' to be appropriately covered at this stage of the Commission's work on the topic. Nonetheless, he left the possibility open of returning to preparedness at the pre-disaster phase later on in the Commission's work. Ultimately, Draft Article 9 addresses disaster risk reduction, imposing a duty on States to reduce the risk of disasters and to undertake the 'appropriate measures, including through legislation and regulations, to prevent, mitigate, and prepare for disasters'.[17] While this Draft Article does go some way in ensuring that a broad disaster management approach is undertaken that embraces the pre-disaster phase. Paragraph 4 of the Commentary on the Draft Article references the obligation to take preventative measures to reduce disaster risk as a corollary of States' human rights obligations, in particular the right to life. It then proceeds to illustrate how such an obligation has been recognised in decisions of international tribunals, in particular the European Court of Human Rights.

Draft Articles 1 and 2 concern the general scope and purpose of the Draft Articles.[18] In determining the general scope of the project and the meaning of protection of persons in the event of disasters, the ILC grappled with the extent to which a rights-based approach should imbue its work on the topic. Already in the Preliminary Report provided to the ILC, the Special Rapporteur outlined his view concerning the meaning of such an approach:

> The essence of a rights-based approach to protection and assistance is the identification of a specific standard of treatment to which the individual, the victim of a disaster, *in casu*, is entitled. To paraphrase the Secretary-General, a rights-based approach deals with situations not simply in terms of human needs, but in terms of society's obligation to respond to the inalienable rights of individuals, empowers them to demand justice as a right, not as a charity, and gives communities a moral basis from which to claim international assistance when needed.[19]

In an early plenary session of the ILC, there was a debate concerning the role of what it described as a 'rights-based approach' to the topic of the protection of persons in the event of disaster. Support was expressed by some members of the ILC for a rights-based approach, 'at least as a starting point' and that 'the human rights protection mechanism provided the best protection for the alleviation of the suffering of victims'.[20] However, some ambiguity arose concerning the pitting of a rights-based approach against a needs-based approach. Some members of the ILC considered that a focus on rights to the detriment of needs within the work of the Commission on the topic might hinder a 'pragmatic response that the topic needs since in emergency situations certain human rights are derogable' and that a rights-based approach might compel an affected State to 'always accept international aid, an obligation that was not based on State practice'.[21] Ultimately, these competing arguments appear to have been reconciled on the basis of agreement around the assertion that a rights-based approach ought to be taken in the Commission's work but that such an approach must be adopted 'in light of the principles of sovereignty and non-intervention'.[22] The commentary to Draft Article 1 ultimately states that, while the scope of the Draft Articles primarily corresponds to the rights and obligations of States to one another in the context of disasters and to persons affected by disaster, another axis of rights and responsibilities of concern to the Draft Articles is the rights of individuals 'as established by international law'.[23] Having detailed some of the key dimensions of the ILC's work on this topic from a human rights perspective, the following sections address individual Draft Articles. While necessarily selective and not intended to be exhaustive, the selection of Draft Articles to further analyse is guided by the concern to convey the particular approach to human rights adopted by the Commission.

Draft Article 4 – human dignity

The provision with one of the most important human rights origins and implications is Draft Article 4, which reads as follows:

> The inherent dignity of the human person shall be respected and protected in the event of disasters.[24]

The first paragraph to the Commentary to the Draft Article states that the ILC 'recognises human dignity as the core principle that informs and underpins international human rights law'.[25] The following paragraph also highlighted the role of dignity in the protection of persons 'as the ultimate foundation of human rights law'.[26] Some members of the ILC did suggest before the stand-alone human rights article (Draft Article 5 on final reading) was adopted that the recognition of human dignity 'could be supplemented by the obligation to respect human rights as set out in existing international instruments, so as to reinforce the applicability of rights'.[27] It should be noted that, while some delegates in the Sixth Committee were supportive of the inclusion of the stand-alone Draft Article on human dignity when it was initially introduced, other delegates in the Sixth Committee suggested that it might be better placed in the preamble.[28] Nonetheless, a dedicated Draft Article addressing human dignity was ultimately retained by the Commission, which would indicate a strong preference on the part of the ILC to ensure that human dignity was prominent within its work on the protection of persons in the event of disaster.

Draft Article 5 – human rights

The most obviously human rights-inspired of the Draft Articles is Draft Article 5. It reads as follows:

> Persons affected by disasters are entitled to the respect for and protection of their human rights in accordance with international law.[29]

The ILC Plenary Session that discussed this Article as originally submitted by the Special Rapporteur noted that the Special Rapporteur had indicated that the principles of sovereignty and non-intervention were a 'point of departure' and not a 'point of conclusion' in determining how the extent to which international human rights instruments and customary law should influence the protection of persons in the event of disaster.[30] This would signify that at least towards the beginning of his work, the Special Rapporteur was not opposed to challenging the pre-existing balance between human rights and sovereignty concerns.

However, some of the effect of the human rights Draft Article appears to have been diluted somewhat through the course of the ILC's work on the topic. The Draft Article adopted on first reading read as follows:

> [p]ersons affected by disasters are entitled to respect for their human rights.[31]

A point of contention concerning the draft Article adopted on first reading is that the Draft Article did not adequately take into account the right of States to derogate and impose limitations on human rights during times of emergency and that some further elaboration would be required within the Draft Article.[32] While the ILC did recognise in the commentary to the first reading of the Draft Article that the Draft Article does not prejudice a State's freedom to derogate and limit in accordance with international human rights instruments and customary international law,[33] it had been argued that further clarity would have been beneficial. The wording of the Draft Article on final reading removed some ambiguity concerning the nature of the human rights obligations imposed and emphasised that human rights ought to be respected and protected 'in accordance with international law'.[34] Nonetheless, further clarity would have been welcome concerning the process by which derogations may be made rather than limitations, limitations of course often being sufficient in the context of natural and similar disasters.[35]

Another call for greater clarity that emerged from the Sixth Committee and which was reported by the ILC was that the wording of the Draft Article as adopted on first reading was excessively general and vague and that the particular human rights relevant during disasters be referenced in the commentary.[36] This view was shared by the International Federation of the Red Cross and Red Crescent Societies (IFRC) in its written submission on the Draft Articles.[37] In its commentary on the Draft Article adopted on final reading, the Commission declined to draw up an exhaustive list of relevant rights due to a concern that such a list could lead to an interpretation that rights not mentioned might thereby not be applicable.[38] However, it did proceed to enumerate some of the most pertinent civil and political rights (the right to life) and economic, social and cultural rights (relating to the provision of essential foodstuffs, essential health care, basic shelter and housing and education for children).[39]

The general wording and broad scope of application of the Draft Article as adopted on first reading allowed for differing obligations to be placed on States, NGOs and inter-governmental organisations.

In so doing it could be argued that the Draft Article directed itself not only towards State actors but also towards non-state actors who do not fall under direct human rights obligations imposed by international human rights instruments but who may as a result of the wording of the Draft Article be placed under a certain obligation to adhere to human rights norms. This intention is confirmed in the Commentary to the Draft Article as adopted on first reading.[40] The ILC did not limit itself to human rights obligations under international agreement and customary international law but included 'assertions of best practices for the protection of human rights included in non-binding texts on the international level'.[41] This approach arguably reinforces developments within the humanitarian sector whereby self-regulation and regulation by donors towards the promotion of the human rights of disaster-affected persons and the enhancing of downwards accountability towards such persons have been increasingly promoted.[42] Consequently, the newly inserted wording, 'in accordance with international law', can be regarded as somewhat disappointing from a human rights perspective and as a missed opportunity for the progressive development of international law insofar as it removes the latent encouragement of non-state humanitarian actors to continue and consolidate their efforts in promoting a human rights-based approach to their work that occurs in the absence of formal international legal processes. The explicit reference to international law also removes human rights provisions as contained in national constitutions from the purview of the Draft Article.

Despite these apparent setbacks in the elaboration of the Draft Article, it should however be noted that the final reading Draft Article revised the previous readings, expanding explicitly the human rights obligations from mere 'respect for' to also embrace 'protection of', thus broadening the scope of the obligation imposed on States.[43]

Draft Article 6 – humanitarian principles

Draft Article 6 concerns the humanitarian principles and reads as follows:

> [r]esponse to disasters shall take place in accordance with the principles of humanity, neutrality and impartiality, and on the basis of non-discrimination, while taking into account the needs of the particularly vulnerable.[44]

While the humanitarian principles pertain mainly to assistance rather than protection as commonly understood within the humanitarian sector, it is nonetheless important to assess the human rights approach adopted by the ILC to them as it is included in its work on the protection of persons in the event of disasters. Although the principles have been mainly inspired by international humanitarian law and the policy and striven-for practice of humanitarian actors in their pursuit of humanitarian space, it is possible to discern a human rights dimension to the approach the ILC takes to them. Thus, the ILC recognises that the principle of humanity is a 'meeting point between international humanitarian law and international human rights law'.[45] Furthermore, the Special Rapporteur in his reports recognises the element of non-discrimination in constituting the principle of impartiality.[46] This inclusion met with the approval of the ILC in one of its plenary sessions at which it stated that:

> [n]on-discrimination, which was initially developed in the context of international humanitarian law, had also become a fundamental provision in human rights law, and was reflected in Article 1, paragraph 3, of the Charter of the United Nations.[47]

Draft Articles 7 through 17 – human rights and the relationship between affected States and third States

With the possible exception of Draft Article 10, Draft Articles 7–17 concern the two-way relationship between the affected State and third States. Obligations in international human rights law permeate the ILC's work in formulating these draft Articles.

Draft Article 7 concerns both directions of the affected State-third State relationship. Third States are placed under a duty to cooperate, as appropriate, as well as the affected State:

> [i]n the application of the present draft articles, States shall, as appropriate, cooperate among themselves, with the United Nations, with the components of the Red Cross and Red Crescent Movement, and with other assisting actors.

A general clause obliges States to cooperate, as appropriate, among themselves and with the United Nations (UN), the Red Cross and Red Crescent Movement and other assisting actors. The latter category is imported from the definition found in Draft Article 3, subparagraph (d). Again, the duty to cooperate is only required to the extent appropriate. In drafting this Draft Article, the ILC relies heavily on a justification based on human rights considerations. It cites the report of the Independent Expert on Human Rights and International Solidarity submitted to the Human Rights Council by the High Commissioner for Human Rights in which it is stated that '[t]he obligations related to international assistance and cooperation are complementary to the primary responsibility of States to meet their national human rights obligations'.[48] International cooperation rests on the premise that developing countries may not possess the necessary resources for the full realisation of rights set forth in human rights instruments, in particular the International Covenant on Economic, Social and Cultural Rights, resulting in a shared responsibility for development.[49] The Commission also cites the Declaration on the Right to Development in which a new international economic order ought to be established based on the observance and realisation of human rights.[50]

The Special Rapporteur reiterates, however, that cooperation should not be understood in a manner that would diminish the sovereignty of States within the international legal regime as laid out in UN General Assembly (UNGA) Resolution 46/182.[51] This is also reflected in the final Commentary on the Draft Article.[52] The Commission therefore refrains from challenging the status quo ante concerning international cooperation contained within Resolution 46/182 in which the sovereignty of the affected State remains central, despite an auxiliary responsibility to seek assistance where national capacities are overwhelmed.[53] Nonetheless, the Commentary to the Draft Article concerning international cooperation does proceed to cite further provisions of UNGA Resolution 46/182:

> [t]he magnitude and duration of many emergencies may be beyond the response capacity of many affected countries. International cooperation to address emergency situations and to strengthen the response capacity of affected countries is thus of great importance. Such cooperation should be provided in accordance with international law and national laws.[54]

This would suggest that the ILC is reflecting in its approach to the Draft Articles the core tension encountered in ensuring compliance with and implementation of human rights law at the domestic level. The nature of this tension is that the effect of international human rights norms is tempered by the demands of the principles of sovereignty and non-intervention. Nonetheless, the Special Rapporteur cites instruments that highlight what he calls the 'internal' aspect of sovereignty, whereby the primary responsibility placed on an affected State may 'may encompass a duty to seek external support where national response capacities are overwhelmed'.[55] This caveat to sovereignty is also reflected in the Commentary to Draft Article 10 concerning the role of the affected State.[56] Of further relevance to cooperation between assisting actors and affected States is that a previous version of the Draft Articles contained a stand-alone Draft Article concerning the different forms of cooperation, which was subsequently removed. It had been noted that neither the wording of the Draft Article nor its Commentary sufficiently reaffirms the relationship with Draft Articles 4 and 5 concerning human dignity and human rights respectively.[57] In particular, the lack of clarity concerning the content of the duty to cooperate does not sufficiently countenance the obligations under international human rights law on third States to lend assistance.

Draft Article 11 concerns the duty of the affected State to seek external assistance:

> [t]o the extent that a disaster manifestly exceeds its national response capacity, the affected State has the duty to seek assistance from, as appropriate, other States, the United Nations, and other potential assisting actors.

In considering the duty to seek external assistance the ILC draws extensively on the obligations on States derived from international human rights instruments and customary international human rights law. Noting that a number of rights are 'directly implicated in the context of a disaster', it lists non-exhaustively, the right to life, the right to adequate food, the right to health and medical services, the right to safe drinking water, the right to adequate housing, clothing and sanitation and the right to be free from discrimination.[58] In the Commentary, the ILC then proceeds to demonstrate on the basis of sources within international human rights law how this obligation has been elaborated.

With respect to an earlier version of this Draft Article, there was considerable debate within the Commission about the rightful balance between sovereignty on the one hand and the protection of human rights on the other. To summarise, several members of the ILC proposed to restate the principles of sovereignty and non-intervention in the domestic affairs of a State within the Article to 'properly reflect both the rights of the affected state vis-à-vis humanitarian assistance, as well as its responsibility for the overall rescue operations'.[59] On the other hand, the ILC indicated that another set of views stated that the Special Rapporteur's report concerning the Draft Article did not adequately capture the contemporary understanding of sovereignty, whereby State sovereignty is to be balanced with the need to protect human rights. It was further noted that 'the purpose of the topic was the protection of persons in the event of disasters, and not the protection of the rights of States'.[60] Interestingly, the ILC noted that a view was expressed amongst its members that a refusal to accept assistance could constitute an internationally wrongful act if such a refusal violated the rights of persons affected by disasters under international law.[61] The Commission ultimately cautioned against making such characterisations as it could have 'adverse consequences for international relations and justify intervention in an affected State'.[62]

A further example of the tension between sovereignty and human rights that can be discerned in relation to the drafting of this Draft Article is the preference expressed by the ILC for choosing the term 'duty', rather than 'responsibility', in discussing the role of the disaster-affected State. This approach is adopted in order to avoid an association with a responsibility to protect. Nonetheless, in spite of the expressly limited application of the responsibility to protect doctrine outside of quite limited circumstances,[63] there were voices in the plenary session of the ILC that cautioned against an approach that would preclude out of hand the possible future development of an obligation similar to the responsibility to protect for disaster contexts of the kind defined in the Draft Articles.[64]

Draft Article 12 concerns offers of external assistance:

> 1. In the event of disasters, States, the United Nations, and other potential assisting actors may offer assistance to the affected State.
> 2. When external assistance is sought by an affected State by means of a request addressed to another State, the United Nations, or other potential assisting actor, the addressee shall expeditiously give due consideration to the request and inform the affected State of its reply.

While human rights do not feature explicitly in this Draft Article nor the Commentary thereto, it should be noted that an early version of the Draft Article accorded States, the UN and other competent inter-governmental organisations a right to offer assistance. NGOs were not bestowed the same right but may have offered assistance to the affected State. In presenting this early draft, the Special Rapporteur noted that the solidarity that underpins the identification of the right to offer assistance has its 'ultimate goal and inspiration' in the protection of the individual, which is reflected in the inherent dignity of the human being and the protection of human rights.[65] The role of the affected State had also been considered by the Commission, which the Special Rapporteur also claimed had been inspired by dignity and human rights.[66] In guiding the ILC's early approach to offers of assistance, the Special Rapporteur noted that the right to offer assistance is recognised by a range of international instruments, including human rights instruments.[67]

The definition of protection of persons and its implications for the human rights approach

It is important to highlight the potentially different usages of the term 'protection' deployed by the ILC on the one hand and humanitarian actors on the other. Such differing usage as deployed by human rights lawyers on the one hand and operational humanitarian actors on the other carries important implications for the nature of the human rights approach adopted by the ILC in its work on the topic. Humanitarian actors consider protection as all those activities that contribute to the respect for the rights of the individual.[68] In the context of humanitarian crises without an armed conflict dimension (in which case international humanitarian law would not be relevant), such rights are derived from international human rights law. Protection activities can involve prevention measures, advocacy in the case of ongoing violations of international human rights law and remedial actions designed to address the effects of violations. Humanitarian actors thus distinguish protection from assistance in their activities, the latter generally relating to all activities whereby material help is provided to persons affected by disaster.

Along similar lines, in its Preliminary Report the Special Rapporteur asserts that protection can be understood in a broad or a narrow manner:

> [p]rotection can be said to be all-encompassing, covering the more specific concepts of response, relief or assistance with which it is often associated. One should, however, differentiate between protection *sensu lato* and protection *sensu stricto*. This may be conceptualized as follows: there is a general, all-encompassing concept of protection which includes protection in a strict sense, denoting a rights-based approach, and other concepts, in particular assistance.[69]

The ILC in its work seems to adopt the broader definition at times, which makes sense from a humanitarian perspective in that the broadest possible approach to the legal issues that arise in the case of disaster is ensured. As a means of illustration, the Special Rapporteur in his Fourth Report stated that '[t]he term "assistance" reflects the broad ambit of operational aspects in the provision of humanitarian protection'.[70] The adoption of this broader definition is arguably also reflected by the inclusion of reference to the humanitarian principles in the scope of protection, notwithstanding the rationale for the principles being primarily grounded in the need for humanitarian actors to establish and maintain access to affected populations in order to provide assistance.[71] However, the adoption of this broader definition can be problematic if the Draft Articles are to be integrated into protection debates within the fields of disaster management and humanitarian action.

The comment by some States in the Sixth Committee that human rights and human dignity provisions should be placed in the preamble or towards the beginning of the Draft Articles as these Articles ought to permeate the entire set of Draft Articles might arguably indicate that the ILC has attempted to address not only human rights but also other legal issues and therefore goes beyond the ordinary definition of protection as understood within humanitarian circles. If protection is to be defined as all those activities that contribute to the enjoyment of human rights, then it could be argued that every aspect of the ILC's approach to the topic can be considered as part of a human rights approach. Adopting such a broad definition of protection draws issues that the ILC addresses such as the protection of relief goods and termination of external assistance into the human rights arena, which may not be merited.

Conclusion

At the heart of the human rights approach to the protection of persons in the event of disaster is a tension between securing the human rights of disaster-affected persons while respecting the principles of sovereignty and non-intervention. This tension arguably maps onto the ILC's mandate to codify and progressively develop international law. Mere codification would present little threat to existing conceptualisations of the principles of sovereignty and non-intervention. In contrast, progressive development of the law on this topic would necessitate a re-appraisal of the principles of sovereignty and non-intervention as currently understood.

This tension between protection on the one hand and the principles of respect for territorial sovereignty and non-interference in the internal affairs of affected States was recognised by the Special Rapporteur in his Fourth Report as central to the ILC's work on the topic and acknowledged by the ILC in its subsequent plenary session.[72] The States in the Sixth Committee perhaps ultimately act as an *eminence grise* in constraining the human rights potential of the Draft Articles.

With greater attention being paid by human rights bodies to disasters, the ILC's human rights approach ought to be more closely integrated with wider developments in the law and policy of disaster management and humanitarian action. Limited though it may be in terms of its ambition, the human rights approach contained within the ILC's Draft Articles ought to be considered and taken into account by and benefit from other, parallel developments within the international legal and policy architecture of disaster management. The concern with persons who are endowed with agency and rights as well as the duties on disaster management actors has been increasingly recognised within broader academic literature and operational policy briefs and best practices over the last twenty years or so.

The Agenda for Humanity issued by the UN Secretary-General ahead of the first World Humanitarian Summit (WHS) in May 2016 had as a central headline the upholding of norms, admittedly primarily in conflict but which nonetheless would be relevant for natural and similar disasters.[73] Other relevant initiatives that feature prominently within the international agenda concern the importance of ensuring that humanitarian action is delivered as locally as possible and as internationally as necessary. Such a combined concern for human rights protection and the role of international as well as regional and national actors reflects the central tension between the protection of human rights and the principles of sovereignty and non-intervention that characterises the ILC Draft Articles. Indeed, the tension has been described by some engaged in the WHS as akin to an emerging subsidiarity principle within the humanitarian aid domain. Similarly, the Sendai Framework for Disaster Risk Reduction, which was formulated in 2015, discusses the importance of adequate legal frameworks for disaster risk reduction at multiple levels of governance. It highlights, in one of its guiding principles, the objective of 'promoting and protecting all human rights' in the management of the risk of disasters.[74]

To date these various initiatives have been taking place at some distance from the work of the ILC. If the human rights approach of the ILC, limited inevitably though it may be by the inescapable precepts of international law outlined above relating to the principles of sovereignty and non-intervention, is to be realised, then a greater connectedness within the debate is required. The consultation with the parallel international processes detailed in the Special Rapporteur's Eighth Report on the topic is therefore to be welcomed as is the broad consultation undertaken with relevant stakeholders prior to the adoption of the Draft Articles on final reading.[75] Ultimately, these processes are essentially related in that they are aimed at promoting human dignity at a period in human history when humanitarian needs are being outstripped by the international community's capacity to meet them. The challenge is to seek a coherent message across policy domains.

In conclusion, the ILC claims to have addressed the topic of the protection of persons in the event of disasters with international human rights law as a core component. This is highlighted in the Secretariat document provided towards the beginning of the ILC's work on the topic and for the most part in the Reports of the Special Rapporteur and from the ILC's plenary sessions. The divergence from the human rights approach that can be discerned is mainly due to the sovereignty considerations and perhaps the realisation that the ILC operates in the shadow of UN member States in the Sixth Committee of the UNGA and their jealous guarding of their sovereignty. Throughout its work on the topic, the ILC is conscious that it is conducting its work either in anticipation of or in reaction to the responses of States. The question arises as to whether and to what extent the ILC has ultimately engaged in codification and/or progressive development respectively. In the sense that disparate bodies of law and policy have been unified and addressed as a whole one could assert that there has indeed been a progressive development. In terms of substance, at least in relation to human rights, the Special Rapporteur, and the ILC generally, have been cautious. And it is in the form of the Draft Articles and their reception at the diplomatic level that the key test of the impact of the largely human rights approach of the ILC in practice will be. Their impact will also depend on how the Draft Articles are articulated *vis-à-vis* similar developments in other aid policy domains. Every effort ought to be made to ensure that the Draft Articles, whatever form they may ultimately take, contribute to a more predictable, coherent and effective international legal order governing humanitarian crises and one which places human rights at the centre.

Selected bibliography

G. Bartolini, T. Natoli and A. Riccardi, 'Report of the Expert Meeting on the ILC's Draft Articles on the Protection of Persons in the Event of Disasters' 3 *International Law and Disasters Working Papers Series* (2015), available at http://disasterlaw.sssup.it/wp-content/uploads/2014/01/Bartolini-Natoli-Riccardi-Report-of-the-Expert-Meeting-2015-DEF.pdf, accessed on 20 June 2017.

J.C. Carmalt and C. Haenni-Dale, 'Human Rights and Disaster' in B. Wisner, J.C. Gaillard and I. Kelman (eds), *The Routledge Handbook of Hazards and Disaster Risk Reduction* (Routledge, 2012) 61.

R. Connolly, E. Flaux and A. Wu, 'Working Paper on the ILC Draft Articles on the Protection of Persons in the Event of Disasters' *Human Rights Centre Working Paper, Queen's University Belfast* (2016), available at http://blogs.qub.ac.uk/amnesties/files/2016/02/QUB-HRC-WP-ILC-Draft-Articles-on-the-Protection-of-Persons-Feb-2016-FINAL.pdf, accessed on 30 May 2016.

F. Zorzi Giustiniani, 'The Works of the International Law Commission on "Protection of Persons in the Event of Disasters": A Critical Appraisal' in A. de Guttry, M. Gestri and G. Venturini (eds), *International Disaster Response Law* (TMC Asser Press, 2012) 65.

Notes

1 ILC, Texts and Titles of the Draft Articles Adopted by the Drafting Committee on First Reading, UN Doc. A/CN.4/L.831 (15 May 2014) draft art 2.
2 ILC, Third Report on the Protection of Persons in the Event of Disasters by Eduardo Valencia-Ospina, Special Rapporteur, UN Doc. A/CN.4/629 (31 March 2010) para 63.
3 ILC, Report of the International Law Commission on the Work of Its Sixty-Eighth Session, UN Doc. A/71/10 (2 May–10 June and 4 July–12 August 2016) para 48, draft art 3.
4 F. Zorzi Giustiniani, 'The Works of the International Law Commission on "Protection of Persons in the Event of Disasters": A Critical Appraisal' in A. de Guttry, M. Gestri and G. Venturini (eds), *International Disaster Response Law* (TMC Asser Press, 2012) 68.
5 ILC (n. 3) commentary to draft art 3, para 9.
6 J.C. Carmalt and C. Haenni-Dale, 'Human Rights and Disaster' in B. Wisner, J.C. Gaillard and I. Kelman (eds), *The Routledge Handbook of Hazards and Disaster Risk Reduction* (Routledge, 2012) 61 ff.; R. Barber, 'Protecting the Right to Housing in the Aftermath of Natural Disaster: Standards in International Human Rights Law' 20 *International Journal of Refugee Law* (2012) 432; R. Carver, 'Is There a Human Right to Shelter after Disaster?' 10 *Environmental Hazards* (2011) 232.
7 ILC, Preliminary Report on the Protection of Persons in the Event of Disasters, UN Doc. A/CN.4/598 (5 May 2008) para 25.
8 W. Kälin, 'The Human Rights Dimension of Natural or Human-Made Disasters' 55 *German Yearbook of International Law* (2012) 119.
9 E. Kujit, 'A Humanitarian Crisis: Reframing the Legal Framework on Humanitarian Assistance' in A. Zwitter, C. Lamont, H.J. Heintze and J. Herman (eds), *Humanitarian Action: Global, Regional and Domestic Legal Responses* (Cambridge University Press, 2015).
10 ILC, Preliminary Report (n. 7) para 54.
11 Ibid.
12 Convention on the Rights of Persons with Disabilities (adopted 13 December 2006, entered into force 3 May 2008) 2515 UNTS 3.
13 African Charter on the Rights and Welfare of the Child, OAU Doc. CAB/LEG/24.9/49 (1990).
14 ILC, Preliminary Report (n. 7) para 26.
15 Ibid.
16 Ibid paras 57–58.
17 ILC (n. 3) draft art 9.
18 Draft Article 1 reads as follows: '[t]he present draft articles apply to the protection of persons in the event of disasters'.
19 ILC (n. 11).
20 ILC, Report of the International Law Commission on the Work of Its 61st Session, UN Doc. A64/10 (2009) (4 May–5 June and 6 July–7 August 2009) para 159.
21 Ibid para 162.
22 Ibid.
23 ILC (n. 3) para 2, commentary to art 1.
24 Ibid draft art 4.
25 Ibid para 1.
26 ILC, Report of the International Law Commission, Sixty-Third Session, UN Doc. A/66/10 (2011) (26 April–3 June and 4 July–12 August 2011) para 289.
27 ILC, Report of the International Law Commission on the Work of Its 62nd Session, UN Doc. A/65/10 (2010) (3 May–4 June and 5 July–6 August 2010).
28 ILC, Fourth Report on the Protection of Persons in the Event of Disasters by Eduardo Valencia-Ospina, Special Rapporteur, UN Doc. A/CN.4/643 (2011) (26 April–3 June and 4 July–12 August 2011) para 17.
29 ILC (n. 3) draft art 5.
30 ILC (n. 27) para 307.
31 ILC (n. 28) para 13.
32 G. Bartolini, T. Natoli and A. Riccardi, 'Report of the Expert Meeting on the ILC's Draft Articles on the Protection of Persons in the Event of Disasters' 3 *International Law and Disasters Working Papers Series* (2015), available at http://disasterlaw.sssup.it/wp-content/uploads/2014/01/Bartolini-Natoli-Riccardi-Report-of-the-Expert-Meeting-2015-DEF.pdf, accessed on 20 June 2017.

33 ILC (n. 1) para 3.
34 ILC (n. 3) draft art 5.
35 E. Sommario, 'Derogation from Human Rights Treaties in Situations of Natural or Man-Made Disasters' in A. de Guttry, M. Gestri and G. Venturini (eds), *International Disaster Response Law* (TMC Asser Press, 2012). See also Sommario's chapter in this volume.
36 ILC, Fifth Report on the Protection of Persons in the Event of Disasters by Eduardo Valencia-Ospina, Special Rapporteur, UN Doc. A/CN.4/652 (2012) (7 May–1 June and 2 July–3 August 2012) para 22.
37 IFRC, Written Submission of the International Federation of Red Cross and Red Crescent Societies to the International Law Commission on the Draft Articles on the Protection of Persons in the Event of Disasters' (January 2016), available at www.ifrc.org/PageFiles/126924/IFRC%20statement%20-%20protection%20of%20persons%20in%20the%20event%20of%20disasters%20(Jan%202016).pdf, accessed on 20 June 2017.
38 ILC (n. 3) commentary to draft art 5, para 5.
39 Ibid para 6.
40 ILC, Report of the International Law Commission, Sixty-Sixth Session, UN Doc. A/69/10 (2014) (5 May–6 June and 7 July–8 August 2014) para 389.
41 ILC (n. 26) draft art 8, para 2.
42 One of the latest developments in this regard is the development of the Core Humanitarian Standard, available at www.corehumanitarianstandard.org/the-standard, accessed on 31 May 2016.
43 ILC (n. 3) commentary to draft art 5, para 4.
44 Ibid draft art 7.
45 ILC (n. 27) para 304.
46 J. Pictet, *Développement et principes du droit international humanitaire* (Pedone, 1983) 78. Pictet identifies three principles common to humanitarian law and human rights law: inviolability, non-discrimination and security.
47 ILC (n. 27) para 303. See also Casolari's chapter in this volume.
48 ILC (n. 28) para 36.
49 ILC (n. 3) commentary to draft art 7, para 2.
50 ILC (n. 28) para 36.
51 Ibid para 38.
52 ILC (n. 3) commentary to draft art 7, para 4.
53 Ibid.
54 ILC (n. 28) Annex.
55 Ibid.
56 ILC (n. 3) commentary to draft art 10, para 2.
57 R. Connolly, E. Flaux and A. Wu, 'Working Paper on the ILC Draft Articles on the Protection of Persons in the Event of Disasters' *Human Rights Centre Working Paper, Queen's University Belfast* (2016), available at http://blogs.qub.ac.uk/amnesties/files/2016/02/QUB-HRC-WP-ILC-Draft-Articles-on-the-Protection-of-Persons-Feb-2016-FINAL.pdf, accessed on 30 May 2016.
58 ILC (n. 3) commentary to draft art 11, para 3.
59 ILC (n. 27) para 31.
60 Ibid.
61 ILC (n. 28) para 22.
62 Ibid.
63 In his 2009 report the Secretary-General clarified that the responsibility to protect doctrine is not applicable to natural and technological disasters. See UNSG, Implementing the Responsibility to Protect: Report of the Secretary-General, UN Doc. A/63/677 (12 January 2009) para 10(b).
64 ILC (n. 41) para 389.
65 ILC (n. 28) para 78.
66 Ibid para 79.
67 Ibid para 93.
68 IASC defines protection as

> a broad term for activities aimed at obtaining full respect for the rights of all individuals in accordance with international law, including international humanitarian, human rights and refugee law, regardless of their age, gender or social, ethnic, national, religious or other background.

69 ILC (n. 10) para 51.
70 ILC (n. 28) para 47.
71 ILC (n. 10) para 52.
72 ILC (n. 26) para 275.
73 The UNSG notes that '[t]here is outrage that national sovereignty and security are being placed above people's rights to protection and assistance and that the most basic tenets of international humanitarian and human rights law are being violated every day without accountability'. See UNSG, One Humanity: Shared Responsibility: Report of the Secretary General for the World Humanitarian Summit, UN Doc. A/70/709 (2016) para 10.
74 UNISDR, 'Sendai Framework for Disaster Risk Reduction 2015–2030', available at www.unisdr.org/files/43291_sendaiframeworkfordrren.pdf, accessed on 20 June 2016 para 19(c).
75 ILC, Eighth Report on the Protection of Persons in the Event of Disasters by Eduardo Valencia-Ospina, Special Rapporteur, UN Doc. A/CN.4/697 (2016).

7

LIMITATION AND DEROGATION PROVISIONS IN INTERNATIONAL HUMAN RIGHTS LAW TREATIES AND THEIR USE IN DISASTER SETTINGS

Emanuele Sommario[*]

Introduction

The Inter-Agency Standing Committee's *Operational Guidelines on the Protection of Persons in Situations of Natural Disasters* remind us that

> people affected by natural disasters do not live in a legal vacuum. They belong to the population of countries that have ratified international and regional human rights instruments and enacted constitutions, laws, rules and institutions that should protect these rights.[1]

Indeed, even in such dire predicaments, individuals affected by calamitous events continue to enjoy the protection of International Human Rights Law (IHRL), and nothing suggests that its safeguards lose force when a community is struck by a disaster. On the contrary, States remain responsible for respecting, protecting and fulfilling the rights of all individuals living under their jurisdiction, especially when they are most in need. While there is currently a general lack of human rights treaties specifically addressing the protection of persons affected by disasters,[2] IHRL remains highly relevant, as are the enforcement mechanisms it offers.

Over the last decade much attention and work has been devoted to exploring the relationship between disaster prevention and response and human rights law.[3] Contributions by international human rights courts and tribunals have mainly focused on obligations concerning the prevention and mitigation of risks connected to hazardous events and on elucidating how human rights provisions can be interpreted in the context of disasters to identify assistance obligations incumbent on the affected States.[4] In addition, IHRL has been used to shape disaster management and response strategies, leading many humanitarian actors to adopt a rights-based approach to disaster relief and reconstruction actions.[5]

The International Law Commission (ILC) has also offered its insights on the subject. In 2006, it identified the topic 'Protection of persons in the event of disasters' for inclusion in its programme of work,[6] and its work culminated in 2016 in the adoption of a set of Draft Articles bearing the same name.[7] Already in his preliminary report, Special Rapporteur Eduardo Valencia-Ospina recognised international human rights law as one of the immediate legal sources regulating international disaster protection and assistance.[8] The focus on human rights led to the inclusion of a specific provision within the final text (Draft Article 5). In its commentary to the article, the ILC considered that the reference to human rights 'incorporates both the rights and limitations that exist in the sphere of international human rights law' and includes 'in particular its treatment of derogable and non-derogable rights'.[9]

This statement recognises that – even in situations of disaster – national and international legal regimes envisage the possibility to restrict or suspend certain rights to safeguard common societal interests, such as public order or public health. The nature and scope of these restrictions varies depending on the prevailing situation, with more serious circumstances calling for more severe limitations. However, so far, scholars have paid little attention to permissible restrictions on human rights in disaster settings. The present contribution aims to fill this gap.

This chapter will start by briefly illustrating the legal framework developed under international law concerning limitations on the enjoyment of human rights in disaster situations. The attention will then shift to the actual practice of treaty monitoring bodies in reviewing situations in which States have made use of the above powers when faced with natural or technological disasters. Considering that, so far, treaty bodies have never formally examined derogations triggered by disaster situations, we will test the compatibility *in abstracto* of the derogation notices presented with the relevant normative framework. The analysis will be based on a perusal of the decisions of the main human rights bodies, and in particular of the European Court of Human Rights (ECtHR or Strasbourg Court) and the United Nations (UN) Human Rights Committee (HRComm). In sketching the norms applicable, reference will also be made to the *Siracusa Principles on the Limitation and Derogation Provisions in the International Covenant on Civil and Political Rights* (Siracusa Principles) that elaborate on the standards developed by treaty monitoring bodies.[10] Finally, while public emergencies may also have profound consequences for the enjoyment of economic, social and cultural rights, their application in disaster settings is addressed elsewhere in this volume,[11] and we will therefore limit our discussion to civil and political rights.

Limitations to the enjoyment of individual rights in human rights treaties

Human rights treaties envisage at least three different techniques to limit the enjoyment of individual rights.[12] The first two allow States to impose *ordinary limitations* on certain rights, without the need to alter the prevailing treaty regime. The third requires instead that the situation reaches a particular threshold of gravity and that State authorities formally suspend the applicability of some treaty provisions, in order to introduce *extraordinary limitations*.

Starting with ordinary limitations, these are usually made possible by including the option to interfere with individual rights when certain qualifying conditions are met. This model draws direct inspiration from the general limitation clause contained in Article 29(2) of the 1948 Universal Declaration of Human Rights (UDHR), according to which

> [i]n the exercise of his rights and freedoms, everyone shall be subject only to such limitations as are determined by law solely for the purpose of securing due recognition and respect for the rights and freedoms of others and of meeting the just requirements of morality, public order and the general welfare in a democratic society.

Such limitations are commonly considered to be the result of the need to balance community interests with the rights and liberties bestowed on individuals.

A second way to impose ordinary limitations is to determine that certain conducts fall outside the protection of the treaty. For instance, Article 8(3)(c)(iii) of the International Covenant on Civil and Political Rights[13] (ICCPR) expressly states that any 'service exacted in cases of emergency or calamity threatening the life or well-being of the community' does not amount to 'forced or compulsory labour', which the provision otherwise prohibits.[14] Similarly, Article 5(1) of the European Convention on Human Rights[15] (ECHR or Convention) features an exhaustive list of circumstances which would not constitute violations of the right to liberty and security, such as the 'lawful detention of persons for the prevention of the spreading of infectious diseases'. Clearly, both these examples are relevant for our purposes, as both 'emergencies and calamities' and 'the spreading of infectious diseases' might, under certain circumstances, meet the threshold of gravity envisaged by the definition of 'disaster'.[16]

Moving to extraordinary limitations, the third option available is to derogate from some of the provisions contained in human rights treaties all together. However, resort to the derogation clause is only possible when authorities face a 'public emergency which threatens the life of the nation'. Again, certain procedural and substantial conditions need to be fulfilled in order to make valid use of this prerogative. The next two sections will deal in turn with ordinary and extraordinary limitations and analyse the practice that emerged in relation to their use in disaster settings.

Ordinary limitations on human rights in case of disaster

As mentioned above, most human rights are amenable to limitations in favour of overriding public or private interests. Yet the drafters of human rights treaties have included specific safeguards, so as to protect those rights against arbitrary or excessive infringements.

The legal parameters

The text of most limitation clauses provides that restrictions on the freedoms they guarantee are only permissible under certain circumstances. The relevant provisions set out the protected rights in their first paragraph, which are then qualified by listing the conditions under which they can be lawfully restricted. These include the requirement that possible limitations (a) are provided by law; (b) pursue a legitimate aim (i.e. that they serve one of the purposes for interference that are enumerated in the specific provision); and (c) are necessary to achieve said aim, which implies a balancing between the rights restricted and the interest that the limitation seeks to protect. As we shall see, although these requirements are not explicitly spelled out with respect to limitations which are realised by excluding certain conducts from the protection provided by the treaties, monitoring bodies have nevertheless used them to assess State conduct even with regards to such types of limitations.

The requirement of a legal basis

Rights can be restricted only if such possibility is provided for by law. In all major human rights treaties, the term 'law' has been understood to indicate a general and abstract act or, in the case of common law systems, an equivalent unwritten norm.[17] The State wishing to impose a given limitation must point to some specific legal rule or regime – recognised in its legal order – which authorises the interfering act.

The 'law' must however possess additional features. First, it must be adequately accessible, so that citizens are 'able to have an indication that is adequate in the circumstances of the legal rules applicable to a given case'.[18] Furthermore, in order to be regarded as a 'law', a norm must be 'formulated with sufficient precision to enable the citizen to regulate his conduct: he must be able – if need be with appropriate advice – to foresee, to a degree that is reasonable in the circumstances, the consequences which a given action may entail'.[19] Furthermore, a law may not confer unfettered discretion for the restriction of individual rights on those charged with its execution. In other words, if the law grants some latitude to public authorities, it must be framed with sufficient clarity and specify the manner in which such discretion will be exercised.[20] In the words of the HRComm, 'the law itself has to establish the conditions under which the rights may be limited'.[21] Moreover, laws imposing limitations on the exercise of human rights shall not be arbitrary or unreasonable.[22]

The need for a legitimate aim

If it wishes to limit individual rights, a State must identify the purpose of its interference. Each provision protecting limitable rights presents an exhaustive list of aims on which restrictions can be based. These include public order (*ordre public*),[23] public health, public morals, national security, public safety and the rights and freedoms of others. The right to property – protected by Article 1 of Protocol No. 1 of the ECHR – mentions 'public interest' and 'general interest' as possible reasons for the imposition of limitations. Of course, limitations are only permitted on the basis of grounds that are explicitly listed in the specific provision.[24] However, the scope of most of the grounds for interference is rather wide, and States can usually make a plausible case that they have a legitimate reason for interfering with the right.

In cases of interference imposed to counter the effects (or to prevent the occurrence) of disasters, the grounds on which these are most commonly based are the maintenance of public order (*ordre public*) and public safety (e.g. to evacuate and prevent movement to a highly contaminated area);[25] the preservation of public health (e.g. compulsory vaccination to prevent the spreading of lethal infectious disease);[26] or, in the case of the right to property, the protection of a 'public' or 'general' interest (e.g. to expropriate land or goods necessary to tackle the effects of a disaster).[27]

Necessity and proportionality of limitations

In addition to being lawful and serving a legitimate purpose, any restriction must be 'necessary' to achieve said purpose. When restrictions are introduced, States 'must demonstrate their necessity and only take such measures as are proportionate to the pursuance of legitimate aims'.[28] To prove that a limitation meets this test, it needs to be shown that the action taken is in response to a 'pressing social need' and that the interference with the rights protected is no greater than is necessary to address such need.[29] The latter element is usually referred to as the test of *proportionality*, through which treaty monitoring bodies balance the severity of the interference against the importance of the public interest. Note, however, that limitation clauses must be interpreted strictly and in favour of the right at stake[30] and cannot be applied or invoked 'in a manner that would impair the essence of a Covenant right'.[31] The relevant provisions also specify that restrictions must be necessary 'in a democratic society'. This qualification imposes further restrictions on the sort of limitations allowed, as national authorities have the burden of proving that they do not impair the democratic functioning of the State.[32]

Under the ECtHR case law, States have been granted a 'margin of appreciation' in deciding on the nature and scope of the limitations required to protect the general interest. In the *Handyside* case, the Strasbourg Court stressed that the Convention leaves 'to each Contracting State, in the first place, the task of securing the rights and liberties it enshrines', adding that

> [b]y reason of their direct and continuous contact with the vital forces of their countries, State authorities are in principle in a better position than the international judge to give

> an opinion on the exact content of these requirements as well as on the 'necessity' of a 'restriction' or 'penalty' intended to meet them.[33]

The margin of appreciation doctrine is applied both with respect to limitations and derogations from the ECHR, but its exact meaning and scope can sometimes be troublesome.[34] The discretion left to States may, in fact, vary depending on the nature of the rights at issue and on the balancing of competing rights.[35] What is clear, however, is that the margin of appreciation is 'not unlimited', and 'it is for the Court to give the final ruling on whether [restrictions] are compatible with the Convention'.[36] Moreover, the margin will be narrower 'where the right at stake is crucial to the individual's effective enjoyment of intimate or key rights'[37] and will disappear with respect to the Convention's non-derogable rights.

Ordinary limitations in the practice of treaty monitoring bodies

There is no abundance of practice concerning ordinary limitations imposed in disaster settings. All of the cases which will be briefly presented have been decided by the bodies tasked with supervising the ECHR, i.e. the ECtHR and the (now extinct) European Commission on Human Rights (ECommHR or Commission). The practice analysed contains examples of the first two kinds of limitations described above, i.e. cases of generic limitations, as well as cases in which a given conduct is explicitly excluded from protection under the relevant article.

Generic limitation clauses

The case of *I v. Italy*[38] concerned the admissibility of a complaint brought in front of the ECommHR for an alleged violation of the right to property, protected by Article 1 of Protocol No. 1 to the ECHR.[39] The applicant owned a flat in Naples, which he had rented out, and was living in another, smaller flat in the same city. Having formed a family, he wished to move into the flat he owned and took proceedings against the tenant to have the lease terminated and secure the use of the property. A domestic court accepted his requests, yet before its decision could be enforced emergency decrees were enacted with regards to areas that had been struck by earthquakes, including the district where the flat was located. The decrees prohibited the forced eviction of tenants living in the disaster-struck areas. Meanwhile the applicant was obliged to leave Naples because the flat he was renting had become too small for him and his family, and he had not found any other suitable accommodation. He complained to the ECommHR that the measures introduced to deal with the housing crisis prevented him from using his flat and thus rendered his right to ownership meaningless. He therefore alleged that his right to property had been unlawfully interfered with.

The relevant parts of the article at stake read as follows:

> Every natural or legal person is entitled to the peaceful enjoyment of his possessions. . . . The preceding provisions shall not, however, in any way impair the right of a State to enforce such laws as it deems necessary to control the use of property in accordance with the general interest or to secure the payment of taxes or other contributions or penalties.

The Commission determined that the application of the decrees represented a restriction on the applicant's right of property, and as such an interference possibly falling under the limitation clause envisaged by the provision. It was thus required to consider two questions: (a) whether the legislation at issue pursued a legitimate aim that was in accordance with the 'general interest' and (b) whether the control thereby exercised over the applicant's use of his property was proportionate to the aim pursued.

As to the first question, the decision found that the suspension of eviction orders came under the emergency legislation which was made necessary by the need to deal with a housing crisis in the aftermath of a natural disaster, a purpose that was both legitimate and 'in accordance with the general interest'. The ECommHR then moved to consider the issue of proportionality. In assessing this element, the Commission noted that the suspension of the eviction orders had only lasted 16 months, during which time the applicant was still able to collect the rent for the flat. It took note of the very serious situation the Italian authorities were confronted with and accepted that their decision to maintain the *status quo* could not be considered unreasonable, also given the limited time which had elapsed. Particular weight was given to the fact that the necessity of the measure was reviewed at regular 6-month intervals.

Having once more stressed 'the special circumstances of the case', and considering the margin of appreciation to which states are entitled, the ECommHR found that the sacrifice demanded of the applicant 'was not unreasonable when weighed against the legitimate aim pursued'.[40] Hence the limitation was proportionate to the general community interest, and the Commission deemed the application inadmissible.[41]

Another case involving the restriction of individual rights to protect common interests concerned compulsory vaccination against diphtheria, a highly infectious and virulent disease. In *Solomakhin v. Ukraine*,[42] the applicant complained, *inter alia*, that there had been no reason for vaccinating him, as there had not been an outbreak of diphtheria in his hometown at the relevant time and the vaccine had been strongly contraindicated for him. The Government agreed that the compulsory vaccination had constituted an interference with the applicant's private life, protected by Article 8 ECHR. However, given the complicated epidemiological situation in the region, it maintained that the interference had been necessary to protect the health of the applicant and of the public at large.

The Court agreed with the Government. It initially noted that the interference was clearly provided by law and pursued a legitimate aim. Elaborating on the issue of proportionality, the Court recalled that the medical staff had checked the applicant's suitability for vaccination prior to carrying it out, which suggests that necessary precautions had been taken to ensure that the medical treatment would not be to his detriment to an extent that could upset the balance of interests between the applicant's personal integrity and the public interest of protecting the health of the population.[43] Another decisive element in the Court's reasoning was the fact that the applicant's allegations had been thoroughly examined by the domestic courts and found to be unsubstantiated and that he had failed to produce any evidence to challenge the findings of the domestic authorities.[44]

Although the cases surveyed had different outcomes, in all of them the monitoring bodies accepted that the rights at stake could be compressed to preserve a public interest threatened by a (present or potential) disaster situation. The decisions analysed are however not univocal when it comes to the standards used to review the conduct of State parties. While in *I v. Italy* the Commission clearly recognised the State's margin of appreciation in deciding how far it could go in limiting individual rights to preserve the public interest, no mention of said doctrine is present in cases decided by the Court. The reasons for such apparent inconsistency may be due to different factors, including the importance of the specific right at stake, the presence of a general consensus among State parties regarding the admissibility of a certain restriction and the weight of the interest to be protected through the interference.[45] Yet the sparsity of practice makes the identification of a general approach to limitations adopted to tackle or avoid the occurrence of disasters rather difficult.

Limitations imposed by excluding certain conducts from the protective scope of IHRL

Certain provisions included in IHRL instruments explicitly exclude a number of situations from the protective scope of the treaty itself. Article 4(3)(c) ECHR, for instance, considers outside the scope of 'forced and compulsory labour' any service that is 'exacted in a case of emergency or calamity threatening the life or well-being of the community'.[46] As recalled above, Article 5 ECHR prohibits deprivation of liberty save in a number of circumstances, which include 'the lawful detention of persons for the prevention of the spreading of infectious diseases' (Article 5(1)(e)). Let us briefly consider the import of both provisions based on the (scant) case law of the ECtHR.

Examining first the forced labour exception, it must be recalled that the provision is clearly inspired by the 1930 Special Convention of the International Labour Organization (ILO) on Forced Labour (ILO Convention).[47] Article 2(d) of this treaty defines the concept of emergency as

> war or . . . calamity or threatened calamity, such as fire, flood, famine, earthquake, violent epidemic or epizootic diseases, invasion by animal, insect or vegetable pests, and in general any circumstance that would endanger the existence or the well-being of the whole or part of the population.

A systemic interpretation of the ILO Convention and of the human rights law provisions banning forced labour would suggest that the imposition of special duties in case of emergency should only be limited to the very serious events listed in the ILO Convention.

In *S v. Federal Republic of Germany*,[48] one of the few cases in which the Strasbourg organs discussed the scope of Article 4(3)(c), the applicant objected to the request of German authorities that he assist in the gassing of foxholes as part of a campaign against a rabies epidemic. The ECommHR argued that, even assuming that the obligation could be considered compulsory labour, the requirement that a hunting tenant participate in measures to control epidemics could be justified under the provision.

The case suggests that treaty monitoring bodies have identified a rather low threshold of gravity with respect to situations that would allow the imposition of compulsory service in case of emergency. Even circumstances considerably less serious than the ones prevailing in times of 'disaster' would entitle public authorities to impose compulsory duties on individuals.[49] Clearly, fully fledged natural or human-made disasters would allow similar sorts of restrictions.

The second type of limitation, i.e. the possibility of forcibly hospitalising individuals carrying infectious diseases, has so far only been scrutinised by the ECtHR. In *Enhorn v. Sweden*,[50] the applicant was a homosexual man who was diagnosed with HIV. After discovering that he had (unknowingly) infected another man, medical authorities issued a number of instructions to the applicant, designed to minimise the risk that he transmitted the virus to others. Among them was the attendance of periodical medical appointments. When the applicant failed to attend a number of them, the Swedish authorities issued an order imposing on him compulsory hospital isolation for 3 months. He was then arrested and interned, and the detention order was renewed several times. However, he frequently absconded thereafter with the result that he was in fact deprived of his liberty for a total of about 18 months over a 7-year period.

Having accepted that Enhorn's detention potentially fell under the exception provided by Article 5(1)(e) ECHR, the ECtHR had to determine whether it was also 'prescribed by law'. The applicant complained that the piece of domestic legislation on which his detention was based was not precise enough and that too much discretion was granted to the medical officers who had to determine whether he posed a risk to society. The Court acknowledged that, if deprivation of liberty is involved, it is particularly important that the principle of legal certainty be satisfied. It was therefore essential that the conditions for detention be clearly defined and that the law be foreseeable in its application. At the same time, however, the Court accepted that it is for national courts to interpret and apply domestic law. In the case at hand, the Swedish courts had carefully examined the instructions given to the applicant and had concluded that the requirements of the relevant domestic legislation were fulfilled. The ECtHR was therefore satisfied on that basis that the detention was prescribed by law.

The Court then turned to the substantive requirements of Article 5 and determined that the essential elements when assessing the 'lawfulness' of the detention of a person for sanitary purposes are (a) whether the disease 'is dangerous to public health or safety' and (b) whether detention of the person infected is 'the last resort in order to prevent the spreading of the disease, because less severe measures have been considered and found to be insufficient to safeguard the public interest'.[51] Regarding the first leg of the test, the Strasbourg judges had no problems in recognising that the HIV virus constituted a serious threat to public health and safety. Yet, with respect to the necessity of the measure, the judgment found that 'the compulsory isolation of the applicant was not a last resort in order to prevent him from spreading the HIV virus because less severe measures had not been considered and found to be insufficient to safeguard the public interest'.[52] Clearly, the judgment attempted to strike a balance between the interference in the right to personal liberty and the need to preserve the general interest of society, thereby mirroring the process adopted to assess the necessity and proportionality of generic limitation clauses.[53]

The brief analysis of these cases shows that treaty monitoring bodies have adopted, with respect to this kind of restriction, the very same approach they developed to assess the legitimacy of generic limitations, i.e. they first look at whether the restriction is prescribed by law, to then assesses if it pursues a legitimate aim (the 'life or well-being of the community' in case of Article 4 ECHR and public health in the case of Article 5 ECHR). Finally, a proportionality test is carried out, weighing the necessity of the interference against the interest of upholding a public interest or the rights of other individuals.

Extraordinary limitations on human rights in case of disaster: using the derogation clause

While calamitous events usually affect a limited portion of a State's territory, certain natural or technological disasters may have exceptionally severe consequences that call for the adoption of extraordinary measures. Some of these may entail restrictions of individual rights and freedoms to an extent which goes beyond what is allowed by limitation clauses and is not compatible with the affected State's international obligations under human rights law treaties. The drafters of human rights conventions acknowledged that the texts needed to provide states facing severe emergencies with a mechanism that would enable them 'to loosen the stranglehold of their obligations without running the risk of their membership of the community of States parties being called into question'.[54] This is why the principal human rights instruments include a provision to that effect. Article 4(1) of the International Covenant on Civil and Political Rights (ICCPR), for instance, provides that:

> In time of public emergency which threatens the life of the nation and the existence of which is officially proclaimed, the States Parties to the present Covenant may take measures derogating from their obligations under the present Covenant to the extent strictly required by the exigencies of the situation, provided that such measures are not

> inconsistent with their other obligations under international law and do not involve discrimination solely on the ground of race, colour, sex, language, religion or social origin.[55]

Paragraph 2 of this provision goes on to list rights that cannot be derogated from, while paragraph 3 sets out the procedural steps states need to take if they intend to avail themselves of the clause. The use of such 'derogation clauses' is of no little import, because it exonerates the State invoking them from international responsibility for failing to fully respect its treaty obligations, provided that certain substantial and procedural rules are complied with.[56]

However, before looking at said rules, it is worth underlining that natural or technological disasters could qualify as 'public emergencies' in the sense of Article 4 and hence fall within the sphere of applicability of derogation clauses. As is apparent from the letter of the provision, the drafters chose to refrain from providing an exhaustive list of situations in which the right to derogate could be invoked. They preferred instead to place the focus on the magnitude and effects of the emergency, irrespective of its nature or origin. Whereas in the vast majority of cases derogations have been justified with reference to situations of armed conflict or terrorist campaigns,[57] there is nothing to indicate that major disasters having the potential to severely undermine the functioning of the State could not amount to 'public emergencies' as understood in human rights treaties. This view is supported by the preparatory works of the derogation clause contained in the American Convention on Human Rights (ACHR)[58] but is also widely reflected in legal scholarship. Joseph, Schultz and Castan, for instance, maintain that 'a severe natural disaster, such as a major flood or earthquake' could qualify as a public emergency for the purposes of Article 4 ICCPR.[59] Commenting on Article 15 ECHR, Boisson de Chazournes expresses the view that '[e]nvironmental disasters can . . . give rise to the right of derogation if the conditions of Article 15 are met'.[60] However, as will be seen, the most important element that militates in favour of the application of derogation clauses to certain disaster is the practice of States which have actually invoked them when struck by earthquakes, hurricanes and other similar calamities.

The normative framework: substantial requirements

Once it has been ascertained that disasters may potentially trigger the application of derogation clauses, it needs to be determined under which exact circumstances this may happen and what substantial rules States must comply with to lawfully invoke them.

The requirement that the State faces an 'exceptional threat'

As the HRComm points out, 'not every disturbance or catastrophe qualifies as a public emergency which threatens the life of the nation'.[61] When it was called on to work out this notion in relation to Article 15 ECHR, the Strasbourg Court held that the natural and customary meaning of the words 'other public emergency threatening the life of the nation' was sufficiently clear and that the expression indicated 'an *exceptional situation of crisis or emergency* which affects the whole population and constitutes a threat to the organised life of the community of which the State is composed' (emphasis added).[62]

In the *Greek* case, the ECommHR elaborated upon the above definition, stating that a 'public emergency' must possess the following features:

1. It must be actual or imminent.
2. Its effect must involve the whole nation.

3. The continuance of the organised life of the community must be threatened.
4. The crisis or danger must be exceptional, in that the normal measures or restrictions, permitted by the Convention for the maintenance of public safety, health and order, are plainly inadequate.[63]

A quick review of these four elements is called for in order to clarify their actual import. The 'actual' or 'imminent' nature of the emergency implies that derogation is not allowed when the threat is merely 'latent' or 'perceived'.[64] The element of 'imminence' might assume particular importance with reference to natural or human-made disasters, as it could warrant suspension of certain rights before the calamity has actually hit a particular territory (e.g. if a hurricane or a radioactive cloud is approaching). In *A and Others v. UK*, the ECtHR further expanded on the notion of latent threats, specifying that '[t]he requirement of imminence cannot be interpreted so narrowly as to require a State to wait for disaster to strike before taking measures to deal with it'.[65]

The requirement that the emergency must involve 'the whole nation' has been loosened as it is accepted that the crisis situation may have a geographically limited scope while still affecting the entire population of the interested area. In *Ireland v. UK*, the respondent State had limited the applicability of the derogation measures to Northern Ireland, and neither the ECtHR nor Ireland contested its right to do so.[66] The *Paris Minimum Standards of Human Rights Norms in a State of Emergency*[67] have also endorsed this view, accepting that the emergency can affect 'the whole population or the population of the area to which the declaration applies'.[68] In other words, disaster situations affecting only part of the State's territory would still justify resorting to the derogation clause.

The third criterion demands that 'the continuance of the organised life of the community must be threatened'. According to Hartman, this implies that 'some fundamental element of statehood, such as the functioning of the judiciary or legislature or the flow of crucial supplies, must be endangered'.[69] In the same vein, the Siracusa Principles establish that the situation must be so serious as to imperil 'the physical integrity of the population, the political independence or the territorial integrity of the State or the existence or basic functioning of institutions indispensable to ensure and protect the rights recognised in the Covenant'.[70] Again, it is quite likely that major natural or technological disasters may reach – at least during their peak phase – the threshold of severity required.

The last condition requires that a crisis be truly 'exceptional', a feature that is assessed on the basis of the quality and scope of the measures required to avert the emergency. Measures that are incompatible with conventional standards must be the last resort and can only be enacted when all ordinary measures are exhausted and have not been adequate to deal with the threat. While considering the prospect of derogation from the ICCPR during a natural catastrophe or a major industrial accident, the HRComm expressed the opinion that

> the possibility of restricting certain Covenant rights under the terms of, for instance, freedom of movement . . . or freedom of assembly . . . is generally sufficient during such situations and no derogation from the provisions in question would be justified by the exigencies of the situation.[71]

Therefore, when (even severe) disasters can be dealt with by resorting to ordinary restrictions, the crisis cannot be deemed to be 'exceptional', and derogation from the treaties would be prohibited.

As recalled when discussing ordinary limitations, the Strasbourg organs have left States a 'wide margin of appreciation' in deciding (a) if a given situation qualifies as a public emergency under

Article 15 and (b) if the measures introduced to tackle it are 'strictly required by the exigencies of the situation'. In *Ireland v. UK*, the Court has spelled out the concept by stating that:

> It falls in the first place to each Contracting State, with its responsibility for 'the life of [its] nation', to determine whether that life is threatened by a 'public emergency' and, if so, how far it is necessary to go in attempting to overcome the emergency. By reason of their direct and continuous contact with the pressing needs of the moment, the national authorities are in principle in a better position than the international judge to decide both on the presence of such an emergency and on the nature and scope of derogations necessary to avert it. In this matter Article 15 para. 1 (art. 15–1) leaves those authorities a wide margin of appreciation.[72]

While the Court was swift to add that it remains responsible for ensuring the observance of the States' engagements and is 'empowered to rule on whether the States have gone beyond the "extent strictly required by the exigencies" of the crisis',[73] it nevertheless conceded that the limits of its power of review 'are particularly apparent where Article 15 . . . is concerned'.[74]

The need for an 'official proclamation'

The ICCPR and the Arab Charter require that a state of emergency must be 'officially proclaimed'.[75] This act usually takes the form of a decision adopted by the political organs of the State and its adoption is normally subordinated to a number of substantive and procedural conditions. The consequences of such a move may involve not only the suspension of certain constitutional guarantees, but also a temporary modification in the allocation of powers and functions among the different State organs. From a human rights law perspective, the act serves the purpose of informing the community about possible extraordinary restrictions on the enjoyment of individual rights and about the changes in the institutional settings prompted by the emergency. The rationale behind its inclusion in the derogation clauses appears to have been the desire to reduce *de facto* emergencies by compelling States that intend to suspend human rights to do so openly, respecting the formalities required by national law.[76] The HRComm emphasises that this requirement 'is essential for the maintenance of the principles of legality and rule of law at times when they are most needed'.[77] Both the HRComm[78] and the Siracusa Principles[79] stress that the act must be adopted by a competent body and in accordance with the relevant domestic legal regime. In all the instances of derogation motivated by natural disasters, the principle of official proclamation appears to have been fully observed, and the derogating authorities have made it a point of indicating that they were acting within the boundaries of municipal law.

Necessity and proportionality of derogation measures

Once it is established that a given event represents a 'public emergency', it must be asked whether the measures adopted to confront it are 'strictly required by the exigencies of the situation'. As with ordinary limitations, the severity of the measures resorted to must strictly depend on – and correspond to – the gravity of the threat. The HRComm has deemed the principle of strict necessity to be 'a fundamental requirement for any measures derogating from the Covenant' and one which relates 'to the duration, geographical coverage and material scope of the state of emergency and any measures of derogation resorted to because of the emergency'.[80]

Looking first at the temporal dimension, the requirement stipulates that derogatory measures can only be kept in place as long as the emergency persists. In the words of the ECommHR:

> Article 15, paragraph 3, clearly means that the measures of derogation which it provides for are only justified in the circumstances defined in paragraph 1, with the result that if they remain in force after those circumstances have disappeared they represent a breach of the Convention.[81]

As to the 'geographic' element, the principle of strict necessity demands that the applicability of any derogation measure be limited to the areas where the emergency actually unfolds,[82] although one could think of situations in which certain rights may be suspended even outside said areas where this is absolutely necessary to counter the effects of the disaster.[83]

Moving to the scope of the derogation measures enacted, States are again required to strike a balance between the rights and freedoms of individuals and the public interest that is imperilled by the emergency. In reviewing state compliance with the principle, treaty bodies have developed a number of criteria. In the first place, it must be asked whether a given measure is required at all, in light of the fact that ordinary measures are insufficient to meet the public danger.[84] A derogation measure would fail this test if a course of action permissible under the substantive provisions of the treaties would accomplish the same end. As recalled above, the HRComm considers that ordinary limitations should generally be sufficient to deal with natural disasters and major industrial accidents. Second, each measure of derogation must bear some relation to the threat and be apt to contribute to the solution of a specific problem that forms part of the emergency. In the words of the ECommHR, '[t]here must be a link between the facts of the emergency on the one hand and the measures chosen to deal with it on the other'.[85] Third, when more than one measure appears acceptable after balancing the right encroached upon with the exigencies of the situation, the least interfering measure must be chosen.[86]

While assessing the requirement of strict necessity, much emphasis has been put on the availability of sufficient safeguards against the abuse of derogation measures. The need for a proper assessment of emergency legislation and for a periodic review of emergency powers by the legislature or by the judiciary have been identified as essential factors in this respect.[87] A continuous review of derogation measures is particularly relevant in emergencies prompted by disasters, which are inherently dynamic phenomena whose gravity varies over time and which call for a continuous readjustment of the nature and scope of emergency measures.[88] Closely linked to this requirement is that effective remedies remain available to persons affected by emergency legislation.[89]

The prohibition on discriminatory measures

The derogation clauses in the ICCPR, the ACHR and the Arab Charter stipulate that emergency measures shall not entail discrimination based 'solely on the ground of race, colour, sex, language, religion or social origin'.[90] The HRComm recalls that neither Article 26 ICCPR (establishing equality before the law) nor other provisions related to non-discrimination are listed among the non-derogable provisions in Article 4. However, it is of the opinion that 'there are elements or dimensions of the right to non-discrimination that cannot be derogated from in any circumstances' and that the prohibition on discrimination 'must be complied with if any distinctions between persons are made when resorting to measures that derogate from the Covenant'.[91]

In the context of disaster response, the prohibition on discrimination would prohibit measures that foresee unreasonable distinctions among individuals or communities with respect to the prioritisation in the provision of assistance. In this sense, non-discrimination can be seen as a facet of the duty of impartiality that States and humanitarian actors owe to disaster-stricken populations.[92]

The conformity of derogation measures with the State's other obligations under international law

Even if specific derogatory measures were found to comply with the criteria set out so far, a State would be barred from resorting to them if their introduction breached other international obligations by which it is bound. These will obviously vary from State to State, depending on their level of participation in multilateral and bilateral treaties. Yet, in assessing State responsibility for failure to comply with obligations stemming from other instruments, it must be borne in mind that these could include provisions allowing for their suspension or that the other parties to the treaty may agree to temporarily exonerate the derogating State from its legal commitments.[93] Furthermore, the treaty obligations could be terminated or suspended if it becomes impossible to perform them[94] or due to a fundamental change of circumstances.[95]

The requirement of consistency has generated very little case law by treaty bodies.[96] Commentators have indicated that the expression would include obligations under the UN Charter, International Humanitarian Law, other universal or regional Human Rights treaties, European Union Treaties, ILO Conventions, Refugee Law treaties and the International Health Regulations.[97] The HRComm includes International Criminal Law as a source of possible obligations.[98] Also relevant are obligations arising under binding UN Security Council resolutions and any rule of international law that should attain the status of *jus cogens*.[99] Treaties pertaining to the field of International Disaster Response Law are obviously also relevant this respect.[100] It would be difficult for States to maintain that these instruments can be suspended during a disaster-related emergency, as they are intended to be applied in exactly those situations.

Reverting to the field of human rights law, a convincing argument can be made that a State derogating from a treaty listing only a limited number of non-derogable rights, which is also a party to another treaty containing a longer catalogue of non-derogable rights, is precluded from derogating from the supplementary rights that are included in the latter treaty.[101]

Non-derogability of certain civil and political rights

One of the cornerstones of the derogation regime is the principle of non-derogability, according to which certain rights can never be suspended, even in the presence of a public emergency. The different derogation clauses contain each a list of these rights, which – mainly due to the lapse of time between the adoption of the instruments – display certain differences.[102] Those which are common to all human rights treaties are: the right to life; the prohibition of torture and cruel, inhuman and degrading treatment and punishment; the prohibition of slavery and the prohibition of retroactive application of criminal law, most of which are considered to reflect norms of *jus cogens*.[103]

The list of non-derogable rights goes beyond the ones here listed[104] and is held to have been expanded through customary international law.[105] However, these aspects are of little consequence for our purposes as no State has in fact ever attempted to derogate from any of the rights that are regarded as non-derogable. Also, no treaty monitoring body has so far claimed the status of non-derogability for the rights and freedoms that States have asked to suspend in times of disaster.

The normative framework: procedural requirements

Article 15 ECHR requires a State invoking the right to derogate to keep the Secretary-General of the Council of Europe 'fully informed' of the measures it has taken and of the reasons for doing so.[106] This is usually done by filing a so-called 'derogation notice', which the Secretary-General then circulates to other member States. The purpose of this procedural safeguard is twofold: on the one hand it allows the monitoring bodies to discharge their surveillance function over the nature and scope of the derogation measures enacted; on the other hand it enables other State parties to monitor compliance with the provisions of the treaties and to exercise their own rights accordingly.[107] As to the timing, a State exercising its right of derogation under the ICCPR must 'immediately inform' the other State parties of the emergency measures undertaken. The ECHR has no requirement of 'immediacy', yet Article 15 EHCR has been interpreted as requiring notification 'without delay' after the entry into force of the measures concerned.[108]

While there are no formal requirements for the notice, the HRComm demands that States provide 'full information about the measures taken and a clear explanation of the reasons for them, with full documentation attached regarding their law'.[109] Further notifications are required when the derogation regime is subject to modifications and when the State intends to withdraw the derogation. More generally, the scope and depth of the information regarding derogation measures must be such as to enable the other State parties and the monitoring bodies 'to appreciate the nature and extent of the derogation from the provisions of the Convention which those measures involve'.[110]

State practice regarding derogations in times of disasters

As mentioned above, practice under the ICCPR and ECHR – although rather scant – suggests the permissibility of derogations in case of major calamitous events. Article 4 ICCPR has been invoked by at least five States in cases of natural disasters. On 23 November 1998, Guatemala notified the UN Secretary-General that it intended to suspend several human rights guarantees in order to tackle the 'public disaster' generated by the passage of hurricane Mitch. The notice of derogation was accompanied by the text of the emergency decree enacted by the President describing the measures implemented. Pursuant to the decree the Government could (a) 'centralize all State and privately owned public services'; (b) 'establish sanitary cordons, change or maintain people's place of residence, limit vehicular traffic and prevent people from entering affected areas'; (c) 'demand the necessary assistance and cooperation from members of the public to help control the affected areas'; (d) 'organize the immediate evacuation of the inhabitants of affected areas'; and (e) 'order the civil and military authorities to take all necessary steps to protect people and property'.[111]

The same State again resorted to the derogation clause when confronted with the effects of hurricane Stan (October 2005). The state of emergency was declared for a period of 30 days, and it restricted 'the right of liberty of movement and the right of freedom of action, except for the right of persons not to be harassed for their opinions or for acts which do not violate the law'.[112] In May 2009, Guatemala again derogated to deal with the 'swine flu' pandemic. On that occasion, a 'public health emergency' was declared throughout the national territory for a period of 30 days, with a view to 'preventing and mitigating the effects of the influenza A (H1N1) epidemic'. The government suspended Article 12 (right to liberty of movement), Article 19 (right to freedom of expression) and Article 21 (right of peaceful assembly) of the Covenant.[113] A few months later (May–June 2010), Guatemala again resorted to Article 4 ICCPR when it had to cope with the eruption of the Pacaya volcano and the devastations caused by tropical storm Agatha. With respect to the volcano eruption, a 'disaster emergency' was declared for 30 days in some of the country's Departments, to safeguard the 'safety and freedom from disturbance of persons and their property . . . and to prevent or reduce the impacts of the eruption'. On 13 November 2012, Guatemala again submitted a notice of derogation in response to a severe earthquake that struck the country one week earlier, asking to suspend the right to freedom of movement.[114]

Jamaica also derogated from Articles 12, 19 and 21 of the Covenant in response to the devastations caused by hurricane Ivan in 2004[115] and hurricane Dean in 2007.[116] Chile filed a derogation notice in March 2010 stating its intention to suspend freedom of movement and freedom of assembly in order to deal with the aftermath of the powerful earthquake that struck some of the country's regions. The measures were publicly announced through the adoption of a decree declaring a '30-day constitutional state of disaster emergency'.[117] In March 2006 it was Georgia's turn to avail itself of Article 4 ICCPR when authorities felt they had to suspend – in one of the country's districts – constitutional guarantees related to freedom of movement and to the right to property in order to prevent further spread of the Avian Flu virus.[118] Lastly, in June 2016, Ecuador decided to suspend Articles 12 and 17 ICCPR in the provinces affected by a violent earthquake, which caused almost 700 deaths and injured more than 16,000 people.[119] According to the Executive Order attached to the notice, suspensions of the rights at stake were necessary to prevent individuals affected by the disaster from returning to their homes, as these were still unstable and potentially dangerous.

The lawfulness of the above derogations has not been tested by the HRComm under the individual communications procedure. However, to this author's knowledge, none of the UN human rights treaty monitoring bodies has so far expressed concern or disapproval at the emergency measures adopted,[120] nor have these been criticised by other State parties to the Covenant.

Conclusions

While human rights treaty monitoring bodies have rarely dealt with cases of limitations or derogations prompted by disasters, States often resort to special powers when faced with such predicaments. The reasons for the scarce involvement of expert bodies are difficult to explain. Certainly, at least in the case of derogations, it helped that States kept the suspension of rights geographically and temporarily limited, so that the proportionality of the exceptional measures introduced could not be called into question. More generally, it is reasonable to assume that individuals that are subject to restrictive measures due to catastrophic events might consider emergency measures with indulgence, since public authorities are confronted with extremely dangerous and volatile situations, which have the potential to severely jeopardise the safety of the population.

One thing limitations and derogations have in common is the balancing exercise between the individual rights curtailed and the general interest that needs to be upheld. This requires the application of the same legal principles (proportionality, non-discrimination, etc.), with the notable difference that, in the case of derogations, States are generally granted a greater leeway in deciding which measures to implement (even more so under the ECHR jurisprudence, which accords them a 'wide margin of appreciation').

One wonders, however, if derogating from human rights conventions in disaster situations is really a necessary step. First of all, international treaties establish minimum standards of protection, and States often have the possibility to depart from their domestic standards without reaching the 'floor' established by international instruments. In other terms, 'abnormal' measures can be used without violating the treaties (and, therefore, without the need to derogate).[121]

Moreover, quite often the rights derogated from in disaster settings have built-in limitation clauses, which are usually sufficient to accommodate restrictive measures.[122] For instance, the need to compel members of the public to assist in dealing with the consequences of hurricane Mitch – which, according to the Guatemalan authorities, made it necessary to derogate from the ICCPR – could probably have been accommodated by invoking Article 8(3)(c)(iii) of the treaty, which allows the imposition of compulsory labour in emergency situations.[123]

However, resort to derogations to counter the effects of calamities seems on the rise. One possible explanation is that some States use the derogation clause as a sort of 'safety net', as they are not completely sure whether the measures they introduce are compatible with normal convention standards. This means that derogation notices are often presented on precautionary grounds, to avoid international responsibility should emergency measures be found to be in conflict with convention obligations. In fact, States often indicate that there 'may be derogation from the rights guaranteed' by the treaties,[124] suggesting that it is not necessarily their intention to suspend them.

Some degree of clarity on these issues could emerge from the practice of treaty monitoring bodies. While, as a scholar, one would usually appreciate the opportunity to examine such practice, in this particular field, we are content with what little has been produced so far, as this means that no disaster has occurred or (more likely) that national authorities have not deemed it necessary to impose extraordinary constraints on individual rights.

Selected bibliography

W. Kälin, 'The Human Rights Dimension of Natural or Human Made Disasters' 55 *German Yearbook of International Law* (2012) 119.

J. Oraà, *Human Rights in States of Emergency in International Law* (Oxford University Press, 1992).

'Siracusa Principles on the Limitation and Derogation Provisions in the International Covenant on Civil and Political Rights' 7 *Human Rights Quarterly* (1985) 3.

A.L. Svensson-McCarthy, *The International Law of Human Rights and States of Exception* (Martinus Nijhoff Publishers, 1998).

Notes

* The author is grateful to Annalisa Creta, Andrea de Guttry and Francesca Spagnuolo for their comments on earlier drafts of this chapter. Any remaining errors or omissions are, of course, entirely the author's responsibility.

1 See IASC, 'Operational Guidelines on the Protection of Persons in Situations of Natural Disasters' (2011) 3, available at www.ohchr.org/Documents/Issues/IDPersons/OperationalGuidelines_IDP.pdf, accessed on 3 March 2017. The IASC is the main mechanism for inter-agency coordination of humanitarian assistance, and involves the principal UN and non-UN humanitarian actors.

2 See W. Kälin, 'The Human Rights Dimension of Natural or Human Made Disasters' 55 *German Yearbook of International Law* (2012) 119–147. A notable exception is the Convention on the Rights of Persons with Disabilities (adopted 13 December 2006, entered into force 3 May 2008) 2515 UNTS 3. Its art 11 imposes on State parties the obligation to take 'all necessary measures to ensure the protection and safety of persons with disabilities in situations of risk, including . . . the occurrence of natural disasters'.

3 By way of example, see D. Cubie and M. Hesselman, 'Accountability for the Human Rights Implications of Natural Disasters: A Proposal for Systemic International Oversight' 33 *Netherlands Quarterly of Human Rights* (2015) 9–41; K. Cedervall Lauta, 'Human Rights and Natural Disasters' in S.C. Breau and K.L.H. Samuel (eds), *Research Handbook on Disasters and International Law* (Edward Elgar Publishing, 2016) 91–110.

4 See, among many, the decisions of the ECtHR in *Budayeva and Others v. Russia*, App. Nos. 15339/02, 21166/02, 20058/02, 11673/02 and 15343/02 (ECtHR, Judgment of 20 March 2008), and *Öneryildiz v. Turkey*, App. No. 48939/99 (ECtHR, Judgment of 30 November 2004). See also M. Hesselman, 'Regional Human Rights Regimes and Humanitarian Obligations of States in the Event of Disaster' in A. Zwitter, C.K. Lamont, H.-J. Heintze and J. Herman (eds), *Humanitarian Action: Global, Regional and Domestic Legal Responses* (Cambridge University Press, 2014) 202–227.

5 See Creta's chapter in this book.

6 UNGA, Official Records, Sixty-First Session, Supplement No. 10, UN Doc. A/61/10 (2006) para 257.

7 For the text final text of the ILC Draft Articles, see ILC, Report of the International Law Commission, Sixty-Eight Session, UN Doc. A/71/10 (2016) (2 May–10 June and 4 July–12 August 2016) ch IV, 13–17.

8 ILC, Report of the International Law Commission, Sixtieth Session, UN Doc. A/63/10 (2008) (5 May–6 June and 7 July–8 August 2008) ch IX, para 223.
9 ILC Report, UN Doc. A/71/10 (n. 7) 32.
10 The Siracusa Principles have been adopted by a group of eminent legal experts in 1984 and are reproduced in 7 *Human Rights Quarterly* (1985) 3.
11 See Nohle and Giacca's chapter in this volume. On the right to derogate from treaties protecting economic, social and cultural rights in times of disaster, see E. Sommario, 'Derogation from Human Rights Treaties in Situations of Natural or Man-Made Disaster' in A. de Guttry, M. Gestri and G. Venturini (eds), *International Disaster Response Law* (Springer, 2012) 323–352.
12 See B. Rainey, E. Wicks and C. Ovey, *Jacobs, White and Ovey: The European Convention on Human Rights* (6th edn, Oxford University Press, 2014) 307.
13 ICCPR (adopted 16 December 1966, entered into force 23 March 1976) 999 UNTS 171.
14 The very same wording is used in art 4(3)(c) ECHR, and in art 6(3)(c) ACHR (adopted 22 November 1969, entered into force 18 July 1978) 1144 UNTS 123.
15 (European) Convention for the Protection of Human Rights and Fundamental Freedoms (as Amended) (adopted 4 November 1950, entered into force 3 September 1953) 213 UNTS 222.
16 The notion of disaster considered is the one contained in the definition developed by the ILC in its work on the protection of persons in the event of disasters. According to draft art 3(a), the term indicates 'a calamitous event or series of events resulting in widespread loss of life, great human suffering and distress, mass displacement, or large-scale material or environmental damage, thereby seriously disrupting the functioning of society'; see ILC Report, UN Doc. A/71/10 (n. 7) 14. See also Bartolini's chapter in this volume.
17 M. Novak, *UN Covenant on Civil and Political Rights: CCPR Commentary* (2nd edn, N.P. Engel Publisher, 2005) 224.
18 *Sunday Times v. UK*, App. No. 6538/64 (ECtHR, Judgment of 26 April 1979) para 49.
19 Ibid. The same principles have been endorsed by the HRComm as valid for limitations imposed under the ICCPR, see HRComm, General Comment No. 34, Article 19: Freedoms of opinion and expression, UN Doc. CCPR/C/GC/34 (2011) para 25.
20 *Maestri v. Italy*, App. No. 39748/98 (ECtHR, Judgment of 17 February 2004) para 30.
21 HRComm, General Comment No. 27: Freedom of movement (Art.12), UN Doc. CCPR/C/21/Rev.1/Add.9 (1999) para 12.
22 Siracusa Principles (n. 10) N. 16.
23 The French term *ordre public* was included in the English text, as the term 'public order' was perceived to have a narrower meaning. *Ordre public* does not merely refer to absence of disorder and the prevention of crime, but includes 'the sum of rules which ensure the functioning of society or the set of fundamental principles on which society is founded', Siracusa Principles (n. 10) N. 22.
24 This requirement in also presupposed by art 18 ECHR, according to which 'restrictions permitted under this Convention to the said rights and freedoms shall not be applied for any purpose other than those for which they have been prescribed'.
25 For instance, in the wake of the March 2011 earthquake which affected the Fukushima nuclear plant, Japanese authorities designated no-access areas on the basis of their proximity to the plant, see HRC, Report of the Special Rapporteur on the Right of Everyone to the Enjoyment of the Highest Attainable Standard of Physical and Mental Health, Anand Grover, UN Doc. A/HRC/23/41/Add.3 (2013) para 45.
26 *Solomakhin v. Ukraine*, App. No. 24429/03 (ECtHR, Judgment of 15 March 2012).
27 IACommHR, *Juan Milla Bermúdez v. Honduras*, Case 11.206, Report N. 46/96 (on admissibility) 17 October 1996, para 8, describing how local authorities expropriated several portions of private land bordering a river to build protective shelters which would minimise the impact of hurricanes affecting the area.
28 HRComm, General Comment No. 31: The Nature of the General Legal Obligation Imposed on States Parties to the Covenant, UN Doc. CCPR/C/21/Rev.1/Add.13 (2004) para 6.
29 *Sunday Times v. UK* (n. 18) para 59.
30 Siracusa Principles (n. 10) N. 3.
31 HRComm, General Comment No. 31 (n. 28) para 6.
32 See Siracusa Principles (n. 10) N. 20; D. Harris, M. O'Boyle, E. Bates and C. Buckley, *Harris, O'Boyle, and Warbrick: Law of the European Convention on Human Rights* (3rd edn, Oxford University Press, 2014) 512–513.
33 *Handyside v. UK*, App. No. 5493/72 (ECtHR, Judgment of 7 December 1976) para 48.

34 See A. Legg, *The Margin of Appreciation in International Human Rights Law* (Oxford University Press, 2012). According to this author, even the IACtHR (at 32) and the HRComm (at 81) while not explicitly endorsing this doctrine – have granted States a certain margin of appreciation when deciding cases before them. However, in one of its more recent General Comments, the HRComm has explicitly dismissed the doctrine. See HRComm, General Comment No. 34 (n. 19) para 36.

35 See Rainey et al. (n. 12) 325–333.

36 *Silver v. UK*, App. Nos. 5947/72, 6205/73, 7052/75, 7061/75, 7107/75, 7113/75 and 7136/75 (ECtHR, Judgment of 25 March 1983) para 97.

37 *Connors v. UK*, App. No 66746/01 (ECtHR, Judgment of 27 May 2004) para 82.

38 *I v. Italy*, App. No. 11381/85 (ECommHR, Decision of 3 March 1986) published in D.R. 46, 210.

39 While the provision is drafted rather differently from other articles allowing for limitations, it has been applied in pretty much the same way, in that interference with the right are only possible if provided by law, justified for pursuing a collective interest and proportionate to said interest. See Rainey et al. (n. 12) 492–493.

40 *I v. Italy* (n. 38) 213.

41 A somewhat similar case was decided by the ECtHR in 2007, when it determined that the destruction of a private house that was damaged by an earthquake and threatened public safety constituted a disproportionate interference with the applicant's right to property as no sort of compensation was foreseen, see *Amato v. Turkey*, App. No. 58771/00 (ECtHR, Judgment of 3 May 2007) para 26.

42 See *Solomakhin v. Ukraine* (n. 26).

43 Ibid para 36.

44 Ibid para 38.

45 On the factors influencing the use of the margin of appreciation doctrine by the ECtHR, see Harris et al. (n. 32) 510–521.

46 As seen above, the exact same language is used in art 8(3)(c)(iii) ICCPR, while art 6(3)(c) ACHR speaks of 'service exacted in time of danger or calamity that threatens the existence or the well-being of the community'.

47 Convention Concerning Forced or Compulsory Labour (ILO Convention No 29) (adopted 28 June 1930, entered into force 1 May 1932) 39 UNTS 55.

48 *S v. Federal Republic of Germany*, App. No. 9686/82 (ECommHR, Decision of 4 October 1984).

49 On a similar note, in *Iversen v. Norway*, two members of the ECommHR held that the possibility that a dentist who had recently completed his studies could be obliged to work for 2 years in the public service and in an area in which there was severe shortage of dentists, fell under the exception provided by art 4(3)(c). See *Iversen v. Norway*, App. No. 1468/62 (ECommHR, Decision of 17 December 1963).

50 *Enhorn v. Sweden*, App. No. 56529/00 (ECtHR, Judgment of 25 January 2005). The case is discussed in detail in R. Martin, 'The Exercise of Public Health Powers in Cases of Infectious Disease: Human Rights Implications' 14 *Medical Law Review* (2006) 132–143.

51 *Enhorn v. Sweden* (n. 50) para 44.

52 Ibid para 55.

53 The ECtHR's conclusions in the *Enhorn* case do not necessarily rule out the legality of temporarily detaining individuals who carry highly dangerous infective diseases. For instance, under the World Health Organization's International Health Regulations, a State Party that has evidence of an 'imminent public health risk' may compel a traveller for whom there is reason to believe that he may be infected to undergo health measures to prevent and control the spread of the disease, 'including isolation, quarantine or public health observation'. See International Health Regulations (IHR), adopted by the World Health Assembly through Resolution WHA 58.3 (23 May 2005, entered into force 15 June 2007) art 31(2)(c), available at www.who.int/ihr/publications/9789241580496/en/, accessed on 3 March 2017. On the relationship between international health emergencies and human rights, see A. Zidar, 'WHO International Health Regulations and Human Rights: From Allusion to Inclusion' 19 *The International Journal of Human Rights* (2015) 505–526.

54 N. Questiaux, *Study of the Implications for Human Rights of Recent Developments Concerning Situations Known as States of Siege or Emergency*, UN Doc. E/CN.4/Sub.2/1982/15 (1982) 11, para 37.

55 Virtually identical provisions can be found in other treaties protecting civil and political rights, such as: ECHR art 15, ACHR art 27, or in the 2004 Arab Charter on Human Rights (adopted 22 May 2004, entered into force 15 May 2008) reprinted in 12 *International Human Rights Reports* (2005) 893, art 4.

56 For a general introduction to the derogation clauses and their operation see R. Ergec, *Les Droits de l'homme à l'épreuve des circonstances exceptionnelles – Etude sur l'article 15 de la Convention européenne des*

droits de l'homme (Editions Bruylant, 1987); J. Oraà, *Human Rights in States of Emergency in International Law* (Oxford University Press, 1992); A.L. Svensson-McCarthy, *The International Law of Human Rights and States of Exception* (Martinus Nijhoff Publishers, 1998); G. Cataldi, 'Art. 15 – Deroga in caso di urgenza' in S. Bartole, P. De Sena and V. Zagrebelsky (eds), *Commentario breve alla Convenzione europea dei diritti dell'uomo* (CEDAM, 2012) 555–564.

57 See for instance the text of the derogation notices filed under the ICCPR, reported in Novak (n. 17) 984–1041.

58 See Conferencia Especializada Interamericana Sobre Derechos Humanos, *San Josè, Costa Rica, 7–22 de noviembre de 1969, Actas y Documentos*, Doc OEA/Ser.K/XVI/1.2, 264–265 (1969), and Sommario (n. 16) 328.

59 S. Joseph, J. Schultz and M. Castan, *The International Covenant on Civil and Political Rights: Cases, Materials and Commentary* (2nd edn, Oxford University Press, 2005) 825.

60 L. Boisson De Chazournes, 'Non-Derogable Rights and the Need to Protect the Environment' in D. Premont (ed), *Droits Intangibles Etetatsd' Exception: Non-Derogable Rights and States of Emergency* (Editions Bruylant, 1996) 465. The same view is held by, among many others, S.R. Chowdhury, *Rule of Law in a State of Emergency: The Paris Minimum Standards of Human Rights Norms in a State of Emergency* (St. Martin's Press, 1989) 16–17; Svensson-McCarthy (n. 56) 215–6; Novak (n. 17) 91.

61 HRComm, General Comment No. 29. States of Emergency (Article 4), UN Doc. CCPR/C/21/Rev.1/Add.11 (31 August 2001) para 3.

62 *Lawless v. Ireland*, App. No. 332/57 (ECtHR, Judgment of 1 July 1961) para 28.

63 *Denmark, Norway, Sweden and the Netherlands v. Greece*, App. Nos. 3321/67, 3322/67, 3323/67 and 3344/67 (ECommHR, Report of 5 November 1969) in 12 *YBECHR* 70, para 113.

64 See J. Hartman, 'Derogation from Human Rights Treaties in Public Emergencies' 22 *Harvard International Law Journal* (1981) 16; Oraà (n. 56) 27–28; and Siracusa Principles (n. 10) N. 39.

65 *A and Others v. UK*, App. No. 3455/05 (ECtHR, Judgment of 19 February 2009) para 177.

66 *Ireland v. UK*, App. No. 5310/71 (ECtHR, Judgment of 18 January 1978) para 205. The Court adopted a similar stance in *Aksoy v. Turkey*, App. No. 21987/93 (ECtHR, Judgment of 18 December 1996) para 70. See also R. Higgins, 'Derogations under Human Rights Treaties' 48 *British Yearbook of International Law* (1976–1977) 289–290, ft 5, listing a considerable number of derogations made by the UK under art 15 with respect to some overseas colonies to which it had extended the application of the Convention in accordance with art 63 of the treaty. Quite clearly, the disorders in those distant territories could hardly be considered to be a threat to the whole population of the UK.

67 The *Paris Minimum Standards* were adopted by the International Law Association at its 61st Conference held in Paris in 1984. The text is reproduced in R. Lillich, 'The Paris Minimum Standards of Human Rights Norms in a State of Emergency' 79 *American Journal of International Law* (1985) 1072–1081.

68 Ibid 1073.

69 Hartman (n. 64) 16.

70 Siracusa Principles (n. 10) N. 39.

71 HRComm, General Comment No. 29 (n. 61) para 5.

72 *Ireland v. UK* (n. 66) para 207.

73 Ibid.

74 Ibid. Interestingly, the drafters of the Siracusa Principles did not seem ready to accord States a margin of appreciation, at least with respect to the necessity and proportionality of the derogation measures. See Siracusa Principles (n. 10) N. 57.

75 While this requirement is not explicitly foreseen by the ECHR, the ECommHR has found that art 15

> requires some formal and public act of derogation, such as declaration of martial law or state of emergency, and that, where no such act has been proclaimed by the High Contracting Party concerned, although it was not in the circumstances prevented from doing so, Art. 15 cannot apply,

See *Cyprus v. Turkey*, App. Nos. 6780/74 and 6950/75 (ECommHR, Report of 10 July 1976) para 527.

76 See Oraà (n. 56) 35.

77 HRComm, General Comment No. 29 (n. 61) para 2.

78 Ibid.

79 Siracusa Principles (n. 10) N. 43.

80 HRComm, General Comment No. 29 (n. 61) para 4.

81 *De Becker v. Belgium*, App. No. 214/56 (ECommHR, Report of 8 January 1960) para 271. The principle was reaffirmed by the IACommHR in its Report on the situation of human rights of a segment of the Nicaraguan population of Miskito origin, OAS/Ser.L./V.II.62, Doc. 10 rev. 3 (29 November 1983) 117–118.

82 Novak (n. 17) 98.
83 Derogation from particular aspects of the right to property, for instance, could under given circumstances be warranted even in areas of the country not directly affected by a calamity, in order to seize private goods and distribute them to the disaster-stricken population.
84 *Lawless v. Ireland* (n. 62) para 36. As observed above, this element is also present within the test adopted to assess the exceptional nature of a public emergency.
85 *Ireland v. UK*, App. No. 5310/71 (ECommHR, Report of 25 January 1976) 97.
86 See, e.g., the Commission's stance in *Lawless v. Ireland*, App. No. 332/57 (ECommHR, Report of 19 December 1959) 123 (Opinion of Mr Waldock).
87 *Ireland v. UK* (n. 66) para 220.
88 Oraà (n. 56) 142.
89 Siracusa Principles (n. 10) Nn. 55–56.
90 The principle of non-discrimination is not mentioned in art 15 ECHR. Yet, as with the principle of official proclamation, it could be argued that, for State parties to the Convention that are also parties to the ICCPR, the prohibition on taking derogatory measures that may discriminate on one of the grounds listed in art 4(1) ICCPR represents one of the 'other obligations under international law' that must be respected when derogating from the ECHR.
91 HRComm, General Comment No. 29 (n. 61) para 8.
92 See H. Spieker, 'The Legal Framework of Humanitarian Action' in P. Gibbons and H.-J. Heintze (eds), *The Humanitarian Challenge* (Springer, 2015) 144–145. But see also Casolari's chapter in this volume.
93 Vienna Convention on the Law of Treaties (adopted 22 May 1969, entered into force 27 January 1980) 1155 UNTS 331, art 57.
94 Ibid art 61.
95 Ibid art 62.
96 But see *Brannigan and McBride v. UK*, App. Nos. 14553/89 and 14554/89 (ECtHR, Judgment of 26 May 1993); and *Marshall v. UK*, App. No. 41571/98 (ECtHR, Decision on Admissibility of 10 July 2001).
97 See Sommario (n. 16) 338–339.
98 HRComm, General Comment No. 29 (n. 61) para 13.
99 Ibid para 11.
100 See A. de Guttry, 'Surveying the Law' in de Guttry, Gestri and Venturini (eds) (n. 11) 3–44.
101 Oraà (n. 56) 205; Harris et al. (n. 32) 844.
102 The longer lists in the ICCPR, the ACHR and the Arab Charter are also explained by the different rationale behind the inclusion of certain rights, which were added not because they were perceived as being absolutely central to the protection of individuals in emergency situations, but rather because their suspension could never be justified in such contexts; see HRComm, General Comment No. 29 (n. 61) para 11; and Hartman (n. 64) 15–16.
103 Questiaux (n. 54) 19.
104 For a detailed description of the catalogues of rights included in the various treaties, see Sommario (n. 16) 342–343.
105 HRComm, General Comment No. 29 (n. 61) paras 13, 15–16.
106 See W. Schabas, *The European Convention on Human Rights: a Commentary* (Oxford University Press, 2015) 602–603. The ICCPR, the ACHR and the Arab Charter include the same type of obligation.
107 HRComm, General Comment No. 29 (n. 61) para 17.
108 *Lawless v. Ireland* (n. 62) para 47.
109 HRComm, General Comment No. 29 (n. 61) para 17.
110 *Lawless v. Ireland* (n. 86) 73.
111 See ICCPR, 'Derogation under Article 4(3): Guatemala, UN Doc. C.N.866.1998.TREATIES-9 (Depositary Notification)' (24 May 1999), available at https://treaties.un.org/doc/Publication/CN/1998/CN.866.1998-Eng.pdf, accessed on 30 March 2017.
112 UN, *Multilateral Treaties Deposited with the Secretary General*, vol. 1 (United Nations, 2009) 242.
113 See ICCPR, 'Notification under Article 4(3) of the Covenant: Guatemala, UN Doc. C.N.347.2009.TREATIES-8 (Depositary Notification)' (20 May 2009), available at http://treaties.un.org/ doc/Publication/CN/2009/CN.347.2009-Eng.pdf, accessed on 30 March 2017.
114 See ICCPR, 'Notification under Article 4(3): Guatemala, UN Doc. C.N.754.2012.TREATIES-IV.4 (Depositary Notification)' (23 November 2012), available at https://treaties.un.org/ doc/Publication/CN/2012/CN.754.2012-Eng.pdf, accessed on 30 March 2017. Guatemala has also on other occasions invoked the derogation clause due to emergencies caused by natural hazards, including a case of drought

in 2001. Peru, on the other hand, resorted to art 4 ICCPR to respond to the effects of multiple weather-related phenomena (2004) and of a violent earthquake (2009). See A. Zwitter, L. Fister and S. Groeneweg, *State of Emergency Mapping Project: Database Phase 2* (2016), available at www.emergencymapping.org, accessed on 30 March 2017.

115 ICCPR, Notification under Article 4(3) of the Covenant: Georgia (7 March 2006) 2363 UNTS 465. In this case, Jamaica also derogated from art 22 (right to freedom of association and to form and join trade unions). The derogation was withdrawn on 27 October 2004, and the public emergency lasted from 10 September to 8 October 2004.

116 ICCPR, Notification under Article 4(3) of the Covenant: Jamaica (24 August 2007) 2466 UNTS 11–20. The derogation measures entered into force on 19 August 2007 and were withdrawn on 24 August 2007. A notification announcing the end of the public emergency was made to the UNSG on 27 August 2007.

117 See ICCPR, Notification under Article 4(3): Chile (23 March 2010) 2659 UNTS 39.

118 See ICCPR, Notification under Article 4(3) of the Covenant: Georgia (7 March 2006) 2363 UNTS 465. Note that, in relation to the same events, Georgia also invoked art 15 ECHR; see Georgia: ECHR, Derogation to the Convention on the Protection of Human Rights and Fundamental Freedoms, Notification – JJ6239C Tr./005–166 (13 March 2006). The derogation was withdrawn about 3 weeks later; see ECHR, Georgia: Withdrawal of Derogation to the Convention on the Protection of Human Rights and Fundamental Freedoms, Notification – JJ6268C Tr./005–168 (7 April 2006). Both notifications are available at https://wcd.coe.int. Neither the ECtHR nor other State parties to the Convention have voiced opposition to Georgia's conduct.

119 See ICCPR, Notification under Article 4(3): Ecuador (6 June 2016) A-14668-Ecuador-080000028049 8bb8.pdf UNTS 1. The measure was then renewed in January 2017, when a 60-day state of emergency was declared; see ICCPR, Notification under Article 4(3): Ecuador (originally received 20 January 2017, further information provided 15 March 2017) A-14668-Ecuador-080000028049d4f5.pdf UNTS 1.

120 In the case of Guatemala, for instance, the concluding observations of the HRComm to the State's periodic report did not even mention the emergency measures enacted to tackle the emergencies in 2009 and 2010. See HRComm, Concluding Observation: Guatemala, UN Doc. CCPR/C/GTM/CO/3 (19 April 2012).

121 C. Warbrick, 'The European Response to Terrorism in an Age of Human Rights' 15 *European Journal of International Law* (2004) 1003.

122 Harris et al. (n. 32) 826.

123 See *supra*, at 104.

124 This is, for instance, the wording of the 2007 Jamaican derogation to the ICCPR, triggered by the violence of hurricane Dean (n. 116).

8

STATES' FAILURE TO TAKE PREVENTIVE ACTION AND TO REDUCE EXPOSURE TO DISASTERS AS A HUMAN RIGHTS ISSUE

Mirko Sossai

Introduction

On 9 October 1963, 260 million cubic metres of rock broke off from the top of Mount Toc on the border between the two regions of Veneto and Friuli Venezia Giulia, in north-east Italy. It fell into the reservoir of the Vajont Dam, producing an enormous wave of at least 50 million cubic metres of water. Although the dam did not suffer any serious damage, flooding destroyed the town of Longarone and other satellite villages in the Piave valley. Nearly 2,000 people died. What at first appeared to be no more than a totally unexpected natural disaster, in reality was the result of a combination of decision-making errors, failures to assess the degree of risk, and lack of effective early warning. The subsequent domestic trial attracted much public attention regarding the predictability of the landslide as well as the specific responsibilities for the tragedy.[1]

In estimating the impact of disasters in modern societies, the application of human rights standards has fostered the paradigm shift from the evaluation of impact of the hazard as such towards the assessment of States' negligence of risks. If the essence of disasters is then lack of preparation and social vulnerability in the first place,[2] preventative action becomes a key element of disaster management. In this regard, the development of the doctrine of positive obligations in the field of human rights law has contributed to clarifying that States have to take all reasonable measures to prevent a foreseeable breach of the rights of those within their jurisdiction.

It is significant that the 2015 Sendai Framework[3] establishes a fundamental link between disaster risk reduction (DRR) and the protection of human rights: the principles contained therein require that, in taking all the necessary measures to prevent and reduce disaster risk, States and all other stakeholders promote and protect all human rights.[4] A focus on international human rights law offers an adequate legal and analytical framework to better understand the trajectory in disaster management from emergency response to DRR. This chapter is aimed at identifying the implications of a human rights-based approach within the context of prevention and DRR, by taking into account the relevant case law, particularly that of the European Court of Human Rights (ECtHR), as well as the solutions found in the relevant provisions of the International Law Commission Draft Articles on the protection of persons in the event of disasters (ILC Draft Articles).

Although one might even agree that a rule imposing States to engage in specific DRR strategies has not yet emerged under general international law,[5] it is still important to assess the role of existing human rights obligations in clarifying the steps States should take in order to prevent and to reduce the exposure to disasters. The concept of due diligence becomes relevant in this regard, since 'an impossible or disproportionate burden must not be imposed'[6] on States' authorities: given that the elements of knowledge of the risk (the State 'knew or ought to have known') and capacity (the State employed all means that were 'reasonably available' and 'within its power') are essential in the assessment of compliance, it is possible to identify standards of conduct expected of States in a more comprehensive way. Still, in determining the appropriate measures to be taken in the pre-disaster phase, what emerges is that States are under an obligation not only to protect the life and property of those under an imminent risk of disasters through timely warnings and evacuations, but also to reduce the risk of disasters, through a variety of measures and policies, including what the Sendai Framework calls 'preparedness'.

Disaster risk reduction as a human rights issue

The elaboration of risk reduction strategies is based on the assumption that disasters could have not only a direct impact on human rights – such as the threat that extreme weather events may pose to the right to life – but also indirect and more progressive effects, particularly on the enjoyment of economic and social rights, like housing, health, land rights and access to food.[7]

The Sendai Framework still follows the fundamental relationship under international human rights law between the human beings affected by disasters as right-holders and the State as the main duty-bearer,[8] by stating that 'each State has the primary responsibility to prevent and reduce disaster risk', although it envisages the involvement of a variety of stakeholders.[9] The reduction of disaster risks is described as 'a common concern for all States', a concept which points not only to the global character of the challenges posed by disasters, requiring collective action, but also to the collective benefits for all States of such an approach.[10] In this respect, the Sendai Framework consolidates a community interest approach in dealing with the prevention of disasters, which combines the international concern with human rights and the protection of the environment.[11] It is not by chance that the United Nations Office for Disaster Risk Reduction (UNISDR) has emphasised the interlinkages between DRR priorities for action and the Sustainable Development Goals.[12]

The utility of adopting a human rights-based approach[13] in relation to DRR has been discussed on the basis of the following statement contained in the Guiding principles of the Sendai Framework: '[m]anaging the risk of disasters is aimed at protecting persons and their property, health, livelihoods and productive assets, as well as cultural and environmental assets, while promoting and protecting all human rights, including the right to development'.[14] In other words, the added value of a human rights perspective lies in 'a more people-centred approach', which recognises that the critical factors to address are the increasing exposure of persons and assets to hazards and the vulnerability of communities in all countries.[15] Therefore, international human rights law should not only be seen as a guiding parameter during the implementation of DRR measures but also as a source of legal obligation to take action in this field.

The two concepts of exposure and vulnerability are interrelated, although the former focuses on a spatial element whereas the latter refers to the specific conditions of certain individuals and groups. Indeed, the notion of vulnerability, which is applied in the field of DRR, focuses on 'the conditions determined by physical, social, economic and environmental factors or processes which increase the susceptibility of an individual, a community, assets or systems to the impacts of hazards'.[16] Suffice here to recall that Article 11 of the Convention on the Rights of Persons with

Disabilities represents one of the first provisions containing explicit protection obligations *vis-à-vis* vulnerable people in disaster situations.[17] In recent years, the issue of the interaction between vulnerability – as a social and ethical notion in the first place – and human rights has attracted much attention in the literature.[18] Even if vulnerability remains a rather kaleidoscopic concept, it has been argued that its appearance in human rights case law has represented a crucial step towards the recognition of equality in a substantive way, in terms of 'participation, transformation, redistribution, and recognition'.[19]

One might wonder to what extent such multi-dimensional characterisation of substantive equality, based on the general principle of non-discrimination, might find application in the realm of DRR. Previous analyses have suggested that effective implementation of human rights law has had an impact on the prevention and reduction of disaster in three critical areas: by developing States' capacity, by promoting the participation of individuals and communities affected and by enhancing greater accountability in case of negligence.[20]

Although human rights law cannot substitute the detailed development of effective regulation, still obligations incumbent on States can foster capacity-building initiatives, by setting out *minimum standards*. A review of the practice concerning the application of human rights to environmental issues *latu sensu* has identified three sets of duties: procedural obligations (which include risk assessment, information and early warning, as well as public participation measures); substantive obligations (taking steps to prevent and reduce exposure to hazards); and obligations relating to those in vulnerable situations.[21]

The existence of procedural obligations suggests how crucial information[22] and participation both are. The Sendai Framework provides for 'inclusive, accessible and non-discriminatory participation, paying special attention to people disproportionately affected by disasters, especially the poorest' and 'inclusive risk-informed decision-making based on the open exchange and dissemination of disaggregated data, including by sex, age and disability'.[23] In this context, United Nations (UN) agencies have relied on the notion of *empowerment* of individuals and communities affected by disasters.[24] A human rights approach not only offers guidance in taking the most appropriate action particularly *vis-à-vis* the most vulnerable groups, including indigenous peoples, with a view to avoiding discrimination based on gender, age, ethnic or social origin, but it also enables such groups to perform DRR initiatives, by portraying them as active agents of change for achieving effective and equitable resilience. DRR has been seen as an enabler of human rights, insofar as they promote participation in political life and consultation of affected groups in decision-making processes. The Expert Mechanism on the Rights of Indigenous Peoples found guidance for DRR activities in this area in the provisions of the UN Declaration addressing the right to self-determination and the right to participation in decision-making, among others.[25]

The key role of empowerment processes has been recently stressed by independent experts of special procedures of the UN Human Rights Council on the occasion of the adoption of the Sendai Framework, as follows:

> [m]oving from words to effective actions requires the full and effective participation and accessibility of individuals and communities affected, including women, persons with disabilities, indigenous peoples, older persons, as well as those displaced internally notably by the effects of climate change, in all phases of disaster risk reduction and building resilience strategies and policies.[26]

The dynamics between the State as the main duty-bearer and individual and collective right-holders in the specific field of prevention and reduction of disaster risks can be therefore envisaged as a complementary relationship between a top-down approach on the part of the State through legislation and other implementation measures and a bottom-up approach in which non-state actors mobilise and strengthen local capacities. Finally, the conceptualisation of a failure to take preventive action as a human rights issue leads to the establishment of responsibility, as already confirmed by existing case law of the ECtHR. Even human rights mechanisms at the UN level – though limited to investigating complaints and issuing legally non-binding decisions – may still have real strengths, particularly as they remain independent of governmental control.[27]

The duty of establishing a legislative and administrative framework

The previous paragraph has demonstrated that awareness has grown on the importance of integrating a human rights-based approach in prevention and reduction of disasters. In addition to the duty of prevention as developed by international environmental law,[28] human rights law has been identified as a fundamental source of obligations for taking preventative measures by the ILC. The current wording of Draft Article 9(1) ILC Draft Articles recognises the existence of a number of obligations aimed at DRR, by establishing that States 'shall reduce the risk of disasters by taking the necessary and appropriate measures, including through legislation and regulations, to prevent, mitigate and prepare for disasters'.[29] The ILC Special Rapporteur had identified prevention, mitigation and preparedness as lying on different points of the continuum of actions for the purpose of DRR, covering measures that need to be taken in the pre-disaster phase.[30] It follows that, in his view, mitigation and preparedness could be regarded as 'specific manifestations of the overarching principle of prevention'.[31]

It is not always an easy task to clarify the content and scope of the obligation to prevent, in order to determine exactly the concrete measures such duty requires. In general terms, there seems to be a trend under current international human rights law towards a more comprehensive understanding of the notion of prevention so that it aims to 'eliminate risk factors and establish a legal, administrative and policy framework which seeks to prevent violations'.[32] This is a relevant element at a time in which the traditional perception of disasters as episodic events has been superseded by the growing consciousness that they are 'events touching upon the "persistent" interests of States to such an extent and with such costly consequences that international legislative action . . . has flourished'.[33]

The case law of relevant human rights courts and mechanisms makes it possible to identify some common features and approaches to prevention,[34] particularly as regards the existence of a 'primary duty' placed upon States to put in place a legislative and administrative framework for both human-made[35] and natural disasters.[36] Awareness is increasing in the sense that the obligation to protect requires States parties of the relevant human rights treaties to adopt a legal framework imposing business entities to exercise human rights due diligence in order to identify, prevent, mitigate and account for the negative impacts caused by their activities.[37]

In this context, the ILC significantly stressed that legislation

> is meant to be understood in broad terms to cover as many manifestations of law as possible, it being generally recognized that such law-based measures are the most common and effective way to facilitate . . . the taking of disaster risk reduction measures at the domestic level.[38]

Following the authoritative position taken by the International Court of Justice (ICJ) with regard to the crime of genocide, one might be tempted to conclude that the duty to prevent, in all circumstances, is an obligation of conduct rather than one of result, as it requires States only to deploy their best efforts,[39] i.e. to do all in their power 'to achieve a result, but without ultimate commitment'.[40] Such distinction between the two categories of obligations is relevant insofar as it may assist in ascertaining when a breach has occurred:[41] it is notoriously based on the crucial concept of due diligence.[42] However, under international human rights law, even the duty to prevent is composed of a number of elements, only some of which are obligations of due diligence:[43] in particular, the duties to adopt both a dedicated legislative framework and an institutional apparatus are positive obligations of result.[44] Even the obligations requiring the 'progressive realisation' of economic, social and cultural rights can be viewed in terms of a combination of immediate obligations of result and obligations of best efforts.[45]

Of course, a matter of due diligence is how the administrative apparatus then functions: whereas both the enactment of laws dealing with all relevant aspects of disaster risk mitigation and the set up of the necessary mechanisms and procedures are the object of an obligation of result, on the contrary the obligation to use that institutional capacity to prevent is one of conduct, in the sense that a State cannot be under an obligation to succeed, whatever the circumstances, in preventing the impairment of human rights stemming from natural and man-made disasters.[46]

Such two-step approach in which legislation anticipates the taking of 'appropriate measures' has also been endorsed by the ILC in the Commentary to Draft Article 9, where it is stated that 'the general obligation to reduce the risk of disasters would also include an obligation to put such a legal framework into place so as to allow for the taking of the "appropriate" measures'.[47] As a corollary, the existence of a legal framework represents a *condicio sine qua non* also for the establishment of an accountability mechanism at a domestic level in case of non-performance.

The 2005 Hyogo Framework for Action considered DRR as 'a national and a local priority with a strong institutional basis for implementation', particularly through 'policy, legislative and institutional frameworks for disaster risk reduction'.[48] As other commentators have already observed, the Hyogo Framework prompted the adoption of a significant amount of legislation in many countries,[49] although the level of priority given to risk reduction in domestic regulation still depends on a variety of variables, including the prevailing risk context, the level of understanding of DRR and the specific regulatory needs and gaps in the country.[50]

It goes without saying that, under International Human Rights Law, States enjoy a certain degree of discretion regarding the content of the normative tools they are required to use. However, in the area of dangerous industrial activities, the ECtHR stated that domestic regulation should include 'the licensing, setting up, operation, security and supervision of the activity'.[51]

Moreover, both hard and soft law instruments in the specific field of DRR could provide clear guidelines for the enactment of further legislative measures.[52] In this respect, the goal of the 2015 Sendai Framework is much more comprehensive than the previous documents, as it is aimed at the 'substantial reduction of disaster risk and losses', through 'the implementation of integrated and inclusive economic, structural, legal, social, health, cultural, educational, environmental, technological, political and institutional measures that prevent and reduce hazard exposure and vulnerability to disaster, increase preparedness for response and recovery, and thus strengthen resilience'.[53] Still, 'national and local framework of laws and regulations' serve a two-fold purpose: not only do they assign clear mandates, tasks and responsibilities and provide for coordination across the relevant institutions, but they are also aimed at reducing risks of exposure and vulnerability by developing 'land use and urban planning, building codes, environmental and resource management and health and safety standards'.[54]

It is important to consider the impact of the growing importance attached to the adoption of a coherent legislative and administrative framework to reduce disaster exposure, as well as of the non-binding efforts taken in specifying which measures are needed. To the extent that the diffusion of a DRR paradigm is able to influence both States' capacity and their knowledge of the risk, this might have implications also for the determination of negligence, and therefore responsibility, in a specific case.

The relevance of the due diligence standard

The mere existence of domestic legislation concerning natural disasters, including legislation relating to DRR, is an essential starting point but may not be sufficient for guaranteeing full compliance with the obligation to prevent. States are required to use such a normative and institutional framework with diligence. This is how the ILC Commentary to the Draft Articles should be read too, where it construes the duty to reduce risk as one of conduct and not result: 'in other words not to completely prevent or mitigate a disaster, but rather to reduce the risk of harm potentially caused thereby'.[55]

Draft Article 9 is consistent with the position taken by the ECtHR as regards the scope of the positive obligation 'to take appropriate steps to safeguard the lives of those within their jurisdiction'.[56] This approach moves from the premise that disasters constitute threats to the right to life.[57] As a consequence, a classical understanding of the duty to prevent, as developed by the *Osman* case, applies in this realm too. The Court individuated the rationale for 'best efforts' obligations as follows: 'an impossible or disproportionate burden must not be imposed on the authorities without consideration being given, in particular, to the operational choices which they must make in terms of priorities and resources'.[58]

The standard of due diligence, which applies to this kind of primary obligations,[59] serves as a criterion for assessing compliance with the specific duty to prevent.[60] Due diligence is linked to the concept of negligence and the general principle *ad impossibilia nemo tenetur.*[61] It has been described as a standard of care, which requires 'a value judgment of what could and should have reasonably been done'[62] in the particular circumstances. Diligence entails using capacity at the disposal of a State in an effective manner to respond to known and knowable threats. It means that, in order to assess whether the State was negligent, two essential factors must be evaluated: whether the State knew or ought to have known the degree of risk; and whether it used all the 'available means'.[63]

The importance of the knowledge of risk,[64] as an element for the evaluation of diligence, found confirmation in the *Öneryildiz* case, which concerned a methane explosion in a municipal rubbish dump. The ECtHR held that Turkish authorities had a positive obligation to prevent as they 'knew or ought to have known that there was a real and immediate risk to a number of persons'.[65] This specific understanding of risk is based on the elements of foreseeability and imminence, given the dangerous character of the industrial activity and the quantity of persons potentially affected.[66] In the subsequent *Budayeva* case, which specifically concerned natural disasters, the Court considered a variety of factors in order to assess the knowledge of risk, including 'the imminence of a natural hazard', whether 'it concerned a recurring calamity', 'the origin of the threat' and 'the extent to which one or the other risk is susceptible to mitigation'.[67] It is noteworthy that the concrete evaluation was again based on the criterion of foreseeability of the mudslide:[68] the Court concluded that the town 'was situated in an area prone to mudslides', that it could be 'reasonably assumed that a mudslide was likely'[69] and that the authorities 'were aware that any mudslide, regardless of its scale, was capable of causing devastating consequences'.[70]

Finally, the relevance of the subsequent case *Kolyadenko v. Russia* lies in the combination of the foreseeability of the hazard with the existence of an obligation to use best efforts to gain knowledge. In relation to a large-scale release of water from a reservoir near the city of Vladivostok, the Court pointed out that the authority 'should have foreseen the likelihood as well as the potential consequences of releases of water from the reservoir', since they had the obligation 'to assess all the potential risks inherent in the operation of the reservoir'.[71] If risk assessment has become part of a specific duty under human rights law, as 'the first step towards any sensible measure to reduce the risk of disasters',[72] greater understanding is nowadays available on the predictability of events. As a consequence, the criteria of 'imminence' and 'visibility' are less important for the knowledge of the threat, and therefore, States have binding obligations under the ECHR to proactively undertake disaster reduction activities, particularly in the field of preparedness measures.

The 'available means' standard is the second factor to be considered in the evaluation of compliance with due diligence obligations: responsibility arises once 'State officials and authorities did not do everything within their power to protect [human rights]'.[73] In other words, if State capacity to prevent constitutes a sort of limit in establishing responsibility, it is important to take into account various aspects, including whether 'a State has the financial, technical or human resources available to put its institutional capacity to good use'.[74] The Inter-American Commission on Human Rights, in granting precautionary measures on behalf of the inhabitants of Omoa in Honduras, at risk because of a liquid petroleum gas storage facility, asked the State

> to take the steps necessary to ensure the . . . company's effective observance of the environmental regulations and laws in place in Honduras, and to adopt the measures needed to reduce the danger to the lives and persons of the inhabitants of the community of Omoa to an acceptable level.[75]

Significantly, capacity has been identified in the DRR framework as '[t]he combination of all the strengths, attributes and resources available within an organization, community or society to manage and reduce disaster risks and strengthen resilience'.[76]

The reasoning of the ECtHR in this series of cases is based on the notion of negligence attributable to the State. In *Budayeva*, the Court found that the State authorities neither allocated financial resources nor took concrete steps for the 'restoration of the defence infrastructure'[77] after the previous mudslide. Moreover, they failed 'to show all possible diligence in informing the civilians and making advance arrangements for the emergency evacuation', as they could have 'set up temporary observation posts in the mountains'.[78] In *Kolyadenko*, the Court established a causal link between the negligence attributable to the State and the endangering of the lives of those living in the vicinity of the reservoir, by finding that the main reason for the flood was the authorities' failure to take measures to keep the river channel clear.[79]

The case law of the ECtHR seems to concur with the view that reasonableness is 'a golden thread in determining which measures States should take to act in a duly diligent manner'.[80] As observed also by the ICJ with respect to the crime of genocide,[81] it is difficult to determine *in abstracto* what a 'reasonable preventive action' is: this leaves States a degree of flexibility in the choice of means and the allocation of resources.[82] In any case, various authors have noted that international law has moved away from the *diligentia quam in suis* principle, to a more objectivised standard,[83] which the obligation to establish a legislative and institutional framework seems to imply, which guarantees a minimum standard to be upheld. The ILC, drawing on principles emanating from international human rights law, has identified three categories of DRR measures, namely: the conduct of risk assessments, the collection and dissemination of risk and past loss information and the installation and operation of early warning systems.[84]

As for the scope of the States' margin of appreciation in taking the most appropriate measures, in the European Court's view, this seems to depend on the importance of the rights involved as well as on the nature of the disaster: first, whether the right to life or a different right might be impaired and, second, whether the specific circumstances are to be qualified as a natural rather than a man-made disaster. The net result is that much more discretion is left to the States when, for instance, they decide 'what measures to take in order to protect private possessions from weather hazards'.[85] One might wonder what the implications of the position taken by the Court are, particularly as it considered that meteorological events do not call for the same extent of State involvement as do dangerous activities of a man-made nature, because they are 'beyond human control'.[86] Criticism has been levelled against this approach, since it might entail a lesser standard of protection for natural disasters under international human rights law, 'especially in the preparedness and prevention stage'.[87]

However, the apparently strong statement made by the Court needs to be read in the light of the definition of disasters as the result of the interaction between hazardous events with conditions of exposure, vulnerability and capacity: it goes without saying then that natural disasters are not as such 'beyond human control'. In this regard, the still limited jurisprudence cannot be said to be definitely settled yet. Moreover, it has been observed that the approach of the Court on the margin of appreciation in the series of cases here considered is understandable, because none of the four events would have fallen within the definition of disasters under the ILC Draft Articles.[88]

To conclude, what emerges for the previous analysis that, even assuming that States are not expected to succeed in preventing the effects of disasters in all circumstances, still the standard of care increases where the risks are known to be particularly significant, in terms of 'harmfulness of the dangerous activities' and 'foreseeability of the risks to life': *rectius*, the specific measures State authorities could reasonably be expected to take vary in accordance with the risks of severe human rights impact.[89] There is no doubt that the merit of the case law of the ECtHR has been that of clarifying the scope of positive obligations particularly vis-à-vis infringements of the right to life in situations of natural and man-made disasters. At the same time, a focus on the right to life might even be counterproductive, insofar as it tends to reduce disaster reduction to the very limited sphere of individual interest, rather than that of the welfare of the society as a whole.[90] It remains that specific obligations to respect, protect and fulfil also arise from economic, social and cultural rights, including the right to an adequate standard of living (food and housing) and the right to health.[91] Finally, the situation changes once a legal framework on DRR exists at an international level: indeed, the degree of flexibility diminishes when specific regulatory regimes provide for specific actions.

Conclusion

Prevention, mitigation and preparedness for disasters represent 'a cornerstone' of the ILC Draft on the protection of persons in the event of disasters, 'rendering it capable of complementing non-binding approaches pursued at the international level such as the Sendai Framework'.[92] As various States expressed doubts as to the existence of an obligation to prevent the risk of disasters under customary international law,[93] case law and the relevant literature concurs with the view that States have positive obligations under international human rights law to take preventive action once they have knowledge of disaster risks. Whereas international environmental law has offered a valuable contribution in identifying procedures which could be applied for preventing the occurrence of disasters, including a duty to cooperate,[94] a human rights approach allows one to address the comprehensive scope of DRR, particularly as regards the reduction of vulnerability.[95]

Identifying the specific conduct required by the duty to prevent was a source of controversy among States for a long time. The ECtHR has contributed to clarifying the scope of positive obligations of prevention, based on a two-step approach in which legislation anticipates the taking of 'appropriate measures'. In addition to approving a legislative framework and establishing an administrative apparatus, States are required to use them with diligence. The ILC too has construed the obligation to reduce disasters as an obligation of conduct, subject to the due diligence standard: it follows that, in order to assess whether a State was negligent, an evaluation must be made on both its knowledge of the risk and on the use of 'all available means'.

The jurisprudence developed by the ECtHR in the series of cases concerning situations qualified as disasters cannot be considered as definitely settled, even though an evolution in the understanding of the concept of risk has already emerged. In particular, the assessment of the foreseeability of a hazard needs to take into account the existence of a specific due diligence obligation to gain knowledge, through a risk assessment activity. As a consequence, if the criteria of 'imminence' and 'visibility' are less relevant in considering a disaster risk as certain, States are not only under a procedural obligation to disseminate information and operate early warning systems, but also must proactively enact DRR measures, in order to reduce exposure and vulnerability.

In the specific area of disaster prevention, international law is still fragmented and presents gaps.[96] On the assumption that 'human vulnerability in a time of disasters can be caused by both immediate pre-disaster, or by long term poor governance',[97] the degree of flexibility still left to States in deciding the most appropriate action is counterbalanced by the increasing acceptance of the specific legislative and policy measures contained in hard and soft law instruments, including the Sendai Framework, particularly those addressing resilience and preparedness for the purpose of preventing new risks.

Selected bibliography

K. Da Costa and P. Pospieszna, 'The Relationship between Human Rights and Disaster Risk Reduction Revisited: Bringing the Legal Perspective into the Discussion' 6 *Journal of International Humanitarian Legal Studies* (2015) 64.

B. Nicoletti, 'The Prevention of Natural and Man-Made Disasters: What Duties for States?' in A. De Guttry, M. Gestri and G. Venturini (eds), *International Disaster Response Law* (TMC Asser, 2012) 177.

D. Fisher, 'Legal Implementation of Human Rights Obligations to Prevent Displacement Due to Natural Disasters' in W. Kälin, R.C. Williams, K. Koser and A. Solomon (eds), *Incorporating the Guiding Principles on Internal Displacement into Domestic Law: Issues and Challenges* (American Society of International Law, 2010) 551.

R. Pisillo Mazzeschi, 'Responsabilité de l'Etat pour violation des obligations positives relatives aux droits de l'homme' 333 *Recueil des Cours* (2008) 175.

C.P. Romano, 'L'obligation de prevention des catastrophes industrielles et naturelles' in D. Caron and C. Leben (eds), *The International Aspects of Natural and Industrial Catastrophes* (Martinus Nijhoff Publishers, 2001) 379.

Notes

1 See *inter alia* G. Di Baldassarre, J.S. Kemerink, M. Kooy and L. Brandimarte, 'Floods and Societies: The Spatial Distribution of Water-Related Disaster Risk and Its Dynamics' 1 *WIREs Water* (2014) 133; in addition, M. Isnenghi, 'Il potere di carta. Il dopo-Vajont e la lotta delle parole' in M. Reberschak (ed), *Il Grande Vajont* (Cierre, 2013) 141.

2 K.C. Lauta, 'Human Rights and "Natural" Disasters' in S.C. Breau and K. Samuel (eds), *Research Handbook on Disasters and International Law* (Edward Elgar Publishing, 2016) 91.

3 UNISDR, 'Sendai Framework for Disaster Risk Reduction 2015–2030' (2015), available at www.unisdr.org/files/43291_sendaiframeworkfordrren.pdf, accessed on 20 June 2017. The Sendai Framework is a 15-year, voluntary, non-binding agreement, adopted by the UN member States on 18 March 2015 at the Third UN World Conference on Disaster Risk Reduction in Sendai City, Japan. The document was endorsed in UNGA, Res 69/283, UN Doc. A/RES/69/283 (23 June 2015).

4 UNISDR, Reading the Sendai Framework for Disaster Risk Reduction 2015–2030 (2015), available at www.unisdr.org/we/inform/publications/46694, accessed on 20 June 2017.

5 Cf. I. Saunders, 'International Disaster Relief Law and Article 38(1)(c) of the Statute of the International Court of Justice: The Forgotten Source of International Law' in D. Caron, M.J. Kelly and A. Telesetsky (eds), *The International Law of Disaster Relief* (Cambridge University Press, 2014) 29.
6 *Budayeva and Others v. Russia*, App. No. 15339/02, 21166/02, 20058/02, 11673/02 and 15343/02 (ECtHR, Judgment of 20 March 2008) para 135.
7 Cf. OHCHR, Report of the Office of the United Nations High Commissioner for Human Rights on the Relationship between Climate Change and Human Rights, UN Doc. A/HRC/10/61 (15 January 2009) para 92.
8 See W. Kälin, 'The Human Rights Dimension of Natural or Human-Made Disasters' 55 *German Yearbook of International Law* (2012) 119; moreover, W. Kälin and J. Künzli, *The Law of International Human Rights Protection* (Oxford University Press, 2009) 77–81.
9 See C. Shucksmith, 'Methods to Incorporate Human Rights Law into Disaster Prevention and Reduction Strategies' *EJIL:Talk!* (2017), available at www.ejiltalk.org/methods-to-incorporate-human-rights-law-into-disaster-prevention-and-reduction-strategies/, accessed on 20 June 2017.
10 Cf. J. Brunnée, 'Common Areas, Common Heritage, and Common Concern' in D. Bodansky, J. Brunnée and E. Hey (eds), *The Oxford Handbook of International Environmental Law* (Oxford University Press, 2007) 550, 553.
11 For the notion of 'community interest', of course, see B. Simma, 'From Bilateralism to Community Interest in International Law' 250 *Recueil des Cours* (1994) 217.
12 UNGA, Res 70/1, Transforming Our World: The 2030 Agenda for Sustainable Development, UN Doc. A/RES/70/1 (25 September 2015); see T. Karimova, 'Sustainable Development and Disasters' in Breau and Samuel (eds) (n. 2) 177.
13 See Creta's chapter in this book.
14 Sendai Framework para 19.
15 On the issue of the human role in the narrative of disasters, see *inter alia*, L. Grow Sun, 'Climate Change and the Narrative of Disaster' in J. Peel and D. Fisher (eds), *The Role of International Environmental Law in Disaster Risk Reduction* (Brill, 2016) 29.
16 Report of the Open-Ended Intergovernmental Expert Working Group on Indicators and Terminology Relating to Disaster Risk Reduction, UN Doc. A/71/644 (1 December 2016), endorsed by UNGA Res 71/276 (13 February 2017).
17 Convention on the Rights of Persons with Disabilities (adopted 13 December 2006, entered into force 3 May 2008) 2515 UNTS 13; See M. Crock, 'The Protection of Vulnerable Groups' in Breau and Samuel (eds) (n. 2) 383.
18 See in general F. Ippolito and S. Iglesias Sánchez, *Protecting Vulnerable Groups: The European Human Rights Framework* (Hart, 2015).
19 L. Peroni and A. Timmer, 'Vulnerable Groups: The Promise of an Emerging Concept in European Human Rights Convention Law' 11 *International Journal of Constitutional Law* (2013) 1056, 1074.
20 See *inter alia* D. Fisher, 'Legal Implementation of Human Rights Obligations to Prevent Displacement Due to Natural Disasters' in W. Kälin, R.C. Williams, K. Koser and A. Solomon (eds), *Incorporating the Guiding Principles on Internal Displacement into Domestic Law: Issues and Challenges* (American Society of International Law, 2010) 551; K. Da Costa and P. Pospieszna, 'The Relationship between Human Rights and Disaster Risk Reduction Revisited: Bringing the Legal Perspective into the Discussion' 6 *Journal of International Humanitarian Legal Studies* (2015) 64.
21 J.H. Knox, Report of the Independent Expert on the Issue of Human Rights Obligations Relating to the Enjoyment of a Safe, Clean, Healthy and Sustainable Environment, Mapping Report, UN Doc. A/HRC/25/53 (30 December 2013); moreover J.H. Knox, 'Afterword: Environmental Disasters and Human Rights' in Peel and Fisher (eds) (n. 15) 453.
22 On the issue of information as a human right, see Riccardi's chapter in this volume.
23 Sendai Framework para 19.
24 See Da Costa and Pospieszna (n. 20) 69.
25 HRC, Promotion and Protection of the Rights of Indigenous Peoples in Disaster Risk Reduction, Prevention and Preparedness Initiatives: Study by the Expert Mechanism on the Rights of Indigenous Peoples, UN Doc. A/HRC/27/66 (7 August 2014) paras 11 ff.
26 'New Framework for Disaster Risk Reduction – UN Experts Urge Move to Effective Action', available at www.ohchr.org/EN/NewsEvents/Pages/DisplayNews.aspx?NewsID=15733, accessed on 20 June 2017.
27 See Knox, 'Afterword' (n. 21) 468.

28 See U. Beyerlin and T. Marauhn, *International Environmental Law* (Hart-Nomos, 2011); P. Sands and J. Peel, *Principles of International Environmental Law* (3rd edn, Cambridge University Press, 2012) 200; L.A. Duvic-Paoli and J.E. Viñuales, 'Principle 2: Prevention' in J.E. Viñuales (ed), *The Rio Declaration on Environment and Development: A Commentary* (Oxford University Press, 2015) 107, 130.
29 See ILC, Draft Articles on the Protection of Persons in the Event of Disasters, with Commentaries, in Report of the International Law Commission, Sixty-Eight Session, UN Doc. A/71/10 (2016) (2 May–10 June and 4 July–12 August 2016) 43, para 4. Cf. D. Cubie, *The International Legal Protection of Persons in Humanitarian Crises: Exploring the Acquis Humanitaire* (Hart, 2017) 268.
30 ILC, Sixth Report on the Protection of Persons in the Event of Disasters, UN Doc. A/CN.4/662 (3 May 2013) para 37.
31 Ibid para 40.
32 OHCHR, The Role of Prevention in the Promotion and Protection of Human Rights, Report of the Office of the United Nations High Commissioner for Human Rights, UN Doc. A/HRC/30/20 (16 July 2015) para 9.
33 B. Nicoletti, 'The Prevention of Natural and Man-Made Disasters: What Duties for States?' in A. De Guttry, M. Gestri and G. Venturini (eds), *International Disaster Response Law* (TMC Asser, 2012) 177, 195.
34 *Velasquez Rodriguez v. Honduras*, IACtHR, Ser. C, No. 4 (1988) paras 174–175. See C. Bakker, 'Climate Change and Right to Life: Limits and Potentialities of the Human Rights Protection System' in O. Quirico and M. Boumghar (eds), *Climate Change and Human Rights: An International and Comparative Law Perspective* (Routledge, 2016) 71.
35 *Öneryildiz v. Turkey*, App. No. 48939/99 (ECtHR, Judgment of 30 November 2004) para 89.
36 *Budayeva* (n. 6) para 129; UN Doc. A/HRC/25/53 (n. 21) paras 44–57: States have a general duty to 'adopt legal and institutional frameworks that protect against, and respond to, environmental harm that may or does interfere with the enjoyment of human rights'.
37 HRC, Guiding Principles on Business and Human Rights: Implementing the United Nations 'Protect, Respect and Remedy' Framework, UN Doc. A/HRC/17/31 (21 March 2011). Regarding human rights obligations for corporations to prevent disasters, see A. Telesetsky, 'Beyond Voluntary Corporate Social Responsibility: Corporate Human Rights Obligations to Prevent Disasters and to Provide Temporary Emergency Relief' 48 *Vanderbilt Journal of Transnational Law* (2015) 1003.
38 ILC Commentary to draft art 9, para 12.
39 *Application of the Convention on the Prevention and Punishment of the Crime of Genocide (Bosnia-Herzegovina v. Serbia and Montenegro)* [2007] ICJ Rep. 43, 221, para 430.
40 ILC, Second Report on State Responsibility, UN Doc. A/CN.4/498 (17 March 1999) para 57.
41 ILC, Draft Articles on Responsibility of States for Internationally Wrongful Acts, with Commentaries' 2(2) *Yearbook of the International Law Commission* (2001) 31, 56.
42 See P.-M. Dupuy, 'Reviewing the Difficulties of Codification: On Ago's Classification of Obligations of Means and Obligations of Result in Relation to State Responsibility' 10 *EJIL* (1999) 371, 378; R. Wolfrum, 'Obligation of Result Versus Obligation of Conduct: Some Thoughts about the Implementation of International Obligations' in M.H. Arsanjani, J. Katz Cogan, R.D. Sloane and S. Wiessner (eds), *Looking to the Future: Essays on International Law in Honor of W. Michael Reisman* (Brill, 2010) 369.
43 Cf. ILA Study Group on Due Diligence in International Law, 'First Report' (7 March 2014) 16, available at www.ila-hq.org/index.php/study-groups, accessed on 20 June 2017.
44 See R. Pisillo Mazzeschi, 'Responsabilité de l'Etat pour violation des obligations positives relatives aux droits de l'homme' 333 *Recueil des Cours* (2008) 175, in particular ch III, 311.
45 Ibid 442.
46 Kälin (n. 8) 139.
47 ILC Commentary to draft art 9, para 12.
48 UNISDR, Hyogo Framework for Action 2005–2015: Building the Resilience of Nations and Communities to Disasters, World Conference on Disaster Reduction (18–22 January 2005), available at www.unisdr.org/we/inform/publications/1037, accessed on 20 June 2017.
49 Da Costa and Pospieszna (n. 20) 65–66; in addition, UNISDR, Implementation of the Hyogo Framework for Action: Summary of Reports 2007–2013 (2013), available at www.unisdr.org/we/inform/publications/32916, accessed on 20 June 2017.
50 IFRC and UNDP, *Effective Law and Regulation for Disaster Risk Deduction: A Multi Country Report* (UN, 2014); in addition, IFRC, Better Laws, Safer Communities? Emerging Themes on How Legislation Can Support Disaster Risk Reduction (2013), available at www.ifrc.org/PageFiles/118981/IFRC_better-laws-safer-communities_2013.pdf, accessed on 20 June 2017.

51 *Öneryildiz* (n. 35) para 90.
52 See the comprehensive presentation of the international instruments covering disaster prevention in E. Valencia-Ospina (n. 30) 25 ff. The ILC Commentary to draft art 9 too contains a list of multilateral, regional and bilateral instruments concerned with reducing the risk of disasters.
53 Sendai Framework para 17.
54 Ibid para 27.
55 ILC Commentary to draft art 9, para 10.
56 *Budayeva* (n. 6) para 128.
57 See W. Schabas, *The European Convention on Human Rights: A Commentary* (Oxford University Press, 2015) 131.
58 *Osman v. the United Kingdom*, App. No. 23452/94 (ECtHR, Judgment of 28 October 1998) para 116.
59 The ICJ too recognised the connections between the principle of prevention, as a customary rule, and the due diligence standard: see *Pulp Mills on the River Uruguay (Argentina v. Uruguay)* [2010] ICJ Rep 14, para 101.
60 See R. Barnidge, 'The Due Diligence Principle under International Law' 8 *International Community Law Review* (2006) 81; J. Kulesza, *Due Diligence in International Law* (Brill, 2016) 266–270; see also C.P. Romano, 'L'obligation de prévention des catastrophes industrielles et naturelles' in D. Caron and C. Leben (eds), *The International Aspects of Natural and Industrial Catastrophes* (Martinus Nijhoff Publishers, 2001) 379, 388.
61 It is not necessary in this context to discuss the traditional problem concerning the relevance of fault as a *condicio sine qua non* of wrongfulness and responsibility: see G. Palmisano, 'Fault' in R. Wolfrum (ed), *Max Planck Encyclopedia of Public International Law* (Oxford University Press, 2014); see *inter alia* UNGA, Force Majeure and Fortuitous Event as Circumstances Precluding Wrongfulness: Survey of State Practice, International Judicial Decisions and Doctrine – Study Prepared by the Secretariat, UN Doc. A/CN.4/315 (27 June 1977).
62 R. Kolb, *The International Law of State Responsibility: An Introduction* (Edward Elgar Publishing, 2017).
63 See G. Bartolini, T. Natoli and A. Riccardi, 'Report of the Expert Meeting on the ILC's Draft Articles on the Protection of Persons in the Event of Disasters' 3 *International Law and Disasters Working Papers Series* (2015) 44. See also *Kichwa Indigenous People of Sarayaku v. Ecuador*, IACtHR, Ser. C, No. 245 (2012) para 155:

> it is clear that a State cannot be held responsible for all situations in which the right to life is at risk. Bearing in mind the difficulties involved in the planning and execution of public policies and the operational choices that must be made according to priorities and the resources available, the State's positive obligations must be interpreted in such a manner that an impossible or disproportionate burden is not imposed upon the authorities. For this positive obligation to arise, it must be determined that, at the time the events occurred, the authorities knew or should have known about the existence of a situation that posed an immediate and certain risk to the life of an individual or of a group of individuals, and that they did not take the necessary measures available to them that could be reasonably expected to prevent or avoid such risk.

64 See *Corfu Channel (United Kingdom v. Albania) (Merits)* [1949] ICJ Rep. 18.
65 *Öneryildiz* (n. 35) para 101.
66 See C. Hilson, 'Risk and the European Convention on Human Rights: Towards a New Approach' 11 *Cambridge Yearbook of European Legal Studies* (2009) 353–354; O.W. Pedersen, 'Environmental Risks, Rights and Black Swans' 15 *Environmental Law Review* (2013) 55.
67 *Budayeva* (n. 6) para 137.
68 Cf. M. Ambrus, 'The Role of the European Court of Human Rights in Governing Risk' in M. Ambrus, R. Rayfuse and W. Werner (eds), *Risk and the Regulation of Uncertainty in International Law* (Oxford University Press, 2017) 99, 105–112; in addition see also K.C. Lauta and M. Faure, 'Disaster Risk Management' in A. Burgess, A. Alemanno and J. Zinn (eds), *Routledge Handbook of Risk Studies* (Routledge, 2016) 179.
69 *Budayeva* (n. 6) para 147.
70 Ibid para 149.
71 *Kolyadenko and Others v. Russia*, App. Nos. 17423/05, 20534/05, 20678/05, 23263/05, 24283/05 and 35673/05 (ECtHR, Judgment of 28 February 2012).
72 ILC Commentary to draft art 9, para 20.
73 *Öneryildiz* (n. 35) para 135.

74 Cf. K. Trapp, *State Responsibility for International Terrorism* (Oxford University Press, 2011) 71.
75 OAS, 'Inter-American Commission on Human Rights, PM 17/10 – Inhabitants of the Community of Omoa, Honduras' (8 November 2011), available at www.oas.org/en/iachr/decisions/precautionary.asp, accessed on 20 June 2017.
76 UN Doc. A/71/644 (n. 16) 12.
77 *Budayeva* (n. 6) para 149.
78 Ibid para 154.
79 *Kolyadenko* (n. 71) para 215.
80 ILA Study Group on Due Diligence in International Law, 'Second Report' (2016) 8, available at www.ila-hq.org/index.php/study-groups, accessed on 20 June 2017.
81 *Genocide* (n. 39) para 430.
82 See E. Ferris, 'How Can International Human Rights Law Protect Us from Disasters?' 108 *ASIL Proceedings* (2014) 177.
83 Those supporting an objective standard of due diligence usually refer to A.V. Freeman, 'Responsibility of States for Unlawful Acts of Their Armed Forces' 88 *Recueil des Cours* (1955-II) 263, 277–278; such a standard would require 'nothing more nor less than the reasonable measures of prevention which a well-administered government could be expected to exercise under similar circumstances'.
84 ILC Commentary to draft art 9, para 17. See also the analysis of the substantive elements of state regulation in Fisher (n. 20) 567.
85 *Hadzhiyska v. Bulgaria*, App. No. 20701/09 (ECtHR, Decision of 15 May 2012, inadmissible) 15.
86 See also *Budayeva* (n. 6) para 135.
87 Cf. M. Hesselman, 'Regional Human Rights Regimes and Humanitarian Obligations of States in the Event of Disaster' in A. Zwitter, C.K. Lamont, H.-J. Heintze and J. Herman (eds), *Humanitarian Action: Global, Regional and Domestic Legal Responses* (Cambridge, 2015) 202, 223.
88 See Cubie (n. 29) 171. On the argument that the four situations examined by the ECtHR could hardly fall within the definition of disaster under the ILC draft articles, see G. Bartolini, 'La definizione di disastro nel progetto di articoli della Commissione del diritto internazionale' 98 *Rivista di diritto internazionale* (2015) 155, 159.
89 Cf. 'Guiding Principles on Business and Human Rights' (n. 37).
90 This paraphrases the argument developed by F. Francioni, 'International Human Rights in an Environmental Horizon' 21 *EJIL* (2010) 41, 55.
91 HRC, Report of the Special Rapporteur on the Human Right to Safe Drinking Water and Sanitation, Catarina de Albuquerque, UN Doc. A/HRC/27/66 (7 August 2014) para 53; see also M. Aronsson-Storrier and H. Salama, 'Tackling Water Contamination: Development, Human Rights and Disaster Risk Reduction' in Breau and Samuel (eds) (n. 2) 319.
92 See G. Bartolini, 'The Draft Articles on "The Protection of Persons in the Event of Disasters": Towards a Flagship Treaty?' *EJIL:Talk!* (2016), available at www.ejiltalk.org/author/gbartolini/, accessed on 20 June 2017.
93 ILC, Eighth Report on the Protection of Persons in the Event of Disasters, UN Doc. A/CN.4/697 (17 March 2016) para 193; in addition see S. Murphy, 'Protection of Persons in the Event of Disasters and Other Topics: The Sixty-Eighth Session of the International Law Commission' 110 *AJIL* (2016) 718.
94 See Romano (n. 60) 397.
95 See Nicoletti (n. 33) 196.
96 See E. Sommario, 'One Law to Bind Them All: International Law and Disaster Resilience' in A. Herwig and M. Simoncini (eds), *Law and the Management of Disasters: The Challenge of Resilience* (Routledge, 2016) 245, 247.
97 V. Popovski, 'State Negligence before and after Natural Disasters as Human Rights Violations' in C. Hobson, P. Bacon and R. Cameron (eds), *Human Security and Natural Disasters* (Routledge, 2014) 94, 97.

9

INTEGRATING HUMAN RIGHTS INTO DISASTER MANAGEMENT

Normative, operational and methodological aspects

Annalisa Creta

Introduction

The integration of human rights into all phases of the disaster management cycle has been repeatedly called for in several international forums.[1] The latest, although timid, references are those contained in the Sendai Framework for Disaster Risk Reduction 2015–2030, where human rights are listed amongst its Guiding Principles. In particular, paragraph 19, letters (c), (d) and (h), contain the essential elements of a 'human rights-based approach' to disaster management. Letter (c) states that '[m]anaging the risk of disasters is aimed at *protecting persons* and their property, health, livelihoods and productive assets, as well as cultural and environmental assets, *while promoting and protecting all human rights, including the right to development*', and letter (d) calls for an '*all-of-society engagement and partnership, empowerment* and *inclusive, accessible and non-discriminatory participation*, paying *special attention to people disproportionately affected* by disasters' (emphasis added).[2]

The aim of this contribution is to explain *how* human rights standards and principles can be mainstreamed into disaster management to increase the enjoyment of rights by victims of such disasters, by fostering 'awareness and ownership by duty-bearers to meet their obligations towards vulnerable communities'[3] and ensuring that 'rights-holders are empowered to demand greater levels of safety before, during and after disasters'.[4]

After some terminological clarifications, the chapter will survey different sets of documents – recommendations of United Nations (UN) human rights treaty and Charter-based mechanisms, UN Inter-Agency Standing Committee (IASC) and UN Development Group (UNDG) policy documents, deliberations of inter-governmental bodies and policy-making organs – thus highlighting three different ways in which human rights are being integrated into disaster management to strengthen prevention, response and recovery efforts:

(a) Normative: the UN human rights machinery's focus on States' obligations in relation to the enjoyment of specific rights in disaster setting;
(b) Operational: an analysis of guidelines and tools developed for humanitarian actors (applicable at all levels, from national to international) as a means to contribute to better translating human rights law into concrete actions in disaster situations; and

(c) Methodological: examining the human rights-based approach as a methodology that can enable more successful programming by informing the way disaster responses are designed, implemented, monitored and evaluated.

The analysis will be circumscribed to the UN practice in this regard. This narrow focus is motivated by the fact that it is precisely at the UN level that the most significant attempts to apply a Human Rights-Based Approach (HRBA) to disaster management are taking place, influencing and shaping not only the work on this topic of that same Organisation – its agencies, offices, departments and programmes – but also that of its member States.

Towards a human rights-based approach to disaster management?

Defining key terms

For the purposes of the present work, disaster management will be defined as 'the organization and management of resources and responsibilities for dealing with all humanitarian aspects of emergencies, in particular preparedness, response and recovery, in order to lessen the impact of disasters'.[5] This wording encompasses all phases of the disaster cycle: from prevention and preparation, to emergency response and the post-disaster/recovery phase.

An HRBA is:

> a conceptual framework for the process of human development that is normatively based on international human rights standards and operationally directed to promoting and protecting human rights. It seeks to analyse inequalities which lie at the heart of development problems and redress discriminatory practices and unjust distributions of power that impede development progress.[6]

In 2003, the Stamford Interagency Workshop on a Human Rights-Based Approach in the Context of UN Reform reached a common understanding and consensus on the definition of HRBA and also defined six key principles of HRBA to guide programming: (a) universality and inalienability, (b) indivisibility, (c) inter-dependence and inter-relatedness, (d) non-discrimination and equality, (e) participation and inclusion and (f) accountability and the rule of law.[7] An HRBA is therefore a 'framework of action as well as a methodological tool' to apply international human rights principles, values, standards and goals into all stages of programming.[8]

In an HRBA, the relationship between rights-holders and duty-bearers is shaped by human rights norms and plans, policies and programmes that are grounded on a set of rights and correlating legal obligations enshrined in international law norms. Such a framework helps to promote the sustainability of interventions[9] by empowering right-holders – especially the most vulnerable – to actively participate in the formulation of policies and to claim their rights and seek redress.[10]

The progressive integration of human rights in disaster management

Disasters occurring in the last 10 to 15 years have shown the mounting importance of integrating human rights into all phases of disaster management for ensuring the most appropriate response for affected populations. If we take the 2004 Indian Ocean tsunami as a starting point, the need to implement rights-based approaches in disaster management became clear and was also evident in the adoption of a series of key policy documents and guidelines in this regard.

Indeed, it was precisely in the aftermath of the Indian Ocean tsunami that, following input from the then Representative of the Secretary-General on the Human Rights of Internally Displaced Persons (Representative of the Secretary-General on IDPs), Walter Kälin, a process was triggered for providing advice to humanitarian organisations on the application of an HRBA for developing and implementing a response to natural disasters. Kälin paid a working visit to Asia to meet with various actors from the region affected by the tsunami, to discuss the human rights situation of internally displaced persons (IDPs) so as to recommend possible next steps in the international, regional and national response to that disaster.[11] As a result, he flagged several practical issues and concerns arising in situations of displacement due to natural disasters and *inter alia* recommended to use the Guiding Principles on Internal Displacement as a blueprint for the development of national, regional and international policies for protecting and assisting those displaced by disasters.[12] In the same vein, he also called for the development of a set of more general guidelines for the protection of the human rights of persons affected by disasters.[13] The latter recommendation resulted in the preparation and presentation, in 2006, of draft guidelines to the IASC on Protection of Persons in Natural Disasters,[14] which were revised and finally adopted by the IASC in 2010. This document represents the first of a series of explicit guidance tools for humanitarian actors on how to apply an HRBA throughout the disaster management cycle.

In parallel, regional and international human rights treaty-based monitoring bodies have started applying and interpreting their respective treaties in disaster situations thus clarifying that the integration of human rights into disaster management is a legal obligation and hence reinforcing the need for applying an HRBA.[15]

There have also been several initiatives to improve protection in disaster settings that have taken the form of standard setting exercises[16] or inter-governmental deliberations.[17] The Human Rights Council (HRC) has initiated discussions over the promotion and protection of human rights in post-disaster and post-conflict situations[18] and has started discussing human rights aspects of specific disaster-induced situations, such as in the special session of January 2010 focused on an HRBA to support the recovery process in Haiti.[19] Also within the Universal Periodic Review process, attention has been given to rights-sensitive actions in disaster management. Recommendations to several countries, such as Vietnam, Kuwait, El Salvador, Cuba, Bangladesh, Mozambique, Nepal, Oman, Pakistan, Palau, the Philippines, Solomon Islands and the United States of America, put emphasis on measures and programmes aimed at providing protection and assistance to victims of natural disasters thus emphasising the importance of taking into account protection concerns in all phases of the disaster cycle.[20]

The issue of integrating human rights into disaster management has also been part of the discussions within the International Law Commission (ILC) prior to the adoption of the first reading of the Draft Articles on the protection of persons in the event of disasters (Draft Articles).[21] Indeed, when commenting on Draft Article 2[22] of the draft, several States elaborated on a rights-based approach versus a need-based one.[23] The final view, embedded in the Commentary to Draft Article 2, reflects the prevailing sense of the ILC, namely that the two approaches are not necessarily 'mutually' exclusive but 'complementary'. The formulation settled upon, indeed puts emphasis on the importance of a response to a disaster, and the reduction of the risks thereof, 'that adequately and effectively meets the "needs" of the persons concerned' and that 'has to take place with full respect for the rights of such persons'.[24]

These efforts represent an initial engagement with the human rights' implications of disasters;[25] however, a systematic analysis of the subject is yet to take place and there is limited doctrinal examination of the subject.[26]

Integrating human rights into the disaster management cycle: the work of the UN human rights machinery

A survey of UN treaty bodies' concluding observations and recommendations of thematic and country-specific HRC special procedures shows an increasing trend in analysing States obligations vis-à-vis vulnerable groups and in relations to the enjoyment of specific rights in disaster contexts. This paragraph, focused on the UN practice in this regard, highlights how the UN human rights machinery – treaty- and Charter-based – reaffirms the integration of human rights into disaster management thus calling for an HRBA as a tool to ensure that protection concerns are taken into account in such situations. In the concluding observations to State parties reports, there are various specific recommendations of UN treaty monitoring bodies towards rights-sensitive measures in disaster preparedness, response and recovery.[27]

The Committee on the Protection of the Rights of Persons with Disabilities (CPRD) has emphasised the need for comprehensive plans on disaster risk reduction that are fully accessible and fully inclusive.[28] At its third session, the Committee also decided to establish a working group to follow up the situation in Haiti and other similar disasters around the world, in order to more closely follow issues related to the protection of persons with disabilities in disaster-prone countries in compliance with Article 11 of the Convention on the Rights of Persons with Disabilities that establishes for States parties the obligation to ensure the protection and safety of persons with disabilities in situations of risk, including natural disasters.[29]

The Committee on Economic, Social and Cultural Rights (CESCR) has underlined the need for preventive action to ensure that housing is built in accordance with the rules applicable to earthquake-prone areas, also avoiding construction in areas prone to natural disasters.[30] It has also recommended the adoption of an HRBA to disaster response, risk mitigation and reconstruction efforts, making sure in particular that disaster management plans do not discriminate or lead to discrimination in the enjoyment of economic, social and cultural rights.[31]

On disaster response, the major treaty body deliberations are contained in the General Comments of the CESCR, in particular in General Comment n. 3 on the nature of obligations of States Parties to the International Covenant on Economic, Social and Cultural Rights (ICESCR) that introduces the concept of 'core obligations' to apply at all times regardless of any constraints, including in disaster situations.[32]

Both the Committee on the Elimination of Racial Discrimination (CERD) and the Human Rights Committee (CCPR) have stressed the need to ensure genuine consultation and participation of victims of natural disasters in the design and implementation of all decisions affecting them and to guarantee that rights of the most marginalised groups are fully taken into account in reconstruction plans with particular attention to access to housing, education and healthcare.[33]

The Committee on the Rights of the Child (CRC) has, in various concluding observations, elaborated on the need for States parties to develop strategies and plans aimed at reducing vulnerabilities of and risks for children and families that may be caused or exacerbated by natural disasters, including by incorporating child-specific and child-sensitive risk and vulnerability reduction strategies into national plans on disaster preparedness. It has also stressed the importance of ensuring that the special physical and psychological vulnerabilities and needs of children, as well as their views, are taken into account and that children are fully involved in such policy dialogues.[34] The importance of defining strategic budgetary lines for children in disadvantaged or vulnerable situations who may require affirmative social measures has also been underlined together with the need to ensure that those resources are protected and preserved even in situations of natural disasters in particular as they relate to health and education.[35]

Particular emphasis is also repeatedly given to the need to increase children's awareness and preparedness for climate change and natural disasters by incorporating it into school curricula and teacher training programmes.[36]

The Committee on the Elimination of Discrimination against Women (CEDAW) has stressed that the promotion of gender equality and sensitisation to gender equality issues must be an explicit component of national plans and policies, including in particular those aimed *inter alia* at natural disaster management, and has underlined the importance for such plans to include the concerns of women, particularly those living in rural areas.[37] This treaty body has also pointed to the importance for those plans to target women not only as victims but also as active participants in their development and enactment.[38] It has also called for appropriate measures to eliminate all forms of discrimination against women in relation to access to housing and food aid in natural disaster situations and to ensure that women in such situations are adequately protected from violence.[39]

Special procedures of the HRC have also elaborated on human rights protection in all phases of the disaster management cycle providing specific recommendations both in country-specific reports and thematic studies. Such elaborations constitute a useful reference for clarifying what a human approach to disaster management entails.

The Representative of the Secretary-General and the Special Rapporteur on IDPs have dealt with the issue thoroughly, devoting a specific report to the protection of IDPs in situations of natural disasters[40] and by issuing specific recommendations during visits to disaster-prone countries[41] calling for an HRBA to sustainable development that integrates issues of internal displacement caused by natural disasters. The Special Rapporteur on adequate housing as a component of the right to an adequate standard of living, and on the right to non-discrimination in this context, has also urged for disaster prevention and post-disaster reconstruction processes to be designed within an HRBA explaining how such processes must be carried out in consultation and with the active participation of concerned communities, 'be gender-sensitive, draw upon local knowledge and be culturally appropriate' giving special attention to groups at risk of discrimination and exclusion.[42] This special procedure has also elaborated on the need to integrate human rights standards, and particularly the right to adequate housing, in post-disaster and post-conflict reconstruction processes and has devoted a specific thematic report to measures to improve prevention, relief and rehabilitation efforts in disaster settings.[43] The Special Rapporteur on the sale of children, child prostitution and child pornography has also developed a thematic study on the protection of children from sale and sexual exploitation following a humanitarian crisis due to natural disasters.[44] This report contains a 'detailed outline for the creation and strengthening of comprehensive child protection systems in relation to natural disasters'[45] and provides guidance for better assisting all involved actors 'to effectively evaluate and address the varying levels of risk and vulnerability faced by children in natural disasters'.[46]

While these recommendations all suggest that 'States have specific human rights obligations with regard to all phases of disaster response including disaster prevention and preparedness, evacuation, emergency assistance and relief measures, as well as return and reintegration of those displaced',[47] they also contain specific indications on how to address human rights issues in disaster management and constitute a guidance tool for all stakeholders involved in planning and implementation. Importantly, they also provide evidence of the fact that responses to natural disasters are still too focused on humanitarian assistance and emergency management activities that mainly aim to meet the immediate survival needs of affected groups, and all their recommendations go in the direction of affirming the need to integrate protection issues more systematically so as to ensure a full 'cycle of protection'[48] in disaster management.

A snapshot of disaster management-related policy documents upholding an HRBA

In the late nineties, the UN embarked on a process towards the systematic mainstreaming of human rights into the work of the Organisation. In his 1998 Report on the Work of the Organisation, the then UN Secretary-General Kofi Annan emphasised that 'the promotion of human rights is the common thread running through all activities of the Organization, particularly through every stage of its work on peace and security'[49] and also reported on the implementation by the UN of a rights-based approach to development, which he detailed as being a tool that:

> describes situations not simply in terms of human needs, or of developmental requirements, but in terms of society's obligation to respond to the inalienable rights of individuals, . . . empowers people to demand justice as a right, not as charity, and gives communities a moral basis from which to claim international assistance where needed.[50]

It took a little bit longer for the human rights implications of disaster response to be recognised since 'natural disasters have traditionally been seen as situations that create challenges and problems mainly of a humanitarian nature'.[51]

The IASC Operational Guidelines on the protection of persons in situations of natural disasters (2007)

The IASC Operational Guidelines represents the first policy document containing 'instructions' for humanitarian actors for the full integration of human rights into humanitarian assistance in situations of natural disasters. Adopted by the IASC in 2007, following feedback from their field-testing, they were revised in 2010 through incorporating lessons learned from the field and expanding the rights-based approach to include also preparedness measures.[52]

What are the reasons behind the adoption of an HRBA in situations of natural disaster? The *Introduction* to the Guidelines clarifies that a rights-based approach can help protect persons in situations of natural disasters by grounding the basis for humanitarian action in universal principles, such as human dignity and non-discrimination and a set of universally accepted human rights standards and by considering individuals as rights-holders who can claim their rights from duty-bearers and not as simple passive beneficiaries and recipients of relief. Emphasis is put on the protection role that humanitarian and development actors (the latter more in the recovery phase) 'play to ensuring that the rights of affected individuals under international human rights law, are respected, protected and fulfilled without discrimination'.[53] This perspective of humanitarian action in situations of natural disasters entails a shift from a purely needs-based approach to a rights-based one: rights entail corresponding legal obligations and responsibilities while needs do not. Rights cannot be addressed without questioning who holds the obligations in relation to those rights and can be held accountable.

The IASC Operational Guidelines aim at providing practical guidance to humanitarian actors for adopting a rights-based approach in situations of natural disasters so as to ensure that protection standards are integrated into any disaster response and recovery effort and to identify mechanisms for the consultation and participation of affected persons and their communities in all disaster response phases, in compliance with their human rights. With an operational focus, they are 'informed by and draw on relevant international human rights law, existing standards and policies pertaining to humanitarian action, and human rights guidelines on humanitarian standards in situations of natural disasters'.[54] They encompass the response and recovery phase in situations of natural disasters while they only touch upon, where relevant, issues related to preparedness and risk reduction – since these phases are beyond the scope of the policy document. They also serve the purpose of providing humanitarian actors with a 'basis when entering into dialogue with governments about their obligations towards affected people under human rights law'.[55] Indeed, under human rights law, States have a fourfold obligation to respect human rights, to protect and fulfil them and to discharge these obligations without discrimination.[56] The IASC Operational Guidelines, addressed primarily to humanitarian actors[57] that are not necessarily State entities, influence the above rights-duties relationship by attributing to the international community an important role to play in supplementing and complementing State efforts in those instances where the capacity or/and willingness of the authorities to fulfil their duties are inadequate. The concept of human rights protection in the humanitarian action endeavour, moreover, entails that humanitarian actors play a role with regard 'to ensuring that the rights of affected persons under international human rights law are respected, protected and fulfilled without discrimination'.[58]

Protection activities must respect the principles of humanity, impartiality and neutrality and combat discrimination. Such activities should be structured so as to do no harm[59] to beneficiary populations nor to expose them to further risks; to ensure access to relevant goods, services and opportunities; and to avenues for affected persons to claim their rights. After having set over-arching general principles, the Guidelines spell out key principles relevant for the protection of human rights of persons affected by disasters by grouping them into four sections:

(a) Protection of rights related to the protection of life, personal security and physical integrity; and the protection of family ties in the context of evacuations;
(b) Protection of rights related to the provision of food, health; shelter and education;
(c) Protection of rights related to housing, land and property; and livelihoods;
(d) Protection of rights related to documentation, free movement in the context of durable solutions for IDPs; re-establishment of family ties, expression and opinion; and elections.[60]

As indicated in the *Introduction* to the policy document, users 'may limit themselves to consult category A and B during the immediate emergency phase and turn to C and D at a later stage. This does not entail in any case a hierarchy among relevant rights but it is meant to help quickly identifying those rights primarily relevant during a given phase of a disaster'.[61] For each principle listed under A, B, C and D, the Guidelines provide for a set of practical activities that can be considered in order to ensure the protection of the relevant rights of the persons affected by disasters. This non-exhaustive, non-binding list constitutes a useful pathway for actors planning interventions in disaster situations in designing, developing and implementing actions through a human rights lens.

Policy into 'tools for action': the OHCHR checklists for Integrating Human Rights in Natural Disaster Management in the Pacific *(2007)*

One of the expected results of a workshop jointly organised by OHCHR and UNDP Pacific Centre in Suva, Fiji, on 9 to 11 May 2007 was that of 'developing human rights checklists, specific to the Pacific region, to be used by concerned actors in situations of natural disaster response and preparation'.[62] These Checklists would be a 'dynamic tool that would be revised and expanded as necessary'.[63] The event, titled *Integrating Human Rights in Natural Disaster Management in the Pacific*, saw the participation of UN staff and national and regional counterparts, especially those involved in disaster relief and recovery operations and programming. The Checklists discussed and consolidated during the workshop were then piloted during the Red Cross' Regional

Disaster Management Forum Simulation Exercise on 28 and 30 July 2007 in Suva, Fiji. Feedback from this exercise was incorporated into the final version of the Checklists.[64]

This instrument, tailored for the Pacific region, aims at facilitating the integration of human rights issues in natural disaster management. It is meant to serve as a 'memory trigger' regarding key human rights issues to take into account in the different phases of natural disaster management. As such, it presents a non-exhaustive list of human rights issues that might emerge articulated into three different checklists to help identify them:

(a) Emergency response: contains a set of key 'survival-related' rights that require immediate attention during the emergency response and assessment.[65]
(b) Response and recovery: contains a detailed checklist applicable both during response and recovery. It is structured in four sections based on the key principles relevant for the protection of the human rights of persons affected by disasters as identified in the IASC Operational Guidelines.[66]
(c) Preparedness: provides guidance regarding the key human rights issues to which disaster management teams (at all levels, UN, regional and national) should be alert during natural disaster preparedness activities.[67]

The tools are complemented by a 'companion note on vulnerability'[68] that outlines issues related to vulnerable groups in situations of natural disasters and provides examples for disaster responders of preventive and protective measures to mitigate vulnerability factors.

The added value of the Checklists lies in their practical approach. They translate the IASC Operational Guidelines into a concrete working tool for members of disaster management teams to undertake human-rights sensitive assessments during the different phases of disaster management. Their role as a reminder of the human rights issues to take into consideration during emergency, recovery assessment and operations and to identify potential human rights violations (so-called 'red flags') makes them a flexible and user-friendly tool for incorporating human rights issues into the disaster management cycle. The Checklists also constitute a valuable instrument for further raising awareness of human rights issues in disaster management and a good example of an assessment/information-gathering methodology on human rights issues.

The UNDG Guidance Note for UNCTs on integrating Disaster Risk Reduction into the Common Country Assessment and United Nations Development Assistance Framework (2009)

In 2009 the UNDG[69] adopted a Guidance Note for United Nations Country Teams (UNCTs) on integrating Disaster Risk Reduction (DRR) into the Common Country Assessment (CCA) and UN Development Assistance Framework (UNDAF),[70] as a follow up to the adoption of revised *Guidelines for UN Country Teams on Preparing a CCA and UNDAF*, where the importance of DRR as a crosscutting theme had been repeatedly highlighted.

The Guidance Note is meant to 'provide advice, including links to resources, on how to integrate DRR into the process of CCA/UNDAF preparation, formulation, monitoring and evaluation'.[71] The focus of the document is primarily on disasters caused by vulnerability to natural hazards. The Note provides directions on how to mainstream DDR into the UN system's practice at the national level through a reflection of disaster risk considerations at all stages of the CCA/UNDAF process. In particular, the country analysis phase should 'include the recognition of the risks of crises and natural disasters, as well as capacities for crisis prevention and disaster preparedness'; and during the programme design and planning phase, UNDAFs should 'reflect risks of crises and natural disasters, as well as capacity gaps for crisis prevention and disaster preparedness, as identified in the analysis'.[72]

The *CCA/UNDAF Guidelines* identify five interrelated principles that must be applied throughout the UNDAF: one of these is an HRBA. The Guidance Note specifies that

> [i]ncorporating HRBA into DRR interventions helps to foster awareness and ownership by DRR 'duty-bearers' to meet their obligations towards vulnerable communities. It also helps to ensure that 'rights-holders', particularly the most vulnerable whose rights are often ignored, are empowered to demand greater levels of safety before, during and after disasters.[73]

In relation to this principle, the Guidance Note highlights the advantages of using an HRBA in the context of disaster risk, explaining that this entails a risk analysis based on human rights. The document reaffirms the process and result-oriented nature of an HRBA in disaster settings as it introduces human rights standards and principles[74] into the programming cycle by stressing an express linkage to rights; non-discrimination; and attention to vulnerable groups, participation, empowerment and accountability.

How to integrate an HRBA into the disaster management programming cycle

The 2003 UN Common Understanding on an HRBA to development cooperation identified three complementary criteria that characterise such an approach. The first criterion requires that 'all programmes should further the realization of human rights'.[75] The second establishes that human rights standards and principles[76] should 'guide all programming in all sectors and all phases of the programming process'.[77] The third criterion affirms that programming should 'contribute to the development of capacities of duty-bearers to meet their obligations and of rights-holders to claim their rights'.[78] Based on these three criteria the document lists the '*necessary, specific and unique*' (emphasis added)[79] elements to an HRBA to programming:

(a) Assessment and analysis in order to identify the human rights claims of right-holders and the corresponding human rights obligations of duty-bearers as well as the immediate, underlying and structural causes of the non-realization of rights.
(b) Programmes assess the capacity of right-holders to claim their rights and of duty-bearers to fulfil their obligations. They then develop strategies to build these capacities.
(c) Programmes monitor and evaluate both outcomes and processes guided by human rights standards and principles.
(d) Programming is informed by the recommendations of international human rights bodies and mechanisms.[80]

The UNDG Guidance Note on integrating DRR into the CCA/UNDAF explains the added value of applying an HRBA in disaster risk reduction. An HRBA contributes to the identification of the disasters that can constitute the bigger risks, the areas most likely to be affected and the most vulnerable segments of the population (what is the risk and who is most at risk). It allows for an analysis of the underlying and root causes of the vulnerabilities identified (what are the origins of the problem) and a mapping of actors and institutions responsible for mitigating risks (who are the duty-bearers). It also permits an evaluation of the capacities needed to address disaster risk, both for potential victims of human rights violations due to disaster vulnerability and for those responsible for addressing such issues (what are the capacities needed to address/redress the situation).[81]

In particular, the application of an HRBA to programming helps answering four critical questions:

(a) Who has been left behind and why?
(b) What are they entitled to?
(c) Who has to do something about it?
(d) What capacity do they need to take action?[82]

The first stage of any programming is the carrying out of a *situation analysis.*[83] The carrying out of such an assessment through a human rights lens helps determine the extent of a potential problem and the affected groups. An HRBA adds value to such an assessment by making a correlation between the challenge identified and the human rights obligations stemming from the international instruments ratified by the country at stake. Such an assessment helps to identify possible discrimination and inequality patterns and gives an overview of the situation of marginalised and vulnerable groups.

Once the existence of a problem has been ascertained, the *causality* analysis from a human rights standpoint entails the identification of the causes of the problem through establishing its immediate, underlying and root causes and identifying which rights are at stake. This will result in a list of potential or actual human rights violations, the major factors contributing to such infringements and the actors involved.

A *role-pattern analysis* then allows the identification of the claim/duty on the basis of the causality analysis, determining who the rights-holders and duty-bearers are in relation to specific rights.[84] A *capacity gap analysis* indicates the capacities necessary for duty-bearers to respond to claims and for rights-holders to advocate for the enjoyment of their rights. Such analysis should lead to the identification of 'candidate actions' contributing to reducing the capacity gaps of right-holders and duty-bearers.

Integrating human rights in disaster settings: concluding remarks

The past decade has witnessed an increasing awareness of the importance to support the protection of persons from human rights violations as a central element of the international response to humanitarian crises. This has *inter alia* included the drafting and adoption of new human rights standards, the clarification by UN human rights bodies of the extent of human rights obligations and the strengthening of international coordination for preventing and responding to crises.

At the operational level, the IASC has reaffirmed the fundamental importance of protection in humanitarian action through ensuring respect for international human rights and international humanitarian law. The 2005 humanitarian reform brought the creation of the cluster approach within which the Protection Cluster plays an instrumental role in coordinating the protection response during humanitarian assistance actions. An HRBA to programming, human rights language and protection requirements are contained in most IASC policy guidelines and standards. Furthermore, policy documents of UN agencies and funds have further internalised human rights as a crosscutting element of their mandates and operational work-plans. In 2013, the IASC and UNDG adopted the 'Common Framework For Preparedness',[85] an instrument to ensure coherence and coordination of the international efforts to enhance preparedness in the disaster risk management context[86] that requires all actors, whether focused on humanitarian assistance or development, to develop national and local capacities for preparedness.[87] The aim of preparedness is that of reducing vulnerability and enhancing resilience and protection by applying an HRBA, including through consultation with the affected population and through laws and policies that mitigate the human rights consequences of crises. This instrument is yet another which seeks to foster the application of an HRBA in a disaster management context. Within the Protection Cluster, a set of tools has been developed to this end, with the aim of strengthening protection in natural disaster response.[88] This constitutes a further attempt to provide practical guidance to international and national protection workers for improving their understanding of the rights and vulnerabilities of different groups affected by disasters, identifying and responding to common protection threats and supporting protection and rights-sensitive approaches to post-disaster recovery and rehabilitation.

In December 2013, the IASC Principals,[89] while reaffirming the centrality of protection in humanitarian action, underlined that the imperative for the UN to protect people lies at the heart of humanitarian action and explained that:

> in practical terms this means identifying who is at risk, how and why at the very outset of a crisis and thereafter taking into account the specific vulnerabilities that underlie these risks, including those experienced by men, women, girls and boys, and groups such as IDPs, older person, persons with disabilities, and persons belonging to sexual and other minorities.[90]

In other words an HRBA should be taken towards humanitarian action.

The UN human rights machinery, both treaty- and Charter-based bodies and the Universal Period Review (UPR) system, all call for an HRBA to disaster management, through recommendations that provide guidance on specific actions to undertake in the various disaster management phases. Issues related to disaster management have also been raised and discussed by States during the UPR process. The ILC, in its work on the protection of persons affected by disasters, has also restated the importance of addressing the needs of concerned persons with full respect for their rights. As per States' obligations and role in disaster settings, both the Hyogo and Sendai Framework for Action call for a reinforced attention to human rights implications. Such a trend shows the increasing importance paid to the human rights aspects related to all phases of disasters.

The lessons learned from responses to recent disasters have blatantly shown the need to prioritise capacity building, participation, accountability, non-discrimination and transparency for contributing directly to the realisation of rights. Lessons from the humanitarian response to the Haiti earthquake represent a case in point through having highlighted how the decision to invest in direct service delivery instead of in local capacity development can result in the creation of a 'blank space where help can be infused'.[91] The disaster response and reconstruction phases in that country were indeed not founded on an HRBA, but rather international actors neglected existing infrastructures and created parallel structures,[92] and there was no access for key stakeholders to forums where decisions directly relating to them were taken.

Critics of the Haiti emergency response converge on the fact that aid was largely 'delivered outside the human rights framework, with a focus on distributions to meet immediate needs at the cost of investing in long-term infrastructure and structural reform'.[93] The Independent Expert on the situation of human rights in Haiti stressed several times that:

> [t]he rights-based approach is not a conceptual approach, but rather one that requires a change of paradigm, as it calls first and foremost for special attention to be paid to those who are the most vulnerable, women, children and disabled persons. It also systematically involves civil society organizations, in particular those representing women,

> farmers and vulnerable groups, in the reconstruction effort, and includes gender-specific analyses and concrete gender-equality targets in reconstruction plans and budgets. . . . The rights-based approach is aimed firstly at taking into consideration the needs and aspirations of Haitians themselves so as to restore a more decentralized and sustainable development capable of protecting the population against natural hazards. It is also an approach that makes it possible to ensure that reconstruction is equitable, specifically seeking equality between the wealthiest and the less prosperous regions, with the objective of creating a more fair society.[94]

In order to be successful, disaster responses must place human rights at their core.

An HRBA programming methodology that identifies rights and duties, explores why these cannot be realised, evaluates the extent of the capacity gap and seeks to close such gaps by developing sustainable local capacity[95] represents a valuable tool for the practical integration of human rights into the disaster management programme cycle. The progressive boost towards the systematic upholding of such an approach given by UN treaty bodies, special procedures and policy-making organs such as the HRC, is building to a gradual affirmation and recognition of the fact that an HRBA to disaster management is a result of international obligations. This is also sustained by the steady introduction of an HRBA to disaster management as a programming tool into national regulatory frameworks and into national and international policies for humanitarian aid and assistance.

Notes

1 See the debates in HRC sessions on best practices and challenges in the promotion and protection of human rights in post-disaster situations and the adoption by such organ of HRC, Res 22/16: Promotion and Protection of Human Rights in Post-Disaster and Post-Conflict Situations, UN Doc. A/HRC/RES/22/16 (10 April 2013), or discussions at the Third UN World Conference on Disaster Risk Reduction.

2 UNGA, Res 69/283, UN Doc. A/Res/69/283 (15 June 2015) Annex II, Sendai Framework for Disaster Risk Reduction 2015–2030.

3 UNDG, Guidance Note for UN Country Teams (UNCTs) on Integrating DRR into the Common Country Assessment (CCA) and United Nations Development Assistance Framework (UNDAF) (2009) 11.

4 Ibid.

5 IFRC, 'About Disaster Management', available at www.ifrc.org/en/what-we-do/disaster-management/about-disaster-management/, accessed on 6 June 2017; UNISDR, 'UNISDR Terminology on Disaster Risk Reduction', available at www.unisdr.org/files/7817_UNISDRTerminologyEnglish.pdf, accessed on 6 June 2017.

6 OHCHR, 'Frequently Asked Questions on a Human Rights-Based Approach to Development Cooperation (2006)', available at www.ohchr.org/Documents/Publications/FAQen.pdf, accessed on 6 June 2017, 15.

7 IASC, 'The Human Rights-Based Approach to Development Cooperation: Towards a Common Understanding among the United Nations Agencies'. Second Inter-Agency Workshop, Stamford, USA (May 2003), available at https://undg.org/wp-content/uploads/2015/05/6959-The_Human_Rights_Based_Approach_to_Development_Cooperation_Towards_a_Common_Understanding_among_UN1.pdf, accessed on 6 June 2017.

8 UN Evaluation Group (UNEG), Integrating Human Rights and Gender Equality in Evaluations, Guidance Document (2014) 10.

9 M. Darrow and A. Tomas, 'Power, Capture, and Conflict: A Call for Human Rights Accountability in Development Cooperation' 27(2) *Human Rights Quarterly* (2005) 486, 506.

10 OHCHR (n. 6) 15.

11 OHCHR, 'Protection of Internally Displaced Persons in Situations of Natural Disaster: A Working Visit to Asia by the Representative of the United Nations Secretary-General on the Human Rights of

Internally Displaced Persons Walter Kälin', 27 February to 5 March 2005 (2005), available at www.ohchr.org/Documents/Issues/IDPersons/Tsunami.pdf, accessed on 6 June 2017, 5.

12 Ibid 6, 28–30.

13 Ibid 30.

14 HRC, Report of the Representative of the Secretary-General on Human Rights of Internally Displaced Persons, Walter Kälin: Addendum, Operational Guidelines on Human Rights and Natural Disasters, UN Doc. A/HRC/4/38/Add.1 (23 January 2006). The Guidelines were endorsed by the IASC Working Group in June 2007.

15 For a thorough analysis through this lens, see M. Hesselman, 'Establishing a Full "Cycle of Protection" for Disaster Victims: Preparedness, Response and Recovery According to Regional and International Human Rights Supervisory Bodies' 18 *Tilburg Law Review* (2013) 106–132.

16 See in this regard the analytical guide on the work of the ILC Special Rapporteur Valencia-Ospina and the discussions in the ILC to date available at http://legal.un.org/ilc/guide/6_3.shtml, accessed on 6 June 2017. Or, the African Union Convention for the Protection and Assistance of Internally Displaced Persons (adopted 23 October 2009, entered into force 6 December 2012).

17 See UNGA, Hyogo Framework for Action 2005–2015: Building the Resilience of Nations and Communities to Disasters, UN Doc. A/CONF.206/6, Resolution 2 (16 March 2005), available at www.unisdr.org/2005/wcdr/intergover/official-doc/L-docs/Hyogo-framework-for-action-english.pdf, accessed on 6 June 2017.

18 See HRC, Res 22/16 (n. 1). Refer also to HRC, Final Research-Based Report of the Human Rights Council Advisory Committee on Best Practices and Main Challenges in the Promotion and Protection of Human Rights in Post-Disaster and Post-Conflict Situations, UN Doc. A/HCR/28/76 (10 February 2015); HRC, Progress Report on the Research-Based Report of the Human Rights Council Advisory Committee on Best Practices and Main Challenges in the Promotion and Protection of Human Rights in Post-Disaster and Post-Conflict Situations, UN Doc. A/HRC/27/57 (11 August 2014).

19 The resolution adopted, the reports presented and the statements issued at that session are available at www.ohchr.org/EN/HRBodies/HRC/SpecialSessions/Session13/Pages/13thSpecialSession.aspx, accessed on 6 June 2017.

20 Such recommendations were made during consideration of those countries within the first and second UPR cycle. A summary of them is available through a search in the UPR database of recommendations, available at www.upr-info.org/database/, accessed on 23 October 2016.

21 ILC, Eight Report on the Protection of Persons in the Event of Disasters, UN Doc. A/CN.4/697 (17 March 2016). This issue is only briefly mentioned here since it is the subject of specific analysis of McDermott's chapter in this volume.

22 Art 2 reads as follows: '[t]he purpose of the present draft articles is to facilitate the adequate and effective response to disasters and reduction of risks of disasters, so as to meet the essential needs of the persons concerned, with full respect for their rights'. UNGA, Report of the International Law Commission, Sixty-Eight Session 2016, UN Doc. A/71/70 (18 August 2016) paras 49, 19.

23 A summary of the views of States in this regard is reported in A/CN.4/697 (n. 21) para 39:

> The Nordic States, Austria, the Russian Federation, Spain, Thailand, France, Slovenia, Poland, Ireland, New Zealand, the European Union and IFRC expressed their satisfaction with the balance the Commission struck by emphasizing the importance of meeting the victims' needs while affirming their entitlement to full respect for their rights. The Netherlands, the United States, the United Kingdom, Myanmar, Malaysia, the Islamic Republic of Iran and Israel doubted the practical value of a rights-based approach and emphasized the importance of taking into account the victims' needs in disaster situations. Conversely, Portugal, Greece and Romania supported a rights-based approach. China and Japan expressed the need to clarify the content of the rights-based approach. Austria, the Islamic Republic of Iran, Pakistan and Spain pointed to the need to take into account the rights and obligations of States as well. Chile, the Russian Federation and Thailand recalled the importance of referring to all categories of human rights, including economic, social and cultural rights.

A/71/70 (n. 22) paras 49, 20.

24 Ibid.

25 On this issue see also E. Ferris, 'How Can International Human Rights Law Protect Us from Disasters?' Paper prepared for the ASIL Annual Meeting (10 April 2014) 21, available at www.brookings.edu/wp-content/uploads/2016/07/EFerris-ASIL-Human-Rights-and-Disasters-20140410.pdf, accessed on 6 June 2017.

26 Indeed the analysis carried out in the present chapter is mainly based on UN operational and policy documents, on reports of UN Charter- and treaty-based mechanisms and on the deliberations of policy-making organs.

27 The main recommendations by treaty bodies are reproduced by relevant treaty.

28 CRDP, Concluding Observations on the Initial Report of Azerbaijan, UN Doc. CRDP/C/AZE/CO/1 (2 May 2014) para 25; CRDP, Concluding Observations on the Initial Report of Australia, UN Doc. CRPD/C/AUS/CO/1 (21 October 2013) para 23.

29 CRPD, Report of the Third Session of the Conference of States Parties to the Convention on the Rights of Persons with Disabilities, UN Doc. CRPD/CSP/2010/3 (16 December 2010).

30 CESCR, Concluding Observations of the Committee on Economic, Social and Cultural Rights Morocco, UN Doc. E/C.12/MAR/CO/3 (4 September 2006) para 51; CESCR, Concluding Observations of the Committee on Economic, Social and Cultural Rights: El Salvador, UN Doc. E/C.12/SLV/CO/2 (27 June 2007) para 39.

31 CESCR, Concluding Observations on the Third Periodic Report on Japan, UN Doc. E/C.12/JPN/CO/3 (10 June 2013) para 24.

32 CESCR, General Comment No. 3: The Nature of States Parties' Obligations (Article 2) para 1, UN Doc. E/1991/23 (14 December 1990). Also the CEDAW in its General Recommendation 27 states that State parties should ensure that climate change- and disaster risk-reduction measures are gender-responsive and sensitive to the needs and vulnerabilities of older women and that they should also facilitate the participation of older women in decision-making for climate change mitigation and adaptation. See CommEDAW, General Recommendation No. 27 on Older Women and Protection of Their Human Rights, UN Doc. CEDAW/C/GC/27 (16 December 2010) para 35. CESCR has dealt with the issue also in other General Comments. These are respectively: UNCESCR, General Comment No. 12: The Right to Adequate Food (Article 11), UN Doc. E/C.12/1999/5 (12 May 1999) paras 12–13; CESCR, General Comment No. 14: The Right to the Highest Standard of Health, UN Doc. E/C.12/2000/4 (11 August 2000) paras 6, 15, 17; CESCR, General Comment No. 15: The Right to Water (Articles 11 and 12), UN Doc. E/C.12/2002/11 (20 January 2003) paras 16, 60; CESCR, General Comment No. 4: The Right to Adequate Housing (Article 11 (1) of the Covenant), Contained in UN Doc. E/1992/23 (1 January 1992) para 8.

33 CCPR, Concluding Observations of the Human Rights Committee United States of America, UN Doc. CCPR/C/USA/CO/3/ Rev.1 (18 December 2006) para 26; CommERD, Concluding Observations of the Committee on the Elimination of Racial Discrimination on the United States of America, UN Doc. CERD/C/USA/CO/6 (8 May 2008) para 28.

34 CommRC, Concluding Observations on the Combined Third and Fourth Periodic Reports of Jamaica, UN Doc. CRC/C/JAM/CO/3–4 (10 March 2015) para 51; CommRC, Concluding Observations on the Combined Second to Fourth Periodic Reports of Fiji, UN Doc. CRC/C/FJI/CO/2–4 (13 October 2014) para 56; CommRC, Concluding Observations: The Philippines, UN Doc. CRC/C/PHL/CO/3–4 (22 October 2009) paras 20, 60.

35 CommRC, Concluding Observations on the Combined Third and Fourth Periodic Reports of Jamaica, UN Doc. CRC/C/JAM/CO/3–4 (10 March 2015) para 51; CommRC, Concluding Observations: Guatemala, UN Doc. CRC/C/GTM/CO/3–4 (25 October 2010) para 26; CommRC, Concluding Observations: Madagascar, UN Doc. CRC/C/MDG/CO/3–4 (8 March 2012) para 18.

36 CommRC, Concluding Observations on the Initial Report of Tuvalu, Adopted by the Committee at Its Sixty-Fourth Session, UN Doc. CRC/C/TUV/CO/1 (30 October 2013) para 56; CommRC, Concluding Observations on the Combined Second to Fourth Periodic Reports of Fiji, UN Doc. CRC/C/FJI/CO/2–4 (13 October 2014) para 56; CommRC, Concluding Observations: The Philippines, UN Doc. CRC/C/PHL/CO/3–4 (22 October 2009) paras 20, 60.

37 CommEDAW, Concluding Comments of the Committee on the Elimination of Discrimination against Women: Indonesia, UN Doc. CEDAW/C/IDN/CO/5 (10 August 2007) para 39; CommEDAW, Concluding Observations of the Committee on the Elimination of Discrimination against Women Grenada, UN Doc. CEDAW/C/GRD/CO/1–5 (23 March 2012) para 36; CommEDAW, Concluding Observations on the Fifth and Sixth Periodic Reports of Chile, UN Doc. CEDAW/C/CHL/CO/5–6 (2 November 2012) para 39; CommEDAW, Concluding Observations of the Committee on the Elimination of Discrimination against Women Jamaica, UN Doc. CEDAW/C/JAM/CO/6–7 (6 August 2012) para 32 (b); CEDAW, Concluding Observations of the Committee on the Elimination of Discrimination against Women Tuvalu, UN Doc. CEDAW/C/TUV/CO/2 (7 August 2009) paras 55–56; CommEDAW, Concluding Observations of the Committee on the Elimination of Discrimination against Women Jamaica, UN Doc. CEDAW/C/JAM/CO/6–7 (6 August 2012) para 32(b).

38 CommEDAW, Concluding Observations on the Combined Initial to Third Periodic Reports of Solomon Islands, UN Doc. CEDAW/C/SLB/CO/1–3 (14 November 2014) para 41.
39 CommEDAW, Concluding Comments of the Committee on the Elimination of Discrimination against Women: Indonesia, UN Doc. CEDAW/C/IDN/CO/5 (10 August 2007) para 39.
40 See HRC, Report of the Representative of the Secretary-General on the Human Rights of Internally Displaced Persons, Walter Kälin: Addendum Protection of Internally Displaced Persons in Situations of Natural Disasters, UN Doc. A/HRC/10/13/Add.1 (5 March 2009).
41 See for all HRC, Report of the Special Rapporteur on the Human Rights of Internally Displaced Persons, Chaloka Beyani Addendum, Mission to Maldives, UN Doc. A/HRC/19/54/Add.1 (30 January 2012).
42 HRC, Report of the Special Rapporteur on Adequate Housing as a Component of the Right to an Adequate Standard of Living, and on the Right to Non-Discrimination in This Context, Raquel Rolnik, on Her Mission to Maldives (18–26 February 2009), UN Doc. A/HRC/13/20/Add.3 (11 January 2011) para 71. On these aspects, see Rolnik's chapter and Nifosi's chapter in this volume.
43 HRC, Report of the Special Rapporteur on Adequate Housing as a Component of the Right to an Adequate Standard of Living, and on the Right to Non-Discrimination in This Context, Raquel Rolnik, UN Doc. A/HRC/16/42 (20 December 2010).
44 HRC, Report of the Special Rapporteur on the Sale of Children, Child Prostitution and Child Pornography, Najat Maalla M'jid, UN Doc. A/HRC/19/63 (21 December 2011).
45 Ibid para 12.
46 Ibid.
47 HRC, Report of the Representative of the Secretary-General on the Human Rights of Internally Displaced Persons, Walter Kälin: Addendum Protection of Internally Displaced Persons in Situations of Natural Disasters, UN Doc. A/HRC/10/13/Add.1 (5 March 2009) para 7.
48 Ibid paras 21–27. This expression has been used by Walter Kälin who has been calling for the establishment of a 'cycle of protection that constantly adapts to the challenges posed by natural hazards and optimizes protection to those affected in order to mitigate the impact of disasters, prevent displacement and other negative consequences, and find durable solutions'.
49 UNSG, Report of the Secretary-General on the Work of the Organization, UN Doc. A/53/1 (27 August 1998) para 172.
50 Ibid para 174.
51 IASC, *Operational Guidelines on the Protection of Persons in Situations of Natural Disasters* (The Brookings – Bern Project on Internal Displacement, 2011) 2.
52 Ibid v.
53 Ibid 6.
54 Ibid 9.
55 Ibid 8.
56 Ibid 5–6.
57 Though, as explained in the document, the Operational Guidelines are also useful for those governmental actors, in particular disaster management institutions, primarily tasked with providing protection and humanitarian assistance to affected persons, and can also inform national laws and policies. Ibid 6.
58 Ibid.
59 The 'do no harm' principle, developed by M.B. Anderson in the 1990s, has developed into an approach, being then embedded in various sets of principles that constitute an operational framework for humanitarian actors. The essence of such principle entails that all those involved in humanitarian response must do all they reasonably can to avoid exposing people affected by disaster or armed conflict to further harm. See The Sphere Project, Humanitarian Charter and Minimum Standards in Humanitarian Response (2011), available at www.spherehandbook.org/en/the-humanitarian-charter/, accessed on 6 June 2017.
60 Ibid 9 and 15 ff. The activities all have the aim to prevent or stop harm; to ensure that victims have access to goods, services and opportunities and can claim their rights; and to avoid or combat discrimination.
61 Ibid 10.
62 OHCHR and UNDP Pacific Centre, Regional Office for the Pacific, Integrating Human Rights in Natural Disaster Management in the Pacific (2007), available at http://pacific.ohchr.org/docs/CD_Booklet_final.pdf, accessed on 6 June 2017.
63 Ibid 3.
64 OHCHR and UNDP, Regional Office for the Pacific, Checklists for Integrating Human Rights in Natural Disaster Management in the Pacific (2007), available at www.undp.org/content/dam/rbap/docs/Research%20&%20Publications/CPR/PC_Checklist_HR_DRM.pdf, accessed on 6 June 2017.

65 Ibid 1, 7 ff.
66 Ibid 2, 10 ff.
67 Ibid 2, 18 ff.
68 Ibid 28 ff.
69 Details on its mandate and composition are available at https://undg.org/home/about-undg/, accessed on 6 June 2017.
70 UNDG (n. 3).
71 Ibid 8.
72 Ibid.
73 Ibid 12.
74 The principles are those identified in the Common Understanding: universality and inalienability, indivisibility, inter-dependence and inter-relatedness, non-discrimination and equality, participation and inclusion, accountability and the rule of law. As stated in Stamford, they should 'guide all programming in all phases of the programming process, including assessment and analysis, programme planning and design (including setting of goals, objectives and strategies); implementation, monitoring and evaluation'. IASC (n. 7) 2.
75 IASC (n. 7) 1.
76 Human rights *standards* – contained in human rights instruments – define the benchmarks for desirable outcomes, while human rights *principles* – universality and inalienability, indivisibility, inter-dependence and inter-relatedness, equality and non-discrimination, participation and inclusion, accountability and the rule of law – constitute the conditions for the process.
77 IASC (n. 7) 1.
78 Ibid.
79 Ibid 3.
80 Ibid.
81 UNDG (n. 3) 19. See also OHCHR (n. 6) 27.
82 UNDG, Guidance Note on the Application of the Programming Principles to the UNDAF (January 2010) 9, available at https://undg.org/wp-content/uploads/2016/09/Five-Programming-Principles.pdf, accessed on 6 June 2017.
83 A situational analysis refers to a process of gaining understanding of the current situation in the area/theme/location of interest. Typically this is done by identifying the key factors influencing the situation considered, problems and their causes, as well as the needs, interests, capacities and constraints of the various relevant stakeholders.
84 See UNDP, Human Rights-based Reviews of UNDP Programmes Working Guidelines (2003); UNFPA, HRBA Checklist of Questions, a Human Rights-Based Approach to Programming: Practical Implementation Manual and Training Materials (2010), available at https://undg.org/wp-content/uploads/2015/02/HRBA-Checklist-UNFPA.pdf, accessed on 6 June 2017.
85 IASC/UNDG, Common Framework for Preparedness (18 February 2013).
86 The Framework is 'common' in the sense that it requires all actors (whether development or humanitarian ones) to develop national and local capacity for preparedness at the country level taking into account both national and international capacities for preparedness.
87 This represents a commitment by the IASC, the International Strategy for Disaster Reduction and UNDG to make the development of preparedness capacity at the country level more systematic and coherent.
88 It encompasses several areas of protection in the context of disaster response: evacuations, children, women and girls, persons with disabilities, older persons, mental disorders and psychosocial stress, the rule of law, housing, land and property. See Global Protection Cluster, Strengthening Protection in Disaster Response, GPC Natural Disaster Reference Sheets, available at www.globalprotectioncluster.org/en/tools-and-guidance/essential-protection-guidance-and-tools/protection-in-natural-disasters-essential-guidance-and-tools.html, accessed on 6 June 2017.
89 The IASC Principals are the heads (or designated representatives) of the UN operational agencies (UNDP, UNICEF, UNHCR, WFP, FAO, WHO, UN-HABITAT, OCHA and IOM). In addition, there is a standing invitation to ICRC, IFRC, OHCHR, UNFPA, the Special Rapporteur on the Human Rights of IDPs and the World Bank. The NGO consortia ICVA, InterAction and SCHR are also invited on a permanent basis to attend. The IASC is chaired by the ERC.
90 IASC, The Centrality of Protection in Humanitarian Action: Statement by the Inter-Agency Standing Committee (IASC) Principals (17 December 2013). Such a statement follows the Report of the Secretary

General's Internal Review Panel on United Nations Action in Sri Lanka of 2012 that unveils 'significant challenges that the United Nations may face in retaining the essential support of a government to help in delivering assistance while at the same time responding to serious violations of international law'. Although referred to an armed conflict situation – that of Sri Lanka – the report discloses critical issues the humanitarian community faces in addressing human rights concerns while delivering humanitarian assistance that are applicable to any humanitarian crisis – from armed conflicts, to situations of violence and insecurity including natural and human-made disasters – and that can lead to a protection implementation gap. At the core of the Sri Lanka report's main finding there is the lack of an adequate and shared sense of responsibility for responding to international human rights violations within the United Nations system. See in this regard IASC, The Centrality of Protection in Humanitarian Action. Statement by the Inter-Agency Standing Committee (IASC) Principals (17 December 2013) 3.

91 B. Concannon and B. Lindstrom, 'Cheaper, Better, Longer-Lasting: A Rights-Based Approach to Disaster Response in Haiti' 25 *Emory International Law Review* (2011) 1191.

92 Ibid 1177.

93 Ibid 1148.

94 HRC, Report of the Independent Expert on the Situation of Human Rights in Haiti, Michel Forst, UN Doc. A/HRC/20/35 (23 April 2012) paras 64–65.

95 World Bank and Organisation for Economic Co-Operation and Development, *Integrating Human Rights into Development: Donor Approaches, Experiences, and Challenges* (2nd edn, World Bank, 2013) 85–86, available at https://openknowledge.worldbank.org/bitstream/handle/10986/12800/9780821396216.pdf, accessed on 7 June 2017.

10

NON-STATE HUMANITARIAN ACTORS AND HUMAN RIGHTS IN DISASTER SCENARIOS

Normative role, standard setting and accountability

Tommaso Natoli

Setting the scene: the legal position of Non-State Humanitarian Actors in disaster-related human rights issues

Despite the huge number of relevant studies on the subject,[1] the complex analysis concerning the role of Non-State Actors (NSAs) in the international protection of human rights still poses several challenges, and no appropriate methodology seems to have been found yet, which would generally assess from a theoretical perspective the role played by those actors in contemporary international legal system.[2]

Nevertheless, in order to move ahead on this track, a focus on the distinction between 'subjects' and 'actors' seems to be crucial.[3] Assuming that the second category includes the first, this would encompass both those entities formally bounded by international norms and those which actively operate within the social base of the international legal order, gaining a relevant role in it by conducts and initiatives which are reflected in its (ascendant and descendant) normative processes. Therefore, a shift from the traditional concept of international legal personality, setting the theoretical framework as the 'theory of actors in international law' as suggested by some scholars, appears instrumental to a consistent analysis of the conduct of those actors within the International Disaster Law (IDL) domain. In fact, even if eventual hesitancies against this perspective are comprehensible, it has to be considered that IDL represents a context where theory profoundly merges with practice. In disaster-related issues, the agency of non-state entities is likely to have relevant consequences on proper systemic dynamics as law-making and liability, also in the light of their capacity to carry out public-like functions in emergency situations in which the host State could temporarily fail.

In any case, to reduce the gap between theory and practice does not necessarily support the putative existence of a broader constitutional order formed by different actors in terms of 'factors and forces', in which public-private partnership would have a well-established role in a multi-level normative system. On the contrary, it demonstrates that we are dealing with a wavering process that still presents a 'set of failings' and structural deficiencies.[4] Accordingly, in the absence of effective enforcement mechanisms, to impose international obligations on NSAs would be a vain effort that would also weaken States' responsibilities to ensure compliance with international law, still based on a more effective State-centred paradigm.[5]

Having said that, the above-mentioned shift in the *subject-actors* discourse seems today not so astonishing as it might have appeared a few decades ago, and it appears as even more necessary if the emphasis is put on the respect and application of human rights, as legally recognised, in the course of disaster management activities. Without a doubt, reasoning on human rights law is reasoning on the need to promote the implementation of their core values, and this inevitably pushes to reconsider the importance of the notion of *subject*, 'to focus more pragmatically on the actual scope of application of international obligations'.[6]

Even if the category of NSAs comprises several type of entities, the present analysis will focus on some major humanitarian actors involved in disaster relief – Non-Governmental Organisations (NGOs) and Red Cross/Red Crescent entities, here defined as Non-State Humanitarian Actors (NSHAs)[7] – in the light of their increasing role in international law-making (both *soft* and *hard*)[8] and accountability processes. As proved in the past, the normative role of non-governmental entities appears as most effective when specific fields of law pass through a phase of innovation, as was for Amnesty International in the development of international legal standards prohibiting torture in the 1970s, for the International Campaign to Ban Landmines (ICBL) successes in the 1990s and for the 'crucial role' of a group of NGOs in the negotiation of the International Criminal Court's statute.[9]

As will be demonstrated, this influential position looks even brighter for the IDL, still considered as an emerging sector of international law. The aim of this contribution is, in fact, to assess if the implementation of consistent practices by private humanitarian actors, and the legitimacy that their engagement can acquire, may ultimately integrate the States' monopoly in the production and application of international norms concerning the protection of individual rights in disaster scenarios. Since the agency of NSHAs in this respect includes several projects and initiatives, where the different aspects – law-making, standard setting, compliance and accountability – blend into each other, the chapter will focus on three selected examples, each of which deals with one of those specific functions.

The role of the International Federation of Red Cross and Red Crescent Societies as (soft) law-maker and its impact on human rights protection

As generally recognised, IDL currently represents a fragmented and amorphous sector of public international law, due to the lack of a so-called 'flagship treaty' which would shape its general framework and systematise rights and duties of the involved actors.[10] According to that, it is not possible to mention substantial examples of how the international civil society participated in a formal interstate normative process, as was the case for instance of the Ottawa Mine Ban Treaty (1997).[11]

Even so, thanks to their noteworthy advocacy techniques and the incomparable expertise gained in the field, some humanitarian organisations are effectively contributing to the creation, development and interpretation of this field of law, exerting a considerable influence on its scope and dictates and thus having a direct impact on the protection of concerned peoples. One of the most significant examples of this dynamic is represented by the direct involvement of the International Federation of the Red Cross and Red Crescent Societies (IFRC)[12] within the work of the United Nations International Law Commission (ILC), which – since 2007 – is committed to a codification effort on the *Protection of Persons in the Event of Disasters*, recently approved in second reading after a consultation phase with States and relevant international organisations.[13]

Since the preliminary phase, as evidenced by the content of a *Background Study* produced by the UN Secretariat and mainly intended to provide an overview of the legal framework on the subject, several instruments developed by the Red Cross Movement, have been cited as key points of references.[14] Consequently, the eight reports drawn up by Eduardo Valencia-Ospina, the Special Rapporteur (SR) on the topic, clearly demonstrate his intention to directly involve within the process, from its early stage, the most relevant humanitarian actors. In the attempt to identify the basic assumptions that should have informed the work of the ILC, the SR described how he undertook to establish initial contacts with representatives of the governmental and non-governmental organisations concerned, including senior officials of the International Disaster Response Laws, Rules and Principles Programme of the IFRC, and how he took into account several findings of the IFRC's research outcomes and documents.[15]

In this regard, we can state that the contribution of the IFRC, which in 2007 was committed to the publication of a set of operational guidelines for disaster response and therefore pushed for the elaboration of a different but complementary tool,[16] has been crucial in defining the perspective of the Draft Articles, such as the one on individual protection in disaster contexts and therefore in suggesting a definite rights-based approach aimed at the identification of a specific standard of treatment to which an individual is entitled. This approach – representing among others one of the main postulates of the Project – has been clearly described by the SR who, paraphrasing the Secretary-General, reported that

> a rights-based approach deals with situations not simply in terms of human needs, but in terms of society's obligation to respond to the inalienable rights of individuals, empowers them to demand justice as a right, not as a charity, and gives communities a moral basis from which to claim international assistance when needed.[17]

Sharing the assumptions contained in a Desk Study of the IFRC on the subject,[18] the SR recognised that 'IDRL draws on international human rights law and international law on refugees and internally displaced persons'.[19] Another excerpt of one of the Reports describes how: 'IFRC has suggested that a rights-based approach to the topic may be complemented by considering the relevance of needs in the protection of persons in the event of disasters. The Special Rapporteur believes that such an exercise can be usefully undertaken in this context' and that 'a reasonable, holistic approach to the topic seems to require that both rights and needs enter the equation, complementing each other when appropriate'.[20] Also, in the SR's view 'defining a new, comprehensive legal framework for all actors involved in a post-disaster response would seem unnecessary, for it could overlap with work already done in the [IFRC] Guidelines' and thus

> the Commission could usefully start by focusing its efforts on rights and duties of States for guaranteeing the protection of persons in the event of disasters . . . without prejudice to specific provisions that [it] would discuss at a later stage, applicable to non-State actors.[21]

In the formulation of a specific duty for a State to seek assistance when its national capacity to respond to a catastrophic event is overstretched, considered as an element of the fulfilment of its primary responsibilities under international human rights law, the SR once again made reference to the IFRC Guidelines, which affirm that '[i]f an affected State determines that a disaster situation exceeds national coping capacities, it should seek international and/or regional assistance to address the needs of affected persons'.[22] Moreover, the IFRC's Guidelines inspired the SR in expanding the notion of quality conditions in order to include coordination efforts and the quality of personnel beyond that of the goods themselves, as well as in binding the affected State's selectivity to the respect of human dignity of the affected people, all elements with obvious repercussions on the fulfilment of people's rights.[23]

But the consideration of the role and expertise of the IFRC has not been limited to the work of the SR. In fact, for the first time in its history, the Federation has been invited to participate to the process of analysis and comment held within the Sixth Committee of the United Nations General Assembly (UNGA), with an analogous role of that of the other member States. Among the comments expressed in that guise, the one on the purpose of the Project is particularly relevant for the present analysis, considering the Federation's appreciation of 'the Commission's acknowledgement of [its] traditional approach to disaster response, which was based on needs but informed by rights'. Moreover, the IFRC stated that

> [h]uman rights must be considered a critical component of the regulatory framework for disaster response; in particular, humanitarian assistance was a fundamental right, as affirmed in the Principles and Rules for Red Cross and Red Crescent Disaster Relief. At the same time, not all practical problems could be solved using a rights-based approach, as the Commission acknowledged in its report.[24]

Likewise, in relation to the above-mentioned 'duty to seek' assistance for the affected State, the IFRC's comment presented within the sixth Committee highlighted that

> it strongly supported the Commission's conclusion that affected States had a duty to seek international support if their domestic capacity was exceeded. . . . However, States were not required under general human rights law to seek assistance from any specific actor. The draft article should be reworded to make it clear that States were free to request assistance from any of the enumerated actors or from others not mentioned.[25]

IFRC presented its observations on almost each of the 21 Draft Articles, which became 18 in second reading.[26] Of course not every position expressed has been reflected within the final text, as for instance the need to determine the scope of an individual right to humanitarian assistance 'plainly implied in numerous human rights instruments'.[27] In the Federation's view, '[m]uch depended . . . on the nature of such assistance and the form that it took, *not having an international actor carte blanche to respond to a natural disaster without regard to domestic authorities and laws*' (emphasis added).[28] In the consultation phase preceding the adoption of the final text in second reading, the IFRC made further remarks on the issues concerning the protection of human rights and human dignity, the emphasis on which has been considered as a strong element of the Project.[29] Contextually, it observed that 'certain rights issues that were of frequent concern in disaster settings' could usefully be 'underlined' in order to provide additional operative specifications for the stakeholders and improve the real impact of those provisions during the operations.[30]

The above reconstruction of the incisive role that the IFRC had in the codification process undertaken by the ILC is a meaningful example of how a humanitarian organisation can affect the production of international norms, by providing an 'external' perspective based on its peculiar set of values and experience. In this respect, as demonstrated in relation to the issue of the existence of an individual right to humanitarian assistance, such dynamic could represent a fruitful counterbalance for the States, usually taking positions shaped on political considerations and national interests. At the same time, while this type of 'interference' could pave the way for progressive evolutions of positive law, it can also be a source of headlong rushes and inconsistencies which could lead to dysfunctional outcomes, as demonstrated in the following paragraph.

The role of NSHAs as (aspirational) standard-setters and the risk of inconsistencies

The relationship between the law as positively stated in the black letter of the treaties and the way in which individual rights are interpreted and implemented by NSHAs, through the autonomous identification of specific standards, is an element deserving particular consideration. Their role has not, in fact, been limited to participation in traditional dynamics of codification and progressive development of international law, but it has been very incisive also in horizontal regulatory initiatives, the importance of which is obviously stressed by the fact that the international legal order cannot directly address their conducts.

As generally known, self-standard-setting is a significant function that has been widely put in practice in humanitarian-related issues since the mid-1990s, a period of rapid expansion of the sector and of the budget allocated to it.[31] The first systematic attempt to increase the professional skills and reliability of humanitarian organisations by the establishment of common standards can be detected in the aftermath of the Rwandan crisis of 1994, which was a momentous event in this sense, highlighting all the drawbacks and weaknesses of the humanitarian system and in particular its shortcomings in terms of efficiency and accountability. For the first time, the unconditioned acceptance of the 'good work' done by humanitarian agencies was severely questioned.[32]

A significant attempt to enhance the coherence and professional skills of the sector came from the Red Cross and Red Crescent Movement. In 1994 the IFRC, in collaboration with Oxfam and under the auspices of the Steering Committee for Humanitarian Response (SCHR),[33] presented the 'Code of Conduct for the International Red Cross and Red Crescent Movement and NGOs in Disaster Relief' (Code).[34] The Code represents one of the first self-policing instruments, conceived to establish a set of written principles and rules that would have lead the humanitarian personnel in disaster-response scenarios.

In this regard, it should be pointed out that the text makes no references to human rights *per se*, since its ethical framework is based on the seven principles of the Red Cross Movement and in particular those extrapolated by the landmark UNGA Resolution 46/182 of 1991 (namely humanity, neutrality and impartiality).[35] In this important, as well as relatively 'rudimentary', instrument,[36] the humanitarian imperatives are the underlying values and its whole text – even if the principle of impartiality implies the right of not being discriminated and the respect of culture and custom can be connected to certain individual rights – represents the typical needs-based approach to humanitarian endeavour.[37]

In just a few years, several initiatives took their example from the Code. Among them the Sphere Project, established in 1997 following a wide and inclusive process which comprised some of the main non-governmental consortium active at that time, is particularly relevant for this analysis also for the importance that still has today.[38] The 'Sphere Handbook', published in the current form in 2011 after three revisions and consisting of the 'Humanitarian Charter' and the 'Minimum Standards in Humanitarian Response', represents its main outcome.[39] While the former is aimed at establishing the rights and duties of the actors involved, the latter represents the first attempt to accurately determine specific goals for each field of intervention (namely Water Supply, Sanitation and Hygiene Promotion; Food Security, Nutrition and Food Aid; Shelter, Settlement, and Non-Food Items; Health Services) in order to guarantee a satisfactory fulfilment of the related individual rights. Accordingly, in the Humanitarian Charter (presented in 2000 as the ethical framework of the Project), the *needs-based* approach is distinctly integrated with a *rights-based* configuration, intended to be the driving force of the humanitarian action in disaster response and the basis for verifying the impact and the quality of its performances.

This amalgam of the two approaches has not been straightforward. In fact, in the tenets of the different versions of this new 'humanitarian manifesto', a series of inconsistencies of both formal and substantial nature can be detected. One of the most questioned elements was contained in the text of the first editions, in which it was asserted that '[t]he Charter defines the *legal responsibilities of states* and parties to guarantee the right to assistance and protection. When states are unable to respond, *they are obliged to allow* the intervention of humanitarian organisations' (emphasis added).[40] Even if this controversial affirmation disappeared in the following editions, published in 2004 and 2011, the Charter still expresses the 'conviction . . . that all people affected by disaster or conflict have a right to receive protection and assistance to ensure the basic conditions for life with dignity', underlining that the principles described in it are 'universal, applying to all those affected by disaster' and – most surprisingly – 'reflected in international law'.[41]

Furthermore, in another paragraph it includes, among the rights of the victims, 'the rights to protection and assistance reflected in the provisions of international humanitarian law, human rights and refugee law', outlining a legal cauldron formed instead by different regimes each of which entails specific characteristics.[42] In particular, three rights are mentioned and underlined: the right to life with dignity, the right to receive humanitarian assistance and the right to protection and security. In illustrating the first right, it is affirmed that 'implicit in this is the duty not to withhold or frustrate the provision of life-saving assistance',[43] presumably including the assistance provided by external actors. Moreover, for the Charter, '[d]ignity entails more than physical well-being; it demands respect for the whole person, including the values and beliefs of individuals and affected communities, and respect for their human rights, including liberty, freedom of conscience and religious observance'.[44]

Therefore, if compared with the positive provisions arranged by international human rights law, an amplified (and somehow distorted) conception of human rights is asserted here, with particular reference to the right to liberty, not further explained or argued, the right to humanitarian assistance, not explicitly stated in any binding instruments currently adopted by States,[45] and to the right to protection and security, described as being '*rooted* in the provisions of international law, in resolutions of the United Nations . . . , and in the sovereign responsibility of states to protect all those within their jurisdiction' (emphasis added).

In the same text we can read that

> *As the law recognises*, some people may be particularly vulnerable to abuse and adverse discrimination due to their status such as age, gender or race, and may require special measures of protection and assistance. To the extent that a state lacks the capacity to protect people in these circumstances, we believe *it must seek international assistance to do so.*
> *(emphasis added)*

Likewise, in the language of the Charter, 'where the state or non-state actors are not providing such assistance themselves, [we believe] they must allow others to help do so'.

As described above, the document contains a doubtful juxtaposition of well-established elements of positive law and progressive elements biased by ethical considerations, thus portraying a blurred landscape: from a legal perspective, the simple acknowledgment of the existence of 'moral rights' and 'moral duties' appears as problematic.[46] In this respect, the Sphere initiative can be considered as an activity of 'aspirational' standard setting, dressed with real legal elements.

Fortunately, in an official commentary on the Charter, which was deemed necessary to accompany the 2011 edition, the most problematic elements emphasised above are clarified thanks to the introduction of some explanatory observations, like the one explaining that '[i]nternational NGOs, for their part, have no formal rights or responsibilities in international law other than the right to offer assistance' and that 'ultimately, the basis for engagement by non-governmental agencies remains a moral rather than a legal one'.[47] This document describes how the 'interplay between the legal and moral is a feature of the Charter' and that 'the Common Principles it articulates are not found as such in international law, but are based on an amalgam of legal and moral elements and have a strong basis in both'.[48]

Nowadays, even if the Sphere Handbook is still one of the most relevant points of reference for the humanitarian community worldwide, some doubts concerning its theoretical set-up remain. In particular, the formal link between operational standards, quantitative indicators and the connected individual rights to protect, apparently under-utilised on field,[49] could still entail the risk of defining the latter as merely instrumental to the fulfilment of professional performances, weakening their inner value.[50] In addition, its configuration could underpin the idea that the humanitarian relief activities, if successfully accomplished in a quantifiable sense, are sufficient to maintain that individual rights obligations are correctly enforced. But what about the situations in which the local authorities, or the economic or security conditions, do not allow the fulfilment of the foreseen standards: would it be a reason to not even launch relief operations, running the risk of being labelled as unaccountable? And then, is it really possible to establish minimum standards that are universally applicable? The risk of putting the responsibilities of the territorial authorities, which from a legal perspective are the real subject of the human rights obligations, in a subordinate position must also be taken into account.[51]

The alignment of the humanitarian 'galaxy' on the basis of shared standards and harmonised theoretical premises is undoubtedly to be considered as a positive advancement. Nevertheless this cannot undermine the assumption that each post-disaster scenario has its own peculiarities, and thus any humanitarian activity request a specific advance analysis dealing with its overall impact on local communities and individuals as well as with the consideration of the specific international, regional and national legal framework, including human rights obligations.[52]

Hence, the impact of any standard-setting activity is closely connected with the existence and functioning of a monitoring mechanism of compliance, as illustrated in the following example.[53]

The accountability of NSHAs: the rise of a 'people-based' compliance mechanism

Recent developments related to the normative role of humanitarian NGOs in disaster scenarios deal with the issues of compliance and accountability, two aspects which, due to the increasing heterogeneity of this category of actors in terms of capability and efficacy, have become pivotal in the last 20 years.

If 'accountability' generally refers to any method or procedure that can be used to assess the responsible conduct of a specific legal 'performer', we must first recognise that the legal notion of 'responsibility', as internationally conceived, can be properly attributed in this context only to the activities of intergovernmental and governmental entities.[54] As for NSHAs, we could take into consideration the State's role in preventing (and eventually prosecuting) harmful conducts which entail the violation of the core rights of the affected people in its territory, on the base of its duty to protect human rights. Nevertheless, this is not the central issue of this analysis, assuming that humanitarian organisations normally intervene in disaster scenarios in good faith, with the sole aim of alleviating human suffering. Given this premise, the 'accountability' of private humanitarian entities in relief activities can be considered as having a milder content, formed by elements ranging from behavioural to procedural standards, with ill-defined responsibilities connected to the correct management of their 'dominant position', as regard to vulnerable peoples.[55] Compliance with those standards, developed in order to provide a tool for the actors themselves, as well as for both the affected communities and monitoring agencies, is thus a basis for supervising and evaluating the humanitarian outcomes and impacts of any intervention.

Consequently, humanitarian accountability is not an inherently a univocal concept. It is a characteristic of power dynamics aimed at altering behaviours over time, the relevance of which has to be determined by 'the eye of the beholder', on the base of the specificities of each situation.[56] International law seems playing an increasing role in these dynamics, at least as reference general framework, so that nowadays we can assert that the scope of application of certain of its provisions is informally extended when relating to the humanitarian sector. In particular, and with due regard to the theoretical premises made in the introduction of the present work, human rights law seems to have gained, in the last 20 years, a 'normative role' that goes beyond the formalistic interpretation of its content, affecting the way in which the conduct of the private actors in disaster-related scenarios is addressed.

In this respect, the point of reference for accountability and compliance is currently represented by the 'Core Humanitarian Standard on Quality and Accountability (CHS)', presented in December 2014 in Copenhagen – exactly 20 years after the Code of Conduct.[57] Once again, this document is the result of the joint effort of several humanitarian policy makers and organisations, aimed at unifying the pre-existing instruments in a unique tool and endorsing new, shared, well-embedded criteria that would combine their strong points and overcome eventual inconsistencies.[58]

The classic humanitarian principles still underpin the CHS, a lightweight document (twenty pages) drafted on nine specific commitments, each of which is supported by quality criteria, key actions and organisational responsibilities indicating how humanitarian organisations and staff should perform in order to meet them. Organisations and individuals involved in humanitarian response (but also governments, the militaries and the private sector) can use it to assess the quality and effectiveness of the assistance they provide, while, on the other hand, the beneficiaries can consider it as a point of reference for what they should expect from organisations and individuals delivering humanitarian relief: 'knowing what humanitarian organisations have committed to, will enable them to hold those organisations to account'.[59]

As regard to its approach, in comparison with the Code of Conduct and the Sphere Handbook, the main innovation introduced seems to be the inclusive and people-centred nature of the document. The CHS claims to be conceived from the point of view of crisis-affected communities, with the aim of empowering individuals to request appropriate assistance and to have access to a responsive compliant mechanism. Moreover, a parallel initiative currently being developed, spearheaded by the SCHR, should enable certification and verification of agencies on the base of the CHS.[60]

Regarding this configuration, it is interesting to evaluate the position on human rights, generically mentioned in the introduction of the CHS, stating the intention of the humanitarian endeavour to uphold their promotion and respect. More specifically, the document is underpinned by the right to life with dignity and the right to protection and security 'as set forth in international law', including the 'International Bill of Human Rights'.[61] The latter two facets, a significant legacy of the Sphere's perspective, still appear as problematic from a strictly legal point of view. The textual references to the concept of protection and security within the core human rights instruments cover a vast spectrum of situations basically framed in a non-emergency dimension, from the protection from arbitrary arrest or detention[62] to social security for working mothers,[63] and which in post-disaster scenarios, while maintaining their relevance, are hard to construe (and thus enforce) as unitary rights.

Apart from that, and unlike the *Sphere Humanitarian Charter*, the theoretical background is stated very briefly and is limited to the recognition of the usual sources (International Humanitarian

Law, International Human Rights Law and International Refugee Law) setting the overall legal standards relating to the protection of persons involved. Moreover, the respective legal responsibilities between public and private entities are outlined in a clearer and more consistent way:

> those who apply the *Core Humanitarian Standard* recognise the primary responsibility of states and other relevant authorities to protect and assist those affected by disasters or armed conflicts within their territories. Humanitarian action should not undermine these responsibilities; indeed, whenever possible, it should complement them.[64]

Having said that, it seems worthwhile to note that, in this new humanitarian policy tool, no other particular right is mentioned, and no explicit connection between operational issues and the correspondent right is established. Instead, general references to individual rights are foreseen by Key Action 3.6, which calls upon actors to 'identify and act upon potential or actual unintended negative effects in a timely and systematic manner, including in the areas of . . . people's safety, security, dignity and rights';[65] and in the fourth commitment, aimed at guaranteeing that 'Communities and people affected by crisis know their rights and entitlements, have access to information and participate in decisions that affect them',[66] introducing the important dimension of the right to transparency and to information, which is an essential element of any accountability mechanism.[67]

As a result, what can be observed in the CHS's approach is that human rights are still there, but they lie in the background, not constituting anymore the main theoretical counterpart as was the case for the Sphere Project. The focus shifts instead to the affected community, no longer conceived merely as a group of individuals in need or as a collectivity of right holders. In this 'people-based' approach, the beneficiaries assume a proactive role, as clearly demonstrated by the extensive use of terms such as participation, awareness, information-sharing, consultation, feedback mechanisms, open communications, complaints-handling processes and accessibility.

Somehow, human rights are less distinctly considered as part of the operational plan of NSHAs response, but rather as a basis of action for the victims, whose initiative gains a decisive prominence as accountability dynamic. In this regard, it can be pointed out that, in one of the first monitoring actions drawn up on the basis of the CHS, the 'Nepal earthquake appeal response review' by the Disaster Emergency Committee (September 2015), no explicit references are made to specific human rights. On the contrary, the recommendation n. 5 calls upon the humanitarian actors to 'Build the right housing based on listening people's realities and supporting traditional practices'.[68] Also in other reports on the earthquake in Nepal of 2015, containing 'lessons learnt' on the base of evaluations processes, human rights are never mentioned, even if the need to guarantee and adequate housing has been at the centre of the analysis.[69]

However, this does not obviously mean that human rights protection is now considered as irrelevant in relation to disaster context, as demonstrated by the work of Freedom Fund and three other Nepali organisations on the strengthening of community-based capacities in preventing gender violence and child trafficking phenomena after the earthquake.[70] On the contrary, the relevance of human rights in post-disaster humanitarian assistance has been described as ever-increasing and recognised as an essential element, but with a focus properly placed on the responsibilities of the affected authorities.[71]

The actual impact of the CHS can only be assessed over the coming years. At present, it can only be noted that their innovative approach seems to facilitate a more coherent and reliable positioning of human rights law within the activities put in place by the 'responders' cauldron'.[72] Their endorsement during the first World Humanitarian Summit held in Istanbul in May 2016, in which they have been recognised as 'as a way to improve humanitarian effectiveness' and 'to ensure people affected by crises are not only informed and consulted, but put at the centre of the decision-making processes',[73] appears as a clear intention to definitively go beyond the beneficiaries needs-rights discourse.

Final remarks – NSHAs, human rights and disaster law: filling the gap or creating an autonomous soft regime?

As stated in the introduction, the aim of this contribution was not to address the general theory of subjectivity in the creation/application of the law, which characterise – in all its complexity – an international legal order in constant mutation. On the contrary, the intention was to emphasise how contemporary practices show that IDL has to be considered as a normative process which tends to conform to societal changes in a pragmatic way, rather than a purely theoretical one, built on a set of clear-cut legal premises. Accordingly, the range of participating entities inevitably expanded in order to include humanitarian NSAs. IDL is, in this sense, 'at the frontier' of international law, being a model for the elaboration of norms on how public and private institutions can work together to solve multinational problems. The most evident example of this can be found in one of the few multilateral binding treaties currently in force in this field of law, the Tampere Convention of 1998, which covers extensively the cooperation among States and non-state entities in facilitating the deployment and use of telecommunication equipment to predict, monitor and provide information concerning natural hazards, health hazards and disasters.[74]

As demonstrated by the analysis of three specific cases, such dynamics have consistently addressed the international protection of individual rights. Given the assumption that the territorial State is still the central actor 'around which all other entities revolve',[75] a humanitarian organisation like the IFRC effectively contributed to the production and interpretation of (potential) international norms, as in the case of the ILC's Draft Articles, with a clear impact on the purposes of guaranteeing the fundamental human rights of the disaster victims. This is because its expert knowledge – deriving from research activities and practice in the field – has been considered as an indispensable 'source' for that normative process.

Moreover, thanks to their capacity to gather information, provide expertise, mobilise resources – both human and economic – in the course of relief activities, it has been underlined how the most relevant humanitarian entities currently contribute to enhance the overall effectiveness of multilateral human rights provisions in post-disaster scenarios, also by the creation of operative standards shaped by the necessity of guaranteeing their content.[76] However, this kind of activity, as in the case of the Sphere Handbook, is accompanied by the risk of discrepancies and headlong rushes, with potential counterproductive effects and other setbacks.

Private actors can also complement the states in related compliance or enforcement mechanisms, making eventual violations of human rights more transparent. This complementary activity can be possible not only by the gathering and disclosing of information, but also through the development of internal regulatory tools, aimed at creating compliance mechanism and framing multiple accountabilities (to the victims, the territorial authorities and the donors) within national systems in which the exercise of the public authority can be seriously undermined. Only the time will tell if the Core Humanitarian Standards (2014) are suitably paving the way in this respect.

The above-mentioned examples show how, from a normative perspective, NSHAs are strengthening their capacity to contribute to 'the functioning of international guarantee procedures, the identification of more advanced preventive, protective and reparatory mechanism and the definition of standards to interpret in practice the rights formally recognized'.[77] While in an early phase their activity was characterised by the affirmation of the basic humanitarian principles, with the so called 'new humanitarianism' the focus has shifted – though not without frictions[78] – in order to include other operational perspectives such as human rights protection. It is thus, currently evolving again with the rise of a new participative approach, in which the conduct of the humanitarian entities, and somehow its 'legitimacy', is evaluated in terms of compliance with informal (soft) regimes, procedural patterns and monitoring systems.

The relevance of this process cannot be underestimated, as it casts a new light not only on the way in which NSHAs operate internationally, but also, and perhaps most importantly, on the changing modes by which the distinction legal/illegal is perceived and applied by relevant actors in contemporary international society. In certain cases, such as for the presumed individual right to humanitarian assistance, it creates a communicative practice whereby the conduct of states is no longer assessed in terms of acting in compliance with specific rules, but by some basic understanding of certain human values the respect of which is perceived to be essential.

The need for new conceptual tools, as well as a new assessment of the social forces that structure a wider community whose members have 'values, identities and roles distinct from the geographic limitations of states',[79] therefore seems increasingly necessary. Considering the humanitarian practice, the risk of a greater marginalisation and the subsequent loss of authority of international law appears rather concrete, and the use of terms and categories 'borrowed' from other fields of studies stands as a clear warning.

To conclude, the role of NSHAs as contextualised in the present work should not be seen as a demonstration of a supposed redistribution of legitimacy and powers in international law, nor as a claim for a self-contained democratic regime 'coming from below'.[80] On the contrary, what emerges is the need to deal with the increasing capabilities of 'unconventional' actors to affect the regulatory patterns of the formal interstate system. For these reasons, the attempts at worldwide harmonisation via traditional international law-making mechanisms and the self-regulatory dynamics of the transnational civil society should not be regarded as competing processes of a completely different nature, but rather as a converging mechanism aimed at reinforcing the value of human dignity and thus its protection.

Selected bibliography

M. Noortmann, A. Reinisch and C. Ryngaert (eds), *Non-State Actors in International Law* (Hart Publishing, 2015).

N. Rodley, 'Non-State Actors and Human Rights' in S. Sheeran and N. Rodley (eds), *Routledge Handbook of International Human Rights Law* (Routledge, 2013) 523.

A. Bianchi, 'Introduction: Relativizing the Subjects or Subjectivizing the Actors: Is That the Question?' in A. Bianchi (ed), *Non-State Actors and International Law* (Routledge, 2009) xiv.

M. Palma, 'The Possible Contribution of International Civil Society to the Protection of Human Rights' in A. Cassese (ed), *Realizing Utopia: The Future of International Law* (Oxford University Press, 2012) 76.

Notes

1 See, among others, M. Noortmann, A. Reinisch and C. Ryngaert (eds), *Non-State Actors in International Law* (Hart Publishing, 2015); N. Rodley, 'Non-State Actors and Human Rights' in S. Sheeran and N. Rodley (eds), *Routledge Handbook of International Human Rights Law* (Routledge, 2013); A. Clapham, *Human Rights and Non-State Actors* (Edward Elgar Publishing, 2013); J. d'Aspremont (ed), *Participants in the International Legal System: Multiple Perspectives of Non-State Actors in International Law* (Routledge, 2011); P. Alston, 'The "Not-a-Cat" Syndrome: Can the International Human Rights Regime Accommodate Non-State Actors?' in P. Alston (ed), *Non-State Actors and Human Rights* (Oxford University Press, 2005) 3–36.

2 See A. Bianchi, 'Introduction: Relativizing the Subjects or Subjectivizing the Actors: Is That the Question?' in A. Bianchi (ed), *Non-State Actors and International Law* (Routledge, 2009) xiv.

3 Ibid xii, for which

> [t]he term "actor" comes from the language of political science. This may attest to an ever-increasing cross-fertilization between the two disciplines. Or, perhaps, it is simply evidence that once the border of interdisciplinarity is crossed, what lies ahead is a barren plain with no landmarks or other distinctive signposts.

4 See A. Peters, 'Are We Moving towards Constitutionalization of the World Community?' in A. Cassese (ed), *Realizing Utopia: The Future of International Law* (Oxford University Press, 2012) 126–135.

5 See C. Ryngaert, 'Non-State Actors: Carving Out a Space in a State-Centred International Legal System' 63 *Netherlands International Law Review* (2016) 183–195; N. Butha, 'The Role International Actors Other Than States Can Play in the New World Order' in Cassese (n. 4) 75.

6 See Bianchi (n. 2) xvii, citing the work of A. Clapham and A. Bianchi, 'Globalization of Human Rights: The Role of Non-State Actors' in G. Teubner (ed), *Global Law without a State* (Dartmouth, 1997) 181–182 for whom

> [o]ver time, the shaping of the doctrine of international human rights has proved to be a catalyst for a process which has progressively led not only to the steady erosion of the positivist notion of state sovereignty, but also to the practical necessity of framing international law in a different context.

7 For an overview of the organisational, human and financial resources devoted to humanitarian aid, see ALNAP, *The State of the Humanitarian System* (ODI, 2015) 38–44.

8 For an interesting analysis of the relation between hard and soft law in the international legal order, see A. Pronto, 'Understanding the Hard/Soft Distinction in International Law' 48 *Vanderbilt Journal of Transnational Law* (2015) 941 ff.

9 M.J. Struett, 'NGOs, the International Criminal Court, and the Politics of Writing International Law' in I.F. Dekker and W.G. Werner (eds), *Governance and International Legal Theory* (Springer, 2004) 351–353.

10 See A. de Guttry, 'Surveying the Law' in A. de Guttry, M. Gestri and G. Venturini (eds), *International Disaster Response Law* (Springer, 2012) 3 ff.

11 Convention on the Prohibition of the Use, Stockpiling, Production and Transfer of Anti-Personnel Mines and on Their Destruction (adopted 18 September 1997, entered into force 1 March 1999) 2056 UNTS 211. See K. Anderson, 'The Ottawa Convention Banning Landmines, the Role of International NGO and the Idea of International Civil Society' 11 *European Journal of International Law* (2000) 91–120.

12 This contribution will not address the issue of the special status of the IFRC as regard to other non-governmental humanitarian entities. It will be generally considered as a private humanitarian organisation 'with functional international legal personality'; see S. Mehring, *International Federation of Red Cross and Red Crescent Societies* (MPEPIL, 2010).

13 An analytical guide to the work of the ILC on this topic and all the links to relevant documents are available at http://legal.un.org/ilc/guide/6_3.shtml, accessed on 13 March 2017.

14 See ILC, Protection of Persons in the Event of Disasters, Memorandum by the Secretariat, UN Doc. A/CN.4/590 (2007), note 8, citing the IFRC's World Disaster Report (2000) paras 58, 117, note 12, 197, 203 and 206 citing D. Fisher, *Law and Legal Issues in International Disaster Response: A Desk Study* (IFRC, 2007) para 6, citing the resolution of the International Conference of the Red Cross on 'Measures to expedite international relief of 1977' (also cited in paras 164, 198 and 201) and the IFRC 'Guidelines for the Domestic Facilitation and Regulation of International Disaster Relief and Initial Recovery Assistance' (IDRL Guidelines, 2007), available at www.ifrc.org/en/what-we-do/idrl/idrl-guidelines/ and the relative note 20 citing, as several following notes, the 'Principles and Rules for Red Cross and Red Crescent Disaster Relief', prepared by IFRC in consultation with ICRC, reprinted in 310 *International Review of the Red Cross* (29 February 1996), Annex IV (also cited in paras 117, 183, 198, 248 and 258), the 'Code of Conduct for the International Red Cross and Red Crescent Movement and Non-Governmental Organizations in Disaster Relief', Annex VI to the report entitled 'Principles and Response in International Humanitarian Assistance and Protection' Doc. 95/C.II/2/1, 26th International Conference of the Red Cross and Red Crescent, Geneva, 3–7 December 1995 (cited also in paras 182, 200 and 222) paras 13, 15, 16 together with note 33, 40, 46, 48 citing the seven fundamental principles of the International Red Cross and Red Crescent Movement.

15 ILC, Preliminary Report on the Protection of Persons in the Event of Disasters, UN Doc. A/CN.4/598 (2008) para 6; see also, among other references to the works of the IFRC, para 18 for which

> According to IFRC, the legal core of international disaster relief law consists of the laws, rules and principles applicable to the access, facilitation, coordination, quality and accountability of

> international disaster response activities. . . . Moreover, the primary focus of IDRL is on the operational side of protection, namely, assistance.

16 See IDRL Guidelines (n. 14).
17 ILC, Preliminary Report (n. 15) para 12, which makes reference to the Official Records of the General Assembly, Fifty-third Session, Supplement No. 1, UN Doc. A/53/1, para 174.
18 Fisher (n. 14), available at www.ifrc.org/PageFiles/125639/11360 0-idrl-deskstudy-en.pdf, accessed on 13 March 2017.
19 ILC, Preliminary Report (n. 15) paras 18–20.
20 ILC, Second Report on the Protection of Persons in the Event of Disasters, UN Doc. A/CN.4/615 (2009) para 17.
21 Ibid para 28.
22 ILC, Fourth Report on the Protection of Persons in the Event of Disasters, UN Doc. A/CN.4/643 (2011) paras 42–43, for which

> The formulations of the duty in the [IFRC Guidelines presents] attributes that can be linked to the foregoing discussion. First, a duty to seek international assistance only arises in cases where national incapacity is demonstrated. . . . Second, the duty is framed as a duty to 'seek' rather than a duty to 'request' assistance.

It is worth to say that the final formulation of the article on the Duty to seek assistance (art 11), inspired by para 3(2) of the IFRC Guidelines, cites 'other potential assisting actors' as legitimate recipient of the request (see paras 45–46).
23 ILC, Fifth Report on the Protection of Persons in the Event of Disasters, UN Doc. A/CN.4/652 (2012) paras 154, 156, 160, 166. In some cases, the IFRC Guidelines are even cited among other international treaties without formal distinctions (see i.e. para 184 on the 'Termination of assistance'). See also ILC, Seventh Report on the Protection of Persons in the Event of Disasters, UN Doc. A/CN.4/668 (2014) para 22 addressing the safety and security of humanitarian personnel.
24 See ILC, Sixth Committee: Summary Record of the 22nd Meeting, UN Doc. A/C.6/64/SR.22 (2 November 2009) para 30.
25 See ILC, Sixth Committee Summary Record of the 25th Meeting, UN Doc. A/C.6/66/SR.25 (31 October 2011) para 41. For an insight of the debate on the article's content see G. Bartolini, T. Natoli and A. Riccardi, 'Report of the Expert Meeting on the ILC's Draft Articles on the Protection of Persons in the Event of Disasters' 3 *International Law and Disasters Working Papers Series* (2015) 50–52, available at http://disasterlaw.sssup.it/pubblications/working-papers/, accessed on 7 June 2017.
26 See, among others, ILC Sixth Committee Summary Record(s): UN Doc. A/C.6/65/SR.25 para 47 on draft art 1 (Scope); UN Doc. A/C.6/64/SR.22 para 31 on draft art 3 (Definition of disaster); UN Doc. A/C.6/69/SR.21 paras 73–74 on draft art 4 (Use of terms); UN Doc. A/C.6/64/SR.22 para 32 on draft art 8 (Duty to cooperate); UN Doc. A/C.6/67/SR.20 paras 60–61 on draft art 9 (Forms of cooperation); UN Doc. A/C.6/67/SR.26 paras 16–18 on draft art 10 (Cooperation for Disaster Risk Reduction) and art 11 (Duty to reduce the risk of disasters); UN Doc. A/C.6/66/SR.25 para 23 on draft art 14 (Consent of the affected State to external assistance); UN Doc. A/C.6/67/SR.20 paras 62–63 on draft art 15 (Conditions on the provision of external assistance); UN Doc. A/C.6/66/SR.25 para 24 on draft art 16 (offers of external assistance); UN Doc. A/C.6/67/SR.20 para 62 on draft art 17 (Facilitation of external assistance); UN Doc. A/C.6/67/SR.20 para 64 on draft art 19 (Termination of external assistance); UN Doc. A/C.6/65/SR.25 para 49 on draft art 21 (Relationship to international humanitarian law) and para 46 including general observations.
27 See ILC, Sixth Committee Summary Record of the 22nd Meeting, UN Doc. A/C.6/63/SR.22 (November 2008) para 68.
28 Ibid.
29 See ILC, Eighth Report on the Protection of Persons in the Event of Disasters, UN Doc. A/CN.4/697 (2016) paras 23, 103.
30 Ibid para 119, for which

> [the IFRC] was conscious of the fact that it would be impossible to enunciate every right that could prove relevant in a disaster operation and that mentioning some examples might be misread to imply that rights not enunciated do not apply. Nonetheless, there existed certain rights issues that were of frequent concern in disaster settings and could usefully be underlined in the draft articles, such as: the right to receive humanitarian assistance; the rights of particularly vulnerable

groups (such as women, children, seniors, and disabled persons) to have their special protection and assistance needs taken into account; the right of communities to have a voice in the planning and execution of risk reduction, response and recovery initiatives; and the right of all persons displaced by disasters to non-discriminatory assistance in obtaining durable solutions to their displacement.

31 See E. Davey, with J. Borton and M. Foley, 'A History of the Humanitarian System: Western Origins and Foundations' *HPG Working Paper* (2013) 14.
32 See M. Buchanan-Smith, *How the Sphere Project Came into Being: A Case Study of Policy-Making in the Humanitarian Aid Sector and the Relative Influence of Research*, Working Paper 215 (ODI London, 2003) vi, according to which the first 'embryonic NGO initiative to develop performance standards' after Rwanda was the *Joint Evaluation of Emergency Assistance to Rwanda: Study III Principal Findings and Recommendations*, Relief and Rehabilitation Network, Paper n. 16 (ODI London, 1996).
33 Founded in 1972, SCHR brings together nine of the world's leading humanitarian organisations to share analysis and learning and promote greater accountability and impact of humanitarian actions. See http://schr.info/about.
34 See The Code of Conduct for the International Red Cross and Red Crescent Movement and Non-Governmental Organisations (NGOs) in Disaster Relief, prepared jointly by the International Federation of Red Cross and Red Crescent Societies and the ICRC, 1994. For more information and documentations, see the page www.ifrc.org/en/publications-and-reports/code-of-conduct/, accessed on 13 March 2017.
35 UN Doc. A/RES/46/182, *Strengthening of the Coordination of Humanitarian Emergency Assistance of the United Nations* (19 December 1991) Annex I Guiding Principles, para 2. To those three principles, the Code adds the one of 'Independence', by stating that the signatory organisations 'shall endeavour not to act as instruments of government foreign policy' (principle 4).
36 It has to be noted that 'The Code of Conduct' was published with no steering tools as guidelines for implementation, or training practices, and that it lacked any mechanism to monitor compliance.
37 See The Code of Conduct (n. 34), principles 1, 2, 8.
38 For a comprehensive analysis of the origins of the Project, see M. Buchanan-Smith (n. 32) passim.
39 For more information and documentation, see the page www.sphereproject.org/about/, accessed on 13 March 2017.
40 The Sphere Project – Humanitarian Charter and Minimum Standards in Disaster Response, first final edition (2000) 2.
41 The Sphere Handbook (ed. 2011) 20; The Sphere Handbook (ed. 2004) para 2.2.
42 Ibid 21.
43 Ibid 22.
44 Ibid.
45 The right to humanitarian assistance will therefore imply several problematic issues on the subjectivity, the responsibilities and the eventual enforcement measures. See C. Dufour, V. de Geoffroy, H. Maury and F. Gruenwald, 'Rights, Standards and Quality in a Complex Humanitarian Space: Is Sphere the Right Tool?' 28(2) *Disasters* (2004) 131.
46 See The Sphere Project, '2011 Edition of the Sphere Handbook: What Is New?' (2012) para 4(a). The document recalls that the new edition was considered as necessary in order to 'clarify the definition and the use of principles included in the Charter' and define it as an 'aspirational and a statement of belief rather than a straightforward statement of legal norms'.
47 J. Darcy, *User Guidance and Commentary on the Humanitarian Charter* (Sphere Project, 2011) 3.
48 Ibid 5.
49 See M. Van Dyke and R. Waldman, *The Sphere Project Evaluation Report*, Center for Global Health and Economic Development, Columbia University (2004) 5, 33, according to which

> [t]he rights-based approach, the cornerstone of the Sphere Project's philosophical approach to humanitarian assistance, is not as well-understood as the more technical aspects presented in the Handbook and some donors seem to choose to concentrate on and to acknowledge the technical portion of the Project while 'opting out' of the rights-based approach.

50 See Dufour (n. 45) 128–129.
51 On this topic, see J. Darcy, 'Locating Responsibility: The Sphere Humanitarian Charter and Its Rationale' 28(2) *Disasters* (2004) 115–122, according to whom '[t]he mechanisms for accountability against these standards remain undefined, and there is an ambiguity between individual and collective responsibility for the achievement of the specified outcomes'.

52 See C. Gribbin and I. Maiolo, 'Legal Framework Applicable to Humanitarian Actors Responding to Disasters in Weak and Fragile States' in D. Caron, M. J. Kelly and A. Telesetsky (eds), *The International Law of Disaster Relief* (Cambridge University Press, 2014) 157, according to whom '[i]n spite of the success of initiatives such as Sphere, the HA community has recognized that it is difficult to set universal objective standards for humanitarian responses'.

53 For an overview on the rise of the firsts evaluation and monitoring systems see D. Hilhorst, 'Being Good at Doing Good? Quality and Accountability of Humanitarian NGOs' 26(3) *Disasters* (2002) 206–209.

54 See G. Bartolini, 'Attribution of Conduct and Liability Issues Arising from International Disaster Relief Missions: Theoretical and Pragmatic Approaches to Guaranteeing Accountability' 48 *Vanderbilt Journal of Transnational Law* (2015) 1029 ff.

55 With reference to the 'Standard in Accountability and Quality Management', Humanitarian Accountability Partnership (HAP, 2010) 5, accountability is defined as 'the means through which power is used responsibly. It is a process of taking account of, and being held accountable by, different stakeholders, and primarily those who are affected by the exercise of power'.

56 See A. Davis, 'Concerning Accountability of Humanitarian Action' 58 *HPN Network Paper* (2007) 5.

57 For a brief introduction to the instrument and its content, see www.corehumanitarianstandard.org/the-standard, accessed on 13 March 2017.

58 As affirmed by M. Casey-Maslen, executive director of HAP International, following the humanitarian responses to the Haiti earthquake and the Pakistan floods in 2010,

> [there was] a widespread sense among many humanitarians and organisations that there was limited interoperability between these different initiatives [i.e. HAP International, People in Aid and the Sphere Project], and that the sector lacked a key statement of what people could expect from humanitarian organisations.

See K. Purvis, 'Core Humanitarian Standard: Do NGOs Need Another Set of Standards?' *The Guardian* (11 June 2015). The CHS brings together the main elements of the Sphere Core Standards and HAP Standard in Accountability and Quality Management (2010), the Red Cross and Red Crescent Code of Conduct, the People in Aid Code of Good Practice and criteria from the OECD's DAC and from the Quality COMPAS developed by Groupe URD. The CHS Alliance currently includes 266 organisations in more than 160 countries, supporting the implementation of the document with training, tools and advice.

59 CHS Alliance, Group URD and the Sphere Project, 'Core Humanitarian Standard on Quality and Accountability' (2014) 2.

60 See www.chsalliance.org/verification, accessed on 13 March 2017. The CHS Verification Scheme, currently under testing phase, should become a structured, systematic process to assess the degree to which an organisation is working to achieve the CHS.

61 Namely: UNGA, Res 217(III): Universal Declaration on Human Rights, UN Doc. A/RES/217(III) (10 December 1948); International Covenant on Economic, Social and Cultural Rights (adopted 16 December 1966, entered into force 3 January 1976) 993 UNTS 3; and the International Covenant on Civil and Political Rights (adopted 16 December 1966, entered into force 23 March 1976) 999 UNTS 171. See CHS (n. 59) 2.

62 Art 9 ICCPR.

63 Art 10.2 ICESCR.

64 See CHS (n. 59) 8, *Principled Humanitarian Action.*

65 Ibid 12.

66 Ibid 13.

67 See A. Featherstone, 'Improving Impact: Do Accountability Mechanisms Deliver Results?' in Christian Aid, *Save the Children and the Humanitarian Accountability Partnership* (Christian Aid and Save the Children, 2013) 27, observing that

> A modest investment in information sharing (in terms of financial resources, staff time and agency commitment), involvement by project participants in the design and delivery of programmes, and ensuring there is a means of listening to and acting on feedback, brings a significant return – not only in participant satisfaction and engagement in projects, but also in the tangible success of projects.

On the right to information see also A. Riccardi's chapter in this book.

68 D. Sanderson, A. Rodericks, N. Shresta and B. Ramalingam, *Nepal Earthquake Appeal Response Review* (DEC, 2015) 13.

69 See ALNAP Lessons Paper, *Nepal Earthquake Response: Lessons for Operational Agencies* (ODI, 2015); F. Grünewald and A. Burlat, *Nepal Earthquake: A Rapid Review of the Response and a Few Lessons Learnt* (Groupe URD, 2015).

70 See G. Baumann, 'After the Earthquake: Lessons in Using Local Capacities to Protect Human Rights, from Community Workers in Nepal' *CHS Alliance Blog* (23 May 2016); M. Dharel, W. Bhatta Rai and N. Thapa, 'Understanding Vulnerabilities and Strengthening Response: Community-Based Integration of Anti-Trafficking and Human Rights Protections within Post-Earthquake Recovery Efforts in Sindhupalchok District' *Nepal* (2015).

71 See International Commission of Jurists (ICJ), *Nepal: Human Rights Impact of the Post-Earthquake Disaster Response: A Preliminary Report* (Geneva, 2016) 31–33.

72 A. Katoch, 'The Responders' Cauldron: The Uniqueness of International Disaster Response' 59(2) *Journal of International Affairs* (2006) 153.

73 World Humanitarian Summit, Istanbul 23–24 May 2016, *Chair's Summary Standing Up for Humanity: Committing to Action Advance Unedited Version*, 5–6. For an overview of the other expression of support made during the Summit, see www.chsalliance.org/news/latest-news/high-engagement-with-chs-at-whs, accessed on 13 March 2017.

74 See Tampere Convention on the Provision of Telecommunication Resources for Disaster Mitigation and Relief Operations (adopted 18 June 1998, entered into force 8 January 2005) 2296 UNTS 157, signatories 60, parties 48. In particular, art 5 of the Convention provides necessary privileges and immunities to be afforded by the State to persons (other than its nationals) and to organisations (other than those headquartered within its territory), representing the first provision of its kind which attributes privileges and immunities to non-State entities and their personnel. These individuals are also to be exempted from taxation and duties related both to disaster relief functions and those charges that may be incurred on the telecommunications equipment that they are required to transport into a disaster-stricken country.

75 See Alston (n. 1) 3. See also Butha (n. 5) 61 highlighting that 'This remain true although at present numerous state functions appear to be disaggregated and delegated to, or calibrate by reference to, a variety of non-state entities'.

76 See HPG, *Time to Let Go: Remaking Humanitarian Action for the Modern Era* (ODI, 2016) 5, for which the current dynamics within the humanitarian system show that 'most organisations engaged in humanitarian assistance, the so-called multi-mandate organisations, both UN agencies and NGOs, combine their humanitarian work with development and human rights or conflict-resolution work'.

77 See M. Palma, *The Possible Contribution of International Civil Society to the Protection of Human Rights*, in Cassese (n. 4) 81.

78 For an in-depth analysis of this theoretical evolution, see S. Gordon and A. Donini, 'Romancing Principles and Human Rights: Are Humanitarian Principles Salvageable?' 97 *International Review of the Red Cross* (2016) 897, 898.

79 R. McCorquodale, 'Beyond State Sovereignty: The International Legal System and Non-State Participants' 8 *Revista colombiana de derecho internacional* (2006) 149.

80 See Butha (n. 5) 71, for whom

> the value of democratic legitimacy in International politics – and indeed, its very meaning – remain uncertain where no clear demos can be identified, and where the actors claiming to represent democratic values (NGOs) are themselves rarely created and maintained in a democratic manner.

PART III

(Categories of) rights of particular significance in a disaster context

11
MAPPING BASIC SUBSISTENCE RIGHTS IN POST-DISASTER SCENARIOS

*Marco Inglese**

Introduction

Considering that catastrophes keep striking States and their population – thereby jeopardizing their development and enjoyment of human rights – the international community has begun to lay out a set of potential rapid responses whose aim is, on the one hand, to foster a network of institutional and non-governmental actors[1] and, on the other, quite obviously, to develop remedies specifically tailored to the nature of each disaster. In any case, the need for cooperation amongst States, as well as the protection of victims' basic subsistence rights, are steadily emerging as priorities.

This specific domain of International Disaster Response Law (IDRL) has been rapidly evolving, starting from the United Nations General Assembly (UNGA) Resolution 46/182,[2] but not limited to that development. Indeed, under its paragraph 6, States providing humanitarian assistance are required to guarantee a supply of food, medicines, shelter, and health care. Furthermore, the so-called Bruges Resolution, adopted by the Institute of International Law and representing the opinion its members have formed independently of governmental interests, seeks to shed light on some IDRL concepts, especially regarding the protection of victims.[3] It bears pointing out in this connection that humanitarian assistance is often 'the first necessary step' in alleviating the consequences of a disaster.[4] The Bruges Resolution then acknowledges the existence of 'essential needs' but without providing a definition of them, linking them to the very concept of 'humanitarian assistance'.[5] This, in turn, refers to goods and services that are indispensable for 'the survival and fulfilment of the essential needs'[6] of the victims of disasters, on an approach already endorsed in two other UNGA resolutions.[7]

Taking stock of the aforementioned UNGA and Bruges Resolutions, the more recent Draft Articles on the Protection of Persons in the Event of Disasters (from here on out, Draft Articles), adopted by the UN International Law Commission in 2016, attempt to codify victims' rights and States' duties in a disaster scenario. While it is accepted that disaster law is composed of three intertwined parts – the first being the (*ex ante*) prevention of potential disaster events; the second, the concrete (*ex post*) response; and the third, recovery – this chapter, for reasons of space constraints, deals only with the second. However, being fully aware of the inherent difficulty of considering these parts in isolation, reference will occasionally be made to the *ex ante* part, so as to show that it would be problematic to evaluate basic subsistence rights individually rather than as part of an integrated strategy.

This chapter takes a top-down approach, looking at the practice of international organizations as well as the interpretation of some rights set forth in treaty-based bodies in order to first map out a pool of basic subsistence rights, provisionally including the rights to life, shelter, health,[8] food, and water. However, because the right to life is uniquely distinctive, it will not be treated here, while the right to shelter will be dealt with elsewhere in this book, in Chapter 12.[9] The practice of regional organizations and forums will be considered in passing in order to assess whether the instruments they promote include the same pool of rights. Once we have a set of rights, we will consider whether they can be helpful as a theoretical basis for basic subsistence needs. Thirdly, and finally, it will be argued that IDRL still lacks a proper analysis of basic subsistence rights and that further work is needed, especially in emergency scenarios, if States and relief personnel are to be able to make meaningful decisions in the effort to ensure the protection of victims. Note that the analysis will not take account of the distinction between natural and man-made disasters; moreover, as the commentary specifies, armed conflicts are excluded from the notion of disaster.[10]

Mapping basic subsistence rights in universal instruments

In chronological order, the three UNGA Resolutions 43/131, 45/100, and 46/182 paved the way for the concepts underpinning the protection of victims' basic subsistence rights, stressing that States in need of humanitarian assistance have to facilitate the work of organizations by providing, in particular, a supply of food, medicines, and healthcare.[11] These elements are not expressly defined as basic subsistence rights, even though the emphasis placed on them suggests a recognition that they are more imperative than the others.[12]

The Bruges Resolution explicitly states that the concept of humanitarian assistance encompasses the provision of goods and services 'indispensable for the survival and the fulfilment of the essential needs of the victims'.[13] As a way of simplification and perhaps as an open list, these goods and services include foodstuffs, medical supplies – including medical services, decontamination tools, and psychological assistance – vehicles, tents, and temporary shelters. Again, concrete actions are spelled out, but no definition of basic subsistence needs is attached. Article I (3) describes victims as 'groups of human beings whose fundamental human rights or whose essential needs are endangered'. The recitals are not helpful either since they essentially repeat that 'disaster[s] endanger . . . fundamental human rights'.[14]

The Draft Articles are the most recent attempt to assert victims' rights in a disaster scenario. Article 2 of the Draft Articles, defining their purpose, distinguishes between 'essential needs' and 'rights', wedging in a dichotomy that is difficult to grasp. The commentary specifies that the former refers to 'survival or similarly basic needs in the aftermath of a disaster',[15] while the latter consists of human rights and rights acquired under national law.[16] Apart from that, it seems to be at odds with the purpose of the Draft Articles that basic subsistence needs have not been defined in Draft Article 3 ('Use of terms'), while the same norm defines the concepts of disaster, affected State, assisting State, other assisting actors, external assistance, relief personnel, and equipment and goods. In particular, goods encompass 'foodstuffs, drinking water, medical supplies, means of shelter, clothing, bedding, vehicles, telecommunications equipment, and other objects for disaster relief assistance', which is therefore consistent with the approach taken in the UNGA resolutions. Although this list offers an idea of what might be termed 'basic subsistence needs', there remains the problem that the latter concept is not accurately defined. A reason for this choice could be that other provisions specifically deal with human dignity and human rights.

Draft Article 4 provides for the respect and protection of human dignity. The commentary on this Article considers human dignity a 'core principle'[17] of victims' protection, and so a matter deserving a separate provision. The commentary further recalls the instruments devoted to the protection of human rights, stressing that the affected State bears the duty to protect persons in its territory or under its jurisdiction.

The most important provision for our purposes is Draft Article 5, for it states that '[p]ersons affected by disasters are entitled to the respect for and protection of their human rights in accordance with international law'. The reason why there is not an exhaustive list of rights is that such a list would have established a hierarchy of rights (something the framers wanted to avoid) and, even more importantly, that any rights not in the list would not have been protected.[18] The commentary, however, does not refrain from enumerating some of such rights, with an emphasis on the rights to life, food, health, shelter, and humanitarian assistance.[19] The problem of their enforcement and that of the derogations they may be subject to are left open, with the caveat that these situations should be treated under the rules of international law.[20]

In light of this brief survey, it seems possible to maintain that the Draft Articles took a neutral attitude to the identification of basic subsistence rights. This choice has a beneficial and a downside effect at the same time. The former essentially lies in the fact that there is no hierarchy of basic subsistence rights, leaving them open-ended enough that they can be invoked by victims in different situations and protected by affected States as well as other assisting actors with a sufficient margin of discretion. The latter instead lies in the fact that certain rights could be disregarded or sidelined, thereby introducing a *de facto* hierarchy. In other words, naming some human rights as basic subsistence rights would have been helpful in identifying them in a disaster scenario and guaranteeing a quicker and targeted intervention by relief agents. In any case, again, the duty to cooperate is constantly highlighted.[21]

What the foregoing analysis suggests is that basic subsistence rights encompass at least the rights to health, food, water, shelter, and life – all of them underpinned by human dignity as a sort of meta-principle. Considering that the last three are addressed in other chapters of this book, we will focus on the first three.

In the Draft Articles, the words *health*, *food*, and *water* appear twelve, fourteen, and six times, respectively, and are qualified through their basic components, namely, access to essential medicines and healthcare facilities, access to safe and sufficient foodstuff, and access to safe water. At the international level, these rights have been enshrined in different instruments, starting from the International Covenant on Social, Economic and Cultural Rights (ICESCR).[22] Therefore, we will now turn to the General Comments of the ESCR Committee to determine whether these rights – owing to their substantive nature – have been interpreted as having a privileged role in disaster scenarios.

The right to health

The right to health has several overlapping dimensions commonly referred to as its 'social determinants'.[23] These are preconditions of sorts that can be useful in making sure that this right can be enjoyed or else that it is not jeopardized. Thus, for example, access to health education and the right to education could serve both purposes.

General Comment No. 14,[24] on the right to the highest attainable standard of health, explicitly interprets Article 12(2)(c) ICESCR as also encompassing the provision of disaster relief,[25] while linking this dimension to the general obligation of signatory States to cooperate with the United Nations and the World Health Organization.[26] Furthermore, it needs to also be borne in mind that a specific component of the right to health is access to medicine. If we combine this element with the general obligation to cooperate – as expressed in the UN Charter and in the ICESCR,[27] among other places – we can infer, on the one hand, that assisting States have a duty to provide medicines and, on the other, that, amongst several corollary measures, for instance, intellectual property rights might be suspended in order to produce a specific medicine if, and only if, the affected State's facilities are no longer able to manufacture it. At least theoretically and indirectly, this reading seems to be supported by Article 31(b) of the Agreement on Trade Related Aspects of Intellectual Property Rights (TRIPs), which lists the conditions to be complied with to exploit a patent without the right-holder's authorization.[28] A broad understanding of this provision may encompass natural and man-made disasters. Unfortunately, there is no relevant practice to support this idea, and until further developments, it remains purely theoretical.

The importance of the right to health is also evidenced by the practice of international organizations and other treaty-based bodies. For instance, the Inter-American Commission on Human Rights recognized that the Haitian population's right to health was severely affected by the tropical storm Jeanne and thus recommended making all the necessary efforts to restore an efficient health service.[29] The Committee on the Elimination of Discrimination against Women, in its concluding observations on Indonesia, highlights the need to protect the right to health of women living in rural areas affected by the 2005 tsunami.[30] Similar conclusions are present in the reports on the assessment of post-Chernobyl Belarus[31] as well as post-Fukushima Japan.[32] In addition, the Committee on the Rights of the Child, in its concluding observations on Kazakhstan, stressed the need to protect children's health after the shrinking of the Aral Sea and the closure of a nuclear testing site.[33] Furthermore, General Comment No. 15, on the right of the child to enjoy the highest attainable standard of health, underscores the need for States to ensure unhindered access to health services and facilities, including psychological assistance for their families.[34] The Human Rights Committee, for its part, has recommended to the United States that it take further steps to ensure access to essential healthcare facilities for the African American population in the aftermath of Hurricane Katrina.[35]

As concerns the practice of States, the Djibouti Combined Initial and Periodic Reports under the African Charter on Human and Peoples' Rights finds that, in setting up a national health system, specific actions need to be taken to ensure access to health care in disaster-prone areas, so as to protect potential victims by taking the essential needs of vulnerable people into account.[36] Moreover, in the concluding observations on Chile, the Committee on the Elimination of Discrimination against Women regrets that a national plan on natural disaster management has not included the specific health needs of women.[37]

In what concerns the UN system, the World Health Organization has been very active enacting a plethora of instruments by which to tackle the different layers of the right to health over the entire course of a disaster's lifecycle.[38] These instruments are essentially operational and so do not contain any statement that the right to health is a basic subsistence right, nor do they mention its relation to other rights. However, an interesting step forward has been taken by the UN Security Council in declaring that the Ebola outbreak 'constitutes a threat to international peace and security'.[39] This instrument on the one hand emphasizes the duty of States and multilateral organizations to cooperate in providing specialized health care assistance, while at the same time acknowledging the relevant role the World Health Organization needs to play in coordinating joint efforts and in providing technical resources and personnel.

Looking at the practice of regional organizations, the Association of Southeast Asian Nations (ASEAN)[40] has adopted the Manila Declaration on Mutual Assistance on Natural Disasters, aimed at promoting closer cooperation amongst States in order to enhance the 'dissemination of medical supplies'.[41] In addition, the Vientiane Agreement on Disaster Management and Emergency Response acknowledges that the increased frequency and scale of disasters in the region is a major concern.[42] Although the agreement does not address the right to health directly, it provides for a comprehensive strategy to protect disaster victims. These instruments are entirely operational in that they deal with aspects such as prevention and mitigation, preparedness, emergency response, rehabilitation, technical cooperation, and scientific research. Although these instruments do not say much on the concept of basic subsistence rights, it is noteworthy that they seem to favour a practical rather than a theoretical approach to the subject matter at hand.

Another interesting example of this practical approach may be found in the European Union (EU). The EU is equipped with an administrative framework for coping with disasters centrally managed by the Directorate General European Civil Protection and Humanitarian Aid Operations (DG ECHO) – a European Commission service – deriving from the fact that the EU as a whole enjoys a competence to support and complement the action of Member States and if need be to enact measures based on Article 196 of the Treaty on the Functioning of the European Union (TFEU).[43] The EU is currently looking for a comprehensive crisis planning strategy,[44] while actions are still being carried out on a case-by-case basis.[45] Against this general backdrop, we need to stress the recent establishment of European Medical Corps (EMC), established in response to the Ebola outbreak.[46] The EMC, created under the auspices of the EU Civil Protection Mechanism,[47] can be deployed on short notice to act in disaster scenarios offering specific types of assistance, such as providing medical equipment, vaccinations, and logistical support meeting the quality standard set out by the World Health Organization. The EMC thus contributes to the reinforced protection of the right to health in disaster scenarios, highlighting the duty of international organization to cooperate with the affected and the assisting State.

The discussion so far shows that the right to health has several implications – acknowledged at different levels – whose main components include access to essential health care facilities and essential medicines, as well as prevention and control of epidemic diseases.[48] The overlapping dimensions of the right to health have to be considered together, forming as a whole a comprehensive right, having a prominent role in disaster scenarios and, as such, a right to be protected.

The right to food

The ESCR Committee has interpreted the right to food in General Comment No. 12,[49] identifying it as an independent concept and highlighting its relation to the right to health.[50] However, these two dimensions overlap to the extent that, in the aftermath of a disaster, foodstuff must be provided as quickly as possible. This point is linked to the concept of safety, given that stocked foodstuffs may have been contaminated through water and soil, especially in case of human-made disasters. Indeed, the lack of immediate available scientific evidence makes it difficult to foresee how a disaster can concretely affect the right to food in its component of access to safe foodstuffs. This reading is confirmed by General Comment No. 12, where, in considering the concept of physical accessibility to food, it is stated that 'victims of natural disasters . . . in disaster-prone areas . . . may need special attention'.[51] Moreover, in virtue of the consolidated tripartite nature of the obligation of States to ensure human rights, States have a duty to respect, protect, and fulfil the right to food by providing it in disaster situations. Finally, General Comment No. 12 once more underlines the fact that States have a joint and individual responsibility to cooperate in the event of catastrophes by offering the necessary assistance to ensure that the right to food is guaranteed.[52]

These findings are corroborated by the practice of States as well as that of international organizations and treaty-based bodies. In what concerns the former, the second Combined Periodic Report of Niger on the Implementation of the African Charter on Human and Peoples' Rights highlights that hunger reduction is a goal to be achieved especially in response to natural or other disaster in order to improve the resilience of the Nigerian population.[53] To this end, the government has put in place a national mechanism for disaster and food-crisis prevention and management.[54] Nigeria, by contrast, endorsed a different approach: on the one hand, it recognized the right to food as a 'non-health factor' affecting the population; on the other, as a member of international organizations, it highlighted its contribution in delivering food in post-disaster scenarios.[55] As for the latter, the Committee on the Rights of the Child, in its concluding observations on Kazakhstan, stresses the need to guarantee safe access to food, especially in response to the shrinking of the Aral Sea.[56]

In the same vein as the World Health Organization, the Food and Agriculture Organization has promoted several operational instruments to guide relief agents and States in implementing disaster response activities.[57] However, it is important to stress that these instruments prefer the term 'basic subsistence needs'[58] to a right-based approach, thereby contributing to the terminological confusion surrounding this category.

The African Union (AU)[59] presents an interesting framework on disaster law and the protection of basic subsistence needs, with particular emphasis on the rights to food and water. Indeed, the African Regional Strategy for Disaster Risk Reduction was enacted in 2004 under the auspices of the Executive Council.[60] Significantly, the strategy contributes 'to the attainment of sustainable development and poverty eradication by facilitating the integration of disaster risk reduction into development'.[61] The integrated approach foresees a different attitude to basic subsistence rights in that their protection must take the peculiarities of AU Member States into account; therefore, interventions need to be based on the principles of sustainable development and non-risk accumulation. These actions include 'cash-for relief instead of food, voucher-based seed programmes at seed fairs, small-scale water harvesting and integrated food, health and functional education programmes'[62] as endorsed in 2010 at the second ministerial conference on disaster risk reduction.[63]

The right to food, in its predominant component of ensuring safe foodstuffs, has thus been considered as a priority in disaster scenarios, thereby enriching the obligations that States bear vis-à-vis their population, especially in what concerns the resilience of agricultural and productivity systems.

The right to water

The foregoing considerations are applicable, *mutatis mutandis*,[64] to the right to water,[65] as well as to the preservation and restoration of water resources.[66] However, a different, rather practical, aspect needs to be added, insofar as this right is expressed not only in the obligation to sanitize water but also in the obligation to avoid water shortages.[67] Indeed, the ICESCR Committee's General Comment No. 15 specifically stipulates that the right to water has to be ensured for 'groups facing difficulties with physical access',[68] with an emphasis on victims of natural disasters or people living in disaster-prone areas. Moreover, General Comment No. 15 goes on to highlight that, in disaster-relief scenarios, all the rights enshrined in the ICESCR need to be given priority, with particular emphasis on the right to water,[69] while international assistance needs to be provided in compliance with the ICESCR itself.[70] Finally, on a more general level, States are required to comply with the obligations to respect and protect the right to water.[71]

Looking at the practice on the ground, three elements bear mention. Firstly, the High Commissioner for Human Rights has stressed the impact that climate change can have on weather-related disaster, thereby envisaging a potential breach of the right to water.[72] Secondly, in the concluding observations regarding Uzbekistan, the Committee on the Rights of the Child considers the right to water a component of 'environmental health', a matter closely bound up with the ecological disaster in the Aral Sea.[73] Thirdly, the World Health Organization has put out a set of guidelines designed to ensure safe water in disaster scenarios.[74] From these three elements, it could be inferred that the right to water should not be regarded as isolated from the rights to health and food.

The theoretical account contained in General Comment No. 15 and the practice concerning the right to water make it possible to conclude that this right constitutes a basic need to be protected and ensured in a disaster scenario. In doing so, States have to insert these protections in legislative acts, especially those aimed at implementing a disaster response framework.

The foregoing combined analysis of the rights to health, food, and water has shown that these rights are the main elements to be taken into account in disaster scenarios, thereby contributing to their identification as basic subsistence rights. However, the practice of States and international organizations seems to suggest that they should never be interpreted separately but in as a whole, thereby supporting the idea that they all constitute a sort of *basket* of basic human needs.

Identifying the concept of basic subsistence rights

Despite some attempts,[75] legal theory has not yet come up with a comprehensive analysis of basic subsistence rights, even if the problem has captured the attention of many philosophers. A detailed account of the philosophical debate on the concept of human rights, and of basic subsistence rights amongst them, falls outside the scope of this chapter and is well beyond my own capacity. However, before delving into the legal dimension of these rights, it may be helpful to provide a brief overview of that debate so as to better delineate our findings.

In his seminal monograph, Henry Shue argues that the right to subsistence is a basic human right whose full enjoyment is needed as a condition for the enjoyment of other rights.[76] The broad scope of this premise has led other commentators to accept or criticize it, thereby sparking an intense academic debate.[77] This theory has been fine-tuned in such a way as to support the view that

> on an objective ranking of interests, the interest in subsistence is so important that . . . lacking subsistence is unsustainable, and . . . , the right-holders' interest in subsistence is likely to outweigh their interest in the substances of any other right.[78]

Furthermore, it has been argued that 'coordinated action[s]' are a decisive feature for the enjoyment of basic subsistence rights.[79]

Nonetheless, a consensus on the core content of basic subsistence rights is still lacking. Departing again from Shue's theory, a decisive contribution to the debate has identified the content of these rights as including, at least, 'clean water, adequate food and shelter, and basic health care',[80] whose enjoyment, according to this argument, has to be guaranteed *in rem*.[81]

Having looked at these arguments – in combination with the relative practice and the interpretation that treaty-based bodies have given of the rights to health, food, and water – we are now in a position to identify the basic subsistence rights that States need to protect in disaster scenarios.

What emerges from the interpretation of treaty-based bodies, and from the practice of regional and universal organizations and that of States, is that we still lack a general understanding of basic subsistence rights. At least two different reasons can account for this shortcoming. First and foremost, at a more theoretical level, there seems to emerge a trend that equates basic subsistence rights with human rights, laying special emphasis on the rights to life, health, water, food, and shelter. Therefore, considering the copious amount of instruments protecting these rights and the abundant interpretation and relative practice, it would seem redundant to include their specification in instruments devoted to protecting victims of disasters. This approach seems to be endorsed by the ILC's Draft Articles to the extent that, as discussed, Draft Article 5 closes with the open-ended statement 'in accordance with international law'. Indeed, the commentary on this provision clearly states that these human rights encompass 'human rights obligations expressed in relevant international agreements' and in 'customary international law'.

Secondly, the analysis done in the previous sections brings a contrast into focus: whereas, on the one hand, treaty-based bodies have provided a sound theoretical account of the rights in question, on the other the practice of organizations and States is more focused on concrete intervention.

The main consequence of this finding is that the standard for the protection of basic subsistence rights in a disaster scenario can operate on two different levels. This difference does not entail a hierarchy between the two different approaches: any discrepancies between the two can ideally be overcome to the benefit of victims through the duty to cooperate, which in turn stands as an obligation of all States. On the other hand, the lack of a theory of basic needs, at both the universal and the regional level, means that these needs essentially overlap with the rights to life, shelter, health, food, and water, but the overlap does not negatively impact disaster-relief operations and recovery actions – this to the extent that these actions and operations are in any case taken care of by the affected State itself, if need be with the support of assisting States and relief personnel.

In sum, as much as a better specification of basic subsistence rights would probably be useful at the theoretical level, such a specification seems less crucial than expected when it comes to the practice on the ground.

Conclusion

Research has made it possible to identify three different trends in the protection of basic subsistence rights in the aftermath of a disaster. Firstly, basic subsistence rights essentially overlap, or rather, they belong in the wider category of human rights, with a marked focus on the rights to life, health, food, water, and shelter. Secondly – with the exception of the right to life – this in turn entails that States have an obligation to respect, protect and fulfil these rights, realizing them progressively and using all available economic resources. In any case, it has to be stressed that their core content – such as it can be gleaned from the general comments – must be guaranteed immediately, even in emergency situations, and *a fortiori* in a disaster scenario. This finding is corroborated by the recent Sendai Framework for Disaster Risk Reduction,[82] an instrument promoted as the successor to the Hyogo Framework.[83] They both include the rights to health, water, and food within the wider category of human rights as key elements to be taken into account in the *ex ante* phase of a disaster. As we have seen, this also confirms that it is almost impossible to isolate the protection of basic subsistence rights in the lifecycle of a disaster. Thirdly, the vast majority of instruments analyzed in this chapter are mainly operational, that is, rather than insisting on the need to define basic subsistence rights, they focus on ensuring that concrete actions and strategies are deployed in a disaster scenario. This becomes especially apparent in the recitals of these instruments, where rights are quickly invoked before setting out the principles to be observed in relief operations.

The international and regional disaster relief system is thus based on the concrete actions to be taken by all of the agents involved. This is one of the reasons why a proper categorization of basic subsistence rights is still lacking, so much so that it would be extremely difficult to transplant a hierarchy of rights into a hierarchy of actions. In any case, the lack of a theoretical statement has never affected the practicability of interventions; on the contrary, the absence of specific constraints tied to any instruments makes for a good deal of flexibility – the more the better – and this can be pointed out as the outcome that clearly needs to be safeguarded.

Another issue needs to be stressed. To date, there is no international litigation regarding the enforcement of basic subsistence rights. Even though certain elements could be inferred from the Hurricane Katrina case,[84] it remains difficult for treaty-based bodies to hear complaints alleging a violation of basic subsistence rights.[85]

In light of the piecemeal framework that has been sketched out, and considering that disaster scenarios require a practical rather than a theoretical approach, the lack of a proper theory of basic subsistence rights does not seem a big issue. Indeed, these rights are included in ICESCR general comments and constantly referred to as well in the practice of international organizations. Moreover, the review mechanisms established under universal treaties entail that treaty-based bodies will assess the legislative and operational framework that States put into practice to cope with disasters.

A full-fledged list of basic subsistence rights seems to amount to a theoretical exercise to the extent that, in one way or another, these rights are already in place as State obligations. It can thus be concluded that basic subsistence rights enjoy a very practical dimension singled out in both the *ex ante* and the *ex post* phase – a dimension that is key to ensuring the protection of victims provided for in the ILC's Draft Article 5.

Selected bibliography

O. De Schutter and K. Cordes, *Accounting for Hunger: The Right to Food in the Era of Globalization* (Hart Publishing, 2011).

H. Shue, *Basic Rights: Subsistence, Affluence and US Foreign Policy* (2nd edn, Princeton University Press, 1996).

B. Toebes, *The Right to Health as a Human Right in International Law* (Intersentia-Hart, 1999).

A. Trhlj, 'Water for All? Developing a Human Right to Water in National and International Law' 65 *International and Comparative Law Quarterly* (2016) 771.

F. Zorzi Giustiniani, 'The Works of the International Law Commission on "Protection of Persons in the Event of Disasters": A Critical Appraisal' in A. de Guttry, M. Gestri and G. Venturini (eds), *International Disaster Response Law* (TMC Asser Press-Springer, 2012) 65.

Notes

* The research for this chapter was mostly carried out at the Sarajevo University School of Law and financed through a postdoctoral grant awarded by the University of Graz. Responsibility for any errors rests with me.

1 S.F. Ali, 'Crowd-Sourced Governance in a Post-Disaster Context' 64 *International and Comparative Law Quarterly* (2015) 211.

2 UNGA, Res 46/182, UN Doc. A/RES/46/182 (19 December 1991), available at www.un.org/documents/ga/res/46/a46r182.htm, accessed on 7 June 2017.

3 Institute of International Law, Bruges session, 2 September 2003, 16th Commission, Humanitarian Assistance, Rapporteur: M. Budislav Vukas, available at www.ifrc.org/Docs/idrl/I318EN.pdf, accessed on 7 June 2017.

4 Ibid 2.

5 Ibid para 1(1): '"Humanitarian assistance" means all acts, activities and the human and material resources for the provision of goods and services of an exclusively humanitarian character, indispensable for the survival and the fulfillment of the essential needs of the victims of disasters'.

6 Ibid letters (a) and (b).

7 UNGA, Res 43/131, UN Doc. A/RES/43/131 (8 December 1988) and Res 45/100, UN Doc. A/RES/45/100 (14 December 1990), available at www.un.org/documents/ga/res/43/a43r131.htm and www.un.org/documents/ga/res/45/a45r100.htm, accessed on 7 June 2017.

8 See also Adinolfi's chapter in this volume.

9 See also Rolink's chapter in this volume.

10 According to art 3 of the Draft Articles on the Protection of Persons in the Event of Disasters, adopted by the International Law Commission at its 68th session in 2016, '"disaster" means a calamitous event or series of events resulting in widespread loss of life, great human suffering and distress, mass displacement, or large-scale material or environmental damage, thereby seriously disrupting the functioning of society'. Subparagraph 10 of the Draft Articles commentary expressly excludes armed conflicts from this definition. See also UN Doc. A/71/10, 24. For a comment on this definition see G. Bartolini and P. Benvenuti, 'Is There a Need for New International Humanitarian Law Implementation Mechanisms?' in R. Kolb and G. Gaggioli (eds), *Research Handbook on Human Rights and Humanitarian Law* (Edward

Elgar Publishing, 2013) 590; G. Bartolini, 'La Definizione di Disastro nel Progetto di Articoli della Commissione del Diritto Internazionale' 98 *Rivista di Diritto Internazionale* (2015) 155; F. Zorzi Giustiniani, 'The Works of the International Law Commission on "Protection of Persons in the Event of Disasters": A Critical Appraisal' in A. de Guttry, M. Gestri and G. Venturini (eds), *International Disaster Response Law* (TMC Asser Press-Springer, 2012) 65.

11 UNGA, Res 43/131 (n. 7) para 4; UNGA, Res 45/100 (n. 7) para 4; UNGA, Res 46/182 (n. 2) para 6.

12 For instance, UNGA, Res 43/131 acknowledges that 'in providing humanitarian assistance, in particular the supply of food, medicines or health care, for which access to victims is essential, rapid relief will avoid a tragic increase in their number'. Annex 1 to UNGA Res 46/182 stipulates that 'the United Nations should continue to make appropriate arrangements with interested Governments and intergovernmental and non-governmental organizations to enable it to have more expeditious access, when necessary, to their emergency relief capacities, including food reserves'.

13 Art 1, letters (a) and (b).

14 R. Kolb, 'De l'assistance humanitaire: la resolution sur l'assistance humanitaire adoptée par l'Institut de Droit International à sa session de Bruges en 2003' 86 *Revue Internationale de la Croix-Rouge* (2004) 856.

15 ILC, Report of the International Law Commission, Sixty-Eighth Session (2 May–10 June and 4 July–12 August 2016), UN Doc. A/71/10 (2016) art 2, para 6.

16 Draft Articles commentary (n. 15) art 2, para 8.

17 Ibid art 4, para 1.

18 Ibid art 5, para 5.

19 Ibid art 5, para 6.

20 E. Sommario, 'Derogation from Human Rights Treaties in Situations of Natural and Man Made Disasters' in de Guttry et al. (eds) (n. 10) 323. See also the Sommario's chapter in this volume.

21 See art 7 of Draft articles: 'in the application of the present draft articles, States shall, as appropriate, cooperate among themselves, with the United Nations, with the components of the Red Cross and the Red Crescent Movement, and with other assisting actors'. In particular, para 3 of the commentary recalls that the obligation to cooperate was already present in UNGA, Res 46/182. See also G. Bartolini, T. Natoli and A. Riccardi, 'Report on the Expert on the ILC's Draft Articles on the Protection of Persons in the Event of Disasters' 3 *International Law and Disasters Working Paper Series* (2015) 36.

22 See the Giacca's chapter in this book. See also A. Muller, *The Relationship between Economic, Social and Cultural Rights and International Humanitarian Law* (Brill, 2013) 127.

23 See E. Riedel, 'Health, Right to, International Protection' in *Max Planck Encyclopedia of Public International Law* (Oxford University Press, 2011); J. Tobin, *The Right to Health in International Law* (Oxford University Press, 2012); B. Toebes, 'The Right to Health' in B. Toebes, M. Hartlev, A. Hendriks and J.R. Heermann (eds), *Health and Human Rights in Europe* (Intersentia, 2012) 213; B. Toebes, *The Right to Health as a Human Right in International Law* (Intersentia-Hart, 1999).

24 CESCR, General Comment No. 14: The Right to the Highest Attainable Standard of Health, UN Doc. E/C.12/2000/4 (2000).

25 Ibid para 16.

26 Ibid para 40:

> States parties have a joint and individual responsibility . . . to cooperate in providing disaster relief . . . Priority in the provision of international medical aid, distribution and management of resources, such as safe and potable water, food and medical supplies, and financial aid should be given to the most vulnerable or marginalized groups of the population.

27 Art 1 UN Charter:

> [t]he purposes of the United Nations are . . . to achieve international co-operation in solving international problems of an economic, social, cultural, or humanitarian character, and in promoting and encouraging respect for human rights and for fundamental freedoms for all without distinction as to race, sex, language, or religion'

In the ICESCR see arts 1(2), 2(1), 11, 11(2), 15(4). See also UNGA, Res 25/2625, UN Doc. A/RES/25/2625 (24 October 1970).

28 Art 31(b) TRIPs stipulates that the requirement to obtain a prior authorization may be waived in case of 'national emergency or other circumstances of extreme urgency'. See, in general, M. Hestermayer,

Human Rights and the WTO: The Case of Patents and Access to Medicines (Oxford University Press, 2007); M. Sognigbe, 'Le Droit d'Accès aux Médicaments et l'Accord sur les ADPIC: une Lecture à la Lumière des Droits de l'Homme' 21 *Revue de Droit Sanitaire et Social* (2011) 501.

29 Annual Report of the Inter-American Commission on Human Rights 2004, Chapter IV (Haiti), OEA/Ser.L/V/II.122 Doc. 5 rev. (25 February 2005) para 117.

30 CommEDAW, Concluding Comments of the Committee on the Elimination of Discrimination against Women: Indonesia, UN Doc. CEDAW/C/IDN/CO/5 (2007) para 38.

31 CommEDAW, Report of the Committee on the Elimination of Discrimination against Women, UN Doc. A/59/38 (12–30 January 2014) paras 355–356.

32 See, for instance, the HRC, Report of the Special Rapporteur on the Right of Everyone to the Enjoyment of the Highest Attainable Standard of Physical and Mental Health, Addendum, Mission to Japan, UN Doc. A/HRC/23/41/Add.3 (2013). The country visit was needed to ascertain the Japanese situation in the wake of the Fukushima nuclear plant disaster.

33 CommRC, Concluding Observations of the Committee on the Rights of the Child: Kazakhstan, UN Doc. CRC/C/15/ADD.213 (10 July 2003) paras 7 and 59.

34 CommRC, General Comment No. 15 on the Right of the Child to the Enjoyment of the Highest Attainable Standard of Health (art. 24), UN Doc. CRC/C/GC/15 (2013) para 40.

35 HRComm, Consideration of Reports Submitted by States Parties Under Article 40 of the Covenant Concluding Observations of the Human Rights Committee: United States of America, UN Doc. CCPR/C/USA/CO/3/Rev.1 (18 December 2006) para 26. See also the US Response, 12 February 2008, CCPR/C/USA/CO/3/Rev.1/Add.1, detailing the concrete measures taken to respond to the Committee's observations.

36 Djibouti: Combined Initial and Periodic Reports (1993–2013), 3 May 2014, available at http://disasterlaw.sssup.it/human-rights-protection-and-disasters-list-of-documents/, accessed on 7 June 2017.

37 CommEDAW, Concluding Observations on the 5th and 6th Periodic Reports of Chile, UN Doc. CEDAW/C/CHL/CO/5-6 (1–19 October 2012).

38 WHO, Strengthening National Health Emergency and Disaster Management Capacities and Resilience of Health Systems, UN Doc. EB128.R10 (22 January 2011). This instrument urges States to include health protection in the aftermath of a disaster in their national health plans (sec. 1(1)) and to allocate sufficient resources for this purpose. WHA58.1, 58th World Health Organisation meeting, urging States to ensure access to health care, in particular for vulnerable groups such as women and children and those affected by communicable diseases or disability (art 2(7)). See also the WHO, Emergency Response Framework, providing a set of guidelines enabling States and other organizations to ascertain whether the affected State is suffering a public health threat taking into account the scale of the disaster and the urgency of the response. See also the WHO, Technical Report: Health Systems in Urban Disasters 2013, offering case studies drawn from disasters affecting specified countries (37–61). On mental health, see WHO, Assessing Mental Health and Psychosocial Needs and Resources: Toolkit for Humanitarian Settings (2012) 8.

39 UNSC, Res 2177(2014), UN Doc. S/RES/2177 (2014), 18 September 2014. See F. Casolari, 'La reazione alla diffusione del virus Ebola: verso un nuovo paradigma nella governance internazionale delle pandemie?' in L.P. Tronconi (ed), *Unione europea e diritto alla tutela della salute: problematiche giuridiche comparate* (Maggioli, 2016) 177.

40 ASEAN has been established through the Declaration constituting an agreement establishing the Association of South East Asian Nations (ASEAN) (adopted 8 August 1967, entered into force 8 August 1967) I-22342 UNTS. See P. Nguitragool and J. Rüland, *ASEAN as an Actor in International Fora: Reality, Potential and Constraints* (Cambridge University Press, 2015). For a historical account of ASEAN see also S. Narine, 'Institutional Theory and Southeast Asia: the Case of ASEAN' 161 *World Affairs* (1998) 33.

41 ASEAN Socio-Cultural Community, ASEAN Committee on Disaster Management, ASEAN Declaration on mutual assistance on natural disasters, Manila (26 June 1976) art 1(d), available at http://asean.org/?static_post=asean-declaration-on-mutual-assistance-on-natural-disasters-manila-26-june-1976, accessed on 7 June 2017.

42 ASEAN, ASEAN Agreement on Disaster Management and Emergency Response, Vientiane (adopted 26 July 2005, entered into force 24 December 2009), available at http://agreement.asean.org/media/download/20140119170000.pdf, accessed on 7 June 2017. On cooperation between Asian States and non-ASEAN members, see S. Jiang, 'International Disaster Response Law and Policy in China: Evolution, Problem and Resolution' 12 *Chinese Journal of International Law* (2013) 455.

43 See M. Gestri, 'EU Disaster Response Law: Principles and Instruments' in de Guttry et al. (n. 10) 105; M. Broberg, 'Legal Basis of EU Council Regulation 1257/96 Concerning Humanitarian Aid: Time for Revision?' in H.J. Heintze and A. Zwitter (eds), *International Law and Humanitarian Assistance: A Crosscut through Legal Issues Pertaining to Humanitarianism* (Springer, 2011) 71.
44 C. Dany, 'Politicization of Humanitarian Aid in the European Union' 20 *European Foreign Affairs Review* (2015) 419; A. Mattelaer, 'The Empty Promise of Comprehensive Planning in EU Crisis Management' 18 *European Foreign Affairs Review* (2016) 125; N. Pavlov, 'Conceptualizing EU Crisis Management' 20 *European Foreign Affairs Review* (2015) 23; F. Pusterla and E. Pusterla, 'The Uniqueness of EU Humanitarian Aid Policy Between Sovereignty and Humanitarian Concerns' 20 *European Foreign Affairs Review* (2015) 247.
45 M. Glasius, 'The EU Response to the Tsunami and the Need for a Human Security Approach' 11 *European Foreign Affairs Review* (2006) 353.
46 See http://ec.europa.eu/echo/what-we-do/civil-protection/european-medical-corps_en, accessed on 7 June 2017.
47 Decision No 1313/2013/EU of the European Parliament and of the Council on a Union Civil Protection Mechanism, OJ L 347/924 (2013).
48 General Comment No. 14 (n. 24) paras 43–45. For a medical approach, see K.L. Koenig, H.C.S. Lim and S.H. Tsai, 'Crisis Standard of Care: Refocusing Health Care Goals during Catastrophic Disasters and Emergencies' 3 *Journal of Experimental and Clinical Medicine* (2011) 159.
49 CESCR, General Comment No. 12: The Right to Adequate Food (Art. 11 of the Covenant), UN Doc. E/C.12/1999/5 (1999).
50 See P. Alston and K. Tomasevski, *The Right to Food* (Martinus Nijhoff Publishers, 1984); O. De Schutter and K. Cordes, *Accounting for Hunger: The Right to Food in the Era of Globalization* (Hart Publishing, 2011); K. Mechlem, 'Food, Right to, International Protection' in *Max Planck Encyclopedia of Public International Law* (Oxford University Press, 2008); S. Raponi, 'A Defense of the Human Right to Adequate Food' 23 *Res Publica* (2016) 99.
51 General Comment No. 12 (n. 49) para 13.
52 Ibid paras 38–39.
53 Combined Periodic Report of the Republic of Niger on the Implementation of the African Charter on Human's and People's Rights, 2003–2014, para 301.
54 Ibid para 303.
55 Nigeria's 5th Periodic Country Report (2011–2014) on the Implementation of the African Charter on Human and Peoples' Rights, 109.
56 CommRC (n. 33) para 59.
57 *Ex multis*, FAO, The Impact of Disasters on Agriculture and Food Security (2015).
58 FAO, Resilient Livelihoods. Disaster Risk Reduction for Food and Nutrition Security (2013) 91.
59 Constitutive Act of the African Union (adopted 11 July 2000, entered into force 26 May 2001), 37733 UNTS.
60 Africa Regional Strategy for Disaster Risk Reduction, July 2004, available at www.unisdr.org/files/4038_africaregionalstrategy1.pdf, accessed on 7 June 2017.
61 Ibid para 3.1.
62 Ibid para 3.3.6.
63 African Union Commission, United Nations International Strategy for Disaster Reduction: Extended programme of action for the implementation of the Africa regional strategy for disaster risk reduction (2006–2015) and declaration of the 2nd African Ministerial Conference on Disaster Risk Reduction 2010, available at www.preventionweb.net/files/19613_bookletpoaenglish.pdf, accessed on 7 June 2017.
64 This approach is also endorsed in P. Thielbörger, 'Re-Conceptualizing the Right to Water: A Pledge for a Hybrid Approach' 15 *Human Rights Law Review* (2015) 225.
65 See E. Benvenisti, 'Water, Right to, International Protection' in *Max Planck Encyclopedia of Public International Law* (Oxford University Press, 2010).
66 CESCR, General Comment No. 15: The Right to Water (Arts. 11 and 12 of the Covenant), UN Doc. E/C.12/2002/11 (2003).
67 K. Ellis and L. Feris, 'The Right to Sanitation: Time to Delink from the Right to Water' 36 *Human Rights Quarterly* (2014) 607.
68 General Comment No.15 (n. 66): 'Groups facing difficulties with physical access to water, such as . . . victims of natural disasters, persons living in disaster-prone areas . . . are provided with safe and sufficient water' (para 16(g)).
69 Ibid para 34.

70 Ibid.

71 Ibid para 22. S. Salman and S. McInerney-Lankford, *The Human Right to Water: Legal and Policy Dimensions* (Open Knowledge Repository, 2004); A. Trhlj, 'Water for All? Developing a Human Right to Water in National and International Law' 65 *International and Comparative Law Quarterly* (2016) 771.

72 HRC, Report of the Office of the United Nations High Commissioner for Human Rights on the Relationship between Climate Change and Human Rights, UN Doc. A/HRC/10/61 (2009) paras 28–30.

73 CommRC, Concluding Observations: Uzbekistan, UN Doc. CRC/C/UZB/CO/2 (2006) para 54.

74 WHO, Household Water Treatment and Safe Storage Following Emergencies and Disasters: Southasia Earthquake and Tsunami (2002).

75 A. Eide, A. Eide, C. Krause and A. Rosas (eds), *Economic, Social and Cultural Rights: A Textbook: Second Revised Edition* (Martinus Nijhoff Publishers, 2001); M. Ssenyonjo, *Economic, Social and Cultural Rights in International Law* (Hart Publishing, 2009); E. Riedel, G. Giacca and C. Golay (eds), *Economic, Social and Cultural Rights in International Law: Contemporary Issues and Challenges* (Oxford University Press, 2016).

76 H. Shue, *Basic Rights: Subsistence, Affluence and US Foreign Policy* (2nd edn, Princeton University Press, 1996).

77 A criticism of Shue has been put forward by T. Pogge, 'Shue on Rights and Duties' in C.R. Beitz and R.E. Goodin (eds), *Global Basic Rights* (Oxford University Press, 2009) 113 – who in turn has been criticized in E. Ashford, 'In What Sense Is the Right to Subsistence a Basic Right?' 40 *Journal of Social Philosophy* (2009) 488.

78 Ashford (n. 77) 501.

79 J. Lichtenberg, 'Are There Any Basic Rights?' in Beitz and Goodin (n. 77) 71, 91.

80 C. Jones, 'The Human Right to Subsistence' 30 *Journal of Applied Philosophy* (2013) 57, 61.

81 S. Hope, 'Subsistence Needs, Human Rights, and Imperfect Duties' 30 *Journal of Applied Philosophy* (2013) 87, 89.

82 Sendai Framework for Disaster Risk Reduction 2015–2030, Third UN World Conference, 2015. The Sendai Framework has also been endorsed by UNGA, Res A/71/230. See also A. Aitsi-Selmi, S. Egawa, H. Sasaki, C. Wannous and V. Murray, 'The Sendai Framework for Disaster Risk Reduction: Renewing the Global Commitment to People's Resilience, Health and Wellbeing' 6 *International Journal of Disaster Risk Science* (2015) 164.

83 Hyogo Framework for Action: Building the Resilience of Nations and Communities to Disasters, 2005–2015. The Hyogo Framework has also been endorsed by UNGA, Res 60/195: International Strategy for Disaster Reduction, UN Doc. A/RES/60/195 (2 March 2006).

84 HRC (n. 32).

85 G. Ulfstein, 'Individual Complaints' in H. Keller and G. Ulfstein (eds), *UN Human Rights Treaty Bodies: Law and Legitimacy* (Cambridge University Press, 2012) 73; U. Khaliq and R. Churchill, 'The Protection of Economic and Social Rights: A Particular Challenge?' in H. Keller and G. Ulfstein (eds), *UN Human Rights Treaty Bodies: Law and Legitimacy* (Cambridge University Press, 2012) 199.

12

THE HUMAN RIGHT TO ADEQUATE HOUSING IN POST-DISASTER CONTEXTS*

Raquel Rolnik

Introduction

The appointment of the first Special Rapporteur (SR) on adequate housing as a component of the right to an adequate standard of living dates back to 2000, when the Commission on Human Rights (CHR) adopted resolution 2000/9 by consensus.[1] In 2007, when the Human Rights Council (HRC) replaced the CHR, the former extended the mandates of all the latter thematic special procedures, including that of this particular SR;[2] specifically, it requested that the SR promote the full realization of adequate housing, identify protection gaps and connect practical solutions and the provision of technical assistance.[3] The first SR appointed by the CHR (and subsequently by the HRC), Miloon Kothari, drawing upon the interpretation of the right to adequate housing offered by the Committee on Economic, Social and Cultural Rights (CESCR),[4] proposed a broad interpretation of the right to adequate housing based on the indivisibility and universality of human rights, defining it as '[t]he right of every women, man, youth and child to gain and sustain a safe and secure home and community in which to live in peace and dignity'.[5] During his mandate, he advocated for better support and response from States, focusing in particular on the lack of legislation and implementation of the right to housing and on the issues of homelessness, forced evictions, discrimination, affordability and the human right to water and sanitation.[6]

The attention of the first SR was first focused on the link between disasters and the right to housing when he visited Iran in 2004, following the earthquake that shocked the country in December 2003. Specifically, the SR paid a visit to Bam, a city situated at the epicentre of the Iranian earthquake which was completely destroyed. He reported that, in disaster-prone areas, the accessibility element of the right to adequate housing is particularly relevant, entailing States' obligations to adopt both prevention and reconstruction measures.[7] The disastrous effects of subsequent natural phenomena such as the Indian Ocean tsunamis of 2004, the South Asia earthquake and United States hurricane of 2005 and the earthquake in Peru of 2007, convinced SR Kothari in his final Report to propose that the next mandate holder further consider, *inter alia*, the issue of the impact of natural disasters, humanitarian emergencies and climate change on the right to adequate housing. In this regard, he notably underlined that the effect of natural disasters on individuals' right to adequate housing requires the integration of human rights standards into the entire disaster cycle, namely into prevention, relief and rehabilitation efforts.[8]

It is indeed a reality that the right to housing can be severely compromised by disasters; through damage and destruction; loss of records; and displacement of individuals, families and communities. The impact of severe natural phenomena can be devastating upon affected persons, causing the destruction of their homes and property, and public infrastructure; disruption or termination of essential services; and the prolonged and sometimes even permanent forced displacement from land, home and community. Although wealth and power do not offer immunity from such impact, it is in most cases the poor and socially disadvantaged persons who are the worst affected. The poor notably stand to lose most in disaster contexts for they usually settle on fragile and exposed land highly susceptible to the effects of disasters. When destructive phenomena strike, their pre-existing vulnerabilities are exacerbated. In the aftermath of disasters, they often find their attempts to return to their homes officially denied on the grounds that return would be unsafe. In addition, vulnerable victims of disasters are often exposed to grave human rights violations, invariably including the right to adequate housing. Their return may be denied when displaced individuals do not have official proof of a right to live in a given land or home in the first place.

The need to focus on the interplay between disasters and the right to housing is therefore compelling. The urgency of such necessity is enhanced by the increasing prevalence of natural phenomena worldwide that have more devastating effects than ever before; by the likelihood that this trend will continue as a result of climate change, rapid urbanization and population growth; and as a result of the comparatively less experience and guidance available to address issues related to the right to adequate housing in the wake of disasters, compared to post-conflict settings.[9]

These are the reasons why, upon appointment as SR to the right to housing, the present author decided to answer the plea of the preceding SR. In the 2008 report, this author notably underlined that both post-disaster situations and climate change were of particular relevance to the SR's mandate.[10] These themes emerged as central in this author's work, and subsequent reports were devoted to the integration between human rights standards in post-disaster and post-conflict reconstruction processes,[11] to the right to adequate housing in disaster relief efforts,[12] and to the impact of climate change for the fulfilment of the right to adequate housing.[13] The following pages describe and further expand on the three reports mentioned, proceeding in two steps. First, a definition of the right to housing in disaster scenarios is provided. Then, the main consequences stemming from this definition in terms of obligations incumbent upon States are delineated. In particular, this contribution focuses on (i) due diligence obligations in the pre-disaster phase, (ii) specific obligations concerning property restitution in the aftermath of disasters and (iii) the issue of discrimination in disaster settings.[14]

Towards a broad notion of the right to adequate housing and property restitution in disaster contexts

The right to housing as a component of the right to an adequate standard of living is clearly recognized in Article 11 of the International Covenant on Economic, Social and Cultural Rights (ICESCR).[15] Pursuant to this provision, States have unambiguous obligations to respect, protect and fulfil the right to adequate housing. This implies that States are called to implement the right to housing by taking steps, individually or through international assistance and cooperation, to the maximum of their available resources, with a view of progressively achieving its full realization.[16] The CESCR underlined in its General Comment No. 4 that the right shall be interpreted broadly. In other words, it cannot be simply equated to the right to have a 'roof over one's head',[17] but – on the contrary – it must be seen as the right to live in security, peace and dignity.[18] The CESCR identified seven aspects of the right to adequate housing that States must progressively realize, namely: security of tenure; availability of services, material, facilities and infrastructure;

affordability; habitability; accessibility; location; and cultural adequacy.[19] Therefore, housing is not simply a shelter commodity but, rather, has an inherent social value.

Although the CESCR was therefore clear in generally expanding the scope of the right to housing, in disaster settings it is too often still looked at from a strict viewpoint, i.e. as simply entailing obligations for States to provide a shelter in the aftermath of disasters. Indeed, even though the right to housing has attracted growing consideration in the United Nations (UN) system[20] and doctrine, notably due to the increase of the world population, disparities in standards of living, the phenomena of homelessness and poverty clusters,[21] so far little attention has been paid to the intricacies of its enjoyment in disaster scenarios. This state of affairs originated from two sequential causes.

First, it has taken time for the human rights implications of disasters to be clearly recognized. According to the Inter-Agency Standing Committee (IASC), natural disasters have traditionally 'been seen as situations that create challenges and problems mainly of a humanitarian nature',[22] although the CESCR explicitly included victims of natural disasters and people living in disaster-prone areas among the disadvantaged groups that 'should be ensured some degree of priority consideration in the housing sphere'.[23] During the past decade however, there have been important and welcomed shifts in this approach. According to the IASC, '[i]ncreasingly, it has come to be recognized that human rights protection also needs to be provided in these contexts' given that '[h]uman rights have to be the legal underpinning of all humanitarian work pertaining to natural disasters'.[24] Yet, the relative youth of the international community's interest in the human rights' implications of disasters has resulted in scarce studies and international guidelines on this issue. This is particularly true for the right to housing.

Second – as anticipated – in disaster contexts, the right to housing has been too often narrowly interpreted (contrary to the opinion expressed by the CESCR in its General Comment No. 4 to broadly construe its contents) which has led on occasions to violations of the right. Existing international guidance has so far made limited reference to the right at hand and narrowed it to the need to provide shelter, housing, or to aspects related to protection. The elaboration of the right to housing in disaster settings therefore often remained at the level of generalities[25] or was addressed only from a specific angle.[26] In 2012, the HRC adopted a resolution on the right to adequate housing in the context of disaster settings,[27] which constitutes today the most authoritative international effort to delineate States' human rights obligations vis-à-vis the right to housing and disasters. Yet, this and other isolated attempts to discuss the right in a more comprehensive manner were seemingly never translated into policies of broad application.

The most worrying consequence of adhering to a strict interpretation of the right to housing is that the impact of calamitous events is usually measured merely in quantitative terms. Although it is true that the number of people affected by disasters are often staggering, the right to housing should also and perhaps primarily be understood in terms of the extent of the disruption of social relationships, networks and assets; destruction of home-centred livelihoods built up over many years; and the undermining of complex, multilayered land tenure rights.[28] Broadening the scope of the right would allow the recognition that States are not only bound to address the destruction of housing as a physical asset through repair, rehabilitation and reconstruction, but that authorities are also under an obligation to address the destruction of housing as a social asset and are therefore required to establish more multifaceted and longer-term responses based on a deeper understanding of the tenure system and histories of the affected settlements and, in particular, of their poorer and marginalized residents. Moreover, a broad understanding of the right to housing in disaster settings would also require vigilance in the course of restoration and reconstruction, in order to ensure that previously held tenure is not undermined or diminished in any way but is, instead, protected and where possible strengthened.

In light of these considerations, a definition of the right to adequate housing in disaster contexts shall comprise the right to live in safety and security, in conditions deemed adequate on grounds of security of tenure; availability of services, materials, facilities and infrastructure; affordability; habitability; accessibility; location; and cultural adequacy. Only by employing such a broad interpretation of the right at hand can States abide to the obligations stemming from Article 11 ICESCR in the reading given to it by the CESCR and thus allow the full realization of the right to housing both prior to and in the aftermath of disasters.

Acting with due diligence in order to prevent violations of the right to housing

A human rights approach to disasters has a lot to offer in terms of reduction of risks. While some disasters are unavoidable, much can be done to avoid their negative impacts on human rights. With respect specifically to the right to housing, the implementation of a human rights approach entails a number of due diligence obligations incumbent upon States, relating in particular to the pre-disaster phase.

First, of particular importance is the obligation to adopt measures aimed at strengthening the resilience and capacity to adapt of individuals and groups most vulnerable to the impacts of disasters. In this vein, Disaster Risk Reduction (DRR) plays a pivotal role, as recognized by the HRC, which encouraged States to respect, protect and fulfil the right to housing 'in their broader disaster risk reduction, prevention and preparedness initiatives'.[29] Examples of projects that can be adopted within a DRR strategy include conducting risk assessment in urban planning, rural development projects and the design of housing. Also, warning information must be communicated to all communities at risk in order to allow dwellers to seek protection and to take risk reduction actions. In this respect, the European Court of Human Rights has already had occasion to underline that States have a human rights obligation to reduce disaster risks and vulnerabilities by setting up, *inter alia*, alarm and evacuation systems if a disaster is foreseeable. Also, if the State is able to prevent ensuing threats to life and property, it has to take appropriate action in conformity with its human rights obligations under both the right to life and the right to private life and property.[30] Successful examples include the evacuation of hundreds of thousands of people from Cuba when the 2004 Hurricane Charley started approaching the country.[31] Similarly, various effective measures were adopted in many central American States, partly in response to the devastation caused by Hurricane Mitch in 1998.[32]

Second, States have an obligation to implement DRR activities in a manner that respects human rights. For instance, when States adopt so called 'constructive forced evictions'[33] – namely evictions rendered necessary by public security and safety concerns – these are legitimate only in so far as the regulations introducing them are in line with human rights standards, in particular the strict procedural requirements relating to the conduct of evictions per se and the right to redress and remedy.[34] Also, evictions should not result in individuals becoming homeless. In this respect, when those affected by disasters are unable to provide for themselves, States must take measures to ensure that alternative housing, resettlement or access to productive land is available.[35] Moreover, restrictive measures affecting an individual's freedom of movement must always conform to the principle of proportionality.[36] This implies that a balance must be struck between the rights of those affected and the obligation of the State to mitigate the anticipated damage and ensure public safety. Accordingly, in adopting restrictive measures – such as for instance a regulation preventing residents from returning to beachfront areas in order to prevent the effects of a tsunami – States shall show that the adopted measure is the least restrictive means of achieving the sought objective, by demonstrating that other safety measures are not available or are ineffective.

States are therefore under an obligation to adopt DRR legislation respecting the right to adequate housing. Special attention shall be given to those who may face discrimination and exclusion, including on the grounds of tenure status, and measures must be devised to protect them.[37]

Third, States shall guarantee all affected persons and groups access to information and grant them the ability to participate meaningfully in the planning and implementation of the various stages of disaster response. Human rights law mandates the participation of groups that stand to be affected in the design and implementation of mitigation measures. In this regard, the HRC urged States to 'ensure access to information and meaningful consultation and participation of affected persons and communities in the planning and implementation of shelter and housing assistance'.[38] Informed and effective participation, in turn, requires that information about the mitigation targets and decisions related to these goals are managed transparently. The principle of participation in the context of mitigation initiatives should be implemented to ensure that those who stand to be most directly affected have a say in its design and implementation, which could help anticipate, and thus avert, new rights violations that could result from the measure under discussion. The informed participation of people in the development of national- and local-level responses to disasters requires efforts from States to build the capacity of populations to take part in such decisions through public awareness and mitigation. This approach will ensure that the individuals whose rights are most directly threatened by disasters (as well as by the response actions undertaken) become central authors in the implementation of urban planning initiatives and projects aimed at the development of new infrastructures. The participation of right-holders will increase the likelihood of States being more responsive to human rights vulnerabilities and of being better positioned to effectively strengthen the resilience of communities, homes and infrastructure systems. In the undertaking of DRR, human rights standards and obligations would call for the consultation and participation of concerned communities, the recognition of local knowledge and paying special attention to marginalized groups and those who face discrimination and exclusion. In this vein, a number of reconstruction projects worldwide have attempted to see the reconstruction process 'as an opportunity to promote a local development process' rather than being limited to restoring pre-disaster conditions – the participation of communities being essential in that regard.[39]

The right to housing, land and property restitution: recognizing all forms of tenure equally

The right to housing, land and property (HLP) restitution finds its most specific elaboration in the 2005 Principles on Housing and Property Restitution for Refugees and Displaced Persons (Pinheiro Principles or the Principles),[40] which recognized a distinct 'right to restitution' – covering housing, land and/or other property – for refugees and displaced persons.[41] The Pinheiro Principles constituted in this sense the culmination of a shift that commenced in the early 1990s from essentially humanitarian-driven responses to rights-based approaches to return.[42]

Yet it is not unanimously accepted that the Pinheiro Principles may also apply in disaster scenarios. Some commentators held that they are explicitly limited to the 'arbitrary or unlawful deprivation' of individuals' homes, lands or places of habitual residence following displacement.[43] In this respect, it should be underlined that the Principles' scope of application extends to all those displaced 'regardless of the nature or circumstances by which displacement originally occurred';[44] this implies that the Principles do apply in all cases of unreasonable failure by States in allowing displaced persons their right to return. Also, it may be argued that the Principles apply when the destruction of property could have been avoided, had the State implemented measures aimed at disaster preparedness and mitigation, e.g. it fell short of installing early warning systems.[45]

Moreover, the Principles can be applied as a specification of existing standards pertaining to the rights of displaced persons and refugees to return to their homes. In fact, the Principles provide relevant guidance on how best to manage the technical and legal issues associated with housing, land and property restitution, guidance which has since been reflected to varying degrees in States' policies and practice.[46]

Although the content of the Pinheiro Principles may find application in the case of disasters, they however need to be reoriented in order to be adapted to disaster contexts. In particular, a disaster-oriented re-interpretation of the Principles should encompass the refusal of the opinion – expressed by some doctrine – that the Principles do not put the rights of tenants and the rights of non-owners on equal footing,[47] for tenure security for all is central to the right to adequate housing in a post-disaster context.[48] The Principles shall therefore be understood as embracing a wide ambit of situations and as extending to any right to tenure related to housing or land prior to disasters, irrespective of the tenure status or whether the land or housing is formally registered, as confirmed by recent State practice. This line of thinking has been upheld by the HRC which, in its 2012 resolution on the right to adequate housing and disasters, maintained that 'all affected persons, irrespective of their pre-disaster tenure status and without discrimination of any kind, have equal access to housing'.[49] Furthermore, the HRC urged States to ensure that the 'tenure rights of those without individual or formally registered property ownership are recognized in restitution, compensation, reconstruction and recovery programmes'.[50] Therefore the notion of tenure security and corresponding restitution rights shall not simply be equated to the right to private ownership, nor shall it be limited to the conferral of formal legal titles. On the contrary, provided that States' obligations associated with the right to adequate housing include the obligation to respect and ensure tenure security for all irrespective of the form of tenure, it follows that those who are not registered individual owners must nevertheless be recognized as rights-holders.[51] Accordingly, housing and property restitution must be understood as the recognition and restitution of all tenure rights to housing or land.

The importance of recognizing restitution rights to all forms of tenure is particularly relevant in disaster contexts, where only a minority of victims may have individual, formally registered, ownership rights to their housing or land. If recovery efforts overlook these situations, they can perpetuate or even reinforce pre-existing patterns of vulnerability, disadvantage and discrimination. This is often the case with women: in the wake of the 2004 Indian tsunami, a large number of women had insecure tenure – as they often do because their access to housing and land frequently hinges on a relationship with a man or because they face additional hurdles as sole head of a household.[52] It has been noted that, in most housing reconstruction programmes, tenure documentation and legal proof of rights are prerequisites for establishing beneficiaries' eligibility.[53] The multiplicity of forms of tenure should thus be recognized equally, and security of tenure should be ensured for everyone post-disaster.[54] An example of such an approach can be found for instance in the South Africa Restitution of Land Rights Act and in recent operational guidance on durable solutions.[55]

This underlines that, legally speaking, property restitution should not be merely seen as part of the right to remedy but rather a condition for return and the adoption of other durable solutions.[56] Understanding the equal legitimacy of all forms of tenure is thus not only relevant to restitution but even more so to efforts to ensure durable solutions and recovery.[57] In disaster scenarios, this implies that States have an obligation to assess tenure rights – e.g. by conducting assessments of tenure arrangements, identifying insecure settlements and population groups including the homeless, facilitating participatory settlement mapping and reviewing urban plans in order to integrate settlements – and taking measures to protect and ensure secure tenure post-disaster, whether at a former place of residence or elsewhere, should individuals be unable or unwilling to return.

The right to tenure is indeed not dependent on the actual re-occupancy of a former place of habitual residence. Moreover, the principle of non-discrimination requires States to prioritize assistance and strengthen tenure security for those with weak, ambiguous or vulnerable tenure, a responsibility often overlooked in relief and recovery efforts, as further illustrated in the following paragraph.

Combating discrimination in access to adequate housing in disaster settings

As noted above, the most vulnerable – such as the poor and those living with insecure tenure – are more likely to live in disaster-prone areas. As a result, they are at a greater risk of displacement and often hardly recover from the consequences of disasters.[58] Although natural hazards do not distinguish between vulnerable and non-vulnerable individuals when they strike, it has been accepted that the losses originating from disasters are to a large extent man-made.[59] This is the result of the fact that vulnerability and discrimination are usually intertwined and that disasters, albeit not causing discrimination, do exacerbate it.[60] Two consequences stem from the inherent link between discrimination and vulnerability in disaster contexts: first, that disadvantaged groups are the most affected by disasters and, second, that actions taken by States to recover from disasters may perpetuate pre-existing patterns of discrimination against some groups.

In general terms, States are under an obligation to address housing inequalities in all phases of the disaster cycle. This stems from Articles 2 and 11 ICESCR, according to which the right to adequate housing shall be exercised without discrimination of any kind based on race, colour, sex, language, religion, political or other opinion, national or social origin, property, birth or other status.[61] It follows that States shall engage with securing the right to housing in a non-discriminatory manner, including in times of disaster. Although the HRC underlined that States shall respect, protect and fulfil the right to adequate housing without discrimination making explicit reference only to post-disaster response and recovery efforts,[62] it can be safely maintained that public authorities are under an obligation to respect equality and non-discrimination in all phases of the disaster cycle, including prevention and preparedness.

In pre-disaster settings specifically, this obligation would originate from States' general duty to undertake measures to protect vulnerable members of society and secure for disadvantaged groups the full and equal enjoyment of their human rights, even in times of severe resource constraints.[63] This viewpoint has been recognized, *inter alia*, within the European and Mediterranean Major Hazard Agreement (EUR-OPA), a platform for cooperation between European and Southern Mediterranean countries in the field of major natural and technological disasters. In 2012, EUR-OPA promoted the adoption of a document incorporating ethical principles relating to disaster risk reduction and contributing to people's resilience to disasters. The principles notably upheld that measures to prevent, reduce and prepare for disasters shall be secured and implemented without discrimination and that disaster prevention measures must be tailored to existing vulnerabilities.[64] Also, fruitful discussions have specifically taken place in relation to disaster resilience, gender equality[65] and disability.[66] A human rights-oriented approach to discrimination and the right to housing in pre-disasters would therefore entail that, in the undertaking of mitigation activities, States are called to implement, *inter alia*, gender-sensitive project designs and culturally adequate policies, the recognition of local knowledge and the adoption of measures attentive to the necessities of marginalized groups and those who face discrimination and exclusion.

In post-disaster situations, hidden discrimination and vulnerabilities usually surface, as emergency situations may highlight long-entrenched patterns of discrimination and neglect. Recovery and reconstruction shall therefore be undertaken with the aim of progressively realizing the right to housing taking particular account of pre-disaster vulnerabilities. If the right to housing is interpreted broadly – i.e. as also encompassing housing as a social asset – then States would be bound to rebuild with a view to ensuring an adequate standard of living for all.[67] In other terms, recovery should not be seen as merely including the obligation to restore pre-disaster living conditions, but also as an opportunity to promote local development processes. Following the Indian Ocean tsunami the Special Envoy of the UN Secretary-General noted that post-disaster recovery should allow authorities to 'build back better' and break out of inequitable development patterns in a sustained way.[68] In the aftermath of the Pakistan floods, it was similarly affirmed that the disaster should have been seen as 'an opportunity to build back better lives and to step up to the task of brining dignity to the millions who live on the margins of society'.[69] Among other affected vulnerable groups, special consideration in recovery programmes shall also be given to disaster-induced displaced persons, who are frequently victims of discrimination when it comes to the right to housing. In fact, the realization of their rights is often limited by marginalization and intolerance, cultural barriers and obstacles stemming from their legal status. Nevertheless, States are under an obligation to ensure non-discrimination and equal treatment of displaced persons in the enjoyment of ICESCR rights, as per Articles 2 and 11 ICESCR.[70]

In conclusion, the duty not to discriminate in post-disaster efforts means that States' interventions must aim to progressively realize the right to adequate housing for all, by improving the overall living and housing conditions in the settlements affected by disasters. The approach should thus focus on settlements and communities, not on individual constructions, with the aim to create places where people can have an adequate standard of living. With the view of implementing such an approach, States should be keen to link relief and development, in turn contributing to reducing people's vulnerability and increasing their resilience to future shocks.

Recommendations

This contribution has maintained that the right to adequate housing in disaster relief and recovery efforts should not be narrowed down to the right to shelter but should instead be accorded a broad interpretation.[71] Accordingly, the right to housing shall encompass both the adequacy of physical structures and individual property ownership, and the right of individuals to have an adequate standard of living. This expansive interpretation of the right at hand in disaster contexts entails that States' duties to realize it in pre- and post-disaster phases shall not only be seen as an obligation, but foremost as an opportunity. While DRR and disaster response activities should not replace development efforts, they may provide a timely occasion to redress the inequalities and vulnerabilities exacerbated by disasters and progressively realize the right to adequate housing for all.[72] Consequently, States should adopt an approach to disasters deliberately and comprehensively integrating the right to adequate housing both at a legal and policy level.

On the other hand – and given the actual situation of tenure systems in the world – a narrow approach to property restitution, based on the existence of registered individual freeholds in the name of affected individuals and families in order to rebuild homes and infrastructures, fails to address the actual situation of the majority of urban and rural populations, especially of the most vulnerable. In this regard, States should promote, protect and strengthen a variety of tenure forms in reconstruction efforts, including tenures deriving from statutory, customary, religious and other hybrid tenure systems.[73] Several instruments, apart from freehold, can be used in this regard: for instance possession rights, use rights and rental and collective arrangements. Non-discrimination on the basis of tenure must be guaranteed and protected in law, policy and practice. Non-discrimination on the basis of tenure must be guaranteed in the context of access to basic services and facilities, and humanitarian assistance, including access to shelter in the context of post-disaster reconstruction.

Non-discrimination on the basis of gender should also direct post-disaster reconstruction efforts. Indeed, both *de jure* and *de facto* gender equality are essential to the enjoyment of the right to adequate housing. In this regard, States must strengthen and protect women's security of tenure, regardless of age, marital, civil or social status and independently from their relationship with male householders or community members.[74]

Tenure should be secured *in situ* unless there are exceptional circumstances justifying evictions and displacements consistent with international human rights law. Public health, safety and environment risks for the population should not be used as an excuse to undermine security of tenure. *In situ* solutions should be found whenever it is possible, to: mitigate and manage risks of disasters and threats to public health and safety, or balance environmental protection and security of tenure, except when inhabitants choose to exercise their right to resettlement.[75]

Additionally, considering the importance of the role of multilateral and bilateral development agencies in post-disaster reconstruction efforts, these institutions should ensure that their operations and projects promote rather than undermine the human right to adequate housing, including by adopting safeguard policies directed to that aim.

Selected bibliography

C. Gould, 'The Right to Housing Recovery after Natural Disasters' 22 *Harvard Human Rights Journal* (2009) 169.

R. Barber, 'Protecting the Right to Housing in the Aftermath of Natural Disasters: Standards in International Human Rights Law' 20 *International Journal of Refugee Law* (2008) 432.

J.G. Sprankling, *The International Law of Property* (Oxford University Press, 2014).

A. Durand-Lasserve and L. Royston (eds), *Holding Their Ground: Secure Land Tenure for the Urban Poor in Developing Countries* (Earthscan, 2002).

H.M. Valdes, 'A Gender Perspective on Disaster Risk Reduction' in E. Enarson and P.G. Dhar Chakrabarti (eds), *Women, Gender and Disasters: Global Issues and Initiatives* (SAGE Publications, 2009) 18.

Notes

* This text was based on the reports on adequate housing and disasters presented to the Human Rights Council as Special Rapporteur on the right to adequate housing during my mandate (2008–2014). Although they are focused on natural disaster scenarios, the same findings and principles could – *mutatis mutandis* – be applied to technological disasters. The tireless work of Alice Riccardi, post-doctoral fellow at Roma Tre University was essential in the preparation of this chapter. I express my deepest gratitude to her and also to Emanuele Sommario, and the other editors of this book for their support and help.

1 CHR, Res 2000/9: Question of the Realization in All Countries of the Economic, Social and Cultural Rights Contained in the Universal Declaration of Human Rights and in the International Covenant on Economic, Social and Cultural Rights, and Study of Special Problems which the Developing Countries Face in Their Efforts to Achieve Human Rights, UN Doc. E/CN.4/ RES/2000/9 (17 April 2000). Subsequent resolutions confirming the mandate of the Special Rapporteur were CHR, Res 2001/28: Adequate Housing As a Component of the Right to an Adequate Standard of Living, UN Doc. E/ CN.4/RES/2001/28 (20 April 2001); CHR, Res 2002/21: Adequate Housing As a Component of the Right to an Adequate Standard of Living, UN Doc. E/CN.4/2002/21 (22 April 2002); CHR, Res 2003/27: Adequate Housing As a Component of the Right to an Adequate Standard of Living, UN Doc. E/CN.4/2003/27 (22 April 2003); and CHR, Res 2004/21: Adequate Housing As a Component of the Right to an Adequate Standard of Living, UN Doc. E/CN.4/2004/21 (16 April 2004).

2 HRC, Res 5/1: Human Rights Council: Institution-Building, UN Doc. A/HRC/RES5/1 (18 June 2007).

3 HRC, Res 6/27: Adequate Housing as a Component of the Right to an Adequate Standard of Living, UN Doc. A/HRC/RES/6/27 (14 December 2007).

4 CESCR, General Comment No. 4: The Right to Adequate Housing (Art 11(1) of the Covenant), UN Doc. E/1992/23 (13 December 1991); CESCR, General Comment No. 7: The Right to Adequate Housing (Art 11.1): Forced Evictions, UN Doc. E/1998/22 (20 May 1997).

5 HRC, Report of the Special Rapporteur on Adequate Housing as a Component of the Right to an Adequate Standard of Living, and on the Right to Non-Discrimination in This Context, UN Doc. A/HRC/7/16 (13 February 2008) para 4.
6 M. Kothari, 'The Global Struggle for the Right to a Place to Live' 7 *Development in Practice* (1997) 5–16; see also M. Kothari, S. Karmali and S. Chaudhry, 'The Human Right to Adequate Housing and Land' *National Human Rights Commission* (2006), available at https://rwi.lu.se/NHRIDB/Asia/India/Housing.pdf, accessed on 13 April 2017; M. Kothari and P.I. Vasquez, 'Policy Debate: The UN Guidelines on Forced Evictions: A Useful Soft-Law Instrument?' 6(2) *International Development Policy/Revue Internationale de politique de développement* (2015), available at https://poldev.revues.org/2188#quotation, accessed on 13 April 2017.
7 CHR, Report of the Special Rapporteur on Adequate Housing as a Component of the Right to an Adequate Standard of Living, Miloon Kothari: Mission to the Islam Republic of Iran, UN Doc. E/CN.4/2006/41/Add.2 (21 March 2006) paras 61–73.
8 HRC, Report of the Special Rapporteur on Adequate Housing as a Component of the Right to an Adequate Standard of Living, and on the Right to Non-Discrimination in This Context, Miloon Kothari, UN Doc. A/HRC/7/16 (13 February 2008) paras 2, 81–86.
9 See ICRC, Customary IHL Database (ICRC 2016), Rule 133, available at www.icrc.org/customary-ihl/eng/docs/v1_cha_chapter38_rule133, accessed on 13 April 2017, according to which '[t]he property rights of displaced persons must be respected'. For a recollection of resolutions adopted by both the UNGA and UNSC on the right to property restitution post-conflict, see M.J. Ballard, 'Post-Conflict Property Restitution: Flawed Legal and Theoretical Foundations' 28 *Berkley Journal of International Law* (2010) 462, fn 15; see also S. Leckie and C. Huggins, *Conflict and Housing, Land, and Property Rights: A Handbook on Issues, Frameworks and Solutions* (Cambridge University Press, 2011) 53–91.
10 UNGA, Report of the Special Rapporteur on Adequate Housing as a Component of the Right to an Adequate Standard of Living, and the Right to Non-Discrimination in This Context, UN Doc. A/63/275 (13 August 2008) paras 28–38.
11 HRC, Report of the Special Rapporteur on Adequate Housing as a Component of the Right to an Adequate Standard of Living, and the Right to Non-Discrimination in This Context, Raquel Rolnik, UN Doc. A/HRC/16/42 (20 December 2010).
12 UNGA, Report of the Special Rapporteur on Adequate Housing as a Component of the Right to an Adequate Standard of Living, UN Doc. A/66/270 (5 August 2011) (Report on right to housing and disaster response).
13 UNGA, Report of the Special Rapporteur on Adequate Housing as a Component of the Right to an Adequate Standard of Living, and on the Right to Non-Discrimination in This Context, UN Doc. A/64/255 (6 August 2009).
14 In order to develop the reports and subsequent resolutions derived from them, the SR benefitted from dialogue as well as conceptual and practical exchanges with the IFRC, the Norwegian Refugee Council and the International Development Research Centre and with the UN agencies directly related to post-disaster reconstruction, namely UN Habitat and the International Organization for Migration.
15 Art 11 ICESCR asserts 'the right of everyone to an adequate standard of living for himself and his family, including adequate food, clothing and housing, and to the continuous improvement of living conditions'. See also UNGA, Res 217A: Universal Declaration of Human Rights (10 December 1948) art 25; Convention on the Rights of the Child (adopted 20 November 1989, entered into force 2 September 1990) 1577 UNTS 3, art 27(3); Convention on the Elimination of All Forms of Discrimination against Women (adopted 18 December 1979, entered into force 3 September 1981) 1249 UNTS 13, art 14(2)(h); International Convention on the Elimination of All Forms of Racial Discrimination (adopted 7 March 1966, entered into force 4 January 1969) 660 UNTS 195, art 5(e); International Convention on the Protection of the Rights of All Migrants Workers and Members of Their Families (adopted 18 December 1990, entered into force 1 July 2003) 2220 UNTS 3, art 43(1)(d); Convention on the Rights of Persons with Disabilities (adopted 13 December 2006, entered into force 3 May 2008) 2515 UNTS 3, art 28. At the regional level, the right to adequate housing is recognized in the European Social Charter (adopted 18 October 1961, entered into force 26 February 1965) ETS No. 035, art 31; the American Convention on Human Rights (adopted 22 November 1969, entered into force 18 July 1978) OAS TS No. 36, art 21; and the African Charter on Human and Peoples' Rights (adopted 27 June 1981, entered into force 21 October 1986) OAU Doc. CAB/LEG/67/3 Rev. 5, art 14.
16 ICESCR art 2(1).
17 CESCR, General Comment No. 4 (n. 4) para 7.

18 See M.C.R. Craven, *The International Covenant on Economic, Social and Cultural Rights: A Perspective on Its Development* (Clarendon, 1998) 329–349.
19 CESCR, General Comment No. 4 (n. 4) para 8.
20 Among other initiatives, see the establishment of the UN Habitat and Human Settlements Foundation (UNHHSF) and the strengthening of UN Habitat mandate through UNGA, Res 56/206: Strengthening the Mandate and Status of the Commission on Human Settlement and the Status, Role and Function of the UN Centre for Human Settlements (Habitat), UN Doc. A/RES/56/206 (1 January 2002).
21 See M.E. Stone, 'Housing Affordability: One-Third of a Nation Shelter Poor' in R.G. Bratt, M.E. Stone and C. Hartman (eds), *A Right to Housing: Foundation for a New Social Agenda* (Temple University Press, 2006) 38 ff.
22 IASC, *Human Rights and Natural Disasters: Operational Guidelines and Field Manual on Human Rights Protection in Situations of Natural Disasters* (Brookings-Bern Project on Internal Displacement, 2008) 1.
23 CESCR, General Comment No. 4 (n. 4) para 8(e).
24 IASC (n. 22) 1–2.
25 The few exceptions are constituted by E. Harper, *International Law and Standards Applicable in Natural Disaster Situations* (IDLO, 2009). See also various reports of the UN Representative of the Secretary-General on the human rights of internally displaced persons, among others HRC, Report of the Representative of the Secretary-General on the Human Rights of Internally Displaced Persons, Walter Kälin, UN Doc. A/HRC/10/13/Add.2 (13 February 2009).
26 This is for instance the case of OCHA, Guiding Principles on Internal Displacement, UN Doc. E/CN.4/1998/53/Add.2 (11 February 1998), and of the mentioned IASC Operational Guidelines, both recognizing the right of persons displaced to durable solutions, namely, a return to their homes or places of habitual residence, relocation elsewhere or local integration.
27 HRC, Res 19/4: Adequate Housing as a Component of the Right to Adequate Standard of Living in the Context of Disaster Settings, UN Doc. A/HRC/RES/19/4 (3 April 2012).
28 As to tenure rights specifically, see HRC, Report of the Special Rapporteur on Adequate Housing as a Component of the Right to an Adequate Standard of Living, and on the Right to Non-Discrimination in This Context, Raquel Rolnik, UN Doc. A/HRC/22/46 (24 December 2012), dealing with mapping and framing security of tenure; see also HRC, Guiding Principles on Security of Tenure for the Urban Poor, UN Doc. A/HRC/25/54 (30 December 2013).
29 HRC, Res 19/4 (n. 27) para 3.
30 Among others, see *Budayeva and Others v. Russia*, App. Nos. 15339/02, 21166/02, 20058/02, 11673/02 and 15343/02 (ECtHR, Judgment of 20 March 2008).
31 BBC News, 'Hurricane Charley Slams into Cuba' (13 August 2004), available at http://news.bbc.co.uk/2/hi/americas/3557180.stm, accessed on 13 April 2017.
32 C. Moser and D. Satterthwaite, 'Human Settlement Discussion Paper Series, Theme: Climate Change and Cities' 3 *IIED Climate Change and Cities Discussion Paper Series* (2008) 22.
33 M. Langford, 'The Right to Return and Resettlement after the Tsunami Disaster' 2 *Disaster Brief* (2005) 2.
34 See CESCR, General Comment No. 7 (n. 4).
35 Ibid. See also IASC (n. 22) C.2.4 and C.2.5.
36 HRComm, General Comment No. 27: Article 12 (Freedom of Movement), UN Doc. CCPR/C/21/Rev.1/Add.9 (2 November 1999) para 14.
37 See Report on Right to Housing and Disaster Response (n. 12) Operational principles 7, 25.
38 HRC, Res 19/4 (n. 27) para 4(e).
39 See for instance the projects described in M. Lyons and T. Shilderman (eds), *Building Back Better: Delivering People-Centred Housing Reconstruction at Scale* (Practical Action, 2010) 307–344.
40 UN Sub-Commission on the Promotion and Protection of Human Rights, Res 2005/21: Resolution 2005/21 on Housing and Property Restitution for Refugees and Displaced Persons, UN Doc. E/CN.4/Sub.2/RES/2005/21 (11 August 2005), endorsing CHR, housing and property restitution in the context of the return of refugees and internally displaced persons. Final report of the Special Rapporteur, Paulo Sérgio Pinheiro. Principles on Housing and Property Restitution for Refugees and Displaced Persons, UN Doc. E/CN.4/Sub.2/2005/7 (28 June 2005).
41 Ibid principle 2.2. On whether the right to property restitution in international law is a self-standing right, see M. Langford and K. Moyo, 'Right, Remedy or Rhetoric? Land Restitution in International Law' 28 *Nordic Journal of Human Rights* (2010) 143–176.
42 See in general R.C. Williams, 'Guiding Principle 29 and the Right to Restitution' *FMReview – GP 10* (2008) 23–24.

43 See C. Gould, 'The Right to Housing Recovery after Natural Disasters' 22 *Harvard Human Rights Journal* (2009) 169–204; R. Barber, 'Protecting the Right to Housing in the Aftermath of Natural Disasters: Standards in International Human Rights Law' 20 *International Journal of Refugee Law* (2008) 432–468; contra see E. Harper, *International Law and Standards Applicable in Natural Disaster Situations* (IDLO, 2009) ch 4.

44 Pinheiro Principles (n. 40) principle 1.2.

45 Following the reasoning of *Budayeva* (n. 30); see also Supreme Court of Pakistan, *Constitution Petition no 62 of 2010 and Suo Moto Case no 17 of 2010 and Human Rights case no 52220-P of 2010 and Human Rights case no 57247-A of 2010 and Human Rights case no 69622-S of 2010* (Floods Commission case) (7 June 2011), available at www.supremecourt.gov.pk/web/user_files/File/Const.P.NO.62OF2010_orderdt06062011.pdf, accessed on 13 April 2017.

46 See J.G. Sprankling, *The International Law of Property* (Oxford University Press, 2014) 143–150.

47 See B. McCallin, 'The Role of Restitution in Post-Conflict Situations' in J. Unruh and R. Williams (eds), *Land and Post-Conflict Peacebuilding* (Earthscan, 2013).

48 A tendency to give precedence to the rights of tenants in post-disaster scenarios has also been evidenced by European human rights bodies. In the case of *I v. Italy*, App. No. 11381/85 (ECommHR, Admissibility Decision of 3 March 1986), the European Commission of Human Rights was asked to rule on an alleged violation of the right to property. The applicant had instituted legal proceedings against his tenant to regain possession of a flat he owned into which he intended to move with his family. He was granted an eviction order by the judicial authorities, but the Italian government issued emergency regulations suspending the execution of the order, as the area had been repeatedly affected by earthquakes and the authorities wanted to prevent a housing crisis. The Commission acknowledged that the suspension constituted an interference with the applicants' property rights, but maintained that a proper balance was struck between the general community interest and the requirements of safeguarding the applicant's individual rights.

49 HRC, Res 19/4 (n. 27) para 4(a).

50 Ibid para 4(f).

51 See for instance the Commission on Real Property Claims emerging from the Dayton Peace Accords in Bosnia-Herzegovina, which gave fully equal rights to both formal owners and individuals holding social-occupancy rights; the South African Land Reform Programme for Restitution of Land Rights and the Commission for the Resolution of Real Property Disputes in Iraq. In general see A. Durand-Lasserve and L. Royston (eds), *Holding Their Ground: Secure Land Tenure for the Urban Poor in Developing Countries* (Earthscan, 2002); R. Neuwirth, *Shadow Cities: A Billion Squatters: A New Urban World* (Routledge, 2005).

52 E. Ferris and D. Petz, *A Year of Living Dangerously: A Review of Natural Disasters in 2010* (The Brookings Institution-London School of Economic Project on International Displacements, 2011).

53 UN Special Envoy for Tsunami Recovery, Key Propositions for Building Back Better. A Report by the UN Secretary-General Special Envoy for Tsunami Recovery, William J Clinton (Office of the UNSG, December 2006).

54 Report on right to housing and disaster response (n. 12) Recommendation A(2), para 22.

55 South Africa Office of the President, Restitution and Land Rights Act No. 22 of 1994, Ch I (1)(xi); IASC, *Framework on Durable Solutions for Internally Displaced Persons* (The Brookings Institution, 2010) 35.

56 See in this respect UN Habitat, *Land and Natural Disasters: Guidance for Practitioners* (UN Human Settlement Programme, 2010).

57 In this respect see HRC, Report of the Special Rapporteur on adequate housing as a component of the right to adequate standard of living, and on the right to non-discrimination in this context, Raquel Rolnik. Guiding principles on security of tenure for the urban poor, UN Doc. A/HRC/25/54 (30 December 2013) 3 ff.

58 The HRC noted in this respect that 'any deterioration in the general housing situation disproportionately affects persons living in condition of poverty, low-income earners, women, children, persons belonging to minorities and indigenous people, migrants, internally displaced persons, tenants, the elderly and persons with disabilities'. See HRC, Res 19/4 (n. 27) 2.

59 UNGA, Res 60/227: International Migration and Development, UN Doc. A/Res/60/227 (7 April 2006).

60 See IFRC, *World Disasters Report: Focus on Discrimination* (IFRC, 2007) 10–20. Cf. also Casolari's chapter in this volume.

61 These provisions are complemented at the universal level by International Convention on the Elimination of All Forms of Racial Discrimination (n. 15) art 5.

62 HRC, Res 19/4 (n. 27) para 4.
63 CESCR, General Comment No. 3: The Nature of States Parties' Obligations (Art. 2, para. 1, of the Covenant), UN Doc. E/1991/23 (14 December 1990) para 12. In general see U. Oswald Spring, 'Social Vulnerability, Discrimination and Resilience-Building in Disaster Risk Reduction' in H.G. Brauch, Ú. Oswald Spring, C. Mesjasz, J. Grin, P. Kameri-Mbote, B. Chourou, P. Dunay and J. Birkmann (eds), *Coping with Global Environmental Change, Disasters and Security* (Springer, 2011) 1169–1188.
64 M. Prieur, *Ethical Principles on Disaster Risk Reduction and People's Resilience* (EUR-OPA, 2009) 25.
65 See H.M. Valdes, 'A Gender Perspective on Disaster Risk Reduction' in E. Enarson and P.G. Dhar Chakrabarti (eds), *Women, Gender and Disasters: Global Issues and Initiatives* (SAGE Publications, 2009) 18–28. In 2016, CommEDAW launched initiatives towards the consolidation of a General Recommendation on gendered-dimensions of DRR and climate change to be adopted by the CommEDAW in the near future, available at www.ohchr.org/EN/HRBodies/CEDAW/Pages/ClimateChange/aspx, accessed on 13 April 2017.
66 See UNGA, Implementation of the International Strategy for Disaster Reduction: Report of the Secretary-General, UN Doc. A/69/364 (3 September 2014) 57–60; see also D. Alexander and S. Sagramola, *Guidelines for Assisting People with Disabilities during Emergencies, Crises and Disasters* (EUR-OPA, 2013).
67 See M. Cernea and C. McDowell (eds), *Risks and Reconstruction: Experiences of Resettlers and Refugees* (World Bank, 2000).
68 UN Special Envoy for Tsunami Recovery (n. 53) 7. For a similar approach to the Myanmar and Haiti cases, see L. Fan, 'Disasters as Opportunity?' *HPG Working Paper* (November 2013).
69 Government of Pakistan, Asian Development Bank and World Bank, *Pakistan Floods 2010: Preliminary Damage and Needs Assessment* (November 2010) paras 7 ff.
70 See also CommERD, General Recommendation XXX on Discrimination against Non Citizens (1 October 2002).
71 Report on right to housing and disaster response (n. 12) Recommendation A(1), para 22.
72 Ibid VII.
73 See Reports on security of tenure (n. 28).
74 HRC, Report of the Special Rapporteur on Adequate Housing as a Component of the Right to an Adequate Standard of Living, and on the Right to Non-Discrimination in This Context, Raquel Rolnik, UN Doc. A/HRC/19/53 (26 December 2011).
75 Reports on security of tenure (n. 28).

13

ADDRESSING DISCRIMINATION IN DISASTER SCENARIOS

An international and EU law perspective

*Federico Casolari**

Introduction

Equality is a common cornerstone of many contemporary democracies. In this respect, it acts as a structural principle guiding decision-makers in adopting decisions that are likely to influence the enjoyment of human rights.[1] On the other hand, however, the equality principle is fully incorporated into human rights law, acting as a source of procedural and substantive obligations. Viewed from this angle, not only does the principle imply a formal equality of individuals before the law, requiring a uniform implementation of the law by public authorities, but it also imposes a substantive equality, thus serving as a tool in the fight against discrimination, that is, unlawful differentiation among individuals,[2] and particularly among the most disadvantaged in society.[3]

In this latter dimension lies the indissoluble intertwinement between equality and non-discrimination – two principles representing two sides of the same coin.[4] And, clearly, in virtue of that connection, we can appreciate the decisive role that equality takes on in disaster scenarios. Not only is it apparent that when a disaster strikes it becomes imperative to ensure instant and full relief for *everyone*, taking into account the particular challenges faced in protecting the human rights of vulnerable groups, but it is also increasingly evident that this imperative must inform *all stages* in the disaster-management lifecycle (thus also including the prevention, preparedness, mitigation, and recovery stages).

In light of the foregoing, this chapter intends to reflect broadly on the role that equality and non-discrimination *in fact* plays or *should* play in disaster settings in both international and European Union law. Due to space constraints, the discussion cannot consider in any depth the different forms of discrimination based on prohibited grounds that may be encountered in a disaster scenario.[5] Rather, it highlights the most significant general approaches to non-discrimination set forth in International Disaster Law (IDL), as well as the legal implications stemming from this set of rules. To this end, the analysis proceeds in three consecutive steps. The second section describes the general approaches taken in international practice to ensure that disaster victims (potential or actual) are not discriminated against. In this connection particular emphasis will be placed on the solutions enshrined in the Draft Articles on the Protection of Persons in the Event of Disasters (hereinafter 'Draft Articles'), adopted in 2016 by the International Law Commission and to date representing the most authoritative effort to codify IDL into a set of universal rules. The analysis will highlight the way that IDL stands to benefit from an emphasis on non-discrimination (third section), while also offering a general reflection on the legal status and scope of the equality and non-discrimination principles in IDL. The main outcomes of this legal analysis carried out are summarised in the fourth section.

Setting the scene: the main approaches to non-discrimination in disaster scenarios and their rationale

Due in particular to the paramount importance the protection of vulnerable groups has in disaster scenarios,[6] it does not come as a surprise that IDL instruments make recurrent reference to the need not to discriminate among victims of disasters. In this respect, three general approaches may be distinguished: (1) non-discrimination is written into IDL instruments as an *implicit* attribute of classic principles governing humanitarian assistance (the 'humanitarian approach'); (2) non-discrimination is *explicitly* recognised among the constitutive elements of the human rights-based approach to disaster management (the 'human rights-based approach'); and (3) the two previous trends are merged, with the same instrument making reference to both the humanitarian and human rights-based approaches to non-discrimination (coexisting in a 'mixed approach'). Let us consider the main features of these three trends in the following subsections.

The humanitarian approach to non-discrimination: incorporating humanitarian principles into international disaster law

A first clear trend in IDL consists in straightforwardly incorporating the basic principles of humanitarian assistance into the relevant instruments. These are the principles of humanity, impartiality, and neutrality. In fact the latter two principles (impartiality and neutrality) are commonly considered inherent in non-discrimination discourse. More to the point, while neutrality is considered a macro-level principle requiring that humanitarian assistance be provided without taking sides in any controversy of a political, racial, religious, or ideological nature,[7] impartiality is considered a micro-level principle requiring that assistance be provided non-discriminatorily solely on the basis of the victim's needs and in proportion to such needs. Drawing on Jean Pictet's well-known systematisation of humanitarian principles,[8] impartiality can thus be conceived as a principle containing three intertwined but separate subprinciples: the principle of non-discrimination, that of proportionality, and that of impartiality *stricto sensu*.[9] So, even though the principle of non-discrimination is not expressly mentioned, it figures as *an implied element* of humanitarian assistance, as it is rooted in International Humanitarian Law (IHL).[10] The implied relevance of the principle of non-discrimination has also been confirmed by the International Court of Justice in the *Nicaragua* case,[11] where at issue were the conditions that had to be met in order for humanitarian assistance to be delivered to persons in need in Nicaragua in conformity with international law. In light of the fundamental principles declared at the Twentieth International Conference of the Red Cross, the Court found that

> if the provision of 'humanitarian assistance' is to escape condemnation as an intervention in the international affairs of Nicaragua, not only must it be limited to the purposes allowed in the practice of the Red Cross, namely 'to prevent and alleviate human suffering', and 'to protect life and health and to ensure respect for the human being'; it must also, and above all, be given without discrimination to all in need in Nicaragua, not merely to the *contras* and their dependents.[12]

Turning to the instruments and provisions that may be included in the IDL category, traces of this trend can be found in the first place in the resolutions adopted by the United Nations General Assembly (UNGA) *in subiecta materia*, starting from the UNGA Resolution 46/182 – a veritable cornerstone in the establishment of the foundational principles of humanitarian assistance. Indeed, according to this resolution '[h]umanitarian assistance must be provided in accordance with the principles of humanity, neutrality and impartiality'.[13] More recently, the UNGA has reaffirmed the paramount role of these principles in its Resolution 71/128 on International Cooperation on Humanitarian Assistance in the Field of Natural Disasters.[14]

Exclusive reference to the humanitarian principles has also been made in some international treaties.[15] Not surprisingly, due to the commitment the International Red Cross and Red Crescent Movement has made to the improvement of the humanitarian agenda, the same approach is incorporated into the Guidelines for the Domestic Facilitation and Regulation of International Disaster Relief and Initial Recovery Assistance, adopted in 2007 by the International Federation of Red Cross and Red Crescent Societies (IFRC).[16] In particular, Guideline No. 4 ('Responsibilities of Assisting Actors') states that '[a]ssisting actors should ensure that their disaster relief and initial recovery assistance is provided in accordance with the principles of humanity, neutrality and impartiality'.[17] Similar solutions are present in other soft-law instruments, such as the Guidelines on the Use of Military and Civil Defence Assets to Support United Nations Humanitarian Activities in Complex Emergencies of 2003,[18] as well as the Guidelines on the Use of Foreign Military and Civil Defence Assets in Disaster Relief of 2006 (the so-called 'Oslo Guidelines').[19]

The human rights-based approach to non-discrimination: international disaster law making direct recourse to non-discrimination clauses elaborated under International Human Rights Law

Next to the humanitarian approach, clearly revealing how permeable IDL is to the core principles of IHL,[20] it is possible to discern another approach, which as mentioned consists in relevant international-law instruments and provisions making direct reference to the principle of non-discrimination. This means that, on this approach, non-discrimination is *not conceived as a derived principle* contained in that of impartiality but *enjoys a freestanding status*. Unlike the humanitarian approach, this one is firmly rooted in International Human Rights Law (IHRL) – hence the idea of a human rights-based approach to disaster management.[21]

As is well known, different techniques have been developed under IHRL to promote equality and non-discrimination among individuals. The great majority of IHRL instruments, starting from that milestone instrument which is the Universal Declaration of Human Rights (UDHR),[22] contain an accessory non-discrimination clause mentioning an open list of prohibited grounds on which there can be no discrimination in respecting the human rights protected by the instrument at stake.[23] Sometimes the IHRL instruments also explicitly mention the principles of non-discrimination and equality in relation to specific individual rights.[24] In other cases, freestanding non-discrimination clauses have also been formulated, some in the diplomatic practice,[25] others through the practice of relevant monitoring bodies.[26] Lastly, several issue-specific conventions have been developed for the purpose of eliminating discrimination on one particular ground – evidence that discrimination on that ground is especially reprehensible or that those who are discriminated against on that ground are particularly vulnerable.[27] These treaties generally do not make explicit reference to disaster scenarios. The most significant exception is the Convention on the Rights of Persons with Disabilities, under which

> States Parties shall take, in accordance with their obligations under international law, including international humanitarian law and international human rights law, all necessary measures to ensure the protection and safety of persons with disabilities in situations of risk, including situations of armed conflict, humanitarian emergencies *and the occurrence of natural disasters*.[28]

However, as is clearly demonstrated in different contributions to this volume,[29] just because an instrument makes no explicit reference to any disaster scenario does not mean that such scenarios fall outside the scope of the instrument in question. On the contrary, it is very much the practice of human rights monitoring bodies to take a human rights-based approach to disaster management, and, most importantly for our purposes here, to clearly invoke the non-discrimination clauses enshrined in relevant treaties, stressing the need to protect the vulnerable members of society, as well as their full enjoyment or exercise of rights and freedoms, in either pre- or post-disaster settings.

Quite instructive, in this respect, is the practice of the Committee on Economic, Social and Cultural Rights (CESCR) established under the corresponding Covenant. In its General Comment on the right to the highest attainable standard of health, for instance, the CESCR has stated that

> States parties have a joint and individual responsibility . . . to cooperate in providing disaster relief . . . Priority in the provision of international medical aid, distribution and management of resources . . . should be given to the most vulnerable or marginalized groups of the population.[30]

This obligation is claimed to stem directly from the accessory non-discrimination clause (Article 2, para 2) in combination with the Covenant's right-to-health clause (Article 12) – a combination in virtue of which there can be no discrimination on any ground in providing access to healthcare, and hence no intent to nullify the equal enjoyment of the right to healthcare. Similarly, in its General Comment on the right to adequate food, the CESCR has highlighted the need to ensure the most vulnerable populations are given priority in food aid on a need basis – a priority that follows from the prohibition on any discrimination in access to food (under Article 2, para 2 of the Covenant, to be read in conjunction with Article 11).[31] The same attitude, which the CESCR has also taken to the right to adequate housing,[32] as well as the right to water,[33] is also present in the activity of other monitoring bodies, such as the Committee on the Elimination of Racial Discrimination (CERD)[34] and the Committee on the Elimination of All Forms of Discrimination against Women (CEDAW).[35]

Turning to IDL, it is interesting to note that the need to ensure non-discriminatory treatment for people in need had already been recognised in the instrument that to some extent stands as the progenitor of this branch of international law, that is, the International Convention and Statute Establishing an International Relief Union.[36] Indeed, Article 3 of this Convention expressly provides that '[t]he International Relief Union shall operate for the benefit of all stricken peoples, whatever their nationality or their race, and irrespective of any social, political or religious distinction'. Although the Convention prohibits only a select number of discriminatory grounds, in line with the understanding of the limited discrimination practices of the time, it clearly reflects the need to ensure prompt assistance for *all* persons in need, thus anticipating – albeit in a narrow and rather primitive fashion – some of the constitutive elements of the current human rights-based approach to non-discrimination.

More robust (and recent) elements of a human rights-based approach to non-discrimination in disaster settings can be found in the framework established under the 2003 Bruges Resolution of the International Law Institute on Humanitarian Assistance.[37] In particular, the Bruges Resolution contains a provision on the right to humanitarian assistance stating that such 'assistance shall be offered and, if accepted, distributed *without any discrimination on prohibited grounds*, while taking into account the needs of the most vulnerable groups'.[38] In the same vein, under the Agreement among the Governments of the Participating States of the Black Sea Economic Cooperation on Collaboration in Emergency Assistance and Emergency Response to Natural and Man-Made Disasters, 'the goods of assistance shall be distributed without any discrimination based on race, religion, language, political or other factors'.[39]

Needless to say, this kind of approach does not apply only to disaster response. This is especially apparent in the range of instruments adopted internationally to develop a climate change adaptation and mitigation system. In a resolution adopted in 2009 on human rights and climate change, the Human Rights Council (HRC) stresses that 'the effects of climate change will be felt most acutely by those segments of the population who are already in vulnerable situations owing to factors such as geography, poverty, gender, age, indigenous or minority status and disability'.[40]

The emphasis on the need to protect vulnerable groups is also present in the Sendai Framework for Disaster Risk Reduction, where this protection is listed among the guiding principles of the Framework's implementation.[41] As the document starts:

> Disaster risk reduction requires an all-of-society engagement and partnership. It also requires empowerment and inclusive, accessible and non-discriminatory participation, paying special attention to people disproportionately affected by disasters, especially the poorest. A gender, age, disability and cultural perspective should be integrated in all policies and practices, and women and youth leadership should be promoted.[42]

Quite significantly, a human rights-based approach to non-discrimination is also enshrined in the Paris Agreement adopted under the United Nations Framework Convention on Climate Change,[43] even if in the preambular section.[44] In that section – and for the first time ever in a binding multilateral treaty[45] – the Paris Agreement recognises the need to protect human rights in managing climate change internationally, stating that such protection must in particular take the position of vulnerable individuals and groups into account.[46]

Mixing the humanitarian and human rights-based approaches in managing discrimination in disaster settings

Far from representing two alternative approaches, the incorporation of humanitarian principles and that of non-discrimination clauses are two *complementary* ways to go about ensuring the protection of vulnerable groups in disaster scenarios. This explains why these two approaches have also been merged, thus giving rise to a third, mixed approach, on which classic humanitarian principles and non-discrimination clauses seamlessly coexist. Importantly, this attitude is increasingly visible in international-law instruments dealing with disaster settings.

A first example of this mixed approach can be found in the 2000 Framework Convention on Civil Defence Assistance:[47] having established that the contracting parties may not discriminate in providing the assistance needed to prevent disasters or mitigate their consequences,[48] Article 3 of the Convention clarifies that the same assistance must also be governed by the principles of humanity and impartiality.[49]

The same attitude can also be found in EU law. Worthy of mention in primary law is the legal basis of EU humanitarian aid, namely, Article 214 of the Treaty on the Functioning of the European Union (TFEU).[50] The provision, introduced with the Lisbon Treaty,[51] is meant to establish the legal framework for *ad hoc* financial assistance and relief protection for people in third countries who fall victim to natural and man-made disasters, and it enumerates three principles of EU humanitarian assistance: impartiality, neutrality, and non-discrimination. As is apparent, this list does not perfectly correspond to that of the above-mentioned humanitarian principles:[52] on the one hand, the principle of humanity is not expressly mentioned; on the other, the principle of non-discrimination – which, as we have seen,[53] works as a sub-principle of that of impartiality – is listed next to the other guiding principles, suggesting that the drafters of the EU Treaties understood it as having primary legal standing. The fact that humanity is not present in the Treaty provision does not in itself seem particularly relevant. As I have discussed elsewhere,[54] the very same provision also states that EU humanitarian aid operations 'shall be conducted in compliance with the principles of international law'. It is thus possible to conclude that the principle of humanity in any case stands as a guiding principle of EU action in the domain in question insofar as it constituted a well-established core principle of humanitarian assistance, whose customary nature under international law cannot easily be questioned. By contrast, the inclusion of non-discrimination among the guiding principles of the EU humanitarian aid does not seem irrelevant. For it suggests that reference is made here to the EU general principle of non-discrimination: this is a veritable cornerstone of the EU integration process,[55] and more importantly where we are concerned, it stands as an essential piece of the standard for protecting fundamental rights – a standard now codified in the EU Charter of Fundamental Rights.[56] In other words, the reference made in Article 214 TFEU seems to express the Union's adherence to a human rights-based understanding of non-discrimination.[57] This conclusion is supported by the European Consensus on Humanitarian Aid,[58] an important document outlining the policy framework for EU action in response to humanitarian crises. Indeed, the list of classic 'fundamental humanitarian principles' contained in this document only includes humanity, neutrality, impartiality, and independence.[59] It is thus evident that the non-discrimination principle is not deemed by the drafters of the European Consensus a constitutive element of what in this chapter is being called the 'humanitarian approach'.

Moreover, and quite significantly, the same dual attitude expressed in the legal basis of EU humanitarian aid may be found in the EU's international agreements,[60] as well as in EU secondary law dealing with disaster management.[61]

At the regional level, traces of this mixed approach can also be found in the African Union Convention for the Protection and Assistance of Internally Displaced Persons in Africa (Kampala Convention),[62] which not only mentions the non-discrimination principle together with equality and equal protection before the law,[63] but also stresses the need to ensure respect for the humanitarian principles of humanity, neutrality, and impartiality and the independence of humanitarian actors.[64]

More importantly for our purposes, however, a similar attitude seems to also emerge from the work the International Law Commission (ILC) has devoted to the topic of the protection of persons in the event of disasters. Worthy of mention in this respect is Draft Article 6, which the ILC adopted in 2016 on second reading.[65] The Draft Article – titled 'Humanitarian Principles', and, also noteworthy, located immediately after the provision devoted to human rights – merges the two trends analysed in previous subsections, echoing in particular the solutions adopted in both UNGA Resolution 46/182 and the Bruges Resolution of the Institute of International Law. It reads as follows:

> Response to disasters shall take place in accordance with the principles of humanity, neutrality and impartiality, and on the basis of non-discrimination, while taking into account the needs of the particularly vulnerable.

Importantly, the final version of this provision differs from the one originally proposed by the Special Rapporteur, where only classic humanitarian principles were listed.[66] The rationale behind the ILC's amendment is explained in the Commentary to the Draft Articles, where it is stated that the

> principle of non-discrimination, applicable also in the context of disaster risk reduction, reflects the inherent equality of all persons and the determination that no adverse distinction may be drawn between them. Prohibited grounds for discrimination are non-exhaustive and include ethnic origin, sex, nationality, political opinions, race, religion and disability. The Commission determined that non-discrimination should be referred to as *an autonomous principle in light of its importance to the topic at hand.*[67]

As is apparent from the ILC's arguments, the importance of the non-discrimination principle mainly lies in its indissoluble link to the principle of equality and thus derives from a human rights-based approach to disaster management.[68] Moreover, the fact that the Commentary makes express reference to the context of disaster-risk reduction suggests that the human rights element in non-discrimination comes into play at all stages of disaster management, including the pre-disaster stage.[69]

Quite significantly, the ILC's choice to expressly mention both the principle of impartiality and that of non-discrimination has been warmly received by States.[70] This can be appreciated, for example, in the positions expressed by Austria,[71] Greece,[72] Indonesia,[73] and Ireland[74] in the Sixth Committee of the UNGA, as well as in the United States' comments on the ILC's Draft Articles.[75] On the contrary, when it came to the concept of neutrality, several States questioned the wisdom of mentioning it,[76] arguing that the concept is closely bound up with situations of armed conflict, which are supposed to fall outside the scope of the topic.[77]

What can be concluded, also in light of the previously mentioned elements of practice, is that there seems to be a significant and broad consensus on the idea that non-discrimination in disaster management can be more effectively ensured when the relevant instruments expressly make reference not only to humanitarian principles but also to the non-discrimination principle *stricto sensu*.

The potential added value of the 'mixed approach' to non-discrimination in disaster scenarios

Far from being a mere linguistic issue, the additional recourse to non-discrimination clauses in IDL instruments may significantly add to the protection of persons who are (or may be) affected by disasters. Generally speaking, it must first be noted that such recourse strengthens the need to avoid discrimination against vulnerable groups in disaster scenarios, as well as the consequent idea that a central purpose of this set of rules is to help those who are most disadvantaged.[78] More to the point, three major features are worthy of note.

First, as can be appreciated by a closer inspection of the elements of practice mentioned in the previous section,[79] the incorporation of non-discrimination clauses into the relevant instruments makes it possible to extend to IDL the working definitions and tools elaborated in IHRL to implement equality and non-discrimination among the beneficiaries of human rights. As for the working notions, reference can be made not only to the classic distinction between 'direct and indirect discriminations',[80] but also to concepts such as 'multiple or intersectional discrimination'[81] and 'discrimination by association',[82] which significantly extend the scope of application of anti-discrimination law.[83] On the other hand, recourse to non-discrimination clauses gives the actors concerned a chance to have access to the 'toolkit' so far developed to implement anti-discrimination law. In this respect, an essential role is played by so-called 'positive actions' (or 'affirmative actions') aimed at addressing historical and/or structural disadvantages in order to further the goal of substantive and genuine equality.[84] The role of positive actions is even stronger once we consider that according to the practice of human rights monitoring bodies, failure to take such measures to ensure substantive equality can amount to discrimination under IHRL.[85] Quite significantly, this understanding has been codified in the most recent universal convention for fighting discrimination, that is, the UN Convention on the Rights of Persons with Disabilities, whose Article 2 in fact makes it clear that '"[d]iscrimination on the basis of disability" . . . includes all forms of discrimination, *including denial of reasonable accommodation*'.[86]

Second, as can be appreciated from the comments made to the ILC's Draft Articles,[87] non-discrimination clauses, and thus the human rights-based approach they express, seem to be better suited to ensuring an adequate protection of vulnerable groups *before* disasters occur. This is probably because humanitarian principles are traditionally linked to the assistance provided *in response* to man-made crises and natural disasters. Like a through-line connecting all stages of disaster management, the inclusion of non-discrimination clauses into the IDL instruments could thus facilitate a more unitary (and coherent) approach to human rights protection in disaster scenarios.

Third, the inclusion of a human rights-based approach in shaping non-discrimination in IDL should logically lead to the reconstruction of a veritable right not to be discriminated against in disaster settings. In other words, similarly to what may be observed in the implementation of human rights instruments containing non-discrimination clauses,[88] the human rights-based approach can be expected to prompt a shift toward substantive equality in disaster settings that in turn should prompt us to reframe our understanding of the corresponding duty not to discriminate. From this perspective, this duty should be understood not only as an ancillary obligation needed to ensure a full respect for other human rights (such as the right to humanitarian assistance),[89] but also as *a self-standing duty*, thus entailing *a corresponding autonomous right*.

If a similar right can already be considered as existing in the human rights treaty-based systems containing a general non-discrimination clause,[90] a question arises about the possible identification of a corresponding international customary rule.

In this connection, it is important to first point out the clear statement the Inter-American Court of Human Rights has made in its advisory opinion on the juridical condition and rights of undocumented migrants,[91] holding that

> the principle of equality before the law, equal protection before the law and non-discrimination belongs to *jus cogens*, because the whole legal structure of national and international public order rests on it and it is a fundamental principle that permeates all laws. Nowadays, no legal act that is in conflict with this fundamental principle is acceptable, and discriminatory treatment of any person, owing to gender, race, color, language, religion or belief, political or other opinion, national, ethnic or social origin, nationality, age, economic situation, property, civil status, birth or any other status is unacceptable. This principle (equality and non-discrimination) forms part of general international law. At the existing stage of the development of international law, the fundamental principle of equality and non-discrimination has entered the realm of *jus cogens*.[92]

As correctly highlighted in the literature,[93] although the acknowledgment of the peremptory status of the principles of equality and non-discrimination is indeed significant (and desirable), this view does not seem to have yet achieved a general consensus. More precisely, it seems that only the prohibition against racial discrimination, and against practices directly associated with it, may be deemed peremptory.[94] In all other cases, wherever human rights monitoring bodies have acknowledged the essential role that non-discrimination and equality play in the protection of human rights,[95] this acknowledgment – coupled with these bodies' extensive practice of seeking to enlarge the scope of the protection afforded by the principles at issue – has paved the way for a process *leading* to the formation of corresponding (ordinary) international customary rules. It is interesting to note in this regard that, on the one hand, considering the different ways in which States understand the relevant grounds of discrimination, scholars are usually reluctant to view this process as having been on the whole completed,[96] thus arguing that the principle of non-discrimination has yet to achieve the status of international customary law, while, on the other hand, the practice in disaster settings,[97] as well as the favour that States and the actors concerned have shown to inserting an express reference to non-discrimination in the ILC's Draft Articles,[98] suggests that both the practice of States and *opinio juris* could be regarded as already established as far as non-discriminatory conduct in disaster scenarios is concerned. In other words, the pressing need to give assistance to potential disaster victims might have speeded up the process leading to the formation of an international customary rule prohibiting discriminatory treatment in disaster settings.

Be that as it may, considering that some human rights treaty-based regimes already recognise a self-standing right to non-discrimination,[99] the further question is raised of whether limits to, and derogations from, this right may be considered admissible in the event of disasters. As is well-known, human rights treaties do recognise the possibility of limiting, and derogating from, the vast majority of protected rights. This possibility may also be invoked in a disaster scenario.[100] Having said that, however, it is obvious that the practice of invoking limits to, and derogations from, non-discrimination clauses in disaster settings may risk undermining (or even nullifying) the very rationale behind these clauses in disaster events, that is, the need to recognise the special challenges faced in the protection of the human rights of vulnerable groups affected by humanitarian emergencies. In other terms, the possibility of significantly limiting (or derogating from) non-discrimination duties in disaster scenarios – except for the case of racial discrimination, which is prohibited under peremptory international norms – could lead to the striking conclusion that similarly situated vulnerable groups or persons in deep need of assistance enjoy only a limited protection, if any.

Such a conclusion, however, neglects to consider that human rights treaty provisions allowing limitations and derogations – and the relative practice of monitoring bodies – impose specific requirements that must be met in order to lawfully trigger the corresponding mechanisms. These requirements generally provide that limitations must be compatible with the nature of the right in question,[101] and derogations cannot involve unjustifiable discriminations,[102] nor can they involve discriminations solely based on the ground of race, colour, sex, language, religion, or social origin.[103]

In light of the foregoing, it may be argued thus that (1) the essence of the right not to be discriminated against cannot be undermined by way of limitations introduced by States in dealing with disaster scenarios and (2) any related derogations introduced for the same purpose cannot *in any case* give rise to unjustified discrimination.[104] In light of the principle of proportionality, however, this does not exclude that a 'reasonable balance between States' and individuals' interests'[105] must be reached, taking also into account the capacity of affected States before and after a disaster strikes.[106]

Concluding remarks

A number of conclusions can be drawn from the foregoing analysis. A first element that deserves to be mentioned is that different approaches inform the way relevant IDL instruments frame the imperative not to discriminate among (actual or potential) disaster victims. Increasingly strong in this regard is the approach that consists in combining the classic humanitarian principles with explicit references made to the non-discrimination principle as understood in IHRL. As this chapter has highlighted, this approach seems to be the one best suited to disaster settings, for on the one hand it makes it possible to better cover all the stages in a disaster's lifecycle, while at the same time it opens the door to the concepts and tools that human rights monitoring bodies have so far developed to better achieve substantive equality among individuals.

From this perspective, although the solution the ILC adopted in the Draft Articles could be further improved,[107] this solution, and the reactions of the actors concerned, importantly consolidate the trend just mentioned, thus facilitating the process toward the formation of an international customary rule prohibiting discriminatory treatment in disaster scenarios, while underscoring the point that – in spite of some caveats the Commission formulated in working on the topic – if the rights of individual disaster victims are to be genuinely protected, a dialogue needs to be pursued among IDL, IHRL, and IHL.

Selected bibliography

M. Bizzarri, 'Protection of Vulnerable Groups in Natural and Man-Made Disasters' in A. de Guttry, M. Gestri and G. Venturini (eds), *International Disaster Response Law* (Springer, 2012) 381.

J. Clifford, 'Equality' in D. Shelton (ed), *The Oxford Handbook of International Human Rights Law* (Oxford, 2013) 421.

M. Crock, 'The Protection of Vulnerable Groups' in S.C. Breau and K.L.H. Samuel (eds), *Research Handbook on Disasters and International Law* (Edward Elgar Publishing, 2016) 383.

L.S. Rossi and F. Casolari (eds), *The Principle of Equality in EU Law* (Springer, 2017).

Notes

* Unless otherwise indicated, this contribution takes into account developments in practice and legislation until 30 June 2017.

1 J. Clifford, 'Equality' in D. Shelton (ed), *The Oxford Handbook of International Human Rights Law* (Oxford, 2013) 421–422.

2 According to the Human Rights Committee (HRComm),

> the term 'discrimination'. . . should be understood to imply any distinction, exclusion, restriction or preference which is based on any [prohibited] ground . . . and which has the purpose or effect of nullifying or impairing the recognition, enjoyment or exercise by all persons, on an equal footing, of all rights and freedoms.

Cf. HRComm, General Comment No. 18: Non-Discrimination, UN Doc. HRI/GEN/1/Rev.9 (10 November 1989).

3 For a general discussion of the multifaceted notions of equality and non-discrimination in international law, see, *ex multis*, S. Farrier (ed), *Equality and Non-Discrimination under International Law* (Ashgate, 2015); K. Henrard, 'Equality of Individuals', *Max Planck Encyclopedia of Public International Law*, online edition, 2008; W. Vandenhole, *Non-Discrimination and Equality in the View of the UN Human Rights Treaty Bodies* (Intersentia, 2005).

4 Clifford (n. 1) 427. The close interaction between the two notions explains why they are usually treated as overlapping legal concepts: cf. HRC, General Comment No. 18: Non-Discrimination, para 1; Committee on Economic, Social and Cultural Rights, General Comment No. 20: Non-Discrimination in Economic, Social and Cultural Rights (art. 2, para 2, of the International Covenant on Economic, Social and Cultural Rights), UN Doc. E/C.12/GC/20 (2009) paras 2–3. According to the Court of Justice of the European Union, equality and non-discrimination 'are simply two labels for a single general principle of . . . [EU] law, which prohibits both treating similar situations differently and treating different situations in the same way unless there are objective reasons for such treatment'. Cf. Judgment of 27 January 2005, *Europe Chemi-Con (Deutschland) GmbH v. Council and Commission*, Case C-422/02 P, ECLI:EU:C:2005:56, para 33. Similarly, the Inter-American Court of Human Rights has made it clear that '[t]he element of equality is difficult to separate from non-discrimination. Indeed, when referring to equality before the law, . . . this principle must be guaranteed with no discrimination'. Cf. Advisory opinion of 17 September 2003, *Juridical Condition and Rights of Undocumented Migrants*, OC-18/03, para 83.

5 The main internationally 'prohibited grounds' are race, colour, sex, language, religion, political or other opinion, national or social origin, property, and birth or other status. Cf. International Covenant on Civil and Political Rights (adopted 16 December 1966, entered into force 23 March 1976) 999 UNTS 171, art 26. A legal analysis of the management of single prohibited grounds in a disaster scenario can be found in F. Acar and G. Ege, 'Women's Human Rights in Disaster Contexts: How Can CEDAW Help?', Paper prepared on the Occasion of Expert Meeting on Environmental Management and Mitigation of Natural Disasters in a Gender Perspective, (Ankara, Turkey, 6–9 November 2001) Doc. EGM/NAT-DIS/2001/EP.4, 25 October 2001, available at www.un.org/womenwatch/daw/csw/env_manage/documents/EP4-2001Oct25.pdf, accessed on 30 June 2017; P.K. Shah, 'Assisting and Empowering Women Facing Natural Disasters: Drawing from Security Council Resolution 1325' 15 *Columbia Journal of Gender and Law* (2006) 711; J. Todres, 'Mainstreaming Children's Rights in Post-Disaster Settings' 25 *Emory International Law Review* (2011) 1233; A. Ito, 'Disasters, International Law, and Persons with Disabilities' in D.D. Cameron, M.J. Kelly and A. Telesetsky (eds), *The International Law of Disasters Relief* (Cambridge University Press, 2014) 208; and M. Le-Ngoc, 'Normative Frameworks' Role in Addressing Gender – Based Violence in Disaster Settings', IFRC Disaster Law Working Paper Series, No 3, January 2015, available at www.ifrc.org/PageFiles/189264/Mireille%20Le%20Ngoc%20Working%20Paper%20GBV%20(final).pdf, accessed on 30 June 2017.

6 This point has recently been reiterated in General Assembly Resolution 71/128 on international cooperation on humanitarian assistance in the field of natural disasters, from relief to development, where the General Assembly notes '*with concern* that persons with disabilities, older persons, women and children are disproportionately affected in natural disasters'. Cf. UNGA, Res 71/128, UN Doc. A/Res/71/128 (8 December 2016). In this regard see M. Bizzarri, 'Protection of Vulnerable Groups in Natural and Man-Made Disasters' in A. de Guttry, M. Gestri and G. Venturini (eds), *International Disaster Response Law* (Springer, 2012) 381; M. Crock, 'The Protection of Vulnerable Groups' in S.C. Breau and K.L.H. Samuel (eds), *Research Handbook on Disasters and International Law* (Edward Elgar Publishing, 2016) 383; and chapters contained in Part IV, in this volume.

7 Cf. K. Mačák, 'A Matter of Principle(s): The Legal Effect of Impartiality and Neutrality on States as Humanitarian Actors' 97 *International Review of the Red Cross* (2016) 157, esp 161; K. Mačák, 'Principles of Neutrality and Impartiality of Humanitarian Action in the Aftermath of the 2011 Libyan Conflict' in A. Zwitter, C.K. Lamont, H.-J. Heintze and J. Herman (eds), *Humanitarian Action: Global, Regional and Domestic Legal Response* (Cambridge University Press, 2014) 447.

8 J. Pictet, 'The Fundamental Principles of the Red Cross: Commentary' 19 *International Review of the Red Cross* (1979) 130. Cf also Mačák (n. 7) 161.

9 See also the Third Report on the protection of persons in the event of disasters, presented by the Special Rapporteur Eduardo Valencia-Ospina, UN Doc. A/CN.4/629 (31 March 2010) 11. The distinction between the principle of non-discrimination and that of impartiality has been stated as follows by the International Committee of the Red Cross:

> [N]on-discrimination means disregarding objective differences between individuals. Impartiality in its true sense requires that subjective distinctions be set aside as well. To illustrate the difference between the two notions: a National Society that refuses to provide its services to a specific group of people, because of their ethnic origin, fails to observe the rule of non-discrimination; whereas a National Society staff member who, in the exercise of his functions, favours a friend by giving him better treatment than that given to others, contravenes the principle of impartiality.

International Committee of the Red Cross, *The Fundamental Principles of the Red Cross and the Red Crescent* (Geneva, 1996), available at www.icrc.org/eng/assets/files/other/icrc_002_0513.pdf, accessed on 30 June 2017.

10 It is in fact undisputed that humanitarian principles are grounded in International Humanitarian Law: cf. G. Venturini, 'International Disaster Response Law in Relation to Other Branches of International Law' in de Guttry et al. (eds) (n. 6) 45, esp 52; and G. Bartolini, T. Natoli and A. Riccardi, 'Report of the Expert Meeting on the ILC's Draft Articles on the Protection of Persons in the Event of Disasters (Roma Tre University Department of Law – 8 and 9 June 2015)' 3 *International Law and Disasters Working Papers Series* (2015) 88, available at http://disasterlaw.sssup.it/wp-content/uploads/2014/01/Bartolini-Natoli-Riccardi-Report-of-the-Expert-Meeting-2015-DEF.pdf, accessed on 30 June 2017.

11 *Military and Paramilitary Activities in and against Nicaragua (Nicaragua v. United States of America), Merits, Judgment* [1986] ICJ Rep 14.

12 Ibid para 243.

13 UNGA, Res 46/182, UN Doc. A/RES/46/182 (19 December 1991).

14 UNGA, Res 71/128 (n. 6). The leading role of those principles was also stressed by the General Assembly in its Resolutions 43/131 and 45/100 on humanitarian assistance to victims of natural disasters and similar emergency situations, as well as in the more recent Resolution 68/102, on the strengthening of the coordination of emergency humanitarian assistance of the United Nations. Cf. UNGA, Res 43/131, UN Doc. A/RES/43/131 (8 December 1988), Res 45/100, UN Doc. A/RES/45/100 (14 December 1990), and Res 68/102, UN Doc. A/RES/68/102 (13 December 2013), respectively.

15 Cf. for instance the Food Aid Convention (adopted 13 April 1999, entered into force 1 July 1999), art VIII(d). The Convention expired on 1 January 2013 and was replaced by the Food Assistance Convention (adopted 25 April 2012, entered into force 1 January 2013) 2884 UNTS 4. The new Convention only mentions the 'fundamental humanitarian principles' in its Preamble. For a first comment on the new instrument, see A. La Chimia, 'Food Security and the Right to Food: Finding Balance in the 2012 Food Assistance Convention', 65 *International and Comparative Law Quarterly* (2016) 99.

16 International Federation of Red Cross and Red Crescent Societies, *Introduction to the Guidelines for the Domestic Facilitation and Regulation of International Disaster Relief and Initial Recovery Assistance* (Geneva, 2011), available at www.ifrc.org/PageFiles/125652/1205600-IDRL%20Guidelines-EN-LR%20(2).pdf, accessed on 30 June 2017.

17 To be sure, this IFRC guideline also specifies that disaster relief and assistance must be provided 'without any adverse distinction . . . to disaster-affected persons' (guideline 4, para 2(b)) and thus makes express mention of the principle of non-discrimination in disaster settings. However, as is apparent from the wording of the provision, this principle is understood in this guideline as a specific expression of the principle of impartiality, for it is listed among the criteria that humanitarian assistance needs to satisfy in order to be consistent with the principles of humanity, neutrality, and impartiality.

18 Available at www.refworld.org/pdfid/3f13f73b4.pdf, accessed on 30 June 2017. Cf. in particular guideline No. 22 ('Core principles').

19 Office for the Coordination of Humanitarian Affairs, Oslo Guidelines – Revision 1.1 November 2007 (Geneva, 2008), available at https://docs.unocha.org/sites/dms/Documents/Oslo%20Guidelines%20ENGLISH%20(November%202007).pdf, accessed on 30 June 2017. See in particular the guideline No. 20 ('Core principles').

20 Cf. Venturini (n. 10) 51 and Simm and Williams' chapter in this volume.

21 For some general considerations on the human rights-based approach, see McDermott's chapter in this volume. Worthy of note is also the position expressed by Cubie, who includes the 'non-discrimination and prioritisation of vulnerable groups' among the four cardinal principles on which a rights-based approach to humanitarian action needs to be founded (the other principles are the empowerment of rights-holders, participation in decision-making processes, and the duty-bearers' accountability to rights-holders). Cf. D. Cubie, *The International Legal Protection of Persons in Humanitarian Crises- Exploring the* Acquis Humanitaire (Hart Publishing, 2017) 85.

22 Universal Declaration of Human Rights, art 2. UNGA, Res 217 A (10 December 1948).

23 Cf. International Covenant on Civil and Political Rights (n. 5), art 2, para 1; International Covenant on Economic, Social and Cultural Rights (adopted 16 December 1966, entered into force 3 January 1976) 993 UNTS 3, art 2, para 2; Convention for the Protection of Human Rights and Fundamental Freedoms (adopted 4 November 1950, entered into force 3 September 1953) 213 UNTS 222, art 14; American Convention on Human Rights (adopted 22 November 1969, entered into force 18 July 1978) 1144 UNTS 123, art 1, para 1; African Charter on Human and Peoples' Rights (adopted 28 June 1981, entered into force 21 October 1986) art 2.

24 Cf., for instance, International Covenant on Civil and Political Rights (n. 5) art 3; and International Covenant on Economic, Social and Cultural Rights (n. 23) arts 3, 7 and 13.

25 UDHR (n. 22) art 7; International Covenant on Civil and Political Rights (n. 5) art 26; African Charter on Human and Peoples' Rights (n. 23) arts 3 and 19; Protocol No. 12 to the Convention for the Protection of Human Rights and Fundamental Freedoms (adopted 4 November 2000, entered into force 1 April 2005) ETS No. 177, art 1, para 1; Charter of Fundamental Rights of the European Union (adopted 7 December 2000), OJ C 202/389 (2016) art 21.

26 This is the case, for instance, of the European Court of Human Rights' case law that, in spite of the relatively low number of ratifications of Protocol No. 12 (n. 25), significantly put in perspective the ancillary character of the non-discrimination clause enshrined in art 14 of the European Convention for the Protection of Human Rights and Fundamental Freedoms. Cf. G.P. Dolso, 'Art. 14' in S. Bartole, P. De Sena and V. Zagrebelsky (eds), *Commentario breve alla Convenzione europea dei diritti dell'uomo* (CEDAM,

2012) 519–520; and W.A. Schabas, *The European Convention on Human Rights: A Commentary* (Oxford University Press, 2015) 555, esp 563.

27 See, *inter alia*, the Convention on the Elimination of All Forms of Racial Discrimination (adopted 7 March 1966, entered into force 4 January 1969) 660 UNTS 195; the Convention on the Elimination of All Forms of Discrimination against Women (adopted 18 December 1979, entered into force 3 September 1981) 1249 UNTS 13; the Convention on the Rights of the Child (adopted 20 November 1989, entered into force 2 September 1990) 1577 UNTS 3; and Convention on the Rights of Persons with Disabilities (adopted 13 December 2006, entered into force 3 May 2008) 2515 UNTS 3.

28 Convention on the Rights of Persons with Disabilities (n. 27) art 11; emphasis added. See also UNGA, Res 63/150, UN Doc. S/RES/63/150 (11 February 2009 para 9, urging 'States to take, in accordance with their obligations under international law, . . . all necessary measures to ensure the protection and safety of persons with disabilities in situations of risk, including situations of armed conflict, humanitarian emergencies and the occurrence of natural disasters', and UNGA, Res 71/128 (n. 6), para 48, emphasising 'the importance of mainstreaming the perspective of persons with disabilities in disaster risk reduction'. On that topic, see Ito (n. 5).

29 See in particular the chapters in Parts III and IV.

30 CESCR, General Comment No. 14: The Right to the Highest Attainable Standard of Health (Art. 12), UN Doc. E/C.12/2000/4 (2000), para 40. See Inglese's chapter in this volume.

31 CESCR, General Comment No. 12: The Right to Adequate Food (Art. 11), UN Doc. E/C.12/1999/5 (1999), paras 38–39. See Inglese's chapter in this volume.

32 CESCR, General Comment No. 4: The Right to Adequate Housing (Art. 11(1) of the Covenant), Un Doc. E/1992/23 (1991) para 8(e). Cf. Rolnik's chapter in this volume.

33 CESCR, General Comment No. 15: The Right to Water (Arts. 11 and 12 of the Covenant), UN Doc. E/C.12/2002/11 (2003), para 16(h). See again Inglese's chapter in this volume.

34 See, for instance, CERD, Concluding Observations on the United States of America, UN Doc. CERD/C/USA/CO/6 (2008) para 31, where the Committee expresses its concerns about the impact that Hurricane Katrina had on low-income African American residents, recommending that state intensify its effort to help those displaced by the hurricane to return to their homes.

35 CommEDAW, Concluding observations on the Solomon Islands, UN Doc. CEDAW/C/SLB/CO/1–3 (14 November 2014) paras 40–41; Concluding observations on Peru, UN Doc. CEDAW/C/PER/CO/7–8 (24 July 2014) paras 37–38; Concluding observations on Guinea, UN Doc. CEDAW/C/GIN/CO/7–8 (14 November 2014) para 53; Concluding observations on Grenada, UN Doc. CEDAW/C/GRD/CO/1–5 (23 March 2012) paras 35–36; Concluding observations on Togo, UN Doc. CEDAW/C/TGO/CO/6–7 (8 November 2012) para 17; Concluding observations on Algeria, UN Doc. CEDAW/C/DZA/CO/3–4 (23 March 2012) paras 42–43; Concluding observations on New Zealand, UN Doc. CEDAW/C/NLZ/CO/7 (27 July 2012) paras 9, 36–37; Concluding observations Jamaica, UN Doc. CEDAW/C/JAM/CO/6–7 (27 July 2012) paras 31–32; Concluding observations on Chile, UN Doc. CEDAW/C/CHI/CO/5–6 (24 October 2012) paras 38–39; Concluding observations on Belarus, UN Doc. CEDAW/C/BLR/CO/7 (6 April 2011) paras 37–38, Concluding observations on Sri Lanka, UN Doc. CEDAW/C/LKA/CO/7 (8 April 2011) paras 38–39; Concluding observations on Tuvalu, UN Doc. CEDAW/C/TUV/CO/2 (7 August 2009) paras 55–56. See also, CommEDAW, General Recommendation No. 27 on Older Women and the Protection of Their Human Rights, UN Doc. CEDAW/C/GC/27 (16 December 2010) para 25, and General Recommendation No. 28 on the Core Obligations of States Parties under Article 2 of the Convention, UN Doc. CEDAW/C/GC/28 (16 December 2010) para 11.

36 Convention establishing an International Relief Union (adopted 12 July 1927, entered into force 27 December 1932) 135 LNTS 247.

37 Yearbook of the Institute of International Law, Volume 71, Part II, 262. As is well known, the resolution aims to establish a common legal framework for humanitarian assistance to be deployed in both peacetime and wartime. Even so, the resolution may be considered an IDL instrument to the extent that the understanding of 'humanitarian assistance' it espouses covers 'all acts, activities and human and material resources for the provision of good and services of an exclusively humanitarian character, indispensable for the survival and the fulfillment of the essential needs of the victims of *disasters*' (art I, para 1; emphasis added). See also B. Vukas, 'Humanitarian Assistance in Cases of Emergency', *Max Planck Encyclopedia of Public International Law*, online edition, 2013.

38 Art II, para 3; emphasis added.

39 Art 3, para 4. Text available at www.bsec-organization.org/documents/LegalDocuments/agreementmous/agr4/Documents/Emergencyagreement%20071116.pdf, accessed on 30 June 2017.

40 HRC, UN Doc. A/HRC/RES/10/4 (25 March 2009).
41 Available at www.unisdr.org/files/43291_sendaiframeworkfordrren.pdf, accessed on 30 June 2017.
42 Ibid art 19(d).
43 Paris Agreement (adopted 12 December 2015, entered into force 4 November 2016), available at https://treaties.un.org/doc/Publication/UNTS/No%20Volume/54113/Part/I-54113-0800000280458f37.pdf, accessed on 30 June 2017.
44 It need scarcely be mentioned that, under the 1969 Vienna Convention on the Law of Treaties, the preamble of a treaty may be relevant to its interpretation. Cf. Vienna Convention on the Law of Treaties (adopted 23 May 1969, entered into force 27 January 1980), 1155 UNTS 331, art 31(2).
45 The significance of the reference made to human rights protection in the Paris Agreement is highlighted, *inter alia*, by B. Mayer, 'Human Rights in the Paris Agreement' 6 *Climate Law* (2016) 109; O. Quirico, 'Systemic Integration between Climate Change and Human Rights in International Law?' 35 *Netherlands Quarterly of Human Rights* (2017) 31. See also Sossai's chapter in this volume.
46 The Preamble expressly states that

> Parties should, when taking action to address climate change, respect, promote and consider their respective obligations on human rights, the right to health, the rights of indigenous peoples, local communities, migrants, children, persons with disabilities and people in vulnerable situations and the right to development, as well as gender equality, empowerment of women and intergenerational equity.
>
> *(eleventh paragraph)*

47 Framework Convention on Civil Defence Assistance (adopted 22 May 2000, entered into force 23 September 2001). Text available at www.icdo.org/files/2014/3642/8279/EN-Convention-Cadre.pdf, accessed on 30 June 2017.
48 Ibid art 3(c).
49 Ibid art 3(d).
50 OJ C 202/47 (2016).
51 Treaty of Lisbon amending the Treaty on European Union and the Treaty establishing the European Community (adopted 13 December 2007, entered into force 1 December 1999) 2702 UNTS 3.
52 *Supra*, first subsection.
53 Ibid.
54 F. Casolari, 'The External Dimension of the EU Disaster Response' in A. de Guttry, M. Gestri and G. Venturini (n. 6) 129, 152.
55 T. Tridimas, *The General Principles of EU Law* (2nd edn, Oxford University Press, 2006) 60. Among the most recent works offering an overview of the EU principles of equality and non-discrimination, see L.S. Rossi and F. Casolari (eds), *The Principle of Equality in EU Law* (Springer, 2017); J. Croon-Gestefeld, *Reconceptualizing European Equality Law: A Comparative Institutional Analysis* (Hart, 2017); P. Watson (ed), *EU Anti-Discrimination Law* (2nd edn, Oxford University Press, 2012).
56 In particular, the non-discrimination principle is codified in the Charter's art 21, which reads as follows:

> 1. Any discrimination based on any ground such as sex, race, colour, ethnic or social origin, genetic features, language, religion or belief, political or any other opinion, membership of a national minority, property, birth, disability, age or sexual orientation shall be prohibited. 2. Within the scope of application of the Treaties and without prejudice to any of their specific provisions, any discrimination on grounds of nationality shall be prohibited.

57 But see also P. Van Elsuwege and J. Orbie, 'The EU's Humanitarian Aid Policy after Lisbon: Implications of a New Treaty Basis' in I. Govaere and S. Poli (eds), *EU Management of Global Emergencies – Legal Framework for Combating Threats and Crises* (Brill Nijhoff, 2014) 21, 33, maintaining that the non-discrimination principle mentioned in art 214 TFEU may be considered as a 'derived principle' insofar as its substance follows from the principle of impartiality.
58 Cf. Joint Statement by the Council and the Representatives of the Governments of the Member States meeting in the Council, the European Parliament and the European Commission, OJ C 25/1 (2008).
59 Ibid para 2.1.10.
60 See, for instance, the Partnership Agreement between the Members of the African, Caribbean and Pacific Group of States of the one part, and the European Community and its Member States, of the other part (adopted 23 June 2000, entered into force 1 March 2003) OJ L 317/3 (2000), art 72, para 4.

A consolidated version of the Agreement is available at http://eur-lex.europa.eu/legal-content/EN/TXT/HTML/?uri=CELEX:02000A1215(01)-20170101&from=FR, accessed on 30 June 2017.

61 Decision No. 1313/2013 on a Union Civil Protection Mechanism, OJ L 347/924 (2013). The decision, providing for civil protection assistance in the event of disaster inside and outside the European Union, makes it clear that, in all cases where assistance under the Union Mechanism contributes to a Union humanitarian response, it needs to be consistent with humanitarian principles (art 26, para 3). However, as with any other piece of EU legislation, this decision needs to also be implemented by both EU institutions and Member States in keeping with the Charter of Fundamental Rights (thereby including the non-discrimination clause enshrined in its art 21).

62 African Union Convention for the Protection and Assistance of Internally Displaced Persons in Africa (adopted 23 April 2009, entered into force 6 December 2012). Text available at https://treaties.un.org/doc/Publication/UNTS/No%20Volume/52375/Part/I-52375-08000002803f0260.pdf, accessed on 30 June 2017.

63 Ibid art 3, para 1(d). The non-discrimination principle is also mentioned in arts 5, para 1, and 9, para 2(c), of the Kampala Convention.

64 Ibid arts 5, para 8, and 6, para 3.

65 UN Doc. A/CN.4/L.871 (27 May 2016).

66 Third Report on the Protection of Persons in the Event of Disasters, presented by the special rapporteur Eduardo Valencia-Ospina (n. 9), Draft Article 6 ('Humanitarian principles in disaster response'): 'Response to disasters shall take place in accordance with the principles of Humanity, Neutrality and Impartiality.' The insertion of the non-discrimination principle dates back to 2010, when the ILC considered the special rapporteur's third report. As noted by the special rapporteur himself, some ILC members suggested the insertion of the non-discrimination principle because of its close link to IHRL. See the Provisional summary record of the 3057th meeting, UN Doc. A/CN.4/SR.3057 (1 July 2010) 9. The actual wording of the provision was confirmed in 2014, when the ILC adopted the Draft Articles on first reading: Report of the International Law Commission, Sixty-Sixth Session (5 May–6 June and 7 July –8 August 2014), Supplement No. 10 (A/69/10).

67 Commentary to Draft Article 6, in Report of the International Law Commission, Sixty-Eighth Session (2 May–10 June and 4 July–12 August 2016), Supplement No. 10 (A/71/10) 34.

68 This is the reason why the Nordic countries have proposed to amend the Draft Article 5, devoted to the respect of human rights in the event of disaster, according to the following formula: 'States must ensure that the rights of affected persons under international human rights law are respected, protected and fulfilled without discrimination.' Cf. Joint comments by the Nordic countries on the Report of the International Law Commission on the work of its sixty-sixth session (Chapter V: Protection of persons in the event of disasters) 3, available at http://legal.un.org/docs/?path=../ilc/sessions/68/pdfs/english/pop_finland_nordic.pdf&lang=E, accessed on 30 June 2017.

69 See also, in the same vein, the International Organization for Migration (IOM) Comments and observations on the International Law Commission Draft articles on the protection of persons in the event of disasters with commentaries, 11 (text available at http://legal.un.org/docs/?path=../ilc/sessions/68/pdfs/english/pop_iom.pdf&lang=E, accessed on 30 June 2017), highlighting the fact that the non-discrimination principle also plays a pivotal role in the context of disaster prevention. Indeed, according to the IOM,

> [t]he principle of non-discrimination is particularly relevant . . . in the context of the prevention of disasters. In addition, a specific attention to vulnerable groups, in terms of ensuring accessibility of information, participation in the decision making process and preparedness to respond to their specific needs when the disaster strikes should be key considerations in the prevention of disasters or their consequences.

As is apparent, the Organization lays particular emphasis on the need for positive actions to ensure substantive equality among individuals *in subiecta materia*. On that tool and the role played by non-discrimination at a pre-disaster stage, see *supra*, second subsection, and *infra*, n. 107.

70 This warm reception cannot be taken for granted, considering the strong reactions that emerged in the debate on other solutions written into the Draft Articles.

71 UNGA, Sixth Committee, Summary Record of 23rd Meeting, UN Doc. A/C.6/65/SR.23 (1 December 2010) 6–7.

72 UNGA, Sixth Committee, Summary Record of 22nd Meeting, UN Doc. A/C.6/65/SR.22 (1 December 2010) 8.

73 UNGA, Sixth Committee, Summary Record of 24th Meeting, UN Doc. A/C.6/65/SR.24 (1 December 2010) 12.
74 Ibid 10.
75 Comments from the United States on the International Law Commission's Draft Articles on 'Protection of persons in the event of disasters' as adopted by the Commission in 2014 on First Reading, 8, available at http://legal.un.org/docs/?path=../ilc/sessions/68/pdfs/english/pop_usa.pdf&lang=E, accessed on 30 June 2017.
76 They include Greece (UNGA, UN Doc. A/C.6/65/SR.22 (n. 72) 8), Ireland (UNGA, UN Doc. A/C.6/65/SR.24 (n. 73) 10), the United Kingdom (ibid 11), Portugal (UNGA, UN Doc. A/C.6/65/SR.23 (n. 71) 3), Austria (ibid 6–7), and Estonia (ibid 11).
77 But see the position expressed by the European Nordic countries, arguing, by contrast, that respect for neutrality should more coherently be written into all relevant Draft Articles: Joint comments by the Nordic countries on the Report of the International Law Commission (n. 68) 2. In fact, as the ILC itself has rightly stressed in its Commentaries on the Draft Articles, the principle of neutrality, though rooted in the context of armed conflict, has taken on a broader meaning, requiring those subject to it to conduct themselves apolitically, which makes it applicable to other branches of international law. Cf. Commentary to Draft Article 6, in Report of the International Law Commission, Sixty-Eighth Session (n. 67) 33–34. See also, in the same vein, Bartolini, Natoli, and Riccardi (n. 10) 35.
78 For a concrete illustration of the corresponding operative implications, cf. Inter-Agency Standing Committee (IASC), IASC Operational Guidelines on the Protection of Persons in Situations of Natural Disasters, January 2011, available at www.ohchr.org/Documents/Issues/IDPersons/Operational Guidelines_IDP.pdf, accessed on 30 June 2017.
79 *Supra*, second section.
80 Direct discrimination takes place when one is treated less favourably than others in a similar situation for a reason tied to a prohibited ground. Indirect discrimination, by contrast, designates practices that (unlike overt discrimination on prohibited grounds) appear neutral on the surface but then wind up disproportionately affecting the ability of some to exercise a right they are entitled to.
81 Multiple discrimination is discriminatory treatment that is based on multiple grounds but specifically impact on individuals in different and unique ways.
82 As the term suggests, discrimination by association takes place when people are discriminated against because of their association with others who have a protected characteristic, or because they are mistakenly perceived to have one such characteristic and are treated accordingly.
83 While the former are well-established in IHRL (see, for instance, CESCR, General Comment No. 20 (n. 4), paras 7–17), the concept of 'discrimination by association' is a recent development. See in this respect Judgment of 17 July 2008, *S. Coleman v. Attridge Law and Steve Law*, Case C-303/06, EU:C:2008:415, para 56. Cf. Clifford (n. 1) 439–440, correctly maintaining that '[h]uman rights bodies . . . are increasingly taking an expansive approach to the definition of discrimination'. Cf. also C. Karagiorgi, 'The Concept of Discrimination by Association and Its Application in the EU Member States' (18) *European Anti-Discrimination Law Review*, July 2014, 25, available at www.equalitylaw.eu/downloads/825-law-review-18, accessed on 30 June 2017.
84 ILC's Commentary to Draft Article 6 (n. 67) para 7, stressing that the 'principle of non-discrimination is not to be taken as excluding the prospect of "positive discrimination" as appropriate. The phrase "while taking into account the needs of the particularly vulnerable" in draft article 6 reflects this position.'
85 *Thlimmenos v. Greece*, App No. 34369/97 (ECtHR, Judgment of 6 April 2000) para 44: 'The right not to be discriminated against in the enjoyment of the rights guaranteed under the Convention is also violated when States without an objective and reasonable justification fail to treat differently persons whose situations are significantly different.'
86 Emphasis added. A further example of a measure involving a legitimate differential treatment can be found in art 2, para 3, of the International Covenant on Economic, Social and Cultural Rights (n. 23), providing that: '[d]eveloping countries, with due regard to human rights and their national economy, may determine to what extent they would guarantee the economic rights recognized in the present Covenant to non-nationals'. Cf. B. Saul, D. Kinley and J. Mowbray, *The International Covenant on Economic, Social and Cultural Rights-Commentary, Cases and Materials* (Oxford University Press, 2014) 214.
87 *Supra*, second section.
88 Clifford (n. 1) 443–444.

89 This to the extent that such a right is recognised internationally. On this question see Hesselman's chapter in this volume.
90 *Supra* n. 25.
91 Advisory opinion of 17 September 2003 (n. 4).
92 Ibid para 101.
93 M. Gestri, 'Obblighi internazionali di protezione dello straniero e tutela dei diritti "universali" della persona' in A.M. Calamia, M. Di Filippo and M. Gestri (eds), *Immigrazione, Diritto e Diritti: profili internazionalistici ed europei* (CEDAM, 2012) 279, esp 298.
94 See in this respect the ILC's Commentary on Draft Article 26 of the Draft Articles on 'Responsibility of States for Internationally Wrongful Acts', where the Commission finds that '[t]hose peremptory norms that are clearly accepted and recognized include the prohibitions of aggression, genocide, slavery, *racial discrimination*, crimes against humanity and torture, and the right to self-determination' (Report of the International Law Commission, Fifty-Third Session (23 April–1 June and 2 July–10 August 2001), UN Doc. A/CN.4/SER.A/2001/Add.1 (Part 2) 85; emphasis added). In the *Barcelona Traction Case*, the International Court of Justice also indicated that *erga omnes* obligations derive from 'the principles and rules concerning the basic rights of the human person, including protection from . . . *racial discrimination*' (*Barcelona Traction, Light and Power Co Ltd (New Application: 1962) (Belgium v. Spain) (Second Phase)* [1970] ICJ Rep. 3, para 34; emphasis added).
95 See, for instance, Human Right Committee, General Comment No. 18 (n. 2), para 1: 'Non-discrimination, together with equality before the law and equal protection of the law without any discrimination, constitute a basic and general principle relating to the protection of human rights.'
96 Cf. Henrard (n. 3). But see, *contra*, Clifford (n. 1) 443, arguing that '[h]olistic consideration of international human rights jurisprudence leads to a strong presumption that a right to equality exists.'
97 *Supra*, second section.
98 Ibid.
99 *Supra*, n. 25.
100 Commentary to Draft Article 5, in Report of the International Law Commission, Sixty-Eighth Session (n. 67) 32. Cf. Sommario's chapter in this volume.
101 International Covenant on Economic, Social and Cultural Rights (n. 23) art 4. The practice of the CESCR stresses that *in any case* minimum essential levels of the following rights must be ensured for *everyone*: (1) minimum essential food – sufficient, nutritionally adequate, and safe – so as to ensure freedom from hunger (see CESCR, General Comment No. 3: The Nature of States Parties' Obligations (Art. 2, para 1, of the Covenant) (1 January 1991), and General Comment No. 12 (n. 31)); (2) essential primary healthcare, including essential drugs (see CESCR, General Comment No. 3, and General Comment No. 14 (n. 30)); (3) essential basic shelter and housing, including sanitation (see CESCR, General Comment No. 3, and General Comment No. 4 (n. 32)) and the right not to be arbitrarily evicted from one's home (see CESCR, General Comment No. 7: The right to adequate housing (Art. 11(1) of the Covenant: Forced evictions (20 May 1997)); and (4) access to a minimum essential amount of water – sufficient and safe for personal and domestic uses – so as to prevent disease (see CESCR, General Comment No. 15 (n. 33)). See also the Charter of Fundamental Rights of the European Union (n. 25) art 52, para 1.
102 *A. and Others v. The United Kingdom*, App No. 3455/05 (ECtHR, Judgment of 19 February 2009) paras 182–190. The European Court has elaborated that condition in light of the principle of proportionality. See Schabas (n. 26) 600.
103 International Covenant on Civil and Political Rights (n. 5), art 4, para 1; American Convention on Human Rights (n. 23) art 27, para 1.
104 For the reasons outlined above, I do not entirely share the opinion of some scholars who have underscored a twofold structure of Draft Article 6, arguing that, while its first part, devoted to humanitarian principles, should enjoy an absolute standing, the second part, devoted to non-discrimination, may be limited or derogated in view of its link to the human rights dimension. Cf. Bartolini, Natoli and Riccardi (n. 10) 37.
105 E. Cannizzaro and F. De Vittor, 'Proportionality in the European Convention of Human Rights' in R. Kolb and G. Gaggioli (eds), *Research Handbook on Human Rights and Humanitarian Law* (Edward Elgar Publishing, 2013) 125.
106 See in this respect the comments made by China: UNGA, UN Doc. A/C.6/65/SR.22 (n. 72) 10. On the assessment made by human rights' monitoring bodies on the impact of resource constraints caused

by disasters on the States' compliance with treaty-based obligations, see Nohle's and Giacca's chapter in this volume.

107 As currently worded, the Draft Article 6 is subject to two lines of criticism. The first one is that the principles governing assistance to persons in need are explicitly restricted to disaster *response*: although the Commentary makes it clear that other stages of the disaster cycle may also be considered to be covered, it would have been better to more clearly frame the scope of the provision's timeframe. The second line of criticism is that Draft Article 6, as currently worded, does not clarify its subjective scope. On this question, see Natoli's chapter in this volume.

14

THE RIGHT TO A HEALTHY ENVIRONMENT

Delineating the content (and contours) of a slippery notion

Giovanna Adinolfi

Introduction

Policy and scholarly debates devote much attention to the relationship between environmental protection and human rights, suggesting diverse approaches to explore their synergies and solve their conflicts.[1] There is an open discussion on a very preliminary issue, which is whether the environment deserves protection functionally, as the natural milieu wherein individuals live and interact, or whether the health of the environment should be protected as such, irrespective of its function in sustaining human life.[2] A less polarizing approach suggests that human rights and environmental protection share some common goals. Consequently, the debate is centred on the contribution that international environmental law could make in achieving higher standards of human rights protection and, vice versa, on the impact that a proper implementation of international human rights instruments could have on the fight against environmental degradation. Potential conflicts between the two regimes are not overlooked; rather, their solution is sought by trying to establish criteria by which to balance competing interests.

On the basis of this third approach, the purpose of the present contribution is to assess to what extent the integration of environmental considerations into human rights litigation may affect policies addressing disaster risk reduction and response.[3] It is beyond any doubt that disasters may be due to environmental degradation and that, in a disaster scenario, the effective enjoyment of human rights is put at risk.[4] Accordingly, the adoption of environmental policies could complement measures by which to counter the likelihood or the detrimental impact of natural or human-made hazards, as they would indirectly reduce exposure and vulnerability to disasters and disaster risk,[5] while at the same time addressing major threats to human rights in a post-disaster situation. However, the issue could also be considered from a reverse perspective: a proper protection of certain human rights may be deemed to contribute to establishing, maintaining, or improving environmental safety, thus avoiding disasters or reducing their magnitude.

The conceptual assumption behind the idea that environmental degradation triggers disasters (and vice versa) and that it consequently impacts negatively on human rights, is that a safe environment is a *sine qua non* for an effective enjoyment of human rights. This connection was first proclaimed in the 1972 Stockholm Declaration on the Human Environment, affirming that '[m]an has the fundamental right to freedom, equality and adequate conditions of life, in an environment of a quality that permits a life of dignity and well-being'.[6] In quite similar terms, the International Court of Justice (ICJ) held in 1996 that 'the environment is not as abstraction but represents the living space, the quality of life and the very health of human beings, including generations unborn'.[7]

This anthropocentric perspective has encouraged the recognition of a right to a healthy environment within the realm of international human rights law.[8] Under positive law, this evolution has shaped the regimes established under the 1969 American Convention on Human Rights,[9] as well as the 1981 African Charter on Human and Peoples' Rights.[10] The second section of this contribution introduces an analysis of the (limited) case law developed under these two treaties, with the purpose of assessing the extent to which it may influence national policies, and in particular the design and implementation of disaster adaptation measures. The third section tackles those international human rights regimes that do not expressly recognise environmental rights. This lacuna has not prevented relevant treaty bodies from acknowledging an environmental dimension of 'general' human rights whose scope does not extend to the protection of the environment,[11] but which in certain circumstances may call for the adoption of environmental measures. In this regard, some of the main decisions also concern human rights violations that have taken place in a disaster situation, and they give evidence of the indirect influence that the enforcement of human rights regimes has on national strategies aimed at improving resilience in the face of disasters. A brief overview of the pertinent case law will reveal that both the normative content of the right to a healthy environment and the environmental interpretation of 'general' human rights have been framed in view of other branches of international law, in particular international environmental law and, most importantly for our purposes, major instruments of disaster risk reduction (such as the Hyogo Framework for Action approved in 2005 or the 2015 Sendai Framework).[12] The contribution concludes with an analysis of the human rights approach to climate change, so as to assess whether its implementation would strengthen the degree of protection of the human rights of individuals living in areas prone to weather-related disasters.

The bearing of the right to a healthy environment on disaster policies

The adoption of the 1972 Stockholm Declaration on the Human Environment has resulted in the progressive opening of human rights catalogues to environmental rights. At the national level, most constitutions endow individuals with a right to a healthy environment or provide for environmental responsibilities of public authorities.[13] At the same time, in some international human rights instruments, an obligation has been included to secure a right to a healthy environment.

More to the point, in 1988 the parties to the American Convention on Human Rights approved the San Salvador Additional Protocol,[14] whose Article 11.1 declares that '[e]veryone shall have the right to live in a healthy environment'. The right that each individual considered in isolation has to environmental protection is recognized, but its effective enforcement suffers from the exclusion of the Protocol from the jurisdiction of the Inter-American Commission and the Inter-American Court on Human Rights.[15]

In this regard, the American Convention deviates from the 1981 African Charter on Human and Peoples' Rights, whose Article 24 affirms the collective right of '[a]ll peoples . . . to a general satisfactory environment favourable to their development'. Indeed, the implementation of this provision was originally placed under the control of the African Commission on Human Rights, and was further strengthened in 2005, when the Court of Justice of the Economic Community of Western African States (ECOWAS) was granted jurisdiction over 'cases of violation of human rights that occur in any Member State'.[16] Given both the nature of ECOWAS as an organization for economic integration and the absence of a prescribed catalogue of human rights to be enforced by it, the Court has extensively interpreted its jurisdiction as covering the human rights instruments binding upon all ECOWAS member states, including the 1981 African Charter.[17]

The decisions adopted in the well-known *Ogoni* case[18] (concerning the heavy environmental disaster caused by oil activities carried out by the Nigerian government and foreign oil companies in the region of the Niger River delta) offer some useful guidance as to the approach to be followed in interpreting a broad provision such as the one enshrined in Article 24. In *Ogoni*, both the African Commission and the ECOWAS Court ruled in favour of the claimants. In particular, in 2001, delivering a decision taking also into account the right to health as set forth in Article 16 of the African Charter, the Commission found that Article 24 requires states to 'take reasonable and other measures to prevent pollution and ecological degradation, to promote conservation and to secure an ecologically sustainable development and use of natural resources'.[19] Furthermore, they may not carry out, sponsor, or tolerate 'any practice, policy, or legal measures violating the integrity of the individual'.[20] According to the Commission, these substantive obligations of means are accompanied by procedural obligations to carry out environmental impact studies, monitor environments threatened by industrial activities, and provide the communities exposed to hazardous activities with appropriate information and meaningful opportunities to be heard.

In a slightly different vein, a few years later the ECOWAS Court judged exclusively on the basis of Article 24. Even though the claimants had also alleged the violation of other 'general' human rights, the Court considered it had to 'shape out the dispute along its essential lines' and to focus on the violations which constituted the core of the grievance brought before it,[21] that is, Article 24. The autonomy of the right to a healthy environment from other human rights has been acknowledged, and its violation has been ascertained without assessing whether poor environmental quality had undermined human health or life. The behaviour required under Article 24 was subsequently determined in light of the opening clause of the African Charter, which under Article 1 binds states 'to adopt legislative or other measures to give effect' to the rights enshrined in the Charter itself. Accordingly, Article 24 has been understood to have two prongs to it, on the one hand requiring states to 'take every measure to maintain the quality of the environment',[22] while at the same time requiring effective enforcement of all applicable laws and regulations:[23]

> the adoption of the legislation, no matter how advanced it may be . . . , may still fall short of compliance with international obligations in matters of environmental protection if these measures just remain on paper and are not accompanied by additional and concrete measures aimed at preventing the occurrence of damage or ensuring accountability, with the effective reparation of the environmental damage suffered.[24]

There are some general considerations that can be extracted from the *Ogoni* ruling, also as concerns the way its express recognition of human environmental rights can impact policies aimed at addressing disaster situations.

One of the main difficulties of expressly recognizing a right to a healthy environment lies in the vagueness of its contours, leaving to the interpreter the onus of determining its normative content. This job may prove complex, as it may require gathering scientific evidence. At the same time, arriving at a normative choice by interpreting a vague provision implies making value judgments that may not be in the states' interest, particularly when they seek to achieve a balance between competing societal interests (such as environmental protection vs. economic development).[25] This consideration weakens the guiding influence of a provision like Article 24 of the African Charter on States' policies aimed at addressing disaster risk reduction. However, in the *Ogoni* case, compelling evidence was presented showing that the environmental impact of the oil activities carried out in the Niger region was severe, and since Nigeria had not challenged this evidence, there was no need to establish general criteria on whose basis to ascertain whether the claimants were actually living in a 'generally unsatisfactory' environment. In other less clear circumstances, human rights bodies may be required to determine preliminarily the elements of a suitable environment in abstract terms. In these cases, it may prove appropriate to refer to applicable international standards.[26]

The decisions by the African Commission and the ECOWAS Court also provide some guidance on what states are required to do to ensure the right to an environment of a given quality. Article 24 of the African Charter has been interpreted as enshrining both substantive and procedural environmental rights – an interpretation that finds support not only in the practice of other human rights bodies but also in international environmental law. Implicit reference is made to the principle of prevention as stated in the final documents of both the 1972 Stockholm Conference on the Human Environment and the 1992 Rio de Janeiro Conference on Environment and Development.[27] On its basis, the African Commission and the ECOWAS Court have inferred from Article 24 an obligation of states to adopt all suitable measures necessary to maintain the quality of the environment, to prevent pollution and degradation, and to regulate hazardous activities. Furthermore, the ECOWAS Court has clarified that these measures need to be effective and accompanied by implementing regulations so that the same measures do not 'remain on paper'.[28] It follows that a legislative framework addressing environmental and disaster risk cannot stand in isolation: it must be integrated by proper regulatory, administrative, and judicial actions aiming at making it effective. Due weight is given to judicial measures, for it is not ruled out that environmental accidents will take place or that they will have a greater magnitude than expected; in that case, the effective implementation of Article 24 will require fulfilling a further obligation of result, meaning that the damage incurred will have to be redressed.

As concerns the procedural component of the right to a healthy environment, the decisions by the African Commission and the ECOWAS Court are implicitly underpinned by the 1992 Rio de Janeiro Declaration and the multilateral environmental agreements recognizing procedural environmental rights. In the 2010 decision about the admissibility of the *Ogoni* claim, the ECOWAS Court did not ignore the 1998 Aarhus Convention on Access to Information, Public Participation in Decision-Making and Access to Justice in Environmental Matters,[29] notwithstanding that it was not legally binding upon African countries, as the Court itself expressly acknowledged.[30]

A final consideration pertains to the justiciability of the right to a healthy environment. The ECOWAS Court rejected Nigeria's argument that the 1966 International Covenant on Economic, Social and Cultural Rights (ICESCR)[31] (whose violation was also alleged by the plaintiff) was not justiciable,[32] since its fulfilment depends upon the resources available to a state. According to the Court, Nigeria's assertion had to be considered on a case-by-case basis, and it could not be ruled out that, in some situations, the implementation of economic and social rights merely requires states to enforce the law they have already adopted and to 'prevent powerful entities from precluding the most vulnerable from enjoying the right granted to them'.[33] This line of reasoning has also informed the judgment over the justiciability of the right to a satisfactory environment, whose 'core content' lies in the adoption and implementation of appropriate and effective legislation and regulations, which states must uphold in all circumstances.

'Indirect' environmental rights: the environmental dimension of 'general' human rights

The approach adopted by the African human rights bodies has also been endorsed in other contexts, even though the human rights treaties in question do not expressly recognize a freestanding right to a safe environment. As mentioned, according to relevant case law, national environmental policies are deemed to fall within the scope of 'general' human rights, whose violation has been also alleged in the aftermath of disasters (both natural and human-made).

The UN approach

The UN system fully supports the idea that 'the protection of the environment is . . . a vital part of contemporary human rights doctrine, for it is a *sine qua non* for numerous human rights such as the right to health and the right to life', and that 'damage to the environment can impair and undermine all the rights spoken of in the Universal Declaration of Human Rights and other human rights instruments'.[34] In 1994, the then Special Rapporteur on Human Rights and the Environment proposed the adoption of a set of draft principles on the environmental content of human rights.[35] Significantly departing from the 1972 Stockholm Declaration, the document in its opening paragraphs acknowledged that '[a]ll persons have the right to a secure, healthy and ecologically sound environment':[36] this right was unequivocally affirmed, and everyone ('all persons') was recognized as a right-holder in that regard. However, the proposal failed to secure the backing of states. As a result, UN human rights bodies took the different approach of 'greening general rights', interpreted as prescribing the adoption of measures also aimed at protecting the environment.

The Committee on Economic, Social and Cultural Rights has repeatedly stated that a genuine enjoyment of some social rights may require measures for improving the quality and safety of the environment in which individuals live and work. The Committee has determined that the core content of the right to adequate food, as set forth in Article 11 ICESCR, also entails the 'availability of food in a quantity and quality sufficient to satisfy the dietary needs of individuals, free from adverse substances'.[37] Its implementation is made conditional on the adoption of protective means 'to prevent contamination of foodstuff'.[38] Along the same lines, the right to health enshrined in Article 12 ICESCR has been interpreted as entailing the right to enjoy conditions 'necessary for the realization of the highest attainable standard of health',[39] including 'healthy environmental conditions'.[40] More in detail, states are placed under an obligation to adopt measures for the 'prevention and reduction of the population's exposure to . . . detrimental environmental conditions that directly or indirectly impact upon human health'.[41]

A similar approach has also been taken by the Human Rights Committee in its interpretation of Article 27 of the 1966 International Covenant on Civil and Political Rights (ICCPR),[42] acknowledging the right of persons belonging to ethnic, religious, or linguistic minorities to enjoy their own culture, including the right to a particular way of life associated with the use of land resources. For instance, as has been held in the *Poma Poma* ruling, Article 27 obligates states to adopt 'positive legal measures of protection and measures to ensure the effective participation of minority communities in decisions which affect them'.[43] Therefore, a measure designed to promote national economic development (at issue in *Poma Poma* was a project to divert the course of a mountain river to provide water to coastal cities) will be found to be illegitimate if it has 'substantive' negative impacts on the enjoyment of minorities' rights (in the case at hand, this was due to the environmental damage caused by depriving indigenous lands of water).

In its more recent resolutions on the relationship between human rights and the environment, the Human Rights Council has not distanced itself from the approach followed by the UN treaty bodies. On the basis of the reports submitted by the independent expert and the then Special Rapporteur on human rights obligations relating to the enjoyment of a healthy environment,[44] in a 2016 resolution, the Council does not recognize any right to an environment of a given quality.[45] Rather, it calls upon states 'to respect, protect and fulfil human rights, including in actions relating to environmental challenges'[46] and 'to adopt an effective normative framework for the enjoyment of a safe, clean, healthy and sustainable environment'.[47] Environmental rights are expressly taken into account, but only as procedural rights.[48] On a substantive level, the prevailing trend remains that a proper implementation of international human rights instruments and national legislation is adequate for protecting individuals from any threat due to unsafe environmental conditions.

The regional context: the case law of the European Court of Human Rights

The foregoing developments under the UN system run parallel to those in regional contexts where the protection of the environment has been clearly advocated as a component of policies aimed at achieving social human rights. In this regard, reference can be made to the 2004 Arab Charter on Human Rights[49] and to the 2012 ASEAN Human Rights Declaration.[50] Both documents recognize the right to a healthy environment as part of the right to an adequate standard of living.[51]

In general terms, the practice under the European system of human rights is perfectly aligned with the UN approach. The 1950 European Convention for the Protection of Human Rights and Fundamental Freedoms (ECHR)[52] does not include a right to a healthy environment, nor is any reference to it made in its protocols or in the European Social Charter.[53] Some proposals have been put forward by the Parliamentary Assembly of the Council of Europe,[54] recommending that an additional protocol to the ECHR on environmental rights be drawn up, but the Committee of Ministers did not deem it crucial.[55] In fact, the Committee held that environmental protection is already secured under the case law the European Court of Human Rights (ECtHR) has issued on 'general' rights.[56]

The ECtHR's case law on the environment has been mainly based on the right to life and to private and family life, respectively set forth in Articles 2 and 8 ECHR.[57] In that regard, alleged victims have also brought complaints relating to disaster situations, where the respondent state has been found in violation of 'general' rights for having neglected to adopt disaster risk reduction measures that could have avoided a catastrophe (human-made or natural) or that could have mitigated its devastating consequences.[58]

It is the settled jurisprudence of the Court that Article 2 ECHR sets forth a positive obligation of states to take appropriate actions to protect the life of individuals within their jurisdiction. In what concerns hazardous industrial activities, states are obligated to regulate them bearing in mind the risk they pose to human lives and to govern their 'licensing, setting up, operation, security and supervision', while at the same time making it compulsory 'for all those concerned to take practical measures to ensure the effective protection of citizens whose lives might be endangered by the inherent risks'.[59] While it is recognized that the choice of means in principle falls within the parties' margin of appreciation, and that consideration must also be given to the states' priorities and resources, the Court has nonetheless acknowledged that preventive measures are definitely required under Article 2 when the competent public authorities have full knowledge of the risks individuals are exposed to and have all the necessary powers and resources to reduce disaster vulnerability.[60]

The Court followed a similar line of reasoning also in dealing with natural disasters. In these cases, however, the Court is prone to grant states a wider margin of discretion than in the event of disasters owed to dangerous *human* activities, taking into account that natural hazards are beyond human control. Nevertheless, in view of the origin of the threat, the proneness of a given area to a recurring identifiable natural hazard, and the potential effectiveness of adaptation measures designed to lessen its devastating consequences, the Court has held that Article 2 entails a duty of states to take preventive measures.[61] Article 2 was found to have been violated in *Budayeva*,[62] as Russia had failed to adopt traditional measures under disaster risk reduction policies (it had failed to properly construct and maintain engineering facilities), even though the national authorities were fully aware of the risk of mudslides in the affected region. At the same time, the establishment of effective monitoring posts and of early warning systems to collect information and make it available to the population was also considered to fall within the scope of the positive obligation under Article 2 to adopt appropriate steps to safeguard the life of individuals: 'in exercising their discretion as to the choice of measures required to comply with their positive obligations, the authorities ended up by taking no measures at all up to the day of the disaster'.[63]

In less serious cases, where the deprivation of life is not at issue, the Court's environmental case law is grounded on the right to private and family life under Article 8 ECHR. In fact, in the very first environmental cases brought before the Court, it was this Article 8 whose violation was being alleged, and this gave the Court an opportunity to take its first steps toward interpreting the Convention in light of environmental concerns, almost exclusively with respect to harmful human activities. Since *Lopez Ostra v. Spain*, the Court has consistently recognized that 'severe environmental pollution may affect individuals' well-being and prevent them from enjoying their homes in such a way as to affect their private and family life adversely, without, however, seriously endangering their health'.[64] Therefore, positive obligations are also inferred from Article 8, calling for the adoption of measures commensurate with the risks posed to the enjoyment of the right to private and family life owing to hazardous activities occurring within the jurisdiction of state parties.[65] In this regard, the language used by the Court closely resembles the judgments under Article 2, showing that there is much overlap between the two provisions when it comes to the scope of the positive obligations they entail in connection with dangerous activities.[66]

Apart from substantive obligations, the Court's case law has also highlighted that an effective enjoyment of both the right to life and the right to private and family life implies procedural aspects. Indeed, the ECtHR has aligned itself with the 1998 Aarhus Convention even with respect to states that have not adhered to it.[67] It has consistently held that, under Articles 2 and 8, states are required to take effective measures by which to provide potential victims of environmental disasters with reliable information about those risks, as well as to promote the participation of the public in the framing of policies and measures having a direct or indirect impact on the environment, and, finally, to provide access to justice. In this last regard, the Court has endorsed two different standards of protection. The first one pertains to the right of individuals to access proper judicial procedures for lodging claims alleging a violation of their right to environmental information and participation in decision-making.[68] This practice is in line with the aforementioned 1998 Aarhus Convention. A further strand is focused on the right to an 'effective judicial system' guaranteeing that any breach of substantive rights will be prosecuted and punished through the criminal, civil, administrative, or disciplinary remedies made available to victims.[69]

The human rights approach to climate change and its impact in a disaster scenario

Scientific evidence underlines the existence of a causal relationship between climate change and natural disasters. Relevant data point to a steady increase in greenhouse gas (GHG) emissions since the pre-industrial era, its effect on global warming, and, in sequence, on natural and human systems.[70] Climate change is considered to be a dominant cause of natural disasters, as evidenced by the increase in the number of weather-related events and, indirectly, by its more general effect on environmental degradation.[71]

The detrimental consequences of climate change on living conditions may affect the enjoyment of human rights.[72] Therefore, any progress in international climate change law may have a positive impact for potential or actual victims of global warming. Bearing in mind the differences in national circumstances, the goal pursued under international environmental law is to involve the highest number of states in apportioning among all of them the unavoidable costs of climate change policies, in making collective action as effective as possible, and in avoiding free-riding problems. As a result, in the 1992 United Nations Framework Convention on Climate Change,[73] the later 1998 Kyoto Protocol,[74] and the 2015 Paris Agreement,[75] a common strategy has been designed requiring parties to implement both mitigation and adaptation policies. For our purposes, addressing climate change directly through mitigation measures reducing GHG emissions could lessen the probability of climate change-related disasters and, as a consequence, their impact on human rights. As for adaptation measures, they may be aimed at strengthening resilience in the face of climate change or at addressing climate-change harm once it has already struck human or natural systems.[76] Their proper implementation is implicitly beneficial to the fullest realization of human rights, whether by strengthening their protection, limiting their violation, or providing proper redress in case of infringement.

However, the response under international environmental law has come up against a number of hurdles. Therefore, scholars of international law have started to debate a human rights approach to climate change that would place additional pressure on states to design effective environmental policies.[77] Political arenas would not be the only forums of debate: litigation would raise public concern and give victims a voice. Furthermore, in line with an evolutionary approach to the interpretation of human rights treaties (regarded as 'living instruments'), courts and other relevant bodies would be called on to enforce such treaties by also taking account of the threats to the effective enjoyment of human rights originating from one of the main challenges states have to cope with in the modern era.

Within this framework, this section seeks to ascertain whether the adoption of a human rights approach to climate change could strengthen the enjoyment of human rights of people living in areas prone to weather-related disasters.

Any analysis has to start from the peculiarities of climate change as an environmental issue. It is beyond any doubt that states are legally responsible for dealing with environmental degradation happening within their borders and affecting their population. As discussed, participation in human rights regimes requires states to duly consider infringements resulting from possible environmental disasters. In the case of transboundary environmental damage, the protection granted by human rights treaties to people living in third countries may be disputed, as doubts arise about whether a state has any 'jurisdiction' or 'effective control' over individuals living in neighbouring countries where it has failed to adequately address environmental harm (or any related disaster) within its territory.[78] The complexity increases with respect to environmental issues like climate change, considered by the international community to be a 'common concern of mankind'[79] or, as explored in more recent legal literature, a 'global public good'. This latter expression refers to goods (either positive or negative) which benefit (or harm) all countries, peoples, and generations but which can be produced (or tackled) only by the combined efforts of all States.[80]

One of the arguments that has been raised as an overall criticism of a human rights approach to climate change points out the limited powers of international tribunals, which lack the power to bind states to their rulings.[81] Then, too, the availability of human rights litigation needs to also reckon with the nature of the applicable treaty regimes. First, as has been observed in the legal literature,

> human rights law primarily imposes vertical duties, that is, duties owed by a State to those primarily within its jurisdiction. Extending those duties diagonally, to those outside the State's jurisdiction, may seem necessary in order to apply human rights law to the global aspects of climate change, but such an extension faces serious obstacles, both legal and practical.[82]

Furthermore, as the following analysis will illustrate, international human rights law follows a so-called 'personal injury approach': litigation may start to the extent that applicants prove *prima facie* that a state's action or inaction has infringed a protected human right of one or more victims.[83] Therefore, strict limits are imposed on litigation for a public and collective interest in environmental protection as such.

Most human rights treaties are premised by a jurisdiction clause under which parties are obligated to secure the protected rights for anyone living under their jurisdiction or control. As is well known, Article 1 of the European Convention has been interpreted quite narrowly, as the ECtHR has acknowledged its extraterritorial application only in exceptional circumstances (when the respondent state exercises public powers 'through effective control of the relevant territory and its inhabitants abroad as a consequence of military occupation or through the consent, invitation or acquiescence of the Government of that territory'):[84] to do otherwise would be 'tantamount to arguing that anyone adversely affected by an act imputable to a Contracting State, wherever in the world that act may have been committed or its consequences felt, is thereby brought within the jurisdiction of that State'.[85] A similar approach also prevails with the Human Rights Committee: in its interpretation of Article 2.1 ICCPR,[86] the Committee acknowledges that the protected rights are owed by states to anyone within their (or their agents') power or effective control, even if such persons are not situated in their territory.[87] The case law has not yet tackled the issue of the reach of human rights obligations in cases involving transboundary or global environmental harm. However, the practice hardly supports the idea that individuals living in countries suffering the impact of climate change are under the control of states implementing inappropriate mitigation policies.[88]

A second obstacle stems from the rules on standing before human rights bodies.[89] Under Article 34 ECHR, a complainant has to qualify as a 'victim' of a violation of a protected right. *Actio popularis* is precluded,[90] and plaintiffs must substantiate that the contested conduct has impacted on them. In the *Di Sarno* case, however, the Court adopted a softer reading of the 'victim' requirement: in order for a claim to be admitted, the Court found, it is sufficient that the harm suffered by the population of the area affected by environmental damage be manifest, even though the applicants, in the case at hand, had not submitted any evidence that they lived or worked close to the materials allegedly impairing their conditions of life.[91]

Even though the victim prerequisite is interpreted by other treaty bodies in different ways, it always figures as a general feature of human rights litigation. Article 44 of the 1969 American Convention does not require complainants to be victims of a violation of a human right. In its practice, however, the Inter-American Commission has repeatedly affirmed that claims may not concern abstract victims but have to concern one or more identifiable individuals or a group having a protected right that has been infringed.[92] *Actio popularis* seems to be excluded in this case, too.

Under the African system, communications submitted by individuals (and NGOs) to the African Commission have to refer to an alleged violation of the African Charter and to its victims (who may be different from the applicants themselves).[93] In the case of the ECOWAS Court, the rule on the admissibility of claims seems to be far more restrictive, as it refers to 'individuals' recognized as having the right to initiate litigation for a violation of 'their' human rights.[94] However, a broad interpretation of this provision has prevailed in the practice, an interpretation based on the 'collective' nature of the right to a healthy environment as enshrined in the African Charter,[95] as well as on the 1998 Aarhus Convention. The latter has been considered 'persuasive evidence' that the international community generally favours the legal standing of NGOs in what concerns the protection of human rights related to the environment, enabling NGOs to appear before the ECOWAS Court to represent the interests of groups.

On closer scrutiny, the relevant case law reveals a further feature of environmental case law, particularly in the European and American contexts. The ECtHR has made it clear that no right to nature preservation as such is secured under the ECHR or its Protocols[96] and that claims under Article 8 must point to 'severe' environmental degradation having a 'direct' link to the alleged infringement and significantly impairing the enjoyment of a human right above a certain minimum level (to be ascertained on a case-by-case basis).[97] In *Kyrtatos*, for instance, the Court excluded violation of Article 8, as complainants had not brought sufficient evidence that the alleged environmental harm (to a wetland owing to an urban development project) was of such a nature as to 'directly affect' their rights: had they been living closer to the area in question, a direct effect on their well-being would have been easier to ascertain.[98] In similar terms, the case law under the American Convention acknowledges that a mere situation of environmental degradation is not *per se* sufficient to support a claim for the violation of the Convention, unless it impairs the ability of identifiable individuals to enjoy a protected right.[99]

The African regime, by contrast, has undergone a significant evolution with the *Ogoni* case. In the African Commission's decision, the encroachment of the right to a satisfactory environment was considered in conjunction with the violation of the right to health. A few years later, the ECOWAS Court accepted the idea that circumstances of environmental degradation may well support the analysis of the merits of the case exclusively on the basis of Article 24, maintaining the autonomy of the right to a healthy environment from other protected rights.[100]

The combination of jurisdiction clauses with the limitations imposed on *locus standi* before human rights treaty bodies seems to seriously hamper the influence of a human rights approach to climate change on national disaster policies. It is very unlikely that the states' inadequate design of mitigation measures, considered to be the main culprit of GHG emissions, may be the basis for a claim of human rights violations by people residing in third countries and hit by weather-related disasters. The most contentious issues concern the polluting state's exercise of jurisdiction/effective control over such people and the existence of a link between high emissions recorded in that state, global warming, a consequent weather-related disaster, and the serious impairment of a protected human right.[101] Would it be possible, in the aftermath of a weather-related event, to substantiate the claim that the inhabitants of State A are the victims of a violation of their human rights by State B on the grounds that State B has not adopted appropriate mitigation measures by which to lower GHG emissions within its territory?[102]

As for adaptation measures, they are by definition 'local'. Under human rights case law, access to litigation may not be precluded, irrespective of any state's contribution to global warming. Every state is bound to secure protected rights for any individual living under its jurisdiction and therefore to design and implement all necessary policies and measures by which to reduce the magnitude of weather-related disasters.[103] There is, furthermore, the prohibition on discriminating against individuals in their enjoyment of protected rights,[104] from which it follows that, in crafting and applying adaptation measures, states may not differentiate their potential beneficiaries on any ground. On a positive reading of the prohibition, states are also obligated to take into special consideration the position of more vulnerable groups and individuals, so that they will not suffer *de facto* discrimination owing to such vulnerability.

Conclusion

The adoption of the Hyogo and Sendai Frameworks on disaster risk reduction has been one of the main outcomes of intergovernmental negotiations on disaster law. Both documents draw attention to the design and implementation of measures aimed at improving states' preparedness and resilience in responding to disasters, both natural and human-made. The 2015 Sendai Framework acknowledges that these policies may well contribute to higher standards of protection of human rights within disaster-prone communities.[105]

In view of the impact that climate change can have on the effective enjoyment of human rights, a further improvement could come from strategies for disaster risk reduction that integrate measures on adaptation to climate change, as provided for under international environmental law.[106]

The overlap between adaptation and risk reduction also emerges in international human rights case law. Human rights courts and bodies have identified two components that the environmental policies of states need to take into account with a view to strengthening the protection of human rights in a disaster context. On a substantive level, the case law draws attention to the duty to implement preventive measures aimed at avoiding disasters or at reducing the harm they can cause. The normative content of this duty is (or may be) determined by reference to the following: the adoption of legislation and regulation on human hazardous activities and of procedures for authorizing, licensing, and monitoring those activities, coupled with technical safety standards; the obligation to carry out environmental impact assessments to weigh in advance the effects that planned activities may have on the natural systems and communities which the same activities put at risk; the establishment of early warning systems to monitor industrial activities or natural events, so as to inform individuals of the dangers they are exposed to; the planning of disaster response strategies to provide the population with prompt relief in the event of a disaster; the prohibition on discriminating among affected individuals on any ground; and the duty to implement special measures supporting most vulnerable people. If disaster policies are absent or if they prove to be inconsistent with the above-mentioned requirements, or if the respondent state is aware that a given community is exposed to a natural hazard or is aware of the intrinsic dangers of hazardous human activities, then a claim can be brought to court alleging the violation of human rights in a disaster scenario.

Human rights environmental litigation highlights a second component of human rights protection in a disaster scenario. States are understood to be under an obligation to guarantee procedural environmental rights consistently with the 1998 Aarhus Convention: these include the right to be informed about the environmental risk deriving from potential and actual disaster events; the right to participate in the decision-making process by different means of involvement, so as to give voice to potential victims; and the right to have access to justice, both when procedural environmental rights are infringed and when failure by the state to comply with positive environmental obligations triggers a violation of substantive rights (such as the rights to life, to private and family life, or to a healthy environment or the right to live according to one's own culture and traditions).

The approach is very similar, irrespective of whether rulings and decisions foster a 'green' interpretation of 'general' human rights or uphold an expressly recognized right to a healthy environment, as under the 1981 African Charter. However, in this second case, human rights bodies are called on to determine the legal standards according to which the ecosystem may be considered safe for human life and dignity. In order to tackle this issue, scientific evidence needs to be coupled with value judgments, and these may not necessarily correspond to the states' interests.

However, as the case law relative to Article 24 of the African Charter does not depart from the rulings that other treaty bodies have issued on 'general' human rights, the question arises as to what the benefit is of integrating human rights treaties with a provision requiring states to guarantee an independent right to a healthy environment.

A first advantage stems from the impact of such a right on the implementation of the 'margin of discretion' principle. A common characteristic of human rights environmental case law is that, to the extent that procedural guarantees have been secured for interested individuals, the measures being challenged are deemed to be legitimate. Unless these measures invalidate or consistently impair the enjoyment of a protected right, states will retain discretion in striking a balance between environmental protection and their other interests (such as economic development or urbanization).[107] The integration of a right to a healthy environment would set a new equilibrium, as the substantive value of environmental protection would be granted legal protection.[108] For our purposes, disaster risk reduction strategies could become an integral component of environmental policies, particularly for countries with a high level of exposure and vulnerability to disasters, either preventing the potential harm that individuals may suffer as a result of hazardous activities or disaster event or reducing the impact of such events once they happen.

Furthermore, when coupled with proper rules on standing before human rights treaty bodies, the integration of a freestanding substantive environmental right would strengthen public interest human rights litigation. In the context of the African Charter, it was by combining three elements that the ECOWAS Court of Justice recognized the justiciability of the right to a healthy environment irrespective of the impact of environmental degradation on human health or life. The first of these elements was that the Charter protected not only individual rights but also collective ones; the second one was the express recognition of the right to a satisfactory environment in Article 24; and the third was the rule on standing, broadly interpreted according to other developments in international environmental law. In a disaster scenario, the obligation to secure a healthy environment would put pressure on states to frame climate change policies aimed at improving or preserving the quality of the environment considered as a public good, thereby strengthening the ability of communities to cope with disaster events.

Selected bibliography

A. Boyle, 'Human Rights and the Environment: Where Next?' 23 *European Journal of International Law* (2012) 613.

D. Bodanski, 'Climate Change and Human Rights: Unpacking the Issues' 38 *Georgia Journal of International and Comparative Law* (2010) 511.

R. Pavoni, 'Environmental Jurisprudence of the European and Inter-American Courts of Human Rights', in B. Doer (ed), *Environmental Law Dimensions of Human Rights* (Oxford University Press, 2015) 69.

J. Peel and D. Fisher, *The Role of International Environmental Law in Disaster Risk Reduction* (Brill Nihoff, 2016).

E.A. Posner, 'Climate Change and International Human Rights Law: A Critical Appraisal' 155 *University of Pennsylvania Law Review* (2007) 1925.

Notes

1 D. Shelton, 'Human Rights, Environmental Protection, and the Right to Environment' 28 *Stanford JIL* (1991) 103; HRC, Analytical Study on the Relationship between Human Rights and the Environment, UN Doc. A/HRC/19/34 (2011) paras 7–10.

2 See K. Bosselmann, 'Environmental Ethics' in *MPEPIL* (Oxford University Press, 2009).

3 For the definition of disaster risk reduction and response, see the terminology used within the United Nations Office for Disaster Risk Reduction: www.unisdr.org/we/inform/terminology, accessed on 25 November 2016.

4 For instance, disasters may have devastating effects on the natural environment, impairing the capacity of individuals to enjoy even the more fundamental human rights; states may decide to suspend some human rights to facilitate the provision of humanitarian assistance (see Sommario's chapter in this volume), or their ability to comply with positive obligations under international human rights law could be jeopardized because of the lack of sufficient resources. See HRC, Report of the Office of the United Nations High Commissioner for Human Rights on the relationship between climate change and human rights, UN Doc. A/HRC/10/61 (2009) and HRC, Report of the Independent Expert on the issue of human rights obligations relating to the enjoyment of a safe, clean, healthy, and sustainable environment. Mapping Report, UN Doc. A/HRC/25/53 (2013).

5 For an analysis of the interaction between international environmental law and international disaster law, see J. Peel and D. Fisher, *The Role of International Environmental Law in Disaster Risk Reduction* (Brill Nijhoff, 2016).

6 UN Conference on the Human Environment, Report of the United Nations Conference on the Human Environment, Stockholm 5–16 June 1972, UN Doc. A/CONF.48/14/Rev. 1 (1972) 4.

7 *Legality of the Threat or Use of Nuclear Weapons (Advisory Opinion)* [1996] ICJ Rep. (I) 257, para 29.

8 In this expression, the attribute 'healthy' is considered equivalent to other terms recurring in international human rights law to qualify the environment (for instance, *safe*, *clean*, *satisfactory*, or *sustainable*). For our purposes, all these terms are meant to refer to an environment ensuring the dignity of human life.

9 American Convention on Human Rights (adopted 22 November 1969, entered into force 18 July 1978) OAS TS No. 36.

10 African Charter on Human and Peoples' Rights (adopted 27 June 1981, entered into force 21 October 1986) OAU Doc. CAB/LEG/67/3 Rev. 5.

11 P.-M. Dupuy and J.E. Viñuales, *International Environmental Law* (Cambridge University Press, 2015) 304.

12 See, respectively, Resolution 2 in Hyogo Framework for Action 2005–2015: Building the Resilience of Nations and Communities to Disasters, in UN World Conference on Disaster Risk Reduction, Hyogo Declaration, UN Doc. A/CONF.206/6 (2005) and UNGA, Res 69/283, Sendai Framework for Disaster Risk Reduction 2015–2030, UN Doc. A/RES/69/283 (23 June 2015).

13 Analytical Study (n. 1) para 30. For more recent developments, see D.R. Boyd, 'The Implicit Constitutional Right to Live in a Healthy Environment' 20 *RECIEL* (2011) 171. For the practice by the Council of Europe Members, see Council of Europe, *Manual on Human Rights and the Environment* (2nd edn, Council of Europe, 2012).

14 Additional Protocol to the American Convention on Human Rights in the Area of Economic, Social, and Cultural Rights (Protocol of San Salvador) (adopted 17 November 1988, entered into force 16 November 1999) OAS TS No. 69.

15 See art 19.

16 See art 9, para 4, of the Protocol on the Community Court of Justice, ECOWAS doc. A/P.1/7/91 (adopted 6 July 1991), as amended by the Supplementary Protocol, ECOWAS doc. A/SP.1/01/05 (adopted 19 January 2005). For a comment, see K.J. Alter, L.R. Helfer and J.R. McAllister (eds), 'A New International Human Rights Court for West Africa: The ECOWAS Community Court of Justice' 107 *AJIL* (2013) 737.

17 For instance, see *Aliyu Tasheku v. Federal Republic of Nigeria* (Judgement of 12 June 2012) para 16.

18 *Social and Economic Rights Action Center (SERAC) and Center for Economic and Social Rights v. Nigeria*, Comm. 155/96 (ACHPR, Decision of 27 October 2001) (hereinafter SERAC Decision); for a comment, see F. Coomans, 'The *Ogoni* Case before the African Commission on Human and Peoples' Rights' 52 *ICLQ* (2003) 749; *SERAP v. Federal Republic of Nigeria*, ECOWAS Court of Justice doc. ECW/CCJ/JUD/18/12 (Judgment of 14 December 2012) (hereinafter, SERAP Judgment); for a comment, see L. Pineschi, 'Un'evoluzione imperfetta nella tutela del diritto a un ambiente soddisfacente: la sentenza

della Corte di giustizia dell'ECOWAS nel caso SERAP c. Nigeria' 8 *Diritti Umani e Diritto Internazionale* (2014) 103.

19 SERAC Decision (n. 18) paras 52–53.

20 Ibid.

21 SERAP Judgment (n. 18) para 93.

22 Ibid para 101.

23 Ibid para 108.

24 Ibid para 105.

25 See A. Boyle, 'Human Rights and the Environment: Where Next?' 23 *EJIL* (2012) 613, 626.

26 See UN Doc. A/HRC/25/53 (n. 4) para 54.

27 1972 Stockholm Declaration (n. 6) principle 7; Report of the United Nations Conference on Environment and Development, Rio de Janeiro, 3–14 June 1992, UN Doc. A/CONF.151/26 (Vol. I) (3–14 June 1992) 874, principle 11.

28 SERAP Judgment (n. 18) para 105.

29 Convention on Access to Information, Public Participation in Decision-Making and Access to Justice in Environmental Matters (adopted 26 June 1998, entered into force 30 October 2001) 2161 UNTS 447.

30 See *Socio-Economic Rights and Accountability Project (SERAP) v. President of the Republic of Nigeria & ORS*, ECOWAS Court of Justice doc. ECW/CCJ/APP/07/10 (Ruling of 10 December 2010), para 58. For a critical account of the 2012 judgment in light of the 1998 Aarhus Convention, see Pineschi (n. 18) 129.

31 International Covenant on Economic, Social and Cultural Rights (adopted 16 December 1966, entered into force 3 January 1976) 993 UNTS 3.

32 ECOWAS Court of Justice doc. ECW/CCJ/JUD/18/12 (n. 18) para 24.

33 Ibid para 32.

34 *Gabčíkovo-Nagymaros Project (Hungary v. Slovakia) (Merits)*, Separate opinion of Vice-President Weeramantry [1997] ICJ Rep. 88, 91 ff.

35 CESCR, Review of Further Developments in Fields with Which the Sub-Commission Has Been Concerned: Human Rights and the Environment, UN Doc. E/CN.4/Sub.2/1994/9 (1994).

36 Similar proposals were also put forward at the 1972 Stockholm Conference, but they met with resistance from most states: L.B. Sohn, 'The Stockholm Declaration on the Human Environment' 15 *HILJ* (1973) 423, 451.

37 CESCR, General Comment No. 12; The Right to Adequate Food (Art. 11 of the Covenant), UN Doc. E/C.12/1999/5 (1999) para 8.

38 Ibid para 10.

39 CESCR, General Comment No. 14: The Right to the Highest Attainable Standard of Health, UN Doc. E/C.12/2000/4 (2000) para 9.

40 Ibid para 11.

41 Ibid para 15.

42 International Covenant on Civil and Political Rights (adopted 16 December 1966, entered into force 23 March 1976) 999 UNTS 171.

43 HRC, Views. Comm. No. 1457/2006, UN Doc. CCPR/C/95/D/1457/2006 (2009) para 7.3.

44 See HRC, Res 19/10: Human Rights and the Environment, UN Doc. A/HRC/RES/19/10 (2012) para 2(a) and HRC, Res 28/11: Human Rights and the Environment, UN Doc. A/HRC/RES/28/11 (2015) para 4.

45 HRC, Res 31/8: Human Rights and the Environment, UN Doc. A/HRC/RES/31/8 (2016).

46 Ibid para 4(a).

47 Ibid para 5(a).

48 Ibid para 4(b) and (c).

49 Arab Charter on Human Rights (adopted 22 May 2004, entered into force 15 May 2008).

50 The Declaration was adopted in Phnom Penh on 12 November 2012, available at http://aichr.org/documents, accessed on 17 June 2017.

51 Respectively, in art 38 and art 28(f).

52 Convention for the Protection of Human Rights and Fundamental Freedoms (as amended) (adopted 4 November 1950, entered into force 3 September 1953) 213 UNTS 222.

53 European Social Charter (adopted 18 October 1961, entered into force 26 February 1965) ETS No. 035.

54 Recommendation 1614 (2003) (27 June 2003) and Recommendation 1885 (2009) (30 September 2009).

55 CM/AS(2004)Rec1614 final (23 January 2004) and CA/AS(2010)Rec1883–1885-final (18 June 2010).
56 CM/AS(2004)Rec1614 final (n. 54) para 4. For an extensive analysis of the ECtHR case law, see E. Ruozzi, *La tutela dell'ambiente nella giurisprudenza della Corte europea dei diritti umani* (Jovene Editore, 2011).
57 In some cases, the Court also delivered its judgment under art 1 of Protocol No. 1 to ECHR (adopted 20 March 1952, entered into force 18 May 1954) 213 UNTS 262, finding that material damages to the claimants' belongings due to environmental degradation could substantiate its violation (*Öneryildiz v. Turkey*, App. No. 48939/99 (ECtHR, Judgment of 30 November 2004) paras 133 ff.) and that environmental considerations may legitimately justify restrictions of the right to property: *Turgut and Others v. Turkey*, App. No. 1411/03 (ECtHR, Judgment of 8 July 2008).
58 See Council of Europe (n. 13).
59 *Öneryildiz v. Turkey* (n. 57) para 90. The case involved a methane explosion at a municipal rubbish tip, an incident as a result of which thirty-nine people died.
60 Ibid para 107.
61 Compare that with *Hadzhiyska v. Bulgaria*, App. No. 20701/07 (ECtHR, Decision of 15 May 2012), on positive obligations arising from art 1 of Protocol No. 1, on the right to property.
62 *Budayeva and Others v. Russia*, Apps. No. 15339/02, 21166/02, 20058/02, 11673/02 and 15343/02 (ECtHR, Judgment of 20 March 2008). For a comment, see J.H. Knox, 'Environmental Disasters and Human Rights' (1 November 2015), available at https://ssrn.com/abstract=2687265, accessed on 7 June 2017, also published in Peel and Fisher (n. 5) 453.
63 Ibid para 156. See also *Kolyadenko and Others v. Russia*, App. No. 17423/05 (ECtHR, Judgment of 28 February 2012).
64 *Lopez Ostra v. Spain*, App. No. 16798/90 (ECtHR, Judgment of 9 December 1994) para 51.
65 See, among others, *Di Sarno v. Italy*, App. No. 30765/08 (ECtHR, Judgment of 10 January 2012) para 106.
66 *Budayeva and Others v. Russia* (n. 62) para 133 and *Öneryildiz v. Turkey* (n. 57) para 160.
67 *Taskin and Others v. Turkey*, App. No. 46117/99 (ECtHR, Judgement of 10 November 2004) para 99. For further references, see R. Pavoni, 'Environmental Jurisprudence of the European and Inter-American Courts of Human Rights' in B. Doer (ed), *Environmental Law Dimensions of Human Rights* (Oxford University Press, 2015) 69, ftn 78.
68 With reference to art 8, see *Taskin and Others v. Turkey* (n. 67) para 119.
69 On natural disasters, see *Budayeva and Others v. Russia* (n. 62) para 142 and *Murillo Saldias and Others v. Spain*, App. No. 76973/02 (ECtHR, Judgment of 28 November 2006). As concerns hazardous human activities, the same principle was upheld in *Öneryildiz v. Turkey* (n. 57), para 91 ff. Ruozzi (n. 56) 245 and Pavoni (n. 67) highlight the uncertainty of the relationship between procedural rights inferred from arts 2 and 8 and the right to a fair trial or to an effective remedy as set forth in arts 6 and 13.
70 See Centre for Research on the Epidemiology of Disasters (CRED), *The Human Cost of Natural Disasters: A Global Perspective* (2015); IPCC, *Climate Change 2014: Synopsis Report* (2015); R. Lyster, *Climate Justice and Disaster Law* (Cambridge University Press, 2015) 139.
71 See International Strategy for Disaster Reduction, *Climate Change and Disaster Risk Reduction*, Briefing Note 01 (2008).
72 See UN Doc. A/HRC/10/61 (n. 4).
73 United Nations Framework Convention on Climate Change (adopted 9 May 1992, entered into force 21 March 1994) 1771 UNTS 107.
74 Kyoto Protocol to the United Nations Framework Convention on Climate Change (adopted 11 December 1997, entered into force 16 February 2005) 2303 UNTS 162.
75 See http://unfccc.int/paris_agreement/items/9485.php, accessed on 5 June 2017.
76 M.J. Hall and D.C. Weiss, 'Avoiding Adaptation Apartheid: Climate Change Adaptation and Human Rights Law' 37 *Yale JIL* (2012) 309, 320.
77 See D. Bodanski, 'Climate Change and Human Rights: Unpacking the Issues' 38 *Georgia Journal of International and Comparative Law* (2010) 511. The same advantage is also acknowledged by scholars critical of a human rights approach to climate change: see E.A. Posner, 'Climate Change and International Human Rights Law: A Critical Appraisal' 155 *University of Pennsylvania Law Review* (2007) 1925.
78 But see Byole (n. 25) 638.
79 See UNGA, Res 43/53: Protection of global climate for present and future generations of mankind, UN Doc. A/RES/43/53 (6 December 1988) para 1, recalled in the preamble of the 1992 UN Framework Convention on Climate Change (n. 72) and of the 2015 Paris Agreement (n. 74) (where States are recommended, 'when taking action to address climate change' to 'respect, promote and consider their respective obligations on human rights').

80 G. Schaffer, 'International Law and Global Public Goods in a Legal Pluralist World' 23 *EJIL* (2012) 669, 674 and 678 (citing, respectively, I. Kaul et al., 'How to Improve the Provision of Global Public Goods' in I. Kaul, P. Conceição, K. Le Goulven and R.U. Mendoza (eds), *Providing Global Public Goods: Managing Globalization* (Oxford University Press, 2003) 21; S. Barrett, *Why Cooperate? The Incentive to Supply Global Public Goods* (Oxford University Press, 2007).

81 Posner (n. 76) 1927.

82 J.H. Knox, 'Climate Change and Human Rights Law' 50 *Virginia Journal of International Law* (2009) 163, 197.

83 Dupuy and Viñuales (n. 11) 320.

84 *Bankovic and Others v. Belgium and Other States*, App. No. 52207/99 (ECtHR, Decision on Admissibility of 12 December 2001) para 71.

85 Ibid para 75.

86 The provision requires each state party to the ICCPR 'to respect and ensure to all individuals within its territory and subject to its jurisdiction the rights recognized in the present Covenant'.

87 See HRComm, General Comment No. 31: The Nature of the General Legal Obligations Imposed on States Parties to the Covenant, UN Doc. CCPR/C/21/Rev.1/Add.13 (2004).

88 For a more detailed analysis of the practice, see Knox (n. 82) 201.

89 C. Schall, 'Public Interest Litigation Concerning Environmental Matters before Human Rights Courts: A Promising Future Concept?' 20 *Journal of Environmental Law* (2008) 417.

90 *Aksu v. Turkey*, Apps. Nos. 4149/04 and 41029/04 (ECtHR, Judgment of 15 March 2012) para 50.

91 *Di Sarno and others v. Italy* (n. 65).

92 *Metropolitan Reserve Nature v. Panama*, IACtHR, Ser C, No. 88 (2003).

93 African Charter (n. 10) art 55.

94 Protocol A/P.1/7/91 (n. 16) art 10.d.

95 See ECOWAS Court of Justice doc. ECW/CCJ/APP/07/10 (n. 30).

96 *Atanasov v. Bulgaria*, App. No. 12853/03 (ECtHR, Judgment of 2 December 2010) para 66 (with further references).

97 *López Ostra v. Spain* (n. 64), para 51; *Fedayeva v. Russia*, App. No. 55723/00 (ECtHR, Judgment of 30 November 2005) para 70; *Grimkovskaya v. Ukraine*, App. No. 38182/03 (ECtHR, Judgment of 21 July 2011) para 58.

98 *Kyrtatos v. Greece*, App. No. 41666/98 (ECtHR, Judgment of 22 May 2003) para 53. A similar approach has been adopted with respect to dangerous human activities in *Balmer-Schafroth et al. v. Switzerland*, App. No. 67/1996/686/876 (ECtHR, Judgment of 26 August 1997) para 40.

99 *Metropolitan Reserve Nature* (n. 92).

100 *Supra* Section 2.

101 See Dupuy and Viñuales (n. 11) 327. The lack of a link to the violation of a protected right led the American Commission to decide not to process a petition the Inuit filed in 2005 against the United States. According to the claim, the US had not taken concrete steps to reduce its GHG emissions and therefore failed to comply with the human rights obligations it owed to the Inuit population under the 1948 American Declaration of the Rights and Duties of Man (see the text of the petition on www.inuitcircumpolar.com/inuit-petition-inter-american-commission-on-human-rights-to-oppose-climate-change-caused-by-the-united-states-of-america.html, accessed on 6 June 2017). In its reply, the Commission regretted it would not proceed, as the information provided by the petitioner was insufficient 'to determine whether the alleged facts would tend to characterize a violation of rights protected by the American Declaration' (http://graphics8.nytimes.com/packages/pdf/science/16commission letter.pdf, accessed on 6 June 2017). A similar claim was also submitted in 2013 against Canada: for a comment, see V. de la Rosa Jaimes, 'The Arctic Athabaskan Petition: Where Accelerated Arctic Warming Meets Human Rights' 45 *California Wester ILJ* (2015) 213. A case on mitigation policies has been settled by the Civil Section of the District Court in The Hague, which in 2015 ordered the Netherlands to reduce its GHGs more than it had committed to under international and EU law (for the English version of the ruling, see https://uitspraken.rechtspraak.nl/inziendocument?id=ecli:nl:rbdha:2015:7196, accessed on 6 June 2017). However, the Court based its ruling on the duty of care, as established under the Dutch Civil Code. It excluded that the claimant (a private foundation) could also invoke violation arts 2 and 8 ECHR, as neither its physical integrity nor its privacy as a legal person was at stake. However, it assumed that the ECtHR case law could provide adequate guidance in the interpretation of relevant national legislation. For a comment, see L. Bergkamp and J.C. Hanekamp, 'Climate Change Litigation

against States: The Perils of Court-Made Climate Policies' 24 *European Energy and Environmental Law Review* (2015) 102; K.J. de Graaf and J.H. Jans, 'The Urgenda Decision: Netherlands Liable for Role in Causing Dangerous Global Climate Change' 27 *Journal of Environmental Law* (2015) 517.

102 However, some authors argue a that a 'special' responsibility may arise for states contributing the largest amount of GHG emissions, in view of art 2.1 of the 1966 ICESCR (n. 31), requiring state parties to cooperate 'with a view to achieving progressively the full realization of the rights' set forth in the treaty; Knox (n. 82) 206.

103 Ibid 196.

104 ICCPR (n. 42) art 26; ICESCR (n. 31) art 2, para 2; ECHR (n. 51) art 14; African Charter (n. 10) art 2; American Convention (n. 9) art 1, para 1.

105 See 2015 Sendai Framework (n. 12), guiding principle III.

106 Lyster (n. 70) 156.

107 Knox (n. 82) 189.

108 Boyle (n. 25) 629 (making specific reference to the ICESCR).

15
THE RIGHT TO KNOW
The role of transparency, access to information and freedom of expression in overcoming disasters

Alice Riccardi

Introduction: some preliminary reflections on the nature of the right to know

In general terms, the right to know may be defined as the right according to which States must be held accountable for their actions and make information available, accessible and accurate according to the principles of transparency and openness.[1] The nature of the right at hand is currently highly debated and two different positions are maintained.

On the one hand, it is said to be an autonomous, self-standing right,[2] emerging from the States' general duty to protect and guarantee human rights.[3] At the United Nations (UN) level especially, it is affirmed that the right to know, although rooted in the right to freedom of expression provided for in Articles 19 of the Universal Declaration of Human Rights and the International Covenant on Civil and Political Rights (ICCPR), became a 'right in and of itself'.[4] This interpretation portrays the right to know as a value *per se* – as the 'desire to know' is a 'basic human need'[5] – and considers it a right upon which free and democratic societies depend.[6] Particularly, according to the UN Human Rights Committee (HRComm), this autonomous right encompasses two aspects. Firstly, States should 'make every effort to ensure easy, prompt, effective and practical access'[7] to information of public interest, by enacting the necessary procedures;[8] such activity should be guided by the principle of maximum disclosure,[9] whereby the States should provide those seeking information with all the documentation at their disposal, in whatever form expressed, upon request.[10] This stems from the idea that the right to know goes 'beyond simply being passive recipients of information'.[11] Secondly, States should 'proactively put in the public domain Government information of public interest', irrespective of an individual request.[12]

On the other hand, the right to know is construed as a procedural duty upon States in order to prevent the violations or secure the enjoyment of other rights, such as the right to life and the right to private and family life.[13] This perspective is grounded on the posit that the right to know does not originate from the right to freedom of expression. In this opinion, freedom of expression would not be capable of imposing upon States positive obligations, but only negative ones; hence, it would merely entail that States are prevented 'from restricting a person from receiving information that others wish or may be willing to impart to him', but would not 'confer on the individual a right of access . . . [or] embody an obligation on the Government to impart such information to the individual'.[14] Consequently, States would be bound to provide information only when another right is at stake. This understanding of the right to know, which has been labelled as instrumentalist,[15] carries several disadvantages: *inter alia* by requiring a connection with the infringement of other rights, it narrows the array of right holders entitled to invoke it and the circumstances in which the information can be sought.

Although the interpretation of the right to know in terms of autonomy is at present gaining momentum,[16] a general right to know information held by governments is yet to be fully recognised in international human rights law.[17] The described interpretative discrepancy is particularly evident at the regional level. This may have been caused by the dissimilar formulation of the right to freedom of expression embraced by the American Convention on Human Rights (ACHR), on the one hand, and the European Convention of Human Rights (ECHR) together with the African Charter on Human and Peoples' Rights (ACHPR), on the other. Whereas indeed Article 13 ACHR explicitly provides that freedom of expression includes the 'freedom to seek, receive, and impart information', Article 10 ECHR and 9 ACHPR are drafted in a more restrictive manner, providing that this right includes the freedom to 'receive and impart information' – with no mention of a right to seek. As it will be shown in the forthcoming pages, the European Court of Human Rights (ECtHR) is particularly resistant in abandoning an instrumentalist approach to the right to know, although a slow evolution in the opposite direction can be traced in its most recent case law.[18]

This resistance is particularly relevant in the context of International Disaster Law (IDL). In this realm, it is common sense that the recognition of a self-standing right to know would be fundamental, allowing participation of the affected population in all phases of the disaster cycle, fostering a good and transparent conduct of prevention and mitigation activities and enabling civil society to scrutinise the public authorities' actions. Indeed, if the right to know is construed in terms of autonomy, States would have broad positive information obligations towards the public, encompassing not only the duty to give individuals access to information concerning them, but also a set of proactive dissemination obligations concerning information of public interest. In other words, in such a scenario, States would be required to: firstly, establish administrative procedures for allowing the public to ask for disclosure of information held by public authorities, *irrespective* of whether affected or concerned by risks threatening other rights (in order to facilitate the right to know); and secondly, actively disseminate among the public key information, in particular those needed for the exercise of other rights, *irrespective* of an imminent threat or serious risk to such rights (in order to provide the right to know). Arguably, this would entail an expansion of States' traditional prevention duties, as to include also an obligation to disseminate information in the preparedness phase of the disaster cycle.[19]

Should instead an instrumentalist interpretation of the right to know prevail, then the scope of States' obligations would be narrower, for the right to know would be a positive obligation aimed at protecting other human rights. This implies that, firstly, only those having a legal interest in the disclosure of information held by public authorities would be entitled to trigger such a right. Indeed, although States would be required to establish administrative procedures for allowing individuals to ask for disclosure of information, only those affected by the risk would be entitled to activate it. Secondly, following a classical understanding of the notion of due diligence in the human rights context,[20] States would be bound to proactively disseminate information only when they are or should be aware of an imminent and real risk impairing other human rights – thereby excluding a duty to disseminate information meant to mitigate or prepare for disasters.

Against this debate, the aim of this chapter is to unravel the emerging approach to the right to know in IDL, in order to understand whether one of the two described tendencies is currently prevailing. The investigation will be confined to forward-looking information obligations, i.e. information duties incumbent upon States *prior* to the strike of a disaster. This choice has two main reasons: firstly, because forward-looking obligations are particularly capable of revealing whether knowledge in IDL is envisaged as a value in itself or as a means through which the individual is protected and seeks protection from the State in the enjoyment of other rights and, secondly, because human rights bodies and courts have mainly devoted their attention to the right to know prior to the occurrence of a calamitous event. Consequently, the research question that will be studied is the following: in IDL, what is the (developing) nature of the right to know prior to the strike of a disaster? Particularly, is it portrayed as a self-standing right or rather as an obligation instrumental to the prevention of other human rights violations?

In order to answer the above question, this chapter proceeds in two steps, following the approach of the HRComm envisaging the right to know as encompassing (i) the right to access to State-held information and (ii) the right to be proactively informed by States' authorities. Accordingly, the analysis is divided into two sections, each dealing with one of the above components; each section is sub-divided in three paragraphs, specifically looking at (i) hard and (ii) soft law instruments and at (iii) the practice of human rights treaty bodies, special procedures and regional human rights courts to uncover the paths followed so far.

The right to access to information in IDL

The right to access to information in hard law instruments

Positing that all disasters are, at some point, an information crisis, the vast majority of hard law instruments specifically dealing with disasters includes provisions aimed at regulating the flow of information. However, the majority of them merely provide for horizontal rights and obligations, rather than vertical ones. In other words, these instruments envisage the duty to inform as a mere inter-State cooperation obligation and do not identify individual beneficiaries. As to bilateral agreements, the virtual totality of them establishes inter-State information obligations, including them under a general cooperation umbrella.[21] The research conducted for this chapter found no case of bilateral agreements establishing upon the parties an obligation to give access to the information gathered through cooperation.

At the regional level, with the adoption of the Union Civil Protection Mechanism, the European Union (EU) started promoting the dissemination of information related to disasters among the public.[22] However, it has been noted that the obligations stemming thereby are merely directed to Member States and do not identify individual beneficiaries.[23] Moreover, relevant EU instruments provide clauses guaranteeing the non-dissemination among the public of sensitive information, leaving States with a wide margin of discretion.[24] The Association of South East Asian Nations Agreement on Disaster Management and Emergency Response[25] and the Agreement Establishing the Caribbean Disaster Emergency Response Agency[26] are construed in similar terms, whereas both the South Asian Association for Regional Cooperation Agreement on Rapid Response to Natural Disasters[27] and the Association of Caribbean States for Regional Cooperation Agreement on Natural Disasters[28] shape the obligation to exchange information only as an inter-State obligation of cooperation.

Enlarging the investigation to regional instruments not specifically dealing with disasters, two documents are particularly relevant.

The first one is the 1998 Aarhus Convention on Access to Information, Public Participation in Decision-Making and Access to Justice in Environmental Matters (Aarhus Convention).[29] This Treaty crystallises the idea – which traces back to the 1972 Stockholm and 1992 Rio Declarations – that States have a duty to give access to, collect and disseminate environmental information. Notably, the Aarhus Convention provides a wide variety of obligations connected to both the right of access to and dissemination of information. Leaving aside the latter aspect which will be dealt with in the second section of this chapter, Article 4(1) Aarhus Convention establishes a general right to access for the public 'without an interest to be stated', unless the request is manifestly unreasonable or formulated in too general a manner, or concerns material not yet completed or internal communications of public authorities (Article 4(3)).

The second document, namely the Council of Europe Convention on Access to Official Documents (CoE Convention), adopted in 2009 but not yet entered into force,[30] echoes the Aarhus Convention's approach. This Treaty, which is the first one recognising a general right to access to documents held by States, establishes at Article 4 that '[a]n applicant . . . shall not be obliged to give reasons for having access to the official documents', unless the request is too vague or manifestly unreasonable. However, Article 3(1)(j) lists, among other aims that may justify limitations to the right at hand, purposes that may be relevant in disaster-related requests, such as 'the environment'.[31] Yet, limitations are possible only if precisely set down in law, necessary in a democratic society and proportionate to the aim sought. Both the Aarhus and the CoE Conventions hence embrace an interpretation of the right to access to State-held information as an autonomous one.

At the global level, it seems that the above mentioned 'horizontal' scheme is still prevailing. For instance, Article 6 of the UN Framework Convention on Climate Change establishes that the States parties to it, in promoting and cooperating in education, training and public awareness and encouraging the widest participation as established in Article 4(1)(i), shall merely *promote* 'public access to information'.[32] Yet, some exceptions exist. For instance, the 1992 Convention on the Transboundary Effects of Industrial Accidents establishes that State parties shall provide 'natural or legal persons who are being or are capable of being adversely affected by the transboundary effects of an industrial accident . . . with access to . . . administrative and judicial proceedings' with the aim of obtaining relevant information.[33]

In conclusion, on a conventional level, a trend towards the establishment of a State's duty to grant individuals access to Government-held information, irrespective of any legal interest in it of the person claiming disclosure, shall be recognised. This trend is not specific to IDL; rather, it developed in the realms of international environmental law and of the regulation of dangerous activities to eventually go further and reach all State-held information of public interest.[34]

The right to access to information in soft law instruments

The right to access to disaster-related information is confirmed by recent soft law instruments dealing with IDL.[35] Above all, the UN World Conference agreed in 2015 on seven global targets meant to support the achievement of the goals embraced in the Sendai Framework for Disaster Risk Reduction 2015–2030 (Sendai Framework); *inter alia*, one of such targets is to '[s]ubstantially increase the access to . . . disaster risk information and assessment to people by 2030'.[36] Furthermore, with the purpose of helping States to effectively implement the Sendai Framework, the International Federation of the Red Cross and Red Crescent Societies (IFRC) published in 2015 a Checklist on Law and Disaster Risk Reduction. This document affirms that States should establish adequate mechanisms for ensuring accountability, particularly guaranteeing the 'right to access to information on disaster risk . . . [which] has been recognized as a first step in reducing disaster losses'.[37] These documents do not specifically elaborate on the nature of the right at hand; it can be nevertheless inferred an understanding of the right to know as a self-standing right, stemming from these instruments' general tenor and reference to 'people' as the subject entitled to disclosure.

The International Law Commission (ILC or the Commission), conversely, seems to share the opposite view. Draft Article 9(2) of the Draft Articles on the protection of persons in the event of disasters of 2016 enumerates, among other appropriate measures that States shall take to reduce the risk of disasters, the 'collection . . . of risk and past loss information'.[38] Although this formulation appears broad enough to embrace the right to access to information,[39] the ILC seems to validate an instrumentalist view of it, whereby this right would be triggered only when other rights are at stake. Indeed, the Commission heavily relies on the case law of the ECtHR adopting such an approach,[40] further described in the following paragraph. Moreover, it specifies that

> the duty being envisaged is one of conduct and not of result. . . . Accordingly, the reference to 'taking appropriate measures' is meant to indicate the relative nature of the obligation. The fundamental requirement of due diligence is inherent in the concept of 'appropriate'.[41]

Portraying the right to access to information – among other disaster risk reduction (DRR) activities – in terms of due diligence entails *a fortiori* an understanding of it as an ancillary to other rights.

The right to access to information in the practice of human rights treaty bodies and procedures and regional human rights courts

As anticipated in the introduction, UN human rights treaty bodies and procedures have consistently upheld an understanding of the right to access to information as a self-standing right, at least from 2011 onwards. That year, the HRComm adopted General Comment No. 34 establishing that Article 19(2) ICCPR 'embraces a right of access to information held by public bodies'[42] and affirmed in *Toktakunov v. Kyrgyzstan* that 'the information should be provided without the need to prove direct interest or personal involvement in order to obtain it, except in cases in which a legitimate restriction is applied'.[43] The same approach is shared by the African Commission on Human and Peoples' Rights (ACommHPR), as it may be inferred from its 2002 interpretation of Article 9 ACHPR: therein, the ACommHPR affirmed the right of everyone to access to information held by *private* bodies only when 'necessary for the exercise of other rights', whereas no similar qualification is mentioned in the case of access to information held by *public* authorities.[44] This interpretation is confirmed by the words of the ACommHPR Special Rapporteur on Freedom of Expression and Access to Information,[45] who has been maintaining that '[w]hile freedom of information derives its origins from and is interrelated with freedom of expression, it occupies a special place in the human rights family'.[46]

As to the Inter-American Court of Human Rights (IACtHR), it enshrined the same viewpoint in its 2006 leading case on the right to access to environmental information *Claude-Reyes et al. v. Chile*. This case originated from the request of a Chilean NGO for disclosure of information held by public authorities concerning a deforestation project to be implemented by a foreign company. Contrary to the opinion of Chilean courts which denied the NGO access to information for lack of standing, the IACtHR held that Article 13 ACHR includes a right to access to information under the States' control, irrespective of any demonstration on the part of the claimant of a direct interest in receiving the information.[47] The absence of any need to have a direct legal interest in the piece of information requested originates, according to the Court, from the fact that Article 13 ACHR has both an individual and a social dimension. Indeed, '[t]he delivery of information to an individual can, in turn, permit it to circulate in society'.[48] The IACtHR held in this regard that the right to access to information is a crucial tool for controlling States' affairs and public administration, monitoring corruption, guaranteeing good public administration by the State authorities, preventing abuses by public officials and holding public administration accountable. In turn, the right to access to information has been closely linked by the IACtHR to the principle of transparency, which requires a service-oriented approach to public administration.[49] The IACtHR recognised in this respect that the principles informing this right must be that of 'maximum disclosure' and good faith.[50] In conclusion, the Court recognised in this case that knowledge is a value *per se*, hence qualifying the right to know as a self-standing right.

Contrary to the case law of the IACtHR, the ECtHR was for a long time reluctant to interpret Article 10 ECHR (freedom of expression) as encompassing the right to access to information. This state of affairs changed in 2006, in the context of a case concerning the disclosure of State-owned documents and plans regarding a nuclear power station. Therein, the Court affirmed for the first time that the freedom to 'receive' information mentioned in Article 10(2) ECHR also refers to the right to access to State-held information. This provision, for the Court, is meant 'essentiellement à interdire à un État d'empêcher quelqu'un de recevoir des information'.[51] However, in the same occasion, the Court denied that the right to receive information would entail a *general* right to access.[52] This viewpoint was confirmed in 2009, when the ECtHR on the one hand plainly affirmed that 'the public has a right to receive information of general interest'[53] and on the other specified that Article 10 ECHR does not embody a general right to access to information, since a legal interest in the disclosure of information shall in any event be demonstrated by the claimant. In the case at hand, the Court found that the applicant, an NGO the activities of whom were 'an essential element of informed public debate', could be 'characterized, like the press, as a "social watchdog"' and hence had an interest in the disclosure.[54] This interpretation was confirmed in the 2013 case *Youth Initiative for Human Rights v. Serbia*, where the Court established that the applicant could not be refused access, since it was an NGO involved in the legitimate gathering of information of general interest with the intention of imparting it to the public.[55] In conclusion these pronouncements, although eventually recognising that Article 10 ECHR enshrines the right to access to information, depart from the interpretation provided by other human rights bodies and special procedures. In fact, for the ECtHR the entitlement to invoke this right cannot be granted to those who do not show any legal interest in disclosure. As to environmental information specifically, this approach, confirmed in recent case law,[56] is not in line with Article 4(1) Aarhus Convention establishing a general right to access for the public 'without an interest to be stated' although, somehow ironically, the ECtHR has been consistently quoting this provision in the judgments pronounced after the entry into force of the Aarhus Convention itself.[57]

Nevertheless, it shall be positively evaluated that the Court has recognised that, particularly in the environmental context, there is a strong public interest in enabling individuals to contribute to the public debate by disseminating information on matters of general interest.[58] Hence, the development occurring regarding the right to access to information has to be welcomed since it legitimises the necessity of some social control on States' actions addressing matters of public interest. However, the Court has yet to embrace the trend of recognising transparency as a driving value in (re)construing the subjective scope of the right to know. On a positive note, the joint concurring opinions of Judges Sajò and Vučinić in the case *Youth Initiative for Human Rights v. Serbia* recognised that the Court 'should address in due course' some of the implications deriving from the judgment; notably, the idea that '[t]here can be no robust democracy without transparency, which should be served and used by all citizens'.[59] It can thus be expected that, in future cases raising questions of transparency, the ECtHR will scrutinise the repercussions of this principle on States' information obligations.

Interim conclusions

The right to access to disaster-related information held by public authorities is at present undisputed. This principle is entrenched in all analysed sources. However, no general consensus exists on the scope of the legal entitlement to activate such a right, although a clear trend is emerging in granting access to everybody, irrespective of any interest to be stated. Also the ECtHR, although still requiring claimants to demonstrate a legal interest in acceding to a given piece of information, is enlarging the array of right holders, e.g. including among them NGOs and other public watchdogs. This trend stands on at least two grounds. The first is the fact that disaster-related information held by States is inherently of public interest, especially because disasters may affect numerous human rights, and the second is the fact that the right to access to information is progressively recognised as a right *per se* (although the ILC still purports the opposite view, when it states that the obligation to provide access to information is a relative one). It is held that, in light of the considerable evolution of the law on access to information in the past decade, the trend of recognising 'the public' entitlement to the right to access to information will eventually prevail. Such a process of consolidation may be further prompted by developments triggered by consideration of the legal consequences stemming from the principle of transparency. This principle indeed supports a collective dimension of the right to access to information, thereby enlarging the array of potential rights holders. Moreover, it may facilitate the expansion of the scope of States' duties regarding the collection of information, e.g. by requiring States to undertake disaster-oriented information gathering activities or to further strengthen exchange information duties between States and private individuals and entities undertaking inherently risky activities. Generally speaking, the evolution experienced by the right to access to disaster-related information is consonant with other developments in IDL, concerning for instance the involvement of communities in all phases of the disaster cycle. This may in turn prove particularly effective for preventing and mitigating the effect of disasters.

The right to be proactively informed by States' authorities in IDL

The right to be proactively informed in hard law instruments

In the research conducted for this chapter, no case of bilateral agreements was detected providing for an obligation to spread among the public the information gathered through inter-State cooperation. At the regional level instead, both the Aarhus and the CoE Conventions deserve again a closer analysis. As to the former, its Article 5(1) specifically obliges States to proactively disseminate information enabling 'members of the public who may be affected' to adopt 'measures to prevent or mitigate harm'. This duty is triggered only when there is an '*imminent* threat to human health or the environment, whether caused by human activities or due to natural causes' (emphasis added). According to the Implementation Guide of the Aarhus Convention (Guide), this provision binds States to release 'all information' to public likely to be affected, including 'safety recommendations, predictions about how the threat could develop, results of investigation and reporting or remedial and preventive actions taken'.[60] Other provisions of the Aarhus Convention expand States' dissemination duties beyond situations of imminent threats, requiring public authorities to disseminate: (i) environmental information through electronic databases 'easily accessible to the public'; (ii) nationals reports on the state of the environment; and (iii) legislation and policy documents on strategies, policies, programmes and action plans prepared at various levels of government.[61] According to the Guide, these Articles trigger 'a more general requirement for the dissemination of documents that the public has the right to know' compared to Article 5(1). Particularly, the recipients of such information are '*all members of the public*' (emphasis added) – hence exceeding those directly affected by threats.[62]

As to the CoE Convention, its Article 10 construes dissemination in wide terms as well. It indeed establishes that

> [a]t its own initiative and where appropriate, a public authority shall take the necessary measures to make public official documents which it holds in the interest of promoting

the transparency and efficiency of public administration and to encourage informed participation by the public in matters of general interest.

As evident, the use of the expression 'where appropriate' leaves States with a degree of appreciation in choosing *if* to disseminate; in this respect, the Explanatory Report to the Convention recognises that, pursuant to Article 10, '[n]ational rules on proactive publication are thus *encouraged*' (emphasis added).[63]

At the global level, a recent instance of practice explicitly referring to the dissemination of information among the public in the event of disasters is UN Security Council (UNSC) Resolution 2177(2014) on Ebola, which called upon States to 'enhance efforts to communicate to the public . . . the established safety and health protocols and preventive measures to mitigate against misinformation and undue alarm about the transmission and extent of the outbreak among and between individuals and communities'.[64] However, although currently debated in international legal scholarship,[65] it can be doubted that this UNSC resolution would provide for individual rights. On a different note, the 1993 Convention concerning the Prevention of Major Industrial Accidents provides for clear dissemination obligations.[66] Indeed, its Article 16(a) establishes that States parties shall ensure that 'information on safety measures and the correct behaviour to adopt in the case of a major accident is disseminated to members of the public liable to be affected by a major accident without their having to request it'.[67] Interestingly, this duty is kept distinct from the obligation to ensure that 'early warning is given as soon as possible in the case of a major accident' pursuant to Article 16(b). It follows that this instrument does not limit the duty of disseminating relevant information only when the calamitous event is imminent but enlarges it to allow the population to timely prepare to deal with the effects of an accident.

The right to be proactively informed in soft law instruments

Since 2012,[68] the IFRC has been insisting on the idea that States' duty to proactively put information in the public domain would be a 'global political and legal imperative'.[69] In particular, it has been exhorting States to implement measures aiming at 'end-to-end' early warning systems – i.e. systems spanning 'all steps, from hazard detection through to community response knowledge of the risk'.[70] In a similar vein, the 2015–2030 Sendai Framework purports, among other guiding principles, that DRR 'requires a multi-hazard approach and inclusive risk-informed decision-making based on the open exchange and dissemination of disaggregated data . . . as well as on easily accessible, up-to-date, comprehensible, science-based, non-sensitive risk information, complemented by traditional knowledge'.[71] In order for States to implement such principle, the Sendai Framework calls on them to continuously and proactively inform and update the public with 'non-sensitive hazard-exposure, vulnerability, risk, disaster and loss-disaggregated information freely available and accessible'[72] and 'location-based disaster risk information, including risk maps . . . in an appropriate format'.[73] Clearly, both the IFRC and the Sendai Framework are promoting an understanding of the right to know as encompassing the obligation for States to proactively disseminate information among the public irrespective of an individual request in such sense, and not only limited to *stricto sensu* early warning.

As to the ILC, it dealt with dissemination duties in two recent occasions. A careful reading of the language employed by the Commission in such two instances discloses an evolution in its interpretation of the right at hand. The first case is Draft Article 13 of the 2001 Draft Articles on Prevention of Transboundary Harm from Hazardous Activities. This article establishes that States 'shall, by such means as are appropriate, provide the public likely to be affected . . . with relevant information relating to that activity, the risk involved and the harm which might result and ascertain their views'.[74] In the Commentary, the Commission acknowledged that the content of Draft Article 13 constitutes a progressive development of international law. It recognised indeed that it was 'inspired by *new trends* in international law' (emphasis added),[75] such as '[a] number of . . . recent international instruments dealing with environmental issues . . . requir[ing] States to provide the public with information and to give it an opportunity to participate in decision-making processes'.[76] The second instance is Draft Article 9(2) of the 2016 Draft Articles on the protection of persons in the event of disasters – which identifies, among other measures aimed at DRR, the 'dissemination of risk and past loss information'.[77] In the Commentary to this article, the Commission specified that it 'wishes to emphasise the desirability of the dissemination and free availability of risk and past loss information, as it is the reflection of the *prevailing trend* focusing on the importance of public access to information' (emphasis added).[78] As evident, although the ILC was not comfortable proclaiming the right to proactively disseminate information held by public authorities as embedded in customary international law, it nevertheless certified that it does not constitute anymore simply a 'new trend', but certainly a 'prevailing' one.

As to the nature of this right, the ILC says little. In the Commentary to Draft Article 9(2) of the Draft Articles on disasters, it specified that it felt that an explicit reference to information rights 'was best dealt with in the commentary and not in the body of paragraph 2, since making it a uniform legal requirement could prove burdensome for States'.[79] It is here held that this caveat shall be read in light of the fact, already mentioned, that the ILC relied extensively on the case law of the ECtHR adopting an instrumentalist view of, generally speaking, the right to know. Accordingly, it can be argued that the Commission read the obligation to disseminate as, again, a procedural duty incumbent upon States to prevent the infringements of other rights.

The right to be proactively informed in the practice of human rights bodies and special procedures and regional human rights courts

UN human rights treaty bodies and special procedures have seldom addressed the issue of the right to proactively inform the public in the disaster context. The UN Committee on Economic, Social and Cultural Rights adopted a broad interpretation of this right in its 2013 observations on Japan, where it urged the concerned State to 'provide the population with comprehensive, credible and accurate information on *potential* hazards, preventive measures and response plans, and to ensure prompt disclosure of all information when disasters occur' (emphasis added).[80] The UN Special Rapporteur on the Implications for human rights of the environmentally sound management and disposal of hazardous substances and waste similarly affirmed in his 2013 report on Hungary that '[p]eople who reside near hazardous establishments deserve to know the dangers and exercise the option of relocating or remaining to mitigate exposure. Hungary should therefore increase efforts in the public dissemination of this information.'[81] These documents, however, rather than talking about legal obligations, seem to construe States' proactive dissemination activities in terms of good practices.

As to regional human rights courts, the following pages will be devoted to examine the ECtHR case law, lacking any relevant practice before the IACtHR[82] and the ACtHPR. The ECtHR, whereas eventually recognising that Article 10 ECHR encapsulates a right to access to information, so far denied that it would be the legal basis for States' duty to proactively inform the public. According to the ECtHR indeed, Article 10 ECHR on freedom of expression does not impose a general obligation incumbent upon national authorities to collect and disseminate information about potential risks deriving from both natural phenomena and human activities on their own motion.[83] Rather, the Court has constantly maintained that such an obligation would constitute a procedural guarantee stemming from the duty to prevent infringements upon Articles 8 (right to private and family life) and 2 (right to life) ECHR.[84] As recognised by the very same ILC Special Rapporteur on the protection of persons in times of disasters, the ECtHR's 'framed the duty of prevention as one of due diligence'.[85] It is here held that this implies at least three intertwined legal consequences, related to (i) the notion of risk, (ii) the type of information activities that States are bound to undertake and (iii) the legal entitlement to the right at hand.

As to the notion of risk, the Court constantly affirmed that the ECHR shall not be paternalistically interpreted.[86] Therefore, not all risks of violations are covered by its scope – in other words, States' responsibility does not arise vis-à-vis all potential violations.[87] In this respect, a distinction shall be drawn between Articles 2 and 8 ECHR cases. In right to life cases, the Court has generally affirmed that States are under a duty to 'adequately inform the public about any life-threatening emergencies, including natural disasters'.[88] This positive obligation applies to 'any activity, whether public or not, in which the right to life may be at stake', thus including conducts and omissions concerning both man-made and natural hazards.[89] However, according to the ECtHR, States' prevention duties are triggered only when a disaster becomes foreseeable, i.e. when the public authorities knew or ought to have known that there was a *real* and *imminent* risk for the right to life.[90] In Article 8 cases, the Court requires private and family life to be 'directly and seriously affected' by the imminent risk.[91] It hence asks for a minimum threshold of harm,[92] whereby the duty is triggered when the risk reaches a threshold of seriousness, the consequences of which must be intense and repeated.[93] It follows that, at present, under the ECHR States are not bound to proactively provide information about disasters, unless a risk to the right to life or the right to private and family life is imminent.[94] As to the notion of 'imminent' risk, the Court has adopted a casuistic approach linked to the nature of the risk itself. Specifically, it has differentiated between natural risks and risks arising out of dangerous activities. As to the former, it has pointed out that the unforeseeable nature of natural disasters makes States' margin of appreciation broader – and hence the scope of their obligations narrower – than in cases of dangerous activities.[95] In these latter cases, the Court has been able to define States' prevention duties in detail, stating that

> States have an obligation to set in place regulations geared to the special features of the activity in question, particularly with regard to the level of risk potentially involved. They must . . . make it compulsory for all those concerned to take practical measures to ensure the effective protection of citizens whose lives might be endangered by the inherent risks.[96]

It follows that dissemination activities meant to implement DRR duties are for the Court context-dependent: that is to say, they depend on the imminence of a threat which, in turn, is connected to the nature of the risk and the degree of States' knowledge of the probability that the disaster may take place. Only very recently, in the *Özel* case, the ECtHR seemingly changed this approach, by stating that the principles related to dangerous activities 'also lend themselves to application in the area of disaster relief';[97] however, the *Özel* judgment concerned a question of access to justice for natural disaster victims (notably, an earthquake), and it is to be seen whether the Court will be open to apply *all* principles related to dangerous activities to natural disaster situations.

As to the type of information activities that States shall undertake to prevent infringements upon the right to life and the right to private and family life, again the Court has distinguished between risks emerging from natural hazards and those arising out of the conduct of dangerous activities. Until recently, it consistently affirmed that in natural disaster situations States have a wide margin of appreciation due to the unpredictability of natural calamities;[98] the margin would become even wider in peculiar scenarios such as in case of financial difficulties.[99] In *Budayeva and others v. Russia*, for instance, the Court stated that it would have sufficed for the State concerned to adopt '*essential* practical measures' (emphasis added) when 'the circumstances of a particular case point to the imminence of a natural hazard that had been clearly identifiable', such as the launching of an early warning or an evacuation order.[100] In recent years, however, the ECtHR started nuancing this approach. First, in the *Bacila* case, it underlined that preventive measures shall in any case be reasonable and adequate to protect the rights of the individual.[101] Second, in the above mentioned 2015 *Özel* case, it affirmed that, also in the event of natural catastrophes 'over which States have no control', prevention means 'adopting measures geared to reducing their effects in order to keep their catastrophic impact to *a minimum*' (emphasis added).[102] This, arguably, may imply an expansion of the scope of States' prevention obligations: it seems indeed that the Court has put the threshold of State responsibility lower than in previous cases, by affirming that the effects of natural disasters shall be kept 'to a minimum'. This, *inter alia*, may mean that States are bound to adopt preventive measures irrespective of any sign of the imminence of a natural disaster, when the concerned territory is declared to be inherently at risk.[103]

As to the legal entitlement to the right and consequently to its enforceability, the ECtHR has not embraced the above detected trend of granting to the 'public' information rights, i.e. irrespective of whether those ought to be informed may be concerned with or affected by the risk. Indeed, the ECtHR has so far recognised that the positive obligations arising from Article 2 ECHR (right to life) apply vis-à-vis 'those citizens whose lives might be endangered by the inherent risks',[104] whereas those stemming from Article 8 ECHR (right to private and family life) are incurred to persons at real risk of damage to health or family life.[105] In 2012, the Court clearly established that a mere fear of safety and risk was not sufficient for triggering the information duties under Article 8, for a causal link between the risk and the right affected is necessary.[106]

Interim conclusions

When it comes to the second component of the right to know, i.e. the obligation to proactively put in the public domain information concerning disasters, a definitive answer on its nature cannot be given. Only few conventional examples establish that States must disseminate information irrespective of the imminence of a risk. In a similar vein, human rights treaty bodies and special procedures always expressed themselves in terms of 'should' when they discussed alleged duties of proactive dissemination of information going beyond activities related to *stricto sensu* early warning. This should not come as a surprise, in particular if one considers that the recognition of the right at hand as a self-standing right may entail an excessive burden upon States. Furthermore, should the right to be proactively informed be recognised as an autonomous one, it would be highly controversial to clearly define the precise content of States' positive obligations stemming thereby. Although analysed soft law instruments push for broad dissemination activities (just to recall some, the 2015–2030 Sendai Framework encourages the continuous diffusion of 'non-sensitive hazard-exposure, vulnerability, risk, disaster and loss-disaggregated information'),[107] these can hardly be envisaged as a general yardstick for States' responsibility. Moreover, human rights courts practice demonstrates that States' margin of appreciation in disaster scenarios varies depending on the context of the case.[108] The ECtHR has maintained in this respect that States' duties would differ vis-à-vis the probabilities that a given calamitous event may occur; notably, they would be more stringent in case of calamities arising out from the conduct of inherently dangerous activities than in natural disaster scenarios. However, it shall be stressed that recent cases hint at the recognition that principles applicable to dangerous activities may be transplanted to natural disaster scenarios, provided that the risk is inherent to the concerned territory.

In conclusion, although a trend towards an expansion of States' information dissemination duties with the aim of engaging with the population in all phases of the disaster cycle exists, such a trend is currently way more embryonic than that concerning the right to access to disaster information. Thus, at present an (alleged) autonomous right to know in IDL seems not to encapsulate a States' general duty to proactively inform the public continuously irrespective of an imminent threat to other human rights.

Conclusions

This contribution aimed at discussing the nature of the right to know in disaster contexts, elaborating especially on its nature, i.e. whether it is a self-standing right or an obligation instrumental to the protection of other human rights. To incline towards one or the other alternative entails substantial consequences, pertaining particularly to the notion of right holders and the circumstances in which the right is triggered.

In order to provide such answer, this chapter separately investigated the two components of the right to know identified by the HRComm, i.e. the right to access to information, and the right to have information proactively put in the public domain by States.

As to the first component, it cannot be denied that it has progressively gained autonomy and that currently an irreversible trend recognises it as a right *per se*. Not only does this principle today make an unavoidable part of IDL relevant actors' lexicon, but it is also entrenched in some applicable treaties. Furthermore, it is affirmed by all universal and regional human rights treaty bodies. It follows that, as a minimum, States are required to give access to information concerning disasters not only to persons potentially affected by natural and man-made risks, but also to those aiming at disseminating such information to the public and at raising awareness. Arguably, in the near future, it will be generally recognised that States are under an obligation to provide access to disaster information to everybody, irrespective of an interest to be stated. This tendency is consonant with other developments in IDL, notably those regarding the involvement of potentially affected communities in all phases of the disaster cycle, and particularly in preparedness and mitigation activities. Moreover, it is argued that the application of the principle of transparency in the human rights realm will further expand States' duties with respect to the right to access to information; this could for instance entail that States may be required to actively gather disaster information in order to make them available to the public upon request.

As to the second component of the right to know, contrariwise, it cannot be currently said that it has become emancipated yet, and it probably never will. States' proactive information obligations are indeed usually portrayed as procedural duties to prevent infringements upon other rights, above all the right to life and the right to private and family life. Before the ECtHR, this has entailed that States have more stringent dissemination duties when it comes to risks connected to the conduct of inherently dangerous activities than in natural disaster scenarios. This stems from the common assumption that natural hazards are unpredictable and that this characteristic would impinge on the capacity of States to be aware of the risk itself. Two remarks can be made in this respect. Firstly, it shall be stressed that portraying dissemination obligations in terms of due diligence does not relieve States from their responsibility: indeed, in order to respect their prevention duties, States must continuously monitor the hazard exposure of their territory and proactively inform the population when a given threshold of seriousness is reached. Secondly, one may predict that in the future the distinction between natural and man-made disasters from the viewpoint of prevention will wear thin; indeed, it may be argued that the trend of lending principles related to industrial activities to natural disasters will consolidate in situations in which natural risks are inherent to a given territory, as in the case of areas particularly prone to earthquakes. In these situations, posited that the State is aware of the risk, the threat should always be deemed 'imminent'; hence, the affected population should be regularly updated with, for instance, contingency plans and location-based disaster risk information.

In conclusion, although the right to know in IDL shall not be 'utopised' – that is to say, it shall not be interpreted so vastly as to horizontally impose upon States a too high threshold which may induce disengagement and non-compliance – it is at the same time gaining momentum. Further efforts shall be put in clarifying how States shall practically implement their information duties related to disasters, e.g. by elaborating good practices on accessible and effective disclosure procedures.

Selected bibliography

M. McDonagh, 'The Right to Information in International Human Rights Law' 13 *Human Rights Law Review* (2013) 26.

M. Riekkinen and M. Suksi, 'Access to Information and Documents as a Human Right' in *Research Report no. 35, Institute for Human Rights, Abo Akademi University* (2015) available at http://www.abo.fi/fakultet/media/24259/accesstoinformationepub.pdf, accessed on 12 December 2017.

L. Robert (ed), *L'environnement et la Convention européenne des droits de l'homme* (Bruylant, 2013).

D.M. Zillman, A. Lucas and G. Pring (eds), *Human Rights in Natural Resources Development: Public Participation in the Sustainable Development of Mining and Energy Resources* (Oxford University Press, 2002).

H.E. Ruiz Fabri and L. Gradoni (eds), *La circulation des concepts juridiques: le droit international de l'environnement entre mondialisation et fragmentation* (SLC, 2009) 493.

Notes

1 For a general overview of the right to know in the context of public law, see J.M. Ackerman and I.E. Sandovan Ballesteros, 'The Global Explosion of Freedom of Information Laws' 58 *Administrative Law Review* (2006) 85–130.

2 Commission on Human Rights (CHR), Promotion and Protection of Human Rights. Study on the Right to the Truth. Report of the Office of the United Nations High Commissioner for Human Rights, UN Doc. E/CN.4/2006/91 (8 February 2006) para 42.

3 Ibid para 45. See also UNGA, Report of the Special Rapporteur on the Promotion and Protection of the Right to Freedom of Opinion and Expression, UN Doc. A/68/362 (4 September 2013) para 15.

4 CHR, Report of the Special Rapporteur on the Promotion and Protection of the Right to Freedom of Opinion and Expression, Mr. Abid Hussain, Submitted in Accordance with Commission Resolution 1999/36, UN Doc. E/CN.4/2000/63 (18 January 2000) para 42; see also CHR, Civil and Political Rights, Including the Question of the Freedom of Expression: The Right to Freedom of Opinion and Expression: Report of the Special Rapporteur, Ambeyi Ligabo, UN Doc. E/CN.4/2005/64 (17 December 2004) para 39.

5 UNGA, Res 3220 (XXIX) (6 November 1974) para 8. *Verbatim* see UNGA, Res 33/173, UN Doc. A/RES/33/173 (20 December 1978); UNGA, Res 45/165, UN Doc. A/RES/45/165 (18 December 1990); and UNGA, Res 47/132, UN Doc. A/RES/47/132 (18 December 1992). In general see D. Shelton, *Remedies in International Human Rights Law* (3rd edn, Oxford University Press, 2015) 14–22.

6 CHR, Freedom of Expression (n. 4) para 42.

7 HRComm, General Comment No. 34: Article 19: Freedoms of Opinion and Expression, UN Doc. CCPR/C/GC/34 (12 September 2011) para 19.

8 Ibid.

9 CHR, The Public's Right to Know: Principles on Freedom of Information Legislation, in CHR, Freedom of Expression (n. 4) Annex II, principle 1.

10 Ibid principle 2.

11 HRC, Report of the Special Rapporteur on the Promotion and Protection of the Right to Freedom of Opinion and Expression, Mr. Frank La Rue, UN Doc. A/HRC/14/23 (20 April 2010) para 30.

12 HRComm, General Comment No. 34 (n. 7) para 19.

13 Above all, *Guerra and Others v. Italy*, App. No. 14967/89 (ECtHR, Judgment of 19 February 1998) para 53.

14 *Leander v. Sweden*, App. No. 9248/81 (ECtHR, Judgment of 26 March 1987) para 74.
15 M. McDonagh, 'The Right to Information in International Human Rights Law' 13 *Human Rights Law Review* (2013) 26.
16 According to R. Peled and Y. Rabin, 'The Constitutional Right to Information' 42 *Columbia Human Rights Review* (2011) 257, 381 'the international legal community is beginning to recognize freedom of [information] as an autonomous right'.
17 M. Riekkinen and M. Suksi, *Access to Information and Documents as a Human Right* (Institute for Human Rights, Abo Akademi University, 2015) 120.
18 In general see A. Mowbray, *The Development of Positive Obligations under the European Convention on Human Rights by European Court of Human Rights* (Hart Publishing, 2004) 192–193.
19 See Sossai's chapter in this volume.
20 See for instance *L.C.B. v. United Kingdom*, App. No. 23413/94 (ECtHR, Judgment of 9 June 1998) paras 37–40.
21 As a representative account of bilateral agreements establishing inter-State information obligations in case of disasters, see Agreement between the Government of the United Mexican States and the Government of the United States of America on Emergency Management Cooperation in Cases of Natural Disasters and Accidents (adopted 23 October 2008, entered into force 20 March 2011) art II; Agreement between the Government of the Hellenic Republic and the Government of the Russian Federation on Cooperation in the Field of Prevention and Response to Natural and Man-Made Disasters (adopted 21 February 2000, entered into force 19 June 2002) art 3; Protocol of Intentions between the Government of the United States of America and the Republic of the Philippines Concerning Cooperation in Disaster Prevention and Management (adopted 21 November 2001) art 3; Agreement between the Argentine Republic and the Republic of Chile on Cooperation in Case of Disasters (adopted 8 August 1997) art 2. For a complete account of similar agreements, see the Database of the International Disaster Law Project, available at http://disasterlaw.sssup.it/?sfid=1191&_sfm_type_of_international_instrument=BILATERAL&_sfm_prevention_and_preparedness=Information%20sharing&_sfm_recovery_and_reconstruction=Information%20sharing, accessed on 25 May 2017.
22 Above all see Decision No 1313/2013/EU of the European Parliament and of the Council on a Union Civil Protection Mechanism, OJ L 347/924 (2013) arts 4(5), 20(a)-(d).
23 N. de Sadeleer, 'Les droits fondamentaux au secours de la protection de l'environnement: examen du droit de l'UE et de la CEDH' in L. Robert (ed), *L'environnement et la Convention européenne des droits de l'homme, Cahiers de droit international* (Bruylant, 2013) 109.
24 See for instance Decision No 1313/2013/EU (n. 22) art 6.
25 ASEAN Agreement on Disaster Management and Emergency Response (adopted 26 July 2005, entered into force 24 December 2009) art 4(b).
26 Caribbean Community Agreement Establishing the Caribbean Disaster Emergency Response Agency (adopted 26 February 1991, entered into force 19 May 1992) art 18.
27 SAARC Agreement on Rapid Response to Natural Disasters (adopted 26 May 2011) art IV(1).
28 Association of Caribbean States Agreement on Natural Disasters (adopted 17 April 1999) ACS/2010/TRADE/TTCIC, art 4.
29 Convention on Access to Information, Public Participation in Decision-Making and Access to Justice in Environmental Matters (adopted 26 June 1998, entered into force 30 October 2001) 2161 UNTS 447 (Aarhus Convention). See S.Y. Noé, 'The Emerging International Law of Public Participation Affecting Global Mining, Energy, and Resources Development' in D.M. Zillman, A. Lucas and G. Pring (eds), *Human Rights in Natural Resources Development: Public Participation in the Sustainable Development of Mining and Energy Resources* (Oxford University Press, 2002) 30–36.
30 CoE Convention on Access to Official Documents (adopted 18 June 2009) CoE TS No. 205 (CoE Convention).
31 According to CoE, Convention on Access to Official Documents, Explanatory Report (18 June 2009) CoE TSER 2, art 3(1)(j) concerns 'the possibility of limiting the dissemination of information on the environment . . . meant to allow public authorities to carry out effective policies in the area of environmental protection', for instance regarding 'threatened animals or plant species'.
32 UNFCCC (adopted 9 May 1992, entered into force 21 March 1994) 1771 UNTS 107; see also International Atomic Energy Agency, Convention on Early Notification of a Nuclear Accident (adopted 26 September 1986, entered into force 27 October 1986) 1439 UNTS 276.
33 Convention on the Transboundary Effects of Industrial Accidents (adopted 17 March 1992, entered into force 19 April 2000) 2105 UNTS 457.

34 See F. Schram, 'From a General Right of Access to Environmental Information in the Aarhus Convention to a General Right of Access to all Information in Official Documents: The Council of Europe's Tromso Convention' in M. Pallemaerts (ed), *The Aarhus Convention at Ten: Interactions and Tensions between Conventional International Law and EU Environmental Law* (Europa Law Publishing, 2011) 67–89.
35 Previously see UNGA, Res 58/214: International Strategy for Disaster Risk Reduction, UN Doc. A/RES/58/2014 (27 February 2004) para 7(e).
36 UNISDR, Sendai Framework for Disaster Risk Reduction 2015–2030 (2015) para 18(g).
37 *The Handbook on Law and Disaster Risk Reduction* (IFRC-UNDP, 2015) 68, available at www.ifrc.org/Global/Photos/Secretariat/201511/Handbook%20on%20law%20and%20DRR%20LR.pdf, accessed on 25 May 2017.
38 UNGA, Report of the International Law Commission, Sixty-Eight Session (2 May–10 June and 4 July–12 August 2016), Chapter IV, Protection of Persons in the Event of Disasters, UN Doc. A/71/10 (2016) 42 ff.
39 Furthermore, in its commentary to draft art 9(2), although not specifically referring to the right to access to information, the ILC endorses instruments encompassing it. Ibid 43.
40 Ibid.
41 Ibid 48.
42 HRComm, General Comment No. 34 (n. 7) para 19.
43 HRComm, *Toktakunov v. Kyrgyzstan*, Comm. No. 1470/2006, UN Doc. CCPR/C/101/D/1470/2006 (21 April 2011) 8.
44 ACommHPR, Resolution on the Adoption of the Declaration of Principles on Freedom of Expression in Africa, ACHPR/Res.62(XXXII)02 (2002), IV(2).
45 CommHPR, Resolution on the Expansion of the Mandate and Re-Appointment of the Special Rapporteur on Freedom of Expression and Access to Information in Africa, ACHPR/Res.122(IVXX)07 (2007).
46 ACommHPR, Activity Report of the Special Rapporteur on Freedom of Expression and Access to Information in Africa, 44th Ordinary Session of the ACommHPR (10–24 November 2008) para 27.
47 *Claude-Reyes et al. v. Chile*, IACtHR Series C, No. 151 (2006) (Merits, Reparations and Costs) paras 77, 88–99. On art 13 ACHR see in general *Compulsory Membership in an Association Prescribed by Law for the Practice of Journalism (Arts. 13 and 29 of the American Convention on Human Rights)*, IACtHR OC-5/85 Series A, No. 5 (1985) (Advisory Opinion).
48 *Claude-Reyes* para 77.
49 Ibid paras 86–87.
50 Ibid para 77.
51 *Sdruženi Jihočeské Matky v. Czech Republic*, App. No. 19101/03 (ECtHR, Decision on Admissibility of 10 July 2006) para 1.1.
52 Ibid.
53 *Társaság a Szabadságjogokért v. Hungary*, App. No. 37374/05 (ECtHR, Judgment of 14 April 2009) para 26.
54 Ibid para 27. See also *Guja v. Moldova*, App. No. 14277/04 (ECtHR, Judgment, Grand Chamber, of 12 February 2008) para 75, where the Court affirmed that '[t]he interest which the public may have in particular information can sometimes be so strong as to override even a legally imposed duty of confidence'.
55 *Youth Initiative for Human Rights v. Serbia*, App. No. 48135/06 (ECtHR, Judgment of 23 June 2013) para 24.
56 E.g. *Roşiianu v. Romania*, App. No. 27329/06 (ECtHR, Judgment of 24 June 2014); *Guseva v. Bulgaria*, App. No. 6987/07 (ECtHR, Judgment of 17 February 2015).
57 All ECHR States parties are also parties to the Aarhus Convention except the Russian Federation, Turkey and San Marino.
58 *Steel and Morris v. the United Kingdom*, App. No. 68416/01 (ECtHR, Judgment of 15 February 2005) para 89.
59 Moreover, the judges noted that '[t]he case raises the issue of the positive obligations of the State'. See *Youth Initiative for Human Rights*, Joint Concurring Opinion of Judges Sajò and Vučinić.
60 UN Economic Commission for Europe, *The Aarhus Convention: An Implementation Guide* (2nd edn, UN, 2014) 98.
61 Aarhus Convention, art 5(3)-(5). For further analysis see N. Colacino, 'Exploring the Legal Nature of the States' Obligation to Provide Information to the Public in the Case of an Imminent Threat to the Environment: More Than the B-Side of the Individual Right to Access?' 1 *Ordine internazionale e diritti umani* (2014) 454, 467.
62 *Implementation Guide* (n. 60) 108.

63 CoE Convention, Explanatory Report (n. 29).
64 UNSC, Res 2177, UN Doc. S/RES/2177 (2014) (18 September 2014) para 6.
65 In general see A. Peters, *Beyond Human Rights: The Legal Status of the Individual in International Law* (Cambridge University Press, 2016) 94–99.
66 Convention (No. 174) concerning the prevention of major industrial accidents (adopted 22 June 1993, entered into force 3 January 1997) 1967 UNTS 232.
67 See also Convention on the Transboundary Effects of Industrial Accidents (n. 32) art 9, construed in almost identical terms.
68 As to prior soft law instruments, see *inter alia* UN World Conference on Disaster Reduction, Resolution 2. Hyogo Framework for Action 2005–2015: Building the Resilience of Nations and Communities to Disasters, in Report of the World Conference on Disaster Reduction, UN Doc. A/CONF.206/6 (16 March 2005) paras 10(e), 13(e).
69 IFRC, 'Community Early Warning Systems: Guiding Principles' (2012) 18, available at www.ifrc.org/PageFiles/103323/1227800-IFRC-CEWS-Guiding-Principles-EN.pdf, accessed on 25 May 2017; see also *Handbook on Law and Disaster Risk Reduction* (n. 37) 12.
70 Ibid 13, fn 7.
71 2015–2030 Sendai Framework (n. 35) para 19(g).
72 Ibid para 24(e).
73 Ibid para 24(c).
74 ILC, Report of the International Law Commission, Fifty-Third Session (23 April–1 June and 2 July–10 August 2011), Chapter V, International Liability for Injurious Consequences Arising Out of Acts Not Prohibited by International Law, UN Doc. A/56/10 (2011) 165. In the Commentary, ibid, the ILC clarified that States are thereby bound '(a) to provide information to the public regarding the activity and the risk and the harm it involves; and (b) to ascertain the views of the public' and specified that the term *public* 'includes individuals, interests groups (non-governmental organizations) and independent experts'.
75 Ibid 165.
76 *Inter alia*, the ILC mentions the Aarhus Convention, the UNFCCC, the CoE Convention, and the Convention on the Transboundary Effects of Industrial Accidents. Ibid 166.
77 For the ILC, draft art 9(2) draws 'inspiration from . . . principles emanating from international human rights law, including the States' obligation to respect, protect, and fulfill human rights, in particular the right to life'. UNGA, Report of the International Law Commission, Sixty-Eight Session (2 May–10 June and 4 July–12 August 2016), Chapter IV, Protection of Persons in the Event of Disasters, UN Doc. A/71/10 (2016) 42.
78 Ibid 43.
79 Ibid 50.
80 CESCR, Concluding Observations on the Third Periodic Report of Japan, Adopted by the Committee at Its Fiftieth Session, UN Doc. E/C.12/JPN/CO/3 (10 June 2013) (29 April–17 May 2013) para 25.
81 HRC, Report of the Special Rapporteur on the Implications for Human Rights of the Environmentally Sound Management and Disposal of Hazardous Substances and Waste, Calin Georgescu, Addendum, UN Doc. A/HRC/24/39/Add.1 (6 September 2013) para 24.
82 Although the IACtHR has not yet addressed the issue of the proactive dissemination of information, see Inter-American Juridical Committee, Resolution 147 of the 73rd Ordinary Period of Sessions: Principles on the right to access to information (7 August 2008) Principle 10, whereby art 13 ACHR shall be interpreted as encompassing an obligation of 'active transparency'; accordingly, States ought to provide the public with the maximum quantity of information proactively, at least for what concerns the information needed for the exercise of other rights.
83 The leading case in this respect is *Guerra* para 53; see also *Roche v. the United Kingdom*, App. No. 32555/96 (ECtHR, Judgment, Grand Chamber, of 19 November 2005), where the ECtHR Grand Chamber unanimously held that the freedom to receive information does not entail positive dissemination obligations.
84 Ibid para 60.
85 ILC, Sixth Report on the Protection of Persons in the Event of Disasters, UN Doc. A/CN.4/662 (3 May 2013) para 19.
86 See *Prilutiskiy v. Ukraine*, App. No. 40429/08 (ECtHR, Judgment of 26 February 2015) paras 32–33.
87 See L. Seminara, 'Risk Regulation and the European Convention on Human Rights' 4 *EJRR* (2016) 734–736.
88 *Budayeva and Others v. Russia*, App. Nos. 15339/02, 11673/02, 15343/02, 20058/02 and 21166/02 (ECtHR, Judgment of 20 March 2008) para 131.

89 Ibid para 130.

90 See above all *Budayeva* (n. 88) para 131. In other cases, the Court required a 'clear risk', or a 'high degree of risk', or a 'serious and substantial risk' for the right to life of the complainants. See for instance *Kolyadenko and Others v. Russia*, App. Nos. 17423/05, 20534/05, 20678/05, 23263/05, 24283/05 and 35673/05 (ECtHR, Judgment of 28 February 2012); *Makaratzis v. Greece*, App. No. 50385/99 (ECtHR, Judgment, Grand Chamber, of 20 December 2004).

91 *Fadeyeva v. Russia*, App. No. 55723/00 (ECtHR, Judgment of 9 June 2005) para 68. See also *Lopez Ostra v. Spain*, App. No. 16798/90 (ECtHR, Judgment of 9 December 1994) para 51.

92 *Fadeyeva* (91) para 69. See also among others *Taskin and Others v. Turkey*, App. No. 46117/99 (ECtHR, Judgment of 10 November 2004) para 113; *Grimkovskaya v. Ukraine*, App. No. 38182/03 (ECtHR, Judgment of 21 July 2011) paras 58, 62.

93 Ibid 58.

94 See *Dzemyuk v. Ukraine*, App. No. 42488/02 (ECtHR, Judgment, Grand Chamber, of 4 September 2014) para 73, where the Court affirmed that the applicants

> did not for all establish a direct link between the operating condition of the power station . . . as they failed to show that the operation . . . exposed them personally to a danger that was not only serious but specific and, above all, imminent.

Oneryildiz v. Turkey, App. No. 48939/99 (ECtHR, Judgment, Grand Chamber, of 30 November 2004) para 90; *Di Sarno and Other v. Italy*, App. No. 30765/08 (ECtHR, Judgment of 10 January 2012) paras 106, 113. Cf. E. Lamben-Abdelgawad, 'Le principe de precaution dans le système de la Convention européenne des droits de l'homme' in H.E. Ruiz Fabri and L. Gradoni (eds), *La circulation des concepts juridiques: le droit international de l'environnement entre mondialisation et fragmentation* (SLC, 2009) 493.

95 *Budayeva* (n. 88) paras 34–15, 137.

96 *Oneryildiz* (n. 94) para 90.

97 *Özel and Others v. Turkey*, App. Nos. 14350/05, 15245/05 and 16051/05 (ECtHR, Judgment of 17 November 2015) para 189.

98 Above all *Budayeva* (n. 88) para 134. See also, in cases involving environmental issues, *Buckley v. the United Kingdom*, App. No. 20348/92 (ECtHR, Judgment of 25 September 1996) paras 74–77; *Powell and Rayner v. the United Kingdom*, App. No. 9310/81 (ECtHR, Judgment of 21 February 1990) para 44.

99 Ibid para 135. See also *Hatton and Others v. the United Kingdom*, App. No. 36022/07 (ECtHR, Judgment, Grand Chamber, of 8 July 2003) paras 100–101.

100 *Budayeva* (n. 88) paras 152, 136.

101 *Bacila v. Romania*, App. No. 19234/04 (ECtHR, Judgment of 30 March 2010) para 60.

102 *Özel* (n. 97) para 173.

103 For further analysis on the notion of prevention in IDL see Sossai's chapter in this volume.

104 *Oneryildiz* (n. 94) para 90.

105 *Giacomelli v. Italy*, App. No. 59909/00 (ECtHR, Judgment of 2 November 2006) paras 35, 89.

106 *Hardy and Maile v. the UK*, App. No. 31965/07 (ECtHR, Judgment of 14 February 2012) para 187; see also *Budayeva* (n. 88) para 158.

107 2015–2030 Sendai Framework (n. 35) para 24(e).

108 *Buckley* (n. 98) para 74.

16

ECONOMIC AND SOCIAL RIGHTS IN TIMES OF DISASTER

Obligations of immediate effect and progressive realization

Ellen Nohle and Gilles Giacca

Introduction

The basic premise of human rights is to confer legal protection on all individuals in all types of situations. This implies that human rights apply at all times, including before, during and immediately after a disaster. Moreover, 'it is in periods of extreme hardship, whether of an economic or political nature, that human rights guarantees assume their greatest relevance'.[1]

Economic and social rights (ECOSOC rights) have often been downplayed in normative discussions about the applicability of human rights, owing to doctrinal objections based on their perceived lower normative status, compared to civil and political (CP) rights, and practical objections relating to their implementation and enforcement. ECOSOC rights are said to require positive State action and allocation of considerable resources, which cannot be expected in times of disaster. Moreover, ECOSOC rights have been construed as aspirational statements rather than as imposing immediate legal obligations on States, in contrast to CP rights. In times of disaster, aspirations are quickly ranked low on the list of priorities. While this orthodox view of ECOSOC rights is no longer tenable, its influence in the drafting of instruments enshrining these rights has resulted in certain conceptual and procedural peculiarities of ECOSOC rights.

This chapter focuses on the applicability and nature of ECOSOC obligations under the International Covenant on Economic, Social and Cultural Rights (ICESCR),[2] a treaty that sets international standards of global reach. The Covenant comprises a number of provisions relevant to disaster settings, including the principle of non-discrimination (Article 2(2)); the right to work (Articles 6 and 7); the right to social security and assistance (article 9); the right to an adequate standard of living (Article 11), which includes adequate food, water, sanitation and housing; the right to the highest attainable standard of health (Article 12); and the right to education (Articles 13 and 14).

The first part of this chapter explores the nature of the obligations imposed on States Parties to the ICESCR, including the distinction between obligations of immediate effect and rights which may be realized progressively. The second part examines the applicability of ICESCR obligations in disaster situations, including the relevance of resource constraints and the limitation clause in Article 4 ICESCR.

Obligations under the ICESCR

Article 2(1) ICESCR: a programmatic provision?

Today, it is widely recognized that the distinction between CP rights and ECOSOC rights in terms of positive and negative obligations is invalid, as the realization of all human rights requires State action, and that parts of ECOSOC obligations can be achieved through abstention.[3] Still, the understanding of ECOSOC rights that motivated their treatment in a separate Covenant also produced some peculiarities in the provisions of the ICESCR, most notably in Article 2(1). Article 2(1) ICESCR defines the nature of State obligations under the Covenant. It provides:

> Each State Party to the present Covenant undertakes to take steps, individually and through international assistance and cooperation, especially economic and technical, to the maximum of its available resources, with a view to achieving progressively the full realization of the rights recognized in the present Covenant by all appropriate means, including particularly the adoption of legislative measures.

Located in Part II of the Covenant, Article 2(1) forms part of the general provisions of the Covenant which inform the understanding of all substantive provisions laid down in Part III (Articles 6–15). Article 2(1) accordingly gives expression to a general obligation applicable to all substantive rights, similar to the principle of non-discrimination in Article 2(2). The Committee on Economic, Social and Cultural Rights (CESCR) – the international treaty body created to oversee implementation of the ICESCR – has confirmed this understanding, explaining that Article 2(1) has a dynamic relationship with all of the substantive provisions of the Covenant and thus carries fundamental importance for a full understanding of the ICESCR.[4]

The vague formulation of the general obligation in Article 2(1) has lent itself to a wide range of interpretations, some arguing for a legal obligation, others not. In the latter camp, it has been maintained that Article 2(1) implies that the Covenant as a whole merely lays down programmatic objectives as to how ECOSOC rights are to be realized, leaving implementation entirely up to States. This is in contrast with the ICCPR, which imposes direct and enforceable legal obligations.[5]

Defending the normative import of Article 2(1), Alston and Quinn have emphasized that the ICESCR is 'a treaty that gives rise to formal obligations on the part of ratifying or acceding States'.[6] Relying on the principle of good faith in treaty interpretation, articulated in Article 31(1) Vienna Convention on the Law of Treaties (1969), they argued that to dismiss the legal significance of the ICESCR is to suggest that States ratifying the Covenant did not act in good faith. 'In this view, those States have gone through the formal motions of ratifying a treaty that, appearances to the contrary notwithstanding, gives rise to no obligations on their part to do anything of substance'.[7] The CESCR has confirmed in its General Comments and Communications on State reports that Article 2(1) imposes legal obligations on States Parties.[8]

The CESCR has referred to a number of rights of the ICESCR as being self-executing, that is, capable of being applied 'by courts without further elaboration'.[9] The adoption of the Optional Protocol to the ICESCR in 2008 and its entry into force in May 2013, which envisages the CESCR considering complaints and making inquiries into alleged violations of the Covenant, is further confirmation of the general understanding that the ICESCR is comprised of concrete obligations which States can breach and which can lead to certain claims for individuals.[10]

Categories of obligations under the ICESCR

Having affirmed that the ICESCR imposes legally binding obligations on States Parties, the CESCR has further identified different categories of obligations under the Covenant. This has enabled the Committee to move beyond the vague formulation of Article 2(1) to concretize and operationalize Covenant obligations in different contexts. First, a distinction is drawn between obligations of conduct and obligations of result.[11] According to the International Law Commission (ILC), obligations of conduct are those where an organ of the State is obliged to undertake a specific course of conduct, whether through act or omission, which represents a goal in itself, while obligations of result are described as requiring a State to achieve a particular result through a course of conduct the form of which is left to the State's discretion.[12] Second, the CESCR has distinguished between obligations of immediate effect and long-term obligations that are subject to progressive realization.[13] These obligations will be discussed below. Finally, the CESCR has invoked the tripartite typology of obligations to respect, protect and fulfil ECOSOC rights.[14]

The obligation to respect requires States not to arbitrarily interfere with the enjoyment of rights. The obligation to protect requires States to take measures to prevent third parties from interfering with the rights, and the obligation to fulfil requires that States adopt appropriate legislative, administrative, budgetary, promotional and other measures towards the full realization of the rights.[15] While this framework assumes that obligations become increasingly proactive and resource-costly as you move from the obligation to respect to the obligation to fulfil, it bears emphasizing that the implementation of all human rights obligations, including negative obligations, requires the creation and maintenance of an institutional machinery and the resources necessary to sustain it.

Obligations of immediate effect

The consensus view is that the obligation of non-discrimination in Article 2(2)[16] and the principle of equality between women and men in Article 3[17] are of immediate application and enforceable by judicial and other organs. In addition, the CESCR has provided an indicative list of substantive provisions of the ICESCR 'capable of immediate application'.[18] These include Article 7(a)(i) on equal pay, Article 8 on the right to form trade unions and strike, Article 10(3) on the obligation to take special measures of protection and assistance on behalf of children and young persons, Article 13(2) on free and compulsory primary education for all and Article 13(3) on the freedom of parents to choose the type of education provided for their children.

Moreover, whilst Article 2(1) sets out the general obligation of progressive realization of all ECOSOC rights, not every aspect of a particular right is conditioned on progressive achievement. Each right can be translated into a series of obligations, some of which are of immediate and others of progressive nature. In terms of the tripartite typology of respect, protect and fulfil, it is generally agreed that the duty to respect entails obligations of immediate effect. It requires States parties to avoid measures that impede or prevent the enjoyment of ECOSOC rights. This includes a number of negative obligations, which apply fully and immediately.[19] While negative in nature, these obligations – like any human rights obligation – imply the adoption of positive measures to prevent interference with rights, including establishing the required institutions and an effective system of administrative justice to investigate and remedy any deprivation by State agents.

The duty to protect – understood to require a State to prevent third or private parties from interfering with the enjoyment of rights – can also entail obligations of immediate effect, although it may also require 'positive budgetary measures' to be achieved progressively.[20] The exact scope of this duty varies depending on the ECOSOC right in question but will generally require legislative measures and measures to prevent, investigate and punish actions by third parties that impede the enjoyment of rights.[21]

In addition, the general obligation 'to take steps' in Article 2(1) has been construed as imposing obligations of immediate effect to take deliberate and targeted steps and use all appropriate means.[22] According to the CESCR, these steps 'should be deliberate, concrete and targeted as clearly as possible towards meeting the obligations recognized in the Covenant'.[23] Consequently, the undertaking 'to take steps' is an obligation of conduct 'to move as expeditiously and effectively' (i.e. progressively) as possible towards realizing the final result (full realization of the rights).[24]

Another important set of immediate obligations pertains to the 'minimum core' of each of the rights protected under the ICESCR.[25] This minimum core can be understood as a universally defined baseline that must be guaranteed for all individuals in all situations and on the basis of which States should pursue progressive achievement. This minimum core has been referred to by the CESCR as 'non-derogable',[26] suggesting an absolute obligation that cannot be further restricted.

With respect to the content of this 'minimum core', it has been noted in general terms that 'a minimum core obligation to ensure the satisfaction of, at the very least, minimum essential levels of each of the rights is incumbent on every State Party'.[27] Over the years, the CESCR has attempted to define this minimum core by referring, for instance, to essential foodstuffs, essential primary health care, basic shelter and housing or the most basic forms of education.[28] Rather than elaborating on the minimum core content of ECOSOC rights as a theoretical or qualitative notion of 'the essence of a right',[29] the CESCR has focused on the term 'core *obligations*'. To give the example of the right to the highest attainable standard of health, the CESCR has identified a number of core obligations of immediate application that must be complied with in all circumstances, including:

- To ensure the right of access to health facilities, goods and services on a non-discriminatory basis, especially for vulnerable or marginalized groups;
- To ensure access to the minimum essential food which is nutritionally adequate and safe so as to ensure freedom from hunger for everyone;
- To ensure access to basic shelter, housing and sanitation and to an adequate supply of safe and potable water;
- To provide essential drugs, as defined under the World Health Organization (WHO) Action Programme on Essential Drugs;
- To ensure equitable distribution of all health facilities, goods and services; and
- To adopt and implement a national public health strategy and plan of action.[30]

While the notion of minimum core obligations is accepted in legal doctrine and entrenched in the practice of the CESCR, questions arise about the feasibility of determining an internationally defined minimum core that is impervious to questions of resource availability and progressive realization. It is questionable whether even the implementation of the strict minimum core obligations regarding essential foodstuffs or primary health care is affordable for many poor countries, to say nothing of those experiencing a disaster. It might moreover be considered reasonable that developed States should have to meet a higher 'minimum' standard than developing countries that begin at a much lower level of rights realization.[31] Furthermore, Article 2(1) is, as mentioned, a general provision that informs the interpretation of all substantive obligations of the Covenant. It would therefore seem to follow that the qualifier of 'maximum available resources' in Article 2(1) is applicable to all obligations under the Covenant, including the 'minimum core'.[32] Yet, this is in direct contradiction to the very notion of 'non-derogable' minimum core obligations and the objective of identifying obligations of immediate effect that must be ensured by States in all circumstances. This question is still unresolved.[33]

Progressive realization

The concept of progressive realization has been described as the 'linchpin' of the ICESCR.[34] It reflects the idea that most of the Covenant rights depend to varying degrees on the availability of resources and thereby 'mirrors the inevitably contingent nature of State obligations'.[35] This does not, however, mark a difference in kind between rights under the ICCPR and the ICESCR. The full realization of CP rights, such as the rights to fair trial and to free and fair elections, is also heavily dependent on available resources and the development of necessary societal structures. Nor does progressive realization postpone obligations.[36] It has already been demonstrated that States Parties to the ICESCR have obligations of immediate effect, including the duty to immediately start taking steps towards the full realization of the rights. Instead, progressive realization implies a certain flexibility by accommodating the economic realities of each State Party.

The obligation on States Parties to move as expeditiously as possible towards the full achievement of ECOSOC rights can be expressed in terms of the obligation to 'fulfil' these rights, which has been further divided into a duty to facilitate or promote and a duty to provide. The duty to facilitate or promote demands that States take positive measures aimed at enabling and assisting individuals to enjoy ECOSOC rights. While the exact contours of the duty will depend on the specific circumstances of the State, this requires an active role by the State in adopting the necessary measures and devoting material resources to the full realization of ECOSOC rights, using 'all appropriate means'. These means must be 'reasonable and effective' and produce results compatible with the obligations of the Covenant.[37] In general, States Parties are required to create legal, institutional, administrative and procedural conditions and provide resources for the realization of the rights without discrimination. Moreover, the obligation to provide requires the State to provide the right directly whenever an individual or group is unable, for reasons beyond their control, to provide for themselves. For example, inadequate provision of emergency aid to the civilian population in a disaster setting exemplifies a failure of the duty to fulfil the right to an adequate standard of living.

An implication of the notion of progressive realization is that retrogressive measures – that is, measures that imply a step back in the level of rights enjoyment – are impermissible.[38] The CESCR has stressed that there is a 'strong presumption of impermissibility of any retrogressive measure' taken in relation to substantive rights,[39] which constitute prima facie violations of the ICESCR.[40] As a result, States have the burden of proof to justify the legality of any such measure. The CESCR provides two justifications for taking retrogressive measures, namely 'for the purpose of improving the situation with regard to the "totality of the rights in the Covenant" and an economic crisis which makes progression impossible even if all available resources are used'.[41]

It is unclear how expeditiously and effectively States Parties must move towards full realization of the rights or what exact measures must be taken for this purpose. In the end, this must be assessed on a case-by-case basis, taking account of the circumstances of the individual State and examining whether and to what extent it has done all it reasonably can to realize Covenant rights. Still, some guidance is offered in the human rights indicators developed by the UN High Commissioner for Human Rights.[42] These universal indicators enable a focus on measurable outcomes, thereby facilitating assessment of the fulfilment of human rights obligations. Moreover, in elaborating on the minimum core obligations the CESCR has started to call on States Parties to identify appropriate and pragmatic indicators and benchmarks in relation to the substantive rights. The combination of an internationally defined principled baseline developed by the UN High Commissioner for Human Rights and the CESCR and pragmatic thresholds to be defined at the national level in view of individual State circumstances provides a basis of quantitative clarification of States Parties' obligations, against which the progressive realization of ECOSOC rights can be measured.[43]

Maximum available resources

The obligation on States Parties to take steps toward the full realization of the Covenant rights is an obligation 'to the maximum of available resources'. In the preparatory work, it was stressed that having insufficient resources should not be considered as a ground to circumvent obligations.[44] However, the CESCR appears to have treated the phrase 'maximum available resources' as a justification for noncompliance.[45] On this understanding, the maximum use of available resources does not constitute an autonomous obligation on States Parties but is rather the principal means to fulfil the obligation to progressively realize human rights. Still, there are some limitations to the applicability of this justification. These refer to the obligations States have at all times, even when resources are scarce. Thus, States should always make plans and strategies for the full realization of the rights, and in times of 'severe resource constraints', the State must put in place 'relatively low-cost targeted programs' to care for the most vulnerable groups.[46] In addition, the minimum core obligations of each right must be realized at all times, although as mentioned, the CESCR has not always been consistent in this respect, and the actual feasibility of discharging the minimum core obligations is not evident for all countries, including those experiencing disaster.[47]

The scope of what constitutes 'maximum' available resources is left open-ended, which reflects the fact that the nature of resources can change over time and differ depending on the context. The CESCR has generally refrained from providing concrete guidance on this issue, 'fully respecting the authority vested in relevant State organs to adopt what it considers to be its most appropriate policies'.[48] Yet Alston and Quinn concluded, based on the preparatory work, that it was the intention of the drafters not to leave the determination of what constitutes adequate resource allocation entirely to a State Party's subjective determination.

Certain guidance on how resource allocation should be oriented in relation to ECOSOC rights enjoyment can be found in the CESCR's Statement on resources in 2007 that 'in order for a State Party to be able to attribute its failure to meet at least its minimum core obligation to a lack of available resources it must demonstrate that every effort has been made to use all resources that are at its disposition in an effort to satisfy, as a matter of priority, those minimum obligations'.[49] This suggests that Covenant rights should be given priority in the allocation of resources, although it remains unclear how different sectors should be prioritized (e.g. health versus education). Moreover, the CESCR requires that resources be 'adequate' or 'reasonable' when assessing compliance with Covenant obligations. For this purpose, it will *inter alia* consider:

- Whether the State Party's decision (not) to allocate available resources is in accordance with human rights standards;
- Where several policy options are available, whether the State Party adopts the option that least restricts Covenant rights; and
- Whether the steps had taken into account the precarious situation of disadvantaged and marginalized individuals or groups, whether they were non-discriminatory and whether they prioritized grave situations or situations of risk.[50]

These considerations have led some to conclude that 'the obligation to use the maximum available resources implies a prohibition against diverting resources' from ICESCR-related issues.[51] However, a different interpretation is possible, namely that the adequacy of resources allocated to ECOSOC rights will be judged against other expenditures.[52] This more nuanced approach, which permits consideration of other demands on State resources, seems consistent with the below factors identified by the CESCR in relation to assessing a State's compliance with its obligation to take steps to the maximum of available resources in the context of the Optional Protocol:

- The country's level of development;
- The severity of the alleged breach, in particular whether the situation concerned enjoyment of the minimum core content of the Covenant;
- The country's current economic situation, in particular whether the country was undergoing a period of economic recession;
- The existence of other serious claims on the state party's limited resources, for example resulting from a recent disaster or armed conflict;
- Whether the state has sought to identify low-cost options; and
- Whether the state party has sought cooperation and assistance or rejected offers of resources from the international community for the purpose of implementing the provisions of the Covenant without sufficient reason.[53]

International assistance

Article 2(1) ICESCR refers to taking steps 'individually and through international assistance and co-operation'. In addition, international assistance and cooperation is implicit in the phrase 'maximum of its available resources', which has been interpreted to include whatever resources are available nationally as well as internationally.[54] Further to the general provision in Article 2(1), States Parties have also agreed under Article 11(1) to 'take appropriate steps to ensure the realization of this right [to an adequate standard of living], recognizing to this effect the essential importance of international co-operation based on free consent' and in Article 11(2) to take 'individually and through international co-operation' the relevant measures regarding the right to be free from hunger.

These provisions could be read as imposing an obligation on developing and developed States to accept and offer international assistance, respectively, to ensure compliance with Covenant obligations.[55] Alston and Quinn posit that 'in the context of a given right it may, according to the circumstances, be possible to identify obligations to cooperate that would appear to be mandatory on the basis of the undertaking contained in Article 2(1) of the Covenant'.[56] In elaborating on the right to the highest attainable standard of health, the CESCR in General Comment No. 14 stipulates that

> States Parties have joint and individual responsibility, in accordance with the Charter of the United Nations and the relevant resolutions of the UN General Assembly and World Health Assembly, to cooperate in providing disaster relief and humanitarian assistance in times of emergency, including assistance to refugees and IDPs. Each State should contribute to this task to the maximum of its capacities.[57]

However, the exact nature and scope of an international obligation to accept and to offer international assistance have not been fully elaborated,[58] nor is its existence as *lex lata* without controversy.[59] At the very least, the conceptual link between international assistance and cooperation and the notion of 'maximum available resources' suggests that not having sufficient resources for realizing ECOSOC rights can only be invoked as a justification for noncompliance when a State has shown that it has sought international assistance.[60] When a State claims that it has not been able to carry out its obligations for reasons beyond its control, the State has the 'burden of proving that this is the case and that it has unsuccessfully sought to obtain international support'.[61] Proof that such assistance has been sought demonstrates that the State is willing but unable to meet its obligations. This reading is consistent with the comment made by several States that 'if an affected State cannot discharge its obligation to provide timely relief to its people in distress it must have an obligation to seek outside assistance'.[62] Where an unable State receives assistance, it has the further obligation to 'refrain from obstructing international organizations in their legitimate efforts to gain access to individuals under the jurisdiction of the State in order to assist them in the enjoyment of economic, social and cultural rights'.[63]

ECOSOC rights in times of disaster

Applicability of the ICESCR in disaster settings

From a legal standpoint, there is no relevant difference between disasters and other situations with respect to the applicability of human rights, ECOSOC rights included. The applicability of human rights to disaster settings is affirmed in Article 5 ILC's Draft Articles on the Protection of Persons in the Event of Disasters, which provides that 'persons affected by disaster are entitled to respect for their human rights'.

In terms of the applicability of the ICESCR, the CESCR has underscored that

> it is precisely in situations of crisis, that the Covenant requires the protection of all economic, social and cultural rights, in particular of the most marginalized and disadvantaged groups of the society, to the best of its ability under the prevailing adverse conditions.[64]

The CESCR has referred explicitly to duties applicable in the event of disaster.[65] For example, the obligation 'to take the necessary action to mitigate and alleviate hunger' in Article 11(2) applies 'even in times of natural or other disasters',[66] and the requirement of physical and economic access to adequate food or means for its procurement applies 'at all times'.[67] Regarding the duty to respect the right to food, the Committee has stated that a violation can occur by 'the prevention of access to humanitarian food aid in internal conflicts or other emergency situations'.[68] Concerning the duty to fulfil, it has been observed that

> whenever an individual or group is unable, for reasons beyond their control, to enjoy the right to adequate food by the means at their disposal, States have the obligation to fulfil (provide) that right directly. This obligation also applies for persons who are the victims of natural or other disasters.[69]

Several ECOSOC rights, including the rights to food, shelter, sanitation, water and health care, are of direct relevance during the different stages of a disaster cycle. Relevant to the preparedness stage, the CESCR has stated concerning the right to water that 'States Parties should adopt comprehensive and integrated strategies and programs to ensure that there is sufficient and safe water', which 'may include . . . response mechanisms for emergency situations'.[70] 'Failure to adopt mechanisms for emergency relief' is considered a violation of the right to water.[71] Similarly, regarding the right to adequate housing, the CESCR provides that 'people living in disaster prone areas' deserve priority consideration.[72] Likewise, on the right to social services the CESCR stresses that 'particular attention should be paid in this regard to persons . . . living in remote or disaster-prone areas . . . so that they, too, can have access to these services' and 'States Parties should also consider schemes that provide social protection to individuals belonging to disadvantaged and marginalized groups, for example crop or natural disaster insurance for small farmers'.[73] Furthermore, 'special attention should be given to ensuring that the social security system can respond in times of an emergency, for example, during and after a natural disaster, armed conflict and crop failure'.[74] With respect to the right to health, this includes an obligation to create 'a system of urgent medical care in the case of accidents, epidemics and similar hazards'.[75] Compliance with these and similar obligations is a critical component to ensure the State's ability to secure enjoyment of ECOSOC rights should a disaster strike.[76]

Relevant to the immediate disaster response stage, the CESCR refers to a duty to ensure that 'groups facing difficulties with physical access to water, such as . . . victims of natural disasters . . . are provided with safe and sufficient water'.[77] On the right to adequate housing, the CESCR specifies that the legal security of tenure must also apply to emergency housing.[78] Moreover, housing must be 'habitable', which implies protection from 'cold, damp, heat, rain, wind or other threats to health, structural hazards, and disease vectors',[79] and must be 'accessible', which requires special attention for 'victims of natural disasters' and 'people living in disaster prone areas' who can be considered a 'disadvantaged group'.[80] The right to the highest attainable standard of health requires, *inter alia*, 'the provision of disaster relief and humanitarian assistance in emergency situations'.[81]

In the reconstruction phase, there will arguably be an immediate positive obligation on the affected State to repair damaged structures and institutions, such as health care facilities, necessary for the realization of ECOSOC rights. As the State recovers from the disaster, there will concurrently be an increased focus on the necessary steps it must take towards full realization of these rights.

In accordance with the principle of non-discrimination in Article 2(2) ICESCR, these measures must be undertaken without discrimination.[82] In this respect, concern has for example been expressed over the disparate impact of Hurricane Katrina in the US on low-income African American residents[83] and the situation of women affected by the Indian Ocean Tsunami.[84]

Resource constraints

Having sufficient resources for the realization of human rights may prove particularly challenging for a State that is experiencing a disaster.[85] The CESCR acknowledges this, stating that if a country is recovering from a disaster, that particular circumstance will be taken into account when assessing compliance with Covenant obligations.[86] Specifically, the CESCR recognizes that 'external factors can affect the right to a continuous improvement of living conditions'. However, 'despite externally caused problems, the obligations under the Covenant continue to apply'.[87]

As noted, some of the obligations of immediate effect presuppose certain institutional structures. For instance, the immediate application of the right to free primary education is contingent on the existence of an educational system with infrastructure, equipment and resources.[88] In times of disaster, such a system might no longer be available. In this case, States would arguably have an immediate positive obligation to ensure that the educational system is repaired as soon as possible, where performance is measured against a reasonableness standard.[89]

If a disaster constrains the affected State's ability to comply with even its minimum core obligations under the ICESCR, the State must demonstrate that it has done everything in its power to obtain more resources, including by recourse to international cooperation and assistance. With respect to the minimum core content of the right to food, the CESCR provides that

> a State claiming that it is unable to carry out its obligation for reasons beyond its control therefore has the burden of proving that this is the case and that it has unsuccessfully sought to obtain international support to ensure the availability and accessibility of the necessary food.[90]

As for the obligation to take steps towards the full realization of the rights, Sommario considers that the obligation 'might be heavily conditioned in the presence of disaster that severely undermines the capacity of the authorities to provide even basic assistance'.[91] Sommario therefore considers it 'unrealistic to require States to fully implement all ECOSOC rights during a disaster situation of extraordinary intensity which obliterates their material assets and seriously strains their economic and financial resources'.[92] The CESCR might indeed take a more flexible approach to retrogressive measures when a State is recovering from a disaster.[93] As outlined above, one of the relevant criteria when the Committee assesses compliance under the Optional Protocol procedure is 'the existence of other serious claims on the State Party's limited resources, for example resulting from a recent disaster'.[94] This is consistent with the Committee's practice in considering States' periodic reports. For instance, in relation to Mexico the CESCR took note 'of the natural disaster experienced by Mexico and acknowledges the limitations they impose on the government in guaranteeing implementation of economic, social and cultural rights to its population at all times'.[95] Moreover, with respect to Hurricanes Ivan (2004) and Emily (2005) in Grenada, the CESCR recognized that 'these natural disasters, along with the current global financial crisis, have been significant obstacles to the implementation of the Covenant'.[96]

This does not mean that the obligation of progressive realization is inapplicable in times of disaster. Rather, it means that the kind of measures that can realistically be asked of a State is limited by the resources available to it, and those resources can be affected by the occurrence of a disaster.[97] The obligation on the State thus remains the same: to achieve progressive realization to the maximum of its available resources. This is demonstrated in the context of retrogressive measures. In relation to budget cuts on allocations for social assistance following the Great East Japan Earthquake and the Fukushima nuclear accident (2011), the CESCR stated that Japan was obligated to 'ensure that retrogressive measures are taken only in the context of the full use of the maximum available resources'.[98] The Committee has taken a similar approach where other external factors that have reduced a State's capacity to ensure full realization of ECOSOC rights. For example, with respect to austerity measures taken by Greece in response to the economic crisis, the Committee recommended that Greece review its policies and programs 'with a view to ensuring that austerity measures are progressively waived and the effective protection of the rights under the Covenant is enhanced in line with the progress achieved in the post-crisis economic recovery'.[99] Moreover, in its Concluding Observations made with regard to Iraq, the CESCR stated that, despite the sanctions imposed against Iraq, Iraq still had to work on realizing the rights to food and health to the maximum of its available resources.[100]

As Jansen-Wilhelm observes, the occurrence of a disaster might only *partly* affect the obligation to take steps towards full achievement, and even immediately after a disaster, some steps could still be feasible, such as making plans of actions and strategies for fuller realization.[101] There is at least an obligation to move forward and continuously improve. In other words, it is the scope rather than the applicability of the obligation to take steps that is affected by the availability of resources.[102] That scope will vary depending on the nature of the disaster and how well equipped the State is to cope with the consequences of a disaster. It is therefore necessary to remain flexible in terms of what kind of progression can reasonably be expected of a State experiencing disaster. Here, state-identified benchmarks for progression can play a useful function, complementary to the internationally defined human rights indicators, allowing consideration of the individual circumstances of the State when measuring compliance with the obligation to take steps.[103]

Limitation clauses

Distinct from retrogressive measures due to resource constraints under Article 2(1) is the limitation of ECOSOC rights for other reasons. A State's response to a disaster might involve a range of limitations or restrictions on the enjoyment of ECOSOC rights, including restrictions on access to health care, food and shelter. The question is whether the occurrence of a disaster may generate a legitimate reason – other than resource constraints – for limiting ECOSOC rights under the ICESCR.

There is a general presumption that human rights are not absolute in nature.[104] With a few exceptions, human rights can be subject to limitations or restrictions under specific conditions. In contrast to derogations, which are considered exceptional,[105] limitations are construed as a necessary and normal element to balance individual and community interests. They allow the State a level of flexibility to give effect to human rights while pursuing important objectives aimed at solving conflicts between rights or protect society for reasons of public interest, such as public order, public health or national security.

A general limitation clause applicable to the substantive rights of the ICESCR is articulated in Article 4:

> The States Parties to the present Covenant recognize that, in the enjoyment of those rights provided by the State in conformity with the present Covenant, the State may subject such rights only to such limitations as are determined by law only in so far as this may be compatible with the nature of these rights and solely for the purpose of promoting the general welfare in a democratic society.

Guidance on the interpretation of this provision is scant.[106] States rarely mention limitations on ECOSOC rights in their domestic legislations, and the CESCR seldom demands justification on the basis of Article 4 in the event of noncompliance with substantive obligations. Instead, the CESCR tends to address prima facie violations of the Covenant in terms of retrogressive measures States may take when faced with severe or sudden resource constraints, that is, by reference to Article 2(1).[107]

Article 4 ICESCR appears to suggest that the only legitimate purpose for limiting Covenant rights is promotion of the general welfare of a democratic society. This can be contrasted with limitation clauses in other human rights treaties, notably in the field of CP rights, where other purposes include public interest such as public order, national security, public health or the rights and freedoms of others.[108] The preparatory work does not indicate the meaning of 'general welfare', and while the International Court of Justice considered the limitation clause in Article 4 ICESCR in the Wall Advisory Opinion, its reasoning fails to shed light on the meaning of this term.[109] The Court simply observed that the construction of the security barrier failed to meet the general welfare test. Typically, 'general welfare' is understood to mean 'furthering the socio-economic wellbeing of the people as a whole'.[110]

In order to ensure consistency between human rights instruments, there is good reason to construe 'general welfare' as including other purposes such as public order or public health. A narrow interpretation of Article 4 ICESCR could result in a conflict with other human rights treaties. For example, under Article 12(3) ICCPR, the right to freedom of movement may be limited to protect national security, public order, public health or morals or the freedoms of others. Such limitation may directly restrict the enjoyment of ECOSOC rights, including access to education, health care or work. Yet, how can this be read consistently with Article 4 ICESCR, unless 'general welfare' is read to include these other reasons listed in Article 12(3) ICCPR? The CESCR does not seem to take a restrictive approach to the permissible grounds for limiting ECOSOC rights. For instance, in General Comment No. 14 on the right to health, the Committee suggests that a State that

> restricts the movement of, or incarcerates, persons with transmissible diseases such as HIV/AIDS, refuses to allow doctors to treat persons believed to be opposed to a government, or fails to provide immunization against the community's major infectious diseases, on grounds such as national security or the preservation of public order, has the burden of justifying such serious measures in relation to each of the elements identified in Article 4.[111]

Assuming that the disaster-affected State can prove that a limitation on the enjoyment of ECOSOC rights has been imposed in pursuit of the 'promotion of general welfare', the State must moreover prove that the limitation is determined by law,[112] is compatible with the nature of the rights[113] and is proportionate to the legitimate aim pursued. The requirement that the limitation be determined by law entails both formal and substantive requirements.[114] The former specify that the limitation must have a legal basis in domestic law consistent with the Covenant. The domestic legal provision must be sufficiently precise and adequately accessible. Further, there must be a measure of legal protection and effective remedies against the arbitrary or abusive imposition of limitations on ESCR. Regarding the substantive requirements, the domestic provision envisaging limitations on ECOSOC rights must not be arbitrary, unreasonable or discriminatory. In line with the principle of non-discrimination in Article 2(2) ICESCR, any restriction must have an objective and reasonable justification.[115]

Conclusion

This chapter has demonstrated the context-dependent nature of ECOSOC rights, with the result that specification of State obligations inevitably remains at a level of abstraction and generality. Yet, it has also been made clear that States Parties to the ICESCR have assumed legal obligations, some of which are of immediate effect and must be complied with in all situations. Most notably, the minimum core obligations of the Covenant have been characterized by the CESCR as non-derogable and are applicable at all times. If a State affected by disaster is unable to comply with this universal baseline, it has a heavy burden of proving that it has done all in its power to obtain more resources, including by seeking international assistance.

In addition, States Parties have a positive and immediate obligation to take steps toward the full realization of ECOSOC rights. While it is acceptable that States make less progression immediately after a disaster, States should still make plans of action for the full achievement of these rights and these plans should inform the reconstruction phase. ECOSOC rights obligations also play an important function in the preparedness phase, by requiring the putting into place of emergency plans and structures that enable States to cope with a disaster in a manner consistent with at least the core contents of the rights such as essential health care, basic shelter and housing, water and sanitation, foodstuffs and the most basic forms of education.

Selected bibliography

A. Eide, 'Economic, Social and Cultural Rights as Human Rights' in A. Eide, C. Krause and A. Rosas (eds), *Economic, Social and Cultural Rights: A Textbook* (2nd edn, Kluwer Law International, 2001) 9.

M. Sepulveda, *The Nature of the Obligations under the International Covenant on Economic, Social and Cultural Rights* (Intersentia, 2003).

P. Alston and G. Quinn, 'The Nature and Scope of States Parties' Obligations under the International Covenant on Economic, Social and Cultural Rights' 9 *Human Rights Quarterly* (1987) 156.

R. Chapman and S. Russell (eds), *Core Obligations: Building a Framework for Economic, Social and Cultural Rights* (Transnational Publishers, 2002).

S. Jansen-Wilhelm, 'A Duty to Accept Humanitarian Assistance under the ICESCR?' in A. Zwitter, C.K. Lamont, H.-J. Heintze and J. Herman (eds), *Humanitarian Action: Global, Regional and Domestic Legal Responses* (Cambridge University Press, 2015) 174.

Notes

1 P. Alston and G. Quinn, 'The Nature and Scope of States Parties' Obligations under the International Covenant on Economic, Social and Cultural Rights' 9 *Human Rights Quarterly* (1987) 164.

2 International Covenant on Economic, Social and Cultural Rights (adopted 16 December 1966, entered into force 3 January 1976) 993 UNTS 3.

3 See S. Jansen-Wilhelm, 'A Duty to Accept Humanitarian Assistance under the ICESCR?' in A. Zwitter, C.K. Lamont, H.-J. Heintze and J. Herman (eds), *Humanitarian Action: Global, Regional and Domestic Legal Responses* (Cambridge University Press, 2015) 184.

4 CESCR, General Comment No. 3: The Nature of States Parties' Obligations, UN Doc. E/1991/23 (1990) para 1. See also M. Sepulveda, 'Obligations of "International Assistance and Cooperation" in an Optional Protocol to the International Covenant on Economic, Social and Cultural Rights' 24 *Netherlands Quarterly of Human Rights* (2006) 295.

5 Alston and Quinn (n. 1) 159.

6 Ibid 160.

7 Ibid.

8 P. Alston, 'The Historical Origins of "General Comments" in Human Rights Law' in L. Boisson De Charzournes and V. Gowlland-Debbas (eds), *The International Legal System in Quest of Equity and Universality: Liber Amicorum Georges: Abi-Saab* (Martinus Njihoff, 2001) 257.

9 CESCR, General Comment No. 9: The Domestic Application of the Covenant, UN Doc. E/C.12/1998/24 (1998) para 10.

10 See S. Jansen-Wilhelm, *Accepting Assistance in the Aftermath of Disasters: Standards for States under International Law* (Intersentia, 2015) 127.

11 For example, see CESCR General Comment No. 3 (n. 4) para 1.

12 ILC, Report of the International Law Commission on the Work of Its Twenty-Ninth Session, UN Doc. A/32/10 (1977) 27.

13 For example, CESCR General Comment No. 12: The Right to Adequate Food (Art. 11 of the Covenant), UN Doc. E/C.12/1999/5 (1999) para 16.

14 Maastricht Guidelines on Violations of Economic, Social and Cultural Rights, Maastricht (1997) para 6 B.

15 See H.-J. Heintze, 'The ILC Codification Project on the "Protection of Persons in the Event of Disasters"' in P. Gibbons and H.-J. Heintze (eds), *The Humanitarian Challenge: 20 Years European Network on Humanitarian Action (NOHA)* (Springer International Publishing, 2015) 171.

16 ICESCR art 2(2) states:

> The States Parties to the present Covenant undertake to guarantee that the rights enunciated in the present Covenant will be exercised without discrimination of any kind as to race, colour, sex, language, religion, political or other opinion, national or social origin, property, birth or other status.

See on that Casolari's chapter in this volume.

17 ICESR art 3 states: 'The States Parties to the present Covenant undertake to ensure the equal right of men and women to the enjoyment of all economic, social and cultural rights set forth in the present Covenant.'

18 CESCR, General Comment No. 3 (n. 4) para 5.

19 For example, the obligation to respect the right to the highest attainable standard of health (art 12) requires abstention 'from denying or limiting equal access for all persons . . . to preventive, curative and palliative health' and to abstain from enforcing discriminatory practices as State policy. See CESCR, General Comment No. 14: The Right to the Highest Attainable Standard of Health, UN Doc. E/C.12/2000/4 (2000) paras 34 and 50.

20 CESCR, Statement on an Evaluation of the Obligation to Take Steps to the 'Maximum of Available Resources' under an Optional Protocol to the Covenant, UN Doc. E/C.12/2007/1 (2007) para 7.

21 M. Nowak, *Introduction to the International Human Rights Regime* (Martinus Nijhoff Publishers, 2003) 53.

22 See HRC, Report of the Special Rapporteur on the Right of Everyone to the Enjoyment of the Highest Attainable Standard of Physical and Mental Health, Mission to Japan, UN Doc. A/HRC/23/41/Add.3 (2013) para 54.

23 CESCR General Comment No. 3 (n. 4) para 2.

24 Ibid para 9.

25 See generally CESCR General Comment No. 3 (n. 4) and M. Sepulveda, *The Nature of the Obligations under the International Covenant on Economic, Social and Cultural Rights* (Intersentia, 2003) 25–75.

26 CESCR, General Comment No. 14 (n. 19) para 47; CESCR, General Comment No. 15: The Right to Water, UN Doc. E/C.12/2002/11 (2003) para 40; CESCR, Substantive Issues Arising in the Implementation of the ICESCR: Poverty and the ICESCR, Statement Adopted by the CESCR on 4 May 2001, UN Doc. E/C.12/2001/10 (2001) para 16.

27 CESCR General Comment No. 3 (n. 4) para 10. See E. Sommario, 'Derogation from Human Rights Treaties in Situations of Natural or Man-Made Disasters' in A. de Guttry, M. Gestri and G. Venturini (eds), *International Disaster Response Law* (Asser Press, 2012) 348.

28 Ibid. See also CESCR, General Comment No. 12 (n. 13) paras 8–13. For example, the Committee noted that 'immediate and urgent steps may be needed' to ensure the fundamental right of freedom of hunger and malnutrition in art 11(2) and that 'States have a core obligation to take the necessary action to mitigate and alleviate hunger' (para 6).
29 Ibid. See also CESCR, General Comment No. 13: The Right to Education (Art. 13 of the Covenant), UN. Doc: E/C.12/1999/10 (1999) para 57.
30 CESCR, General Comment No. 14 (n. 19) para 43. See also Inglese's chapter in this volume.
31 As Chapman and Russell note 'valid expectations and concomitant obligations of States parties under the Covenant are not uniform or universal, but instead are relative to levels of development and available resources'. See A.R. Chapman and S. Russell (eds), *Core Obligations: Building a Framework for Economic, Social and Cultural Rights* (Transnational Publishers, 2002) 5; A. Eide, 'Economic, Social and Cultural Rights as Human Rights' in A. Eide, C. Krause and A. Rosas (eds), *Economic, Social and Cultural Rights: A Textbook* (2nd edn, Kluwer Law International, 2001) 9–28; Sepulveda, *The Nature of the Obligations* (n. 25) 25–75.
32 The notion 'maximum available resources' has been interpreted to include whatever resources are available nationally as well as internationally. For example, CESCR General Comment No. 3 (n. 4) para 13.
33 Ibid para 10. Compare for instance Principles 25 and 28 of the Maastricht Guidelines.
34 Alston and Quinn (n. 1) 172.
35 Ibid.
36 Jansen-Wilhelm, 'A Duty to Accept Humanitarian Assistance under the ICECSR?' (n. 3) 189.
37 CESCR General Comment No. 3 (n. 4) para 4.
38 Ibid para 9.
39 CESCR General Comment No. 13 (n. 29) para 45; CESCR General Comment No. 14 (n. 19) para 32; CESCR General Comment No. 15 (n. 26) para 19; CESCR General Comment No. 19: The Right to Social Security (Art. 9 of the Covenant), UN Doc. E/C.12/GC/19 (2008) para 42.
40 '[A]ny deliberately retrogressive measures . . . require the most careful consideration and would need to be fully justified by reference to the totality of the rights provided for in the Covenant and in the context of the full use of the maximum available resources.' CESCR General Comment No. 3 (n. 4) para 9.
41 Ibid para 9. See also Jansen-Wilhelm, *Accepting Assistance in the Aftermath of Disasters* (n. 10) 147.
42 See OHCHR, *Human Rights Indicators: A Guide to Measurement and Implementation* (United Nations, 2012). These are divided into structural, process and outcome indicators.
43 See CESCR General Comment No. 14 (n. 19) para 57.
44 Jansen-Wilhelm, *Accepting Assistance in the Aftermath of Disasters* (n. 10) 141.
45 Ibid 141–142.
46 CESCR, 'Statement on an Evaluation' (n. 20) paras 4–5; CESCR General Comment No. 3 (n. 4) paras 11–12.
47 Jansen-Wilhelm, *Accepting Assistance in the Aftermath of Disasters* (n. 10) 141.
48 CESCR, 'Statement on an Evaluation' (n. 20) para 2.
49 Ibid para 4.
50 Ibid para 2.
51 QUB, *Budget Analysis Project Budgeting for Economic and Social Rights: A Human Rights Framework* (QUB, School of Law, 2010) 28.
52 See R. Pisillo Mazzeschi, 'Responsabilité de l'Etat pour violation des obligations positives relatives aux droits de l'homme' 333 *Recueil des Cours* (2008) 466–467.
53 CESCR, 'Statement on an Evaluation' (n. 20) para 10.
54 For example, CESCR General Comment No. 3 (n. 4) para 13.
55 See CESCR General Comment No. 3 (n. 4) para 14. See also K. Sykes, 'Hunger without Frontiers: The Right to Food and State Obligations to Migrants' in D.D. Caron, M.J. Kelly and A. Telesetsky (eds), *The International Law of Disaster Relief* (Cambridge University Press, 2014) 200–206.
56 Alston and Quinn (n. 1) 191.
57 CESCR General Comment No. 14 (n. 19) para 40.
58 However, efforts have been made. See in particular: Institut de Droit International, *Resolution 2003 on Humanitarian Assistance*, Bruges Session, Sixteenth Commission, 2 February 2003, and ILC, *Draft Articles on the Protection of Persons in the Event of Disasters*, Yearbook of the International Law Commission (vol. II, part two, 2016) arts 7, 8, 11–15.
59 For example, see Jansen-Wilhelm, *Accepting Assistance in the Aftermath of Disasters* (n. 10) 150; J. Todres, 'Mainstreaming Children's Rights in Post-Disaster Settings' 25 *Emory International Law Review* (2011) 1244.
60 See CESCR General Comment No. 3 (n. 4) para 13.
61 CESCR, General Comment No. 12 (n. 13) para 17.

62 ILC, Reports of the International Law Commission, Sixtieth Session (5 May–6 June and 7 July–8 August 2008), *Official Records of the General Assembly, Sixty-Third Session, Supplement No 10* (A/63/10) para 243.
63 CESCR, Concluding Observations: El Salvador, UN Doc. E/1997/22 (1997) paras 171 and 185; CESCR, Concluding Observations: Mexico, UN Doc. E/2000/22 (2000) para 271.
64 CESCR, Concluding Observations: Colombia, UN Doc. E/C.12/COL/CO/5 (2010) para 7.
65 See Jansen-Wilhelm, 'A Duty to Accept Humanitarian Assistance under the ICESCR?' (n. 3) 200.
66 CESCR General Comment No. 12 (n. 13) para 6.
67 Ibid.
68 Ibid para 19.
69 Ibid para 15.
70 CESCR General Comment No. 15 (n. 26) para 28.
71 Ibid para 44.
72 CESCR, General Comment No. 4: The Right to Adequate Housing, UN Doc. E/1992/23 (1991) para 8(e). For example, in its Concluding Observations on Morocco, the Committee stated that it

> exhorts the State party to provide assistance to earthquake victims, particularly women and children, and to take preventive action to ensure that housing is built in accordance with the rules applicable to earth-quake prone areas. The State party should redouble its efforts to rehouse the disaster-struck population of Al-Hoceima.

See CESCR, Concluding Observations: Morocco, UN Doc. E/C.12/MAR/CO/3 (2006) para 51.
73 General Comment No. 19 (n. 39) paras 27–28. This was reiterated in relation to Nepal: CESCR, Concluding Observations on the Third Periodic Report of Nepal, UN Doc. E/C.12/NPL/CO/3 (2014) para 28.
74 General Comment No. 19 (n. 39) para 50. See also CESCR, Concluding Observations on the Third Periodic Report of Nepal, UN Doc. E/C.12/NPL/CO/3 (2014) para 50.
75 CESCR General Comment No. 14 (n. 19) para 16. Such a system should take into account the specific needs of women and children. For example, it should include reproductive health. See CommEDAW, Concluding Comments: Indonesia, UN Doc. CEDAW/C/IDN/CO/5 (2007) para 38.
76 For example, in relation to Japan, the CESCR stated that

> the insufficient nationwide community preparation for the prevention and handling of nuclear accidents . . . in the case of the Fukushima nuclear accident, has led to negative impact on the enjoyment of economic, social and cultural rights of victims (arts. 11 and 12).

See CESCR, Concluding Observations on the Third Periodic Report of Japan, UN Doc. E/C.12/JPN/CO/3 (2013) para 25.
77 CESCR General Comment No. 15 (n. 26) para 16.
78 CESCR General Comment No. 4 (n. 72) para 8(a).
79 Ibid para 8.
80 Jansen-Wilhelm, *Accepting Assistance in the Aftermath of Disasters* (n. 10) 179. The CommERD has stressed the importance of the inclusion of the persons affected by housing and other decisions in the decision-making process. See CommERD, Concluding Observations: United States of America, UN Doc. CERD/C/USA/CO/6 (2008) para 31.
81 CESCR, General Comment No. 4 (n. 72) para 8(e). This includes an obligation to mitigate the effects of the disaster on mental health. See for example: HRC, Report of the Special Rapporteur on the Right of Everyone to the Enjoyment of the Highest Attainable Standard of Physical and Mental Health, Mission to Japan, UN Doc. A/HRC/23/41/Add.3 (2013) para 36.
82 For example, in relation to the Great East Japan Earthquake and the Fukushima nuclear accidents the CESCR recommended that Japan 'ensure that disaster management plans do not discriminate or lead to discrimination in the enjoyment of economic, social and cultural rights'. CESCR, Concluding Observations on the Third Periodic Report of Japan (n. 76) para 24. See also HRC Report of the Special Rapporteur on the right of everyone to the enjoyment of the highest attainable standard of physical and mental health (n. 81) para 70 ('The State is . . . under an immediate obligation to prevent discrimination, especially against vulnerable groups in its policies and practices, even during times of resource constraints'). For a general discussion, see again Casolari's chapter in this volume.
83 See CommERD, Concluding Observations: United States of America (n. 80) para 31; HRComm, Consideration of Reports Submitted by States Parties Under Article 40 of the Covenant Concluding Observations of the Human Rights Committee: United States of America, UN Doc. CCPR/C/USA/CO/3/Rev.1 (18 December 2006) para 26.

84 For example, see CommEDAW, Concluding Comments: Indonesia (n. 75) para 38.
85 See Jansen-Wilhelm, *Accepting Assistance in the Aftermath of Disasters* (n. 10) 45.
86 CESCR, 'Statement on An Evaluation of the Obligation' (n. 20) para 10 (d) and (f).
87 General Comment No. 4 (n. 72) para 11.
88 In recognition of this, the Committee made the following comment: 'The plan of action must be aimed at securing the progressive implementation of *the right to compulsory primary education, free of charge*' (emphasis added). CESCR General Comment No. 11: Plans of Action for Primary Education, (Art. 14 of the Covenant), UN Doc. E/1992/23 (1999) para 10.
89 UNESCO, *Protecting Education from Attack: A State-of-the-Art Review* (UNESCO, 2010) 165.
90 CESCR General Comment No. 12 (n. 13) para 17.
91 Sommario, 'Derogation from Human Rights Treaties in Situations of Natural or Man-Made Disasters' (n. 27) 347.
92 Ibid.
93 For example, see Concluding Observations on Honduras, as the country was recovering from Hurricane Mitch: CESCR, Concluding Observations: Honduras, UN Doc. E/C.12/1 Add.57 (2001) para 11.
94 CESCR, 'Statement on An Evaluation of the Obligation' (n. 20) para 10.
95 CESCR, Report on the twentieth and twenty-first sessions, UN Doc. E/2000/22-E/C.12/1999/11 (2000) para 375.
96 CommRC, Concluding Observations: Grenada, UN Doc. CRC/C/GRD/CO/2 (2010) para 3.
97 For example, the Indian Ocean tsunami of December 2004 resulted in losses exceeding 62% of the Maldives' GDP. See HRC, Nineteenth Session, Report of the Special Rapporteur on the Human Rights of Internally Displaced Persons, UN Doc. A/HRC/19/54/Add.1 (2012) para 15.
98 CESCR, Concluding Observations on the Third Periodic Report of Japan (n. 76) para 9.
99 CESCR, Concluding Observations on the Second Periodic Report of Greece, UN Doc. E/C.12/GRC/CO/2 (26 October 2015) para 8. The Committee recommended, *inter alia*, that Greece '[p]rogressively increase health-care expenditure as a proportion of gross domestic product with a view to complying with its obligation to fulfil the right to health under the Covenant' (para 36).
100 CESCR, General Comment No. 7: The Right to Adequate Housing: Forced Evictions (Art. 11 (1) of the Covenant), UN Doc. E/1998/22 (1997).
101 Jansen-Wilhelm, *Accepting Assistance in the Aftermath of Disasters* (n. 10) 159.
102 Ibid 150.
103 For example, see ibid 171–172.
104 Sommario, 'Derogation from Human Rights Treaties in Situations of Natural or Man-Made Disasters' (n. 27) 326; H. Spieker, 'International Norms Informing Domestic Disaster Response Schemes' in A. Zwitter, C.K. Lamont, H.-J. Heintze and J. Herman, *Humanitarian Action: Global, Regional and Domestic Legal Responses* (Cambridge University Press, 2015) 153.
105 A.L. Svensson-McCarthy, *The International Law of Human Rights and States of Exception: With Special Reference to the Travaux Préparatoires and Case-Law of the International Monitoring Organs* (Martinus Nijhoff Publishers, 1998) 49.
106 However, it is generally understood that art 4 deals with limitations other than those that can be imposed under art 2(1) relating to resource availability. See A. Müller, 'Limitations to and Derogations from Economic, Social and Cultural Rights' 9 *Human Rights Law Review* (2009) 570.
107 CESCR, General Comment No. 3 (n. 4) para 9.
108 Many civil and political rights, but also some ESCR, can lawfully be limited for reasons of public order, public morals, public health, national security, public safety or public interest. See ICCPR, arts 12, 18, 19, 21, and 22; ICESCR, art 8; ECHR, art 8; ACHR, art 32(2); and ACHPR, art 14. See also Sommario's chapter in this volume.
109 *Legal Consequences of the Construction of a Wall in the Occupied Palestinian Territory (Advisory Opinion)* [2004] ICJ Rep. 136, para 136.
110 See The Limburg Principles on the Implementation of the International Covenant on Economic Social, and Cultural Rights, UN Doc. E/CN.4/1987/17 (1997) para 52.
111 CESCR, General Comment No. 14 (n. 19) para 28.
112 Ibid.
113 See 'The Limburg Principles' (n. 110) para 56.
114 Ibid paras 48–56.
115 CESCR General Comment No. 20: Non-Discrimination in Economic, Social and Cultural Rights, UN Doc. E/C.12/GC/20 (2009) para 13.

17

CULTURAL RIGHTS IN THE PREVENTION AND MANAGEMENT OF DISASTERS

Eleni Polymenopoulou

Introduction

Akin to catastrophes occurring in situations of armed conflict, disasters may affect not only human lives and households but also cultural heritage: archaeological sites and monuments, memorials, cultural landscapes or even museums, sculptures and precious cultural assets may bear the impact of earthquakes, cyclones, storms, floods and droughts.

The role of culture and cultural rights, however, goes way beyond the need to safeguard tangible cultural heritage. Culture defines the way that people feel, understand and ultimately confront and respond to disasters.[1] The confrontation and management of disasters therefore is not the same in Pakistan and North Carolina, as it is not the same in the Arctic and the islands in the Indian Ocean. In many parts of the world, for instance, people believe that disasters are God- or spirit-sent punishments for their sinful behaviour: the 2004 tsunami, for example, has been perceived as 'divine punishment';[2] the floods of the River Kosi in Northern India as the fault of Goddess Kosi;[3] the earthquake in Haiti as punishment for the *voodoo* ceremonies that were taking place on the island (as a result, almost entirely marginalized after the earthquake struck);[4] and even Hurricane Katrina as 'God's punishment for sinful behaviour in New Orleans'.[5] In other instances, superstition governs the local population's ability to recover. By way of illustration, when the 1985 earthquake hit Mexico, people thought that dead bodies would spread several epidemics, therefore delaying the recovery process.[6]

At the same time, a people's cultural identity as manifested in cultural expressions and living traditions is the feature of 'culture' that is endangered the most when disasters strike. By way of example, following the earthquakes in Yogyakarta in 2006 and Nepal in 2015, the local populations suffered significant damages in their local tourist industry. This encompassed not only important tourist attractions in the destroyed sites (for instance, the temple complexes of the Kathmandu valley) but also local intangible cultural heritage, including the making of *wayang* shadow-theatre puppets and *batik* textiles in Indonesia, as well as the know-how related to mountaineering guides in Nepal.

The role of culture in disasters is therefore twofold. On the one hand, it indicates the impact of disasters and the destruction of cultural heritage visible after every tragedy – including destruction of monuments, impact on tourism and folk industry and the general demoralization of the population affected. On the other hand, it refers to cultural and religious beliefs as well as social representations that are directly relevant to the way that disasters are conceived. Although it seems quite evident that 'without a good understanding of the cultural environment, interventions for risk reduction can fail',[7] the 'cultural factor' is one that has only recently started being explored. This exploration has been based on expertise in different fields, particularly environmental sciences, anthropology, geography, human security, biosciences, ethnology and cultural studies.

The present chapter examines the role of culture in relation to disasters from a legal perspective, focusing on those cultural rights that could be pertinent in disaster risk reduction and responses. It further highlights the links between cultural rights and sustainable disaster management, explaining approaches to prevention and management built upon the notion of cultural resilience. In order to do so, firstly, it underlines the importance of including culture in the disaster discourse. Secondly, it analyses those cultural rights that appear to be more affected in times of disaster – focusing on cultural identities and living traditions, as well as cultural perceptions on gender roles. Then, it explores the preservation of group rights in relation to cultural vulnerabilities, focusing on indigenous livelihoods and indigenous traditional knowledge. Finally, the chapter explains the transition in policy matters from cultural rights to the more generic notion of 'cultural resilience'.

The protection of cultural rights as part of the disaster agenda

Preliminary observations: cultural rights that may be pertinent when disasters strike

It is undisputed that all human rights are applicable in times of natural or other disasters.[8] Distinguishing which rights are pertinent in the wake of natural disasters however is a challenging exercise. The challenge is twofold. Firstly, as Symonides argues already in 1999, the scope of cultural rights depends on the very meaning that one offers to the term 'culture': culture may be perceived as 'creative artistic and scientific activities' as well as, in a broader sense, 'the sum of human activities, the totality of values, knowledge and practice'.[9] Yet, under international law, only five human rights are expressly labelled as 'cultural':

> the right to education; the right to participate in cultural life; the right to enjoy the benefits of scientific progress and its applications; the right to benefit from the protection of the moral and material interests resulting from any scientific, literary or artistic production of which the person is the author, and the freedom of scientific research and creative activity.[10]

From these rights, *prima facie*, only a few are pertinent when disasters strike – the right to education for instance could be one, in the sense of an education that takes into account appropriate disaster management. Secondly, cultural rights have been typically considered as a species of rights entailing obligations that are not immediate but, rather, only 'progressively realized'.[11] As a result, the safeguarding of cultural rights as a whole would not ordinarily be considered urgent in times of disasters – for the very meaning of 'disasters' is commonly associated with something *urgent*, affecting chiefly human security more than anything else.[12]

Including 'cultural heritage' in the definition of 'disasters'

This said, several developments in international human rights law that took place in the new millennium have resulted in the 'enlargement' of cultural rights. The 'right to participate in cultural life' in particular has been gradually interpreted so broadly as to include a right of 'access to and enjoyment of cultural heritage'. This is precisely the case with Article 15 paragraph 1 (a) of the International Covenant on Economic, Social and Cultural Rights (ICESCR) as a starting point that guarantees the right to participate in cultural life.[13] This development coincides with the adoption of General Comment No. 21 by the Committee on Economic, Social and Cultural Rights (CESCR) (the United Nations treaty body that is mandated to monitor the ICESCR),[14] in which it acknowledged a right of access to cultural heritage is included within Article 15 of the CESCR.[15] Such recognition is significant given that the protection of cultural heritage has already been for years part of the process of the States-parties' periodic review in relation to Article 15 of the ICESCR – especially the 'promotion of awareness and enjoyment of the cultural heritage of national ethnic groups and minorities and of indigenous peoples'.[16]

At the same time, the United Nations (UN) agenda on disaster relief has been progressively developed[17] and efforts to include the 'cultural dimension' in the disaster agenda multiplied. These efforts have focused primarily on the safeguarding of (tangible) cultural assets. Thanks to expert advocacy,[18] the protection of the latter has even been included in the definition of disasters. Hence, the ILC Draft Articles that were adopted in a second reading in 2016,[19] contrary to those adopted on first reading in 2014,[20] contain references to the destruction of (tangible) heritage. Firstly, the 'large-scale material or environmental damage' that was included by the Commission in the definition of disasters encompasses wide-scale damage not only to property and livelihoods, but also *inter alia* to cultural assets.[21] Secondly, Draft Article 9 on the 'reduction of the risk of disasters' also contains references to cultural heritage, namely the protection of cultural assets of 'persons, businesses, communities and countries'.[22]

The preservation of (individual) 'cultural assets' is also present among the aims of the more recent the *Sendai Framework for Disaster Risk Reduction 2015–2030* (Sendai Framework'):[23]

> [d]isasters, many of which are exacerbated by climate change and which are increasing in frequency and intensity, significantly impede progress towards sustainable development. Evidence indicates that exposure of persons and assets in all countries has increased faster than vulnerability has decreased, thus generating new risks and a steady rise in disaster-related losses, with a significant economic, social, health, *cultural* and environmental impact in the short, medium and long term, especially at the local and community levels.[24]

Likewise, at the European level, cultural heritage is part of the definition of 'disasters'. Council Decision No. 1313/2013 of the European Union establishing the Union Civil Protection Mechanism defines disaster as 'any situation which has or may have a severe impact on people, the environment, or property, including cultural heritage' (Article 4, paragraph 1). Likewise, the *Ethical Principles on Disaster Risk Reduction and People's Resilience* issued by the Council of Europe (CoE) highlight the fact that disasters pose a major threat 'not only to the survival of populations and societies as a whole, but also to the dignity and safety of individuals and to the preservation of the natural, cultural and environmental heritage'.[25]

While still sparse, the importance of such references should not be overlooked. In fact the very term 'disasters' is relatively new in international law and only sporadically referred in the UN human rights law discourse, while even key soft law instruments on disasters omit references to cultural rights. These include documents such as the 2013 Human Rights Council (HRC) Resolution on post-disaster and post-conflict situations (acknowledging that 'the human rights and fundamental freedoms of millions of people around the world are affected in different ways by humanitarian crises, including armed conflict, natural disasters and man-made disasters, as well as during the stages of recovery, relief and rehabilitation');[26] the HRC Resolution on climate change and human rights and;[27] the more recent 2015 UN General Assembly resolution on 'cooperation on humanitarian assistance in the field of natural disasters'.[28]

Cultural heritage and the disaster agenda

The safeguarding of tangible cultural heritage

Several authors have embraced the idea that the legal framework that is applicable in situations of armed conflicts may provide guidance to disaster responses.[29] This means that instruments such as the 1954 Hague Convention (that addresses 'damage to cultural property belonging to any people whatsoever means damage to the cultural heritage of all mankind')[30] and the provisions of the additional Protocols to the Geneva Convention pertaining to cultural property that are applicable in event of armed conflict,[31] could be applicable by analogy also in times of disasters. As long as there is no overlap between the two regimes (i.e. international humanitarian law and the law on disaster management)[32] such application does not seem to be problematic. It is in fact in this spirit that the HRC Advisory Committee report on disaster prevention highlights the need for accountability mechanisms in both situations: 'a human rights-based approach in post-disaster and post-conflict situations emphasizes measurable and enforceable obligations through mechanisms of accountability'.[33] The same approach is adopted by the CESCR Committee that highlights in General Comment No. 21 that cultural heritage should be protected in times of armed conflict and disasters alike.[34]

Furthermore, provided that the cultural property in question fulfils the requirements of 'great importance to the cultural heritage of every people' or that of 'outstanding universal value from the point of view of history, art or science',[35] the legal regime established by the UNESCO World Heritage Convention could be applied.[36] The benefit of such analogy is obvious as States would benefit from the UNESCO protective regime – including therefore technical assistance in the 'identification, protection, conservation, presentation and rehabilitation of the cultural and natural heritage'[37] and international assistance (including therefore cooperation with civil society actors, NGOs and the International Federation of the Red Cross and Red Crescent Societies).[38]

Initiatives for the safeguarding of heritage that are based on soft law rather than binding legal norms may equally be successful. These are typically based upon the concept of 'cultural resilience' in 'cultural built heritage' (CBH)[39] and urban planning.[40] The latter is in fact an important aspect of cultural heritage management and preservation. At international level, the UN 'Making Cities Resilient' campaign addresses issues of local governance and urban risk, while campaigns on safer schools and hospitals have also developed in the context of the UN-Habitat World Urban Campaign 2009–2013.[41] The Hyogo Framework for Action which set the agenda until 2015 was also one of the key references points, referring to the 'Building the Resilience of Nations and Communities to Disasters' and recommending action by various State holders, including local governors.

Cultural identities: intangible heritage and living traditions

Recent legal initiatives on disaster prevention and management reinforce 'culture' as a dimension that shall be taken into account by the international agenda. Such initiatives were first visible at the European level, not only within the EU (for instance, with the aforementioned Union Civil Protection Mechanism), but also within the aforementioned CoE's ethical principles (2011). In enunciating the principles that should be implemented following a disaster, these principles refer not only to 'the protection of property and cultural heritage', but also to the 'preservation of culture, traditions and customs and restoration of the quality of the environment'.[42] Even the 'ceremonies for the dead' should be organized 'in accordance with the respective traditions and religions'.[43]

At the international level, the guidelines adopted by the International Federation of Red Cross (IFRC), known as the 'IDRL Guidelines', provide that disaster relief and initial recovery assistance should be mindful of 'cultural, social and religious customs and traditions'.[44] Likewise, the ILC Draft Articles adopted on second reading in 2016 (ILC Draft Articles 2016), in addressing the protection of human rights in times of disasters, make reference to communities, specifying that the latter have the right to 'have a voice in the planning and execution of risk reduction, response and recovery initiatives'.[45]

Such references are important given that there is nothing on the protection of intangible heritage and livelihoods in disaster scenarios in the UNESCO 2003 Convention for the safeguarding of intangible cultural heritage (ILC Convention). The ILC Convention omits reference to disasters: while discussing Article 17 in relation to heritage 'in need of urgent safeguarding' in particular, the emphasis was placed on the need to safeguard rather than the nature of the threat.[46]

Limiting cultural identities: the example of gender (in)equality in patriarchal and male-dominated societies

Cultural identities (and traditions) however may also need be reformed or even limited – especially when clashing with the preservation of right to life and other rights associated to a people's survival. In these cases, disaster management should point to the need of reform for such cultural traditions, limiting the rights stemming from 'cultural identities'.

A typical example is gender: in patriarchal societies stroke by natural hazards women have significantly less chances to survive than men. The reason is that emergencies involve dynamism and quick decision-making that are only rarely promoted among women within non-liberal cultural (and religious) traditions. In terms of illustration, it is estimated that, in the 1991 cyclone that hit the regions of Chakaria and Kutubdia in Bangladesh, approximately three or four women died for every one man,[47] as many of those women waited for their husbands and other male relatives to return home prior seeking refuge or taking evacuation decisions.[48] The practice of wearing a *sharee* and having long hair have also been factors blamed for increased vulnerability,[49] while the observation that pregnant women are more vulnerable during disasters also acquires significant cultural weight in poor rural areas where at least one out of six women is either pregnant or breastfeeding[50] or where forced and early-age marriages are common practice, justified by cultural and religious norms.[51] Other problematic cultural and religious traditions include the observation of non-flexible religious norms – especially Muslim norms that prescribe that women should veil or entirely cover themselves, or be accompanied by a male family member when in public and requesting permission to leave home (*purdah*). As noted by the Norwegian Refugee Council following the floods in the Sindh province of Pakistan, 'understanding the practice of *purdah* is key if humanitarian organisations are to ensure that women's right to participate in decisions related to their needs is respected and their access to assistance assured'.[52]

Some regional instruments also make explicit reference to the protection of those individuals that are particularly vulnerable during disasters. For instance, the 2009 African Union Convention for the Protection and Assistance of Internally Displaced Persons in Africa (Kampala Convention, Article 1); the 2006 Great Lakes Protocol on the Protection and Assistance to Internally Displaced Persons (Article 1); and the 1990 African Charter on the Rights and Welfare of the Child (Article 23). Furthermore, while discussing the ILC Draft Articles on first reading and particularly Article 6 (in relation to responses to disasters in accordance with humanitarian principles) delegates have highlighted that 'there exist possible divergences, and conflicts among States', *inter alia*, cultural ones, that 'could impede efforts to deliver timely and effective assistance'.[53] The references became explicit in the ILC Draft Articles adopted on second reading, directly pointing to gender inequalities that exist in different cultural contexts.[54]

In contrast, most binding international legal instruments on the matter do not explicitly address these traditions as clashing with the need for humanitarian assistance, neither do they refer to individuals that are 'particularly vulnerable' – as in the case of Article 6 of the ILC Draft Articles. In terms of enforceable instruments in relation to vulnerable individuals, it is only the Disability Convention (CRPD), adopted in the aftermath of Hurricane Katrina, that explicitly invokes natural disasters and the special needs of persons with disabilities.[55] Instruments that protect the rights of women and children for instance do not have provisions aimed at reducing the increased risks and discrimination that they may suffer in times of natural hazards. Likewise, the Convention on the Elimination of All Forms of Discrimination against Women (CEDAW) omits references to situations of emergency during which women may be either more vulnerable targets or discriminated against. The Committee on the Elimination of Discrimination against Women (CommEDAW) has amended this omission only in relation to armed conflict and subsequent forced displacement by issuing General Recommendation No. 30[56] – yet, there has been no particular effort 'to improve women's ability to participate in rescue and recovery efforts and in community based decision making processes following disasters' and other environmental situations.[57] Likewise, the Convention on the Rights of Child (CRC) contains no relevant provision on disasters – even though it refers to contracting parties' obligations in other emergency scenarios (e.g. armed conflicts).[58]

Group rights: indigenous traditional ecological knowledge and disaster management

Extreme climate change-related phenomena striking rural and coastal areas and other types of natural disasters are endangering not only the life of animals and plants, but also indigenous populations.[59] A relevant example is that of indigenous peoples of the Arctic circle who have been – or will be – forced to resettle due to climate change: the region has experienced the highest annual average air temperature over land since the beginning of the 20th century,[60] affecting indigenous peoples of the region such as Inuit, Yupik and Sami. Culture is again directly affected as indigenous livelihoods are largely based on the maintenance of the ecosystem, as well as the specific geo-morphology and climate of the region where they live. Traditional practices such as fishing and hunting will have to be redefined in an urban context, posing a threat for biodiversity.

This said, indigenous peoples' knowledge of the ecosystem (traditional ecological knowledge or TEK) may be a valuable source of risk reduction and reducing vulnerability. This knowledge has been defined by the Arctic Council (2015) as 'a systematic way of thinking and knowing that is elaborated and applied to phenomena across biological, physical, cultural and linguistic systems'.[61] In fact, in many cases, indigenous traditional knowledge related to the environment appears to have a positive impact on appeasing the impact of climate-change related phenomena. This ranges from practices bringing together community members to survival strategies: in Kenya and Uganda for instance, pastoralists such as the Maasai and the Turkana use praying and traditional ceremonies to boost their ability to cope with drought and other natural hazards,[62] while in Indonesia following the floods, traditional practices and ancient societal forms played an important role in bonding among members of the community.[63] In other cases, indigenous TEK proves to be valuable in responses to tropical cyclones: in the case of Vanuatu, for instance, traditional and indigenous communities live in constructions that are mythically believed to resist the force of cyclones when disasters strike (*namakals*).[64]

Bushfires and fire management plans

A good illustration of the role of indigenous traditional knowledge in disaster management is the debate over fire management plans in Australia. Bushfires, whose risks are increasing due to the extensive heat waves throughout the continent, have sparked an interesting controversy which is also an illustration of a 'conflict' between public interests and indigenous cultural rights. Research reveals that fire risk management plans in many parts of Australia – in terms of reparation, response and recovery – are overall inadequate,[65] not only affecting Aboriginal livelihoods, but further having an adverse effect in the atmosphere, allowing the release of larger amounts of greenhouse gas (GHG) emissions. In contrast, fires have a spiritual meaning for many indigenous Australians.[66] Ancient aboriginal knowledge suggests therefore that it would be better to regularly set small fires to break out in controlled savannah areas, in order to prevent larger and uncontrolled ones.[67] At the same time, this could 'improve forest access and increase the size of hunting grounds'. It would be therefore sensible to develop legislation that allows certain peoples to be exempt from fire regulations, while being in line with sustainable environmental management strategies. Aborigines are in fact already exempt from some Australian regulations related to wildlife hunting and wildlife conservation (apart from endangered species), precisely to be able to continue their 'traditional use' of their lands, for the purpose of hunting, fishing and food gathering.[68] The extent to which these exemptions are valid however are still controversial and a matter of control by national jurisdictions.[69]

Tsunamis and knowledge about the marine environment

Likewise, indigenous knowledge could contribute to the understanding of disasters related to the marine environment and ecosystem, particularly tsunamis and underwater earthquakes. For example, studies of indigenous responses to the 2004 Tsunami in the region of the Asia-Pacific suggest that, most indigenous peoples – most strikingly, living in different islands – identified the Tsunami signs and survived it unharmed.[70] Their survival and admirable management of the disaster was attributed to their know-how and 'ancient wisdom about previous tsunamis' that allowed them 'to act in a coordinated manner and reach high ground before the tsunami struck'.[71]

Certainly these results should be read in context (for instance, non-indigenous local populations, contrary to tourists, may equally have knowledge that enables them to identify signs of disasters) as well as in combination with other aspects of indigenous living (for instance, the fact that indigenous home constructions such as *nakamals* or even longhouses and houseboats made with wood or bamboo may not always be earthquake-resistant). In fact, the risk assessment for the various peoples and ultimately the effective disaster management is largely dependent on various factors – including high poverty rates, illiteracy, lack of infrastructure, governance deficits and corruption, as well as ecological and geographical factors (particularly extreme weather conditions related to climate change or a region's geological position and landscape).[72] It is also indicative that research findings on the matter are controversial: in another case study, regarding the 2007 earthquake in the Solomon Islands, Down suggests that indigenous knowledge and local traditions alone are inadequate and that a hybrid approach to risk reduction is very much preferred.[73] No matter where the truth lies, the only certainty is that disregarding cultural identities in times of disasters leads to unsustainable responses.

From 'cultural rights' to 'cultural resilience'

The consideration of disasters in the human rights law discourse has typically held migration and forced displacement as a starting point (especially by invoking the main instrument, the UN Guiding Principles on Internal Displacement),[74] following up with the preservation of social and economic rights (food, shelter, health). The CESCR, in particular, has highlighted that the rights contained in the ICESCR are applicable even in the event of disasters – focusing however primarily on the right to shelter, the right to health and the right to food as well as the right to alleviate hunger.[75]

Over the last few years, however, there has been a shift towards the inclusion of culture in these responses, particularly given the emerging concepts of cultural resilience and human security. This shift has coincided also with the gradually perceptible claims to hold individuals, or even States, or corporations, criminally accountable in the aftermath of a disaster.[76] Hence, in General Comment No. 21, the CESCR has highlighted that the obligations to protect cultural heritage continue during disasters and that 'such obligations include the care, preservation and restoration of historical sites, monuments, works of art and literary works, among others'.[77] Other obligations stemming from the ICESCR may also be particularly relevant during disasters – for instance, those pertaining to minorities and indigenous rights (including land rights and their right to traditional knowledge and expressions)[78] as well as those to 'persons living in poverty'.[79]

Likewise, the FAO Voluntary Guidelines to Support the Progressive Realisation of the Right to Adequate Food provide that food and other types of assistance should be done 'bearing in mind local circumstances, dietary traditions and cultures'.[80] This means that, in safety operations undertaken by emergency management professionals, enough space should be accorded to cultural considerations, including for instance the respect for gender and religious sensitivities and the accommodation of food preferences. Such guidelines are in fact present in voluntary initiatives such as the Sphere strategic plan. The Sphere Humanitarian Charter (2014) in particular suggests concrete ways to provide humanitarian help in a way that considers local and cultural norms. For instance, the Sphere standards suggest that 'projects [should be designed] wherever possible, to accommodate and respect helpful cultural, spiritual and traditional practices regarded as important by local people'.[81]

In addition, cultural resilience is part of three out of four priorities[82] of the *Sendai Framework*:

- Priority 1(d), on the understanding of disaster risk, mandates that States should 'systematically evaluate, record, share and publicly account for disaster losses and understand the economic, social, health, education, environmental and cultural heritage impacts, as appropriate, in the context of event-specific hazard-exposure and vulnerability information'.[83] This means that States should maintain lists to register their cultural losses.
- Priority 3, on 'Investing in disaster risk reduction for resilience', mandates that 'public and private investment in disaster risk prevention and reduction through structural and non-structural measures are essential to enhance the economic, social, health and cultural resilience of persons, communities, countries and their assets, as well as the environment', and goes on explaining that these measures 'are cost-effective and instrumental to save lives, prevent and reduce losses and ensure effective recovery and rehabilitation'. It further provides that States should take measures to 'protect or support the protection of cultural and collecting institutions and other sites of historical, cultural heritage and religious interest'.[84] While there is no further clarification of the meaning of such 'protection' and 'support', the Framework guidelines do explain that 'managing the risk of disasters is aimed at protecting persons and their property, health, livelihoods and productive assets, as well as cultural and environmental assets, while promoting and protecting all human rights, including the right to development'.[85]

- Priority 4, on 'enhancing disaster preparedness for effective responses' and the '*Build Back Better*' methods in recovery, rehabilitation and reconstruction include *Gender Considerations* in Early Warning Systems according to cultural requirements. According to the Framework, to achieve this at a national and local level it is important:

> to invest in, develop, maintain and strengthen people-centred multi-hazard, multi-sectoral forecasting and early warning systems, disaster risk and emergency communications mechanisms, social technologies and hazard-monitoring telecommunications systems; develop such systems through a participatory process; tailor them to the needs of users, including social and cultural requirements, in particular gender.[86]

A 'cultural perspective' of policies in relation to disaster management is also expressly predicted in its guiding principles:

> [d]isaster risk reduction requires an all-of-society engagement and partnership. It also requires empowerment and inclusive, accessible and non-discriminatory participation. . . . A gender, age, disability and cultural perspective should be integrated in all policies and practices, and women and youth leadership should be promoted.[87]

Conclusion

Earthquakes, cyclones, droughts, floods, hurricanes and other issues associated with climate change and El Niño phenomena should no longer be considered the fault of nature alone: human senselessness, supported by large corporations and business interests, play their part in increasing risks. With few exceptions, such disasters strike unfortunately primarily rural or coastal areas where people live in conditions of extreme poverty. While it is by now clear that 'human beings [should be] at the centre of concerns for sustainable development',[88] it is equally clear that these human beings should be protected not as abstract entities but rather within the social and cultural context they live in. An approach to disaster risk reduction and management that excludes the cultural factor therefore is doomed to be an unsustainable one.

However, not all aspects of culture necessarily correspond to cultural rights: several cultural and religious traditions (particularly those enhancing gender inequality) are the reasons for increased vulnerability of women and children in many parts of the world. At the same time, collective cultural rights such as the right of indigenous to maintain and protect their traditional knowledge[89] with respect to the ecosystem could, eventually, provide an excellent input to risk reduction mechanisms. The examples of bushfire management in Australia and the Indian Ocean tsunami demonstrate however that this input has not been sufficiently explored.

Yet, cultural rights – apart perhaps from the right to access and preservation of cultural heritage – are still not considered 'urgent' ones in environmental and humanitarian emergencies. The protection of collective cultural identities in particular and by extension also to living traditions, until now happens through soft law initiatives. It is a positive trend therefore that notions such as cultural resilience have emerged. Both the ILC Draft Articles adopted on second reading (2016) and the Sphere Humanitarian Charter (2014), as well as the 2015–2030 Sendai Framework marked important steps in this respect. The latter in particular has formally introduced the concept of cultural resilience in the disaster discourse – a concept that allows to local governors more flexibility in order to create more sustainable and culturally resistant cities and peoples. Hopefully more such initiatives will follow.

Selected bibliography

M. Companion (ed), *Disaster's Impact on Livelihood and Cultural Survival: Losses, Opportunities* (CRC Press 2015).

M. Kelly, D. Caron and A. Telesetsky (eds), *The International Law of Disaster Relief* (CUP 2014).

A. Riccardi, 'Protection and Safeguard of Cultural Heritage from Risks Connected to Natural and Man-made Disasters' (2014) ILD Working Paper 01.

S. Borelli and F. Lenzerini (eds), *Cultural Heritage, Cultural Rights, Cultural Diversity* (Brill, 2012).

E. Stamatopoulou, *Cultural Rights in International Law* (Martinus Nijhoff Publishers, 2007).

Notes

1 See, on this, S. Hoffman, 'The Worst of Times, the Best of Times: Toward a Model of Cultural Response to Disaster' in O. Smith and S. Hoffman (eds), *The Angry Earth: Disaster in Anthropological Perspective* (Routledge, 2011) 134; B. Phillips, 'Cultural Diversity in Disasters: Sheltering, Housing, and Long-Term Recovery' 11 *International Journal of Mass Emergencies and Disasters* (1993) 99.

2 IFRC, 'World Disasters Report 2014, Focus on Culture and Risk' (2015) 23 ff. and 53, available at www.ifrc.org/Global/Documents/Secretariat/201410/WDR%202014.pdf, accessed on 28 October 2016. Also generally, J. Rhyner, 'Forword' in German Committee for Disaster Reduction – DKKV (ed), *Detecting Disaster Root Causes: A Framework and an Analytic Tool for Practitioners* (DKKV Publication Series, 2012), available at www.preventionweb.net/files/globalplatform/entry_bg_paper~studydetectingdisasterrootcausesweb.pdf, accessed on 12 January 2016 (hereafter DKKV report) 187; K. Cedervall Lauta, 'New Fault Lines? On Responsibility and Disasters' 5 *European Journal of Risk Regulation* (2014) 137–138.

3 Ibid 14.

4 W. Bertrand, 'Haiti: Threatened Cultural Heritage and New Opportunities' 62 *Museum International* (2010) 34–35.

5 IFRC (n. 2) 11; J. McKernan and K. Mulcahy, 'Hurricane Katrina: A Cultural Chernobyl' 38 *Journal of Arts Management, Law, and Society* (2008) 217.

6 C. de Ville de Goyet, 'Stop Propagating Disaster Myths' 9 *Disaster Prevention and Management: An International Journal* (2000) 5, 5. See also generally, World Disasters Report 2014.

7 F. Thomalla, R. Smith and L. Schipper, 'Cultural Aspects of Risk to Environmental Changes and Hazards: A Review of Perspectives' in M. Companion (ed), *Disaster's Impact on Livelihood and Cultural Survival: Losses, Opportunities* (CRC Press, 2015) 13.

8 See the HRC, Resolution on the Protection of Human Rights in Post-Disaster/Post-Conflict Situations, UN Doc. A/HRC/RES/22/16 (2013) and subsequent HRC, Report of the Advisory Committee on 'Final research-based report of the Human Rights Council Advisory Committee on best practices and main challenges in the promotion and protection of human rights in post-disaster and post-conflict situations', UN Doc. A/HRC/28/76 (2015) paras 44 ff. Also D. Cubie and M. Hesselman, 'Accountability for the Human Rights Implications of Natural Disasters: A Proposal for Systemic International Oversight' 33 *Netherlands Quarterly of Human Rights* (2015) 9, 11.

9 See, as an indication, J. Symonides, 'Cultural Rights, A Neglected Category of Rights' in J. Symonides (ed), *Human Rights: Concepts and Standards* (UNESCO, 1998) 560.

10 E. Stamatopoulou, 'Right to Take Part in Cultural Life' (article 15 (1) (a) of the Covenant), Background paper submitted to the CESCR, E/C.12/40/9 (9 May 2008) and generally, S. Borelli and F. Lenzerini (eds), *Cultural Heritage, Cultural Rights, Cultural Diversity* (Brill, 2012); E. Stamatopoulou, *Cultural Rights in International Law* (Martinus Nijhoff Publishers, 2007).

11 ICESCR, art 2 para 2. See also the relevant discussion the HRC, Report of the Special Rapporteur on the issue of human rights obligations relating to the enjoyment of a safe, clean, healthy and sustainable environment, UN Doc. A/HRC/31/52 (2016) para 47.

12 According to Merriam-Webster dictionary, 'disasters' are 'something (such as a flood, tornado, fire, plane crash, etc.) that happens suddenly and causes much suffering or loss to many people'.

13 ICESCR, art 15:

> 1. The States Parties to the present Covenant recognize the right of everyone: (a) To take part in cultural life; (b) To enjoy the benefits of scientific progress and its applications; (c) To benefit from the protection of the moral and material interests resulting from any scientific, literary or artistic production of which he is the author.

14 CESCR, General Comment No. 21, Right of Everyone to Take Part in Cultural Life, UN Doc. E/C.12/GC/21 (2009).

15 Ibid para 15 (b), in which the CESCR flagged that the right to participate in cultural life contains three key components, namely: participation in, access to, and contribution to cultural life. As the Committee points out, 'access to culture' encompasses 'the right of everyone . . . to know and understand his or her own culture and that of others through education and information, and to receive quality education and training with due regard for cultural identity' and further, a right 'to benefit from the cultural heritage and the creation of other individuals and communities'. See also the relevant HRC, Report of the Independent Expert in the Field of Cultural Rights, UN Doc. A/HRC/17/38 (2011).

16 A. Yupsanis, 'The Meaning of "Culture" in Article 15 (1)(a) of the ICESCR – Positive Aspects of CESCR's General Comment No. 21 for the Safeguarding of Minority Cultures' 55 *German Yearbook of International Law* (2012) 345, 359 and ftn 76.

17 Including by the establishment of the UNISDR, following UNGA Res 56/195 on the 'International Strategy for Disaster Reduction' and that of the 'intergovernmental expert working group on indicators and terminology relating to disaster risk reduction' are two institutions maintaining key roles within this context.

18 The ILC Special Rapporteur on Disasters, Eduardo Valencia-Ospina for instance has pointed to a dimension of cultural rights that includes cultural cooperation. See, ILC Report of the 66th Session (2014), Chapter VII on the Protection of persons in the event of disasters, UN Doc. A/65/10 (Draft Articles with commentary of the ILC Special Rapporteur on Disasters, Mr Eduardo Valencia-Ospina, hereafter ILC draft articles (2014)), adopted by the ILC Drafting Committee at its 66th Session (2014) on first reading and presented at the UNGA on 15 May 2014, UN Doc. A/CN.4/L.831, available at http://legal.un.org/ilc/reports/2014/ at 316, para 309 (presented at the UNGA A/69/10) 309 (while discussing ILC draft art 5 in relation to the duty to cooperate).

19 ILC, Report of the 68th Session (2016), UN Doc. A/71/10 (2016) 23, section 9, Chapter IV on the 'Protection of persons in the event of disasters'.

20 See draft art 3 of the ILC Draft Articles 2014 (n. 18). Cf. also IFRC, Guidelines for the Domestic Facilitation and Regulation of International Disaster Relief and Initial Recovery Assistance (or 'International Disaster Response Laws, Rules and Principles'), adopted by the IFRC on 30 November 2007 (IDRL Guidelines), available at www.ifrc.org/PageFiles/126924/A-CN.4-L.831.pdf, accessed on 10 June 2016.

21 Ibid Draft art 3: 'Use of Terms' and Commentary on art 3, subparagraph (a), 24 (9).

22 Ibid Draft art 9: 'Reduction of the risk of disasters', at 43 and Commentary on art 9, 43 (3).

23 The 'Sendai Framework for Disaster Risk Reduction' (2015–2030), Sandai (Japan) 24–25 June 2015 was adopted following the World Conference on Disaster Risk Reduction, Sandai (Japan) (14–18 March 2015), available at www.unisdr.org/we/coordinate/sendai-framework.

24 Ibid 10 ff. See also J. Fromageau, 'Cultural Heritage and Natural Disasters', intervention at the Sendai World conference on Disasters, 14 March 2015.

25 CoE, 'Ethical Principles on Disaster Risk Reduction and People's Resilience', available at www.coe.int/t/dg4/majorhazards/ressources/pub/Ethical-Principles-Publication_EN.pdf, Introduction, 13.

26 See UN Doc. A/HRC/RES/22/16 (n. 8).

27 HRC, Resolution 32/33, Human Rights and Climate Change, UN Doc. A/HRC/RES/32/33 (2016).

28 See especially UNGA, Res 69/243, UN Doc. A/RES/69/243 (2015).

29 See for instance ILC, Eighth report of the ILC Special Rapporteur on Disasters, Eduardo Valencia-Ospina, 68th session of the ILC, UN Doc. A/CN.4/697 (2016), available at http://legal.un.org/docs/?symbol=A/CN.4/697; D. Cubie, 'Clarifying the Acquis Humanitaire: A Transnational Legal Perspective on the Internalization of Humanitarian Norms' in M. Kelly, D. Caron and A. Telesetsky (eds), *The International Law of Disaster Relief* (Cambridge University Press, 2014) 338; Cubie and Hesselman (n. 8) 9. See also, A. Riccardi, 'Protection and Safeguard of Cultural Heritage from Risks Connected to Natural and Man-Made Disasters' 1 *ILD Working Paper* (2014) 5, available at http://disasterlaw.sssup.it/?page_id=314, accessed on 28 October 2016.

30 Hague Convention for the Protection of Cultural Property in the Event of Armed Conflict (adopted on 14 May 1954, entered into force 7 August 1956) 249 UNTS 240, Preamble.

31 Protocol Additional to the Geneva Conventions of 12 August 1949, and Relating to the Protection of Victims of International Armed Conflicts (adopted 12 December 1977, entered into force 7 December 1978) 1125 UNTS 3, art 53 ('Protection of Cultural Objects and Places of Worship') and art 16.

32 The former would be *lex specialis* in relation to the latter. On the interrelation between the two, see also Commentary on the ILC Draft Articles (n. 20) in relation to arts 3 ('Use of Terms'), 4 ('Human Dignity') and 6 ('Humanitarian principles').

33 See UN Doc. A/HRC/28/76 (n. 17) 11, para 40.
34 CESCR, General Comment No. 21 (n. 14) 19, para 50: 'States have the obligation to respect and protect cultural heritage in all its forms, in times of war and peace, and natural disasters'.
35 UNESCO Convention for the Protection of the World Cultural and Natural Heritage (adopted 16 November 1972, entered into force 17 December 1975) 1037 UNTS 152, art 1.
36 See, on this, also Riccardi (n. 29) 6.
37 UNESCO World Heritage Convention, art 23.
38 Ibid.
39 See e.g. J. MacKee and H. Haugen Askland, 'Recovering Cultural Built Heritage after Natural Disasters a Resilience Perspective' 5 *International Journal of Disaster Resilience in the Built Environment* (2014) 202.
40 See the UNESCO's Venice Declaration, for instance, adopted at the international Conference on Building Cities Resilience to Disasters in Europe: Protecting Cultural Heritage and Adapting to Climate Change, available at http://whc.unesco.org/en/news/869, accessed on 28 October 2016.
41 UNISDR and UN-Habitat, Making Cities Resilient, World Urban Campaign (2009–2013).
42 Ibid 32, 'The ethical principles applied after disasters', Principle 3: 'Protection of economic, social and cultural rights', section 1:

> Efforts to secure respect for [economic, social and cultural rights] should give priority to the right to medical and psychological assistance, education, protection of property and the cultural heritage, housing and means of subsistence, preservation of culture, traditions and customs and restoration of the quality of the environment.

Cf. also HRC, Advisory Committee Report, UN Doc. A/HRC/28/76 (n. 17) paras 76–77 entitled 'Respect for cultural values'.

43 Ibid Principle 3, section 2.
44 IDRL Guidelines (n. 20), art 4 para 3 (d); see also, the subsequent UNGA Resolutions, namely UNGA, Res. 63/139, 63/141, and 63/137 (2008), encouraging States to follow them.
45 Ibid Draft art 5: 'Human Rights', 31 and Commentary on art 5, 32 (6). See also the Sendai Framework (n. 23) paras 5–6.
46 See generally J. Blake, *International Cultural Heritage Law* (Oxford University Press, 2015).
47 See E. Ferris, 'How Can International Human Rights Law Protect Us from Disasters?' Paper prepared for the American Society of International Law, Annual Meeting, 10 April 2014 (2014) 11, ftn 29.
48 M. Rashid and H. Shafie, 'Gender and Social Exclusion Analysis' in R. Shaw, F. Mallick and A. Islam (eds), *Disaster Risk Reduction Approaches in Bangladesh* (Springer, 2013) 353.
49 Ibid.
50 WHO, 'Escalating Crisis in Ethiopia: 2 Million Children and Mothers Face Malnutrition and Disease', available at www.who.int/hac/crises/eth/appeal/december2015/en/, accessed on 12 January 2016.
51 On child marriages, see e.g. S. Syed, 'The Impact of Islamic Law on the Implementation of the Convention on the Rights of the Child: The Plight of Non-Marital Children under Shari'a' 6 *The International Journal of Children's Rights* (1998) 359–393.
52 Norwegian Refugee Council, Briefing paper on flood-displaced women in Sindh Province, Pakistan, Nansen Conference on Climate Change and Displacement in the 21st Century, Oslo, 5–7 June 2011 (2011) 5. See also generally, S. Bradshaw and M. Fordham, 'Women, Girls and Disasters, A Review for the UK's Department for International Development' in *DFID* (2 August 2013), available at www.gov.uk/government/uploads/. . ./women-girls-disasters.pdf, accessed on 12 January 2016.
53 See ILC Draft Articles (n. 18) 316, para 309.
54 See ILC Draft Articles (n. 19) 36 (commentary on art 6).
55 See Convention on the Rights of Persons with Disabilities (adopted 13 December 2006, entered into force 3 May 2008) 2515 UNTS 3, art 11: 'States Parties shall take . . . all necessary measures to ensure the protection and safety of persons with disabilities in situations of risk, including situations of armed conflict, humanitarian emergencies and the occurrence of natural disasters.' Likewise, UNGA, Res 69/243, UN Doc. A/RES/69/243 (2015) affirms that 'persons with disabilities, older persons, women and children are disproportionately affected in natural disasters.'
56 CommEDAW, General recommendation No. 30 on women in conflict prevention, conflict and post-conflict situations, UN Doc. CEDAW/C/GC/30 (2013).
57 See e.g. F. Acar and G. Ege, 'Women's Human Rights in Disaster Contexts: How Can CEDAW help?' (25 October 2001), UN CEDAW< EGM/NATDIS/2001/EP.4, 3. See also CommEDAW, Statement of the CEDAW Committee on Gender and Climate Change, 44th session, New York (20 July–7 August 2009).

58 See Convention on the Rights of the Child (adopted 20 November 1989, entered into force 2 September 1990) 1577 UNTS 3, arts 38–39.
59 T. Bamforth, 'The Social Impact of Typhoon Bopha on Indigenous Communities, Livelihoods, and Conflict in Mindanao' in *Disaster's Impact on Livelihood* (n. 10) (discussing the cultural impact of the typhoon Bopha in the Philippines).
60 National Oceanic and Atmospheric Administration (NOAA), *Arctic Report Card 2015* (2015), available at www.arctic.noaa.gov/reportcard/ArcticReportCard_full_report.pdf, accessed on 10 January 2016.
61 Ibid 83.
62 Thomalla, Smith and Schipper (n. 10) 13.
63 In the example at hand, the research referred to the traditional Javanese practise of *gotong royong* ('mutual help'). *Gotong royong* stems from 'traditional concepts of community members', village leadership practices, religious beliefs and other social and cultural practices – such as the position of the persons affected within the family structure. See H. Taylor and R. Peace, 'Children and Cultural Influences in a Natural Disaster: Flood Response in Surakarta, Indonesia' 13 *International Journal of Disaster Risk Reduction* (2015) 76, 79. See also G. Nugroho Adi and S. Susanto, 'Floods Swamp Homes in Surakarta, Yogyakarta' *The Jakarta Post* (24 April 2015), available at www.thejakartapost.com/news/2015/04/24/floods-swamp-homes-surakarta-yogyakarta.html, accessed on 10 January 2015. On the *goton royong* see J.R. Bowen, 'On the Political Construction of Tradition: Gotong Royong in Indonesia' 45 *The Journal of Asian Studies* (1985) 545, 545.
64 See B. Laboukly and A. Takahashi, 'Post Disaster Needs Assessment of Vanuatu ICH Following Tropical Cyclone Pam' *ICH Courier*, available at http://ichcourier.ichcap.org/en/post-disaster-needs-assessment-of-vanuatu-ich-following-tropical-cyclone-pam/, accessed on 1 November 2016; see also the UNESCO Intergovernmental Committee, File No. 01214, Request for International Assistance from the Intangible Cultural Heritage Fund (22 April 2015) 5, available at www.unesco.org/culture/ich/en/assistances/safeguarding-indigenous-vernacular-architecture-and-building-knowledge-in-vanuatu-01214, accessed on 28 October 2016.
65 See e.g. P. Laidlaw, D. Spennemann and C. Allan, 'Protecting Cultural Assets from Bushfires: A Question of Comprehensive Planning' *Overseas Development Institute* (2007) 66, 71.
66 See S. Heckbert, J. Russell-Smith, A. Reeson and G. James, 'Indigenous Australians Fight Climate Change with Fire' 2 *Solutions* (2001) 50, 56; J. Bradley, 'Working on Country: Contemporary Indigenous Management of Australia's Landsand Coastal Regions' in R. Baker, J. Davies and E. Young (eds), *Landscapes of the Mind, Landscapes of the Spirit: Negotiating a Sentient Landscape* (Oxford University Press, 2001). Also, D. Adam, 'Australian Firestorms Prompt Call to Return to Aboriginal Bush Control' *The Guardian* (9 February 2009), available at www.theguardian.com/environment/2009/feb/09/fire-australia-aborigine, accessed on 10 January 2016.
67 See D. Strain, 'Aboriginal Hunting and Burning Increase Australia's Desert Biodiversity, Researchers Find', available at www.sciencedaily.com/releases/2010/05/100503174030.htm, accessed on 10 January 2016 (regarding the practices of the Martu people in the Australian Western desert-based on research undertaken by Stanford University).
68 See D. Sweenay, 'Fishing, Hunting and Gathering Rights of Aboriginal Peoples in Australia' 16 *UNSW Law Journal* (1993) 97, 100.
69 Ibid 130.
70 See M. Lauer, 'Oral Traditions or Situated Practices? Understanding How Indigenous Communities Respond to Environmental Disasters' 71 *Human Organization* (2012) 176.
71 Ibid.
72 See this complexity in the example of the 2010 earthquake in Haiti, for instance at DKKV Report (n. 2) 11.
73 Ibid 184.
74 Guiding Principles on Internal Displacement, UN Doc. No. E/CN.4/1998/53/Add.2 (1998). See D. Fisher, 'Legal Implementation of Human Rights Obligations to Prevent Displacement Due to Natural Disasters' 1 *Stud. Transnational Legal Policy* (2010) 551, 552; UNESCO, *World Heritage and Cultural Diversity* (German Commission for UNESCO, 2010).
75 CESCR, General Comment No. 4: The Right to Adequate Housing (Art. 11(1) of the Covenant), UN Doc. E/1992/23 (1991); CESCR, General Comment No. 12: The Right to Adequate Food (Art. 11 of the Covenant), UN Doc. E/C.12/1999/5 (1999), in relation to the right to food; CESCR, General Comment No. 14: The Right to the Highest Attainable Standard of Health, UN Doc. E/C.12/2000/4 (2000), in relation to the right to health. See Fisher (n. 74) 556; Cubie and Hesselman (n. 8) 9, 11 and 20.
76 On State accountability from a criminal law perspective, see for instance A. van Aaken and I. Wildhaber, 'State Liability and Critical Infrastructure: A Comparative and Functional Analysis' 2 *European Journal*

of Risk Regulation (2015) 244; *The International Law of Disaster Relief* (n. 33); P. Green, 'Disaster by Design: Corruption, Construction and Catastrophe' 45 *British Journal of Criminology* (2005) 528 (focusing on the earthquakes in Turkey and arguing that it is important to develop 'a political criminology of natural disasters . . . which involves an acknowledgment of State organizational deviance as central to future mitigation strategies'); P. Green and T. Ward, *State Crime: Governments, Violence and Corruption* (Pluto Press, 2004) 52 ff.

77 *Supra* n 39. See also the report prepared by *pro bono* legal experts for the Independent Expert on the issue of human rights obligations relating to the enjoyment of a safe, clean, healthy and sustainable environment in J. Knox, *Mapping Human Rights Obligations Relating to the Enjoyment of a Safe, Clean, Healthy and Sustainable Environment*, Individual Report on the International Covenant on Economic, Social and Cultural Rights (December 2013).

78 Ibid paras 36–7 and also 56.

79 Ibid paras 38–9.

80 D. Fisher, 'Domestic Regulation of International Humanitarian Relief in Disasters and Armed Conflict: A Comparative Analysis' 89 *IRRC* (2007) 345, 347 referring to paragraph 16.6 of FAO, Voluntary Guidelines to Support the Progressive Realisation of the Right to Adequate Food in the Context of National Food Security, reprinted in the Report of the Intergovernmental Working Group for the Elaboration of a Set of Voluntary Guidelines to Support the Progressive Realization of the Right to Adequate Food in the Context of National Food Security, Rome, September 23, 2004, FAO Doc. No. CL 127/10-Sup.1, annex 2 (2004).

81 See T. Kabau and S. Ali, 'A Human Rights-Based Approach to the Global Regulation of Humanitarian Relief: The Emerging Obligation to Incorporate Local Participation' 40 *Brooklyn Journal of International Law* (2015) 791, 819–21 (discussing the Sphere project).

82 The Sendai Framework sets four priorities: (i) understanding disaster risk; (ii) strengthening disaster risk governance to manage disaster risk (for prevention, mitigation, preparedness, response, recovery and rehabilitation); (iii) investing in disaster reduction for resilience and; and (iv) enhancing disaster preparedness for effective response.

83 Sendai Framework (n. 23) 18, para 29.

84 Ibid 18, paras 29 and 30(d).

85 Guiding principles with regard to Priority 3, 19(d)(g).

86 Ibid 21, para 33(b).

87 Sendai Framework (n. 23) 19(c) and (d).

88 UN Conference on Environment and Development, Report of the United Nations Conference on Environment and Development, Rio de Janeiro, UN Doc. A/CONF.151/26 (Vol. I) (3–14 June 1992) Principle 1.

89 This right has been recognized by the UN Declaration on the Rights of Indigenous Peoples (UNDRIP), particularly art 31(1) that proclaims indigenous peoples' right to maintain, protect and develop their traditional knowledge, traditional expressions and intangible cultural heritage (as well as the right to benefit from the corresponding IP rights).

PART IV

Protection of vulnerable groups in disaster settings

18

A HUMAN RIGHTS-BASED VULNERABILITY PARADIGM

Lessons from the case of displaced women in post-quake Haiti

Ingrid Nifosi-Sutton

Introduction

In this essay, I focus on the vulnerability of disaster-affected persons as conceptualised by the United Nations (UN) Committee on Economic, Social and Cultural Rights (CESCR or the Committee), the body that monitors State parties compliance with the 1966 UN International Covenant on Economic, Social and Cultural Rights (ICESCR or the Covenant). I apply the Committee's vulnerability paradigm to the housing situation of internally displaced women in post-quake Haiti. I contend and show that implementation of the paradigm leads to robust legal protection of persons affected by disasters (especially those that are most destructive) and, by extension, more effective disaster management. My essay builds upon a study of mine which explores the practice of UN and regional human rights monitoring bodies relevant to the protection of vulnerable groups.[1] My essay is a continuation of this investigation in the sense that it further canvasses the vulnerability of disaster victims as elaborated by the CESCR, applies it to a post-disaster setting, and underscores its added analytical and operational value *qua* disaster management tool that revolves around human rights protection of persons affected by disasters.

I develop my analysis in four main parts. First, I describe the housing situation of internally displaced women (IDP women) in post-quake Haiti. Since Haiti has ratified the ICESCR in October 2013, my essay specifically and exclusively focuses on governmental efforts aimed at providing housing to IDP women between 2014 and 2015. I deal with IDP women because they constitute more than half of the disaster victims internally displaced by the 2010 earthquake, and because their predicament is particularly suitable to illustrate the complexity of the notion of disaster victims' vulnerability developed by the CESCR. I appraise this notion and its far-reaching legal consequences, as largely elaborated by the Committee in General Comment No. 4 on the right to adequate housing, in the second part of this essay. There I also explore conceptualisation of vulnerability set out in General Comment No. 7 on forced evictions. General Comment No. 7 features in this essay since the prohibition of forced evictions is a fundamental component of the right to adequate housing and because these phenomena, as I show below, have greatly affected Haitian IDP women. I apply the vulnerability paradigm to the housing situation of Haitian IDP women in the third part of this chapter. Based on this exercise, I conclude by emphasising the added value of the CESCR's vulnerability paradigm, and arguing that it should be implemented in the most devastating disaster situations that may affect State parties to the ICESCR.

The housing situation of internally displaced women in post-quake Haiti

The earthquake that struck southern Haiti at the beginning of 2010 destroyed housing of more than 2 million Haitians. Once rendered homeless, a significant number of these persons moved to the metropolitan area of Port-au-Prince where they were housed in camps for Internally Displaced Persons (IDPs). The International Organization for Migration (IOM) estimated that, in the immediate aftermath of the earthquake, there were more than 1.3 million IDPs and that more than 50% of them were women.[2]

The Government of Haiti has adopted various measures to provide housing to the staggering number of IDP women. These measures form part of the overall governmental strategy to address the plight of IDPs in general and include rental subsidies and transitional shelters.

As explained by Amnesty International, the Haitian government has resorted to rental subsidies mainly because by January 2012 about 78% of the people who were still living in IDPs camps had lived in rental accommodations before the earthquake and did not have enough financial means to rent a new house or apartment.[3] Authorities made it plain that the subsidies were not aimed at providing IDPs, including IDP women and their households, with permanent housing. The subsidies were rather meant to restore families, who did not own housing before the earthquake, to a situation similar to the one they were in before the disaster. As governmental officials have put it, the subsidies were meant to 'buy each family some time to help themselves'.[4]

The way the rental subsidy policy works is by giving IDPs living in camps, including IDP women and their households, US$ 500 to pay their rent for 1 year and a smaller amount of money to cover transportation costs. If, after 6 to 8 weeks these persons are still living in the same place, they can receive an additional grant of US$ 125.[5]

A 2014 report published by the IOM and the Brookings Institution and the report of the former Special Rapporteur on the Rights of IDPs, Chaloka Beyani, on his summer 2014 visit to Haiti, have highlighted problems associated with the rental subsidy policy. These documents have denounced that: (a) a significant number of IDPs who benefited from the policy, including IDP women, could not afford paying for rent after the subsidies ended,[6] and (b) as of June 2014, a quarter of camps for IDPs were reoccupied as the result of the return of 'at least 78 per cent of IDPs [including IDP women among them] who, after a year of enjoying rental subsidies, were unable to continue paying their rent'.[7] Moreover, the rental policy did not incorporate elements enabling IDPs in general, and IDP women in particular, to go on with their lives such as the restoration of livelihoods and job opportunities.[8]

Transitional shelters built with significant donor investments are another way through which the housing situation of IDPs has been tackled. Transitional shelters are small dwellings with metallic roofs and frames made of timber, bamboo or steel. They are meant to provide housing solutions for a period of time varying between 3 and 5 years.[9] As Amnesty International has noticed, these shelters 'offer better protection than emergency shelters and can be built much more quickly than permanent houses'.[10]

Problematic aspects have however arisen. Due to difficulties in finding sites that offered security of tenure, the shelters benefited only families who owned land or were in areas 'where secure land was available'.[11] Additionally, concerns have been voiced that the construction of the shelters has been three times more expensive than the expected costs and that it has caused authorities to lose focus on finding permanent housing solutions.[12]

Widespread arbitrary evictions have exacerbated the housing situation of IDP women and their households. The occurrence of these phenomena is well documented by human rights NGOs, the Inter-American Commission on Human Rights, the Special Rapporteur on the rights of IDPs and human rights lawyers.[13]

Evictions have been carried out by State officials and private individuals. State officials have been directly involved in the eviction of around 500 IDP families living in the camp called Camp Teleco Sans Fil when, on 8 August 2015, they closed and demolished the camp. The eviction was the result of competent authorities' decision to allocate rental subsidies to the IDPs living in Camp Teleco Sans Fil. However, the 500 families that were evicted were found ineligible for the subsidies, and on 5 August 2014, they were given 3 days to leave the camp. The families lost all their belongings in the eviction.[14] According to Amnesty International, the families were found ineligible for the rental subsides because they did not appear at unannounced verification visits in 2010 and 2014, the periods of time in which the subsidies were assigned.[15]

Amnesty International also reported that, on 11 January 2015, a fire destroyed the makeshift shelters of Camp Comité du Peuple Progressiste.[16] The IDPs housed there lost not only their shelters but also all their belongings.[17] What is more, three people died in the fire.[18] Some of the IDPs interviewed by Amnesty said that the fire was the result of arson. They further corroborated this point by stating that a few days before the fire a man, who claimed to be the landowner, visited the camp with police officers and made clear that the camp would be destroyed if the IDPs did not leave.[19] Law enforcement officials reported the destruction of the camp, and a Haitian human rights organisation filed a complaint on behalf of the IDPs. As documented by Amnesty International, as of 2015 no thorough investigation had been conducted.[20]

The CESCR and disaster victims' vulnerability

Scholars have amply demonstrated that the CESCR is particularly concerned with vulnerable groups and that this concern informs its overall monitoring activity of State compliance with the ICESCR. The Committee usually refers to vulnerable groups by using the formula: 'vulnerable or marginalized and disadvantaged groups'. Advancing the human rights of these persons is a recurring theme of the Committee's Concluding Observations on periodic reports that State parties to the ICESCR submit to detail what they have done to implement the Covenant rights domestically. By the same token, the Committee discusses the predicament of vulnerable or marginalised and disadvantaged groups, as well as pertinent State obligations, in its General Comments on the scope and import of various provisions of the Covenant.[21]

Unsurprisingly, disaster victims feature among those groups that the Committee regards as vulnerable or disadvantaged. Sufficient for the purposes of this essay is recognition that the Committee labeled disaster victims as a disadvantaged group in General Comment No. 4 of 1991 on the right to adequate housing as implied in paragraph 1 of Article 11 of the ICESCR, setting out the right to an adequate standard of living.[22] In paragraph 8(e) on housing accessibility, the Committee makes clear that, under the ICESCR, disadvantaged groups must be accorded *full and sustainable* access to adequate housing resources. Such groups include, among others, the elderly, children, persons with disabilities and victims of natural disasters. The relevant State obligation is detailed in paragraph 11: it necessitates giving priority consideration to the above groups in the housing sphere through housing legislation and policy. Other groups that the Committee deems to experience particular problems in the field of housing are enumerated in paragraph 13, i.e. the homeless, those who have inadequate housing, those living in 'illegal' settlements, those subject to forced evictions and low-income groups. The above groups are characterised as 'vulnerable and disadvantaged with regard to housing'.

It has been maintained that the Committee's conceptualisation of vulnerable groups is unclear since the Committee does not conclusively determine whether these groups are vulnerable because they are discriminated against or whether these groups are discriminated against because they are vulnerable.[23] With a view to offering an alternative view, I submit that, taken together, paragraphs 8(e) and 13 indicate that the notions of disadvantage and vulnerability appear to coincide. The Committee uses them interchangeably to refer to groups that do not have access to adequate housing on an equal basis with other individuals in comparable situations. Stated differently, the Committee's notion of vulnerability and disadvantage is predicated upon lack of equal and full enjoyment of the right to adequate housing. Furthermore, I take the view that the Committee appears to implicitly suggest that vulnerability to discrimination in the enjoyment of the right to adequate housing is due to certain factors such as age, disability and socio-economic condition.

Based on the above construction of paragraphs 8(e) and 13, for the purposes of the Committee's practice, disaster victims are vulnerable and disadvantaged (hereafter vulnerable) in so far as they do not have access to adequate housing, owing to the widespread damage that powerful natural disasters typically cause to structures and buildings of affected areas, on an equal footing with persons living in regions of the affected State that have not been struck by these emergencies. Powerful natural disasters generate vulnerability because they give rise to *de facto* discrimination in the enjoyment of the right to adequate housing. Persons whose housing has been destroyed or severely damaged by a powerful disaster find themselves in a factual predicament whereby they are deprived of the right to adequate housing to a greater extent than those individuals living in areas that the disaster has spared.

Analysis of General Comments adopted after 1991 corroborate the above interpretations: they yield the conclusion that factors generating unequal enjoyment of rights for vulnerable or marginalised and disadvantaged groups correspond to, or are implied in, the internationally prohibited grounds of discrimination the Committee examines in General Comment No. 20. This Comment deals with paragraph 2 of Article 2 of the ICESCR on the principle of non-discrimination. Prohibited discrimination grounds enumerated in paragraph 2 of Article 2 include race, color, sex, language, religion, political or other opinion, national or social origin, property, birth or other status. Prohibited grounds the Committee has read into the ground 'other status' encompass, although they are not limited to: disability, age and socio-economic situation.[24]

In light of paragraph 34 of Comment No. 20, being affected by natural disasters can be deemed to be a ground that falls under the chapeau of 'place of residence', implied in the expressly listed ground 'other status', as such emergencies typically strike certain regions and areas of a State and may, depending on their severity, make it difficult, if not impossible, for disaster victims to enjoy ESCR, including the right to adequate housing, on an equal basis with individuals living in unaffected areas.

Furthermore, unequal enjoyment of rights for vulnerable or marginalised and disadvantaged groups can also be triggered by the intersectionality of more than one of the prohibited grounds falling within the scope of paragraph 2 of Article 2. In this case, the vulnerability of the persons concerned will be compounded and layered, and indicative that, within vulnerable or marginalised and disadvantaged groups, there are persons who are more vulnerable, disadvantaged, and marginalised than other group members because they experience multiple forms of discrimination preventing them from adequately enjoying ESCR.[25]

Implications of the vulnerability of disaster victims flowing from General Comment No. 4

As set forth in paragraph 11 of General Comment No. 4, the vulnerability of disaster victims does not merely describe their predicament. It has important legal ramifications. It primarily requires giving priority consideration to their housing situation through housing law and policy. One can understand the concrete import of such obligation in light of the State obligation to fulfil/provide spelled out in other General Comments of the CESCR. Specifically, in the General Comments on the rights to food and water, the Committee has unequivocally affirmed that the obligation to fulfil/provide requires State parties to the ICESCR to directly provide the rights to water and food to disaster victims due to the magnitude of the deprivation of these rights that they typically experience.[26] That the obligation to provide is part of the normative content of the right to adequate housing is indirectly borne out by paragraph 10 of General Comment No. 3 on the nature of State obligations under paragraph 1 of Article 2 of the ICESCR. The Committee makes it clear that 'a State party in which any significant number of individuals is deprived of . . . basic shelter and housing . . . is, *prima facie*, failing to discharge its [core] obligations under the Covenant'. Core obligations are duties State parties to the Covenant are expected to implement as a matter of priority 'to ensure the satisfaction of, at the very least, minimum essential levels of each of the [Covenant] rights'.[27] Interpreting paragraph 10, *a contrario*, and taking into account the importance of core obligations, one infers that where a significant number of individuals are homeless, State parties to the Covenant have to urgently implement measures aimed at putting an end to such an extreme deprivation of adequate housing, including by directly providing adequate housing.

Thus, construing the State obligation flowing from the vulnerability of disaster victims under the terms of paragraph 11 of General Comment No. 4 in light of paragraph 10 of General Comment No. 3, it follows that State parties to the Covenant have to give priority consideration to homeless disaster victims by directly providing the right to adequate housing through adoption and implementation of relevant laws and policies. These measures should form part of a general housing policy which aims at progressively realising the right to adequate housing of disaster victims by providing them with temporary housing for a certain period of time and replacing it thereafter with permanent housing. Progressive realisation of economic, social and cultural rights, including the right to adequate housing, is foreseen under the ICESCR provided that, as the Committee has put it, State parties comply with the 'obligation to move as expeditiously and effectively as possible'[28] towards the full realisation of the Covenant rights. Provisions of temporary housing to disaster victims that is progressively upgraded or that is replaced with permanent housing would satisfy the above obligation.

It also is noteworthy that, in paragraph 12 of General Comment No. 4, the Committee asserts that State Parties to the ICESCR have to adopt a national housing strategy which should 'reflect extensive genuine consultation with, and participation by, all those affected, including the homeless, the inadequately housed and their representatives'.[29] By mentioning the homeless and the inadequately housed, the Committee is positively referring to the vulnerable groups enumerated in paragraphs 8(e) and 13 of General Comment No. 4, including disaster victims. Consequently, where State parties to the ICESCR have been struck by a natural disaster that has generated homelessness, competent authorities will have to adopt a housing policy in consultation with affected persons or their representatives, and give them a real opportunity to have a say on it. The relevance of disaster victims' informed participation in the development of disaster response strategies is further borne out by Rolnik's contribution to this volume.

Moreover, paragraph 13 of General Comment No. 4 sets forth an additional State obligation relevant to the vulnerability of disaster victims: as the Committee puts it, paragraph 1 of

Article 11 of the ICESCR requires States parties 'either alone or on the basis of international cooperation' to monitor the situation of the right to housing and to do whatever necessary to determine the extent of homelessness and inadequate housing.

But what is the right to adequate housing about? In General Comment No. 4, the Committee maintains that right to adequate housing, as contained in the ICESCR, is quite a complex entitlement predicated on human dignity and the scope of which goes far beyond the notion of having a roof on one's head.[30] As the Committee has beautifully put it, the right to housing is 'the right to live somewhere in security, peace and dignity'.[31] The Committee goes on to illustrate the concrete meaning of this wording when explaining the import of housing adequacy. In its view the fundamental notion of adequacy is made up of certain essential elements that State parties to the Covenant must take into account 'in any particular context', including, therefore, when formulating and implementing policies conducive to access to housing for disaster victims.[32] Elements that are considered here include affordability, security of tenure and accessibility.

Affordability refers to the economic dimension of housing and necessitates that housing costs should be commensurate to income levels.[33] It also implies that tenants should be protected against unreasonable rent increases.[34] Security of tenure takes various forms, including rental (public and private) accommodation, and also protects from arbitrary eviction and harassment.[35] In the Committee's view, State parties to the ICESCR should take immediate steps concerning security of tenure of persons and households lacking it in consultation with them.[36] Accessibility entails that housing must be accessible to those entitled to it, including disadvantaged groups.[37] Quite relevantly to this investigation, the Committee has expanded the notion of adequate housing by detailing characteristics that housing should have in areas at risk. In 2006, when assessing the second periodic report of El Salvador, the Committee made clear that, in areas at risk, necessary steps for the realisation of the right to adequate housing as spelled out in Comment No. 4 include implementation of 'effective preventive measures, ensuring that housing is constructed in accordance with the standards for resisting earthquakes . . . , and to adopt a national territorial classification plan, avoiding construction in areas prone to natural disasters'.[38]

Rather importantly, as every Covenant right, the right to adequate housing 'must, in accordance with article 2(2) of the Covenant, not be subject to any form of discrimination'.[39]

Before concluding, it is important to recall that, in paragraph 2 of General Comment No. 3, the Committee maintains that State parties to the Covenant are required to adopt measures that are conducive, within a reasonable period of time, to the full realisation of the Covenant rights, including the right to housing. Importantly, such measures must *effectively* contribute to bring about the realisation of the Covenant rights. As the Committee put it, these measures 'should be deliberate, concrete and targeted as clearly as possible towards meeting the obligations recognized in the Covenant'.[40]

The Committee's views shed further light on the scope of the obligation flowing from the vulnerability of disaster victims and necessitating that State parties to the ICESCR address realisation of these persons' right to adequate housing as a matter of priority through adoption and implementation of relevant laws and policies. The Committee's views imply that competent authorities should deal with vulnerable disaster victims by directly providing access to housing through implementation of measures that effectively comply with the core elements of housing adequacy identified in General Comment No. 4.

General Comment No. 7 on forced evictions: further reference to vulnerability (as a layered notion)

The above legal framework has to be complemented by the Committee's analysis of forced evictions. The Committee canvasses forced evictions in General Comment No. 7 and defines them 'as the permanent or temporary removal against their will of individuals, families and/or communities from the homes and/or land which they occupy, without the provision of, and access to, appropriate forms of legal or other protection'.[41] Forced evictions amount to *prima facie* violations of the right to adequate housing as well as infringements of the right of access to justice where the evictees cannot challenge the legality of the evictions.[42]

Thereafter the Comment indicates that forced evictions can occur in different contexts including in situations internal displacement[43] and that they impose duties on States parties to the ICESCR. Contracting States are required to refrain from carrying out forced evictions and adopt legislation providing the greatest possible security of tenure to occupiers of houses and land. Such legislation must also prevent occurrence of forced evictions and detail punishment for individuals, including State agents and private persons, who have engaged in them.[44]

The Committee dwells on vulnerability in paragraph 10 of General Comment No. 7. The Committee affirms that various vulnerable groups such as women suffer 'disproportionately from the practice of forced eviction'. Specifically, '[w]omen in all groups are especially vulnerable given the extent of statutory and other forms of discrimination which often apply in relation to property rights (including home ownership) or rights of access to property or accommodation'.[45] This means that governments must comply with the non-discrimination provisions set out in Article 3 and paragraph 2 of Article 2 of the ICESCR so as to make sure that, where evictions occur, effective measures are taken to avoid that sex-based discrimination is involved.

In General Comment No. 7, the Committee ascribes the *special* vulnerability of women, or a dimension of it, to the fact that they are affected by forced evictions to a greater extent than other evictees or prospective evictees owing to institutionalised sex-based discrimination in the housing field. Women should be specifically protected against sex-based discrimination if evictions occur so as to avoid homelessness, including in disaster and post-disaster settings, given that the principle of equality between men and women and the principle of non-discrimination (enshrined in Article 3 and paragraph 2 of Article 2 of the ICESCR) are, in the Committee's words, 'fundamental components of international human rights law'[46] and 'fundamental to the enjoyment of each of the specific rights enumerated in the Covenant'.[47] As for General Comment No. 4, the term 'vulnerable' in General Comment No. 7 signifies being affected by unequal enjoyment of the right to adequate housing. At the same time, though, the Committee expands upon the point it has made in paragraph 13 of Comment No. 4 indicating that persons affected by forced evictions are vulnerable with regard to housing. The Committee introduces the notion that, among vulnerable groups, there are groups more vulnerable than others, or especially vulnerable, due to the greater extent of the discrimination they experience in the enjoyment of the right to adequate housing.[48]

For the purposes of this essay, the above conclusion further entails that, when a powerful disaster strikes a State where there is legislation setting out sex-based discrimination in relation to property and housing rights, women-heads of households who have been rendered homeless by the disaster and forcibly evicted in its aftermath are especially vulnerable because they have been re-exposed to homelessness as a result of the eviction and encounter significant difficulties in accessing housing after the eviction owing to *de jure* sex-based inequality in the exercise of housing rights.

The prohibition of forced evictions also incorporates precise procedural guarantees which apply to any person affected by forced evictions and *a fortiori* to especially vulnerable groups such as women, including forcibly evicted disaster-affected women. These guarantees include genuine consultation with prospective evictees; adequate and reasonable notice for all affected individuals prior to the scheduled date of eviction; provision of legal remedies; and provision, where possible, of legal aid to persons who are in need of it to seek redress from the courts.[49] The above guarantees are complemented by evictees' 'right to adequate compensation for any property, both personal and real, which is affected'.[50] Finally, in the view of the Committee, evictions should not render individuals homeless or vulnerable to the violation of other human rights. Where the evictees are unable to provide for themselves, State parties to the ICESCR 'must take all appropriate measures, to the maximum of their available resources, to ensure that adequate alternative housing, resettlement or access to productive land, as the case may be, is available'.[51]

Critical assessment of the Committee's notion of vulnerable disaster victims

One could argue that labeling disaster victims 'vulnerable' and forcibly evicted disaster-affected women 'especially vulnerable' is stigmatising since the adjective vulnerable is typically associated with powerlessness and weakness in the face of harm. In the same vein, some commentators have forcefully warned against several 'evils' of notion of vulnerable groups, which include victimisation, paternalism and essentialism.[52] Victimisation and paternalism are disempowering consequences of regarding certain persons as vulnerable. Essentialism may lead to consideration of vulnerable disaster victims as monolithic and overlook the predicament of group members or sub-groups.[53]

It is important to emphasise that the definition of vulnerable groups as elaborated by the CESCR is legal rather than merely descriptive. This point is less obvious than it seems. A legal definition of vulnerable disaster victims escapes a narrative that describes the vulnerability of certain groups of persons in terms of innate characteristics they have or predicaments they are in, thereby sounding judgmental and stigmatising. In other words, the Committee' s paradigm does not ascribe the vulnerability of disaster victims and, by implication the particular vulnerability of forcibly evicted disaster-affected women, to their disaster victim status or to gender/sex coupled with disaster victim status. Rather, the paradigm places more emphasis on the lack of effective legal protection characterising the situation of these persons, and acknowledges powerful natural disasters and sex/gender as elements that should help competent authorities better understand the challenges inherent in implementing these persons' right to adequate housing in conformity with the requirements set forth in the ICESCR.[54] That the vulnerability paradigm of the CESCR is not conducive to stigmatisation and, consequently victimisation and paternalism, is further evident in its empowering reach. The Committee unmistakably regards vulnerable disaster victims as right-holders and main stake-holders who should have a say in the way in which their right to adequate housing is realised in the aftermath of a powerful natural disaster and have access to justice where infringements of it have occurred.

The CESCR is not the only human rights monitoring body that regards vulnerable groups as being made up of persons who are exposed to violations of human rights to a greater extent than other persons in comparable situations. To mention just a few examples, the European Court of Human Rights has considered persons living with HIV/AIDS and the Roma vulnerable in so far as they have suffered considerable historical discrimination, on the grounds of, respectively, health status and race, giving rise to on-going unequal enjoyment of rights.[55] The Inter-American Court of Human Rights has elucidated the vulnerability of women, girls, undocumented migrants, persons with disabilities and indigenous peoples in terms of exposure to discrimination in the enjoyment of rights based on, respectively, gender, undocumented migrant status, disability and ethnicity.[56] Moreover, the UN International Law Commission (ILC) has also referred to persons affected by disasters as vulnerable when drafting the Articles on the Protection of Persons in the Event of Disasters. Draft Article 6 on humanitarian principles states that '[r]esponse to disasters shall take place in accordance with the [principle] of . . . impartiality, and on the basis of non-discrimination, while taking into account the needs of the particularly vulnerable'. In the commentary to Draft Article 6, the ILC affirms that 'those affected by disaster are by definition vulnerable'[57] and that, among them, there are particularly vulnerable individuals such as women.[58] While the ILC's notion of vulnerability is predicated upon exposure to disasters rather than legality, it shares similarities with the main requirement of the vulnerability paradigm of the CESCR necessitating that disaster-affected States tackle the housing situation of homeless disaster victims urgently. The ILC takes the view that the principle of non-discrimination, implied in the humanitarian principle of impartiality, is of special relevance to the situation of those disaster victims who are particularly vulnerable. It requires priority be given to their needs.[59]

The Committee's notion of vulnerability does not lead to essentialism either. On the contrary, its emphasis on lack of full and equal enjoyment of human rights allows additional consideration of a myriad of different situations in which the rights of disaster victims are at stake. Also the paradigm is quite nuanced since it takes into account the predicament of disaster victims who are disproportionately affected by violations of rights and consequently particularly vulnerable.

Applying the vulnerability paradigm to the housing situation of Haitian IDP women

The IDP women in post-quake Haiti are a vulnerable group for the purposes of General Comment No. 4. These persons' vulnerability lies in their exposure to *de facto* discrimination in the enjoyment of the right to adequate housing in paragraph 1 of Article 11 of the ICESCR. Specifically, these women are vulnerable because they could not access the right to adequate housing, on an equal basis with those living in areas that were not affected by the 2010 earthquake, due to the widespread material damage the disaster caused in southern Haiti and ensuing extreme deprivation of housing. Extreme deprivation of housing has to be understood as homelessness.

As underscored, the first implication of the above notion of vulnerability is that State parties to the ICESCR have to address the situation of homeless disaster victims, as a matter of priority, through implementation of relevant measures aimed at directly providing the right to adequate housing. The measures should be part of a strategy that progressively realises the right to adequate housing of disaster victims by providing them with temporary housing for a certain period of time and replacing it after some time with permanent housing. The important *caveat* here is that said measures effectively foster realisation of the right to adequate housing of vulnerable disaster victims if, and only if, they are in line with the essential elements making up housing adequacy under paragraph 1 of Article 11 of the ICESCR. This being so, has Haiti complied with the obligation to timely provide vulnerable IDP women with the right to adequate housing through the adoption of measures that are effectively conducive to adequate accommodation? Has Haiti progressively realised the right to adequate housing of IDP women?

It is undeniable that the government of Haiti has adopted measures to promptly deal with the housing situation of the IDP women, and hence their vulnerability, thereby seeking to implement the obligation to directly provide them with the right to adequate housing. These measures, however, do not conform to the normative content of the right to adequate housing in so far as they fall short of the core elements of this entitlement. The fact that a significant number of IDP women have not been able to pay for rent after the expiration of the rental subsidies and returned to camps for IDPs is manifestly at variance with the notion of affordability; it highlights absence of security of tenure and indicates that competent authorities have failed to guarantee access to adequate housing to the IDP women. Return to IDP camps dramatically points to a recurrence of IDP women's vulnerability. The women concerned experience, once again, unequal enjoyment of the right to adequate housing: this time owing to their socio-economic situation, another prohibited discrimination ground that, as seen above, the CESCR has read into the ground 'other status' set out in paragraph 2 of Article 2 of the ICESCR.[60] This situation prevents them from renting accommodation in the post-disaster phase and therefore enjoying the right to adequate housing on an equal footing with those IDPs who, after having benefited for the rental subsides, had accessed permanent housing. Furthermore, return to IDP camps signals that the government has not realised IDP women's right to adequate housing progressively since their temporary accommodation was not coupled with options leading to permanent housing.

Transitional shelters lack relevant constitutive elements of the right to adequate housing, too. To begin with, their allocation appears to be *prima facie* discriminatory since it has benefited only IDPs who were in areas that offered security of tenure. While the information used for the purposes of this essay does not highlight specific forms of sex/gender-based discrimination, it is submitted that those IDP women who have not benefited from transitional shelters, because they were not in areas that offered security of tenure, appear to have suffered unlawful differential treatment in the enjoyment of the right housing based on the above mentioned prohibited ground 'place of residence'. This type of discrimination augments IDP women's vulnerability by intensifying the pre-existing *de facto* discrimination in access to adequate housing that they were experiencing as a result of the 2010 earthquake, and hence exposing them to greater unequal enjoyment of the right to adequate housing than other Haitians who had been affected by the disaster.

A further failure to account for IDP women's *qua* vulnerable group is evident in the fact that the government of Haiti has not considered these persons as right-holders and, consequently, stake-holders who should have had a say regarding the identification and implementation of measures giving effect to their right to adequate housing in the post-disaster phase.

The evictions described in the first part of this essay squarely fall within the definition of forced evictions the CESCR put forward in General Comment No.7 and engage the responsibility of Haiti which did not prevent them or respond to them. The evictions severely aggravate the vulnerability of IDP women who are heads of households to violations of the right to adequate housing and make them a particularly vulnerable group. The evictions have rendered these women homeless once again and further subjected them to pre-existing statutory gender-based discrimination under domestic legislation denying them the ability to administer property.[61] Their only choice they are left with, to escape homelessness, is to find precarious accommodation somewhere else.

The eviction carried out by State officials when they demolished Camp Teleco Sans Fil is contrary to the requirements flowing from the prohibition of forced evictions since it was carried out without prior consultation with IDP women and without providing them with alternative housing solutions given their ineligibility for rental subsidies. What is more, IDP women did not have access to remedies to challenge the lawfulness of their eviction from Camp Teleco Sans Fil and Camp Comité du Peuple Progressiste and were never compensated for the property destroyed during these evictions.

Final remarks

Highly destructive disasters such as the 2010 earthquake that struck southern Haiti are sobering reminders of the fragility of human existence. They dramatically test the capability of affected States and the international community to safeguard human security, a notion that the UN Commission on Human Security defines as the 'vital core of all human lives'[62] and which encompasses fundamental human rights and freedoms.[63]

Given that protection of human rights is the pivot around which disaster response should revolve, I take the view that the vulnerability paradigm of the CESCR is a formidable analytical and operational tool for fostering adequate protection of disaster victims and, by extension, better disaster management. Its hallmark lies in the fact that it provides guidance on how to actualise human rights in disaster settings. The paradigm breaks new ground since it transcends the idea that disaster response merely entails timely provision of certain goods and logistics to the needy. The paradigm aims at promoting disaster management that is human rights-centric. It has remarkable advantages.

First, the paradigm provides State parties to the ICESCR that have been struck by a disaster, especially a powerful natural disaster, with a better understanding of the scope of the protection needs of disaster victims and how to address them. The emphasis on the vulnerability of persons affected by powerful disasters *qua* exposure to *de facto* discrimination in the enjoyment of the right to adequate housing; the far-reaching State obligations ensuing from it; and the notion that disaster victims' vulnerability is more worrisome when these persons suffer particularly pervasive discrimination or multiple forms of discrimination in access to housing, illuminate for contracting States specific requirements integral to paragraph 1 of Article 11 of the ICESCR that correspond to the unique needs of disaster victims.

Expanding on the above points, the Committee's vulnerability paradigm incorporates a cluster of obligations that, taken together, constitute a road map for State parties to the ICESCR to follow in order to minimise or eliminate disaster victims' exposure to homelessness, and which is conducive to disaster recovery and resilience in the field of housing. Thus, applying the main State obligations flowing from the paradigm to a disaster cycle that begins with the response to the disaster, the relevant road map would necessitate adoption of measures to be implemented in the order outlined below so as to realise the right to adequate housing of disaster victims timely, effectively and progressively:

- Monitoring and collection of information on the situation of homeless disaster victims in order to identify housing needs and challenges to be addressed as a priority matter in the immediate aftermath of the disaster and, subsequently, in the post-disaster phase;
- Genuine consultation with homeless disaster victims or their representatives when devising housing strategies to be implemented in the very aftermath of the disaster and in the reconstruction phase;
- Design and implementation of measures for the provision of adequate housing to homeless disaster victims that are tailored to the outcomes of the consultation with them and which comply with the elements underlying housing adequacy within the meaning of General Comment No. 4, particularly accessibility, affordability, security of tenure and resistance to earthquakes. The measures should form part of a general housing policy which aims at realising the right to adequate housing of disaster victims on a progressive basis by ensuring access to temporary housing for a certain period of time and replacing it thereafter with permanent housing;
- Undertaking of special efforts to make sure that housing measures do not result in a worsening of the vulnerability of disaster victims by adding to the extent of their deprivation of right to adequate housing. This means that the housing measures at hand can never generate discrimination in access to housing based on any of the prohibited grounds of discrimination enumerated or implied in paragraph 2 of Article 2 of the ICESCR or be in contravention to Article 3. Said efforts may also encompass repealing of existing national legislation on the right to housing/property that is discriminatory against groups such as women;
- Where evictions have occurred in the post-disaster phase and the affected State has laws that discriminate against women in the field of housing, additional measures will have to be put in place so as to avoid or minimise the disproportionate impact evictions have on disaster victims who are women and heads of households. Where necessary, the measures must enable these women to exercise housing and property rights without discrimination based on their gender; and
- Ensuring access to justice and reparation where disaster victims' right to adequate housing has been violated.

Some may say that the vulnerability paradigm places an excessive burden on a State party to the ICESCR that has been affected by a powerful disaster and that its requirements are not realistic. Maintaining these points: does not do justice to disaster victims who, as their fellow human beings, 'are born . . . equal in dignity and rights';[64] acquiesces to loose disaster management; and dooms human rights law to irrelevance in the event of disasters. A disaster-affected State that is party to the Covenant should do whatever is in its power to implement the vulnerability paradigm in good faith. This is a requirement that flows from its ratification of the Covenant.[65] If the disaster situation warrants it, the affected State could also seek international assistance. Seeking international assistance for the purposes of implementing the right to adequate housing under the ICESCR is not optional. It is mandatory in cases where a contracting State does not have enough funds to give effect to it[66] and should be used to tackle the predicament of those who are inadequately housed.[67]

Selected Bibliography

S.C. Breau and K.H. Samuel (eds), *Research Handbook on Disasters and International Law* (Edward Elgar Publishing, 2016).

A. de Guttry, M. Gestri and G. Venturini (eds), *International Disaster Response Law* (Springer, 2012).

F. Ippolito and S. Iglesias Sánchez (eds), *Protecting Vulnerable Groups: The European Human Rights Framework* (Bloomsbury Publishing, 2015).

I. Nifosi-Sutton, *The Protection of Vulnerable Groups under International Human Rights Law* (Routledge, 2017).

Notes

1 I. Nifosi-Sutton, *The Protection of Vulnerable Groups under International Human Rights Law* (Routledge, 2017).

2 IOM Shelter Update (August 2014) 11, available at www.iom.int/files/live/sites/iom/files/What-We-Do/docs/IOM-Shelter-Update-August-2014.pdf, accessed on 17 December 2016; and US Department of State, 'Post-Earthquake USG Haiti Strategy' (3 January 2011) 20, available at http://reliefweb.int/sites/reliefweb.int/files/resources/E94EDF448126F7E4852578420075647F-Full_report.pdf, accessed on 17 December 2016. See also: Report the Special Rapporteur on the Human Rights of Internally Displaced Persons, Chaloka Beyani, Mission to Haiti, UN Doc. A/HRC/29/34/Add.2 (2015) para 6.

3 Amnesty International, 15 Minutes to Leave. Denial of the Right to Adequate Housing in Post-Quake Haiti, AMR 36/001/2015 (2015) 15.

4 Ibid.

5 Ibid.

6 Report of the Special Rapporteur on the Human Rights of Internally Displaced Persons (n. 2) para 11.

7 Ibid.

8 Brookings and International Organization for Migration, *Supporting Durable Solutions to Urban, Post-Disaster Displacement: Challenges and Opportunities in Haiti* (2014) 20 and 38, available at www.brookings.edu/wp-content/uploads/2016/07/Supporting-Durable-Solutions-to-DisplacementHaiti-March-4-2014.pdf, accessed on 17 December 2016. See also Bureau des Avocats Internationaux and Institute for Justice and Democracy in Haiti, 'Surveys Indicates Earthquake Victims Who Received Housing Subsidies under Haitian Government's Housing Program Are Still in Crisis One Year Later' (7 January 2014), available at www.ijdh.org/wp-content/uploads/2013/05/Haitis-Housing-Crisis-Jan-2014-Press-Release.pdf, accessed on 17 December 2016.

9 Amnesty International (n. 3) 17.

10 Ibid.

11 Ibid.

12 Ibid 17–18; and IFRC, 'An Evaluation of the Haiti Earthquake 2010, Meeting Shelter Needs: Issues, Achievements and Constraints' (December 2011) 27, available at www.ifrc.org/docs/Evaluations/Evaluations2011/Global/HTShelterClusterReview11.pdf, accessed on 15 December 2016.

13 N. Phillips, K. Bergin, J. Goldsmith and L. Carr, 'Enforcing Remedies from the Inter-American Commission on Human Rights: Forced Evictions and Post-Earthquake Haiti' 19 *Human Rights Brief* (2011) 13; Report of the Special Rapporteur on the Human Rights of Internally Displaced Persons (n. 2) paras 34–36; IACommHR, PM 367–10 – Forced Evictions from Five Camps for Displaced Persons, Haiti (2010).
14 Amnesty International (n. 3) 23.
15 Ibid.
16 Ibid 26.
17 Ibid.
18 Ibid.
19 Ibid.
20 Ibid.
21 Nifosi-Sutton (n. 1) Section 1 of Chapter 4; A.R. Chapman and B. Carbonetti, 'Human Rights Protections for Vulnerable and Disadvantaged Groups: The Contributions of the UN Committee on Economic, Social and Cultural Rights' 33 *Human Rights Quarterly* (2011) 682; and C. Chinkin, *The Protection of Economic, Social and Cultural Rights in Post Conflict* 10 and 30–31, available at www2.ohchr.org/english/issues/women/docs/Paper_Protection_ESCR.pdf, accessed on 15 December 2016.
22 CESCR, General Comment No. 4: The Right to Adequate Housing (Art. 11(1) of the Covenant), UN Doc. E/1992/23 (1991).
23 Chapman and Carbonetti (n. 21) 724–725.
24 See Nifosi-Sutton (n. 1) Sections 1.1. and 1.3. of Chapter 4; CESCR, General Comment No. 20: Non-Discrimination in Economic, Social and Cultural Rights, UN Doc. E/C.12/GC/20 (2009) paras 8 (b) and 18–35.
25 Ibid. See also para 17 of Comment No. 20.
26 CESCR, General Comment No. 15: The Right to Water (Arts. 11 and 12 of the Covenant), UN Doc. E/C.12/2002/11 (2003) para 16(h); CESCR, General Comment No. 12: The Right to Adequate Food (Art. 11 of the Covenant), UN Doc. E/C.12/1999/5 (1999) para 15.
27 CESCR, General Comment No. 3: The Nature of States Parties' Obligations (Art. 2, para 1 of the Covenant), UN Doc. E/1991/23 (1990) para 10. See also, Office of the UN Commissioner for Human Rights, Core Human Rights in the Two Covenants (2013) 2, available at http://nhri.ohchr.org/EN/IHRS/TreatyBodies/Page%20Documents/Core%20Human%20Rights.pdf, accessed on 16 December 2016.
28 General Comment No. 3 (n. 27) para 9.
29 General Comment No. 4 (n. 22) para 12.
30 Ibid para 7.
31 Ibid.
32 Ibid para 8.
33 Ibid para 8(c).
34 Ibid.
35 Ibid para 8(a).
36 Ibid.
37 Ibid para 8(e).
38 CESCR, Concluding Observations on the Second Periodic Report of El Salvador, UN Doc. E/C.12/SLV/CO/ (2007) para 39.
39 General Comment No. 4 (n. 22) para 6. See also para 9.
40 General Comment No. 3 (n. 27) para 2. For further analysis of the international right to housing, see Rolnik's chapter in this volume.
41 CESCR, General Comment No. 7: The Right to Adequate Housing (Art. 11 (1) of the Covenant): Forced Evictions, UN Doc. E/1998/22, annex IV (1997) para 3.
42 Ibid paras 1 and 11.
43 Ibid para 5.
44 Ibid paras 8–9.
45 Ibid para 10.
46 General Comment No. 20 (n. 24) para 2.
47 CESCR, General Comment No. 16: The Equal Right of Men and Women to the Enjoyment of all Economic, Social and Cultural Rights (Art. 3 of the Covenant), UN Doc. E/C.12/2005/4 (2005) para 41.
48 Nifosi-Sutton (n. 1) Sections 1.1.1. and 1.3. of Chapter 4.
49 General Comment No. 7 (n. 41) para 15.

50 Ibid para 13.
51 Ibid para 16.
52 L. Peroni and A. Timmer, 'Vulnerable Groups: The Promise of an Emerging Concept in European Human Rights Convention Law' 11 *International Journal of Constitutional Law* (2013) 1056, 1070–1073; M.A. Fineman, 'Vulnerability, Resilience, and LGBT Youth' 14–292 *Emory Legal Studies Research Paper* (2014) 101, 109; and K. Sandberg, 'The Convention on the Rights of the Child and the Vulnerability of Children' 84 *Nordic Journal of International Law* (2015) 221, 223.
53 Peroni and Timmer (n. 52) 1071.
54 For an alternative analysis of the vulnerability of disaster victims that attaches weight to factors such a gender, age, ethnicity, disabilities, exposure to disasters and harmful practices, see: M. Bizzarri, 'Protection of Vulnerable Groups in Natural and Man-Made Disasters' in A. de Guttry, M. Gestri and G. Venturini (eds), *International Disaster Response Law* (Springer, 2012) 386–388 and 392–395; and M. Crock, 'The Protection of Vulnerable Groups' in S.C. Breau and K.H. Samuel (eds), *Research Handbook on Disasters and International Law* (Edward Elgar Publishing, 2016) 383–385 and 395–402. On a notion of vulnerability that appears to be mainly factual, see also Rolnik's chapter in this volume.
55 Nifosi-Sutton (n. 1) Section 1 of Chapter 6; Peroni and Timmer (n. 52) 1065–1067. For a broader overview of the practice of the European Court of Human Rights relevant to the protection of vulnerable groups, see, generally, F. Ippolito and S. Iglesias Sánchez (eds), *Protecting Vulnerable Groups: The European Human Rights Framework* (Bloomsbury Publishing, 2015).
56 Nifosi-Sutton (n. 1), Sections 5.3, 5.4, 5.5 and 5.6 of Chapter 5. On the IACtHR's use of the notion of vulnerability and its legal implications under the American Convention of Human Rights, see also L. Burgorgue-Larsen and A. Ubeda de Torres, '"War" in the Jurisprudence of the Inter-American Court of Human Rights' 33 *Human Rights Quarterly* (2011) 148, 156.
57 See para 7 of the commentary to Draft Article 6. The commentary is reproduced in the following document: 'Draft Articles on the Protection of Persons in the Event of Disasters, with Commentaries' (2016), available at http://legal.un.org/docs/?path=../ilc/texts/instruments/english/commentaries/6_3_2016.pdf&lang=EF, accessed on 15 December 2016.
58 Ibid. See also para 9.
59 Ibid paras 5 and 7.
60 General Comment No. 20 (n. 24) para 35.
61 OAS, Inter-American Commission on Human Rights, The Right of Women in Haiti to be Free from Violence and Discrimination, OEA/Ser.L/V/II (10 March 2009) para 132; The Haiti Gender Shadow Report (2010) 28, available at www.genderaction.org/publications/2010/gsr.pdf, accessed on 18 December 2016.
62 Human Security Unit, United Nations, Human Security in Theory and Practice (2009) 5, available at www.un.org/humansecurity/sites/www.un.org.humansecurity/files/human_security_in_theory_and_practice_english.pdf, accessed on 12 December 2016.
63 Ibid.
64 Article 1 of the 1948 Universal Declaration of Human Rights, UNGA, Res 217(III), UN Doc A/810, (10 December 1948), 71.
65 See generally General Comment No. 3 (n. 27).
66 General Comment No. 4 (n. 22) para 10.
67 Ibid para 19. For further and complementary analysis of the relevance of the international right to adequate housing in post-disaster settings, see Rolnik's chapter in this volume.

19

INDIGENOUS COMMUNITIES

From victims to actors of disaster management

Kristin Hausler

Introduction

> The more vulnerable the population is, in terms of where they live, their level of knowledge and awareness of and preparedness for the hazards, and the resources they have at their disposal to limit their exposure, the greater the adverse impact will be on their lives and livelihoods.[1]

Indigenous communities are likely to be particularly vulnerable to natural hazards, which occur more and more frequently as a result of global warming.[2] According to the Intergovernmental Panel on Climate Change (IPCC), 'livelihoods and lifestyles of indigenous peoples, pastoralists, and fisherfolk, often dependent on natural resources, are highly sensitive to climate change policies, especially those that marginalize their knowledge, values and activities'.[3] At the national level, the specific risks faced by Indigenous communities in case of disasters have also been recognised. For example, the Canadian Red Cross Emergency Preparedness Guide for Muskego Cree families states that 'First Nation Communities in Ontario are particularly vulnerable to natural disasters and many remote Northern First Nation communities must deal with hazards such as forest fires and floods every year'.[4] Disasters that struck Indigenous communities have resulted in serious damage, including loss of lives. For example, in Honduras, in 1998, Indigenous peoples living in areas exposed to flooding and landslides were particularly affected by Hurricane Mitch, which caused close to 20,000 fatalities.[5] In 2010–2011, floods in Colombia affected especially those who had already been displaced by conflict, most of them being Indigenous peoples living in remote areas subject to violence from armed non-State actors.[6] As a result of these torrential rains, many were left homeless.[7] More recently, in Nepal, in 2014, floods and landslides killed about 260 people. While there is no exact data available, it has been reported that Indigenous peoples, along with the so-called 'Dalits', were the most impacted.[8]

There are, at least, an estimated 370 million Indigenous peoples living in about 70 nations worldwide, amounting to about 5 percent of the world's population but to about 15 percent of the poor population.[9] In accordance with the fundamental criterion of self-determination, to determine whether a particular group of individuals qualifies as 'Indigenous', the group in question should first identify *itself* as Indigenous, as affirmed by the Special Rapporteur of the Sub-Commission on Prevention of Discrimination and Protection of Minorities in his Study on the Problem of Discrimination against Indigenous Populations.[10] While there is no universally agreed definition of 'Indigenous peoples', a number of common factors can generally be observed among them, such as a shared ancestry with pre-colonial societies, as well as a particularly strong relationship with the ancestral lands they inhabit, which contribute to their distinctiveness, along with their specific cultures (including languages, customs, and traditions) and their own social and legal systems, a distinctiveness they generally strive to perpetuate.[11] Almost always, Indigenous peoples are now minority communities on the territory of the State they inhabit.

The factors that place Indigenous peoples at particular risk of being affected by disasters include their place of residence, which is often remote and thus not easily accessible to emergency aid workers. Living remotely from urban centres may also mean that they may not possess identity documents because of a lack of registration at birth, for example, which in turn renders them unaccountable for in a disaster context.[12] In addition, Indigenous communities' places of residence are not necessarily fixed. For example, there are pastoral communities in Africa which are particularly mobile, travelling throughout the year with their livestock, even crossing borders, which makes challenging the identification of the location of such nomadic communities when a natural disaster occurs. While pastoral communities are generally known to be particularly adaptable to difficult climate conditions,[13] they are not immune to the effects of natural disasters. In the North of Kenya, the Turkana community suffered a food crisis as a result of several years of drought which had led to a loss of livestock.[14] Even communities that may have one main residence may spend, for example, summers in other places, such as when they follow their herds' transhumance or where harvesting may take place. For example, the Sámi people in Norway spend the summer months on the coast and coastal islands, and the winter months on the interior plain, moving their reindeer herds to where pastures are available depending on the seasons.[15]

Other factors that exacerbate the vulnerability of Indigenous communities include their economic status, as they often live in relative poverty, as well as a lack of awareness and preparedness, in particular as they are often marginalised, meaning that they often do not participate in the decision-making process of the State which has control over their traditional territories. Despite being close to the environment they have traditionally inhabited and having knowledge of climate patterns, including natural hazards, transferred through generations, the combination of the vulnerability factors mentioned above increase their risk of being negatively affected by natural hazards.

When a natural hazard strikes, it becomes a disaster when the population living in that area suffers from its consequences. Disasters may endanger the lives of Indigenous peoples, as well as have a negative impact on their housing conditions, their health, their access to subsistence resources, including water, and their ancestral lands more in general. While disasters have an immediate negative impact, they can also have a gradual effect and eventually force communities to migrate; this phenomenon is being observed in Alaska, for example, where melting Arctic sea ice and permafrost expose the local native communities to flooding and erosion.[16] Some of these communities have already begun to move their buildings to higher ground, as full relocation has yet to be organised.[17] While the slow-onset damage induced by climate change in general is a real threat for the livelihood of many Indigenous communities, this chapter focuses on the sudden-onset damage caused to those communities as a direct result of natural disasters.

Disasters may be a threat to several human rights which most States must respect, protect, and fulfil, under treaty law, such as the right to life (which has been interpreted to extend to the right to live a decent life, in particular with regard to Indigenous communities),[18] the right to an adequate standard of living, including food, water, and housing, the right to health, and the right to property, among others.[19] If a State they inhabit fails to protect its Indigenous population from the negative impacts of disasters, it may thus be held responsible for human rights violations, including the rights of minorities, as enshrined in Article 27 of the International Covenant on Civil and Political Rights (ICCPR).[20] The provision establishes that minorities shall have the right to 'enjoy their own culture, to profess and practice their own religion, or to use their own language'. The State may also be responsible if it fails to provide its Indigenous population with its right to self-determination and a right to free, prior, and informed consent (FPIC), two key concepts stemming from the Indigenous rights framework, which are also applicable in the context of disaster risk reduction, preparedness, and management.

Despite the risks they face with regard to disasters, in particular as a result of the vulnerabilities derived from their living conditions, Indigenous peoples have generally been left out of initiatives and policy developments concerned with disasters. This is a reflection of their lack of participation in the decision-making process at the national level. While there are many examples of Indigenous decision-making processes in place with regard to issues that relate to their internal affairs,[21] they are most often disregarded when the decision-making involves a State institution. In Nepal, for example, the large Indigenous population has been ignored in the development of 2009 National Strategy for Disaster Risk Management.[22]

This chapter, which focuses on disasters stemming from natural hazards, first presents how the existing legal framework applies (or may apply) to disasters involving Indigenous communities before considering the existing legal basis to include Indigenous peoples in the decision-making processes pertaining to the development of disaster risk reduction, preparedness, and management policies. It also addresses the potential added-value of integrating an Indigenous perspective in the decision-making processes aimed at curbing the effects of disasters, in particular through the use of Indigenous knowledge. Finally, it includes some existing good practice and possible ways forward in order to involve Indigenous peoples, their views and specific knowledge, in all activities regarding disaster risk reduction, preparedness, and management.

International law applicable to indigenous peoples in the event of disaster

International human rights law

All human rights enshrined in treaties, such as the ICCPR and the International Covenant on Economic, Social and Cultural Rights (ICESCR),[23] are applicable to Indigenous persons under the jurisdiction of their States Parties. Under these treaties, human rights are generally deemed to belong to Indigenous as individuals rather than to Indigenous communities as groups, although some of those rights are only recognised to individuals if they relate to the application of a group practice. For example, the right of minorities contained in Article 27 ICCPR can be invoked when it regards the culture, religion, or language, belonging to a particular group. However, under certain treaties, such as the ILO Convention 169 on Indigenous and Tribal Peoples, Indigenous peoples also possess group rights, i.e. rights which attach to a particular group because of its characteristics and can thus only be exercised by the group as a whole.[24]

No matter whether the rights belonging to Indigenous peoples can be categorised as 'individual' or 'group' rights, States have the obligation to respect, protect, and fulfil, the human rights of Indigenous peoples, as contained in the treaties they are party to, and, in case of violation, they have an obligation to repair the harm, both material and moral,[25] suffered as a consequence thereof.[26] As the Expert Mechanism on the Rights of Indigenous Peoples stated,

> [A]ll States have positive human rights obligations to protect human rights. Natural hazards are not disasters, in and of themselves. They become disasters depending on the elements of exposure, vulnerability and resilience, all factors that can be addressed by

> human (including State) action. A failure (by national and local governments, disaster risk reduction agencies, indigenous peoples and other actors) to take reasonable preventive action to reduce exposure and vulnerability and to enhance resilience, as well as to provide effective mitigation, is therefore a human rights issue.[27]

If Indigenous peoples suffer harm as the result of a human rights violation in a disaster context, in particular when it is a consequence of a State's neglect to act against the foreseeable disastrous effects of natural hazards, they may therefore seek reparations before a court. If domestic courts fail in repairing the harm in question, the plaintiffs may then seek reparation at the regional level, when such bodies are available to them, or before the relevant United Nations Treaty Body. As an analysis of domestic courts' jurisprudence in this area goes beyond the remit of this chapter, the following sections focuses on the work of international mechanisms in upholding the human rights of Indigenous peoples in a disaster context, including both the UN mechanisms and the regional human rights courts.

Universal human rights framework

At the international level, alleged violations of most human rights can be the object of petitions (sometimes called 'communications') before the relevant UN Treaty Body, if the defending State has accepted the applicable individual communication procedure. In addition to hearing individual cases, the UN human rights mechanisms, through the Human Rights Council, may also consider patterns of human rights violations, as well as provide insight into certain areas of international human rights law, as it did with the Study it published in August 2014 on the 'Promotion and protection of the rights of indigenous peoples in natural disaster risk reduction and prevention and preparedness initiatives' (the Expert Mechanism Study), which was prepared by the Expert Mechanism on the Rights of Indigenous Peoples.

The Expert Mechanism Study was developed through consultation and cooperation with Indigenous peoples. It explores the links between disaster risk reduction and human rights, stating that the former enables the latter by minimising the negative impacts that natural hazards may have on the realisation of a number of rights such as housing or health, for example.[28] It also considers how Indigenous peoples could further participate in disaster risk reduction efforts. Its advice highlights the relevance of the UN Declaration on the Rights of Indigenous Peoples as a legal framework for the promotion and protection of the rights of Indigenous peoples in this area.[29] In particular, it calls on States to 'secure the input of indigenous peoples in the development and implementation of disaster risk reduction initiatives' in order to, among others, empower their resilience while respecting their rights, including 'their right to self-determination with regard to their lands, territories and natural resources, their right to participate in decision-making, and their right to protect their cultural knowledge'.[30] This input must also be sought by Indigenous peoples themselves through advocacy.[31] In addition, the Expert Mechanism Study also urges States to take into account the vulnerability of Indigenous peoples to disasters when considering the development of infrastructures or extraction activities that may negatively affect it.[32] This means that Indigenous communities should not only be considered in the development of disaster risk reduction and preparedness policies but also in any other governmental activity that may have a negative effect on it. Otherwise, the State may be in breach of its obligation to protect the rights of Indigenous peoples.

Finally, UN Special Procedures, which focus either on human rights violations taking place in a particular State or the implementation of specific rights, have also provided some relevant information or, even, recommendations pertaining to disasters with regard to Indigenous peoples.

For example, the Special Rapporteur on 'adequate housing as a component of the right to an adequate standard of living, and on the right to non-discrimination in this context', whose mandate currently focuses on the most vulnerable populations, including Indigenous peoples, stated that, when addressing the consequences of disasters, pre-existing vulnerability, including land tenure insecurity which is often the norm for Indigenous communities, had to be taken into account for the full realisation of the right to adequate housing.[33] The Special Rapporteur on the issue of human rights obligations relating to the enjoyment of a safe, clean, healthy, and sustainable environment supported the acknowledgment of the Human Rights Council, according to which certain groups are particularly vulnerable to environmental harm,[34] by calling climate change 'inherently discriminatory', adding that States must take the necessary steps to ensure that those in vulnerable positions, including Indigenous peoples, 'are fully informed of the effects of climate actions, that they are able to take part in decision-making processes, that their concerns are taken into account and that they have access to remedies for violations of their rights'.[35] Following its visit to Nicaragua, the Special Rapporteur on the right to food has specifically recommended that rapid alert systems be put in place to protect the Indigenous communities which are particularly vulnerable to the effects of climate change and that these communities should be supported in developing agricultural models more resilient to extreme weather patterns.[36] The particular vulnerability faced by Indigenous communities with regard to disasters have thus been widely acknowledged within the international human rights framework, as well as the need for States to adopt a human rights approach when addressing the potential impacts of natural hazards on such communities.

Regional human rights framework

International human rights law has also been enshrined at the regional level; however, most economic, social, or cultural rights are not directly enforceable before the regional courts. Nevertheless, both the European and the Inter-American Court of Human Rights have indirectly enforced certain economic, social, or cultural rights through the application of civil or political rights. The Inter-American human rights system has been particularly innovative in protecting the rights of Indigenous peoples, including their traditional knowledge, which may be relevant to develop effective disaster risk reduction and prevention initiatives. As a result of the close relation they enjoy with the lands they inhabit, Indigenous peoples have gained an intimate knowledge of natural events, which the Expert Mechanism Study recommended to take into account to successfully reduce the risk of disasters.[37] This special relationship that Indigenous groups have with their traditional lands has been recognised by the Inter-American human rights system in cases which have involved the management of natural resources. In the case of the *Kichwa Indigenous People of Sarayaku v. Ecuador*,[38] where oil exploration threatened the lives of local communities, the Court found violations of the right to life and physical integrity as a result of the placement of high-powered explosives on their land, in addition to violations of their right to prior consultation and consent. It awarded a combination of reparations, including guarantees of non-repetition to ensure effective consultation with regard to any project that may impact local communities, as well as training officials on Indigenous rights.

In general, when awarding reparations, the Court has taken into account the particular customs and traditions of Indigenous peoples, such as their familial structures and cultural practices, when determining the class of victims who may be awarded reparations.[39] When assessing the harm caused by environmental pollution, it has considered the specific ties that Indigenous communities have with their traditional lands.[40] When deciding on the form of reparations to be awarded to a group of victims, the Court has considered the cultural background of the victims. For example,

Guatemala was requested to 'take into account the traditions and customs of the members of the affected communities' when honouring victims publicly.[41] The respect of the affected communities' language was also upheld through the obligation made to the State to translate the judgment into Maya-Achí.[42] All of these measures should also be considered by bodies awarding reparations to Indigenous peoples who had their rights violated in a disaster context.

Furthermore, reparations have been deemed by the Court as an opportunity not only to redress the harm caused but also to improve the context which may have been instrumental in generating the violations.[43] Again, this is relevant for all types of disasters as even those originating from natural forces may cause more or less harm depending on the situation the victims are in. For example, an earthquake is likely to generate a higher number of casualties in areas where housing conditions are poor. Reparations which include, for example, housing and development programmes, as well as the implementation of regulations of dangerous industrial activities or the adoption of warning systems, may support the non-repetition of disasters or a reduction of their harmful consequences. This approach is in line with the concept of 'Build Back Better', which was first established during the reconstruction of Aceh, in Indonesia, following the 2004 tsunami and subsequently adopted within the Hyogo Framework for Action.

In a case involving the Ogoni people in Nigeria, where the activities of an extractive industry contaminated the environment, the African Commission on Human and Peoples' Rights said that States must 'take reasonable and other measures to prevent pollution and ecological degradation, to promote conservation, and to secure an ecologically sustainable development and use of natural resources'.[44] Within the African human rights system, Article 24 of the 1981 African Charter on Human and Peoples' Rights provides all peoples with the 'right to a general satisfactory environment favourable to their development', a right which could potentially be invoked by victims of disasters when States failed to take necessary steps to reduce the risks of disasters and thus protect their environment.[45]

Within the African framework, a unique instrument is worth noting given its direct applicability to victims of disasters: the African Union Convention for the Protection and Assistance of Internally Displaced Persons in Africa (also known as the Kampala Convention) provides for the protection and assistance of persons displaced not only as a result of conflict but also as a result of natural disasters.[46] It provides for the establishment of early warning systems, as well as disaster risk reduction and coordination of humanitarian assistance, at both the national and regional levels.[47] It also establishes the liability of States to repair the damage caused to internally displaced persons when it refrained from protecting and assisting such persons in the event of a natural disaster.[48] Although the Convention does not mention Indigenous peoples specifically, it is clear that African Indigenous communities are particularly at risk of being forcibly displaced as a result of a disaster, including pastoralists who largely depend on their livestock to survive.[49]

Indigenous rights framework

In addition to the general international and regional human rights framework, a few instruments, which have been adopted to address the specificities of Indigenous peoples, are also relevant in the disaster context. The only international binding instrument concerned with Indigenous communities is the International Labour Organization Convention 169 on Indigenous and Tribal Peoples (1989) (ILO Convention 169), which contains, among others, the right of ownership and possession of traditional lands; it also calls repeatedly for the respect of the customs and traditions of Indigenous and tribal peoples.[50] Its Article 4 is particularly pertinent as it provides for special measures to 'be adopted as appropriate for safeguarding the persons, institutions, property, labour, cultures and environment of the peoples concerned'. Article 7, paragraph 1, affirms Indigenous peoples' right to 'decide their own priorities for the process of development', as well as to 'participate in the formulation, implementation and evaluation of plans and programmes for national and regional development which may affect them directly'. With regard to their land, in addition to recognising their 'rights of ownership and possession over the lands which they traditionally occupy',[51] Article 16 states that Indigenous peoples have the right not to be removed from the lands they occupy, providing safeguards for cases where relocation is 'necessary as an exceptional measure', which may be the case when seeking to reduce the risks associated with disasters. However, this treaty has not been widely ratified and, at present, only counts 22 State parties, mostly within Latin America and the Caribbean.[52] In those States that are party to it, it may be invoked before the national courts and both the Inter-American Commission of Human Rights and the Court have referred to it in its judgments.

Like the ILO Convention 169, the 2007 UN Declaration on the Rights of Indigenous Peoples (UNDRIP),[53] the other key international instrument providing rights to Indigenous peoples, albeit not of a binding nature, does also not contain any provision that is specifically aimed at covering disasters. Nevertheless, it contains similar rights as the ILO Convention 169, which may be relevant in disaster scenarios. These include: the right to self-determination (Articles 3 and 4); the right not to be relocated without having given free, prior, and informed consent (FPIC), compensation, and being offered the possibility to return, where possible (Article 10); the right to participate in decision-making in matters which may affect their rights and the obligation for States to obtain their FPIC before adopting legislative or administrative measures that may affect them (Articles 18 and 19); the right to prioritise their development strategies including with regard to their territories and resources (Articles 23 and 32); the right to the lands they have traditionally occupied (Articles 26 and 27); the right to conserve and protect their environment and the obligation for States to establish assistance programmes to support it (Article 29); and the right to maintain and develop their traditional knowledge, including their knowledge of fauna and flora (Article 31). Adopted with 143 States voting in its favour, this Declaration is widely supported. Even the four key States (namely Australia, Canada, New Zealand and the United States) which voted against it at the time of its adoption have now all voiced their support for it. Given its wide acceptance and despite its non-binding nature, UNDRIP may nevertheless serve as guidance when developing disaster risk reduction and management policies which may impact Indigenous peoples.[54]

Within the above two instruments, a number of rights and concepts emerge as particularly relevant in the disaster context, namely the right to internal self-determination, the right to participation in the decision-making process, as well as the special relationship with ancestral lands, and traditional knowledge, thus deserving a more in-depth analysis.

Self-determination

In several States, Indigenous peoples are now able to self-govern at the local level with regard to certain issues that concern them. This is the case in Canada, where there is even an entire territory, Nunavut, which is under Indigenous control. According to Article 4 UNDRIP, Indigenous peoples have 'the right to autonomy or self-government in matters relating to their internal and local affairs'. Thus Indigenous communities may claim decision-making authority over disaster-related policies which apply strictly on their territories.[55]

The right to self-determination also includes the right of Indigenous communities to determine their own development, including on matters related to their lands and resources. Article 23 UNDRIP includes 'the right to be actively involved in developing and determining health, housing and other economic and social programmes affecting them'. While disaster risk reduction and management *per se* are not listed in the programmes they have a right to be involved in, they may potentially be considered as falling within those listed in this provision. Housing programmes, for example, should systematically include disaster risk reduction efforts. For example, Habitat for Humanity, which built houses for the 150 Miskito families which were impacted by Hurricane Felix in 2007, in Nicaragua, integrates disaster risk reduction initiatives into their shelter, housing, and settlement programmes.[56] As a result, Indigenous peoples should have the right to determine how disaster risk reduction initiatives are integrated in housing policies affecting them. This is further supported by Article 32 UNDRIP, which upholds the right of Indigenous peoples to select and develop priorities for the use of their lands and resources, which could include disaster risk reduction initiatives.[57]

Participation in decision-making and FPIC

Notwithstanding the right to self-determination with regard to local matters, initiatives relating to disasters are often established and implemented at the national level or by sub-national organisations, through processes in which the Indigenous population generally lacks any representation. However, as provided for in Article 18 UNDRIP, Indigenous peoples also have a right to participate in decision-making, with their own representatives, when the State establishes and implements laws and policies affecting them, which may be the case of disaster-related instruments. When including Indigenous communities in the decision-making process, it is key to identify their representatives. While it may appear evident to invite elected chiefs, for example, to participate in the decision-making process, elders and spiritual leaders may be the ones with the most relevant traditional knowledge when it comes to disaster-related matters, and thus, communities may wish to involve them in those processes as well. In addition, in order to benefit from Indigenous knowledge in the decision-making process, an Indigenous perspective should be adopted in the decision-making process itself, with protocols developed in accordance with the relevant Indigenous customs and traditions.

The pendant to the right to participate in the decision-making process with regard to all matters that affect them is the obligation of States to consult with them and seek to obtain their FPIC concerning measures which may affect them, including those regarding disaster risk reduction and management. According to the Expert Mechanism Study, risk reduction initiatives are more likely to be successful if Indigenous decision-making processes, including their implementation in culturally appropriate ways, and traditional knowledge are respected.[58]

The importance of respecting the rights of the most vulnerable, including Indigenous peoples, has also been recognised by the 2015 Paris Agreement on climate change.[59] Its Article 12 requires State parties to take appropriate measures to enhance public participation with regard to climate change education, which may be interpreted to include disaster-risk awareness. Under its Article 7, the Agreement further underlines that adaptation efforts should not only be country-driven but also ensure the participation of vulnerable groups, such as Indigenous communities, and that any adaptation action must be 'guided by the best available science and, as appropriate, traditional knowledge, knowledge of indigenous peoples and local knowledge systems'.

Special relationship with the land

As already mentioned, Indigenous peoples are defined by, *inter alia*, their close relationship with the lands they have traditionally inhabited. In addition to having a right to their land, Article 29 UNDRIP also indicates that Indigenous peoples have 'the right to the conservation and protection of the environment and the productive capacity of their lands or territories and resources'.

The conservation and protection of the environment is closely linked to disaster risk reduction and some farming activities, for example, may in fact increase the risk of disasters, by eroding the soil, for example. It is thus key that Indigenous peoples are educated about the potential risks associated with all their land-related activities. According to the Expert Mechanism on the Rights of Indigenous People, their 'close relationship with their natural environment makes them particularly vulnerable to disaster risk',[60] given the potential impact of disasters on this relationship which not only defines them but is also essential to the survival of their traditional way of live.

In accordance with Article 10 UNDRIP, Indigenous peoples 'shall not be forcibly removed from their lands or territories'. Historically, Indigenous peoples have repeatedly been dispossessed of their traditional lands and thus deprived of the resources on which their livelihood depend, which, in turns, reduces their ability to deal with disasters.[61] Nevertheless, in extreme cases, reducing the risk of disasters may necessitate the relocation of Indigenous communities, for example if their traditional lands are situated in areas at high risk of flooding or landslides. However, relocation may only be possible once the community in question has given its FPIC, has agreed on a form of compensation (which could include a relocation package) and been offered, if possible, the option of return. In this regard, the 2005 UN Principles on Housing and Property Restitution for Refugees and Displaced Persons (also known as the Pinheiro Principles) offer some guidance on the procedures and mechanisms necessary to facilitate property restitution. Its Principle 15.3 states that, where appropriate, States should ensure 'that registration systems record and/or recognize the rights of possession of traditional and indigenous communities to collective lands'. At the regional level, the Protocol on the Property Rights of Returning Persons of the International Conference on the Great Lakes Region went even further by providing that traditional authorities themselves, along with the administrative ones, should be addressing property disputes. The Special Rapporteur on 'adequate housing as a component of the right to and adequate standard of living' has also suggested, in line with the Pinheiro Principles, that the restitution of housing or property restitution must abide by any form of right to tenure attached to the property in question before the disaster, even if formal registration was lacking.[62]

In addition, the close relationship to nature entertained by Indigenous groups may sometimes require a culturally sensitive approach to what may otherwise be qualified as a hazard or a risk. For example, volcanoes are often seen as being part of Mother Nature within Indigenous spirituality (sometimes refer to as 'cosmovision'), which means that qualifying them as hazards may be deemed offensive.[63] As a result, it is necessary to define terms carefully when developing disaster-related policies which may affect Indigenous peoples.[64]

Indigenous knowledge

In addition to their special relationship to the land, Indigenous peoples have in common the oral transmission of their histories and their traditional knowledge, which is linked to their closeness to their environment. Article 31 UNDRIP affirms the right of Indigenous peoples to maintain and protect their traditional knowledge, as well as providing safeguards for the protection of this right. Traditional knowledge has a valuable role to play in disaster risk reduction and preparedness, which has now been widely recognised.[65] Having often lived for thousands of years in areas that may be prone to disasters, Indigenous communities have gained a particular insight into extreme weather' patterns. For example, in Swaziland, floods have been predicted with the height at which birds nest near rivers, and droughts with the number of moths in the air.[66] In the Russian Siberian Arctic, the Nenets people also observe the behaviour of animals carefully for any sign of incoming disaster. If a dog rolls on its back in the snow and crows circle in flock before disappearing, it a sign that a blizzard is near.[67]

Indigenous knowledge was reported to have saved lives during the 2004 Indian Ocean earthquake, which provoked a tsunami with devastating consequences for Indonesia and other countries. On Simeulue Island, which counts 78,000 inhabitants and is situated within the province of Aceh, off the Indonesian island of Sumatra, only 7 individuals perished, despite the tsunami reaching its shores. This was explained by the use of a traditional warning system, which had been passed down generations, since the last tsunami hit the island in 1907. Once the earthquake was felt and the ocean was seen receding, people started shouting 'Smong' (or Semong), meaning tsunami in the language of the local Devayan people, which led everyone to run for the nearby hills for shelter.[68] In the province of Aceh, where there was no early warning system, there were 200,000 victims.[69]

In order to be useful, Indigenous knowledge must be recognised and protected accordingly, and then utilised appropriately. According to the Expert Mechanism on the Rights of Indigenous Peoples, '[A]ll too often, mainstream disaster management institutions have ignored indigenous knowledge, and many successful local practices have disappeared as a consequence of non-indigenous influence. At other times, indigenous peoples' practices have adapted to changing environments'.[70] Indigenous knowledge has even been called an 'underused knowledge reservoir'.[71] It must thus be further integrated in the disaster discourse not only as a matter of respect for Indigenous rights but to strengthen disaster risk reduction and preparedness efforts.

Indigenous communities within the International Disaster Law framework

At the international level, there are a number of initiatives specifically dedicated to disaster risk reduction, preparedness, and management. This section considers the inclusion and participation of Indigenous communities in their development and implementation, as well as some good practice examples.

Risk reduction and preparedness

Disaster risk reduction and preparedness policies contribute to the protection of human rights, including the rights of Indigenous peoples, by reducing the likelihood of natural hazards having a negative impact on them. The Hyogo Framework for Action (HFA), the key framework for the period 2005–2015 for disaster risk reduction, did not make any specific reference to Indigenous peoples or the need to ensure their full and effective participation, which was criticised by the Expert Mechanism Study.[72] Nevertheless, the HFA recognised the need to consider 'cultural diversity, age, and vulnerable groups' and the role of traditional knowledge in disaster risk reduction.[73] It also contains a number of strategies that are particularly pertinent for Indigenous peoples, such as the need to develop and strengthen 'institutions, mechanisms and capacities at all levels, in particular at the community level, that can systematically contribute to building resilience to hazards'[74] and the empowerment of communities and local authorities 'to manage and reduce disaster risk by having access to the necessary information, resources and authority to implement actions for disaster risk reduction'.[75] According to consultations, the follow-up to the HFA, HFA2, should follow a human rights-based approach and be centred on community-level involvement, as well as vulnerable populations, including Indigenous peoples.[76]

In May 2013, at the UN International Strategy for Disaster Risk Reduction (UNISDR) Global Platform for Disaster Risk Reduction, there was a side event on engaging Indigenous peoples in the matter, where the need for a dialogue between Indigenous leaders and their non-Indigenous counterparts on this topic was highlighted. The Pan American Health Organization

(PAHO) and the World Health Organization (WHO) have also published some 'Recommendations for Engaging Indigenous Peoples in Disaster Risk Reduction', based on a consultation process with Indigenous delegates from Latin America, the Caribbean, Canada, and the United States, which sought to develop 'culturally sensitive tools to reduce disaster risk and better protect health during and after disasters'.[77] The Expert Mechanism Study, which itself called for submissions from Indigenous peoples,[78] looked at the possible partnerships between Indigenous peoples and governments and the strategies which may improve their participation in disaster risk reduction.[79] A gap could then be identified: the dialogue that may be needed between the Indigenous communities and non-State actors, as many businesses, such as the extractive industry, are likely to have an impact on Indigenous lands and may thus be the source of environmental disasters on their traditional territories. While States should drive disaster risk reduction initiatives at the national level, non-State actors should also be included in such initiatives, when appropriate. This missing link has been somewhat addressed in the Sendai Framework for Disaster Risk Reduction 2015–2030 (Sendai Framework).[80] This non-binding framework recognises the 'leading, regulatory and coordination role' of States in engaging with relevant stakeholders, including Indigenous peoples, but also underlines the need for the public and private sectors to work more closely together and for 'business to integrate disaster risk into their management practices'.[81]

As already mentioned, traditional knowledge can be key in disaster risk reduction and preparedness strategies and should thus be further utilised, including through dissemination, for example by incorporating it into school curricula. This has been recommended by UNEP which, following its project documenting Indigenous knowledge in Kenya, Tanzania, South Africa, and Swaziland, has underlined the need for such knowledge to be taught in schools as well as disseminated among the wider public.[82] For the most efficient use of available data for disaster risk reduction and preparedness, Indigenous knowledge should be blended with scientific and technological means. This has been recognised by the Sendai Framework, which considers the use of traditional knowledge within its guiding principles as it states that disaster risk reduction must be based on scientific information 'complemented by traditional knowledge'.[83] It also underlined the importance of the local context and the 'use of traditional, indigenous and local knowledge and practices . . . to complement scientific knowledge' when conducting disaster risk assessment and developing associated policies and strategies.[84] It adds that Indigenous peoples 'through their experience and traditional knowledge, provide an important contribution to the development and implementation of plans and mechanisms, including for early warning'.[85]

Disaster management

Once a disaster has struck an Indigenous community, many problems may arise including loss of lives, housing, access to potable water, as well as a general lack of functioning facilities which may inhibit the full realisation of a number of human rights. In order to provide relief and facilitate humanitarian assistance to alleviate the impacts of disasters, guidelines have been developed, such as those by the International Federation of the Red Cross.[86] Despite providing recommendations to governments on how to prepare their disaster laws in international disaster operations, including with regard to early warning procedures and preparedness, Indigenous peoples or knowledge are generally not mentioned in such instruments. The Sendai Framework states that local authorities must be empowered 'through regulatory and financial means to work and coordinate with . . . indigenous peoples . . . in disaster risk management at the local level'.[87] The opposite should also be the norm, i.e. empowering Indigenous communities to work with their local authorities on disaster management. Furthermore, Indigenous peoples should also be involved in the development of rules, protocols, or other tools, at the national level when those may impact them, in accordance with the principle of self-determination, as well as participation in decision-making; Indigenous communities must not only be at the receiving ends of such instruments but also become their 'co-authors', not only to respect their rights but also to develop the most efficient disaster relief instruments.

In terms of good practice, the Canadian Red Cross has developed, with the Moose Cree First Nation, emergency preparedness guides, as well as videos and handouts, specifically aimed at remote northern First Nations communities, in particularly the Muskego Cree living in the James Bay area.[88] Those guides, including one for families and another for elders, have been published in the relevant Indigenous languages. The Canadian Red Cross Emergency Preparedness Guide for Muskego Cree families recognises the 'specific and unique needs' of those communities.[89] It explains not only why disaster preparedness is important, but also the steps that should be taken, including knowing the risks, making a plan, and getting emergency kits, including both 'grab and go' bags in case of evacuation and home emergency preparedness kits in case of having to stay at home for a long period after the disaster strikes.[90] When considering the risks, the way of life of the communities is taken into account as it refers to their mobility and the fact they may spend part of the year in a secondary location, such as a 'bush camp' during the spring or fall harvest seasons.[91] With regard to making a plan, it is recommended to communities to select a family emergency contact person outside of the community because it is generally easier to make a long-distance call than a local call following a disaster.[92] Many recommendations are also addressed to those spending time at a 'bush camp', including communicating the location of the camp and the time one plans to spend there, as well as maintaining regular contact with relatives or the local radio to be informed of potential disasters. If someone is known to be at a 'bush camp' during an emergency, this must be communicated to emergency personnel. Preparedness at home also means to have all important documents stored securely in one place, including the status card, but also board games and playing cards.[93] The document dedicated to elders and emergencies recognises their special space within First Nations communities.[94]

Concluding remarks

Indigenous peoples are particularly vulnerable to disaster because of a number of underlying factors, including the fact that they generally live in remote areas and in poor conditions. As States may be held responsible for violating the rights of Indigenous peoples if they fail to protect them against certain effects of disasters, they have advantage in including them in all stages when developing policies regarding disaster risk reduction, preparedness, and management. Such an approach does not only respect the rights of Indigenous peoples to self-determination and to participation in decision-making with regard to matters that impact or may impact them, but it also minimises the risks posed to Indigenous communities and, in turn, the risk of States in violating the rights of its Indigenous population, which include not only their rights as minorities but also the specific rights which have been enshrined in the international legal framework for Indigenous peoples.

As highlighted in this chapter, Indigenous peoples have a special relation with the land they have traditionally inhabited and, given the close proximity they have enjoyed with their living environment, have developed an in-depth knowledge of its functioning, including of possible extreme weather patterns. Throughout the world, there are examples of Indigenous communities able to foresee natural hazards and potential disasters through a fine observation of the fauna and flora around them. While this Indigenous knowledge has now been widely recognised as relevant the disaster context, it has yet to be fully utilised. For this to happen, Indigenous knowledge should be comprehensively documented and integrated in disaster preparedness policies and teaching material, including in schools' curricula.

So far, Indigenous peoples have not been systematically included in the development of policies geared towards disaster risk reduction and preparedness, and management; they have been the audience rather than the content producer. While a number of good practice examples in this area can be highlighted, Indigenous communities would benefit from being involved in a systematic, comprehensive, and culturally sensitive manner, in the development of disaster policies that may impact them and which may benefit from their participation and knowledge, as underlined in the Sendai Framework. In line with the principle of FPIC, there is thus a need to ensure 'that the perspectives of indigenous peoples are adequately integrated into the implementation of all practices and at all stages of the design and implementation of risk reduction projects and activities'.[95] Indigenous peoples must not only be consulted in a culturally appropriate manner but the tools developed must also be culturally sensitive. As mentioned, for some communities, natural hazards, such as volcanoes, may be considered as sacred. Integrating an Indigenous perspective in the disaster dialogue also means taking into account their customary laws.

Therefore, it is important to not only recognise the specific vulnerabilities of Indigenous communities with regard to disasters but also to recognise their strengths and how they can contribute to the development of more effective disaster-related policies, including through the use of their traditional knowledge; when adopting such an approach, Indigenous peoples, traditionally viewed as likely victims of disasters, can become true actors of disaster management.

Selected bibliography

R. Bronen, *Climate-Induced Displacement of Alaska Native Communities* (Brookings LSE, 30 January 2013).

K. Hausler, 'Collective Cultural Rights within the Inter-American Human Rights System' in A. Jakubowski (ed), *Cultural Rights as Collective Rights: An International Law Perspective* (Brill Nijhoff, 2016).

C. Hesse and L. Cotula, *Climate Change and Pastoralists: Investing in People to Respond to Adversity* (IIED, 2006) 1.

J.M. Pasquaulucci, 'The Right to a Dignified Life (Vida Digna): The Integration of Economic and Social Rights with Civil and Political Rights in the Inter-American Human Rights System' 31 *Hastings International & Comparative Law Review* (2008) 1.

Syafwina, 'Recognizing Indigenous Knowledge for Disaster Management: Smong, Early Warning System from Simeulue Island, Aceh' 20 *Procedia Environmental Sciences* (2014) 573.

Notes

1 HRC, Promotion and Protection of the Rights of Indigenous Peoples in Disaster Risk Reduction, Prevention and Preparedness Initiatives: Study by the Expert Mechanism on the Rights of Indigenous Peoples, UN Doc. A/HRC/27/66 (2014) para 3.

2 The frequency of extreme weather events includes rising sea levels, droughts, increasing water shortages, and the spread of tropical and vector-borne diseases, see the International Panel on Climate Change, 'Fourth Assessment Report' (2007), available at www.ipcc.ch/publications_and_data/publications_ipcc_fourth_assessment_report_synthesis_report.htm, accessed on 7 June 2017.

3 Inter-Governmental Panel on Climate Change, Climate Change 2014: Impacts, Adaptation and Vulnerability, Technical Summary, 8.

4 See the webpage of the Canadian Red Cross for First Nations, Métis and Inuit Communities, available at www.redcross.ca/how-we-help/emergencies-and-disasters-in-canada/for-first-nations-metis-and-inuit-communities, accessed on 7 June 2017.

5 See HRC, Report of the Special Rapporteur on Adequate Housing as a Component of the Right to an Adequate Standard of Living, UN Doc. A/66/270 (2011) para 15.

6 Ibid.

7 See, ABColombia, '"We Can Wait No Longer" – Afro Colombian and Indigenous Communities go to Bogota in an Effort to Have Their Basic Human Rights Upheld' (8 February 2012), available at http://reliefweb.int/report/colombia/%E2%80%98we-can-wait-no-longer%E2%80%99-afro-colombian-and-indigenous-communities-go-bogota-effort, accessed on 7 June 2017.

8 IMADR presented its joint oral statement with National Coalition Against Racial Discrimination (NCARD) on 'Indigenous peoples and natural disaster risk reduction in Nepal' at the 27th session of the Human Rights Council (2014), available at http://imadr.org/indigenous-peoples-and-natural-disaster-risk-reduction-in-nepal-hrc-27th-2014-joint-os/, accessed on 7 June 2017.
9 UN, 'Who Are Indigenous Peoples?', United Nations Permanent Forum on Indigenous Issues, 5th session, Fact sheet 1 (2015): *State of the World's Indigenous Peoples* (2009), available at www.un.org/esa/socdev/unpfii/documents/SOWIP_web.pdf, accessed on 7 June 2017. The FAO website states that there are 390–430 million Indigenous peoples worldwide, while UNESCO estimates their population to be anywhere between 370–500 million, see www.fao.org/indigenous-peoples/en/ and www.unesco.org/new/en/indigenous-peoples/, accessed on 7 June 2017.
10 J.R. Martinez Cobo, 'Study on the Problem of Discrimination against Indigenous Populations', UN Doc. E/CN.4/Sub.2/1986/7 and Add. 1–4 (1986), according to whom '[I]ndigenous communities, peoples and nations are those which, having a historical continuity with pre-invasion and pre-colonial societies that developed on their territories, consider themselves distinct from other sectors of the societies now prevailing on those territories, or parts of them'.
11 All of these criteria have been listed in International Law Association, Final Report of the Rights of Indigenous Peoples Committee, Sofia Conference (2012) 2–3.
12 UN Permanent Forum on Indigenous Issues, Fourth Session, UN Doc. E/C.19/2005/2 (2005), Annex III, Item 13.
13 See C. Hesse and L. Cotula, *Climate Change and Pastoralists: Investing in People to Respond to Adversity* (IIED, 2006) 1.
14 Ibid 2.
15 See B. Melkevik, *Law and Aboriginal Reindeer Herding in Norway* (Université Laval Groupe d'études inuit et circumpolaires, 2000) 198.
16 R. Bronen, *Climate-Induced Displacement of Alaska Native Communities* (Brookings LSE, 30 January 2013) i, 5–6.
17 Ibid 9.
18 See, for example, J.M. Pasquaulucci, 'The Right to a Dignified Life (Vida Digna): The Integration of Economic and Social Rights with Civil and Political Rights in the Inter-American Human Rights System' 31 *Hastings International and Comparative Law Review* (2008) 1, see also HRComm, General Comment No. 6: Article 6 (Right to life), Sixteenth session (1982) para 5.
19 HRC, Res 7/23: Human Rights and Climate Change, UN Doc. A/HRC/RES/7/23 (2008), available at http://ap.ohchr.org/documents/E/HRC/resolutions/A_HRC_RES_7_23.pdf, accessed on 7 June 2017. The HRC stated that climate change 'possesses an immediate and far-reaching threat to people and communities around the world'.
20 International Covenant on Civil and Political Rights (adopted 16 December 1966, entered into force 23 March 1976) 999 UNTS 171.
21 See, in general, the HRC, Expert Mechanism on the Rights of Indigenous Peoples, Final study on indigenous peoples and the right to participate in decision-making, Fourth session, 11–15 July 2011 (2011).
22 IMADR presented its joint oral statement with National Coalition Against Racial Discrimination (NCARD) on 'Indigenous peoples and natural disaster risk reduction in Nepal' at the 27th session of the Human Rights Council (2014), available at http://imadr.org/indigenous-peoples-and-natural-disaster-risk-reduction-in-nepal-hrc-27th-2014-joint-os/, accessed on 7 June 2017.
23 International Covenant on Economic, Social and Cultural Rights (adopted 16 December 1966, entered into force 3 January 1976) 993 UNTS 3.
24 Convention (No. 169) concerning Indigenous and Tribal Peoples in Independent Countries (adopted 27 June 1989, entered into force 5 September 1991) 1650 UNTS 383, art 27. See, for example, K. Hausler, 'Collective Cultural Rights within the Inter-American Human Rights System' in A. Jakubowski (ed), *Cultural Rights as Collective Rights: An International Law Perspective* (Brill Nijhoff, 2016) 225–226.
25 ILC, Draft Articles on Responsibility of States for Internationally Wrongful Acts, with commentaries, UN Doc. A/56/10 (2001) art 31.
26 *Case Concerning the Factory at Chorzów* [1927] PJIC Ser A No 9, para 29.
27 HRC, Promotion and Protection of the Rights of Indigenous Peoples in Disaster Risk Reduction, Prevention and Preparedness Initiatives (n. 1) para 10.
28 Ibid paras 7–10.
29 Ibid Annex para 1.
30 Ibid Annex paras 4–5.
31 Ibid Annex para 15.

32 Ibid Annex paras 8 and 13.
33 HRC, Report of the Special Rapporteur on Adequate Housing as a Component of the Right to an Adequate Standard Living, and on the Right to Non-Discrimination in This Context, R. Rolnik, Sixteenth Session, UN Doc. A/HRC/16/42 (2010) para 32. See also Rolnik's chapter in this volume.
34 HRC, Report of the Independent Expert on the Issue of Human Rights Obligations Relating to the Enjoyment of a Safe, Clean, Healthy and Sustainable Environment, Mapping Report, UN Doc. A/HRC/25/53 (2013) paras 69–78.
35 HRC, Report of the Special Rapporteur on the Issue of Human Rights Obligations Relating to the Enjoyment of a Safe, Clean, Healthy and Sustainable Environment, paras 81–82.
36 HRC, Report of the Special Rapporteur on the Right to Food, Olivier De Schutter, Mission to Nicaragua, UN Doc. A/HRC/13/33/Add.5 (2010) para 76.
37 HRC, Promotion and Protection of the Rights of Indigenous Peoples in Disaster Risk Reduction, Prevention and Preparedness Initiatives (n. 1) paras 13–14.
38 *Kichwa People of Sarayaku v. Ecuador*, IACtHR, Ser. C, No. 245 (2012) paras 284 ff.
39 *Case of Aloeboetoe et al. v. Suriname*, IACtHR, Ser. C, No. 15 (1993) 13.
40 See, for example, the *Case of the Saramaka People v. Suriname*, IACtHR, Ser C, No. 172 (2007), which concerned mining concessions which polluted traditional lands and water resources. Note also that the Commission has stated that severe environmental pollution is not consistent with the right to be respected as a human being and may thus constitute violations of the right to life and physical integrity, see ICAHR, Report on the Situation of Human Rights in Ecuador, OEA/Ser.L/ V.II.96 (1997).
41 A public act acknowledging responsibility and commemorating the victims was part of the reparations award; see case of the *Plan de Sánchez Massacre v. Guatemala*, IACtHR, Ser C, No. 116 (2004) paras 100–101.
42 Ibid para 102.
43 See, example, case of the *Plan de Sánchez Massacre v. Guatemala*, IACtHR, Ser C, No. 105 (2004).
44 *The Social and Economic Rights Action Centre and the Centre for Economic and Social Rights v. Nigeria*, ACommHPR, Communication No 155/96 (Decision of 27 October 2001) para 54.
45 While this right is also contained in Article 11 of the San Salvador Protocol, which states that 'Everyone shall have the right to live in a healthy environment and to have access to basic public services', it cannot be the subject of individual petition to the Inter-American Commission on Human Rights.
46 African Union Convention for the Protection and Assistance of Internally Displaced Persons in Africa (Kampala Convention) (adopted 23 October 2009, entered into force December 2012), AU Doc. Ext/Assembly/AU/PA/Draft/Decl.(I)Rev.1, art 1(k).
47 Ibid arts 4, 5(4).
48 Ibid art 12(3).
49 See, for example, N. Schrepfer and M. Caterina, 'On the Margin: Kenya's Pastoralists', Internal Displacement Monitoring Centre, Norwegian Refugee Council (March 2014).
50 See, for example, art 8(1), according to which '[i]n applying national laws and regulations to the peoples concerned, due regard shall be had to their customs or customary laws.'
51 ILO Convention 169, art 15.
52 They include Argentina, Bolivia, Brazil, Central African Republic, Chile, Colombia, Costa Rica, Denmark, Dominica, Ecuador, Fiji, Guatemala, Honduras, Mexico, Nepal, Netherlands, Nicaragua, Norway, Paraguay, Peru, Spain, and Venezuela.
53 UNGA, Res 61/295: United Nations Declaration on the Rights of Indigenous Peoples, UN Doc. A/RES/61/295 (2007).
54 HRC, Promotion and Protection of the Rights of Indigenous Peoples in Disaster Risk Reduction, Prevention and Preparedness Initiatives (n. 1) para 11, where it stated that 'several of [UNDRIP] provisions have implications for the promotion and protection of indigenous peoples' rights in this area, and can provide guidance for the design and implementation of sound disaster risk reduction strategies and interventions'.
55 HRC, Promotion and Protection of the Rights of Indigenous Peoples in Disaster Risk Reduction, Prevention and Preparedness Initiatives (n. 1) para 12.
56 See the website of Habitat for Humanity available at www.habitat.org/disaster/mitigation_preparedness, accessed on 7 June 2017. See also the following webpage at www.habitat.org/disaster/programs/programs_06_10.aspx, accessed on 7 June 2017.
57 HRC, Promotion and Protection of the Rights of Indigenous Peoples in Disaster Risk Reduction, Prevention and Preparedness Initiatives (n. 1) para 15.

58 Ibid para 13.
59 Paris Agreement, FCCC/CP/2015/L.9, Annex (adopted 12 December 2015, entered into force 4 November 2016).
60 HRC, Promotion and Protection of the Rights of Indigenous Peoples in Disaster Risk Reduction, Prevention and Preparedness Initiatives (n. 1) paras 3 and 16.
61 UN Permanent Forum on Indigenous Issues, Report of the Inter-Agency Support Group Meeting on Indigenous Peoples, UN Doc. E/C.19/2013/4 (2013), para 2.
62 HRC, Report of the Special Rapporteur on Adequate Housing as a Component of the Right to an Adequate Standard of Living, UN Doc. A/66/270 (2011) para 29.
63 PAHO Rand WHO Recommendations, 4.
64 The definitions developed by the UNISDR, for example, do not always reflect Indigenous concepts which may be a hurdle when conducting consultation with Indigenous peoples, see UNISDR, *Terminology on Disaster Risk Reduction* (2009).
65 See, for example, the Twelfth Session of the Permanent Forum on Indigenous Issues, 'Valuing Traditional Knowledge: Sharing Intercultural Perspectives from the MDG Experience'. UNESCO has also conducted research on Indigenous knowledge for DRR.
66 J. Kamara, 'Indigenous Knowledge in Natural Disaster Reduction in Africa', citing O.O.G. Amusan, 'The Status of the Application and Use of Indigenous Knowledge' in *Natural Resource Conservation and Hydrological Disaster Management in Swaziland*, available at www.grida.no/publications/et/ep3/page/2608.aspx, accessed on 7 June 2017.
67 See UNEP, 'Disaster Early Warning, Preparedness, and Response', available at www.unep.org/training/programmes/Instructor%20Version/Part_2/Activities/Interest_Groups/Culture/Strategies/Indigenous_Disaster_Early_Warning_Preparedness_and_Response.pdf, accessed on 7 June 2017.
68 Syafwina, 'Recognizing Indigenous Knowledge for Disaster Management: Smong, Early Warning System from Simeulue Island, Aceh' 20 *Procedia Environmental Sciences* (2014) 573. See also 'Saved by Tsunami Folklore' *BBC News* (10 March 2007), available at http://news.bbc.co.uk/2/hi/programmes/from_our_own_correspondent/6435979.stm, accessed on 7 June 2017. It was reported that, given the closeness of Simeulue to the epicentre, a hi-tech tsunami detection system would not have warned the population on time.
69 The tsunami was also more powerful by the time it reached Aceh, where many victims had no higher ground in their vicinity to shelter.
70 HRC, Promotion and Protection of the Rights of Indigenous Peoples in Disaster Risk Reduction, Prevention and Preparedness Initiatives (n. 1) para 14.
71 J. Kamara, 'Indigenous Knowledge in Natural Disaster Reduction in Africa', available at www.grida.no/publications/et/ep3/page/2608.aspx, accessed on 7 June 2017.
72 Expert Mechanism Study, Annex, para 24.
73 Hyogo Framework for Action 2005–2015, para 13.
74 Ibid para 12.
75 HRC, Promotion and Protection of the Rights of Indigenous Peoples in Disaster Risk Reduction, Prevention and Preparedness Initiatives (n. 1) para 22.
76 UNISDR, 'Post-2015 Framework for Disaster Risk Reduction (HFA2)', Report from 2013 Global Platform Consultations (October 2013), available at www.preventionweb.net/files/35070_hfa2consultationsgp2013report.pdf, accessed on 7 June 2017.
77 PAHO and WHO, 'Recommendations for Engaging Indigenous Peoples in Disaster Risk Reduction, Including Approaches and Strategies to Reduce Disaster and Overcome Existing Challenges to Their Implementation'. At this Hemispheric Consultation, which took place in September 2014, there were delegates from Bolivia, Peru, Ecuador, Honduras, Guatemala, Mexico, Dominica, Guyana, the United States, and Canada.
78 Six States (Australia, El Salvador, France, Germany, Guatemala, and Mexico) and from four other stakeholders (ALDET Centre – Saint Lucia, Consejo Nacional Indígena, Guyanese Organization of Indigenous Peoples, and the New Zealand Human Rights Commission) allowed the Expert mechanism to render their submissions available at www.ohchr.org/EN/Issues/IPeoples/EMRIP/Pages/Studyondisasterriskreduction.aspx, accessed on 7 June 2017.
79 HRC, Promotion and protection of the rights of indigenous peoples in disaster risk reduction, prevention and preparedness initiatives (n. 1) para 4.
80 The Sendai Framework was endorsed by the UNGA, following the 2015 Third UN World Conference on Disaster Risk Reduction (WCDRR).

81 Sendai Framework (n. 80) para 7.
82 UNEP, 'Indigenous Knowledge in Disaster Management in Africa' (2008) 105, available at www.icsu.org/icsu-africa/news-centre/news/Appendix9IndigenousBookletUNEP.pdf, accessed on 7 June 2017.
83 Sendai Framework (n. 80) para 19(g).
84 Ibid para 24(i).
85 Ibid para 36(a)(v).
86 The 2007 IFRC Guidelines for the domestic facilitation and regulation of international disaster relief and initial recovery assistance (also known as the 'IDRL Guidelines').
87 Sendai Framework (n. 80) para 27(h).
88 See Canadian Red Cross, For First Nations, Métis and Inuit Communities, Moose Cree First Nation Community, available at www.redcross.ca/how-we-help/emergencies-and-disasters-in-canada/for-first-nations – metis-and-inuit-communities, accessed on 7 June 2017.
89 Canadian Red Cross, Emergency Preparedness Guide for Muskego Cree Families, James Bay First Nation Communities, Be Red Cross Ready, 2.
90 Ibid 3.
91 Ibid 4.
92 Ibid 5.
93 Ibid 11.
94 Ibid 4.
95 HRC, Promotion and Protection of the Rights of Indigenous Peoples in Disaster Risk Reduction, Prevention and Preparedness Initiatives (n. 1) para 6.

20
THE PROTECTION OF MIGRANTS IN DISASTERS

*Alice Sironi and Lorenzo Guadagno**

Introduction: a focus on migrants in disasters

Today's societies, increasingly interconnected and globalized, in which circulation of people, goods and information is faster and easier than ever, are also characterized by an increasing number of people moving abroad for employment, family reasons or education or as a consequence of conflicts and instability, crime and violence and disasters. Globally, some 250 million people reside outside of their country of origin,[1] and many more circulate across borders for shorter periods.[2] Nationals abroad represent double-digit shares of some countries' population, and foreign-born and migrant-background residents compose large shares of many of the world's cities.[3] As a consequence of these intense population flows, originating from (and directed to) countries in the global North as much as in the global South, communities and societies all around the world become ever more diverse, transnational networks tighter and cross-cultural fertilization more intense, all of which further drive and enable migration processes.[4]

Consequently, everywhere in the world, in countries of origin, transit and destination alike, consideration of human mobility trends is becoming integral to the functioning of governmental institutions, public and private providers of basic services, employers and non-governmental entities. This includes efforts aiming to manage disasters[5] and reduce disaster risk: inclusive disaster prevention, mitigation, preparedness, response and recovery efforts increasingly need to account for migrants' presence,[6] for their diverse sets of skills and resources, and for the specific obstacles and barriers they face, compared to the native population. As recently shown by events such as the 2011 floods in Thailand, the Tohoku triple disaster in Japan, and superstorm Sandy in the United States,[7] such characteristics shape the way migrants are affected by hazards – and often make them more vulnerable to short- and long-term negative impacts.

For countries of destination, whether more or less affluent, reducing such impacts means reducing the hazards' overall impacts on affected communities. Migrant-inclusive disaster risk reduction and disaster management are key to this end, as they allow protecting and leveraging all available resources and capacities to reduce risk and cope with and recover from disasters. For countries of origin, reducing the vulnerability to hazards of their nationals abroad helps protect the economic, social and cultural gains their citizens, as well as their whole societies, derive from migration.

Over the last few years, attention to migrants' specific conditions of vulnerability and to the importance of including them in disaster risk reduction and management has increased.[8]

The issue of migrants caught in emergency situations while abroad, both in cases of conflicts or disasters, and the search for effective collaboration mechanisms, were already among the focuses of the 2013 United Nations (UN) High Level Dialogue on International Migration and Development. The following year, a group of Governments, together with international organizations and research institutions, launched the Migrants In Countries In Crisis (MICIC) Initiative.[9] In 2016, as the result of a 2-year multi-stakeholder consultative process, the Initiative produced a set of non-binding, voluntary principles, guidelines and practices.[10] The document aims to guide efforts by both State and non-state actors to improve protection of, and assistance to, migrants before, during and after crises, including disasters. This chapter partially draws from the discussions and outcomes of these consultations.

Migrants' specificities in disasters

Experience from diverse geographical settings shows that migrants are often disproportionately affected by hazards hitting their destinations. Migrants' specific conditions of vulnerability are determined by the interplay of their individual and collective characteristics (i.e. origin, ethnicity, linguistic proficiency) and the social, cultural and political features of their host society and its institutions (including, crucially, its immigration regime). This interaction determines migrants' status, rights, access to resources, services and opportunities in normal times, and consequently their conditions of safety and security, and their needs, in disasters.

Communication barriers (due to limited language proficiency, reliance on non-mainstream media, physical and social isolation) can reduce migrants' access to information on hazards and risk management procedures, their understanding of early warnings and emergency communications and their access to relief and recovery assistance. Lack of knowledge of the social and environmental features of their destination can result in diverse perception of local risks, different reactions in the face of hazards and limited awareness of available options for assistance and support. Reduced participation in local social networks can reduce their access to material and immaterial support needed to anticipate and cope with a hazard's impacts. Lack of trust in local institutions and communities due, for instance, to fear of arrest or to discrimination or xenophobic acts, can reduce migrants' willingness to seek assistance and to comply with official instructions (e.g. for evacuation and sheltering). All these conditions are exacerbated whenever explicit legal provisions exclude (some) migrants from accessing (some forms of) assistance and support.[11]

Characteristics such as gender, age, skill level, census, family situation, origin and migration status determine to what extent different migrants experience such barriers – and therefore their individual vulnerability.[12] Migrants who have access to an extended pool of opportunities and resources (including through local networks, diasporas and home communities and institutions) may well be more resilient than some members of their host communities.

Migration status as a factor of vulnerability

In many geographical contexts, migration status is linked with administrative and legal barriers which contribute to their vulnerability to disasters. Work permits or visas tied to non-nationals' permanence in a certain area or employment in a certain job can reduce their capacity to evacuate and repatriate.[13] Many countries do not guarantee all non-nationals full access to the broad spectrum of measures citizens can leverage to cope with disasters (e.g. unemployment benefits, housing reconstruction assistance, medical care and psychosocial assistance).[14] In general, while disaster management actors all over the world tend (at least formally) to provide relief assistance in a non-discriminatory manner, non-nationals have much more limited access to longer-term assistance and resources and information that are needed for prevention, preparedness and recovery.

Non-citizens lacking legal status can be particularly vulnerable. They are often unregistered and therefore unaccounted for in disaster management efforts by both their countries of origin and of destination. Due to fear of arrest and deportation, they tend to avoid seeking the support of disaster management actors and service providers and reduce movements (including life-saving evacuation) to the minimum. They are more likely to face risky choices during and after disasters (e.g. losing savings or documentation withheld by employers or recruitment agencies, being exposed to increased risk in affected areas that they are not able to flee, being abused while trying to evacuate and having to accept underpaid jobs in exploitative conditions throughout the reconstruction phase). After hurricane Katrina, in 2004, as well as after the 2011 floods in Thailand, for instance, many undocumented migrants stayed in affected areas due to fear of being arrested and deported by police and immigration officials.[15]

Asylum-seekers may be required to stay in a given area due to restrictions linked with the processing of their asylum claim, as was the case in Japan after the 2011 Tohoku triple disaster.[16] Stateless persons might lack the documentation needed for evacuation and for accessing assistance – and might be refused access to third countries in the case of international evacuation. Refugees, instead, do not necessarily represent a particularly vulnerable group in disasters, as they can usually count on legal status and access to protection in their host State.[17]

In the light of the foregoing, this chapter discusses the responses that international law, and more specifically the human rights regime, provide to address the plight of non-nationals in the context of disasters. While recognizing the important role that a variety of actors, such as civil society and international organizations, play in reducing the vulnerability of non-nationals in disasters, this chapter focuses exclusively on State obligations. It explores the role of the State of origin in the protection of its nationals abroad as both a right and an obligation. It then looks at the protection of non-nationals in disasters from the perspective of the affected State and aims at describing the obligations that this State has with regard to non-nationals who are present on its territory when the disaster strikes. Lastly, it describes the articulation of the respective responsibilities of the State of origin and of the affected State, highlighting the need for establishing an effective cooperation among relevant institutions.

Protecting migrants: the role of the State of origin

This section looks at the role of the State of origin in protecting the rights of its nationals abroad in the context of disasters. It explores the theoretical frameworks that could underpin the protection of disaster-affected nationals as both a right of the State and of the individuals.

A State right to protect its nationals abroad

The first institution that may be relevant to the analysis of a State's right to protect its nationals abroad is diplomatic protection.[18] Diplomatic protection can however play a limited role to help States protect their nationals affected by disasters abroad. It is primarily remedial and therefore does not cover the preventive actions that a State could adopt to ensure that the rights of its nationals are taken into account as part of disaster risk reduction, preparedness and response efforts. Secondly, it can only be resorted to after exhaustion of domestic remedies, which can be problematic in contexts in which action is urgently needed, as it implies that a long time elapses between the injury and the remedy. In fact, relevant practice is almost inexistent, even though in a few cases diplomatic protection has been used to address infringements of individual rights in the context of disasters triggered by technological hazards.[19]

Consular assistance seems more suitable for addressing situations in which nationals abroad need support in a disaster. Consular assistance can be both reactive or preventive[20] and is not subject to the rule of the exhaustion of local remedies.[21] It is part of the right of a State to protect its interests and those of its nationals in another State (Article 5.a Vienna Convention on Consular Relations).[22] The right to consular assistance is to be exercised on another State's territory; therefore, in compliance with the principle of State sovereignty, it is subject to the consent of the receiving State (Article 2.1 Vienna Convention on Consular Relations). Article 5 of the Vienna Convention lists the main consular functions, many of which are relevant in disaster situations. These include: (i) the general protection of the interests of the sending State and of its nationals (Article 5.a), which is particularly pertinent to the pre-disaster phase, when it is key to including non-nationals in disaster risk reduction and preparedness measures,[23] and (ii) the disaster assistance States can provide for their nationals abroad (Article 5.e), for example through the targeted delivery of relief goods, emergency cash assistance, replacement of documents lost in the disaster[24] or organization of evacuation operations.

Most consular functions are routinely performed in normal times and can be simply adapted to the circumstances in a disaster, without requiring additional authorizations by the affected State. However, other functions specific to disaster situations risk infringing upon the territorial integrity of the affected State, unless a specific agreement between the affected State and the State of origin regulates them. These 'extraordinary' functions are not specified in the list of Article 5 of the Vienna Convention and would fall under the residual category provided for in Article 5.m, which refers to 'other functions entrusted to a consular post by the sending State'. The affected State retains the possibility to object to these other functions,[25] particularly when they involve the entry into the State of qualified personnel of the State of nationality to provide emergency consular assistance on a large scale or to organize international evacuations.[26] The latter is an option States have resorted to in a number of circumstances. After the 2011 triple disaster in Japan, Korea evacuated its nationals within 20 kilometres of the disaster zone, including using military aircraft and coast guard boats.[27] The USA evacuated over 28,000 people, mainly US citizens, out of Haiti after the 2010 earthquake, 16,700 of which on military planes.[28]

The question whether the State of nationality has a remedy against the refusal of the affected State to consent to such 'extraordinary' consular functions or interventions on its territory should be addressed within the broader doctrine on the protection of nationals abroad. International Law recognizes the right of States to peacefully protect their nationals abroad as a State's population represents an essential component of statehood. The discussions around the protection of nationals abroad have focused on forcible forms of protection, and many authors concur in denying their legality due to the prohibition of the use of force and the difficulty in considering them as a form of self-defence.[29] Evacuations of nationals taken hostages in another State, for instance, are considered forcible measures because they infringe upon the territorial integrity of the host State, even if the operation is not directed against the host State and is strictly limited to what is necessary for saving the nationals' lives. However, evacuations in response to disasters usually involve a larger set of actors who do not operate with the same modalities and rules of engagement. In most cases, hostage interventions are carried out by military or para-military forces using weapons, whereas evacuations out of disaster areas are coordinated under the responsibility of the foreign ministry, and very often, they rely on commercial airlines or vessels. Even when military personnel or equipment are used, the nature of the intervention remains purely humanitarian and does not involve the use of force.[30]

In the absence of sufficient practice, both scholars and States are generally against the recognition of a State right to humanitarian intervention on the territory of another State when the affected State consent is lacking, even in the cases in which these interventions are exclusively directed at saving the lives of the population. The debate in this regard has focused on the applicability of the responsibility to protect doctrine in the context of disasters,[31] which is generally denied, contained within very narrow limits[32] or looked at through the different lens of the existence of a right to humanitarian assistance of the affected population[33] and of the related obligation for the affected State to consent to external assistance if domestic resources are insufficient to adequately protect people.[34]

With regard to interventions aimed at saving a State's own nationals, instead, there is a growing tendency, highlighted by some scholars,[35] to condone or acquiesce to unauthorized operations by States to evacuate and assist their nationals in distress abroad. This tendency is *a fortiori* confirmed in disaster situations, in which outright refusal by the affected State is relatively rare and the more common problems are delays in responding to requests by foreign States or facilitating the movement of foreign relief personnel.[36]

If the affected State fails to protect non-nationals or particular groups of non-nationals, withholding consent to a foreign State's entry in the territory to protect its nationals may be considered as arbitrary and as a possible breach of the right to life of the concerned persons.[37] In its commentary to Draft Article 13 on this topic, the International Law Commission identifies three conditions that should be assessed when verifying whether the withholding of consent to external assistance is arbitrary. Firstly, the withholding of consent is not arbitrary if the State has the capacity and is willing to respond adequately to the disaster with its own resources. Secondly, such consent can be denied with regard to one source of assistance if the assistance provided by other sources is sufficient. Thirdly, the denial of consent is not arbitrary if the offer is not made in accordance with the humanitarian principles of humanity, neutrality, impartiality and non-discrimination.

As the State of nationality of a large group of affected persons has a qualified interest in protecting its own nationals, it should be allowed to provide assistance for its nationals even if the assistance has already been provided for the broader population by other sources. The withholding of consent to the assistance proposed by such a State should then be considered as not arbitrary, only if the affected State has the capacity and is willing to provide sufficient assistance both for the nationals and for the non-nationals who are on its territory[38] or in the cases in which the offer does not comply with humanitarian principles.[39] Nonetheless, the intervention of the State of nationality of affected persons should respect the primary role of the affected State in the direction, control, coordination and supervision of any assistance provided by foreign actors.[40] However, conditions imposed on the assistance provided by the State of origin of non-nationals should take into consideration the qualified interest of this State in protecting its disaster-affected nationals and their specific needs.[41]

The protection of its nationals as an obligation of the State of origin

Human rights law and the Vienna Convention on Consular Relations

Action and inaction by Governments in response to disasters, and in particular large-scale ones, are often thoroughly scrutinized by the media and the public.[42] However, it is debatable whether, or to what extent, States have a legal obligation to protect their nationals in distress abroad under human rights law.[43]

The absence of a general obligation of States to protect their nationals abroad is embedded in the principle of respect for the sovereignty and territorial integrity of other States – which reflects on the territoriality of State obligations under human rights law. An extension of the territorial dimension of human rights obligations is possible only in exceptional cases.[44] Extraterritorial jurisdiction in the human rights domain is based on the concept of effective control[45] and not on the nationality link. Under human rights law, a few rights are granted exclusively to nationals.[46] However, except for these rights there is no consideration of the specific interest of the State of nationality to protect its nationals. The protection of human rights of individuals is a common interest of the international community, which goes beyond the nationality tie, implies objective obligations and is exempted from the application of the principle of reciprocity.

Still, the human rights framework sets forth a few, but significant, obligations for the States of nationality. The International Convention on the Rights of All Migrant Workers and Members of Their Families (Migrant Workers Convention, ICRMW)[47] recognizes the importance of looking at the whole migration process[48] and, specifically, at the role of States of origin in assisting their nationals, including by protecting their rights when they are abroad.[49] Particular emphasis is on the importance of cooperation among the States of origin and of destination to prevent abuses and ensure access to rights (Articles 64, 65.1(b), 67 and 68).

The Migrant Workers Convention only applies to migrant workers but defines this category in extensive terms in line with its consideration of the whole migration process. Migrant workers are persons who are to be engaged, are engaged or have been engaged in a remunerated activity in a State of which they are not nationals (Article 2.1). This definition is likely to capture the great majority of people moving abroad, although article 3 excludes some specific categories (i.e. international civil servants, investors, refugees and stateless persons, students and trainees and seafarers and workers on an offshore installation). The Migrant Workers Convention is poorly ratified,[50] but most of its provisions reflect rights that are already recognized for everyone by other human rights conventions ratified by a more significant number of States.[51] The Convention provides guidance on how rights should be interpreted in the specific situation of migrants.

Critical for the protection of nationals affected by a disaster abroad are: the right to return to one's own country (Article 67.1) and, for regular migrant workers, reintegration upon return (Article 67.2) and the right to have recourse to consular or diplomatic protection and assistance whenever their rights are impaired – coupled with an obligation upon the State of origin and of destination to facilitate the provision of adequate consular and other services (Articles 23 and 65.2). Diplomatic channels, for instance, can help States negotiate exit from the affected country and facilitate the right to return (e.g. by requiring reduction or waivering of relevant exit fees for their nationals).[52] Finally, the right of information and appropriate assistance regarding formalities and arrangements for departure, travel, arrival, stay, exit and return (Articles 65.1(d) and 33.1(b)) may also apply in disasters. It is particularly relevant to ensure effective information on options and requirements for evacuation out of an affected country and back to one's country of origin. The Migrant Workers Committee, in its first General Comment, recommended States to train domestic workers before departure on, *inter alia*, 'contact information for emergency assistance, including embassies and consulates, and relevant civil society organizations in countries of employment'[53] and underlined the active role that embassies and consulates should have in protecting nationals abroad.[54]

A more complex question is whether any of these rights can be considered customary law.[55] The answer is particularly relevant with regard to the right to consular protection and assistance that is only expressly recognized by the Migrant Workers Convention. The question whether the Vienna Convention on Consular Relations[56] recognizes such an individual right (in addition to the right of the State to carry out its consular functions in another State) is debated. The International Court of Justice (ICJ) in the *LaGrand* case recognized that Article 36.1(b) of the Vienna Convention on communication in case of arrest of a national of the sending State protects both a State and an individual right.[57] The ICJ did not pronounce itself on whether Article 36.1(a) on freedom of communication and access to consular officers, apart from the case of arrest and detention, implies an individual right.[58] Nonetheless, in its examination of the violation of Article 36.1 as a whole by the United States, it highlighted that this Article establishes an interrelated regime designed to facilitate the implementation of the system of consular protection and that the breach of Article 36.1(b) implied a violation of Article 36.1 as a whole.[59] The wording of Article 36.1 seems to point to the same conclusion with regard to its let. (a).[60] The Inter-American Court of Human Rights (IACtHR) more clearly considers the whole Article 36 as granting rights directly to individuals.[61] The IACtHR seems to have interpreted in the same way the broader right to consular protection and assistance referred to in Article 5(a) and (e) of the Vienna Convention.[62]

Assistance to own nationals and non-discrimination

Lastly, a sensitive issue arising in disaster situations may be whether it is always justified for the State of nationality to give dedicated disaster assistance to its nationals. The question is particularly relevant because of the risk of unequal treatment among similarly affected persons, namely among nationals of States which have the resources to provide dedicated relief or evacuation assistance and affected locals or nationals of other States with more limited capacities. Can foreign States come into the territory of the affected State, save their nationals and leave all other affected people unassisted?

The discussion is about whether a foreign State's officials in a disaster area can prioritize their nationals in the delivery of assistance, or whether a strict application of the needs-first approach is required in observance with the basic principles of humanitarian interventions (notably the principles of humanity and impartiality).[63] It needs to be considered that the authorities of the State of origin that usually intervene to protect nationals and to provide humanitarian assistance for the broader population are different, as are the rules that apply to these two types of interventions. For interventions by consular authorities, or otherwise under the responsibility of the Ministry of Foreign Affairs, the main objective is to provide assistance to nationals in distress abroad, and not to provide humanitarian assistance to the broader population. Humanitarian principles would still apply, although in a restrictive manner that takes into consideration the primary objective of the intervening State. Therefore, unless the intervention is regulated under a specific agreement between the intervening State and other States concerned, other individuals (nationals of the affected State or of other States) should be prioritized only when there is an imminent threat to their life or physical integrity and the intervening State's nationals are safe. The proposed reasoning does not exclude the possible existence of a responsibility to protect the broader population, which would apply to the States of origin in the same way as to any other State of the international community.[64]

State practice in past disasters seems to have found a fair balance between the States' interest to protect their nationals abroad and the interest of the international community to protect people in general. Rare are the cases when States intervene exclusively to evacuate their nationals; usually, evacuations and assistance for nationals are coupled with the assistance provided for the broader population.[65]

In addition, eligibility criteria for international evacuations are often extended to dependents of the State citizens and to nationals of third States, albeit on a case-by-case decision.[66] In the context of the European Union (EU), Article 23 of the Treaty on the Functioning of the European Union (TFEU) requires Member States to provide diplomatic and consular protection to citizens of any Member State, on the same conditions as the nationals of that State. Decision 95/553 specifies that such consular protection also includes repatriation of distressed EU citizens on an equal footing with nationals.[67] Despite the existence of some positive practice, States have not been exempted from criticism for having selectively chosen whom to evacuate, particularly in cases in which such decisions resulted in the exclusion of some particularly vulnerable individuals.[68]

The evacuation of non-nationals out of affected areas can be a key measure for reducing pressure for assistance on the affected State. However, these efforts need to be coordinated with parallel local or international relief and assistance targeting the whole population.[69]

Protecting migrants: the role of the affected State

The primary responsibility for protecting the population in the event of a disaster rests with the affected State.[70] States' policies and efforts in disasters need to be inclusive and address the specific needs of particularly vulnerable individuals. This includes people whose vulnerability results from their migration status (irregular migrants, asylum-seekers and refugees); individual circumstances (victims of trafficking or exploited, abused and marginalized migrants); and characteristics (unaccompanied migrant children or disabled migrants). This section discusses the extent of the affected State's obligations towards non-nationals in disasters and the implications of an application of the principle of non-discrimination on grounds of nationality or migration status as interpreted by human rights bodies.

The principle of equality and non-discrimination as a baseline for addressing migrants' specific needs

Human rights conventions apply to everyone on the territory or under the jurisdiction of a State, with very few exceptions.[71] In the absence of a human rights convention specifically dealing with all categories of non-nationals, there is often confusion on the exact content and scope of their rights, particularly for those who are in an irregular situation. Specific categories of migrants are expressly or implicitly protected under a number of international instruments, dealing with migrant workers,[72] refugees,[73] victims of trafficking,[74] smuggled migrants,[75] migrant children,[76] migrant women,[77] disabled migrants[78] and even non-nationals caught in an armed conflict.[79] All these instruments help clarify the scope of the application of general human rights conventions to non-nationals. A rich literature exists on the rights of migrants in both regular and irregular situations.[80] In the absence of any express limitation of rights, the residual provision that applies to non-nationals is the principle of equality and non-discrimination. This section elucidates how this principle has been applied to address the situation of migrants in the context of disasters.

National origin is expressly included among the prohibited grounds of discrimination in almost all universal human rights conventions that contain a non-discrimination provision.[81] Nationality[82] is explicitly mentioned in the most recent instruments, including the ICRMW, but it is considered as implicitly included in all other relevant conventions. To be justified under human rights law, any distinctions between nationals and non-nationals in the access to rights, including in the context of disasters, need to be verified against the principle of non-discrimination. Differential treatments need to pursue a legitimate aim, be compatible with the nature of the rights enshrined in the relevant human rights treaty and be aimed at promoting the general welfare in a democratic society. Lastly, there must be a clear and reasonable proportionality between the aim to be achieved and State actions or omissions (and their effects).[83]

The implementation of the principle of equality and non-discrimination to migrants in national contexts

Many countries have adopted laws or regulations that explicitly require disaster management actors to provide assistance in a way that does not discriminate affected persons on the grounds of their nationality, origin, migration status or language proficiency. The 2012 Colombian law on disaster risk management (No. 1523), for instance, recognizes the general principle that all persons have the right to receive the same assistance in the face of a disaster. The Mexican 'Ley General de Población' states that foreigners have the right to disaster assistance, regardless of their legal status.[84] In the United States, the Robert T. Stafford Disaster Relief and Emergency Assistance Act states that disaster assistance should be provided without distinctions on the grounds of race, colour, religion, nationality, sex, age or economic status. In addition, an August 2000 Executive Order directs each Federal Agency to work to ensure that people that are eligible for federally funded programs and services (including those relevant for disaster risk management) are not discriminated on the basis of limited English proficiency.

Even in countries in which this principle is not explicitly stated in legal or administrative provisions, disaster management actors strive to ensure that their efforts are carried out in a non-discriminatory manner.[85] However, making sure that non-nationals actually receive adequate assistance often requires targeted, proactive efforts – in the light of their specific capacities, conditions of vulnerability and needs in times of disaster. Understanding and addressing the obstacles that might prevent non-nationals from accessing information, resources and assistance in disasters is necessary to fulfilling the criterion of substantive equality that underpins international and national legal provisions on this matter. Conversely, failing to adequately address non-nationals' diversity of conditions and behaviours all too often results in their exclusion and marginalization in times of disaster.

Limited linguistic proficiency, use of foreign or minority mass-media and social and physical isolation can reduce non-nationals' capacity to receive and interpret warnings and communications,[86] potentially resulting in their inability to protect themselves, evacuate or access support in the face of a hazard. This was the case of the Spanish-speaking community affected by the 1987 tornado in Saragosa, Texas,[87] as well as of some foreign residents in the areas of Japan affected by the 2011 triple disaster.[88]

Non-nationals are likely to show specific behaviours in disasters, as a consequence of different culturally learned habits, limited trust in warnings and in authorities and fear of leaving their houses.[89] In the face of Hurricanes Katrina (in 2004) and Gustav (in 2008), vulnerable migrants refused to leave at-risk areas due to fear of arrest and deportation, and of losing their house and belongings, with little access to legal remedies.[90]

Adequate delivery of food and non-food items, emergency shelter, healthcare and psychosocial support is dependent on the recipients' preferences and restrictions, which are part and parcel of their cultural background. Whenever cultural diversity is not factored in relief work, these core disaster management responsibilities are likely to go unfulfilled.[91]

Without proactive efforts on the part of disaster management actors, it is likely that non-nationals suffer more significant short-term and long-lasting impacts, which can further exacerbate their vulnerability. The palette of options available in support of such efforts include organizational measures, standards and procedures and operations. Programmes to involve non-nationals and their representatives in disaster management organizations, increase the cultural competence of emergency management personnel, develop targeted awareness-raising materials and work with relevant civil society and private sector actors to deliver more adequate services can all be useful to this end.[92] Measures to provide flexibility on immigration regulations in the aftermath of a disaster (including the possibility to overstay a visa without consequences or simplified procedures and documentation requirements for renewing one's visa) and 'firewalls' between disaster relief efforts and the enforcement of immigration regulations are also important.

Specific efforts may be needed to account for the conditions of specific groups of non-nationals, including those in irregular status, who might be reluctant to seek official assistance, and newcomers and migrants in transit, who are likely to have reduced local knowledge and social networks.

The affected State as a catalyst of other actors' compliance

Despite recent developments, non-state actors are generally not recognized as subjects of international law and therefore cannot be held responsible for wrongdoings against individuals at the international level.[93] With this limitation in mind, this section will briefly outline the central role of Civil Society Organizations (CSOs), employers and recruiters for the protection of migrants in disasters.

The role of civil society in protecting migrants in disaster and States' human rights obligations

Civil Society Organizations, including migrants and diaspora organizations, play a key role in ensuring that all sectors of the population, including marginalized non-nationals, are included in disaster prevention, preparedness, response and recovery. CSOs can facilitate the circulation of information to such groups and contribute to ensuring that they are consulted in planning and operations.[94] In addition, they are key disaster response actors, as they are often able to operate effectively and inclusively on the ground when hazards strike.[95] They may have well-established knowledge of and contacts with non-nationals, including those in irregular status, as they may work with them on a daily basis, and may be perceived as trustworthy actors, more easily approachable than any public authority.[96]

In line with the general approach of this chapter which primarily looks at State obligations, this section briefly outlines the obligations States have under human rights law to ensure that CSOs can contribute to an effective protection of non-nationals in disasters.

Two rights are particularly relevant to this end: the right to freedom of association and the right to information. The right to freedom of association is enshrined in a number of human rights treaties, including Article 22 of the International Covenant on Civil and Political Rights (ICCPR). It is further elaborated with specific regard to migrant workers in Article 26 ICRMW, which stipulates that all migrants, including those who are in an irregular situation, should be able to take part in meetings and activities of associations 'with a view to protecting their economic, social, cultural and other interests' (paragraph 1(a)); to join freely such associations (paragraph 1(b)); and to seek their aid and assistance (paragraph 1(c)).[97]

CSOs, and specifically migrants' associations, may face obstacles in carrying out their activities. Non-nationals in the Gulf region, for instance, are often prevented from organizing and forming associations.[98] Reforming laws, policies and practices that prohibit or limit such freedom is critical to better protecting and assisting migrants in disasters.[99]

The right to seek, receive and impart information, a corollary of the right to freedom of expression, is stipulated in various human rights conventions (Article 19 ICCPR), including the Migrant Workers Convention (Article 13 ICRMW). The right to impart information implies that the State should not restrict or hinder CSOs from carrying out awareness-raising activities targeting specifically the migrant population. In light of the challenges in disseminating emergency warnings and communications to non-nationals through official channels, efforts by CSOs (through social media, community meetings or door-to-door visits) are key to non-nationals' preparedness and response capacity.[100]

The Migrant Workers Convention imposes on States the positive obligation of taking measures to disseminate relevant information to migrants on their rights under the Convention, as well as requisite authorizations, formalities and arrangements for departure, travel, arrival, stay, exit and return (Article 33 and 65 ICRMW). CSOs can effectively support these efforts, as they relate to disaster situations.

Acknowledging the role of private recruiters and employers

Practices by employers and recruiters are a key determinant of migrants' vulnerability. Migrants may work in risky, exploitative or abusive conditions or may be bound to their employers because their residence permit is linked to their contract or because their employer is withholding their documents or salaries. Employment conditions often contribute to determining whether migrants will be able to avoid, cope with and recover from disasters, while employers can help ensure effective evacuation and relief assistance for their migrant employees.[101]

Both in normal times and in times of disasters, States have to adopt measures to prevent migrant workers from being submitted to exploitative conditions or abuses.[102] More specifically, States also have to compel recruiters and employers to prepare for and respond to disasters, including protecting their non-national employees. In order to comply with this obligation, States may choose to include in the relevant national legislation an obligation of due diligence for the recruiters and a proper duty of care for employers vis-à-vis their employees (as well as due diligence in choosing their subcontractors), so that they are accountable for protecting and assisting their migrant workforce in the event of a disaster.[103] Due diligence for the recruiters may imply that they have to check that the prospective employer has an adequate contingency plan, that an appropriate insurance policy is in place and that it covers migrants and includes relevant disaster situations. To this end, governments can set up mandatory insurance schemes for employers that entitle migrant members to repatriation and medical assistance in the event of a disaster.[104] For employers, complying with their duty of care may mean: (i) adopting a risk management policy; (ii) setting up a risk management team; (iii) developing a contingency plan taking into consideration the specific situation of non-national workers; and (iv) establishing systems for tracking and reaching out to their employees in disasters, including with a view to facilitating targeted assistance by response actors.[105]

The State of destination should also promote bilateral agreements with countries of origin to clarify the respective responsibilities in regulating the obligations of the recruiters and employers.[106]

The articulation of the roles of the State of origin and the affected State and the obligation to cooperate

Disaster risk management and response cannot be successful in the absence of effective cooperation among the various actors involved. This is even more evident when it comes to protecting non-nationals. This section will look at the obligation of cooperation in the relevant human rights framework and at examples of good practices of its operationalization. While cooperation can be key to strengthening the overall response system by allowing different State actors to pool resources, capacities and information, coordinating with foreign actors also requires additional efforts on the part of the affected State. The second part of the section will try to draw the fine line between ensuring that such interventions relieve some pressure on the affected State and the risk that they create an additional burden.

States' obligation to cooperate is well established in international law. It is stipulated in Articles 1(3) and 56 of the UN Charter. More specifically, the UN General Assembly, noting that the magnitude and duration of many emergencies is beyond the response capacity of most States, has recognized the crucial role of international cooperation in disaster situations. The same position was recently reiterated with regard to cooperation in disaster risk reduction.[107] Similarly, the international legal instruments applicable to migration accord great importance to the cooperation between States of origin, transit and destination.[108] The ICRMW recognizes 'the importance and usefulness of bilateral and multilateral agreements' and defines the scope of application of some of its provisions based on relevant inter-State agreements.[109] Part VI of the Convention requires States to consult and cooperate to promote sound, equitable and humane conditions of migration.[110] Article 64.2 urges States to pay attention not only to their labour needs but also to 'the social, economic, cultural and other needs of migrant workers and members of their families involved', as well as to the impacts of migration on the communities concerned in the countries of origin and of destination.[111] Furthermore, States need to maintain appropriate services to ensure an exchange of information and consultation with other States concerned by labour migration (Article 65.1(b) ICRMW). These services can play a key role in ensuring effective circulation and verification of information in times of disasters. In line with the right to information set forth in Article 33 ICRMW, which is applicable to all migrants, the relevant information has to reach those concerned. Particularly, non-nationals in irregular situations can be invisible and coordination among the States of origin and of destination often proves critical in locating, identifying and assisting them. Regular consultation between States of origin and of destination should also encompass disaster preparedness and response matters, including contingency planning, access to migrants, emergency communications, evacuation of non-nationals and administrative flexibility for leaving the country and to reissuing lost documents, in order to ensure that migrants are protected when a disaster strikes.[112]

Efforts led by the State of citizenship to evacuate their nationals out of disaster-affected areas, or provide relief assistance to their nationals or to the whole affected populations, can help reduce pressures for assistance on the affected State. However, these efforts need to be coordinated with parallel disaster response efforts by the affected State or other international actors in order to avoid potential logistical challenges,[113] as well as to prevent possible tensions with other affected persons (whether locals or non-nationals) who may lament unequal access to assistance.[114]

Cooperation between actors of the State of origin with the disaster management system of the affected State is also particularly important for addressing some of the non-nationals' specific needs in emergencies. For instance, authorities of the State of citizenship can help circulate and validate emergency communications and early warnings issued by the affected State's authorities to their nationals, thereby improving outreach to potentially hard-to-reach groups. After the 2011 Bangkok floods, joint assistance desks were set up by the Thai authorities and the consular staff of relevant countries of origin within evacuation centres specifically dedicated to migrants, in order to provide information and rapidly (re-)issue lost documents.[115] These coordinated efforts however require information disseminated through multiple channels to be consistent, failing which the trustworthiness of the whole emergency communications system may be undermined, resulting in lack of clear guidance and ineffective preparedness and response for the individuals. Such was the case of the circulation of information on the contamination after the Fukushima accident in 2011, when many foreigners residing in Japan were advised by their home country institutions to leave the country, against the advice of the Japanese government. This resulted in criticism of the Japanese government by the Japanese population itself.[116]

Pre-disaster arrangements and mechanisms that account for, and leverage, the capacities and resources of relevant actors both of the State of citizenship and of the affected State can help maximize benefits. Such tools may include: (i) bilateral agreements/memoranda of understanding with provisions on coordination in disasters (e.g. consular access), (ii) information sharing between capitals, (iii) common alert systems and (iv) preparedness and emergency communication plans that include focal points in foreign posts.[117]

Finally, a number of measures require cooperation to be oriented towards ensuring that migrants, including those in irregular situation, can safely return to their country of origin, if they wish to do so. The ICRMW requires States to cooperate in this regard.[118] The Trafficking Protocol calls upon States of origin to facilitate the return of their nationals who are without proper documentation and to provide them with the necessary travel documents or other authorization for re-entering their territory (Article 8.4). A similar provision is contained in Article 18.4 of the Smuggling Protocol.[119] Returns shall always be carried out in an orderly manner and with due regard for the safety and dignity of the person.[120] Lastly, for migrant workers in a regular situation, the ICRMW obliges States to cooperate 'with a view to promoting adequate economic conditions for their resettlement and to facilitating their durable social and cultural reintegration in the State of origin'.[121] In light of these provisions, the imposition of substantial restrictions on the right to exit by the affected State, such as the imposition of exit visa or exit fees, should be considered as infringing upon the affected State duty to cooperate.[122]

Conclusions and the way forward

If the international legal framework to protect migrants is still somewhat underdeveloped, with no specific convention dealing with all categories of migrants, this is even more true when it comes to protecting migrants in the context of disasters.[123] In particular, migrants are rarely accounted for among vulnerable categories of individuals in the UN human rights treaty bodies jurisprudence in the area of disaster.[124] Nevertheless, a few recently adopted instruments have started to reverse this trend. The Sendai Framework for disaster risk reduction, adopted in 2015, acknowledges that migrants can be a group specifically affected by disasters and highlights the role that they can have in disaster risk management.[125] The Paris Agreement on Climate Change also mentions migrants among the specific groups whose rights have to be considered and promoted when addressing climate change, including all disaster-related work that falls within the scope of climate change adaptation.[126]

This chapter has moved from an acknowledgement of the critical role that the States of origin and destination can play in reducing migrants' vulnerability to disasters, including by regulating or facilitating the intervention of other actors (notably the private sectors and the civil society). It has shown that the interpretation of the relevant legal framework, and notably of how human rights specifically apply to migrants in these situations, requires further elaboration. In line with a general trend towards a more consensual approach to the development of human rights law on environment-related matters – where States prefer to be assisted in adopting effective policy solutions, instead of having to reach an agreement on new binding instruments – the MICIC Initiative represented a key contribution to this elaboration. The stakeholder consultations and the resulting set of guidelines and effective practices shall help States include migrants more systematically and effectively in efforts to prevent, prepare for, respond to and recover from disasters. Alongside broader endorsement and use of the MICIC outcome documents, targeted efforts from human rights bodies, both universally and regionally, could help ensure that the principles described in this paper are further embedded in the human rights framework and that the practices that can effectively reduce migrants' specific conditions of vulnerability to disasters are tied to States' obligations under human rights instruments. The adoption of the Guidelines to Protect Migrants in Countries Experiencing Conflict and Natural Disaster should then be seen as a starting point for incentivizing further development of the human rights framework in protecting migrants in the context of disasters.

Selected bibliography

H. Duncan, 'Immigrant Integration as a Factor in Disaster Preparedness: The Case of the 2011 Tōhoku Earthquake in Japan' 3 *Migration Policy Practice* (April 2013–May 2013) 9.

International Organization for Migration and the Council of Europe 'Migrants in Disaster Risk Reduction Practices for Inclusion'. Geneva and Strasbourg: 2017. https://publications.iom.int/books/migrants-disaster-risk-reduction-practices-inclusion, accessed on January 1 2018.

T. Ruys, 'The "Protection of Nationals" Doctrine Revisited' 13 *Journal of Conflict & Security Law* (2008) 233.

K. Tindall, 'Governments' Ability to Assist Nationals in Disasters Abroad: What Do We Know about Consular Emergency Management?' 20 *Journal of Contingencies and Crisis Management* (2012) 102.

S. Weerasinghe and A. Taylor, 'On the Margins: Noncitizens Caught in Countries Experiencing Violence, Conflict and Disaster' 3 *JMHS* (2015) 26.

Notes

* The authors would like to thank Ms Chiara Milano for her continued support and advice on the practices cited in this chapter.

1 UNDESA, Population Division, International Migration Report 2015 – Highlights, UN Doc. ST/ESA/SER.A/375 (2016) 1, available at www.un.org/en/development/desa/population/migration/publications/migrationreport/docs/MigrationReport2015_Highlights.pdf, accessed on 14 June 2017.

2 C. Tacoli, 'Migration as a Response to Local and Global Transformations: A Typology of Mobility in the Context of Climate Change' in G. Martine and D. Schensul (eds), *The Demography of Adaptation to Climate Change* (United Nations Population Fund, International Institute for Environment and Development and El Colegio de Mexico, 2013) 41.

3 IOM, World Migration Report 2015, 'Migrants and Cities: New Partnerships to Manage Mobility' (2015) 39, available at http://publications.iom.int/system/files/wmr2015_en.pdf, accessed on 14 June 2017.

4 S. Castles, 'Understanding Global Migration: A Social Transformation Perspective' 36 *Journal of Ethnic Migration Studies* (2010) 1565.

5 For the aims of this paper, and in accordance with the definitions elaborated by UNISDR (3 February 2017), a disaster is considered

> A serious disruption of the functioning of a community or a society at any scale due to hazardous events interacting with conditions of exposure, vulnerability and capacity, leading to one or more of the following: human, material, economic and environmental losses and impacts.

6 The term 'migrant' is used in line with IOM's broad understanding of this term to identify any person who is moving or has moved across an international border, regardless of his or her legal status, causes of the movement and length of stay. More specific categories, such as refugees, asylum-seekers, stateless persons, victims of trafficking, unaccompanied migrant children, etc. fall under the umbrella term 'migrants'. IOM's definition of migrants can be found here: www.iom.int/sites/default/files/about-iom/IOM-definition-of-a-migrant-15March2016.pdf, accessed on 7 June 2017. For the sake of avoiding repetition, the term 'non-national' will be also used as a synonymous to 'migrant'.

7 For recent data about disasters and their consequences, see IFRC, *World Disasters Report 2016* (IFRC, 2016).

8 The text of the Paris agreement, in its Preamble, acknowledges the specific vulnerability of migrants and the need to protect their rights in the context of climate change Paris Agreement (adopted on 12 December 2015, entered into force 4 November 2016), UN Doc. FCCC/CP/2015/L.9, Preamble.

The Sendai Framework also recognizes the contribution of migrants 'to the resilience of communities and societies' (para 36 a.vi) and recommends to local authorities to coordinate their disaster risk management efforts at the local level also with migrants (para 27 h). Sendai Framework for Disaster Risk Reduction 2015–2030, available at www.unisdr.org/we/coordinate/sendai-framework, accessed on 14 June 2017.

9 More information about the Initiative is available at www.micicinitiative.iom.int, accessed on 14 June 2017.

10 MICIC Initiative, 'Guidelines to Protect Migrants in Countries Experiencing Conflict or Natural Disasters' (June 2016) (MICIC Initiative Guidelines), available at http://micicinitiative.iom.int/sites/default/files/document/micic_guidelines_english_web_13_09_2016.pdf, accessed on 14 June 2017.

11 S. Weerasinghe and A. Taylor, 'On the Margins: Noncitizens Caught in Countries Experiencing Violence, Conflict and Disaster' 3 *JMHS* (2015) 26, 41; K. Khoser, 'Protecting Non-Citizens in Situations of Conflict, Violence and Disaster' in S.F. Martin S. Weerasinghe and A. Taylor (eds), *Humanitarian Crises and Migration* (Routledge, 2014) 268, 270.

12 L. Guadagno, '"Reducing Migrants" Vulnerability to Natural Disasters through Disaster Risk Reduction Measures' MICIC Issue Brief 1 (Geneva: Migrants In Countries in Crisis Initiative, 2015), available at https://micicinitiative.iom.int/sites/default/files/brief/MICIC%20Issue%20Briefs%201%20%20DRR.pdf, accessed on 14 June 2017.

13 For the case of Thailand, for instance, see A. Beesey, S. Limsakul and E. McDougall, *Hazard Exposure and Vulnerability of Migrants in Thailand* (IOM, 2016), available at http://micicinitiative.iom.int/sites/default/files/resource_pub/docs/micic_thailand_desk_study_web.pdf, accessed on 27 June 2017.

14 Make the Road New York, 'Unmet Needs: Superstorm Sandy and Immigrant Communities in the Metro New York Area' (December 2012), available at www.maketheroadny.org/pix_reports/MRNY_Unmet_Needs_Superstorm_Sandy_and_Immigrant_Communities_121812_fin.pdf, accessed on 14 June 2017.

15 Beesey et al. (n. 13).

16 K. Koike, 'Forgotten and Unattended: Refugees in Post-Earthquake Japan' 38 *Forced Migration Review* (2013) 46.

17 J. Marlowe and L. Lou, 'The Canterbury Earthquakes and Refugee Communities' 25 *Aotearoa New Zealand Social Work Issue* (2013) 58.

18 A. Vermeer-Künzli, *Diplomatic Protection as a Source of Human Rights Law* (Oxford University Press, 2013); G. Di Stefano, 'The Position of Individuals in Public International Law through the Lens of Diplomatic Protection: The Principle and Its Transfiguration' in R. Kolb and G. Gaggioli (eds), *Research Handbook on Human Rights and Humanitarian Law* (Edward Elgar Publishing, 2012) 65, 74.

19 P.N. Bhagwati, 'Environmental Disputes' in P.H. Sand (ed), *The Effectiveness of International Environmental Agreements: A Survey of Existing Legal Instruments* (Grotius Publications Limited, 1992) 449; ILC, Summary records of the meetings of the 54th session, 2712th meeting (30 April 2002), Discussion on Diplomatic Protection, Yearbook of the International Law Commission 2002, vol. I, UN Doc. A/CN.4/SER.A/2002 paras 51, 54 and 55, 10–11.

20 R. Perruchoud, 'Consular Protection and Assistance' in R. Cholewinski, R. Perruchoud and E. MacDonald (eds), *International Migration Law* (TMC Asser Press, 2007) 71, 74.

21 A. Vermeer-Künzli, 'Diplomatic Protection and Consular Assistance of Migrants' in V. Chetail and C. Bauloz (eds), *Research Handbook on International Law and Migration* (Edward Elgar Publishing, 2014) 265, 276.

22 Convention on Consular Relations (adopted 24 April 1963, entered into force 19 March 1967) 596 UNTS 261. See L.T. Lee and J. Quigley, *Consular Law and Practice* (3rd edn, Oxford University Press, 2008) 118.

23 The importance of including migrants in preparedness is also acknowledged in the MICIC Initiative Guidelines (n. 10), Guideline 4: Incorporate migrants in prevention, preparedness, and emergency response systems, 26. Furthermore, paragraph 7 of the Sendai Framework on disaster risk reduction invites governments to 'engage with relevant stakeholders, including . . . migrants . . . in the design and implementation of policies, plans and standards'.

24 The Mexican consulate gave 500 USD, replaced lost documents and provided psychosocial support to its citizens affected by Hurricane Sandy in the US; 24 Horas, 'Entraga consulado mexicano en NY, as de 700 mil dolares a afectado pro hurican Sandy' (3 May 2013), available at www.24-horas.mx/entrega-consulado-mexicanoen-ny-mas-de-700-mil-dolares-a-afectados-por-huracan-sandy/, accessed on 14 June 2017.

25 Art 5(m) of the Vienna Convention on Consular Relations refers to functions entrusted to a consular

> which are not prohibited by the laws and regulations of the receiving State or to which no objection is taken by the receiving State or which are referred to in the international agreements in force between the sending State and the receiving State.

26 K. Tindall, 'Governments' Ability to Assist Nationals in Disasters Abroad: What Do We Know about Consular Emergency Management?' 20 *Journal of Contingencies and Crisis Management* (2012) 102, 106.

27 Asiaone, 'Seoul to Evacuate Koreans If Japan Crisis Worsens' (18 March 2011), available at http://news.asiaone.com/News/Latest%2BNews/Asia/Story/A1Story20110318–268763. Html, cited from Weerasinghe et al. (n. 11) 41. Evacuations were also organized by Belgium, France, Italy, the Philippines and the UK; see J. Groves, 'Japanese Drop Giant Water Bombs on Stricken Reactors as Foreign Office Promises Rescue Charter Flights to Get Britons Out of Tokyo' *Daily Mail* (17 March 2011), available at www.dailymail.co.uk/news/article-1366670/Japan-earthquake-tsunami-Waterbombs-dropped-nuclear-reactors.html#ixzz48C5BgGnR, accessed on 14 June 2017.

28 Office of Refugee Resettlement (US), 'About Repatriation', available at www.acf.hhs.gov/programs/orr/programs/repatriation/about, accessed on 1 May 2017.

29 The use of force is prohibited by art 2(4) of the UN Charter; the only exception being the case of self-defense stipulated in art 51 of the UN Charter. However, self-defense is only considered acceptable if it is used to respond to an armed attack. According to Ronzitti, it is possible that harm to State's citizens could reach the level of armed attack: 'there may be occasions when the threat of danger is great enough, or wide enough in its application to a sizable community abroad, for it to be legitimately construed as an attack on the state itself'. N. Ronzitti, *Rescuing Nationals Abroad through Military Coercion and Intervention on Grounds of Humanity* (Martinus Nijhoff Publishers, 1985) 468. State practice is not sufficiently uniform for the right to rescue to be part of customary international law (ibid 463–464).

30 For a discussion on the use of military assets in humanitarian interventions, see V. Wheeler and A. Harmer, 'Resetting the Rules of Engagement: Trends and Issues in Military – Humanitarian Relations' in V. Wheeler and A. Harmer (eds), *Resetting the Rules of Engagement*, HPG Report (21 March 2006) 5, available at www.odi.org/sites/odi.org.uk/files/odi-assets/publications-opinion-files/273.pdf, accessed on 7 June 2017.

31 See the chapter by Da Costa in this volume and M. Costas Trascasas, 'Access to the Territory of the Disaster-Affected-State' in A. de Guttry, M. Gestri and G. Venturini (eds), *International Disaster Response Law* (TMC Asser/Springer, 2012) 221, 233–236, and the literature cited therein. L. Boisson de Chazournes, 'Responsabilité de protéger et catastrophes naturelles: l'émergence d'un régime?' Société Française de droit international. Colloque de Nanterre (Pedone, 2008) 149.

32 M. Massouri, 'La responsabilité de protéger' in L. Moreillon, A. Bitcovsky and M. Massouri (dir), *Droit pénal humanitaire* (2nd edn, Helbing Lichtenhahn Verlag, 2009) 197. States are also opposed to the applicability of the responsibility to protect doctrine in disaster situations: see the debates within the UNGA on the reports by ILC on the topic, and in particular, among others, UNGA, Summary Record of the 23rd Meeting, UN GAOR, 63d Sess., 23d meeting, UN Doc. A/C.6/63/SR.23 (2008) (China) para 31; USA (2008/23rd) para 86; Japan (2008/23rd) para 42.

33 See A. Creta, 'A (Human) Right to Humanitarian Assistance in Disaster Situations? Surveying Public International Law' in de Guttry et al. (eds) (n. 31) 353 and the chapter by Hesselman in this volume.

34 See also art 13.2 of the Draft Articles of the of the ILC on the Protection of Persons in the Event of Disasters and paras 3–6 of its commentary, UN Doc. A/71/10 (2016).

35 See T. Ruys, 'The "Protection of Nationals" Doctrine Revisited' 13 *Journal of Conflict & Security Law* (2008) 233; T. Gazzini, *The Changing Rules on the Use of Force in International Law* (Manchester University Press, 2005) 170; K. Eichnsher, 'Defending Nationals Aboard: Assessing the Lawfulness of Forcible Hostage Rescues' 48 *Virginia Journal of International Law* (2008) 451, 460. *Contra*, see the Independent International Fact-Finding Mission on the Conflict in Georgia. The report states:

> it is also true that since 1945, numerous states have led military actions by pointing to the need to protect their own nationals abroad. In many cases the legality of these actions was disputed. There is no customary law allowing such actions. If at all, such actions should be limited in scope and duration and exclusively focused on rescuing and evacuating nationals.

Independent International Fact-Finding Mission on the Conflict in Georgia, Report (September 2009), vol. 1, 23.

36 See D. Fisher, 'Domestic Regulation of International Humanitarian Relief in Disasters and Armed Conflict: A Comparative Analysis' 89 *International Review of the Red Cross* (2007) 345, 356. However, see the case of the 2008 Myanmar Cyclone, Costas Trascasas (n. 31) 236–239.
37 UNGA, Res 43/131, UN Doc. A/RES/43/131 (8 December 1988) preambular para 8; UNGA Res 45/100, UN Doc. A/RES/45/100 (14 December 1990), preambular para 6. The Draft Articles of the ILC on the Protection of Persons in the Event of Disasters also recognize a duty on the affected State to seek external assistance (draft art 11). This duty also derives from affected State's obligations under human rights treaties and customary international law (draft art 11, commentary para 3), ILC 2016 (n. 34).
38 In the commentary to draft art 11, it is specified that such a capacity should be verified with regard to its various aspects and not in absolute terms and that '[a]n affected State's national capacity may be manifestly exceeded in relation to one aspect of disaster relief operations, although the State remains capable of undertaking other operations'. Such an aspect could be the State capacity to effectively include the protection of non-nationals in its response. ILC 2016 (n. 34), para 2 of the commentary to draft art 11.
39 For a discussion on the tension between the humanitarian principles and an intervention aimed at assisting only the nationals of a State and on how to resolve it, see the section entitled 'Assistance to own nationals and non-discrimination' below.
40 ILC 2016 (n. 34) draft art 13, para 10 of the commentary and draft art 10, para 2, of the commentary.
41 ILC 2016 (n. 34) draft art 14.
42 K. Tindall (n. 36) 102, 106.
43 The ECtHR in the decision on the case *Treska v. Albania and Italy* stated:

> Even in the absence of effective control of a territory outside its borders, the State still has a positive obligation under Article 1 of the Convention to take the diplomatic, economic, judicial or other measures that it is in its power to take and are in accordance with international law to secure to the applicants the rights guaranteed by the Convention.

Treska v. Albania and Italy, App. No. 26937/04 (ECtHR, Decision on Admissibility of 29 June 2006).
44 M. Milanovic, *Extraterritorial Application of Human Rights Treaties* (Oxford University Press, 2011); K. Da Costa, *The Extraterritorial Application of Selected Human Rights Treaties* (Brill-Martinus Nijhoff Publishers, 2013).
45 *Issa and Others v. Turkey*, App. No. 31821/96 (ECtHR, Judgment of 16 November 2004) paras 69–71; *Öcalan v. Turkey*, App. No. 46221/99 [GC] (ECtHR, Judgment of 12 May 2005) para 91.
46 The right to take part in public affairs, to vote and to be elected (art 25 ICCPR) and the right to return to one's own country (art 12.4 ICCPR), which however has been interpreted as applying also to stateless persons and permanent residents. See HRComm, General comment No. 27: Article 12 (Freedom of Movement), UN Doc. CCPR/C/21/Rev.1/Add.9 (1999); HRComm, *Stewart v. Canada*, Comm. No. 538/1993, U.N. Doc. CCPR/C/58/D/538/1993 (1996); HRComm, *Nystrom v. Australia*, Comm. No. 1557/2007, UN Doc. CCPR/C/102/D/1557/2007 (2011).
47 International Convention on the Protection of the Rights of All Migrants Workers and Members of their Families (adopted 18 December 1990, entered into force 1 July 2003) 2220 UNTS 3.
48 Art 1.2 stipulates that the Convention applies

> during the entire migration process of migrant workers and members of their families, which comprises preparation for migration, departure, transit and the entire period of stay and remunerated activity in the State of employment as well as return to the State of origin or the State of habitual residence.

49 Right to consular assistance (arts 16.7.1, 23 and 65.2), right to vote and participate in elections of the State of origin (art 41), right to transfer their earnings and savings (art 32), right to social security (art 27.1).
50 At the time of writing the Migrant Workers Convention was ratified by 51 States.
51 Notably the International Covenant on Economic, Social and Cultural Rights (adopted 16 December 1966, entered into force 3 January 1976) 993 UNTS 3 and the International Covenant on Civil and Political Rights (adopted 16 December 1966, entered into force 23 March 1976) 999 UNTS 171, which at the time of writing have been ratified by 165 and 169 States, respectively.
52 MICIC Initiative (n. 10), Guideline 10: Facilitate migrants' ability to move to safety, 33 and the relevant practices regarding the Host State, 98. See also Guideline 13: Relocate and evacuate migrants when needed, 36.

53 Committee on Migrant Workers (CMW), General Comment No. 1: Migrant Domestic Workers, UN Doc. CMW/C/GC/1 (2011) 29.i.
54 Ibid 62–64.
55 Lee and Quigley (n. 22) 124. With regard to the right to consular assistance, the authors report a certain number of State practices, which do not consistently recognize an individual's right to request the protection of the consular authorities of their State of nationality.
56 Vienna Convention on Consular Relations (n. 22).
57 *LaGrand (Germany v. United States of America) (Judgment)* [2001] ICJ Rep. 501, para 466.
58 Ibid. The same was reiterated in the following judgment: *Avena and Other Mexican Nationals (Mexico v. United States of America) (Judgment)* [2004] ICJ Rep. (I) 48, para 40.
59 *LaGrand* (n. 57) paras 73–74; *Avena* (n. 58) para 99.
60 'Consular officers shall be free to communicate with nationals of the sending State and to have access to them. *Nationals of the sending State shall have the same freedom* with respect to communication with and access to consular officers of the sending State' (emphasis added).
61 *The Right to Information on Consular Assistance in the Framework of the Guarantees of the Due Process of Law*, IACtHR, Opinion OC-16/99 (1 October 1999) paras 83–84.
62 Ibid paras 79 and 87.
63 The application of these principles also in disaster situations is confirmed in art 6 of the Draft Articles of the ILC 2016 (n. 34).
64 For a discussion on the application of the responsibility to protect in disaster situations, see Da Costa's chapter in this volume.
65 After the 2015 earthquake in Nepal, Israel supported the evacuation of its nationals while setting up field hospitals to assist all affected persons; D. Kamin, 'Israel Evacuates Surrogate Babies from Nepal but Leaves the Mothers Behind' *Time* (28 April 2015), available at http://time.com/3838319/israel-nepal-surrogates/, accessed on 14 June 2017. Indonesia evacuated 26 nationals from the area and sent disaster relief and supplies, as well as a relief team, to support response operations The Jakarta Post, 'National Scene: Indonesians Repatriated from Nepal' (7 May 2015), available at www.thejakartapost.com/news/2015/05/07/national-scene-indonesians-repatriated-nepal.html#sthash.JQYMFuEH.dpuf, accessed on 14 June 2017.
66 E.G. Brown, Jr. (Governor) et al., 'State of California Emergency Repatriation Plan' (February 2014) 8, available at www.caloes.ca.gov/PlanningPreparednessSite/Documents/State%20of%20California%20Emergency%20Repatriation%20Plan.pdf, accessed on 14 June 2017.
67 OJ L 314/73 (1995). F. Forni, 'The Consular Protection of EU Citizens during Emergencies in Third Countries' in de Guttry et al. (eds) (n. 31) 155. See also M. Moraru, 'Securing Consular Protection of the EU Citizens Abroad: What Role for the EU?' in I. Govaere and S. Poli (eds), *EU Management of Global Emergencies* (Brill Nijhoff, 2014) 147.
68 Kamin (n. 65).
69 On the obligation of coordination between the State of origin and the affected State, see the section entitled 'The articulation of the roles of the State of origin and the affected State and the obligation to cooperate' below. See also H. Duncan, 'Immigrant Integration as a Factor in Disaster Preparedness: The Case of the 2011 Tōhoku Earthquake in Japan' 3 *Migration Policy Practice* (April 2013–May 2013) 9.
70 UNGA in its Resolution 46/182 recognised that

> 4. Each State has the responsibility first and foremost to take care of the victims of natural disasters and other emergencies occurring on its territory. Hence, the affected State has the primary role in the initiation, organization, coordination, and implementation of humanitarian assistance within its territory.

UNGA, Res 46/182: Strengthening of the coordination of humanitarian emergency assistance of the United Nations, UN Doc. A/RES/46/182 (19 December 1991) para 4. See also UNGA, Res 70/107, UN Doc. A/RES/70/107 (13 January 2016).
71 The ICCPR recognizes the right to vote and to participate in elections only for nationals (art 25) and the right to return to one's country for nationals and (based on the interpretation by the HRC) for permanent residents (art 12.4). The only express exception to the universal enjoyment of economic rights under the ICESCR is set forth in art 2.3, which states that: '[t]he developing countries, with due regard to human rights and their national economy, may determine to what extent they would guarantee the economic rights recognized in the present Covenant to non-nationals'. However, this exception does not apply to social or cultural rights.

72 ICRMW (n. 47).
73 Convention relating to the Status of Refugees (adopted on 28 July 1951, entered into force 22 April 1954) 189 UNTS 137, and its Protocol relating to the Status of Refugees (adopted 31 January 1967, entered into force 4 October 1967) 606 UNTS 267.
74 Protocol to Prevent, Suppress and Punish Trafficking in Persons, Especially Women and Children, supplementing the United Nations Convention against Transnational Organized Crime (Trafficking Protocol), (adopted 15 November 2000, entered into force 25 December 2003) 2237 UNTS 319.
75 Protocol against the Smuggling of Migrants by Land, Sea and Air, supplementing the United Nations Convention against Transnational Organized Crime (Smuggling Protocol), (adopted 15 November 2000, entered into force 28 January 2004) 2241 UNTS 507.
76 Convention on the Rights of the Child (adopted 20 November 1989, entered into force 2 September 1990) 1577 UNTS 3.
77 Convention on the Elimination of All Forms of Discrimination against Women (CEDAW) (adopted 18 December 1979, entered into force 3 September 1981) 2131 UNTS 83.
78 Convention on the Rights of Persons with Disabilities (ICPRD) (adopted 13 December 2006, entered into force 3 May 2008) 2515 UNTS 3.
79 Arts 35 to 46 of the Convention (IV) relative to the Protection of Civilian Persons in Time of War (adopted 12 August 1949, entered into force 21 October 1950) 75 UNTS 287.
80 See, *ex multis*, V. Chetail, 'The Human Rights of Migrants in General International Law: From Minimum Standards to Fundamental Rights' 28 *Georgetown Immigration Law Journal* 225 (2013); R.D. Weissbrodt and M. Divine, 'International Human Rights of Migrants' in B. Opeskin, R. Perruchoud and J. Redpath-Cross (eds), *Foundations of International Migration Law* (Cambridge University Press, 2012) 152. For a specific discussion on how economic, social and cultural rights apply to migrants in an irregular situation, including in the relevant jurisprudence of the human rights bodies, see OHCHR, 'The Economic, Social and Cultural Rights of Migrants in an Irregular Situation', HR/PUB/14/1 (United Nations Publications, 2014) 31, available at www.ohchr.org/Documents/Publications/HR-PUB-14-1_en.pdf, accessed on 7 June 2017.
81 Except for the CEDAW (n. 77) and ICRPD (n. 78). The role played by non-discrimination in disaster settings is explored in Casolari's chapter in this volume.
82 For a distinction between national origin and nationality see CESCR, General Comment No. 20: Non-discrimination in economic, social and cultural rights (art 2, para 2 of the International Covenant on Economic, Social and Cultural Rights), UN Doc. E/C.12/GC/20 (2009) paras 24 and 30.
83 Ibid para 13. See also Sommario's chapter in this volume.
84 D.J. Cantor, 'Regional Discussion Paper, Focus on the Latin American Experience' MICIC Regional Consultation on Latin America, 17–18 February 2016 (Bruxelles: International Centre for Migration Policy Development), available at https://unfccc.int/files/adaptation/groups_committees/loss_and_damage_executive_committee/application/pdf/djcantor_micic_feb_2016.pdf, accessed on 27 Jun 2017.
85 The importance of the principle of non-discrimination in the provision of humanitarian assistance is also acknowledged in the MICIC Initiative Guidelines; see MICIC Initiative (n. 10) Guideline 11: Provide humanitarian assistance to migrants without discrimination, 34.
86 O. Carter-Pokra, R.E. Zambrana, S.E. Mora and K.A. Aaby, 'Emergency Preparedness: Knowledge and Perceptions of Latin American Immigrants' 18 *Journal of Health Care for the Poor and Underserved* (2007) 465.
87 B.E. Aguirre, 'The Lack of Warnings before the Saragosa Tornado' 6 *International Journal of Mass Emergencies & Disasters* (1988) 65.
88 Duncan (n. 69).
89 R.W. Perry and M.K. Lindell, 'The Effects of Ethnicity on Evacuation Decision-Making' 9(1) *International Journal of Mass Emergencies & Disasters* (1991) 47.
90 The New York Times, '"Never Again," Again', Editorial (20 September 2008), available at www.nytimes.com/2008/09/21/opinion/21sun2.html?_r=1&scp=1&sq=never%20again%20again&st=cse&oref=slogin, accessed on 27 June 2017.
91 B. Bolin, 'Race, Class, Ethnicity, and Disaster Vulnerability' in H. Rodríguez, E.L. Quarantelli and R.R. Dynes (eds), *Handbook of Disaster Research* (Springer, 2007) 113.
92 L. Guadagno, M. Fuhrer and J. Twigg, 'Migrants in Disaster Risk Reduction: Practices for Inclusion' (Geneva and Bruxelles: IOM and CoE, 2017), available at http://micicinitiative.iom.int/sites/default/files/resource_pub/docs/migrants_in_drr_230517_02.pdf, accessed on 27 June 2017.

93 A. Clapham, *Human Rights Obligation of Non-State Actors* (Oxford University Press, 2010).
94 MICIC Initiative (n. 10) Guideline 4, 27.
95 MICIC Initiative (n. 10), Practices to implement Guideline 11: Provide humanitarian assistance to migrants without discrimination, 108–109.
96 Ibid and Guideline 4.
97 The right to freedom of association is also recognised for refugees and stateless persons lawfully resident in the country in art 15 of the 1951 Convention Relating to the Status of Refugees (n. 73) and the Convention Relating to the Status of Stateless Persons (adopted 28 September 1954, entered into force 6 June 1960) 360 UNTS 117.
98 Global Coalition on Migration and MADE, Mid-Term Report: Civil Society Regional Consultations (January 2016) 2–3, see reference to GCC, available at http://gcmigration.org/wp-content/uploads/2016/04/Mid-Term-Civil-Society-Report-MICIC-Regional-Consultations.pdf, accessed on 14 June 2017.
99 MICIC Initiative (n. 10), Practices to implement Guideline 3: Empower migrants to help themselves, their families, and communities during and in the aftermath of crises, 54.
100 MICIC Initiative (n. 10), Practices to implement Guideline 1: Track information on conflict and natural disasters, and the potential impact on migrants, 43–44, and Practices to implement Guideline 4, 50.
101 MICIC Summary Report on Private Sector Consultation states that: 'By Ensuring That Migrants Are Not Exploited during the Recruitment Process, Employers and Recruiters Empower Them to React More Robustly and Effectively as Agents of Their Own Safety/Destiny in the Event of a Crisis' (Geneva, Switzerland, 2–3 December 2015) 5, available at http://micicinitiative.iom.int/sites/default/files/resource_pub/docs/summary-report_private-sector-consultation.pdf, accessed on 14 June 2017.
102 See R. Piotrowicz, 'States' Obligations under Human Rights Law towards Victims of Trafficking in Human Beings: Positive Developments in Positive Obligations' 24 *International Journal of Refugee Law* (2012) 181.
103 MICIC Initiative, Summary Report Private Sector Consultation (Geneva, Switzerland, 2–3 December 2015) 21, available at http://micicinitiative.iom.int/sites/default/files/resource_pub/docs/summary-report_private-sector-consultation.pdf, accessed on 14 June 2017. See also MICIC Initiative (n. 10), Practices to implement Guideline 3, 57 and 58.
104 MICIC Initiative, 'Guidelines and Effective Practices Private Sector Consultation' (Geneva, Switzerland, 2–3 December 2015) 10, available at http://micicinitiative.iom.int/sites/default/files/resource_pub/docs/guidelines-and-practices_private-sector-consultation_0.pdf, accessed on 14 June 2017.
105 MICIC Initiative, Summary Report Private Sector Consultation (n. 103) 9–13.
106 MICIC Initiative, Private Sector Consultation: Guidelines and Effective Practices (n. 104) 6–7.
107 UNGA, Res 70/107 (n. 70) Preamble.
108 ILO Convention No. 97, Convention Concerning Migration for Employment (Revised 1949) (adopted 1 July 1949, entered into force 22 January 1952) 120 UNTS 71, art 3 on countering the misleading propaganda, and Annex II, art 12, on assistance provided to migrants on conditions of employment.
109 Arts 2.2(h), 4, 5, 46 to 48, 52.3(b), 53.2, 59.2, 61.3 and 4, 69.2, 71.2 of ICRMW (n. 47).
110 Ibid., see specifically arts 64 and 65.1(b) on cooperation to provide information to migrants, and 67 on cooperation regarding the return of migrant workers.
111 Ibid., a number of other provisions impose an obligation of cooperation on States, see arts 33.1(b) and 65.
112 MICIC, 'IGC Plus Consultation: Guidelines and Effective Practices' (Geneva, Switzerland, 2–3 February 2015) 11, available at https://micicinitiative.iom.int/sites/default/files/resource_pub/docs/guidelines-and-practices_igc-plus-consultation_0.pdf, accessed on 14 June 2017.
113 National Audit Office, 'Joint Findings on Lessons to be Learned from the Handling of the Response to the Indian Ocean Tsunami' (UK, October 2005), available at www.nao.org.uk/wp-content/uploads/2005/11/tsunami_ll_report.594.pdf, accessed on 14 June 2017.
114 G. Bondi, 'Una scossa all'integrazione – Gli immigrati e il terremoto in Emilia, sei mesi dopo' *Popoli* (6 November 2012), available at www.popoli.info/EasyNe2/Primo_piano/Una_scossa_all_integrazione_-_Gli_immigrati_e_il_terremoto_in_Emilia_sei_mesi_dopo.aspx, accessed on 14 June 2017. See also the section entitled 'Assistance to own nationals and non-discrimination' above.
115 Duncan (n. 69).
116 Beesey et al. (n. 13).
117 MICIC Initiative (n. 10), Practices to implement Guideline 7: Establish coordination agreements in advance to leverage strengths and foster trust, 76–78.

118 ICRMW (n. 47) art 67.1.
119 Smuggling Protocol (n. 75).
120 Ibid art 18.5 and Trafficking Protocol (n. 74), arts 8.1 and 2.
121 ICRMW (n. 47), art 67.2.
122 MICIC Initiative (n. 10), Guideline 10: Facilitate migrants' ability to move to safety, 33.
123 There are also discussions on whether the UN Guiding Principles on internal displacement would apply to non-nationals, see K. Khoser, 'Protecting Non-Citizens in Situations of Conflict, Violence and Disaster' in S.F. Martin, S. Weerasinghe and A. Taylor (eds), *Humanitarian Crises and Migration* (Routledge, 2014) 268, 270.
124 M. Hesselman, 'Establishing a Full "Cycle Protection" for Disaster Victims: Preparedness, Response and Recovery according to Regional and International Human Rights Supervisory Bodies' 18 *Tilburg Law Review* (2013) 106, 122; HRComm, Concluding observations on Thailand, UN Doc. CCPR/CO/84/THA (2005) 23; CommRC, Concluding Observations on the Republic of Korea, UN Doc. CRC/C/KOR/CO/3–4 (2012) para 19(f); CommRC, Concluding Observations on Panama, UN Doc. CRC/C/PAN/CO/3–4 (2011) para 18(f).
125 Sendai (n. 8) paras 7, 27(h), 36(a)(vi).
126 Paris Agreement (n. 8) Preamble.

21

TEMPORARY PROTECTION AFTER DISASTERS

International, regional and national approaches

Flavia Zorzi Giustiniani

Introduction

Environmental degradation has always caused populations to move in search of more habitable places. Nevertheless, it is estimated that the ongoing environmental changes will involve ever increasing numbers of displaced in the near future. Since 2008, an average of 26.4 million of persons have been internally displaced each year by natural hazards.[1] There are no equivalent statistics concerning cross-border movements; nevertheless the Nansen Initiative reported that '50 countries . . . in recent decades have received or refrained from returning people in the aftermath of disasters, in particular those caused by tropical storms, flooding, drought, tsunamis, and earthquakes'.[2] Faced with such a challenge, existing instruments of international refugee law have been shown to be insufficient.

While disaster displacement is mainly internal, the present contribution will rather deal with instruments and arrangements which are devoted to *international* movements of persons. In contrast to slow-paced events, such as desertification and other consequences of climate change, in the case of sudden-onset events like cyclones or earthquakes, it is too late to develop adaptation strategies and migration tends to be a forced choice. Cross-border migration, though, is not necessarily immediate, and more often, it is a result of the inadequate assistance that disaster victims receive within the country.

The 1951 Geneva Convention on the Status of Refugees (Geneva Convention) could in principle be applicable, but its requirement that asylum-seekers risk individual persecution *because of* a disaster would be hard to claim if not accompanied by a discriminatory policy or practice on the basis of a Convention reason. Despite some assertions to the contrary, it is also unlikely that disaster-displaced persons could benefit from regional refugee instruments. Indeed, the only explicit reference to those fleeing 'because of the occurrence of natural disasters' is contained in the Arab Convention on Regulating Status of Refugees in the Arab Countries,[3] which was adopted by the League of Arab States in 1994 but never ratified by any State. As to the corresponding instruments in Africa and Latin America, it will be shown that their application to cross-border disaster displacement is very controversial.

In order to fill the resulting legal gap, various proposals have been submitted by international lawyers, whose common feature is either to amend the Geneva Convention, or to create a brand-new, *ad hoc* instrument.[4] As is well known, the realisation of these proposals is premised on a strong political engagement by States, which unfortunately is still lacking. Taking note of this state of affairs, the present contribution has the modest and more pragmatic objective of conducting an overview of temporary protection measures existing at regional and national level which are, or may be, applicable in a post-disaster scenario. This overview, while necessarily incomplete, will be followed by some considerations on current States attitudes on the subject and explore the advantages – if any – and shortcomings of these measures.

As a preliminary, it is necessary to clarify my understanding of two key terms whose use is crucial for the current analysis. The first one is disaster. The current contribution is concerned mainly with those disasters which are caused by sudden-onset hazards, such as earthquakes, tsunamis, landslides and floods, as well as industrial accidents. This limitation of scope is due to the fact that existing protection frameworks, with some few exceptions, only envisage displacement or migration related to the latter kind of hazards.

Secondly, in order to identify the various instruments which – at national and regional level – address the protection needs of disaster-related migrants, the phrase 'temporary protection' is utilised. Historically, temporary protection, or temporary refuge, has been used as a means to protect against *refoulement* in situations of mass influx due to generalised violence or internal armed conflict, where individual status determination is either impracticable or inapplicable.[5] Developed after the adoption of the Geneva Convention, temporary protection gained particular resonance in 1979, when it was used in the framework of the Comprehensive Plan of Action in South-East Asia and again, more than two decades later, in the context of the conflicts in former Yugoslavia, when a consistent number of displaced people were hosted by various European States. While not being a new concept, nonetheless many aspects of temporary protection remain largely undefined.[6] Moreover, its critics point to the consequences that its (ab)use can entail in terms of the reduction of the scope of refugee protection and the difficulty it causes for the integration of its beneficiaries.[7]

A different protection instrument, which is occasionally associated or confused with temporary protection, is found in so-called 'complementary protection', in its various forms. While equally this last phrase does not have an unequivocal definition, it is generally accepted that it identifies those protection instruments or arrangements which are rooted in international human rights law (in particular the *non-refoulement* obligations), which are applied on an individual case basis and do not have an emergency character. This latter definition can thus be used as a yardstick in order to explain my understanding of temporary protection as applied in the context of disaster displacement or disaster-related migration. It is here argued that, in the said scenarios, temporary protection can be understood as having most of the following features: it is granted on a group basis and not an individual one; it is based on factual conditions prevailing in the country of origin (typically, a disaster caused by a sudden-onset hazard); it has a residual character, being granted to those who are not eligible for refugee status or other forms of complementary protection; it is discretionary, not being based on international obligations; and it is conceived as a strictly temporary, interim solution, whose termination generally implies for its beneficiaries the return to their country of origin.

The foregoing analysis will start by reviewing current practices in Africa and Latin America. The selection of these areas as a first research focus is almost an obligatory choice, considering that both: (1) have a regional refugee law instrument which could at least potentially cover disaster displacement, (2) are disproportionately exposed to natural disasters and (3) have the most of people crossing borders in search of safety and assistance.[8] Subsequently some major regional and national temporary protection statutes will be analysed. Finally, the 2010 Haiti earthquake will serve as a case study for the purpose of scrutinising the international response to the displacement crisis which followed such a mega-disaster.

Hosting disaster-related migrants

An analysis of international practice

Africa

The African continent benefits from a regional refugee treaty – the Organization of African Unity (OAU) Convention Governing the Specific Aspects of Refugee Problems in Africa[9] – whose theoretical importance cannot be underestimated. To begin with, it was the first, and for a long time the only, hard law refugee instrument having regional scope. Moreover, as a regional complement to the Geneva Convention, it enshrines some significant adaptations to the latter which, while necessary to better fit the African displacement context, had an influence well beyond regional boundaries. In particular, a couple of its innovative features are worth recalling here. First of all, the refugee definition is broadened to include more objective circumstances than the universal notion, so as to encompass those who are 'compelled' to flee their countries of origin and seek refuge in another country due to external aggression, occupation, foreign domination and events seriously disturbing public order.[10] Second, all the said events triggering refugee protection share a communitarian approach, since they are phenomena 'which present a generalised threat to an indefinite class of people'.[11]

While disasters are not expressly mentioned, an objective reading of the text would seem to favour their inclusion under the category of events seriously disturbing public order. Such interpretation, though, is not supported by national case law – which is almost non-existent – and has been widely rejected by the doctrine. According to Rankin, for instance, disasters should be excluded for two different reasons. First of all, he considers that '"[e]vents seriously disturbing public order" is a basket clause and should arguably be read *ejusdem generis* to cover events that share some element that is similar to aggression, occupation and foreign domination, which are all clearly manmade events'.[12] Second, and most importantly, in light of the OAU's communitarian perspective he argues that:

> A natural disaster represents a threat to the community, but rather than coming from within, [it] is an event which sees the community confront collective adversity from the outside. Still, it should be made equally clear that this does not licence a government or non-state agent to use "natural disasters" in pursuit of its own agenda. The definition would seem to capture the effects of a famine caused by state action since this is merely using nature as a tool to a political end.[13]

Kälin, on the other hand, while cautioning that 'it is rather unlikely that the states concerned would be ready to accept such an extension of the concept beyond its conventional meaning of public disturbances resulting in violence',[14] argues that the Convention would apply 'if a person sought refuge because of violence such as riots in the aftermath of a disaster, triggered by the government's unwillingness or inability to address certain consequences of the disaster or to provide the necessary assistance to the victims'.[15]

In any case, State practice runs counter to the inclusion of disasters *tout court* under the protective cover of the Convention. As is generally known, on the African continent it has always been common for States to open their borders to displaced populations, even when the displacement results from a disaster. Nevertheless, only in rare occasions have the countries involved in this practice affirmed their intention to apply the African Refugee Convention. This was the case *vis-à-vis* Somali victims of the drought which occurred in 2011–2012, who were admitted by

Kenya, Djibouti and Ethiopia on the basis of the OAU Convention. The opposite attitude was instead shown, *inter alia*, by Uganda in response to the 2002 eruption of Mount Nyiragongo in Goma. In fact Ugandan authorities gave temporary refuge to the Goman displaced but specified that these people were not considered refugees under the OAU Refugee Convention. In a similar vein, Botswana and Tanzania admitted neighbouring populations fleeing floods on the basis of informal arrangements. More generally, 'the practice of providing temporary refuge in these circumstances has been explained by African states with reference to principles of African hospitality and good neighbourliness, rather than legal obligation'.[16] Furthermore, this tradition has been recently threatened by a securitarian attitude that has grown stronger over the continent along with the rise of international terrorism, causing also a certain distrust towards refugees by host communities.[17] While good examples of hospitality are still present, like the open-door policy practiced by Ethiopia between 2009 and 2014, as well as by Uganda, the described development further confirms the impossibility of detecting a regional *customary* norm on temporary refuge.[18]

All the above notwithstanding, it must be highlighted that the African Union (AU) has again been at the forefront in relation to refugee and migratory issues in the last decade, and this time disaster displacement took centre stage. This first happened in 2006, when AU's Member States recognised in the Migration Policy Framework for Africa[19] that disasters and other environmental factors are major sources of displacement and accordingly recommended that this reality be addressed through national and regional migration policies. A few years later, disasters as causes of displacement were mentioned in the Kampala Convention for the Prevention of Internal Displacement and the Protection of and Assistance to Internally Displaced Persons in Africa.[20] This treaty is focused exclusively on internal displacement but, remarkably, enshrines a clear-cut engagement by States parties to protect and assist IDPs, including those fleeing 'as a result of or in order to avoid the effects of . . . natural or human-made disasters'.[21] In addition, one of its key innovative provisions, which calls for the prevention of displacement in particular through early warning systems and disaster risk reduction strategies (art 4.2), if effectively implemented 'will help prevent or mitigate the impact of internal displacement outside the boundaries of the state'.[22] Furthermore, inter-State cooperation, which may be required by the State concerned (art 5.1), could induce States parties to devise regional approaches to cross-border displacement adopting by analogy the normative standards codified in this same treaty.

Latin America

As anticipated, the African Refugee Convention had an influence far beyond the continent's borders, in particular in Latin America. The Cartagena Declaration on Refugees, which was adopted by the Colloquium on the International Protection of Refugees in Central America, Mexico and Panama on 22 November 1984, in fact accepts the expansive refugee definition foreseen by the OAU Convention and further enlarges it by considering as refugees 'persons who have fled their country because their lives, security or liberty have been threatened by generalised violence, foreign aggression, internal conflicts, massive violations of human rights and other circumstances which have seriously disturbed public order' (III 3).

Similarly to the OAU Convention, the Cartagena Declaration was a response to the exigency of addressing new dimensions of mass displacements of persons in need of international protection. Even though it was not intended as a legally binding instrument, many States in the region have incorporated, or adapted, its refugee concept into their internal legislation.[23]

As to the (in)applicability of the said concept in situations of disasters, similar reasons as those already mentioned with respect to the OAU Convention could be invoked. In particular, a report produced by the International Conference on Central American Refugees (CIREFCA) interpreting the Cartagena Declaration indicates that victims of natural disasters are not entitled to protection under the provision on events seriously disturbing the public order, and the majority of the signatory States share the same opinion. Still, at present, Cuba is the only Latin American State whose national legislation classifies as refugees those fleeing their country 'due to cataclysm or other phenomena of nature'.[24] As will be seen in the next paragraph, though, in the case of the 2010 Haiti earthquake, Ecuador and Mexico applied the Cartagena Declaration by accepting some asylum claims from Haitians. Nonetheless, both countries grounded their decision not on the mere occurrence of the earthquake but rather on the effects of such event for the protection and security of the claimants.

As a consequence, within the region, laws, policies and practices on the provision of humanitarian protection on a temporary basis to aliens in the context of disasters are found predominantly at the national level.[25] Within this varied practice, which cannot be examined thoroughly here, a few points merit attention. First of all, there are three States in the region which provide temporary protection in mass influx situations in their refugee legislation. Apart from Panama, whose temporary protection status will be specifically analysed, Venezuela and Peru have similar disciplines. In Venezuela temporary protection is granted to groups of 'persons that wish to remain temporarily in Venezuelan territory and who do not wish to claim asylum as refugees'.[26] Temporary protection can last for ninety days and is renewable once. Moreover, the Venezuelan State is required to engage in the necessary coordination with the country of origin's authorities. Temporary protection status in Peru, rather, has a protective scope which is similar to that of Panama and which is granted for three renewable blocks in cases of 'mass influx in an illegal or irregular manner by persons seeking protection'.[27] Peruvian legislation does not envisage a role for the country of origin but requires, when temporary protection has lasted for a year, that the Ministry of External Relations evaluate the situation in order to find a permanent solution to the mass influx 'with the support of the international community'.[28]

Various other countries instead provide for the temporary entry and stay of groups of people following extraordinary situations in their migration – and not their refugee – legislation. The measures which are most frequently envisaged and utilised are those aimed either at regularising the presence of migrants or at temporarily suspending the removals. Interestingly, both have been applied to migrants fleeing disaster scenarios. The first type of measures, in particular, is generally discretionary, is granted on a collective basis and is focused exclusively on the nationals of the country hit by the disaster.[29]

Regional practice

The European Union

Among the legal instruments which envisage a form of temporary protection for the disaster-induced displaced, the only one having a regional scope is – still at present – the European Union (EU) Directive on 'minimum standards for giving temporary protection in the event of a mass influx of displaced persons and on measures promoting a balance of efforts between Member States in receiving such persons and bearing the consequences thereof' (hereinafter the Directive).[30] This act, adopted by the Council of the EU back in 2001, was meant to serve as the principal framework in the event of a major refugee influx, so as not to replicate the uncoordinated responses of EU Member States during the Yugoslav and Kosovo displacement crises.[31]

The activation mechanism requires a Council decision adopted by a qualified majority following a Commission's proposal, which can be requested by a Member State (Article 5).[32] It can be implemented either in the case of a 'mass influx' or of an 'imminent mass influx' of displaced persons from third countries who are unable to return to their country of origin.[33] The Directive stipulates that a mass influx may be caused by spontaneous arrivals in the Union's territory as well as by evacuation programmes.[34] The meaning of 'mass influx' remains, however, unclear since it is defined – quite tautologically – as 'arrival in the Community of a large number of displaced persons, who come from a specific country or geographical area'. Moreover, past practice shows that such criterion has been interpreted restrictively. For instance, following the mass flow of migrants from Tunisia and Libya which accompanied the Arab spring, Italy and Malta demanded the activation of the Directive; their request, however, was rejected by the European Commission with the argument that the flow did not have the requisite massive character.[35]

In order 'to promote a balance of effort between Member States in receiving and bearing the consequences of receiving (displaced) persons',[36] the Directive envisages a burden-sharing mechanism. As a result, Member States should receive persons eligible for temporary protection 'in a spirit of Community solidarity'.[37] Nonetheless, the efficiency of the mechanism largely lies in the concrete measures that the Council decides to adopt in this respect and on their enforcement by States.[38]

Temporary protection is one year long, with an automatic extension of two six-monthly periods for a maximum of one year (Article 4.1) and the possibility for the Council to extend it, with the same procedure, for an additional year if the reasons for its activation persist (Article 4.2). The Council can also decide to terminate it prematurely if the reasons justifying its application cease to exist, provided that return can happen 'with due respect for human rights and fundamental freedoms and Member States' obligations regarding non-refoulement'.[39] Additionally, the Council has the ability to circumscribe the applicability of TP to specific groups of persons pursuant to Article 5.3 (a), based for instance on the area of origin, or by setting a specific date by which the displaced should have reached the EU territory. Each Member State can, however, expand – but not limit – the personal scope of protection by granting TP to additional groups of people who are displaced for the same reasons and come from the same country or region of origin as those designated by the Council.

EU temporary protection, while being a 'procedure of exceptional character'[40] which is rather precarious if compared with refugee status and subsidiary protection,[41] bears with it an ample range of rights and benefits: temporary residence permits, emergency health care, shelter, social benefits, education for minors, as well as limited access to the labour market and a limited right to family reunification.[42]

Moreover, the Directive's personal scope is quite broad. People qualifying are 'in particular' those 'who have fled areas of armed conflict or endemic violence'[43] or who are 'at serious risk of, or again who have been the victims of systematic or generalised violations of their human rights'.[44] The list being non-exhaustive, it has been suggested that the Directive could conceivably provide protection to disaster-induced displaced persons.[45] In this respect, it should be noted that the possibility of including within the protective scope of the instrument such persons was debated during the *travaux préparatoires*. The Finnish delegation explicitly suggested the addition of a reference to 'persons who have had to flee as a result of natural disasters'. The proposal was not accepted by other Member States and consequently did not make its way in the final text.[46] Nonetheless, following the adoption of the Directive, the then UK Home-Office Minister affirmed that 'The Directive that we are implementing will ensure that each European Member State plays its part in providing humanitarian assistance to people forced from their homes by war and *natural disasters*' (emphasis added).[47]

In conclusion, while during the negotiation process there was a shared understanding that the Directive was not meant to apply to so-called environmental migrants, this does not preclude *a priori* such an application. The latter is also supported by an objective reading of the text. In practice, though, it is quite dubious to suggest that temporary protection will be activated in disaster displacement scenarios. First of all, the fact that the Directive has never been applied does not bode well for the future. Second, the required majority voting of two-thirds renders its activation improbable unless a mass flow affects a significant number of Member States.[48] And yet, neither during the recent, and massive, Syrian refugee crisis has the Directive's implementation been seriously envisaged.

National practice

The United States of America

At the domestic law level, the most prominent example of temporary protection, despite its own peculiarities, is offered by the United States of America (USA). Temporary Protected Status (hereinafter TPS) was created by Congress in 1990 in order to establish a uniform, and less discretionary than previously, system for protecting those unable to return to their home countries because of a political or environmental catastrophe.[49]

The USA Immigration and Nationality Act provides for the possibility to grant TPS to foreign nationals if: (i) there has been an environmental disaster in the foreign State resulting in a substantial, but temporary, disruption of living conditions; (ii) the foreign State is unable, temporarily, to handle adequately the return of its own nationals; and (iii) the foreign State officially has requested such designation.[50]

The authority to designate a country for TPS, originally attributed to the Attorney General, from 1 March 2003 has been attributed to the Secretary of Homeland Security.[51] After a country's TPS designation, its nationals who already resided – even illegally – in the USA at the time of designation are eligible for protection if they satisfy certain requirements (e.g. no serious criminal record, not subject to asylum bars). TPS beneficiaries receive provisional protection against deportation and authorisation to work in the USA for a limited period of time.

The Department of Homeland Security (DHS) grants TPS for an initial period between 6 and 18 months and then can renew it as long as it deems that the conditions for TPS designation continue to be met. Having a temporary character, though, once the DHS decides to end it, TPS holders revert to their prior immigration status and thus eventually to illegality.

Since its first enactment in 1990, TPS has been granted in response to various events, including natural disasters. This was the case, for instance, of the designation of Honduras and Nicaragua in early 1999 after the passage of the devastating Hurricane Mitch. At present, thirteen countries are designated.[52] Interestingly, the majority of those currently granted TPS are due to disasters, in particular earthquakes (El Salvador, Haiti, Nepal and Nicaragua) and the Ebola virus disease (Guinea, Liberia and Sierra Leone). Moreover, with respect to Somalia, the most recent DHS Notices on the Extension of TPS Designation cite drought and food insecurity as additional factors aggravating the country conditions.[53]

This short overview leads to the conclusion that TPS, while being highly discretionary, is a valuable instrument in protecting those who cannot be repatriated because of a catastrophic event in their country. Nonetheless, repeated extensions of TPS expose the beneficiaries to the risk of a permanent precarious status. An emblematic example is offered by the Latin American countries which are currently on the TPS list. Their designation has been regularly extended for almost two decades because of the asserted ongoing 'substantial disruption of living conditions' caused by the original disaster.[54] This practice, which could be seen as almost abusive, is due to the concern of avoiding the deportation of a significant number of TPS holders who are firmly established in the USA In other words, TPS renewals have been utilised to circumvent an express ban – that of adjusting TPS status to permanent resident status – in order to fill a protection gap in domestic immigration law. Such misuse, though, inevitably limits the chances of a proper application of TPS, also in cases of natural disasters, and continues to expose this instrument to strong critiques.[55]

Moreover, in its practical application, the wide discretion enjoyed by the Secretary of Homeland Security in designating a country for TPS has sometimes led to arbitrariness – an outcome which cannot be remedied since decisions on TPS are categorically exempted from judicial review.[56] This happened, for instance, in the case of the volcanic eruptions in Montserrat when, in blatant contradiction with what was decided in other situations, the temporary character was invoked in order to justify the decision to terminate TPS. It was indeed argued that 'it is likely that the eruptions will continue for decades, [and] the situation that led to Montserrat's designation can no longer be considered "temporary" as required by Congress when it enacted the TPS statute'.[57] And yet, in such a situation, the new and recurring eruptions would have allowed a more practicable alternative to TPS extension: re-designation.

To complete the picture, it is worth citing another instrument – deferred action – which, while administrative and not legislative in character, has been used to avoid the repatriation of foreigners whose home country has been struck by a natural disaster. Deferred action is a form of prosecutorial discretion exercised by the USA Citizenship and Immigration Services (USCIS), which accordingly does not place a particular individual in removal proceedings. Similarly to TPS, deferred action is limited in time but its beneficiaries are eligible to employment authorisation.[58] It is generally granted to *individuals* 'whose cases raise compelling humanitarian concerns and to individuals whose removal is not in the best interests of the USA government'.[59] Interestingly, though, in some cases it has been made available to *groups* of aliens, in particular to certain Haitians repatriated to Florida as well as to Hurricane Katrina-affected foreign students.[60] The lack of public guidance and transparency on the procedure renders it, regrettably, scarcely accessible to those who may merit most humanitarian relief.[61]

Panama

Another country whose legislation provides in detail for a temporary protection status is Panama. Despite its limited dimensions, Panama is a crucial connecting point between South and Central America and is both a destination and transit country for migrants.

Introduced in 1998, Temporary Humanitarian Protection (hereinafter THP) status ('Estatuto Humanitario Provisional de Protección') is granted in the case of a mass influx of individuals entering irregularly in the country in search of protection.[62] Its duration is limited to two months, but in exceptional circumstances it can be extended by the executive. During this period, individual beneficiaries are accorded the rights to basic necessities and to the unity of the nuclear family. They do not have, however, the right to work in Panama. Moreover, they are subject to movement restrictions.

Once the required circumstances are in place, the executive is under an obligation to make the necessary determination so as to trigger temporary protection. This guarantees a certain effectiveness to the instrument. Additionally, its broad triggering criteria may also render THP applicable in disaster displacement situations. On the negative side, though, THP beneficiaries do not enjoy the same rights and benefits as those persons who are formally recognised as refugees according to the Geneva Convention.[63] As a consequence, in a mass influx situation, State authorities are expressly allowed to apply temporary protection status *in lieu* of refugee protection.[64]

The Panamanian legislation also assigns a role to the States of origin. The executive is indeed required to establish bilateral mechanisms with such States in order to manage the return of their nationals in dignity and security, as well as to create possibilities for resettling the most vulnerable persons in third countries.[65]

So far, THP has only been applied to Colombian nationals who fled to the province of Darien in Panama from 1998 to 2000, and in fact, its adoption was a direct response to such displacement crisis. Over the last few years, the precarious situation of the Colombians living in Darien has finally reached a conclusion, thanks to the passing of legislation granting them permanent residence[66] and to the increased control by Panama of its border with Colombia. The country has thus begun to question whether to reform THP in a way so as 'to effectively address the new flows of international forced migrants arriving in Panama, such as the Haitians post-2010'.[67]

A case study: the 2010 Haiti earthquake

The 7.0-magnitude earthquake which hit Haiti on 12 January 2010 had a huge and devastating impact, resulting in over 200,000 deaths and 300,000 people injured, as well as the displacement of 1.5 million and the destruction of more than 300,000 buildings. In a country already ravaged by poverty and corruption, it further weakened the government structure, which proved its inability to cope with the disaster. The earthquake indeed was the most destructing one to ever hit an urban setting, and it decimated a great part of government personnel and infrastructure.

Following the disaster, large amounts of international relief assistance reached the country, thanks to the generosity of many donor States, which in some cases also hoped that a rapid recovery would prevent a mass exodus towards their territories. These hopes, however, did not come true as recovery was late to come and many Haitians left their country in search for a better life. As was contended by some authors, this was partly due to a lack of

> a more strategic approach to assistance that channelled development funding to regions outside of the capital . . . Instead, not only was the relief funding overwhelmingly channelled to Port-au-Prince but, perversely, some of the well intentioned and much needed projects made available in Port-au-Prince ultimately exacerbated the problem.[68]

Abroad, Haitians did not generally encounter the same generosity that was shown to them through international relief and donations to their homeland. Let us consider briefly the attitude of the major destination countries.

The USA, which hosts the largest Haitian immigrant community in the world, designated Haiti for TPS just 3 days after the earthquake. TPS status was later accorded to eligible Haitians who arrived before 12 January 2011, and the programme has been extended until 22 July 2019. The USA also decided to temporarily suspend other regulatory requirements, e.g. by granting humanitarian *parole* to Haitian orphans who at the date of the earthquake were in the process of being adopted by American families and by allowing non-immigrant Haitian students to obtain employment authorisation. Additionally, in January 2012, Haitians were added to the list of country nationals who were eligible for H2-A and H2-B visas (for temporary workers in agriculture and non-agricultural sectors, respectively).

The cited measures seemingly marked a new direction in immigration practices *vis-à-vis* Haitians, who during the 1980s and the 1990s had experienced *refoulement* and harsh detention conditions when trying to reach the USA. However, in reality, the picture is quite different. Indeed, already in 2011 a 'Policy for Resumed Removals to Haiti' was enacted despite the continuing critical conditions prevailing in the country. Under the Policy, even those convicted for minor crimes and/or with USA citizenship and legal permanent resident children and spouses were deported, in many cases without due consideration of their medical situation.[69] Moreover, and more crucially, the USA took wide precautions, including a naval blockade, to avoid the mass migration of Haitians towards its territory.

As to Canada, since 2004, it already had in place a Temporary Suspension of Removals (TSR) on Haitian nationals.[70] The TSR program strongly parallels the US TPS, and *ratione personae* is not applicable to those individuals who choose to return voluntarily, those who are viewed as a security threat or who have a criminal record or conviction. In addition to TSR, the Canadian government adopted specific policy measures allowing the expedited immigration processing of existing applications of persons with immediate family members in Canada, as well as of applications *inter alia* for: citizenship certificates, extensions of temporary resident status from in-Canada and work permits for those individuals now unable to support themselves in Canada and in-process applications to adopt children from the affected country.[71] In such cases, immigration officials were thus allowed to exercise their discretion based on humanitarian grounds. The said measures required, however, a personal link to the disaster: the individual applicants in fact had to demonstrate that they were 'negatively affected by the situation'.[72]

France, for its part, had a rather contradictory attitude. While formally supporting Haitian migrants, first of all by suspending removals to Haiti, at the same time, it generally rejected new arrivals based on the assumption that those fleeing were not refugees under the Geneva Convention. Furthermore, the suspension of removals was applied only to its metropolitan territory. Instead, in its overseas territories which had attracted many Haitians (French Guiana and Guadaloupe), borders were quickly closed.[73]

Another destination country, and in fact the primary southern destination after the 2010 disaster, was Brazil. While previously only a small number of Haitians lived in Brazil, after 2004 the link between the two countries grew stronger thanks to the leading role played by the Portuguese-speaking giant within MINUSHTAH, the United Nations (UN) stabilisation mission in Haiti. When Haitians arrived at the border asking for asylum, they received temporary refugee forms authorising their stay in anticipation of a final decision on their situation. The Brazilian authorities then determined that such persons did not meet the refugee definition either under the Geneva Convention or under the Cartagena declaration and the 1997 National Refugee Act.[74] Nonetheless, acknowledging that the displaced Haitians could not be treated as economic migrants, the Brazilian government ultimately put in place *ad hoc* humanitarian protection measures. This special mode of protection was employed in 2011–2012, when through Normative Resolution No. 97 the existing permanent residence permit for humanitarian reasons was applied for the first time to a defined national group and not to individuals. As a result, Haitians were allowed to stay in the country for a period of 5 years and with rights similar to those of refugees. Initially such a permit had to be requested at the Brazilian embassy in Port-au-Prince, and there was a limit on the number of visas which could be issued per month.[75] However, subsequent normative resolutions in 2013 and 2014 removed both restrictions and provided that applications could be presented at Brazilian consulates across the region. To date, more than 50,000 humanitarian visas have been granted, and despite its shortcomings,[76] such a protection mechanism has been praised by the UNHCR.

As to the other Latin American countries, reactions varied with place and time. In fact, within the same region where the Cartagena Declaration arose, there was no coordinated response to the Haitian flight.[77] The Dominican Republic, which had long hosted Haitian migrants, immediately opened the borders and rendered medical assistance to all Haitians in need while providing their families with multiple entry humanitarian visas. Such timely generosity, though, did not last long. On January 2010, the same month of the earthquake, the new Dominican Constitution entered into force with the effect, *inter alia*, of denying citizenship to Dominican-born children of undocumented parents. Such a revision was made harsher by a later decision of the Constitutional Court which rendered its application retroactive.[78] The most affected by this legislation were, not coincidentally, Haitians. In addition, by 2011 Dominicans became increasingly hostile *vis-à-vis* their island neighbours, partly out of fear that the cholera outbreak which hit Haiti would spread in their country. This growing hostility inevitably have resulted in discriminatory policies and deportation practices towards Haitians ever since.

Temporary humanitarian visas were issued by Venezuela and, to a greater extent, by Mexico. The latter granted visas to Haitians with family ties, as well as to all those arriving irregularly, who were allowed to work or study. Contrary to Brazil, though, regular and irregularly arriving Haitians received no official assistance apart from work authorisation, in a labour market which offered limited possibilities for these newcomers. Moreover, the humanitarian visas program, after an extension, expired at the end of 2011 and deportations were resumed immediately after. The same happened in Venezuela, where consequently many Haitians are still living undocumented.

To complete the picture, it bears noting that a few countries – Panama, Peru and Ecuador – granted refugee status to some asylum-seekers from Haiti based on the consequences of the 2010 earthquake 'which caused massive human and material losses *and exacerbated preexisting situations of political instability and insecurity*' (emphasis added).[79]

By way of conclusion, a few points are worth highlighting. As mentioned, the massive humanitarian aid provided to the Haitian capital was not followed by a parallel engagement by States in receiving those displaced. Moreover, the extent and rapidity of the Haitian flight was unexpected at both national and international level. The first reaction by host countries was, however, for the most part quite benevolent and many of the existing immigrant restrictions were suspended in recognition of the huge consequences of the disaster. Among the most utilised measures, there was a halt to deportations[80] and the issuance of humanitarian visas. Additionally, a common feature was the short duration of the various instruments adopted, which were generally revoked despite the fact that the conditions prevailing in Haiti were still extremely difficult.

Concluding remarks

When natural hazards or industrial accidents become 'disasters' in the words of the International Law Commission,[81] international cooperation proves fundamental, both for assisting the affected State and the affected population *sur place* and for protecting those who fled towards other countries. In these situations, temporary protection measures are fairly frequent in time and space, even though they do not match a single model. The overview conducted reveals the existence of three different general schemes: temporary protection *stricto sensu*, a halt to removals and the introduction of informal temporary protection measures. All of them can be grouped together by the fact of being *disaster-related*, while only the first and the third categories specifically concern *disaster-induced displaced* people.

The first approach is exemplified by the European TP Directive and the Panamanian THP status. None of them, though, has ever been applied in practice to a disaster context. Suspension of removals is, on the contrary, the most widely utilised scheme, either as an *ad hoc* measure or as an application of an existing statute, as with the case of TPS in the USA and TSR in Canada. As to the third category, it encompasses more informal arrangements typically used on the African continent, where States do not have regional or national TP mechanisms to address mass influxes. Despite the wide variety existing among and within the three categories, their most common feature is undoubtedly their discretional character. As a consequence the referred practice, despite its widespread character, is not supported by the *opinio juris* necessary to be considered an expression of a customary norm.

Temporary protection measures in general have been described by the UNHCR in the Guidelines on Temporary Protection or Stay Arrangements (hereinafter UNHCRTP Guidelines) as 'pragmatic tools' for 'offering sanctuary to those fleeing humanitarian crises'.[82] Absent an obligation to protect those coming from a disaster-affected country, the discretion that typically characterises such measures could be seen as an advantage, providing host States with a certain flexibility in implementing them. Nonetheless, discretion can easily turn into arbitrariness, as shown by the USA practice, and increases legal uncertainty. Moreover, there are risks of discrimination both between people coming from different States and contexts, and within a same group of selected beneficiaries, since not all nationals of a given country hit by a disaster have the same – or in fact any – protection needs as a consequence of that disaster. Moreover, a specific concern relates to those situations in which the disaster situation and, consequently, the duration of the correlative protection mechanisms are protracted, leaving beneficiaries in a legal limbo. In such situations, however, 'or where transition to solutions is delayed', the UNHCR TP Guidelines recommend that 'the standards of treatment would need to be gradually improved'.[83]

In order to remedy these shortcomings, it would be advisable to devise more predictable and protection-oriented mechanisms, ideally in a multilateral or regional context.[84] But why should States have an interest in limiting their leeway with respect to a category of people which is not protected *as such* by existing international norms? It is a fact that the burden of hosting and protecting these persons falls excessively on neighbouring States in those areas of the world which are the most hit by disasters. It would thus seem profitable, especially for such States, to agree upon regional temporary protection frameworks based on solidarity and burden-sharing. In disaster-prone regions it should prove to be even more true that

> establishing solidarity mechanisms during times of mass influxes . . . is very much like an insurance scheme. If a State comes to the aid of another State which is experiencing an influx of a large number of refugees, certainly the affected state would reciprocate such aid.[85]

To maximise their effectiveness, and attractiveness towards those countries which are generally States of destination and not of origin of mass influxes, the said frameworks should be accompanied by an engagement to set up national disaster risk reduction programmes.

Although in practice effective solidarity mechanisms are still lacking even at the regional level, as the Haitian crisis has sadly shown, there is nonetheless a growing awareness by the international community of the need to tackle disaster-related migration in a spirit of international cooperation. Over the last few years several international consultative processes, such as the Migrants in Countries in Crisis Initiative,[86] the Nansen Initiative and the Platform on Disaster Displacement,[87] have been started precisely to address this huge humanitarian challenge.

Selected bibliography

D. Cantor, 'Law, Policy and Practice Concerning the Humanitarian Protection of Aliens on a Temporary Basis in the Context of Disasters' Background Paper for the Nansen Initiative Regional Workshop on Temporary Protection Status and/or Humanitarian Visas in Situations of Disaster, San José, Costa Rica (10–11 February 2015).

J. Durieux, 'Temporary Protection: Hovering at the Edges of Refugee Law' 445 *Netherlands Yearbook of International Law* (December 2014) 221.

D. Perluss and J. Fitzpatrick, 'Temporary Refuge: Emergence of a Customary Norm' 26(3) *Virginia Journal of International Law* (1986) 551.

J. Fitzpatrick, 'Temporary Protection of Refugees: Elements of a Formalized Regime' 94(2) *American Journal of International Law* (2000) 279.

P. Weiss Fagen, 'Receiving Haitian Migrants in the Context of the 2010 Earthquake' Discussion Paper Nansen Initiative (3 December 2013).

Notes

1 Internal Displacement Monitoring Centre, 'Global Estimates 2015: People Displaced by Disasters', available at www.internal-displacement.org/assets/library/Media/201507-globalEstimates-2015/20150713-global-estimates-2015-en-v1.pdf, accessed on 26 July 2017.
2 Nansen Initiative, 'Agenda for the Protection of Cross-Border Displaced Persons in the Context of Disasters and Climate Change Volume 1' (2015), available at https://nanseninitiative.org/wp-content/uploads/2015/02/PROTECTION-AGENDA-VOLUME-1.pdf, accessed on 26 July 2017.
3 Cf. art 1 para 3.
4 Cf., *inter alia*, the following authors and their respective proposals: M. Conisbee and A. Simms, *Environmental Refugees: The Case for Recognition* (New Economics Foundation, 2003) 39; B. Docherty and T. Giannini, 'Confronting a Rising Tide: A Proposal for a Convention on Climate Change Refugees' 33 *Harvard Environmental Law Review* (2009) 349, 350; D. Hodgkinson, T. Burton, L. Young and H. Anderson, 'Copenhagen, Climate Change "Refugees" and the Need for a Global Agreement' 4(2) *Public Policy* (2009) 155, 160–162.
5 The first theorisation of temporary refuge is due to D. Perluss and J. Fitzpatrick, 'Temporary Refuge: Emergence of a Customary Norm' 26(3) *Virginia Journal of International Law* (1986) 551.
6 UNHCR, *Roundtable on Temporary Protection: 19–20 July 2012* (International Institute of Humanitarian Law, Sanremo, Italy, 2012).
7 As was aptly put by Joan Fitzpatrick,

> [t]emporary protection is like a magic gift, assuming the desired form of its enthusiasts' policy objectives. Simultaneously, it serves as a magic mirror of its observers' fears. For refugee advocates, TP [temporary protection] expands the protection of forced migrants who cannot satisfy the criteria under the 1951 Convention and it promises group-based protection when the determination of an individual's status proves impossible. At the same time, refugee rights organizations fear that informal and discretionary TP may dislodge refugee protection from the realm of enforceable human rights.
>
> *(J. Fitzpatrick, 'Temporary Protection of Refugees: Elements of a Formalized Regime' 94(2) AJIL (2000) 279, 280)*

8 Cf. Nansen Initiative (n. 2).
9 OAU, *Convention Governing the Specific Aspects of Refugee Problems in Africa* (adopted 10 September 1969, entered into force 20 June 1974) 1001 UNTS 45.
10 Art I(2). Hathaway remarks that the OAU definition acknowledges 'that fundamental forms of abuse may occur not only as a result of the calculated acts of the government of the refugee's state of origin but also as a result of that government's loss of authority' (J. Hathaway, *The Law of Refugee Status* (Cambridge University Press, 1991) 17).
11 M. Bond Rankin, 'Extending the Limits or Narrowing the Scope? Deconstructing the OAU Refugee Definition Thirty Years On' *New Issues in Refugee Research* (April 2005) 7.
12 Ibid 20.
13 Ibid 21.
14 W. Kälin, 'Conceptualising Climate-Induced Displacement' in J. McAdam (ed), *Climate Change and Displacement: Multidisciplinary Perspectives* (Hart Publishing, 2010) 81, 88.
15 Ibid 88–89.
16 T. Wood, 'Developing Temporary Protection in Africa' 49 *Forced Migration Review* (May 2015) 23, 24.
17 J.O. Moses Okello, 'The 1969 OAU Convention and the Continuing Challenge for the African Union' 48 *Forced Migration Review* (November 2014) 70. A 'gradual but serious erosion of hospitality towards asylum seekers and refugees in Africa' was already lamented by G. Okoth Obbo in 2001 (see G. Okoth Obbo, 'Thirty Years On: A Legal Review of the 1969 OAU Refugee Convention Governing the Specific Aspects of Refugee Problems in Africa' 20(1) *Refugee Survey Quarterly* (2001) 79–138) and was the result of a combination of political, economic and security considerations (cf. N. Willie and P. Mfubu, 'Responsibility Sharing: Towards a Unified Refugee Protection Framework in Africa' 2(3) *African Human Mobility Review* (September–December 2016) 542, 546).
18 Moses Okello (n. 17) 71–72.
19 African Union Executive Council, The Migration Policy Framework for Africa, Ninth Ordinary Session (25–29 June 2006).
20 Cf. art 1(k).
21 Ibid.

22 A.M. Abebe, 'The Kampala Convention and Environmentally Induced Displacement in Africa' IOM Intersessional Workshop on Climate Change, Environmental Degradation and Migration 29–30 March 2011, Geneva, Switzerland (2011) 7, available at www.iom.int/jahia/webdav/shared/shared/mainsite/microsites/IDM/workshops/climate-change-2011/SessionIII-Paper-Allehone-Mulugeta-Abebe.pdf, accessed on 26 July 2017.
23 They are Argentina, Belize, Bolivia, Brazil, Chile, Colombia, Ecuador, El Salvador, Guatemala, Honduras, Mexico, Nicaragua, Paraguay, Peru and Uruguay.
24 Cuba, Decreto No 26, Reglamento de la Ley de Migración (1978)/ARTICULO 80. – 'Se clasifican como Residentes Temporales, los asilados políticos y los refugiados'.
25 Cf. the comprehensive research undertaken by D. Cantor, 'Law, Policy and Practice Concerning the Humanitarian Protection of Aliens on a Temporary Basis in the Context of Disasters' Background Paper for the Nansen Initiative Regional Workshop on Temporary Protection Status and/or Humanitarian Visas in Situations of Disaster, San José, Costa Rica (10–11 February 2015).
26 Venezuela, Decreto No. 2491: Reglamento de la Ley Orgánica sobre refugiados o refugiadas y asilados o asiladas, 4 July 2003, arts 21–23.
27 Peru, Ley No. 27891, 20 December 2002, art 35.
28 Peru, Reglamento de la Ley del Refugiado, art 39.
29 Cf. Cantor (n. 25) 37–38.
30 Council Directive 2001/55/EC of 20 July 2001 on minimum standards for giving temporary protection in the event of a mass influx of displaced persons and on measures promoting a balance of efforts between Member States in receiving such persons and bearing the consequences thereof, OJ L 212/12 (2001).
31 The Directive explicitly references, in the Preamble, to people 'displaced by the conflict in Yugoslavia' (Recital 3), as well as to the Council's conclusions calling 'on the Commission and the Member States to learn the lessons of their response to the Kosovo crisis' (Recital 6).
32 The European Parliament, instead, has a very limited role to play, which consists of the right to 'be informed of' any Decision taken by the Council (art 5.5).
33 Art 2(a).
34 See art 2(c) and (d).
35 Cf. A. Abass et al., 'Regional Responses to the Libyan Crisis' *UNU-CRIS, Policy Brief, No. 1* (September 2011) 5–6, available at www.cris.unu.edu/Policy-Briefs.508.0.html, accessed on 26 July 2017; B. Nascimbene and A. Di Pascale, 'The "Arab Spring" and the Extraordinary Influx of People Who Arrived in North Italy from North Africa' 13 *European Journal of Migration and Law* (2011) 341, 346–347.
36 Art 1.
37 Art 25.1.1.
38 M. Ineli-Ciger, 'Has the Temporary Protection Directive Become Obsolete? An Examination of the Directive and Its Lack of Implementation in View of the Recent Asylum Crisis in Mediterranean' in C. Bauloz, M. Ineli-Ciger, S. Singer and V. Stoyanova (eds), *Seeking Asylum in the European Union: Selected Protection Issues Raised by the Second Phase of the Common European Asylum System* (Brill, 2015) 223, 231. It should be highlighted that the Directive also allows States to declare their total inability to host beneficiaries of temporary protection (cf. K. Kerber, 'Temporary Protection Directive' 4 *European Journal of Migration and Law* (2002) 193, 198).
39 Art 6.2.
40 *Sic* art 2(a).
41 Indeed these two statuses can be revoked only in a limited number of situations. Moreover, as was remarked by Durieux, the TP mechanism was not conceived as an alternative to the refugee protection regime, but rather as a 'prelude to [its] normal operation' (J. Durieux, 'Temporary Protection: Hovering at the Edges of Refugee Law' 445 *Netherlands Yearbook of International Law* (December 2014) 221).
42 Arts 8–19. It bears noting that the Directive provides only minimum standards (art 1). Member States are thus empowered 'to introduce or maintain more favourable provisions for persons enjoying temporary protection in the event of a mass influx of displaced persons' (Preamble, para 12).
43 Art 2(c)(i).
44 Art 2(c)(ii).
45 Cf., e.g., V. Kolmannskog and F. Myrstad, 'Environmental Displacement in European Asylum Law' 11 *European Journal of Migration and Law* (2009) 313, 316–319.
46 Council Document 6128/01, ASILE (16 February 2001) 15, 4.
47 Press Release, UK Home Office, UK Plans in Place to Protect Victims of Humanitarian Disasters (20 December 2004) 1.

48 According to a study commissioned by the European Parliament's Committee on Civil Liberties, Justice and Home Affairs:

> Considering that this Directive is applicable only in cases of mass influx and thus does not include cases involving individual applications; that 'temporary protection' is seen only as an exceptional response and taking into account the high political thresholds to activate the Directive (see art 5(1)) and considering that the Directive's mechanism has never been used in practice renders the Directive less effective in dealing with migrants displaced by environmental disasters. Indeed, the high thresholds of activating the mechanism call into question whether the temporary protection mechanism will be an effective instrument at all even for situations such as the Yugoslav conflict which provided the original rationale to develop the directive. A flexible and immediate protection mechanism such as subsidiary protection will be more relevant for individuals displaced due to environmental disasters, and indeed other categories of refugees.
>
> *(European Parliament, '"Climate refugees". Legal and Policy Responses to Environmentally Induced Migration' (2011) 55, available at www.europarl.europa.eu/thinktank/en/document.html?reference=IPOL-LIBE_ET%282011%29462422, accessed on 26 July 2017)*

49 Before 1990, the executive branch dealt with this scenario by designating certain countries for Extended Voluntary Departure (EVD), an administrative status that amounted to an exercise of prosecutorial discretion by the Attorney General not to pursue nationals of certain countries for removal if found to be living in the United States without authorisation. However, there were no established criteria explaining how a country might qualify for EVD, and critics alleged that decisions regarding the grant of EVD to nationals of a particular country were often politically motivated. This argument became especially prominent in the late 1980s, when the Reagan administration decided not to designate El Salvador for EVD despite the country's ongoing civil war.

50 USA, Immigration and Nationality Act, as amended 4 March 2010, Act 244: Temporary Protected Status, Section 244.1(b)(1)(B).

51 Cf. USA, Homeland Security Act of 2002, Public Law 107–296. Accordingly, responsibility for administering the TPS program was transferred from the former Immigration and Naturalization Service (INS) to a component of the Department of Homeland Security (DHS): the US Citizenship and Immigration Services (USCIS).

52 El Salvador, Guinea, Haiti, Honduras, Liberia, Nepal, Nicaragua, Sierra Leone, Somalia, South Sudan, Sudan, Syria, Yemen (www.justice.gov/eoir/temporary-protected-status, accessed on 26 July 2017).

53 Cf. Extension of the Designation of Somalia for Temporary Protected Status, 1 November 2013; Extension of the Designation of Somalia for Temporary Protected Status, 1 June 2015.

54 For instance, with respect to El Salvador, in the last Extension Notice it is affirmed: 'There continues to be a substantial, but temporary, disruption of living conditions in El Salvador resulting from a series of earthquakes in 2001, and El Salvador remains unable, temporarily, to handle adequately the return of its nationals' (USA Citizenship and Immigration Services, Extension of the Designation of El Salvador for Temporary Protected Status, Notice, 81 FR 44645, published on 7 August 2016).

55 M. Krikorian, 'There's Nothing as Permanent as Temporary Immigration Status', Center for Immigration Studies Blog (27 September 2012), available at http://cis.org/krikorian/theres-nothing-permanent-temporary-immigration-status, accessed on 26 July 2017.

56 8 U.S.C. para 1254a(5)(A).

57 Termination of the Designation of Montserrat under the Temporary Protected Status Program; Extension of Employment Authorization Documentation, [69 FR 40642] [FR 19–04], 6 July 2004, available at www.uscis.gov/ilink/docView/FR/HTML/FR/0-0-0-1/0-0-0-94157/0-0-0-94177/0-0-0-96204.html, accessed on 26 July 2017.

58 8 C.F.R. para 274a.12(c)(4).

59 Citizenship and Immigration Services Ombudsman, 'Deferred Action: Recommendations to Improve Transparency and Consistency in the USCIS Process' 2, 11 July 2011.

60 R.B. Murray and S.P. Williamson, 'Migration as a Tool for Disaster Recovery: A Case Study on US Policy Options for Post-Earthquake Haiti' Centre for Global Development – Working Paper 255 (June 2011) 39.

61 Cf. Citizenship and Immigration Services Ombudsman (n. 59).

62 Panama, Decreto ejecutivo 23 de 1998, 'Por el cual se desarrolla la Ley No. 5 del 26 del octubre de 1977 que aprueba la Convención de 1951 y Protocolo de 1967 sobre el Estatuto de Refugiados, se derogan el

Decreto No. 100 del 6 de julio de 1981 y la Resolución Ejecutiva No. 461 del 9 de Octubre de 1984, y se dictan nuevas disposiciones en materia de protección temporal por razones humanitarias', 10 February 1998, Title II, Chapter I.

63 Decreto Ejecutivo No. 28, art 81.

64 Not coincidentally, temporary protection is regulated in the national refugee law. In this respect, it must be noted that Panama is one of the few countries, along with Costa Rica, Venezuela, Colombia and Ecuador (which stripped the expanded Cartagena definition from its legislation in 2012), which have not incorporated the Cartagena Declaration in its national framework. Moreover, Panama 'has long affirmed that it does not consider itself bound by the Cartagena definition' (D. Cantor and D. Trimiño Mora, 'A Simple Solution to War Refugees? The Latin American Expanded Definition and Its Relationship to IHL' in D. Cantor and J.-F. Durieux (eds), *Refuge from Inhumanity? War Refugees and International Humanitarian Law* (Brill, 2014) 204, 214 ftn 44).

65 Cf. art 85.

66 Cf. Law 81/2011, which creates a legal mechanism for persons covered by the Temporary Humanitarian Protection regime to apply for permanent residence.

67 Cantor (n. 25) 21.

68 P. Weiss Fagen, 'Receiving Haitian Migrants in the Context of the 2010 Earthquake' Discussion Paper Nansen Initiative (3 December 2013) 7–8.

69 This policy was severely criticised by the Inter-American Commission of Human Rights, which adopted provisional measures calling on the USA to immediately suspend deportations of named Haitian nationals. Cf. Organization of American States, 'IACHR Urges United States to Suspend Deportations to Haiti' (4 February 2011), available at www.oas.org/en/iachr/media_center/PReleases/2011/006.asp, accessed on 26 July 2017.

70 This programme enables the Minister of Public Safety and Emergency Preparedness to temporarily suspend deportation of foreign nationals whose country faces a generalised risk of, *inter alia*, 'an environmental disaster resulting in a substantial temporary disruption of living conditions' (Government of Canada, 'Removal from Canada', available at www.cbsa-asfc.gc.ca/security-securite/rem-ren-eng.html, accessed on 26 July 2017). This stay of removal would not apply to individuals who are inadmissible for criminality, serious criminality, security, violating human or international rights, organised crime or to a person referred to in section F of article 1 of the United Nations Convention Relating to the Status of Refugees (cf. section 230 of the Immigration and Refugee Protection Regulations).

71 See Governement of Canada, Operational Bulletin 179A – June 29, 2010, available at www.cic.gc.ca/ENGLISH/resources/manuals/bulletins/2010/ob179_A1.asp, accessed on 26 July 2017.

72 Canada, Citizenship and Immigration, 'Guidelines for Priority Processing in the Event of Disaster Situations, Operational Bulletins 083' (30 October 2008), available at www.cic.gc.ca/english/resources/manuals/bulletins/2008/ob083.asp, accessed on 26 July 2017.

73 C. Pelletan, *Haiti-France/Migration: Une politique migratoire sévère en Outre-Mer* (Alter Presse, 2012), available at www.alterpresse.org/spip.php?article13192#.VAXiMvldV8E, accessed on 26 July 2017.

74 It bears noting that the National Refugee Act extends the refugee definition to cover those fleeing from 'gross and generalised human rights violations'.

75 Brazil, National Council of Immigration. 'Normative Resolution 97' (CNIg, 12 Jan. 2012), Diário Oficial da União, Section 1, 13 January 2013, 74.

76 Humanitarian visas are provided, as well as revoked, through acts of the Executive and are applied to specific groups of people, thus raising discrimination concerns.

77 Weiss Fagen (n. 68) 29.

78 This legislation raised numerous protests by human rights groups and was strongly condemned by the Inter-American Commission of Human Rights, which affirmed that it was in violation of the Inter-American Convention of Human Rights (ibid 13).

79 Cf. N. Rodriguez Serna, 'Human Mobility in the Context of Natural Hazards-Related Disasters in South America', Background Paper for the Nansen Initiative South America Consultation Quito, Ecuador (15–16 July 2015) 28. See also Cantor (n. 25) 17.

80 A number of States reported to have interrupted forced returns as a consequence of the 2010 earthquake. They included Costa Rica, Denmark, Germany, Paraguay, Romania, Lebanon, the Slovak Republic and Slovenia. However, as was reported by the Independent Expert on the situation of human rights in Haiti, Michel Forst, '[i]t is unclear . . . if any of these countries had in their jurisdiction Haitian nationals subject to deportation' (A/HRC/20/35/Add.1, para 24).

81 Cf. art 3(a) of the ILC Draft on the Protection of Persons in the Event of Disasters and Bartolini's chapter in this volume.

82 UNHCR, 'Guidelines on Temporary Protection or Stay Arrangements' (February 2014) 1, para 3, available at www.refworld.org/docid/52fba2404.html, accessed on 26 July 2017.
83 Ibid 5, para 17.
84 This is what is proposed, not coincidentally, by the UNHCR in the 2014 TP Guidelines.
85 Willie and Mfubu (n. 17) 13.
86 Cf. Guadagno and Sironi's chapter in this volume.
87 Cf. Kälin's chapter in this volume.

22

DISASTER DISPLACED PERSONS IN THE AGE OF CLIMATE CHANGE

The Nansen Initiative's protection agenda

Walter Kälin

Introduction

Every year millions of people are forced to leave their homes in times of disasters linked to natural hazards and effects of climate change. This reality creates specific protection needs for displaced persons and is increasingly recognised by the international community as one of the big humanitarian challenges of the 21st century that needs to be addressed.

These challenges are the topic of the *Agenda for the Protection of Cross-Border Displaced Persons in the Context of Disasters and Climate Change* (hereinafter: Protection Agenda) endorsed by more than 100 States in October 2015 as outcome of 3 years of consultations by the Nansen Initiative. The Agenda is neither an attempt to develop new legal standards nor is it a binding document. Rather, it purports 'to enhance understanding, provide a conceptual framework, and identify effective practices for strengthening the protection of cross-border disaster-displaced persons'.[1] The Protection Agenda does not address all kinds of disasters, only those triggered by or linked to natural hazards (hereinafter disasters).

This contribution first describes the wider context of the Nansen Initiative, as well as the process leading up to the endorsement of the Protection Agenda. The chapter then analyses key conceptual issues that underline the Agenda before moving to a discussion of the effective practices identified within the Agenda to protect cross-border disaster-displaced persons and measures to manage disaster displacement risk in the country of origin. It ends with an assessment of what the Nansen Initiative and its Protection Agenda did and did not achieve.

The context

Disaster displacement: a reality

While numbers change from year to year, it is estimated that, on average, one person is displaced every second due to a disaster. Between 2008 and the end of 2016, some 227.6 million people – an average of more than 25 million per year or 1 person per second – were displaced in the context of sudden-onset disasters triggered by natural hazards such as earthquakes, tropical storms, landslides and floods.[2] During this period, 86% were displaced by weather-related events and 14% by geophysical events.[3] The number of people newly displaced each year in the context of disasters is, on average, larger than that of people fleeing conflict and other forms of violence. In 2016 alone, for instance, some 24.3 million people fled the impacts of disasters while 6.9 million were newly displaced by armed conflict and violence.[4] In contrast, information on the number of those displaced in the context of slow-onset hazards such as drought, desertification or rising sea levels is not systematically gathered.

While dynamics vary from region to region,[5] it is clear that the large majority of disaster-displaced people remain within their countries as internally displaced persons (IDPs). For example, in the aftermath of the 2004 Indian Ocean Earthquake and Tsunami more than 2 million IDPs were identified in multiple affected countries, spanning from Southeast Asia to Eastern Africa.[6] In 2010, the unprecedented Indus River floods in Pakistan displaced an estimated 11 million people within their country.[7]

In some circumstances, disaster-displaced persons also cross borders to find refuge abroad. They may seek to escape life-threatening situations by fleeing to neighbouring countries or beyond, particularly when they live in border areas and the safest escape routes lead across borders. They may also cross international borders when protection and humanitarian assistance is either unavailable or cannot be accessed in their own country. Others may try to reach family members or friends living abroad and ready to shelter them. However, their overall number is unknown[8] as current counting methods focus on how many people have left disaster-affected areas, and not where they go and how long they remain there. The challenge of data collection is further exacerbated by the fact that the distinction between those migrating abroad for predominantly voluntary reasons and those forced to move is often difficult to establish in such situations.

While cross-border disaster-displacement is very rarely identified in Southeast Asia and Europe, a considerable number of examples have been found in Africa and in Central and South America. In Africa, the main driver is flooding whereas in the Americas hurricanes, flooding, landslides and earthquakes primarily trigger cross-border displacement.[9] A broad range of examples have been documented in various parts of the world.[10] For example, following the 2010 earthquake in Haiti, the neighbouring Dominican Republic admitted over 200,000 disaster-displaced Haitians over the course of months following the disaster, as did other States in the Caribbean and throughout the Americas.[11] During the 2011–2012 Horn of Africa drought crisis, some 290,000 displaced people sought protection and assistance abroad,[12] most notably in Kenya, which in 2011 alone received an estimated 160,000 Somalis primarily from the drought-affected regions of south and central Somalia.[13] Severe storms have also resulted in cross-border disaster-displacement, such as in Southern Africa in 2015, when people fled particularly severe flooding in both directions across the border between southern Malawi and northern Mozambique during Cyclone Chedza.[14]

Notably, climate change impacts have been identified as triggering disaster displacement already today.[15] The Intergovernmental Panel on Climate Change (IPCC) expects that, due to the rise of extreme weather events and other climate change effects, the displacement of people will increase in the future. The IPCC highlights that at the same time 'populations that lack the resources for planned migration experience higher exposure to extreme weather events, particularly in developing countries with low income', meaning that such people face a higher risk of being displaced than those who have the means to migrate to safer areas within the country or abroad before disasters strike.[16]

Disaster displacement: specific protection needs

Disasters affect displaced and non-displaced persons alike. The question then arises whether a specific focus on displaced persons is justified. The answer is 'yes' insofar as displaced persons have particular protection and assistance needs not shared with non-displaced people.[17] For example, when a disaster occurs, disaster-displaced people need to be able to reach a safe place either within their own country or in some cases abroad. During flight, family members may become separated, or displaced persons may rely on dangerous modes of transportation, including the use of human smugglers. Once they find a place of refuge, disaster-displaced persons need to find and have access to emergency shelter, life-saving medical care, water and sanitation facilities and food, as well as education, psycho-social counselling and livelihood opportunities in a place that is often unfamiliar to them and where they cannot rely on established community ties and support. Displaced women and children in particular are more likely to face sexual and gender-based violence during flight or in crowded collective centres than under normal circumstances. Away from their homes and social networks, women and children are also more at risk of human trafficking than before. Finally, disaster-displaced people may lack essential legal documents necessary for accessing humanitarian or reconstruction assistance because they fled without such documents or they were destroyed in the disaster.

Although the majority of people displaced in sudden-onset disasters can usually return home after a relatively short period of time, in some cases ongoing humanitarian assistance is necessary during the recovery and reconstruction phase until durable solutions for those displaced can be identified. Insufficient opportunities for durable solutions to displacement have left people in protracted displacement situations for months or years after a disaster.[18] For example, 119,000 IDPs out of the more than 470,000 persons displaced by the 2011 tsunami and Fukushima disaster in Japan still remained in displacement at the end of 2016.[19] Even upon return, disaster-displaced persons may find that their home, land or property has been occupied in their absence, or that their former residences are located in areas which the government has designated as no longer suitable for habitation following a disaster.

Disaster displacement: an increasing concern to the international community

Disaster displacement creates an obvious challenge not only for affected people and their countries, but also for the international community. In April 2009, the heads of organisations belonging to the Inter-Agency Standing Committee (IASC) – the coordinating body of United Nations (UN) humanitarian agencies and large international humanitarian civil society consortia – addressed a letter to the Executive Secretary of the UN Framework Convention on Climate Change (UNFCCC) asking for acknowledgement of and means to address the humanitarian consequences of climate change in the new climate change agreement.[20] Their lobbying efforts were successful insofar as the 2010 UNFCCC Conference of the Parties (COP16) recognised the implications of climate change on human mobility in the so-called Cancun Adaptation Framework. Its paragraph 14(f) called for voluntary 'measures to enhance understanding, coordination and cooperation with regard to climate change induced displacement, migration and planned relocation, where appropriate, at national, regional and international levels'.[21]

In 2011, then UN High Commissioner for Refugees Antonio Gutierrez decided to make disaster- and climate change-related displacement one of the topics of the 60th anniversary year of the 1951 Convention relating to the Status of Refugees (CSR51).[22] In February of that year, an expert roundtable on climate change and displacement was held in Bellagio, Italy.

It acknowledged that the CSR51, in most cases, does not cover cross-border disaster-displaced persons and identified the 'need to develop a global guiding framework or instrument to apply to situations of external displacement other than those covered by the 1951 Convention, especially displacement resulting from sudden-onset disasters'. At the same time the roundtable discouraged using 'the terms of "climate refugee" and "environmental refugee" . . . as they are inaccurate and misleading'.[23]

As a next step, the Government of Norway hosted the 'Nansen Conference on Climate Change and Displacement in the 21st Century' in Oslo in June 2011. The Chairperson's summary called for a 'more coherent and consistent approach at the international level . . . to meet the protection needs of people displaced externally owing to sudden-onset disasters' and identified in this regard

> a normative gap with respect to external displacement resulting from disasters, which needs to be addressed. It was suggested that States, in conjunction with UNHCR and other relevant stakeholders, could develop a guiding framework or instrument for the protection of people displaced externally due to sudden-onset natural disasters, including those related to climate change.[24]

Following these events, it was hoped that the Ministerial Meeting of UN Member States facilitated by UN High Commissioner for Refugees (UNHCR) in December 2011 would give the green light to initiate such a process. However, no consensus was reached during the meeting,[25] with the Ministerial Communiqué only expressing, in somewhat opaque language, a readiness to 'reinforce cooperation . . . to deepen our understanding of evolving patterns of displacement and to agree upon ways to respond to the challenges we face in a changing global context'.[26] In order to ensure that the issue would nevertheless be addressed, the Governments of Norway and Switzerland highlighted during the meeting that a 'more coherent and consistent approach at the international level is needed to meet the protection needs of people displaced externally owing to sudden-onset disasters, including where climate change plays a role'. They pledged to cooperate with interested States and other relevant stakeholders to: (1) obtain 'a better understanding of such cross-border movements at relevant regional and sub-regional levels', (2) identify best practices and (3) develop a 'consensus on how best to assist and protect the affected people'.[27] The pledge was welcomed by several States and formed the basis of the Nansen Initiative.

The Norwegian and Swiss pledge was informed by the realisation of not only 'a general lack of preparedness leading to *ad hoc* responses' to cross-border disaster-displacement, but also the existence of a series of key gaps which the Protection Agenda identifies as (i) knowledge and data gaps, (ii) legal gaps, (iii) institutional and operational gaps and (iv) funding gaps in terms of a 'lack of clarity regarding funding for measures to address cross-border disaster-displacement and find lasting solutions for displacement'.[28]

The process

The Nansen Initiative was conceived as a bottom-up, State-led consultative process with multi-stakeholder involvement to build a consensus on key principles and elements regarding the protection of persons displaced across borders in the context of disasters that sets the agenda for future action at domestic, regional and international levels.[29] It was not set up as a new institution or organisation, but rather as a light structure providing a forum to learn, consolidate knowledge and frame the discussion about cross-border displacement in the context of disasters and climate change.

Creating an organisational structure

The Nansen Initiative, drawing its name from the June 2011 Nansen Conference and thus highlighting the continuity of the process, was launched in October 2012. It ended in December 2015 when Norway and Switzerland concluded that they had fulfilled their pledge with the adoption of the Protection Agenda in October of the same year.[30]

The Nansen Initiative's organisational structure was light. Norway and Switzerland chaired a small Steering Group with Australia, Bangladesh, Costa Rica, Germany, Kenya, Mexico and the Philippines as members. UNHCR and IOM participated as standing invitees. The Steering Group was Geneva based and worked at the technical as well as ambassadorial level. An academic with international experience acted as Envoy of the Chairmanship of the Nansen Initiative on a part-time basis and provided strategic guidance and input. A Consultative Committee, with about 80 members from international organisations, non-governmental organisations, academic institutions and think tanks as well as individual researchers, informed and supported the process with expertise in the areas of displacement, migration, disaster risk management and climate change. A Group of Friends, comprised of more than forty countries and regional organisations interested in the Initiative and co-chaired by the European Union and Morocco, acted as a sounding board and information-sharing network that contributed to the work of the Initiative with comments and feedback. Finally, the Nansen Initiative was supported by a small secretariat based in Geneva. This structure enabled, as observed by McAdam, 'input from a diversity of actors, and created a sense of investment in the process'.[31]

This structure had the advantage of being nimble, very flexible and at the same time inclusive and representative of the specific situations and challenges in different parts of the world.

Consulting and learning

In order to build consensus, the Nansen Initiative led a series of regional and sub-regional consultations. Between May 2013 and October 2015, seven inter-governmental Regional Consultations, with one exception hosted by the respective governments, were held in the Cook Islands for the Pacific region, Costa Rica for Central America, Kenya for the Horn of Africa, the Philippines for Southeast Asia, Bangladesh for South Asia, South Africa for the Southern Africa region and Ecuador for South America. They were complemented by a series of five regional civil society meetings. Overall, about 100 countries, 10 regional organisations, 15 United Nations Agencies and 150 NGOs with a total of more than 1,000 persons having a background in disaster management, displacement and migration, human rights, climate change and other relevant areas participated in these events. Each regional consultation's agenda was developed in consultation with a wide variety of stakeholders in the respective regions based upon pre-visits by the Envoy and background research by the Nansen Initiative Secretariat to ensure that discussions were tailored to each region's specific situation and challenges. This was an essential element to create trust and ownership and making these gatherings relevant. When particular issues related to disaster displacement in a region warranted additional research, the Nansen Initiative commissioned in depth studies to further contribute to discussions.

The Regional Consultations not only contributed to a deeper understanding of the phenomenon of disaster displacement among participants, many of whom were unfamiliar with the issue, but also provided an opportunity to share experiences and enhance knowledge within the region. By bringing together the results from all the Regional Consultations, the Nansen Initiative was able to compile an enhanced knowledge base that allowed for a better understanding of the causes and dynamics of disaster displacement more generally and provided rich information on the diverse challenges as well as effective practices used in the different parts of the world to address disaster displacement.

Framing and feeding

2015 was a particularly intense year for the international community due to several processes and events directly relevant to the issue of disaster displacement. In particular, States participated in the Sendai World Conference on Disaster Risk Reduction, held negotiations on a new agreement on climate change at COP21 in Paris, adopted the UN Sustainable Development Goals and participated in a series of consultations throughout the year in preparation of the 2016 World Humanitarian Summit. The Nansen Initiative did not attempt to duplicate these efforts but rather saw its role in framing relevant messages on how disaster displacement should be addressed within each of these contexts and feeding the messages into these processes by contributing background information and supporting joint negotiating efforts by States particularly active in the Nansen Initiative.

Some of these efforts were successful. Despite strong opposition till the last hour, negotiators managed to have language on the prevention of and response to disaster displacement included in the Sendai Framework for Disaster Risk Reduction 2015–2030 (UNISDR 2015).[32] The UN's 2030 Agenda for Sustainable Development recognises that global challenges which threaten to reverse much of the development progress made in recent decades include more frequent and intense natural disasters as well as the forced displacement of people. In Paris, negotiators at the COP21 agreed to create a Task Force to develop recommendations for integrated approaches to avert, minimise and address displacement related to the adverse impacts of climate change. The World Humanitarian Summit process identified disaster displacement as a current and emerging humanitarian challenge, with the UN Secretary-General Ban Ki-Moon suggesting, as part of this proposed Agenda for Humanity, the adoption of 'an appropriate international framework, national legislation and regional cooperation frameworks by 2025 to ensure countries in disaster-prone regions are prepared to receive and protect those displaced across borders without refugee status'.[33]

The Nansen Initiative also contributed to ongoing processes at the regional level. For example, the 2014 Brazil Declaration and Plan of Action recognises 'the challenges posed by climate change and natural disasters, as well as by the displacement of persons across borders that these phenomena may cause in the region' and the need to 'give more attention to this matter'.[34] The member States of the Regional Conference on Migration went one step further by adopting, in 2016, a guide to effective regional practices to protect cross-border disaster-displaced persons with humanitarian protection measures.[35] A similar endeavour will start in 2017 in South America.

Developing and endorsing the Protection Agenda

Based on the Regional Consultations, commissioned research and the outcomes of relevant international and regional processes, a first draft of the Protection Agenda was prepared and widely distributed in early 2015 and meetings in Geneva and several parts of the world were organised to obtain broad feedback on the draft.

The process culminated in presenting the Protection Agenda to the Global Consultation held in Geneva, Switzerland. On 13 October 2015, the representatives of more than 100 States participating in this event declared to 'endorse the Agenda as a guiding document to better conceptualise cross-border disaster-displacement', highlighting that it 'compiles and analyzes key principles and illustrative examples of effective State practices from around the world, and provides a toolbox of policy options for action'.[36] UN Secretary-General Ban Ki-Moon subsequently called on States to 'give favourable consideration to incorporating into national policies and practices the insights' of the Agenda.[37]

The Protection Agenda is comprised of three main parts. Part One discusses the protection and assistance needs of people who have been displaced across borders in the context of disasters and presents examples of effective practices used by States to either admit cross-border disaster-displaced persons or to refrain from forcibly returning foreigners to their countries of origin that have been affected by disasters. While Part One examines countries of destination, Part Two focuses on how to manage disaster displacement risk in countries of origin by identifying a series of tools to prevent displacement and highlights effective practices to strengthen the protection of Internally Displaced Persons (IDPs) so that they are not compelled to look for protection and assistance abroad. Part Three concludes the Agenda with a list of priority areas for future action at national, sub-regional, regional and international levels.

Conceptual issues

The Nansen Initiative was initially faced with several conceptual issues: how narrow or broad should the scope of the Protection Agenda be? Should it exclusively focus on cross-border disaster-displacement or also address other forms of human mobility, such as voluntary migration and planned relocation? And what about internal displacement? Should it try to conceptualise displacement as something caused by climate change or look for another approach? And would it be appropriate and feasible to call for a new convention on cross-border disaster-displaced persons?

Scope: a holistic approach

Although the Nansen Initiative was triggered by climate change discussions, Norway and Switzerland realised early on in the process that it would be problematic to exclude, by restricting the Protection Agenda's scope to weather-related events, people displaced in the event of earthquakes, tsunamis and other geophysical hazards. Those promoting special protection for 'climate refugees' often refer to concepts of 'climate justice' and argue that most of the people displaced by extreme weather events, sea level rise and other adverse effects of climate change are not responsible for global warming and therefore deserve special protection.[38] However, from a human rights perspective, limiting protection to displaced victims of climate change effects while excluding other disaster-displaced persons would be highly problematic. Human rights entitlements are not a form of compensation for tort victims injured by the recklessness of someone else. Rather, they are grounded in the dignity of the human being and serve to protect fundamental needs of the human person. Because the protection needs of displaced people are basically the same in disasters triggered by hydro-meteorological and geophysical hazards, restricting a protection regime to the former category would risk amounting to unjustified unequal treatment.

The pledge made by Norway and Switzerland in 2011 focused on cross-border movements. In the course of the Nansen Initiative consultations, it quickly became clear that this scope was too narrow. Even during the first Regional Consultation in the Pacific, participants insisted that displacement is not an option and highlighted, as an alternative, facilitating voluntary migration and, if necessary, planned relocation in ways that respect the rights and dignity of those involved.[39] Voluntary migration was a prominent topic in all consultations, as was disaster risk management. The need to better address internal displacement was particularly highlighted in Southeast Asia and the Greater Horn of Africa region. Based on these contributions, the Protection Agenda highlights that a 'comprehensive approach to cross-border disaster-displacement also requires tackling disaster displacement risk in the country of origin'.[40] It therefore also addresses measures related to (i) the prevention of displacement through climate change adaptation, disaster risk reduction and development interventions that build the resilience of people and communities at risk of displacement, as well as (ii) the facilitation of migration and planned relocation as ways to cope with disaster displacement risk and (iii) addressing the protection needs of IDPs in disaster contexts.[41]

Starting point: disaster, not climate change

What is the cause of displacement when natural hazards occur? An understanding emphasising the multi-causality of such displacement has gained ground over the years.[42] It was also highlighted by participants throughout the Nansen Initiative process. According to this understanding, three factors determine whether people can stay or not. Displacement takes place when people are (i) exposed to (ii) a natural hazard and (iii) lack the resilience to withstand its impacts. Exposure risks increase, for instance, when people move into flood-prone river plains or coastal areas that were traditionally only sparsely populated, or when they settle on steep slopes or river ravines in urban areas. Vulnerability has many causes and is not only rooted in individual traits of affected people but also in factors such as a lack of disaster risk reduction and preparedness measures, high population density, a general lack of development and the absence of good governance. Thus, people who are economically and socially vulnerable are, for instance, at particular risk of displacement if they live in densely populated and poorly planned urban neighbourhoods where corruption contributes to weak enforcement of building codes and other measures to reduce disaster risks. As compared to the impacts of the natural hazard itself, demographic, social, economic, institutional and political factors contribute as much as, and sometimes even more, to whether affected people will be able to stay or have to flee.[43]

This understanding underlies the conceptual approach of the Protection Agenda. By using the concept of a 'disaster' as the point of departure, it avoids the pitfalls inherent in notions of 'climate refugees' or 'environmental migrants'. These notions require demonstrating direct causality between global warming and other hazards and ensuing displacement – a causality that can hardly ever be established as a single or the main cause of displacement. According to the UN, a 'disaster' is defined as a 'serious disruption of the functioning of a community or a society involving widespread human, material, economic or environmental losses and impacts, which exceeds the ability of the affected community or society to cope using its own resources'.[44] Thus, people are typically displaced in contexts where their community or country is unable to cope with the impact of natural hazards and therefore experiences a disaster. This approach looks at the socio-economic effects of natural hazards and their ensuing consequences for affected persons rather than the type of hazard that triggered the disaster. The advantage of this approach is the fact that it provides criteria to determine who is in need of protection and assistance abroad.

Ambition: a toolbox, not a convention

There have been several proposals for a convention on 'climate refugees' or 'environmentally displaced persons'.[45] Similarly, the outcome of the 2011 Nansen Conference called for 'a guiding framework or instrument' for protecting cross-border disaster-displaced persons. The Nansen Initiative, as a process outside any international organisation, certainly would not have been an ideal framework for a standard-setting exercise. During the Regional Consultations, it also became clear that most States were not ready to support standard-setting given that the phenomenon of cross-border disaster-displacement still was not fully understood given a lack of data and knowledge. Even more importantly, the very significant differences in terms of challenges and dynamics between the different regions cautioned against the idea of a universal instrument applicable everywhere.

For these reasons, the Protection Agenda suggests that standard-setting activities, for the time being, are more appropriate at domestic, sub-regional or regional levels.[46] Furthermore, instead of suggesting a normative framework, the Protection Agenda presents a series of tools and effective practices derived from experiences in different parts of the world to protect cross-border disaster-displaced persons, as well as prevent and address disaster displacement risk in countries of origin. It is hoped that these practices will not only be applied on an *ad hoc* basis but may also inspire the development of norms and standards at local, national, sub-regional and regional levels.

Protecting cross-border disaster-displaced persons

The core of the Protection Agenda is dedicated to the protection of cross-border disaster-displaced persons. It first identifies criteria to determine who belongs to this category; then looks at the legal tools than can be used to admit such persons, allow them to stay or refrain from sending them back to disaster-affected countries of origin; and finally addresses the issue of durable solutions. The following overview summarises the key messages and sets out some of the ideas that underlie them.

Identifying the displaced

As mentioned above, present international law does not recognise people displaced across borders due to disasters as a distinct category worthy of protection in another country[47] and therefore does not provide any recognised criteria to distinguish between those migrating for predominantly voluntary reasons in disaster contexts and those who are forced to leave their own country. Thus, the central question is determining in what disaster situations a displaced person would be in need of protection *abroad* instead of in his or her home country. This question recognises that, in most situations, disaster-affected countries have at least some capacity to protect and assist their internally displaced persons.

In certain situations, moving across borders is the only reasonable option to seek safety and protection or assistance. In border regions, for instance, the closest path to safety may be in a neighbouring country. In other situations, protection and life-saving assistance may not be available in-country as a result of widespread destruction of infrastructure and basic services. A disaster may also simply overwhelm the response capacities of authorities, international humanitarian actors and civil society alike. Particularly in mixed disaster-conflict scenarios, the delivery of humanitarian assistance may be severely hindered by insecurity, a lack of trust of authorities or discrimination toward certain sub-sets of the population, which could again prompt disaster-affected people to seek assistance and protection abroad.

Slow-onset natural hazards are more challenging. People moving as a consequence of the gradual erosion of resilience and increasing environmental stress usually have some element of choice and thus can be qualified as (voluntary) migrants. However, when slow-onset hazards building up over many years reach an emergency or 'disaster' phase within a short period of time, for example when drought 'suddenly' triggers famine, people may have no other option than to seek food and assistance abroad and thus are displaced. Slow-onset hazards, or the cumulative effect of a series of smaller, sudden-onset hazards, may also compound a community's capacity to withstand what would normally be insignificant sudden-onset hazards. Such disaster scenarios are particularly relevant for low-lying island States where inhabitants may be forced to leave their homes and seek assistance and protection abroad on a temporary or, in extreme cases of the land becoming uninhabitable, permanent basis.

The Protection Agenda suggests as an effective practice to admit, on the basis of respective laws and policies or on an *ad-hoc* basis, persons arriving from disaster-affected countries if the individual concerned is seriously and personally affected by the disaster. This is particularly true for an individual if

> (i.) An on-going or, in rare cases, an imminent and foreseeable disaster in the country of origin poses a real risk to his/her life or safety; (ii.) as a direct result of the disaster, the person has been wounded, lost family members, and/or lost his/her (means of) livelihood; and/or (iii.) in the aftermath and as a direct result of the disaster, the person faces a real risk to his/her life or safety or very serious hardship in his/her country, in particular due to the fact that he/she cannot access needed humanitarian protection and assistance in that country (a.) because such protection and assistance is not available due to the fact that government capacity to respond is temporarily overwhelmed, and humanitarian access for international actors is not possible or seriously undermined, or (b.) because factual or legal obstacles make it impossible for him/her to reach available protection and assistance.[48]

These criteria are derived from actual State practice.[49] States identify cross-border disaster-displaced persons not by looking at the causes but rather by focusing on the effects of a natural hazard and the ensuing disaster on an individual. At their core, these criteria are based on considerations of whether the persons could reasonably be expected to return under the circumstances. This is not the case in the cases contained in the above list.

In addition, States are sometimes ready to also admit persons from disaster-affected countries who do not fulfil these criteria on the basis of 'considerations of solidarity with an affected country that is temporarily unable to adequately protect and assist all of its citizens due to the disaster'. In other cases, 'humanitarian elements, such as strong ties with family members in the country of destination' are the reason why States grant admission.[50]

These criteria are also applicable when a State has to decide whether to return foreigners to their country of origin who were on its territory at the time the disaster occurred or to grant them temporary protection.[51]

Admitting the displaced

Based on an analysis of State practice, the Protection Agenda suggests the following five approaches for admitting cross-border disaster-displaced persons and allowing them to stay temporarily, or not returning foreign nationals outside their country of origin when a disaster has occurred:[52]

- On the basis of *regular migration categories* foreseen in domestic laws regulating admission of foreigners, countries may admit cross-border disaster-displaced persons as regular migrants. For instance, admission may be granted on the basis of providing priority treatment to requests for work or study permits or family reunification or expanding pre-existing temporary work quota for migrants from disaster-affected areas. In the aftermath of the 2010 Haiti earthquake, for example, Canada decided immigration applications from disaster-affected Haiti on a priority basis, while Bolivia granted temporary visas to children allowing them to enter the country pending long-term immigration solutions.

- While bilateral and regional agreements on the *free movement of persons* are not adopted for humanitarian purposes, disaster-displaced persons can profit from them to gain admission, unless documentary and other requirements are too high to be met by them. Examples include regular cross-border movements of pastoralist during times of drought between members of the Economic Community of West African States (ECOWAS) or the open borders between Nepal and India.
- Many countries use *exceptional migration measures* such as 'temporary protection' or 'humanitarian visas' foreseen in their legislation. Others admit disaster-displaced persons on humanitarian grounds through decisions taken on an *ad-hoc* basis. Among others, Argentina, Cuba, Finland, Mexico and Sweden's immigration laws explicitly recognise the impacts of natural hazards as a potential ground for authorising the entry and stay of foreigners. China and the Democratic People's Republic of Korea have a 1964 bilateral agreement which provides that 'those who were forced to cross the border as a result of a disaster will not be treated as illegal border crossers'. In the USA, temporary protected status to citizens of an affected country who were already present on US territory at the time of the disaster may be granted if in a foreign State or parts of it

  > (i) there has been an earthquake, flood, drought, epidemic, or other environmental disaster in the state resulting in a substantial, but temporary, disruption of living conditions, (ii) the foreign state is unable, temporarily, to handle the return to the State of aliens who are nationals of the state, and (iii) the foreign state officially has requested designation under this subparagraph.[53]

- *Pastoralist transhumance arrangements* are an important feature in areas where pastoralists traditionally cross borders in times of drought. ECOWAS, for instance, issues international transhumance certificates that facilitate the cross-border movement of livestock to access grazing lands and water in neighbouring countries. Bilateral transhumance agreements also exist in other parts of Africa.
- *Refugee law* does not normally apply to disaster-displaced persons, as they do not flee persecution or violence from the hands of human actors – a condition that is inherent in all definitions of refugee. However, refugee law may become relevant in specific situations, for instance when violence breaks out in the aftermath of a disaster and the authorities are unwilling or unable to provide protection to the victims. Broader notions of a 'refugee', such as that contained in the article 1 of the 1969 African Refugee Convention which expands refugee protection to persons fleeing owing to . . . events seriously disturbing public order' may allow States to consider disaster victims as refugees if they experience (i) a life-threatening situation, (ii) are not able to receive protection and assistance from their government, and (iii) foreign assistance cannot reach them for instance due to an overall situation of insecurity or because competent authorities deny humanitarian access to international actors.

  On this basis, Djibouti, Ethiopia and Kenya admitted victims of the 2011–2012 Somalia droughts even though they fled famine rather than conflict.

The Nansen Initiative has identified more than 50 States that during the past decades have admitted persons affected by disasters in their country of origin or refrained from sending them back to such countries relying on the categories described above. This indicates that States have a rich set of experiences regarding cross-border disaster-displacement and that such persons may often get protection abroad even in the absence of clear legal obligations. However, existing mechanisms are largely unpredictable because in most countries competent authorities have the discretion as to when to use them in a given situation. Therefore, harmonisation of State practice is called for, preferably at sub-regional or regional levels as most cross-border disaster-displacement takes place within regions.

In most cases, cross-border disaster-displaced persons are admitted on a temporary basis. This raises the question as to how durable solutions ending displacement may be found. The Protection Agenda suggests as effective practices, *inter alia*, to ensure

> cooperation between countries of origin and receiving countries and, where relevant, with international organizations, to ensure that returnees are received with respect for their safety, dignity, and human rights, and under conditions that allow them to find lasting solutions to their displacement.

As an alternative, receiving countries may adopt provisions 'allowing cross-border disaster-displaced persons to apply for renewed or permanent residency, or resettlement to a third country when conditions causing the displacement persist for an extended period of time or become permanent'.[54] In reality, however, such durable solutions are often difficult to achieve.

Managing displacement risks in the country of origin

In line with its holistic approach to cross-border disaster-displacement, the Protection Agenda identifies a series of measures that States 'can take to manage disaster displacement risk in the country of origin to help people stay, move out of areas at risk, and address the specific needs of those that have been internally displaced'.[55]

Helping people to stay

It is often possible to identify areas particularly prone to disasters and assess the expected impact of a natural hazard on affected populations, including displacement risks. Measures building resilience and reducing the vulnerability of people and communities in such areas, thus helping them to stay, include disaster risk reduction, climate change adaptation and overall development measures. The Protection Agenda identifies, in particular, as effective practices: (i) 'to specifically incorporate disaster displacement risks and protection needs' into separate or joint climate change adaptation and disaster risk management strategies, plans or laws; (ii) the prioritisation of 'preparedness and early warning systems that clearly describe the hazards, identify populations most at risk of displacement, determine evacuation corridors and sites, and ensure that information reaches affected communities and can be easily understood by them'; and (iii) the prioritisation of 'infrastructure improvements, such as sea-walls, dams, dykes, and earthquake resistant buildings, in areas where people are most at risk of displacement'.[56]

These would be important steps as, with just a few exceptions, existing disaster risk reduction and climate change adaptation strategies fail to address human mobility.[57] In this regard, the Sendai Framework on Disaster Risk Reduction and the COP21 decision may bring a change in attitude. As mentioned previously, the latter lays the ground for the creation of a Task Force 'to develop recommendations for integrated approaches to avert, minimise and address displacement related to the adverse impacts of climate change'.[58] The Task Force started its work in May 2017 and is tasked with submitting the results of its work to COP24 in November 2018. The Sendai Framework encourages States to adopt, at national and local levels, policies and programmes addressing disaster-induced human mobility to strengthen the resilience of affected people and that of host communities as per national laws and circumstances and calls for trans-boundary cooperation to address displacement risk in areas with common eco-systems, such as river basins or coastlines.

Helping people to move in dignity

Migration that is predominantly voluntary, because people have a relevant degree of choice, is often used by individuals and families to cope with or adapt to environmental changes and natural hazards, particularly when such changes negatively impact livelihood opportunities. Migration in such contexts may be temporary, circular or permanent. Like those who are displaced, most migrants move to another part of their own country, with a smaller number of people travelling abroad. In some parts of the world, cross-border migration is already facilitated by agreements on the free movement of persons.

The Intergovernmental Panel on Climate Change stresses that '[e]xpanding opportunities for mobility can reduce vulnerability' for populations at risk. Thus '[c]hanges in migration patterns can be responses to both extreme weather events and long-term climate variability and change, and migration can also be an effective adaptation strategy'.[59] However, if not properly supported, migration may expose people to exploitation and discrimination and thus further exacerbate the vulnerability of individuals and families by placing them in a more precarious situation than if they had stayed in their place of origin.[60]

The Protection Agenda identifies facilitating 'migration with dignity as a potentially positive way to cope with the effects of natural hazards, environmental degradation and climate change' and highlights a series of effective practices. These include reviewing existing and negotiating new bilateral or regional migration agreements 'to determine how they could facilitate migration as an adaptation measure, including issues such as simplified travel and customs documents'; developing or adapting 'national policies providing for residency permit quotas or seasonal worker programs in accordance with international labour standards to prioritise people from countries or areas facing natural hazard or climate change impacts'; and facilitating 'pastoralists' traditional practice of moving internally and across international borders to access water, pasture and regional markets during times of drought, such as through the development of transhumance agreements or special travel permits to facilitate the cross-border movement of livestock'. The Protection Agenda also highlights the need to provide

> training and education, including through qualification and accreditation alignment, to enable people from countries facing natural hazard or climate change impacts to compete for skilled employment opportunities in a regional or global labour market, and in this regard to cooperate closely with employers.[61]

The planned relocation of communities or groups of people in disaster-prone areas is another instrument to move people out of harm's way before disaster displacement occurs.[62] Such relocation may be used as a preventative measure within the country of origin to reduce the risk of displacement in the future by moving people out of areas particularly at risk of sudden-onset disasters or becoming inhabitable in the face of environmental degradation and impacts of climate change. They may also provide a durable solution within the country of origin to allow displaced persons to rebuild their lives in another location if the disaster rendered their place of origin inhabitable. Only in very exceptional cases, such as in the case of Small Island Developing States losing substantial parts of their territory, would planned relocation to other countries be an option. As planned relocation often leads to impoverishment and loss of community ties, it is often regarded as a measure of last resort.

The Protection Agenda suggest as effective practices, *inter alia*, the development of

> international and regional guidance, as well as national and local level laws and public policies, to support effective and sustainable planned relocation processes adapted to the local context and with full respect for the rights of affected persons or groups of persons, including members of host communities.[63]

The Agenda furthermore identifies the consultation and participation of affected communities, the provision of suitable land and living space and the provision of adequate livelihood opportunities. Guidance on planned relocation has been developed in 2016 by UNHCR in collaboration with academic institutions.[64]

Addressing internal displacement

The Protection Agenda recognises the protection of IDPs as particularly important as most disaster displacement takes place within countries. It also highlights that adequate protection and assistance for IDPs and the provision of durable solutions reduces their need to move abroad.

At the normative level, the protection of internally displaced persons is rather well developed. The 1998 UN Guiding Principles on Internal Displacement,[65] which have been recognised by the international community as an 'important international framework for the protection of internally displaced persons',[66] as well as the binding African Union Convention on the Assistance and Protection of Internally Displaced Persons in Africa of 22 October 2009 (Kampala Convention)[67] and the 2006 Great Lakes IDP Protocol all include the protection and assistance needs of IDPs in disaster contexts.[68] For this reason, the Protection Agenda provides less detail on IDP protection as compared to other issues.[69] In essence, the Protection Agenda suggests explicitly incorporating the Guiding Principles on Internal Displacement and other applicable instruments within domestic legislation in ways that disaster IDPs are adequately covered. It also suggests incorporating IDP protection within relevant disaster risk reduction, climate change adaptation, humanitarian response and development plans to address the specific needs of IDPs. The Protection Agenda also mentions several effective practices to find durable solutions for internal displacement.

What the Nansen Initiative did and did not achieve

There have been voices questioning the added value of the Nansen Initiative in light of discussions in other fora and processes, such as the Sendai World Conference on Disaster Risk Reduction, the climate change negotiations or the work done by organisations such as IOM and UNHCR.

The Protection Agenda responds to these queries in an implicit way by highlighting its key contributions in four points. First, the Protection Agenda conceptualises a comprehensive approach to cross-border disaster-displacement that understands disaster displacement, not as something directly caused by climate change and other hazards, but as a complex process that allows for interventions that may prevent displacement and mitigate it. Second, it compiles 'a broad set of effective practices used by States and other actors' suitable for ensuring future responses to cross-border disaster-displacement that are more effective than many of today's *ad-hoc* actions'. Third, it highlights 'the need to bring together and link policies and action areas' such as 'humanitarian assistance and protection, human rights protection, migration management, disaster risk reduction, climate change adaptation, and development' in order to address more comprehensively 'cross-border disaster-displacement and its root causes that to date have been relatively uncoordinated'. Finally, it stresses that by taking the form of an agenda, it identifies key areas where future action is needed.[70]

The particular strength of the Nansen Initiative was not only that it was able to solidly anchor disaster displacement on the international agenda, but also the fact that a large number of States with participants representing many different backgrounds (from disaster risk management to environment to migration and human rights) came together to work across silos and agree, albeit in an informal manner, on how to conceptualise displacement in the context of disasters and climate change in a holistic and, at the same time, differentiated manner. It was also able to contribute substantially to the disaster risk and climate change discussions and other relevant international and regional processes. The Nansen Initiative's consultations and commissioned research, as well as the contributions by members of the Consultative Committee, certainly helped to address the knowledge and data gap identified at the Initiative's inception. While the Nansen Initiative was not a standard-setting exercise, the Protection Agenda contains a wealth of information and insight on how to close legal gaps at domestic and regional levels.

What the Nansen Initiative did not – and did not attempt to – achieve was to ensure that necessary action at normative and operational levels is taking place. However, as an 'agenda', it identified three priority areas of action. These are (i) enhanced data collection and knowledge, (ii) enhanced use of humanitarian protection measures for cross-border disaster-displaced persons and (iii) enhanced action to manage disaster displacement risk in the country of origin. For each of these action areas, the Protection Agenda lists a series of key actions that should be given priority.[71]

In terms of actors, the Protection Agenda calls on stakeholders at all levels, from local communities and authorities to the United Nations and other international organisations, to work on these priority areas. At the same time, recognising the variation of displacement dynamics from region to region, the Protection Agenda highlights the roles of regional and (sub-)regional organisations as particularly important for developing future responses to cross-border disaster-displacement. It also recognises the need for actors at all levels to work together across silos and implement 'coordinated approaches to cross-border disaster-displacement that bring together and link humanitarian action, human rights protection, migration management, refugee protection, disaster risk reduction, climate change adaptation, and development interventions'.[72]

Thus, the Protection Agenda is just a first, albeit important step in what will be a long path towards an effective international regime on cross-border disaster-displacement. To ensure that the Protection Agenda would not become another document gathering dust on a bookshelf, the Platform on Disaster Displacement (PDD) was launched at the World Humanitarian Summit in May 2016 as successor to the Nansen Initiative. With Germany as previous and Bangladesh as present Chair, the Platform's purpose is following up on the Protection Agenda and promoting the implementation of its recommendations. Its organisational structure and membership is similar to that of the Nansen Initiative. The Platform's ambitious workplan focuses on action (i) addressing knowledge and data gaps; (ii) enhancing the use of identified effective practices and strengthen cooperation among relevant actors to prevent, when possible, to reduce and to address cross-border displacement at the national, regional and international levels; (iii) promoting policy coherence and mainstreaming of human mobility challenges in, and across, relevant policy and action areas; and (iv) promoting policies and measures in areas where gaps exist.[73] Among its many activities, the Platform is represented in the Task Force on Displacement set up by COP21 and actively engages in the elaboration of the Global compact for safe, orderly and regular migration to be adopted in 2018. At the same time, it puts a particular emphasis on regional developments as it is at regional levels where hope for progress is the most realistic. In this sense, the Platform will be a strong voice in the ongoing quest for adequate responses to the challenge of cross-border disaster displacement. However, as Susan Martin cautions, efforts such as those of the Nansen Initiative and Platform on Disaster Displacement 'in the long term, . . . will only be as effective as the willingness of States and other stakeholders to implement the recommendations and offer protection on a nondiscriminatory basis to all who flee life-threatening situations'.[74]

Selected bibliography

Foresight, *Migration and Global Environmental Change: Final Project Report* (The Government Office for Science, 2011).

W. Kälin and N. Schrepfer, 'Protecting People Crossing Borders in the Context of Climate Change: Normative Gaps and Possible Approaches' (2012) 21, available at www.unhcr.org/4f33f1729.pdf, accessed on 7 June 2017.

J. McAdam (ed), *Climate Change and Displacement: Multidisciplinary Perspectives* (Hart Publishing, 2010).

Nansen Initiative, 'Agenda for the Protection of Cross-Border Displaced Persons in the Contexts of Disasters and Climate Change' (2015), available at www.nanseninitiative.org/global-consultations/, accessed on 7 June 2017.

R. McLeman and F. Gemenne, *Routledge Handbook of Environmental Displacement and Migration* (Routledge, 2018).

B. Meyer and F. Crépeau (eds), *Research Handbook on Climate Change, Migration and the Law* (Edward Elgar, 2017).

Notes

1 Nansen Initiative, 'Agenda for the Protection of Cross-Border Displaced Persons in the Contexts of Disasters and Climate Change' (2015), available at www.nanseninitiative.org/global-consultations/, accessed on 7 June 2017.

2 IDMC/NRC, *GRID 2017 – Global Report on Internal Displacement* (Internal Displacement Monitoring Centre, 2017).

3 Ibid 32.

4 Ibid 10.

5 Nansen Initiative (n. 1) Annex I; E. Piguet and F. Laczko (eds), *People on the Move in a Changing Climate: The Regional Impact of Environmental Change on Migration* (Springer, 2014).

6 WHO, *Tsunami 2004: A Comprehensive Analysis*, vol. I (World Health Organization, Regional Office for South-East Asia, 2013) 21.

7 IDMC, *Displacement Due to Natural Hazard-Induced Disasters: Global Estimates for 2009 and 2010* (Internal Displacement Monitoring Centre, 2011) 13.

8 IDMC/NRC (n. 2) 53.

9 Nansen Initiative (n. 1) Annex I.

10 Ibid.

11 P. Weiss Fagen, 'Receiving Haitian Migrants', available at www.nanseninitiative.org/central-america-consultations-intergovernmental, accessed on 7 June 2017.

12 UNHCR, 'UNHCR Global Trends 2014: World at War' 95, available at www.refworld.org/docid/558292924.html, accessed on 7 June 2017.

13 M. Achour and N. Lacan, 'Drought in Somalia: A Migration Crisis' in F. Gemenne, P. Brucker and D. Ionesco (eds), *The State of Environmental Migration 2011* (Institute for Sustainable Development and International Relations and International Organization for Migration, 2011) 75, 83.

14 Nansen Initiative (n. 1) Annex I, 9 ff.

15 Foresight, *Migration and Global Environmental Change: Final Project Report* (The Government Office for Science, 2011); K. Warner, T. Afifi, K. Henry, T. Rawe, C. Smith and A. de Sherbinin, *Where the Rain Falls: Climate Change, Food and Livelihood Security and Migration: Global Policy Report* (UNU-EHS, 2012).

16 IPCC, *Summary for Policymakers: Climate Change 2014: Impacts, Adaptation and Vulnerability, Contribution of Working Group II to the Fifth Assessment Report of the Intergovernmental Panel on Climate Change* (Cambridge University Press, 2014).

17 HRC, Report of the Representative of the Secretary-General on the Human Rights of Internally Displaced persons, Walter Kälin, Addendum, Protection of Internally Displaced Persons in Situations of Natural Disasters, UN Doc. A/HRC/10/13/Add. 1 (2009) paras 28–65.
18 IDMC, *Global Estimates 2015: People Displaced by Disasters* (Internal Displacement Monitoring Centre, 2015) 47.
19 IDMC/NRC (n. 2) 44.
20 W. Kälin and N. Schrepfer, 'Protecting People Crossing Borders in the Context of Climate Change: Normative Gaps and Possible Approaches' (2012) 21, available at www.unhcr.org/4f33f1729.pdf, accessed on 7 June 2017.
21 UNFCCC, Decision 1/CP.16, The Cancun Agreements: Outcome of the Work of the Ad Hoc Working Group on Long-Term Cooperative Action under the Convention, UN Doc. FCCC/CP/2010/7/Add.1 (2011).
22 Convention Relating to the Status of Refugees (adopted on 28 July 1951, entered into force 22 April 1954) 189 UNTS 137.
23 UNHCR, 'Summary of Deliberations on Climate Change and Displacement', 1, available at www.unhcr.org/4da2b5e19.pdf, accessed on 7 June 2017.
24 IDMC (n. 7) 19.
25 J. McAdam, 'From the Nansen Initiative to the Platform on Disaster Displacement: Shaping International Approaches to Climate Change, Disasters and Displacement' 39 *UNSW Law Journal* (2016) 1518, 1521.
26 UNHCR, Intergovernmental event at the ministerial level of Member States of the United Nations on the occasion of the 60th anniversary of the 1951 Convention relating to the Status of Refugees and the 50th anniversary of the 1961 Convention on the Reduction of Statelessness (7–8 December 2011), Ministerial Communique, UN Doc. HCR/MINCOMMS/2011/6 (2011) para 10, available at www.unhcr.org/4ee210d89.html, accessed on 7 June 2017.
27 Nansen Initiative (n. 1) endnote 7.
28 Ibid para 28.
29 Ibid para 8.
30 Nansen Initiative, The Nansen Initiative Global Consultation Conference Report, Geneva, 12–13 October 2015 (2015) 65, available at www.nanseninitiative.org/global-consultations/, accessed on 7 June 2017.
31 McAdam (n. 25) 1523.
32 Ibid 1530 ff.
33 UNSG, One Humanity: Shared Responsibility. Report of the Secretary-General for the World Humanitarian Summit Contents, UN Doc. A/70/709 (2016), Annex: Agenda for Humanity, viii.
34 Brazil Declaration, 'A Framework for Cooperation and Regional Solidarity to Strengthen the International Protection of Refugees, Displaced and Stateless Persons in Latin America and the Caribbean' (2014) 3, available at www.unhcr.org/54b533fa9.pdf, accessed on 7 June 2017.
35 D.J. Cantor, 'Law, Policy and Practice Concerning the Humanitarian Protection of Aliens on a Temporary Basis in the Context of Disasters: States of the Regional Conference on Migration and Others in the Americas' (2014), available at www.nanseninitiative.org/central-america-consultations-intergovernmental/, accessed on 7 June 2017.
36 Nansen Initiative (n. 30) 59.
37 UNSG, In Safety and Dignity: Addressing Large Movements of Refugees and Migrants. Report of the Secretary-General, UN Doc. A/70/59 (2016) para 106.
38 P. Penz, 'International Ethical Responsibilities to "Climate Change Refugees"' in J. McAdam (ed), *Climate Change and Displacement: Multidisciplinary Perspectives* (Hart Publishing, 2010) 151, 162.
39 Nansen Initiative, 'Human Mobility, Natural Disasters and Climate Change in the Pacific, Outcome Report' (2013) 24, available at www.nanseninitiative.org/pacific-consultations-intergovernmental/, accessed on 7 June 2017.
40 Nansen Initiative (n. 1) para 12.
41 Ibid paras 34 ff.
42 Foresight (n. 15); Warner et al. (n. 15).
43 IDMC (n. 18) 27.
44 UNISDR, *2009 UNISDR Terminology on Disaster Risk Reduction* (UNISDR, 2009).
45 B. Docherty and T. Giannini, 'Confronting a Rising Tide: A Proposal for a Convention on Climate Change Refugees' 33 *Harvard Environmental Law Review* (2009) 349 and M. Prieur, 'Draft Convention on the International Status of Environmentally-Displaced Persons' 42/43 *The Urban Lawyer* (2011) 247.

46 Nansen Initiative (n. 1) para 110.
47 McAdam (n. 25) 39.
48 Nansen Initiative (n. 1) para 33.
49 Ibid Annex II; Cantor (n. 35).
50 Ibid para 33.
51 Ibid para 65.
52 Ibid paras 47–57 and Annex II with examples.
53 USA, Immigration and Nationality Act 2002, section 244.1.
54 Nansen Initiative (n. 1) para 71.
55 Nansen Initiative (n. 1) para 76.
56 Ibid para 78.
57 Ibid para 84.
58 UNFCCC, Adoption of the Paris Agreement, Decision 21, UN Doc. FCCC/CP/2015/L.9/Rev.1 (2015) para 50.
59 IPCC (n. 16) 20.
60 Warner et al. (n. 15) 17.
61 Nansen Initiative (n. 1) para 88.
62 Ibid paras 94–98.
63 Ibid para 95.
64 Brookings/Georgetown University/UNHCR, 'Guidance on Protecting People from Disaster and Environmental Change through Planned Relocation', available at www.unhcr.org/en-us/protection/environment/562f798d9/planned-relocation-guidance-october-2015.html, accessed on 7 June 2017.
65 CHR, Report of the Representative of the Secretary-General, Mr. Francis M. Deng, submitted pursuant to Commission resolution 1997/39. Addendum: Guiding Principles on Internal Displacement, UN Doc. E/CN.4/1998/53/Add.2 (1998).
66 UNGA, Res 60/01: World Summit Outcome, UN Doc. A/RES/60/1 (2005) para 132.
67 AU, Convention for the Protection and Assistance of Internally Displaced Persons in Africa (Kampala Convention) (adopted 23 October 2009, entered into force December 2012) AU Doc. Ext/Assembly/AU/PA/Draft/Decl.(I)Rev.1.
68 International Conference on the Great Lakes Region, 'Protocol on the Protection and Assistance to Internally Displaced Persons' (30 November 2006), available at www.refworld.org/docid/52384fe44.html, accessed on 7 June 2017.
69 Nansen Initiative (n. 1) paras 99–105.
70 Ibid para 29.
71 Ibid paras 114–124.
72 Ibid para 108.
73 Platform on Disaster Displacement, PDD Workplan (2016–2019), available at http://disasterdisplacement.org/the-platform/our-response/, accessed on 7 June 2017.
74 S.F. Martin, 'New Models of International Agreement for Refugee Protection' 4 *Journal on Migration and Human Security* (2016) 60, 72.

23
CONCLUSIONS

Gabriella Venturini

Human Rights Law (HRL) first developed in domestic jurisdictions and, second, in the international legal system through treaties and customary law. It is based on the rule of law, meaning that States have a precise set of obligations to respect towards individuals under their jurisdiction. The primacy of international law over national laws on human rights matters largely derives from the extensive and detailed elaboration developed by human rights bodies and courts, which over the years have set principles and rules common to the universal and regional systems.

The normative framework of disaster response has also primarily developed under the domestic laws, and it has only recently been covered by a variety of international law instruments to form the present body of International Disaster Law (IDL).

The encounter of HRL and IDL has given rise to a number of issues which continue to provide challenges to the international, national, municipal and community actors as well as topics for discussion among scholars.

Indeed, that human rights must be respected and protected in the event of a disaster sounds like a truism. Of course, human rights matter much, and the more so when life and security are seriously endangered by natural or human-made calamities. Therefore, the respect for human rights shall guide all actions to be taken in response to disasters. Yet things are not so simple, as past, recent and current disastrous events demonstrate.

One critical issue is the multiplicity of rights that are at risk in times of disaster. Some of them, such as the rights to life, liberty, security of person, freedom of movement or freedom of assembly, belong to the catalogue of civil and political rights; others, equally or even more numerous, are economic, social and cultural rights such as the right to work; the right to social security and assistance; the right to an adequate standard of living, which includes adequate food, water, sanitation and housing; the right to the highest attainable standard of health; and the right to education. The need to prioritise emergency response as well as recovery and restoration of activities can lead, if not to competing options, at least to selective choices that ultimately privilege some and not others.

The International Covenant on Civil and Political Rights (ICCPR) imposes upon States the obligation to achieve specific results, i.e. to respect and to guarantee to all individuals the rights recognised in the Covenant. The International Covenant on Economic, Social and Cultural Rights (ICESCR), instead, contains duties of best efforts, meaning that economic, social and cultural (ESC) rights are to be realised progressively through steps taken to the maximum of a State's resources. Moreover, both civil/political and ESC rights have certain inherent limitations. They allow restrictions to safeguard the public interest that are typically invoked in times of disaster. In this respect, it is of paramount importance that the States abide by the opinion of the Human Rights Committee and avoid, as far as possible, using derogations, even in cases where these would be permissible.

It is an open question whether individuals have a right to humanitarian assistance in times of disaster, resulting in the legal entitlement of certain persons, being identified as the victims of a disaster, to receive certain services, as defined in the appropriate legal instruments. The core human rights treaties do not mention such a right; however, it could be inferred from the existing obligations by way of interpretation. There can be no doubt that the government of a State affected by a disaster has an obligation to provide assistance and relief to all persons under its jurisdiction. Should it fail to meet its obligations the usual means of redress would be available at the domestic level. But what if the affected State's response capacity is inadequate? Would the victims of a disaster be entitled to assistance from third States, international intergovernmental or non-governmental organisations, or even the international community as a whole?

As a matter of law, obligations stipulated in bilateral and multilateral treaties relating to humanitarian assistance are typically owed to other States, not to individuals. Therefore recognising that individuals are entitled to claim international assistance directly would extend the scope of international law too far, and it is not currently supported by State practice. The force of HRL, however, gives ground for envisaging that international law should evolve towards a more individual-centred approach whereby disaster victims would have the right to request and receive humanitarian assistance, not only from their government, but also from third States and international organisations. This path is already traced by some international agreements concerning the protection of internally displaced persons, as well as by a number of soft law instruments. The more a true right-based approach focusing on the situation and the needs of individual victims is adopted, the more all institutions and entities will be held accountable towards those who are vulnerable to and affected by disasters.

Disaster exacerbates vulnerabilities of individuals and groups. Women, children and adolescents, older persons, persons with disabilities and those living with chronic illnesses, minority groups and indigenous peoples, internally displaced persons, refugees and migrants all have different situations and problems – and especially intersectional vulnerabilities such as those of disabled children, older migrants and similar – that need to be addressed in response to disasters by targeted actions based on previous assessment, specialised training of relief personnel and timely response.

To give an example, gender inequalities are likely to cause a higher death toll among women while risks of rape and other forms of violence increase when gender-blind assistance does not meet the needs of women. The remedy is to address their concerns by way of measures of organisation such as the inclusion of women in planning, design and implementation of food distribution, shelter and housing programs; the provision of safe sanitation facilities in camps and collective shelters; and other actions that are recommended, not only by the main soft law instruments, but also by the human rights bodies and especially by the Committee on ESCR.

Another aspect which must not be neglected is the vulnerability of disaster victims caused by the loss of their cultural heritage. Not unlike armed conflict, disaster often involves the destruction of buildings and monuments of religious or historic significance representing the cultural heritage of peoples, communities and groups which are also deprived of those objects and spaces that define their sense of identity and continuity as an essential dimension of their human rights. Such situations require not just special care in emergency relief, but also continued attention during the restoration, rehabilitation and reconstruction phases.

One of the most interesting aspects of the human rights-based approach in disaster-related issues is the role of soft law as a set of rules and procedures that define the behaviour of those whose task is to provide help to disaster victims – domestic authorities, foreign States, intergovernmental organisations or private actors. These rules consist of principles incorporated in United Nations General Assembly (UNGA) resolutions on humanitarian emergency assistance, strategic frameworks endorsed by States as a result of international conferences concerning the prevention of disasters, operational standards and guidelines adopted by intergovernmental bodies as well as codes of conduct developed by non-governmental organisations. In fact, based on the current trend, both IGOs and NGOs show great resourcefulness not only in providing help – thus performing a role complementary to that of States – but also in fostering compliance with the rules applied domestically and even in influencing the development of international norms to guarantee the rights of disaster victims. The comprehensive and detailed guidelines and codes of conduct governing their actions in the areas affected by a disaster represent the most comprehensive framework for humanitarian activities. As such, they also contribute to an improvement in the provision of humanitarian assistance in armed conflicts that is governed by International Humanitarian Law (IHL) on the basis of international conventions, but it is often hindered by the reluctance of States to allow humanitarian organisations to carry on their activities in the conflict areas. Since IHL and IDL share the fundamental principles of humanitarian assistance, the relevant sets of rules should evolve in parallel and eventually merge to ensure that the victims of both disaster and armed conflict are given the best possible care.

The Human Rights-Based Approach (HRBA) to disaster response therefore results from a series of factors that effectively involve civil society organisations alongside States, public authorities and intergovernmental organisations. Conceptualising the HRBA was the task of human rights bodies and special rapporteurs who analysed the relevant practice and highlighted not only the immediate needs of those affected by disasters, but also their legitimate aspirations to regain a new hope for a better quality of life in the future. In this context, the work of the International Law Commission (ILC) on the Protection of persons in the event of disasters has become central. Although the overall result does not represent something revolutionary, it nonetheless makes a fundamental contribution to the progressive development of IDL insofar as it has addressed in a systematic way the main legal questions pertaining to the dialectics between human rights protection and the principles of State sovereignty and non-intervention. In deciding to recommend to the UNGA the elaboration of a convention on the basis of the Draft Articles, the ILC reminds States of their inherent responsibility to 'meet the essential needs of the persons concerned, with full respect for their rights'. Stating the duty of affected States to seek external assistance whenever a disaster exceeds their national response capacity, and the duty of all States to cooperate in the response to disasters, the Commission adopts a vision focusing on a solidaristic approach in international relations. By introducing the obligation to take appropriate measures to prevent, mitigate and prepare for disasters, it keeps IDL at the forefront of international law, and it constructively challenges government and domestic authorities in order to open new paths for protection of people against natural and human-made catastrophes.

As is often the case for international norms, IDL implementation mainly relies upon the adoption of domestic measures by national authorities. Without this support, any international discipline loses most of its effectiveness. The ILC Draft Articles on the protection of persons in the event of disasters explicitly require the affected State to 'take the necessary measures, within its national law, to facilitate the prompt and effective provision of external assistance' (Article 15, paragraph 1) and to 'ensure that its relevant legislation and regulations are readily accessible, to facilitate compliance with national law' (Article 15, paragraph 2). All States shall take 'appropriate measures', including legislation and regulations, to reduce the risk of disasters through 'the conduct of risk assessments, the collection and dissemination of risk and past loss information, and the installation and operation of early warning systems' (Article 9). The two Articles not only impose obligations of means, but they also set out in detail the national measures to be taken (to ensure accessibility of domestic legislation; to conduct risk assessments, etc.). While complying with these obligations, States are expected to behave with due diligence so as to fulfil the standards and principles of good governance. Therefore, the implementation of the international norms effectively fosters the improvement of living conditions for the benefit of individuals.

Whatever form the ILC Draft Articles will take following their consideration by States and by the UNGA in 2018, what matters the most is that they have a significant impact on the way in which governments shape their policies and law-makers set their priorities in the domestic systems, with a view to ensuring a better level of human rights protection even in the most difficult disaster situations.

TABLES OF DOCUMENTS

List of treaties

Universal treaties

Convention concerning Forced or Compulsory Labour (ILO Convention No 29) (adopted 28 June 1930, entered into force 1 May 1932) 39 UNTS 55

Convention concerning Migration for Employment (ILO Convention No. 97, Revised 1949) (adopted 1 July 1949, entered into force 22 January 1952) 120 UNTS 71

Convention establishing an International Relief Union (adopted 12 July 1927, entered into force 27 December 1932) 135 League of Nations Treaty Series 247

Convention for the protection of the world cultural and natural heritage (adopted 16 November 1972, entered into force 17 December 1975) 1037 UNTS 152

Convention (No. 169) concerning Indigenous and Tribal Peoples in Independent Countries (adopted 27 June 1989, entered into force 5 September 1991) 1650 UNTS 383

Convention (No. 174) concerning the Prevention of Major Industrial Accidents (adopted 22 June 1993, entered into force 3 January 1997) 1967 UNTS 232

Convention on Assistance in the Case of a Nuclear Accident or Radiological Emergency (adopted 26 September 1986, entered into force 26 February 1987) 1457 UNTS 134

Convention on Consular Relations (adopted 24 April 1963, entered into force 19 March 1967) 596 UNTS 261

Convention on Facilitation of International Maritime Traffic (adopted 9 April 1965, entered into force 5 March 1967) 591 UNTS 265

Convention on the Elimination of All Forms of Discrimination against Women (adopted 18 December 1979, entered into force 3 September 1981) 1249 UNTS 13

Convention on the Prohibition of the Use, Stockpiling, Production and Transfer of Anti-Personnel Mines and on their Destruction (adopted 18 September 1997, entered into force 1 March 1999) 2056 UNTS 211

Convention on the Rights of Persons with Disabilities (adopted 13 December 2006, entered into force 3 May 2008) 2515 UNTS 3

Convention on the Rights of the Child (adopted 20 November 1989, entered into force 2 September 1990) 1577 UNTS 3

Convention on the Transboundary Effects of Industrial Accidents (adopted 17 March 1992, entered into force 19 April 2000) 2105 UNTS 457

Convention Relating to the Status of Refugees (adopted 28 July 1951, entered into force 22 April 1954) 189 UNTS 137

Convention Relating to the Status of Stateless Persons (adopted 28 September 1954, entered into force 6 June 1960) 360 UNTS 117

Food Aid Convention (adopted 13 April 1999, entered into force 1 July 1999)

Food Assistance Convention (adopted 25 April 2012, entered into force 1 January 2013) 2884 UNTS 4
Framework Convention on Civil Defense Assistance (adopted 22 May 2000, entered into force 23 September 2001)
Geneva Convention Relative to the Protection of Civilian Persons in Time of War (adopted 12 August 1949, entered into force 21 October 1950) 75 UNTS 287
Hague Convention for the Protection of Cultural Property in the Event of Armed Conflict (adopted 14 May 1954, entered into force 7 August 1956) 249 UNTS 240
Hague Convention (IV) Respecting the Laws and Customs of War on Land and its annex: Regulations concerning the Laws and Customs of War on Land (adopted 18 October 1907, entered into force 26 January 1910) 205 CTS 277
International Atomic Energy Agency, Convention on Early Notification of a Nuclear Accident (adopted 26 September 1986, entered into force 27 October 1986) 1439 UNTS 276
International Convention on Oil Pollution Preparedness, Response and Cooperation (adopted 30 November 1990, entered into force 13 May 1995) 1891 UNTS 78
International Convention on the Elimination of All Forms of Racial Discrimination (adopted 7 March 1966, entered into force 4 January 1969) 660 UNTS 195
International Convention on the Protection of the Rights of All Migrants Workers and Members of Their Families (adopted 18 December 1990, entered into force 1 July 2003) 2220 UNTS 3
International Covenant on Civil and Political Rights (adopted 16 December 1966, entered into force 23 March 1976) 999 UNTS 171
International Covenant on Economic, Social and Cultural Rights (adopted 16 December 1966, entered into force 3 January 1976) 993 UNTS 3
Kyoto Protocol to the United Nations Framework Convention on Climate Change (adopted 11 December 1997, entered into force 16 February 2005) 2303 UNTS 162
Optional Protocol to the Convention of the Rights of Persons with Disabilities (adopted 13 December 2006, entered into force 3 May 2008) 2518 UNTS 283
Optional Protocol to the Convention on the Rights of the Child on a communication procedure (adopted 19 December 2011, entered into force 14 April 2014) UNGA Res 66/138, UN Doc. A/RES/66/138 (27 January 2012)
Optional Protocol to the Covenant on Economic, Social and Cultural Rights (adopted 10 December 2008, entered into force 5 May 2013) C.N.869.2009.TREATIES-34
Paris Agreement (adopted 12 December 2015, entered into force 4 November 2016) FCCC/CP/2015/L.9, Annex
Protocol Additional to the Geneva Conventions of 12 August 1949, and relating to the Protection of Victims of International Armed Conflicts (adopted 12 December 1977, entered into force 7 December 1978) 1125 UNTS 3
Protocol Additional to the Geneva Conventions of 12 August 1949, and relating to the Protection of Victims of Non-International Armed Conflicts (adopted 8 June 1977, entered into force 7 December 1978) 1125 UNTS 609
Protocol against the Smuggling of Migrants by Land, Sea and Air, supplementing the United Nations Convention against Transnational Organized Crime (adopted 15 November 2000, entered into force 28 January 2004) 2241 UNTS 507
Protocol to Prevent, Suppress and Punish Trafficking in Persons, Especially Women and Children, supplementing the United Nations Convention against Transnational Organized Crime (adopted 15 November 2000, entered into force 25 December 2003) 2237 UNTS 319
Protocol to the Convention for the Protection of Cultural Property in the Event of Armed conflict (adopted 14 May 1954, entered into force 7 August 1956) 249 UNTS 358
Second Protocol to the Hague Convention of 1954 for the Protection of Cultural Property in the Event of Armed Conflict (adopted 26 March 1999, entered into force 9 March 2004) 2253 UNTS 172
Tampere Convention on the Provision of Telecommunication Resources for Disaster Mitigation and Relief Operations (adopted 18 June 1998, entered into force 8 January 2005) 2296 UNTS 5
UNESCO Convention for the Protection of the World Cultural and Natural Heritage (adopted 16 November 1972, entered into force 17 December 1975) 1037 UNTS 152
United Nations Framework Convention on Climate Change (adopted 9 May 1992, entered into force 21 March 1994) 1771 UNTS 107
Vienna Convention on the Law of Treaties (adopted 22 May 1969, entered into force 27 January 1980) 1155 UNTS 331

Regional treaties

Additional Protocol to the American Convention on Human Rights in the Area of Economic, Social, and Cultural Rights (Protocol of San Salvador) (adopted 17 November 1988, entered into force 16 November 1999) OAS TS No. 69

African Charter on Human and Peoples' Rights (adopted 27 June 1981, entered into force 21 October 1986) OAU Doc. CAB/LEG/67/3 Rev. 5

African Union Convention for the Protection and Assistance of Internally Displaced Persons in Africa (Kampala Convention) (adopted 23 October 2009, entered into force 6 December 2012) AU Doc. Ext/Assembly/AU/PA/Draft/Decl.(I)Rev.1

Agreement among the Governments of the Participating States of the Black Sea Economic Cooperation (BSEC) on Collaboration in Emergency Assistance and Emergency Response to Natural and Man-Made Disasters (adopted 15 April 1998, entered into force 11 March 2003)

Agreement establishing the Caribbean Disaster Emergency Management Agency (adopted 1 July 2008, provisional application 4 July 2008)

Agreement on the Establishment of the Civil-Military Emergency Planning Council for Southeastern Europe (adopted 3 April 2001)

American Convention on Human Rights (adopted 22 November 1969, entered into force 18 July 1978) 1144 UNTS 123

Arab Charter on Human Rights (adopted 22 May 2004, entered into force 15 May 2008)

Association of Caribbean States Agreement on Natural Disasters (adopted 17 April 1999) ACS/2010/TRADE/TTCIC

Association of Southeast Asian Nations Agreement on Disaster Management and Emergency Response (adopted 26 July 2005, entered into force 24 December 2009)

Caribbean Community Agreement Establishing the Caribbean Disaster Emergency Response Agency (CDERA) (adopted 26 February 1991, entered into force 19 May 1992)

Convention for the Protection of Human Rights and Fundamental Freedoms (as amended) (adopted 4 November 1950, entered into force 3 September 1953) 213 UNTS 222

Convention Governing the Specific Aspects of Refugee Problems in Africa (adopted 10 September 1969, entered into force 20 June 1974) 1001 UNTS 45

Convention on Access to Information, Public Participation in Decision-Making and Access to Justice in Environmental Matters (adopted 26 June 1998, entered into force 30 October 2001) 2161 UNTS 447

Council of Europe Convention on Access to Official Documents (adopted 18 June 2009) CoE TS No. 205

European Social Charter (revised) (adopted 3 May 1996, entered into force 1 July 1999) ETS No. 163

Inter-American Convention to Facilitate Disaster Assistance (adopted 7 June 1991, entered into force 16 October 1996) A-54 OAS

International Conference on the Great Lakes Region, Protocol on the Protection and Assistance to Internally Displaced Persons (adopted 30 November 2006, entered into force 21 June 2008)

Protocol on the Community Court of Justice, ECOWAS doc. A/P.1/7/91 (adopted 6 July 1991), as amended by the Supplementary Protocol, ECOWAS doc. A/SP.1/01/05 (adopted 19 January 2005)

Protocol No. 1 to the Convention for the Protection of Human Rights and Fundamental Freedoms (adopted 20 March 1952, entered into force 18 May 1954) ETS No. 009

Protocol No. 12 to the Convention for the Protection of Human Rights and Fundamental Freedoms (adopted 4 November 2000, entered into force 1 April 2005) ETS No. 177

South Asian Association for Regional Cooperation, Agreement on Rapid Response to Natural Disasters (adopted 11 November 2011)

Treaty of Lisbon amending the Treaty on European Union and the Treaty establishing the European Community (adopted 13 December 2007, entered into force 1 December 1999) 2702 UNTS 3

Bilateral treaties

Accord de coopération entre le Gouvernement de la République française et le gouvernement du Royaume de Maroc en matière de protection et de sécurité civiles (adopted 21 April 1981, entered into force 21 April 1981) 1264 UNTS 453

Agreement between the Argentine Republic and the Republic of Chile on cooperation in case of disasters (adopted 8 August 1997)

Agreement between the Government of the Hellenic Republic and the Government of the Russian Federation on cooperation in the field of prevention and response to natural and man-made disasters (adopted 21 February 2000, entered into force 19 June 2002)

Agreement between the Government of the Republic of Latvia and the Cabinet of Ministers of Ukraine on the co-operation in the field of prevention of disasters and elimination of their consequences (adopted 27 April 2006, entered into force 8 August 2008) 2619 UNTS 95

Agreement between the Government of the Republic of Lithuania and the Government of the Republic of Belarus on cooperation in the field of prevention and elimination of consequences of catastrophes, natural disasters and serious accidents (adopted 16 December 2003, entered into force 27 July 2004) 2339 UNTS 203

Agreement between the Government of the United Mexican States and the Government of the United States of America on emergency management cooperation in cases of natural disasters and accidents (adopted 23 October 2008, entered into force 20 March 2011)

Agreement between the Republic of Austria and the Republic of Albania on mutual assistance in the case of disasters or serious accidents (adopted 27 January 2010, entered into force 1 July 2011) 2771 UNTS 307

Agreement between the Republic of Austria and the Republic of Croatia on mutual assistance in the event of disasters or serious accidents (adopted 17 September 2004, entered into force 1 August 2006) 2486 UNTS 277

Agreement on cooperation on disaster preparedness and prevention, and mutual assistance in the event of disasters (Argentina and Spain, adopted 3 June 1988, entered into force 1 September 1992) 1689 UNTS 23

Austria and Federal Republic of Germany agreement concerning mutual assistance in the event of disasters or serious accidents (adopted 23 December 1988, entered into force 1 October 2002)

Convention between the Kingdom of the Netherlands and the Kingdom of Belgium on mutual assistance in combating disasters and accidents (adopted 14 November 1984, entered into force 1 November 1988) 1526 UNTS 42

Convention on mutual assistance in the event of disasters or serious accidents (Federal Republic of Germany and Luxembourg, adopted 2 March 1978, entered into force 1 December 1981) 1320 UNTS 123

Convention on mutual assistance in the event of disasters or serious accidents (Federal Republic of Germany and Switzerland, adopted 28 November 1984, entered into force 1 December 1988) 1554 UNTS 155

Partnership Agreement between the Members of the African, Caribbean and Pacific Group of States of the one part, and the European Community and its Member States, of the other part (adopted 23 June 2000, entered into force 1 March 2003), OJ L 317/3 (2000)

Protocol of intentions between the Government of the United States of America and the Republic of the Philippines concerning cooperation in disaster prevention and management (adopted 21 November 2001)

United Nations documents

Commission on Human Rights

Reports and studies

CHR, Report of the Representative of the Secretary-General, Mr. Francis M. Deng, submitted pursuant to Commission resolution 1997/39. Addendum: Guiding Principles on Internal Displacement, UN Doc. E/CN.4/1998/53/Add.2 (11 February 1998)

CHR, Promotion and Protection of Human Rights. Study on the right to the truth. Report of the Office of the United Nations High Commissioner for Human Rights, UN Doc. E/CN.4/2006/91 (8 February 2006)

Resolutions

CHR, Res 2000/9: Question of the realization in all countries of the economic, social and cultural rights contained in the Universal Declaration of Human Rights and in the International Covenant on Economic, Social and Cultural Rights, and study of special problems which the developing countries face in their efforts to achieve human rights, UN Doc. E/CN.4/ RES/2000/9 (17 April 2000)

CHR, Res 2001/28: Adequate housing as a component of the right to an adequate standard of living, UN Doc. E/CN.4/RES/2001/28 (20 April 2001)

CHR, Res 2002/21: Adequate housing as a component of the right to an adequate standard of living, UN Doc. E/CN.4/2002/21 (22 April 2002)

CHR, Res 2003/27: Adequate housing as a component of the right to an adequate standard of living, UN Doc. E/CN.4/2003/27 (22 April 2003)
CHR, Res 2004/21: Adequate housing as a component of the right to an adequate standard of living, UN Doc. E/CN.4/2004/21 (16 April 2004)

Committee on Economic, Social and Cultural Rights

Concluding observations

CESCR, Concluding Observations of the Committee on Economic, Social and Cultural Rights on Mongolia, UN Doc. E.C12./1/ADD.47 (1 September 2000)
CESCR, Concluding Observations of the Committee on Economic, Social and Cultural Rights: Japan, UN Doc. E/C.12/1/ADD.67 (24 September 2001)
CESCR, Concluding Observations on the second periodic report of El Salvador, UN Doc. E/C.12/SLV/CO/2 (27 June 2007)
CESCR, Concluding Observations of the Committee on Economic, Social and Cultural Rights: Republic of Korea, UN Doc. E/C.12/KOR/CO/3 (17 December 2009)
CESCR, Concluding Observations on the third periodic report of Japan, adopted by the Committee at its fiftieth session (29 April–17 May 2013), UN Doc E/C.12/JPN/CO/3 (10 June 2013)
CESCR, Concluding Observations on the fifth period report of Norway, UN Doc. E/C.12/NOR/CO/5 (13 December 2013)
CESCR, Concluding Observations on the sixth periodic report of Finland, UN Doc. E/C.12/FIN/CO/6 (16 December 2014)
CESCR, Concluding Observations on the second periodic report of Greece, UN Doc. E/C.12/GRC/CO/2 (2015)

General comments

CESCR, General Comment No. 3: The Nature of States Parties' Obligations (Art. 2, para 1, of the Covenant), UN Doc. E/1991/23 (14 December 1990)
CESCR, General Comment No. 4: The Right to Adequate Housing (Art. 11(1) of the Covenant), UN Doc. E/1992/23 (13 December 1991)
CESCR, General Comment No. 7: The right to adequate housing (Art. 11 (1) of the Covenant): Forced evictions, UN Doc. E/1998//22 (20 May 1997)
CESCR, General Comment No. 9: The domestic application of the Covenant, UN Doc. E/C.12/1998/24 (3 December 1998)
CESCR, General Comment No. 11: Plans of Action for Primary Education (Art. 14 of the Covenant), UN Doc. E/1992/23 (10 May 1999)
CESCR, General Comment No. 12: The Right to Adequate Food (Art. 11 of the Covenant), UN Doc. E/C.12/1999/5 (12 May 1999)
CESCR, General Comment No. 13: The Right to Education (Art. 13 of the Covenant), UN Doc. E/C.12/1999/10 (8 December 1999)
CESCR, General Comment No. 14: The Right to the Highest Attainable Standard of Health, UN Doc. E/C.12/2000/4 (11 August 2000)
CESCR, General Comment No. 15: The Right to Water (Arts. 11 and 12 of the Covenant), UN Doc. E/C.12/2002/11 (20 January 2003)
CESCR, General Comment No. 16: The Equal Right of Men and Women to the Enjoyment of all Economic, Social and Cultural Rights (Art. 3 of the Covenant), UN Doc. E/C.12/2005/4 (11 August 2005)
CESCR, General Comment No. 19: The Right to Social Security, (Art. 9 of the Covenant), UN Doc. E/C.12/GC/19 (4 February 2008)
CESCR, General Comment No. 20: Non-Discrimination in Economic, Social and Cultural Rights (Art. 2, para. 2, of the Covenant), UN Doc. E/C.12/GC/20 (2 July 2009)
CESCR, General Comment No. 21: Right of everyone to take part in cultural life (Art. 15, para. 1(a), of the Covenant), UN Doc. E/C.12/GC/21 (21 December 2009)

Other documents

CESCR, The Limburg Principles on the Implementation of the International Covenant on Economic Social, and Cultural Rights, UN Doc. E/CN.4/1987/17 (1987)

CESCR, Review of further developments in fields with which the Sub-Commission has been concerned. Human Rights and the environment, UN Doc. E/CN.4/Sub.2/1994/9 (6 July 1994)

Committee on the Elimination of All Forms of Discrimination against Women

Concluding comments and observations

CommEDAW, Concluding comments on Indonesia, UN Doc. CEDAW/C/IDN/CO/5 (10 August 2007)

CommEDAW, Concluding observations on Tuvalu, UN Doc. CEDAW/C/TUV/CO/2 (7 August 2009)

CommEDAW, Concluding observations on Belarus, UN Doc. CEDAW/C/BLR/CO/7 (6 April 2011)

CommEDAW, Concluding observations on Sri Lanka, UN Doc. CEDAW/C/LKA/CO/7 (8 April 2011)

CommEDAW, Concluding observations on Grenada, UN Doc. CEDAW/C/GRD/CO/1–5 (23 March 2012)

CommEDAW, Concluding observations on Algeria, UN Doc. CEDAW/C/DZA/CO/3–4 (23 March 2012)

CommEDAW, Concluding observations on New Zealand, UN Doc. CEDAW/C/NLZ/CO/7 (27 July 2012)

CommEDAW, Concluding observations on Jamaica, UN Doc. CEDAW/C/JAM/CO/6–7 (27 July 2012)

CommEDAW, Concluding observations on the 5th and 6th periodic reports of Chile, UN Doc. CEDAW/C/CHL/CO/5–6 (1–19 October 2012)

CommEDAW, Concluding observations on Chile, UN Doc. CEDAW/C/CHI/CO/5–6 (24 October 2012)

CommEDAW, Concluding observations on Togo, UN Doc. CEDAW/C/TGO/CO/6–7 (8 November 2012)

CommEDAW, Concluding observations on Peru, UN Doc. CEDAW/C/PER/CO/7–8 (24 July 2014)

CommEDAW, Concluding observations on Guinea, UN Doc. CEDAW/C/GIN/CO/7–8 (14 November 2014)

CommEDAW, Concluding observations on the Solomon Islands, UN Doc. CEDAW/C/SLB/CO/1–3 (14 November 2014)

General recommendations and reports

CommEDAW, General Recommendation No. 28 on the Core Obligations of States Parties under Article 2 of the Convention, UN Doc. CEDAW/C/GC/28 (16 December 2010)

CommEDAW, General Recommendation No. 27 on Older Women and the Protection of their Human Rights, UN Doc. CEDAW/C/GC/27 (16 December 2010)

CommEDAW, Report of the Committee on the Elimination of Discrimination against Women, UN Doc. A/59/38 (12–30 January 2014)

Committee on the Elimination of Racial Discrimination

CommERD, Concluding observations on the United States of America, UN Doc. CERD/C/USA/CO/6 (8 May 2008)

Committee on the Rights of the Child

Concluding observations

CommRC, Concluding observations: Ukraine, UN Doc. CRC/C/15/Add.191 (9 October 2002)

CommRC, Concluding observations: Kazakhstan, UN Doc. CRC/C/15/ADD.213 (10 July 2003)

CommRC, Concluding observations: Uzbekistan, UN Doc. CRC/C/UZB/CO/2 (2 June 2006)

CommRC, Concluding observations: Mozambique, UN Doc. CRC/C/MOZ/CO/2 (4 November 2009)

CommRC, Concluding observations: Norway, UN Doc. CRC/C/NOR/CO/4 (3 March 2010)

CommRC, Concluding observations: Grenada, UN Doc. CRC/C/GRD/CO/2 (11 June 2010)
CommRC, Concluding observation: Japan, UN Doc. CRC/C/JPN/CO/3 (20 June 2010)
CommRC, Concluding observations: Singapore, UN Doc. CRC/C/SGP/CO/2–3 (4 May 2011)
CommRC, Concluding observations: Italy, UN Doc. CRC/C/ITA/CO/3–4 (30 October 2011)
CommRC, Concluding observations: Panama, UN Doc. CRC/C/PAN/CO/3–4 (11 December 2011)
CommRC, Concluding observations: The Republic of Korea, UN Doc. CRC/C/KOR/CO/3–4 (2 February 2012)
CommRC, Concluding observations: Australia, UN Doc. CRC/C/AUS/CO/4 (28 August 2012)
CommRC, Concluding observations on the initial report of Tuvalu, UN Doc. CRC/C/TUV/CO/1 (29 October 2013)
CommRC, Concluding observations on the combined second to fourth periodic reports of Fiji, UN Doc. CRC/C/FJI/CO/2–4 (12 October 2014)
CommRC, Concluding observations on the combined third to fifth periodic reports of Mauritius, UN Doc. CRC/C/MUS/CO/3–5 (26 February 2015)

General comments

CommRC, General Comment No. 15 on the right of the child to the enjoyment of the highest attainable standard of health (art. 24) UN Doc. CRC/C/GC/15 (1 February 2013)
CommRC, General Comment No. 19 on public budgeting for the realization of children's rights (art. 4), UN Doc. CRC/C/GC/19 (20 July 2016)

Human Rights Committee

Concluding observations

HRComm, Concluding observations on Thailand, UN Doc. CCPR/CO/84/THA (8 July 2005)
HRComm, Consideration of Reports Submitted by States Parties Under Article 40 of the Covenant Concluding Observations of the Human Rights Committee: United States of America, UN Doc. CCPR/C/USA/CO/3/Rev.1 (18 December 2006)

General comments

HRComm, General Comment No. 6, Article 6: Right to life, Sixteenth session (30 April 1982)
HRComm, General Comment No. 18: Non-discrimination, Adopted at the Thirty-seventh Session of the Human Rights Committee (10 November 1989), in UN Doc. HRI/GEN/1/Rev.9 (2004)
HRComm, General Comment No. 27, Article 12: Freedom of Movement, UN Doc. CCPR/C/21/Rev.1/Add.9 (2 November 1999)
HRComm, General Comment No. 29, State of Emergency (Article 4), UN Doc. CCPR/C/21/Rev.1/Add.11 (31 August 2001)
HRComm, General Comment No. 31: The Nature of the General Legal Obligation Imposed on States Parties to the Covenant, UN Doc. CCPR/C/21/Rev.1/Add.13 (26 May 2004)
HRComm, General Comment No. 34, Article 19: Freedoms of opinion and expression, UN Doc. CCPR/C/GC/34 (12 September 2011)

Human Rights Council

Reports and studies

HRC, Report of the Office of the United Nations High Commissioner for Human Rights on the relationship between climate change and human rights, UN Doc. A/HRC/10/61 (15 January 2009)
HRC, Report of the Working Group on the Universal Periodic Review: Bangladesh, UN Doc. A/HRC/11/18 (5 October 2009)
HRC, Report of the Independent Expert in the field of cultural rights, UN Doc. A/HRC/17/38 (21 March 2011)

HRC, Guiding Principles on Business and Human Rights: Implementing the United Nations 'Protect, Respect and Remedy' Framework, UN Doc. A/HRC/17/31 (21 March 2011)
HRC, Report of the Working Group on the Universal Periodic Review: Cuba, UN Doc. A/HRC/24/16 (8 July 2013)
HRC, Report of the Independent Expert on the issue of human rights obligations relating to the enjoyment of a safe, clean, healthy, and sustainable environment. Mapping Report, UN Doc. A/HRC/25/53 (30 December 2013)
HRC, Communications report of Special Procedures, UN Doc. A/HRC/26/21 (2 June 2014)
HRC, Report of the Working Group on Universal Periodic Review: Bhutan, UN Doc. A/HRC/27/8 (1 July 2014)
HRC, Promotion and protection of the rights of indigenous peoples in disaster risk reduction, prevention and preparedness initiatives: Study by the Expert Mechanism on the Rights of Indigenous Peoples, UN Doc. A/HRC/27/66 (7 August 2014)
HRC, Final research-based report of the Human Rights Council Advisory Committee on best practices and main challenges in the promotion and protection of human rights in post-disaster and post-conflict situations, UN Doc. A/HRC/28/76 (10 February 2015)
HRC, Report of the Working Group on the Universal Periodic Review: Kuwait, UN Doc. A/HRC/29/17 (13 April 2015)

Resolutions

HRC, Res 6/27: Adequate housing as a component of the right to an adequate standard of living, UN Doc. A/HRC/RES/6/27 (14 December 2007)
HRC, Res 5/1: Human Rights Council: Institution-building, UN Doc. A/HRC/RES5/1 (18 June 2007)
HRC, Res 7/23: Human Rights and Climate Change, UN Doc. A/HRC/RES/7/23 (28 March 2008)
HRC, Res 10/4: Human rights and climate change, UN Doc. A/HRC/RES/10/4 (25 March 2009)
HRC, Res 19/4: Adequate housing as a component of the right to adequate standard of living in the context of disaster settings, UN Doc. A/HRC/RES/19/4 (3 April 2012)
HRC, Res 19/10: Human rights and the environment, UN Doc. A/HRC/RES/19/10 (19 April 2012)
HRC, Res 25/53: Resolution on the protection of human rights in post-disaster/post-conflict situations, UN Doc. A/HRC/RES/22/16 (21 March 2013)
HRC, Res. 28/11: Human rights and the environment, UN Doc. A/HRC/RES/28/11 (7April 2015)
HRC, Res 31/8: Human rights and the environment, UN Doc. A/HRC/RES/31/8 (23 March 2016)
HRC, Res 32/33: Human rights and climate change, UN Doc. A/HRC/RES/32/33 (1 July 2016)

International Law Commission

ILC, Report of the International Law Commission on the work of its twenty-ninth session, UN Doc. A/32/10 (9 May–29 July 1977)
ILC, Draft Articles on Responsibility of States for Internationally Wrongful Acts, with commentaries, UN Doc. A/56/10 (6–9 August 2001)
ILC, Report of the International Law Commission, Fifty-sixth session (3 May–4 June and 5 July–6 August 2004), UN Doc. A/59/10 (16 September 2004)
ILC, Fragmentation of international law: difficulties arising from the diversification and expansion of international law, Report of the Study Group of the International Law Commission, Finalized by Martti Koskenniemi, UN Doc. A/CN.4/L.682 (13 April 2006)
ILC, Report of the International Law Commission, Fifty-eight session (1 May–9 June and 3 July–11 August 2006), UN Doc. A/61/10 (2006)
ILC, Protection of persons in the event of disasters, Memorandum by the Secretariat, UN Doc. A/CN.4/590 (11 December 2007)
ILC, Preliminary report on the protection of persons in the event of disasters, by Mr. Eduardo Valencia-Ospina, Special Rapporteur, UN Doc. A/CN.4/598 (5 May 2008)
ILC, Reports of the International Law Commission, Sixtieth session (5 May–6 June and 7 July–8 August 2008), UN Doc. A/63/10 (2008)
ILC, Second report on the protection of persons in the event of disasters, by Mr. Eduardo Valencia-Ospina, Special Rapporteur, UN Doc. A/CN.4/615 (7 May 2009)

ILC, Report of the International Law Commission, Sixty-first session (4 May–5 June and 6 July–7 August 2009), UN Doc. A/64/10 (2009)
ILC, Third report on the protection of persons in the event of disasters, by Eduardo Valencia-Ospina, Special Rapporteur, UN Doc. A/CN.4/629 (31 March 2010)
ILC, Provisional summary record of the 3057th meeting, UN Doc. A/CN.4/SR.3057 (1 July 2010)
ILC, Report of the International Law Commission, Fifty-third session (23 April–1 June and 2 July–10 August 2011), Chapter V, International liability for injurious consequences arising out of acts not prohibited by international law, UN Doc. A/56/10 (2011)
ILC, Report of the International Law Commission, Sixty-third Session (26 April–3 June and 4 July–12 August 2011), UN Doc. A/66/10 (2011)
ILC, Draft articles on the effects of armed conflicts on treaties, with commentaries, UN Doc. A/66/10 (2011)
ILC, Fifth report on the protection of persons in the event of disasters, UN Doc. A/CN.4/652 (9 April 2012)
ILC, Sixth Report on the protection of persons in the event of disasters, UN Doc. A/CN.4/662 (3 May 2013)
ILC, Seventh report on the protection of persons in the event of disasters, UN Doc. A/CN.4/668 (27 February 2014)
ILC, Protection of persons in the event of disasters, Comments and observations received from Governments and international organizations, UN Doc. A/CN.4/696 (14 March 2016)
ILC, Eighth report on the protection of persons in the event of disasters, by Mr. Eduardo Valencia-Ospina, Special Rapporteur, UN Doc. A/CN.4/697 (17 March 2016)
ILC, Protection of persons in the event of disasters, Additional comments and observations received from Governments and international organizations, UN Doc. A/CN.4/696/Add.1 (28 April 2016)
ILC, Titles and texts of the ILC Draft Articles on the Protection of Persons in the Event of Disasters, UN Doc. A/CN.4/L.871 (27 May 2016)
ILC, Report of the International Law Commission: Sixty-eighth session (2 May–10 June and 4 July–12 August 2016), Draft Articles and Commentaries on the protection of persons in the event of disasters, UN Doc. A/CN.4/871 (2016)
ILC, Report of the International Law Commission: Sixty-eighth session (2 May–10 June and 4 July–12 August 2016), UN Doc. A/71/10 (2016)

Reports of Special Rapporteurs

CHR, Report of the Special Rapporteur on the promotion and protection of the right to freedom of opinion and expression, Mr. Abid Hussain, submitted in accordance with Commission resolution 1999/36, UN Doc. E/CN.4/2000/63 (18 January 2000)
CHR, Civil and Political Rights, Including the Question of the Freedom of Expression: The Right to freedom of opinion and expression. Report of the Special Rapporteur, Ambeyi Ligabo, UN Doc. E/CN.4/2005/64 (17 December 2004)
CHR, Housing and property restitution in the context of the return of refugees and internally displaced persons. Final report of the Special Rapporteur, Paulo Sérgio Pinheiro. Principles on housing and property restitution for refugees and displaced persons, UN Doc. E/CN.4/Sub.2/2005/7 (28 June 2005)
CHR, Report of the Special Rapporteur on right to food, Jean Ziegler, UN Doc. E/CN.4/2006/44 (16 March 2006)
CHR, Report of the Special Rapporteur on adequate housing as a component of the right to an adequate standard of living, Miloon Kothari: Mission to the Islam Republic of Iran, UN Doc. E/CN.4/2006/41/Add.2 (21 March 2006)
CHR, Report of the Special Rapporteur on adequate housing as a component of the right to an adequate standard of living, and on the right to non-discrimination in this context, Miloon Kothari, Mission to the Islamic Republic of Iran, UN Doc. E/CN.4/2006/41/Add.2 (21 March 2006)
HRC, Report of the Special Rapporteur on adequate housing as a component of the right to an adequate standard of living, and on the right to non-discrimination in this context, UN Doc. A/HRC/7/16 (13 February 2008)
HRC, Report of the Special Rapporteur on the Right of Everyone to the Enjoyment of the Highest Attainable Standard of Physical and Mental Health, Paul Hunt. Addendum: Missions to the World Bank and the International Monetary Fund in Washington, D.C. (20 October 2006) and Uganda (4–7 February 2007), UN Doc. A/HRC/7/11/Add.2 (5 March 2008)

HRC, Report of the Special Rapporteur on adequate housing as a component of the right to an adequate standard of living, and the right to non-discrimination in this context, UN Doc. A/63/275 (13 August 2008)

HRC, Report of the Representative of the Secretary-General on the Human Rights of internally displaced persons, Walter Kaelin, UN Doc. A/HRC/10/13/Add.2 (13 February 2009)

HRC, Report of the Representative of the Secretary-General on the Human Rights of internally displaced persons, Walter Kälin, Addendum, Protection of Internally Displaced Persons in Situations of Natural Disasters, UN Doc. A/HRC/10/13/Add. 1 (5 March 2009)

HRC, Report of the Special Rapporteur on adequate housing as a component of the right to an adequate standard of living, and on the right to non-discrimination in this context, UN Doc. A/64/255 (6 August 2009)

HRC, Report of the Special Rapporteur on the right to food, Olivier De Schutter, Mission to Nicaragua, UN Doc. A/HRC/13/33/Add.5 (19 February 2010)

HRC, Report of the Special Rapporteur on the promotion and protection of the right to freedom of opinion and expression, Mr. Frank La Rue, UN Doc. A/HRC/14/23 (20 April 2010)

HRC, Report of the Special Rapporteur on adequate housing as a component of the right to an adequate standard of living, and the right to non-discrimination in this context, Raquel Rolnik, UN Doc. A/HRC/16/42 (20 December 2010)

UNGA, Report of the Special Rapporteur on adequate housing as a component of the right to an adequate standard of living, UN Doc. A/66/270 (5 August 2011)

HRC, Report of the Special Rapporteur on adequate housing as a component of the right to an adequate standard of living, and on the right to non-discrimination in this context, Raquel Rolnik, UN Doc. A/HRC/19/53 (26 December 2011)

HRC, Report of the Special Rapporteur on adequate housing as a component of the right to an adequate standard of living, and on the right to non-discrimination in this context, Raquel Rolnik, Addendum, Mission to Algeria, UN Doc. (26 December 2011)

HRC, Report of the Special Rapporteur on the Human Rights of Internally Displaced Persons, Chaloka Beyani, Addendum, Mission to Maldives, UN Doc. A/HRC/19/54/Add.1 (30 January 2012)

HRC, Report of the Special Rapporteur on adequate housing as a component of the right to an adequate standard of living, and on the right to non-discrimination in this context, Raquel Rolnik, UN Doc. A/HRC/22/46 (24 December 2012)A/HRC/19/53/Add.2

HRC, Report of the Special Rapporteur on the right of everyone to the enjoyment of the highest attainable standard of physical and mental health, Mission to Japan, UN Doc. A/HRC/23/41/Add.3 (2 May 2013)

HRC, Report of the Special Rapporteur on the right of everyone to the enjoyment of the highest attainable standard of physical and mental health, Addendum, Mission to Japan (15–26 November 2012), UN Doc A/HRC/23/41/Add.3 (31 July 2013)

UNGA, Report of the Special Rapporteur on the promotion and protection of the right to freedom of opinion and expression, UN Doc. A/68/362 (4 September 2013)

HRC, Report of the Special Rapporteur on the implications for human rights of the environmentally sound management and disposal of hazardous substances and waste, Calin Georgescu, Addendum, UN Doc. A/HRC/24/39/Add.1 (6 September 2013)

HRC, Report of the Special Rapporteur on adequate housing as a component of the right to an adequate standard of living, and on the right to non-discrimination in this context, Raquel Rolnik. Report of the country visit in Indonesia, UN Doc. A/HRC/25/54/Add.1 (26 December 2013)

HRC, Report of the Special Rapporteur on adequate housing as a component of the right to adequate standard of living, and on the right to non-discrimination in this context, Raquel Rolnik. Guiding principles on security of tenure for the urban poor, UN Doc. A/HRC/25/54 (30 December 2013)

HRC, Report of the Special Rapporteur on the human rights of internally displaced persons, Chaloka Beyani, Addendum, Follow-up mission to Georgia, UN Doc. A/HRC/26/33/Add.1 (4 June 2014)

HRC, Report of the Special Rapporteur on the human rights of internally displaced persons, Chaloka Beyani, Addendum, Mission to Haiti, UN Doc. A/HRC/29/34/Add.2 (8 May 2015)

HRC, Report of the Special Rapporteur on adequate housing as a component of the right to an adequate standard of living, and on the right to non-discrimination in this context on her mission to Cape Verde, UN Doc. A/HRC/31/54/Add.1 (23 December 2015)

HRC, Report of the Special Rapporteur on the right to food on her mission to Philippines, UN Doc. A/HRC/31/51/Add.1 (29 December 2015)

HRC, Report of the Special Rapporteur on the issue of human rights obligations relating to the enjoyment of a safe, clean, healthy and sustainable environment, UN Doc. A/HRC/31/52 (1 February 2016)

HRC, Report of the Special Rapporteur on the human rights of internally displaced persons on his mission to the Philippines, UN Doc. A/HRC/32/35/Add.3 (5 April 2016)
HRC, Report of the Special Rapporteur on the human rights of internally displaced persons on his mission to Afghanistan, UN Doc. A/HRC/35/27/Add.3 (12 April 2017)

United Nations General Assembly

Reports and other documents

UNGA, Draft Convention on Expediting the Delivery of Emergency Assistance, UN Doc. A/39/267/ Add.2-E/1984/96/Add.2 (18 June 1984)
UNGA, Report of the third session of the Ad Hoc Committee on a Comprehensive and Integral International Convention on the Protection and Promotion of the Rights and Dignity of Persons with Disabilities, UN Doc. A/AC.265/2004/5 (9 June 2004)
UNGA, A More Secured World: Our Shared Responsibility, Report of the High-level Panel on Threats, Challenges and Change, UN Doc. A/59/565 (2 December 2004)
UNGA, Sixth Committee, Agenda Item 75: Report of the International Law Commission on the work of its sixtieth session, UN Doc. A/C.6/63/SR.23 (2008)
UNGA, Sixth Committee, Summary record of 22nd meeting, UN Doc. A/C.6/65/SR.22 (1 December 2010)
UNGA, Sixth Committee, Summary record of 23rd meeting, UN Doc. A/C.6/65/SR.23 (1 December 2010)
UNGA, Sixth Committee, Summary record of 24th meeting, UN Doc. A/C.6/65/SR.24 (1 December 2010)
UNGA, Report of the open-ended intergovernmental expert working group on indicators and terminology relating to disaster risk reduction, UN Doc. A/71/644 (1 December 2016)

Resolutions

UNGA, Res 217(III): Universal Declaration on Human Rights, UN Doc. A/RES/217(III) (10 December 1948)
UNGA, Res 377(V): Uniting for Peace, UN Doc. A/RES/377(V) (3 November 1950)
UNGA, Res 25/2625: Declaration on Principles of International Law concerning Friendly Relations and Co-operation among States in accordance with the Charter of the United Nations, UN Doc. A/ RES/25/2625 (24 October 1970)
UNGA, Res 3220 (XXIX): Assistance and cooperation in accounting for persons who are missing or dead in armed conflicts (6 November 1974)
UNGA, Res 33/173: Disappeared persons, UN Doc. A/RES/33/173 (20 December 1978)
UNGA, Res 43/53: Protection of global climate for present and future generations of mankind, UN Doc. A/RES/43/53 (6 December 1988)
UNGA, Res 43/131: Humanitarian assistance to victims of natural disasters and similar emergency situations, UN Doc. A/RES/43/131 (8 December 1988)
UNGA, Res 45/100: Humanitarian assistance to victims of natural disasters and similar emergency situations, UN Doc. A/RES/45/100 (14 December 1990)
UNGA, Res 45/165: Question of enforced or involuntary disappearance, UN Doc. A/RES/45/165 (18 December 1990)
UNGA, Res 46/182: Strengthening of the coordination of humanitarian emergency assistance of the United Nations, UN Doc. A/RES/46/182 (19 December 1991)
UNGA, Res 47/132: Question of enforced or involuntary disappearance, UN Doc. A/RES/47/132 (18 December 1992)
UNGA, Res 56/206: Strengthening the mandate and status of the Commission on Human Settlement and the status, role and function of the UN Centre for Human Settlements (Habitat), UN Doc. A/ RES/56/206 (1 January 2002)
UNGA, Res 58/214: International Strategy for Disaster Risk Reduction, UN Doc. A/RES/58/2014 (27 February 2004)
UNGA, Res 60/01: World Summit Outcome, UN Doc. A/RES/60/1 (24 October 2005)

UNGA, Res 60/195: International Strategy for Disaster Reduction, UN Doc. A/RES/60/195 (2 March 2006)

UNGA, Res 60/227: International migration and development, UN Doc. A/Res/60/227 (7 April 2006)

UNGA, Res 61/295: United Nations Declaration on the Rights of Indigenous Peoples, UN Doc. A/RES/61/295 (2 October 2007)

UNGA, Res 63/150: Realizing the Millennium Development Goals for persons with disabilities through the implementation of the World Programme of Action concerning Disabled Persons and the Convention on the Rights of Persons with Disabilities, UN Doc. S/RES/63/150 (11 February 2009)

UNGA, Res 68/102: Strengthening the coordination of emergency humanitarian assistance of the United Nations, UN Doc. A/RES/68/102 (13 December 2013)

UNGA, Res 58/214: International Strategy for Disaster Risk Reduction, UN Doc. A/RES/58/2014 (27 February 2014)

UNGA, Res 69/243: International cooperation on humanitarian assistance in the field of natural disasters, from relief to development, UN Doc. A/RES/69/243 (11 February 2015)

UNGA, Res 69/283: Sendai Framework for Disaster Risk Reduction 2015–2030, UN Doc. A/RES/69/283 (23 June 2015)

UNGA, Res 70/1: Transforming our world: the 2030 Agenda for Sustainable Development, UN Doc. A/RES/70/1 (25 September 2015)

UNGA, Res 70/107: International cooperation on humanitarian assistance in the field of natural disasters, from relief to development, UN Doc. A/RES/70/107 (13 January 2016)

UNGA, Res 71/128: International cooperation on humanitarian assistance in the field of natural disasters, from relief to development, UN Doc. A/Res/71/128 (8 December 2016)

UNGA, Res 71/140: Report of the International Law Commission on the work of its sixty-eighth session, UN Doc. A/RES/71/140 (19 December 2016)

UNGA, Res 71/141: Protection of persons in the event of disasters, UN Doc. A/RES/71/141 (19 December 2016)

UNGA Res 71/276: Report of the open-ended intergovernmental expert working group on indicators and terminology relating to disaster risk reduction, UN Doc. A/RES/71/276 (13 February 2017)

United Nations Secretary-General

UNSG, Report of the Secretary-General: In Larger Freedom – Towards Development, Security and Human Rights for All, UN Doc. A/59/2005 (21 March 2005)

UNGA, Report of the Secretary-General: Implementing the Responsibility to Protect, UN Doc. A/63/677 (12 January 2009)

UNSG, One Humanity: Shared Responsibility. Report of the Secretary-General for the World Humanitarian Summit Contents, UN Doc. A/70/709 (31 January 2016), Annex: Agenda for Humanity

UNSG, In Safety and dignity: addressing large movements of refugees and migrants. Report of the Secretary-General, UN Doc. A/70/59 (21 April 2016)

United Nations Security Council

UNSC, Res 1973, UN Doc. S/RES/1973 (17 March 2011)

UNSC, Res 2177, UN Doc. S/RES/2177 (18 September 2014)

United Nations Special Envoys

UN Special Envoy for Tsunami Recovery, Key Propositions for Building Back Better. A Report by the UN Secretary-General Special Envoy for Tsunami Recovery, William J Clinton (Office of the UN Secretary-General, December 2006)

Other United Nations documents

Committee on Migrant Workers, General Comment No. 1: Migrant Domestic Workers, UN Doc. CMW/C/GC/1 (2011)

FAO, Voluntary Guidelines to Support the Progressive Realisation of the Right to Adequate Food in the Context of National Food Security (2004)
IASC, Human Rights and Natural Disasters: Operational Guidelines and Field Manual on Human Rights Protection in Situations of Natural Disasters (The Brookings-Bern Project on Internal Displacement, 2008)
IASC, Operational Guidelines on the Protection of Persons in Situations of Natural Disasters (The Brookings-Bern Project on Internal Displacement, 2011)
International Covenant on Civil and Political Rights, Notification under article 4(3): Ecuador (6 June 2016) A-14668-Ecuador-0800000280498bb8.pdf UNTS 1
International Covenant on Civil and Political Rights, Notification under article 4(3): Ecuador (originally received 20 January 2017, further information provided 15 March 2017) A-14668-Ecuador-080000028049d4f5.pdf UNTS 1
International Covenant on Civil and Political Rights, Notification under article 4(3) of the Covenant: Georgia (7 March 2006) 2363 UNTS 465
International Covenant on Civil and Political Rights, Notification under article 4(3) of the Covenant: Guatemala, UN Doc. C.N.347.2009.TREATIES-8 (20 May 2009)
International Covenant on Civil and Political Rights, Notification under article 4(3): Guatemala, UN Doc. C.N.754.2012.TREATIES-IV.4 (23 November 2012)
International Covenant on Civil and Political Rights, Notification under article 4(3) of the Covenant: Jamaica (27 October 2004) 2283 UNTS 249–251
International Covenant on Civil and Political Rights, Notification under article 4(3) of the Covenant: Jamaica (24 August 2007) 2466 UNTS 11–20
International Covenant on Civil and Political Rights, Notification under article 4(3): Chile (23 March 2010) 2659 UNTS 39
OCHA, Oslo Guidelines. Guidelines on the use of foreign military and civil defence assets in disaster relief (1 November 2007)
OHCHR, Report of the Office of the United Nations High Commissioner for Human Rights on the relationship between climate change and human rights, UN Doc. A/HRC/10/61 (15 January 2009)
OHCHR, Human Rights Indicators. A Guide to Measurement and Implementation (2012)
OHCHR, The Role of Prevention in the Promotion and Protection of Human Rights, Report of the Office of the United Nations High Commissioner for Human Rights, UN Doc. A/HRC/30/20 (16 July 2015)
UN Conference on Environment and Development, Report of the United Nations Conference on Environment and Development, Rio de Janeiro, 3–14 June 1992, UN Doc. A/CONF.151/26 (Vol. I) (3–14 June 1992)
UN Conference on the Human Environment, Report of the United Nations Conference on the Human Environment, Stockholm 5–16 June 1972, UN Doc. A/CONF.48/14/Rev. 1 (5–16 June 1972)
UNDESA, Population Division, International Migration Report 2015 – Highlights, UN Doc. ST/ESA/SER.A/375 (2016)
UNESCO, Protecting Education from Attack: A State-of-the-Art Review (UNESCO, 2010)
UNFCCC, Adoption of the Paris Agreement, Decision 21, UN Doc. FCCC/CP/2015/L.9/Rev.1, 12 December 2015
UNFCCC, Decision 1/CP.16, The Cancun Agreements: Outcome of the work of the Ad Hoc Working Group on Long-term Cooperative Action under the Convention, UN Doc. FCCC/CP/2010/7/Add.1 (15 March 2011)
UNHCR, Guidelines on temporary protection or stay arrangements (February 2014)
UNISDR, Sendai Framework for Disaster Risk Reduction 2015–2030 (2015)
UNISDR, Terminology on Disaster Risk Reduction (2009)
UN Permanent Forum on Indigenous Issues, Fourth Session, UN Doc. E/C.19/2005/2, Annex III, Item 13 (16–27 May 2005)
UN World Conference on Disaster Risk Reduction, Hyogo Framework for Action 2005–2015: Building the Resilience of Nations and Communities to Disasters, in UN World Conference on Disaster Risk Reduction, Hyogo Declaration, UN Doc. A/CONF.206/6 (22 January 2005)
WHO, Strengthening National Health Emergency and Disaster Management Capacities and Resilience of Health Systems, UN Doc. EB128.R10 (22 January 2011)

Documents of regional organizations

African Union

Reports

ACommHPR, Activity Report of the Special Rapporteur on Freedom of Expression and Access to Information in Africa, 44th Ordinary Session of the ACommHPR (10–24 November 2008)

Resolutions

ACommHPR, Resolution on the Adoption of the Declaration of Principles on Freedom of Expression in Africa, ACHPR/Res.62(XXXII)02 (2002)

ACommHPR, Resolution on the Expansion of the Mandate and Re-Appointment of the Special Rapporteur on Freedom of Expression and Access to Information in Africa, ACHPR/Res.122(IVXX)07 (2007)

Council of Europe

Convention for the Protection of Human Rights and Fundamental Freedoms, Georgia: Derogation to the Convention on the Protection of Human Rights and Fundamental Freedoms, Notification – JJ6239C Tr./005–166 (13 March 2006)

Convention for the Protection of Human Rights and Fundamental Freedoms, Georgia: Withdrawal of derogation to the Convention on the Protection of Human Rights and Fundamental Freedoms, Notification – JJ6268C Tr./005–168 (7 April 2006)

European Union

Legislation

Decision No 95/553/EC of the Representatives of the Governments of the Member States meeting within the Council of 19 December 1995 regarding protection for citizens of the European Union by diplomatic and consular representations, OJ L 314/73 (1995)

Council Regulation (EC) No 1257/96 of 20 June 1996, OJ L 163/1996 (1996)

Council Directive 2001/55/EC of 20 July 2001 on minimum standards for giving temporary protection in the event of a mass influx of displaced persons and on measures promoting a balance of efforts between Member States in receiving such persons and bearing the consequences thereof, OJ L 212/12 (2001)

Decision No 1313/2013/EU of the European Parliament and of the Council on a Union Civil Protection Mechanism, OJ L 347/924 (2013)

Decision No 1082/2013/EU of the European Parliament and of the Council on serious cross-border threats to health and repealing Decision No 2119/98/EC, OJ L 293/1 (2013)

Council Decision of 24 June 2014 2014/415/UE on the arrangements for the implementation by the Union of the solidarity clause, OJ L 192/53 (2014)

Council Directive 2013/59/EURATOM laying down basic safety standards for protection against the danger arising from exposure to ionizing radiation and repealing Directives 89/618/Euratom, 90/643/Euratom, 96/29/Euratom, 97/43/Euratom and 2003/122/Euratom, OJ L13/1 (2014)

Other documents

European Consensus on Humanitarian Aid, Joint Statement by the Council and the Representatives of the Governments of the Member States meeting in the Council, the European Parliament and the European Commission, OJ C 25/1 (30 January 2008)

Organization of American States

IACommHR, 2004, Chapter IV (Haiti), OEA/Ser.L/V/II.122 Doc. 5 rev. (25 February 2005)
IACOmmHR, The Right of Women in Haiti to be Free From Violence and Discrimination, OEA/Ser.L/V/II (10 March 2009)

Other soft law documents

AU, NEPAD, AfDB, UNISDR, Africa Regional Strategy for Disaster Risk Reduction (July 2004)
ALNAP, The State of the Humanitarian System (ODI, 2015)
Code of Conduct for the International Red Cross and Red Crescent Movement and Non-Governmental Organisations (NGOs) in Disaster Relief, Prepared jointly by the International Federation of Red Cross and Red Crescent Societies and the International Committee of the Red Cross (1994)
Humanitarian Accountability Partnership, *Standard in Accountability and Quality Management* (HAP, 2010)
IFRC, Guidelines for the Domestic Facilitation and Regulation of International Disaster Relief and Initial Recovery Assistance (IFRC, 2007)
IFRC, Law and Legal Issues in International Disaster Response: A Desk Study (IFRC, 2007)
International Strategy for Disaster Reduction, *Climate Change and Disaster Risk Reduction*, Briefing Note 01 (2008)
Institute of International Law, *Sixteenth Commission: Humanitarian Assistance. Resolution* (Bruges session, 2 September 2003)
Maastricht Guidelines on Violations of Economic, Social and Cultural Rights, Maastricht (1997)
MICIC Initiative, Guidelines to Protect Migrants in Countries Experiencing Conflict or Natural Disasters (June 2016)
Nansen Initiative, Agenda for the Protection of Cross-Border Displaced Persons in the Contexts of Disasters and Climate Change (2015)
Sphere Project, Humanitarian Charter and Minimum Standards in Disaster Response (2000); (2004); (2011)
QUB, Budget Analysis Project Budgeting for Economic and Social Rights: A Human Rights Framework (2010)
The Brookings Institution, Georgetown University, Institute for the Study of International Migration, UNHCR, *Guidance on Protecting People from Disaster and Environmental Change through Planned Relocation* (2015)

Documents of national authorities

Brazil, National Council of Immigration. Normative Resolution 97 (CNIg, 12 Jan. 2012), Di.rio Oficial da Uni.o, Section 1, 13 January 2013
Colombia, law on disaster risk management, no. 1523/2012
Cuba, Decreto No 26: Reglamento de la Ley de Migración (19 July 1978)
Panama, Decreto ejecutivo 23 de 1998, 'Por el cual se desarrolla la Ley No. 5 del 26 del octubre de 1977 que aprueba la Convención de 1951 y Protocolo de 1967 sobre el Estatuto de Refugiados, se derogan el Decreto No. 100 del 6 de julio de 1981 y la Resolución Ejecutiva No. 461 del 9 de Octubre de 1984, y se dictan nuevas disposiciones en materia de protección temporal por razones humanitarias', 10 February 1998
Peru, Ley No. 27891, 20 December 2002
Peru, Reglamento de la Ley del Refugiado, Decreto Supremo No. 119–2003-RE (23 December 2002)
South Africa, Office of the President, Restitution and Land Rights Act No. 22 of 1994, Ch I (1)(xi) (1994)
USA, Homeland Security Act of 2002, Public Law 107–296 (25 November 2002)
USA, Immigration and Nationality Act (2002)
USA, Immigration and Nationality Act, as amended 4 March 2010, Act 244: Temporary Protected Status (2010)
Venezuela, Decreto No. 2491: Reglamento de la Ley Orgánica sobre refugiados o refugiadas y asilados o asiladas, 4 July 2003

List of cases

International cases

Human Rights Committee

Stewart v. Canada, HRComm, Comm. No. 538/1993, UN Doc. CCPR/C/58/D/538/1993 (16 December 1996)

Toktakunov v. Kyrgyzstan, HRComm, Comm. No. 1470/2006, UN Doc. CCPR/C/101/D/1470/2006 (21 April 2011)

Nystrom v. Australia, HRComm, Comm. No. 1557/2007, UN Doc. CCPR/C/102/D/1557/2007 (11 September 2011)

International Court of Justice

Corfu Channel (United Kingdom v. Albania) (Merits) [1949] ICJ Rep. 18

Barcelona Traction, Light and Power Co Ltd (New Application: 1962) (Belgium v. Spain) (Second Phase) [1970] ICJ Rep. 3

Military and Paramilitary Activities in and against Nicaragua (Nicaragua v. United States of America) (Merits) [1986] ICJ Reports 14

Legality of the Threat or Use of Nuclear Weapons (Advisory Opinion) [1996] ICJ Rep. (I) 257

Gabčíkovo-Nagymaros Project (Hungary v. Slovakia) (Merits) Separate opinion of Vice-President Weeramantry [1997] ICJ Rep. 88

LaGrand (Germany v. United States of America) (Judgment) [2001] ICJ Rep. 501, para 466.

Avena and Other Mexican Nationals (Mexico v. United States of America) (Judgment) [2004] ICJ Rep. (I) 48

Legal Consequences of the Construction of a Wall in the Occupied Palestinian Territory (Advisory Opinion) [2004] ICJ Rep. 136

Armed Activities on the Territory of the Congo (Democratic Republic of the Congo v. Uganda) (Merits) [2005] ICJ Rep. 168

Application of the Convention on the Prevention and Punishment of the Crime of Genocide (Bosnia-Herzegovina v. Serbia and Montenegro) [2007] ICJ Rep. 43

Pulp Mills on the River Uruguay (Argentina v. Uruguay) [2010] ICJ Rep. 14

International Criminal Courts and Tribunals

The Prosecutor v. Tadić (Decision on the Defence Motion for Interlocutory Appeal on Jurisdiction) (ICTY, Appeals Chamber, Case No IT-94–1-A, 2 October 1995)

The Prosecutor v. Kunarac, Kovač and Vuković (Judgement) (ICTY, Appeals Chamber, Case No IT-96–23 & IT-96–23/1-A, 12 June 2002)

The Prosecutor v. Semanza (Judgement and Sentence) (ICTR, Trial Chamber III, Case No. ICTR-97–20-T, 15 May 2003)

Permanent Court of International Justice

Factory at Chorzów [1927] PJIC Ser A No 9

Regional cases

African Commission on Human and Peoples' Rights

Social and Economic Rights Action Center (SERAC) and Center for Economic and Social Rights v. Nigeria, Comm. 155/96 (ACommHPR, Decision of 27 October 2001)

Court of Justice of the Economic Community of Western African States

Socio-Economic Rights and Accountability Project (SERAP) v. President of the Republic of Nigeria & ORS, ECOWAS Court of Justice doc. ECW/CCJ/APP/07/10 (Ruling of 10 December 2010)
Aliyu Tasheku v. Federal Republic of Nigeria, ECOWAS Court of Justice doc. ECW/CCJ/RUL/12/12 (Judgement of 12 June 2012)
SERAP v. Federal Republic of Nigeria, ECOWAS Court of Justice doc. ECW/CCJ/JUD/18/12 (Judgment of 14 December 2012)

European Commission of Human Rights

Lawless v. Ireland, App. No. 332/57 (ECommHR, Report of 19 December 1959)
De Becker v. Belgium, App. No. 214/56 (ECommHR, Report of 8 January 1960)
S v. Federal Republic of Germany, App. No. 9686/82 (ECommHR, Decision of 17 December 1962)
Iversen v. Norway, App. No. 1468/62 (ECommHR, Decision of 17 December 1963)
Denmark, Norway, Sweden and the Netherlands v. Greece, App. Nos. 3321/67, 3322/67, 3323/67 and 3344/67 (ECommHR, Report of 5 November 1969)
Ireland v. UK, App. No. 5310/71 (ECommHR, Report of 25 January 1976)
Cyprus v. Turkey, App. Nos. 6780/74 and 6950/75 (ECommHR, Report of 10 July 1976)
I v. Italy, App. No. 11381/85 (ECommHR, Admissibility Decision of 3 March 1986)

European Court of Human Rights

Lawless v. Ireland, App. No. 332/57 (ECtHR, Judgment of 1 July 1961)
Sunday Times v. UK, App. No. 6538/64 (ECtHR, Judgment of 26 April 1976)
Handyside v. UK, App. No. 5493/72 (ECtHR, Judgment of 7 December 1976)
Ireland v. UK, App. No. 5310/71 (ECtHR, Judgment of 18 January 1978)
Silver v. UK, App. Nos. 5947/72, 6205/73, 7052/75, 7061/75, 7107/75, 7113/75 and 7136/75 (ECtHR, Judgment of 25 March 1983)
Leander v. Sweden, App. No. 9248/81 (ECtHR, Judgment of 26 March 1987)
Brannigan and McBride v. UK, App. Nos. 14553/89 and 14554/89 (ECtHR, Judgment of 26 May 1993)
Lopez Ostra v. Spain, App. No. 16798/90 (ECtHR, Judgment of 9 December 1994)
Aksoy v. Turkey, App. No. 21987/93 (ECtHR, Judgment of 18 December 1996)
Balmer-Schafroth et al. v. Switzerland, App. No. 67/1996/686/876 (ECtHR, Judgment of 26 August 1997)
Guerra and others v. Italy, App. No. 14967/89 (ECtHR, Judgment of 19 February 1998)
L.C.B. v. United Kingdom, App. No. 23413/94 (ECtHR, Judgment of 9 June 1998)
Osman v. the United Kingdom, App. No. 23452/94 (ECtHR, Judgment of 28 October 1998)
Thlimmenos v. Greece, App. No. 34369/97 (ECtHR, Judgment of 6 April 2000)
Marshall v. UK, App. No. 41571/98 (ECtHR, Decision on admissibility of 10 July 2001)
Bankovic and others v. Belgium and other States, App. No. 52207/99 (ECtHR, Decision on Admissibility of 12 December 2001)
Kyrtatos v. Greece, App. No. 41666/98 (ECtHR, Judgment of 22 May 2003)
Maestri v. Italy, App. No. 39748/98 (ECtHR, Judgment of 17 February 2004)
Connors v. UK, App. No 66746/01 (ECtHR, Judgment of 27 May 2004)
Taskin and others v. Turkey, App. No. 46117/99 (ECtHR, Judgment of 10 November 2004
Issa and others v. Turkey, App. No. 31821/96 (ECtHR, Judgment of 16 November 2004)
Öneryildiz v. Turkey, App. No. 48939/99 (ECtHR, Judgment, Grand Chamber, of 30 November 2004)
Makaratzis v. Greece, App. No. 50385/99 (ECtHR, Judgment, Grand Chamber, of 20 December 2004)
Enhorn v. Sweden, App. No. 56529/00 (ECtHR, Judgment of 25 January 2005)
Steel and Morris v. the United Kingdom, App. No. 68416/01 (ECtHR, Judgment of 15 February 2005)
Öcalan v. Turkey, App. No. 46221/99 (ECtHR, Judgment, Grand Chamber, of 12 May 2005)
Fadeyeva v. Russia, App. No. 55723/00 (ECtHR, Judgment of 9 June 2005)
Roche v. the United Kingdom, App. No. 32555/96 (ECtHR, Judgment, Grand Chamber, of 19 November 2005)
Treska v. Albania and Italy, App. No. 26937/04 (ECtHR, Decision on Admissibility of 29 June 2006)
Sdruženi Jihočeské Matky v. Czech Republic, App. No. 19101/03 (ECtHR, Decision on admissibility of 10 July 2006)
Giacomelli v. Italy, App. No. 59909/00 (ECtHR, Judgment of 2 November 2006)

Murillo Saldias and others v. Spain, App. No. 76973/02 (ECtHR, Judgment of 28 November 2006)
Amato v. Turkey, App. No. 58771/00 (ECtHR, Judgment of 3 May 2007)
Guja v. Moldova, App. No. 14277/04 (ECtHR, Judgment, Grand Chamber, of 12 February 2008)
Budayeva and others v. Russia, App. Nos. 15339/02, 21166/02, 20058/02, 11673/02 and 15343/02 (ECtHR, Judgment of 20 March 2008)
Turgut and others v. Turkey, App. No. 1411/03 (ECtHR, Judgment of 8 July 2008)
A and Others v. UK, App. No. 3455/05 (ECtHR, Judgment of 19 February 2009)
Társaság a Szabadságjogokért v. Hungary, App. No. 37374/05 (ECtHR, Judgment of 14 April 2009)
Atanasov v. Bulgaria, App. No. 12853/03 (ECtHR, Judgment of 2 December 2010)
Grimkovskaya v. Ukraine, App. No. 38182/03 (ECtHR, Judgment of 21 July 2011)
Di Sarno v. Italy, App. No. 30765/08 (ECtHR, Judgment of 10 January 2012)
Hardy and Maile v. the UK, App. No. 31965/07 (ECtHR, Judgment of 14 February 2012)
Kolyadenko and Others v. Russia, App. Nos. 17423/05, 20534/05, 20678/05, 23263/05, 24283/05 and 35673/05 (ECtHR, Judgment of 28 February 2012)
Aksu v. Turkey, Apps. Nos. 4149/04 and 41029/04 (ECtHR, Judgment of 15 March 2012)
Solomakhin v. Ukraine, App. No. 24429/03 (ECtHR, Judgment of 15 March 2012)
Hadzhiyska v. Bulgaria, App. No. 20701/09 (ECtHR, Decision of 15 May 2012)
Youth Initiative for Human Rights v. Serbia, App. No. 48135/06 (ECtHR, Judgment of 23 June 2013)
Roşiianu v. Romania, App. No. 27329/06 (ECtHR, Judgment of 24 June 2014)
Dzemyuk v. Ukraine, App. No. 42488/02 (ECtHR, Judgment, Grand Chamber, of 4 September 2014)
Hassan v. United Kingdom, App. No.29750/09 (ECtHR, Judgment, Grand Chamber, of 16 September 2014)
Guseva v. Bulgaria, App. No. 6987/07 (ECtHR, Judgment of 17 February 2015)
Prilutiskiy v. Ukraine, App. No. 40429/08 (ECtHR, Judgment of 26 February 2015)
Özel and others v. Turkey, App. Nos. 14350/05, 15245/05 and 16051/05 (ECtHR, Judgment of 17 November 2015)

Court of Justice of the European Union

Judgment of 27 January 2005, *Europe Chemi-Con (Deutschland) GmbH v. Council and Commission*, Case C-422/02 P, ECLI:EU:C:2005:56
Judgment of 17 July 2008, *S. Coleman v. Attridge Law and Steve Law*, Case C-303/06, EU:C:2008:415

Inter-American Commission on Human Rights

Juan Milla Bermúdez v. Honduras, IACommHR, Case 11.206, Report N. 46/96 (on admissibility) (17 October 1996)
Inhabitants of the community of Omoa, Honduras, IACommHR, Precautionary Measure 17/10 (8 November 2011)

Inter-American Court on Human Rights

Velasquez Rodriguez v. Honduras, IACtHR, Ser C, No. 4 (1988)
Aloeboetoe et al. v. Suriname, IACtHR, Ser C, No. 15 (1993)
Metropolitan Reserve Nature v. Panama, IACtHR, Ser C, No. 88 (2003)
Juridical Condition and Rights of Undocumented Migrants, IACtHR (Advisory Opinion), OC-18/03 (17 September 2003)
Plan de Sánchez Massacre v. Guatemala, IACtHR, Ser C, No. 116 (2004)
Claude-Reyes et al. v. Chile, IACtHR, Ser C, No. 151 (2006) (Merits, Reparations and Costs)
Saramaka people v. Suriname, IACtHR, Ser C, No. 172 (2007)
Kichwa People of Sarayaku v. Ecuador, IACtHR, Ser C, No. 245 (2012)

National cases

Supreme Court of Pakistan, *Constitution Petition no 62 of 2010 and Suo Moto Case no 17 of 2010 and Human Rights case no 52220-P of 2010 and Human Rights case no 57247-A of 2010 and Human Rights case no 69622-S of 2010* (Floods Commission case) (7 June 2011)

INDEX

Note: To look up where treaties, cases, soft law instruments and other relevant documents have been mentioned in this volume, please refer to the Table of Documents.

For Product Safety Concerns and Information please contact our EU
representative GPSR@taylorandfrancis.com
Taylor & Francis Verlag GmbH, Kaufingerstraße 24, 80331 München, Germany

www.ingramcontent.com/pod-product-compliance
Ingram Content Group UK Ltd.
Pitfield, Milton Keynes, MK11 3LW, UK
UKHW050053200926
475702UK00019B/2815

* 9 7 8 0 3 6 7 5 8 0 7 9 7 *